BARRON'S

How to Prepare for the
GED® TEST

Christopher M. Sharpe
Joseph S. Reddy

BARRON'S

GED® is a registered trademark of the American Council on Education (ACE) and administered exclusively by GED Testing Service LLC under license.

This material is not endorsed or approved by ACE or GED Testing Service.

About the Authors

Christopher M. Sharpe is the Director of the English Language Arts and English Language Learners Department at a career and technical education charter school in New York City. Throughout his professional career, he has worked to prepare students for success on the GED® test and in college at a variety of organizations. These organizations include Community Impact at Columbia University, Nassau BOCES, and 1199 SEIU Training and Employment Funds. He has also worked at the regional and state level as a provider of professional development to teachers and administrators through the Long Island Regional Adult Education Network/Adult Career and Continuing Education Services (LI-RAEN/ACCES).

Joseph S. Reddy has been a professional test preparation teacher and tutor for over 20 years, and is the founder of JSR Learning, a test preparation services company. He has also helped hundreds of students prepare for the GED® test through the Community Impact GED program at Columbia University.

GED® is a registered trademark of the American Council on Education (ACE) and administered exclusively by GED Testing Service LLC under license. This material is not endorsed or approved by ACE or GED Testing Service.

All inquiries should be addressed to:
Barron's Educational Series, Inc.
250 Wireless Boulevard
Hauppauge, New York 11788
www.barronseduc.com

ISBN: 978-1-4380-0267-5 (book only)
ISBN: 978-1-4380-7369-9 (book with CD-ROM)

ISSN 2329-5295 (book only)
ISSN 2329-5325 (book with CD-ROM)

PRINTED IN THE UNITED STATES OF AMERICA
9 8 7 6 5 4 3

**10%
POST-CONSUMER
WASTE**
Paper contains a minimum
of 10% post-consumer
waste (PCW). Paper used
in this book was derived
from certified, sustainable
forestlands.

CONTENTS

Introduction 1

Steps to Success—Our Approach.. 2

Our Preparation Philosophy... 4

The 2014 General Education Development (GED®) Test..............................5

Computer-Based Testing.. 7

Question Types... 8

Focus on Reasoning... 9

Blended Subjects.. 13

Study Plan.. 14

Test-Taking Strategy... 16

UNIT 1: REASONING THROUGH LANGUAGE ARTS

Pretest 23

1 Reading 31

Lesson 1: Identifying Main Ideas and Supporting Details........................ 33

Lesson 2: Summarizing Details and Ideas.. 37

Lesson 3: Drawing Conclusions and Making Generalizations...................43

Lesson 4: Making Inferences and Assumptions... 46

Lesson 5: Analyzing Language... 50

Lesson 6: Identifying Plot Elements.. 54

Lesson 7: Analyzing Relationships of Ideas...59

Essential Vocabulary... 63

Review Test 67

2 Language 79

Lesson 1: Parts of Speech.. 81

Lesson 2: Parts of the Sentence.. 85

Lesson 3: Independent and Subordinate Clauses..................................... 89

Lesson 4: Types of Sentences.. 91

Lesson 5: Agreement.. 97

Lesson 6: Capitalization.. 99

Lesson 7: Punctuation... 101

Lesson 8: Commonly Confused Words.. 103

Lesson 9: Editing... 105

Review Test 109

3 Extended Responses 121

    Lesson 1: Format and Planning 123

    Lesson 2: Beginning 124

    Lesson 3: Middle 125

    Lesson 4: End 126

    Lesson 5: Planning 127

    Lesson 6: Constructing Your Response 129

    Review Test 131

UNIT 2: MATHEMATICAL REASONING

Pretest 145

4 Mathematical Reasoning Overview 157

5 Numbers and Operations 161

    Lesson 1: Digits and Numbers 161

    Lesson 2: The Number Line 162

    Lesson 3: Inequalities 164

    Lesson 4: Absolute Value 170

    Lesson 5: Place Values 171

    Lesson 6: Rounding 173

    Lesson 7: Operations 174

    Lesson 8: Signed Number Operations 179

    Lesson 9: Factors and Multiples 182

    Lesson 10: Exponents 185

    Lesson 11: Roots 188

    Lesson 12: Order of Operations 191

    Lesson 13: Fractions 192

    Lesson 14: Decimals 197

    Lesson 15: Scientific Notation 200

    Lesson 16: Percentages 202

    Lesson 17: Converting Fractions, Decimals, and Percents 203

6 Ratios, Proportions, and Rates 207

    Lesson 1: Ratios 207

    Lesson 2: Unit Rates 211

    Lesson 3: Proportions 212

    Lesson 4: Ratio Box Variations 219

7 Measurement and Geometry 221

    Lesson 1: Measurement 221

    Lesson 2: Dimensions, Lines, and Angles 226

    Lesson 3: Two-Dimensional Figures 237

    Lesson 4: Three-Dimensional Figures 253

8   Data Analysis..261

   Lesson 1: Interpreting Data Presentations..261

   Lesson 2: Statistics...274

   Lesson 3: Probability..276

   Lesson 4: Counting Methods..278

9   Algebra..281

   Lesson 1: Expressions...281

   Lesson 2: Equations...290

   Lesson 3: Functions...296

   Lesson 4: Graphing and Coordinate Geometry.....................................297

   Lesson 5: Graphing Functions...311

   Essential Vocabulary...323

   Review Test..335

UNIT 3: SOCIAL STUDIES

   Pretest...349

10   Social Studies Skills...353

   Lesson 1: Drawing Conclusions and Making Inferences........................355

   Lesson 2: Identifying Central Ideas and Drawing Conclusions..............360

   Lesson 3: Analyzing Events and Ideas...365

   Lesson 4: Analyzing Language...371

   Lesson 5: Integrating Content Presented in Different Ways...................375

   Lesson 6: Evaluating Reasoning and Evidence.......................................381

   Lesson 7: Writing Analytic Responses to Source Texts..........................385

   Essential Vocabulary...391

   Review Test..395

UNIT 4: SCIENCE

   Pretest...421

11   Science Overview..431

   Scientific Reasoning: Think Like a Scientist...431

   Subject Matter..432

   College and Career Readiness Anchor Standards for Reading..............433

12   Fundamental Concepts..435

   Life Science Topics..435

   Physical Science Topics...436

   Earth and Space Science Topics..436

13   Life Science..437

   Cells..437

   Energy and Respiration..439

Photosynthesis 440
Ecosystem and the Food Chain 441
Species 442
Theory of Evolution 444
DNA 445

14 Physical Science 449
The Atom 449
The Periodic Table 450
The Laws of Motion 453

15 Earth and Space Science 457
The Solar System 457
Earth 457

16 Understanding Science 459
Lesson 1: Scientific Theories 460
Lesson 2: Reading and Interpreting Scientific Findings 463
Lesson 3: Planning and Conducting Investigations 470
Lesson 4: Reasoning from Evidence 478
Lesson 5: Communicating and Evaluating Scientific Findings 480
Essential Vocabulary 481

Review Test 489

MODEL TESTS

Model Test 1 501
Reasoning Through Language Arts 503
Answer Key and Answer Explanations 527
Mathematical Reasoning 535
Answer Key and Answer Explanations 546
Social Studies 553
Answer Key and Answer Explanations 573
Science 581
Answer Key and Answer Explanations 594

Model Test 2 599
Reasoning Through Language Arts 601
Answer Key and Answer Explanations 626
Mathematical Reasoning 633
Answer Key and Answer Explanations 642
Social Studies 649
Answer Key and Answer Explanations 670
Science 677
Answer Key and Answer Explanations 694

Introduction

You deserve to be congratulated—twice, actually. First, you've decided to pursue your GED® test credential, which is a very important and positive decision. Taking this exam is usually the first major step on the path to continuing education or career development. Many students who have moved on to college, graduate school, or career-level employment point to passing this test and receiving their diplomas as the first part of a life-changing process. You've made a very positive choice, it's a big deal, and we congratulate you for it!

You've also decided to prepare for the exam using this book. That was another very smart decision because it means you're not preparing alone. We will guide you every step of the way. Who are we? We're Christopher Sharpe and Joseph Reddy. We're test preparation teachers. We've spent many years helping countless students prepare for the GED® test, and this book holds all of our advice. We'll show you how to organize your time, what to focus on the most, and how to develop the study habits that will lead to success. You've chosen your support team well, and so we congratulate you for that too!

The GED® test is intended to show that a person has the skills and knowledge necessary to pursue post-secondary education, which means college and graduate school, or to pursue professional employment, which means a career path. Post-secondary means "after high school." Since the GED® test is testing at a high school level, you need to reach a high school level of skill and knowledge to pass the exam. If you have some gaps in your prior education, you may need to do some extra studying to fill them. You won't need to learn *everything* that's currently being taught in high school. However, you will want to be well prepared in the material that makes up the core of a high school education.

We'll help, of course. Our book will help you learn or review some of the most important things you'll need to know to pass the exam. It will also help you make the most of what you know when you take the exam. It will even help you identify the gaps you need to fill.

What this book will NOT do is replace a secondary-level education. Depending on your strengths and weaknesses when you start preparing, you might need to budget some additional time to study certain subjects. We'll have some advice for you on this as well.

Over the years that we've spent working with students, we've found that some habits and actions really help students become prepared for the exam:

- Relax
- Learn about the test
- Follow a plan
- Prepare every day
- Strengthen core skills

Relax!

This is very important. Most students build up a lot of stress worrying about the GED® test. Some students just really don't like to take tests. Plus the fact that they have to take a test to get their diplomas is stressful. Some students have heard horror stories from others about how hard the exam is, and that adds some stress. Some students are worried about gaps in their education or the years that have passed since they left school. These worries can add even more stress. Many students have goals in life that depend on passing the test. Those goals can add stress on top of stress. (In fact, reading this is probably adding stress right now!)

Just relax. This exam is not nearly as hard or as scary as you might think. Most of the stress (and yes, even fear) that you may feel is just worry about the unknown. You don't know the test. You don't know how to take it or prepare for it. You don't have a clear plan to follow. Without having any information, about the only thing you can do is worry. Just remember that worrying has never increased an exam score. All worry does is make it more difficult to learn and remember. That's the bad news.

The good news is that fear of the unknown has a simple cure: **knowledge**. When you learn about the GED® test, you will find that you don't have much to worry about. When you have a plan to prepare for and a strategy to take the test, you can stop being so scared. You will develop confidence and good study habits, which always raise exam scores.

You must stay relaxed. As you prepare, you will certainly struggle from time to time as you try to master new topics. This is a natural part of the learning and preparation process. However, struggling doesn't feel good when it's happening. You can easily get worried in these moments. If you start to struggle and worry, just remember that progress takes work and that we're here to help you make progress. Then go and study.

Learn About the Test

To succeed on any test, you need to learn more than just the material on the test. You also need to learn about the test itself. The more you know about what the test measures, how it is designed, and what will be expected of you, the more likely you will be to pass. By the time we're done with you, you will be an expert about the test's contents.

Follow a Plan

The GED® test is a big exam. It covers a wide range of content across multiple subjects. To be ready, you'll need to study and practice a lot of material. If you tried to prepare for everything at once, you would quickly find yourself overwhelmed. The only way to complete a process this large successfully is to break it down into smaller, more manageable pieces.

As you complete each piece, you'll feel a sense of accomplishment. You'll also see yourself making progress.

We'll help you build your study plan. We've got some general guidelines that will help shape a good plan. Since every student is different and has his or her own strengths and weaknesses, you will have to adapt these guidelines to fit your individual needs. Tools like the pretests and the section on developing a study plan on pages 14–16 will help you.

Prepare Every Day

To be honest, creating an individual study plan is the easy part. The more difficult part for most people is consistently using a study plan. The best plan ever created will do you no good if you don't have the self-discipline to follow it. You might need to make a real effort to continue working through your plan, so be ready to push yourself a little. The effort will definitely pay off.

Plan to spend some time preparing **every day** between today and the day you take the test. This may sound extremely difficult or even impossible, but it really isn't. The amount of time you spend each day doesn't always have to be the same. You can spend an hour or 2 one day and then can spend 20 minutes the next day. You can study 5 or 10 minutes at a time 3 times in a day. The important thing is to spend some time each and every day. This will keep your knowledge fresh, your skills sharp, and your forward progress nice and steady.

You can prepare in lots of ways, even when you don't have time to spend an hour with this book. Having a strong knowledge of vocabulary is important. You can learn a few words at a time by working with a list or from flash cards. Your mental math skills need to be sharp. You can practice calculations when you buy things or pay bills. Your reading skills are critical. You can develop them by reading a book, newspaper, or magazine a few pages at a time. Later on, we will discuss a number of easy ways to make test preparation a part of every day.

The important thing here is to make daily preparation a habit. If daily preparation is part of your routine, you'll achieve much faster results.

Strengthen Core Skills

Successful GED® test preparation requires you to have a strong foundation. The mental attitudes and habits we've just described form the first layer of this foundation. The next layer is made up of several very important and fundamental skills. Every student and test taker needs these skills because they are essential for understanding and learning new things. Without these skills, your chances of success on the GED® test will be much worse. Carefully read the following information about these 7 core skills.

READING Much of what we learn is written down. So having strong reading skills is essential. To succeed on the GED® test, you will need to read comfortably and actively. You will need to read at the correct pace, not too fast and not too slowly.

WRITING The ability to communicate clearly in writing is another essential skill. Succeeding in educational or professional settings is impossible if you don't have strong writing skills. A good command of grammar and mechanics is required, as is the ability to organize information clearly and efficiently.

VOCABULARY The common link between the first two skills on this list, reading and writing, is that they both involve words. Even though you can often figure out the meaning of a word, there is just no substitute for knowing what a word actually means. If you learn more words, your reading and writing will be more effective.

INTERPRETING GRAPHIC INFORMATION In addition to the written word, a lot of what we learn is presented in visual or graphic forms. These include charts, graphs, models (diagrams), pictures, maps, illustrations, and other nontext formats. As the popularity of television, the Internet, and mobile wireless technology increases, more and more information will be presented to us in these graphic forms. The ability to interpret data presented in these forms is another essential skill.

USING A COMPUTER The 2014 GED® test is computer based. This move from paper-based to computer-based testing reflects the transition that has taken place in our society as a whole. Computers are everywhere. They are here to stay. In fact, they are a part of virtually every professional and academic role. Most areas of the workforce require that employees have high levels of computer literacy. Postsecondary education and academic research now involve an almost constant reliance on computers and related information technology. Your computer skills must be strong, and this includes the ability to type comfortably.

USING A CALCULATOR The 2014 GED® test provides you with an online scientific calculator. Although you may not need to use all features of the calculator, you should definitely learn the basics of how to use one so that you can take advantage of it during the test.

TAKING TESTS EFFECTIVELY Advancement in education or along a career path usually involves taking tests. Certain commonsense habits can help to increase test performance. Knowing how to approach passages, graphics, and test questions strategically will help you make the most of what you know.

OUR PREPARATION PHILOSOPHY

We love learning. As lifelong teachers, we love to be there when students learn new things. We believe that a lifetime of learning is something that every person should have. We especially want it for all of our students. We hope that once you pass the GED® test, you will continue your pursuit of learning in college, graduate school, and career education; in your local libraries and bookstores; and in all the other places you can find things to learn. We hope that you inspire the same love of learning in your family and friends.

We're also realistic. We know that you bought this book to help you pass a test. Learning is good, as we all can agree, but right now you need to learn how to pass the GED® test. After you've earned your diploma, you can choose what to learn next. That's part of the reward.

Our approach is pretty simple. We're going to teach you about the test. We're also going to teach you the things that you absolutely need to know in order to pass the test. If we don't think you need to know something to succeed on the test, we probably won't cover it. This doesn't mean that we don't think the topic is important or that you should never learn the information. It just means that we don't think you need to know the topic now. On the other hand, if we do cover something, you need it. Period. Don't take shortcuts with the material in this book. You'll need to know everything we present.

The General Education Development (GED®) test is an assessment of high school equivalency. It compares the skills of those who take the test with the skills of recent high school graduates. For more than 70 years, adults have been taking the test as a first step to entering the workforce or pursuing higher education.

Throughout its history, the GED® test has focused on fundamental skills and subjects: language arts (reading and writing), math, science, and social studies. This makes sense since these subjects have long been the foundation of an American high school education. They still are today. As a result, the 2014 GED® test covers these four subjects:

→ **REASONING THROUGH LANGUAGE ARTS (RLA)**
→ **MATHEMATICAL REASONING**
→ **SOCIAL STUDIES**
→ **SCIENCE**

Although the subjects covered on the GED® test have not changed much over the years, a number of other things about the test have changed. Since the standards for high school equivalency and workforce readiness have changed, the test has changed and evolved in order to match those changing standards. The 2014 GED® test is the newest step in this evolution.

For example, when the exam was first established, the majority of jobs did not require the applicant to have a college education. A high school credential (diploma) was sufficient for most people looking for a good job at a good wage. Today, though, most jobs require applicants to have a postsecondary credential from a college, university, or graduate school. As a result, a growing number of students are seeking a GED® test credential as a way to show that they are ready to enter college. In response to this trend, the 2014 version of the exam measures both high school equivalency and college/career readiness.

Another big change affecting the exam is the increasing role that technology plays in our society. Seventy years ago, computers and other forms of information technology were barely even imagined by the average person unless that person collected science fiction. Today computers, tablets, and smartphones, which are all connected to the global Web, play a major role in everyday life. Very few jobs exist today that do not require the employee to have some level of comfort with technology.

To address this, the 2014 GED® test introduces one of the biggest changes in the history of the test: computer-based testing. Students will take their test using a computer rather than the paper-and-pencil format used in past versions. Taking a computer-based test allows students to show that they have the fundamental computer skills required for today's careers and colleges.

Perhaps the most important change to the test since it was first introduced in 1942 is the shift from testing recall (remembering memorized facts) to testing reasoning (using evidence to support answers). This shift was made in response to an early effect of technology on our society: rapid innovation. Since at least the 1960s, information technology has been speeding up the rate at which we learn new things, develop new abilities, and overcome new challenges. Landing on the moon was just one early example of revolutionary discovery and accomplishment. Prior to this time, the pace of innovation was slower because the tools available were not as powerful.

This increase in the rate or pace of innovation had a dramatic effect on our definition of high school equivalency and workforce readiness. Prior to this time, if a student in high school memorized a large volume of facts in a given field, like science or social studies, he or she would almost certainly be asked to remember and use those facts in college or in the workforce because new information and new fields of study were slower to develop. In the early 1970s, however, educators and employers realized that this approach to learning was not going to serve future generations of students. Rapid innovation was leading to a growing number of new fields of study and work. So it was becoming more important that students know how to learn and apply new information quickly and correctly. The ability to think logically and figure out new things was becoming far more important than the ability to repeat memorized facts. As a result, for the last 40 years, the GED® test has been a test of reasoning skills, or the ability to figure things out using new information. This aspect of the test is probably the most important thing for students to remember, which is why we will talk about it constantly throughout this book. The exam is designed to measure *how you think*, NOT *what you remember.*

Sections of the Test

The exam is made up of four parts, which we call subject tests. Each subject test is focused on one area of subject matter, or content.

1. The **REASONING THROUGH LANGUAGE ARTS (RLA)** subject test measures reading, writing, and grammar skills.
2. The **MATHEMATICAL REASONING** subject test measures fundamental knowledge and problem-solving skills in arithmetic and algebra.
3. The **SCIENCE** subject test measures the ability to apply reasoning skills to content taken from life science, physical science, earth science, and space science.
4. The **SOCIAL STUDIES** subject test measures the ability to apply reasoning skills to material that deals with civics and government, U.S. history, economics, geography, and the world.

Test Sequence and Timing

Since the GED® test has been changed for 2014, some of the details about it either weren't available or weren't finalized while this book was being written. Below is a list of approximate timings for each of the subject tests.

NOTE

The actual test may include some unscored questions at the end that are presented for field testing.

	Time
RLA	150 min. (including 10 minute break)
Social Studies	90 min.
Science	90 min.
Math	90 min.
Field Testing	15 min.
Total	Approximately 7¼ hr.

Focus on Fundamentals

Each subject test assumes that students are familiar with the fundamental concepts in that subject. The RLA subject test assumes that you can read and write carefully and that you know the basic rules of grammar in standard written English. The Math subject test assumes you can perform basic operations in arithmetic and algebra and can work with things like proportions, equations, and geometric figures. The Science and Social Studies tests assume you are familiar with the core concepts in these subjects, such as knowing that all living things are made up of cells (life science) or knowing the process by which laws are made (civics and government). To pass the subject tests, students need a strong understanding of the fundamental, big-picture concepts being tested.

More subject matter details for each subject test will be provided in the sections of this book that cover each test. For now, it is enough to know that part of your job in preparing for the GED® test will be to review the fundamentals in each area. The majority of these fundamentals, particularly those related to reading, writing, and math, are covered in this book. Many of the central science and social studies concepts are addressed here as well. Since these two subject tests cover fairly wide areas of content, though, it isn't practical for us to cover all of them in depth, even in a book this large. When you read the content summaries for the Science and Social Studies tests, you may find that some subjects are not familiar. If you think you need to spend some time reviewing them, we suggest you go to the following websites:

BARRON'S

http://www.barronseduc.com/study-guides.html

WIKIPEDIA

http://www.wikipedia.org/

GED® TESTING SERVICE

http://www.gedtestingservice.com/ged-testing-service

COMPUTER-BASED TESTING

The 2014 GED® test is computer based. Although taking a test on the computer may be a new experience for many students, the required computer skills are easy to develop. They include basic keyboard (typing) and word-processing (cut, copy, paste) skills plus the ability to use a mouse (point, click, drag, drop). If you use a computer for things like e-mail, Web browsing, or word processing, then you probably already have the skills you need. If your computer skills are not very strong yet, now is the time to start building them. Practice using online resources like Google, Wikipedia, or the Barron's Educational Series, Inc. websites to find information and sharpen your skills.

As you may have heard, the computer-based format of the 2014 GED® test will evaluate your skills in some new ways. It will ask you to perform interactive tasks that can be performed only using a computer. Some of these tasks will feel similar to ones you've seen on paper-and-pencil tests in the past, but some might be a bit new to you. Some questions ask students to choose answers from a list, fill in a short answer, or give an extended written response. These tasks are essentially the same ones found on traditional tests. The main difference is that students click answers instead of filling in bubbles, or they type text instead of writing by hand. New types of questions ask students to point at things on the screen or to move things around on the screen. These questions can be used to test your ability to sort, organize, or sequence pieces of information. You might also be asked to build a graph or point to a relevant piece of information in a chart or diagram. The good news is that even the questions that involve new kinds of tasks are really quite easy to work with. Although you may not have previously used some of the new tasks on the exam, you've probably used point-and-click and drag-and-drop skills on a computer, smart phone, or tablet.

QUESTION TYPES

In this section, we provide more details on each of the question types found on the exam.

Multiple Choice

The multiple-choice question is perhaps the most familiar type of standardized test question. It consists of a text-based prompt followed by a number of possible answer choices. In some cases, the question may refer to a passage or graphic. On the computer-based 2014 GED® test, these questions will each have four answer choices. Test takers will use a mouse to click the answer they select. Approximately 80% of the questions on the exam will be multiple-choice questions.

Fill in the Blank

A type of fill-in question has been part of more recent paper-based versions of the exam. These questions include a prompt, but do not provide answer choices. So test takers must work out the answer themselves. On the new test, rather than writing in an answer, test takers will use a keyboard to type a number, word, phrase, or sentence into a text box on the computer screen. These questions may also refer to a stimulus.

Short Answer

The short answer question is new for this version of the test. It presents the test taker with a prompt and/or stimulus. The question requires that the student type a brief answer. This answer will often require the student to type more than one sentence.

Drop-Down Items

This is a new type of question that combines multiple-choice and fill-in-the-blank elements. Test takers are presented with a question that includes text with drop-down lists embedded in one or more locations. Each list will contain options for completing, or filling in, that portion of the text. Test takers must choose the best option.

Interactive Items

These new question types make the most significant use of the new testing technology, specifically the computer mouse. The **hot spot** question type will require test takers to click one or more locations on a graphic based on information in the question. The **drag-and-drop** question type will require test takers to move words or graphics into target locations on the screen based on information in the question.

Extended Response

This is another relatively familiar question type. An extended response is just a question that requires students to write a long answer. Test-takers will be required to type a well-structured written response to a prompt. Time limits for these questions are estimated to be 25 minutes.

Question Type Summary

	Language Arts	Mathematics	Science	Social Studies
Multiple Choice	Y	Y	Y	Y
Drop Down	Y	Y	Y	Y
Fill in the Blank	Y	Y	Y	Y
Drag and Drop	Y	Y	Y	Y
Hot Spot		Y	Y	Y
Short Answer	Y		Y	
Extended Response	Y			Y

FOCUS ON REASONING

As we've said previously, the modern-day GED® test is an assessment of reasoning skills. On a reasoning skills test, the way you think is much more important than the list of facts you remember. Some fundamental knowledge of facts and concepts is required. However, the majority of the questions on the test will require you to do more than just recall a fact. They will present you with new facts and ask you to use those facts as evidence to support answers. This process of thinking about new information and using it as a basis to answer questions is called reasoning. The vast majority of questions on the test will require you to use your reasoning skills, explain your reasoning for an answer, or both.

Standardized tests have a very specific way of testing reasoning skills. They begin by presenting you with new information. On the RLA test, this may be a reading passage, a sentence to be edited, or the stated topic (or prompt) for a writing exercise. On the Math test, you will encounter a word problem, graph, or equation. In the Science and Social Studies tests, you may see a passage or other form of text, a visual presentation (graph, chart, diagram, map, cartoon), or both. The information presented is called a **stimulus**. The questions to be answered will be based on the information in the stimulus. The student's job is to read and understand the stimulus, apply the information contained in it to the questions, and then choose or provide answers to the questions. This process is called testing subject matter knowledge in context because students can figure out the meaning of a term, symbol, or concept by using the surrounding information (context) as a guide. People do this every day when they work out the meaning of one unfamiliar word in a sentence using the words around it.

Although it may not seem very important on first glance, the method that the GED® test uses to measure reasoning skills in context is really a very big deal. Let's take a moment to think about what this means. **Almost all of the information you'll need to answer a question on the GED® exam will be provided to you as part of the test.**

Information Tested in Context

The test will never require you to use the definition of an important term without first providing you with enough information in context to figure out the definition. As long as you can read, understand, and use the information provided in the stimulus, you should be able to find most or all of the information you need to answer the questions. Since understanding how reasoning skills are tested is extremely important, let's take a look at this right away.

To illustrate how reasoning skills are tested, we'll use an example taken from life science. First, here is a list of questions you will never ever see on the Science test:

- What is photosynthesis?
- What is glucose?
- What are the chemical symbols for glucose, water, oxygen, and carbon dioxide?
- Briefly explain the roles that water, oxygen, carbon dioxide, and glucose play in photosynthesis. Include a discussion of the Calvin cycle and the light reactions.

You will never see questions like these on the test because they don't provide any stimulus information or context. These questions test your ability to recall facts, not your ability to use facts. A GED® test question on the same subject works a bit differently.

A question might begin by presenting a diagram as a stimulus. Never forget that questions and answer choices will always be based on the information provided in the stimulus. If you carefully analyze the information provided, you will usually find everything you need to answer the questions. Here's an example.

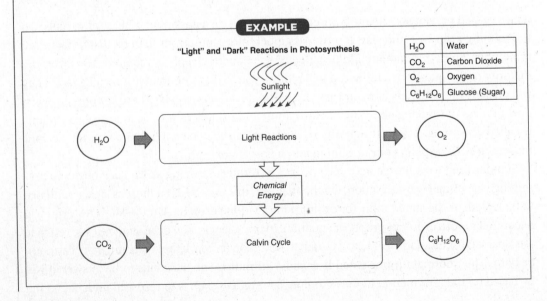

EXAMPLE

"Light" and "Dark" Reactions in Photosynthesis

H_2O	Water
CO_2	Carbon Dioxide
O_2	Oxygen
$C_6H_{12}O_6$	Glucose (Sugar)

Sunlight

H_2O → Light Reactions → O_2

Chemical Energy

CO_2 → Calvin Cycle → $C_6H_{12}O_6$

This diagram describes the process of photosynthesis, which is the process by which plants convert light into nutrients. This is a good example of what we mean when we talk about the fundamentals on a subject test. The Science test will assume that you may have heard of photosynthesis or that you may know that plants can make their own food. It does not assume that you know all the details and definitions about photosynthesis.

Even though photosynthesis itself is quite a complicated process, this diagram describing it is actually not that complicated. After looking closely at the graphic, you will see that photosynthesis is fairly easy to understand. Note that the diagram contains quite a few facts.

- Photosynthesis is divided into two parts: light reactions and the Calvin cycle.
- Three compounds enter the process of photosynthesis: sunlight, H_2O, and CO_2.
- H_2O is water, and CO_2 is carbon dioxide. (These are defined in the legend, but you might already know the definitions.)
- Two compounds are products of photosynthesis: O_2 and $C_6H_{12}O_6$.
- O_2 is oxygen. $C_6H_{12}O_6$ is glucose, which is sugar. (These are also shown in the legend.)
- Sunlight and H_2O are used by the light reactions to produce chemical energy and O_2.
- Chemical energy and CO_2 are used by the Calvin cycle to produce $C_6H_{12}O_6$.

This process of listing the facts you find in new information is crucial for success on the test. If you develop your ability to analyze new information confidently, you'll find that the questions themselves become much easier to answer. Use the facts taken from the diagram to answer this sample question.

EXAMPLE

Which statement best describes the process shown in the diagram?

(A) Glucose and oxygen are broken down into water, carbon dioxide, and sunlight by the light reactions and the Calvin cycle. This process also creates chemical energy.

(B) Water, carbon dioxide, and sunlight are used to produce oxygen and glucose. The light reactions produce chemical energy used by the Calvin cycle.

(C) The Calvin cycle uses water, carbon dioxide, and sunlight, along with chemical energy from the light reactions, to produce oxygen and glucose.

(D) The light reactions use carbon dioxide and water to produce chemical energy used by the Calvin cycle. The Calvin cycle produces oxygen and glucose.

Remember that the questions and answers will always be connected to the source information. In this example, the second answer choice is the correct one because it agrees with the diagram. The other choices are all incorrect because they all contain information that conflicts with the diagram.

The first answer choice reverses the process. It confuses the inputs and outputs. Choice A says that glucose and oxygen are converted into water, carbon dioxide, and sunlight. Photosynthesis actually works in the other direction.

The third answer choice says that the Calvin cycle uses water and sunlight. This disagrees with the diagram. The graphic shows that water and sunlight are used by only the light reactions. It also shows that the Calvin cycle uses only carbon dioxide and the chemical energy produced by the light reactions.

The fourth answer choice says that the light reactions use carbon dioxide. This disagrees with the diagram, which shows that carbon dioxide is used by only the Calvin cycle.

This example illustrates working with science information in context. The question tests your ability to summarize a process presented in a diagram accurately. It uses content from life science for that purpose. The question assumes you are able to read a diagram and understand the meaning of symbols (like arrows) and other components of the diagram (like the legend). It also assumes that you have a basic familiarity with the concept of photosynthesis, such as knowing that plants use light to make food. All of the other information needed to test your reasoning skills is provided in the diagram.

Question–Answer Relationship Strategy

The GED® test will ask you three different kinds of reasoning questions.

REMEMBER AND REPEAT (R) These questions don't require a lot of thought. They will ask you to find information in the source material and then select an answer choice that matches the information.

ANALYZE AND APPLY (A) These questions require a bit more thought. To answer them, you will need to break down the information in the source material and identify some new relationships or uses for the information.

EXPLAIN AND EXTEND (E) These questions take the most thought and effort because they ask you to explain the reasoning that leads to your answer. To answer them fully, you will need to do more than simply analyze the information in the source material and use it to support an answer. You will also need to explain how the evidence in the source material supports the answer.

Approach every question by looking at the relationship between the question and the answer:

→ What is the question asking you to do? Is it an R, an A, or an E question?
→ What steps should you take to answer it?

QAR and RAE

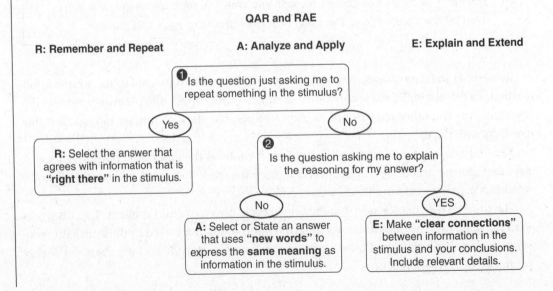

R: Remember and Repeat   A: Analyze and Apply   E: Explain and Extend

❶ Is the question just asking me to repeat something in the stimulus?

Yes → **R:** Select the answer that agrees with information that is **"right there"** in the stimulus.

No → ❷ Is the question asking me to explain the reasoning for my answer?

No → **A:** Select or State an answer that uses **"new words"** to express the **same meaning** as information in the stimulus.

YES → **E:** Make **"clear connections"** between information in the stimulus and your conclusions. Include relevant details.

STEP 1 Is the question just asking you to repeat information as it is presented in the stimulus?

- If Yes, this is a remember and repeat (R) question, and you can expect it to be fairly easy. The answer will be right there in the stimulus. Select or state the answer that agrees with the information in the stimulus.
- If No, go to Step 2.

STEP 2 Is the question asking you to explain your reasoning?

- If No, this is an analyze and apply (A) question. To answer it, you will need to break down the information in the stimulus and work out the relationships among the parts. The correct answer will agree in meaning with the stimulus but will express that meaning in a new or different way. Your job will be to reassemble the parts into an answer that means the same thing as described in the stimulus but uses different words.
- If Yes, this is an extend and explain (E) question. To answer it, you will need to go beyond just the answer and explain your reasoning process. Since all reasoning on the test is based on effective use of evidence, your job will be to make clear connections among what the stimulus says, what the stimulus means, and how that relates to your answer or conclusion. The correct answer will agree in meaning with the stimulus but will express that meaning in a new or different way. Your job will be to reassemble the parts into an answer that means the same thing as described in the stimulus but uses different words.

BLENDED SUBJECTS

A very interesting part of the new test is an increase in subject matter integration. Previous versions of the test, for the most part, isolated the various content areas. This means the Social Studies section tested only social studies subjects, the Science section tested only science subjects, and so on.

The 2014 GED® test blends subject matter across sections. This is a definite improvement in the test, because it reflects the way these skills are used in the real world. In life, we use many of our skills together. Reading, writing, and math are almost always combined. The 2014 exam does a much better job of testing these skills the way you actually use them in day-to-day activities than did previous versions of the exam.

- The Math test contains questions based on graphics previously found only in the Science test.
- The Science test contains questions that require you to use math to produce a numerical answer. Calculators are almost always provided for these questions.
- The RLA test includes historical texts previously found only in the Social Studies test.
- The Social Studies test includes an extended written response.

A study plan has two parts: time and materials. You need to know how much time you can spend studying. You also need to know what you'll be doing with that time and what materials you'll need.

Types of Studying

There are four types of studying:

- **BOOK WORK** Reading the lesson material in this book
- **PRACTICE** Doing practice questions or taking practice exams from the book or disc
- **REVIEW** Reexamining practice questions you missed or skipped and also reading the explanations
- **DRILLS** Using study aids (like flash cards) to test and improve memorization

---

Study Environments

Most types of studying require you to have a study friendly environment. This environment is quiet, well lit, and free from distractions (music, TV, mobile devices, and other people making noise). It has enough space for you to work and includes a firm, flat surface to lean on when writing. When doing book work, practice, or review, you'll want to be in a study friendly environment.

Drills are a different story, however. You can do drills in many environments where other kinds of study wouldn't work: on the bus or train, during a break at work, at the gym, or in similar settings. Most of the study aids used for drills (like flash cards or worksheets) are small and portable, making them easier to use when space is limited. Since most drills test memorization, like the definitions of vocabulary words or the factors of numbers, they require shorter periods of concentration. Unlike reading a paragraph or passage, which takes a long and uninterrupted span of time, a drill question is asked and answered quickly. So interruptions are easier to manage.

The Planning Process

When planning your study schedule, use the following suggestions. They will help you prepare for the test in the time available. Using a spreadsheet, a planning calendar, or good old pen and paper, create a template that you can use to show a weekly schedule. It might look like the one on the next page.

	Monday	Tuesday	Wednesday	Thursday	Friday	Saturday	Sunday
7:00–7:30 am							
7:30–8:00 am							
8:00–8:30 am							
8:30–9:00 am							
9:00–9:30 am							
9:30–10:00 am							
10:00–10:30 am							
10:30–11:00 am							
11:00–11:30 am							
11:30–12:00 pm							
12:00–12:30 pm							
12:30–1:00 pm							
1:00–1:30 pm							
1:30–2:00 pm							
2:00–2:30 pm							
2:30–3:00 pm							
3:00–3:30 pm							
3:30–4:00 pm							
4:00–4:30 pm							
4:30–5:00 pm							
5:00–5:30 pm							
5:30–6:00 pm							
6:00–6:30 pm							
6:30–7:00 pm							
7:00–7:30 pm							
7:30–8:00 pm							

Use this template to lay out your general schedule for two or three weeks. Include work, classes, commuting time, meals, sleep, and other scheduled activities. This will give you an initial picture of your potential study time. Review the schedule. Identify blocks of time that you could use for quiet, focused book work, practice, and review. These blocks should be at least 30 minutes long and no more than 2 hours in length. Note the number of hours per week you'll be able to spend on each activity.

Review your schedule a second time, this time looking for opportunities for drills. These might be while commuting or during breaks in your work or school schedule.

Don't worry if some days do not have study time scheduled. You will be able to find ways to use your daily activities as part of your preparation. Many work tasks provide a chance for reading and analyzing information. Tracking all of your daily expenses is a great way to spend a few minutes doing calculations. Conversations with other people will frequently give you a chance to explain the reasoning you used to form a particular opinion. Work tasks involving e-mails or creating reports are great opportunities to practice writing skills. Writing personal e-mails and journal entries are also good ways to practice writing. On days when you don't have enough time for a lot of formal studying, you can still make progress.

Find Your Strengths and Weaknesses

We have provided some general guidelines for studying subject matter on pages 14–15. Based on our experience, you should study certain topics early in the process and address other topics later. Once you have your pretest results, you'll know which areas to address first.

Create Some Study Aids

Study aids are things like flash cards, magazines, newspapers, journals, and similar items that you can carry with you. You'll use these for studying wherever you may be—at work, on the bus, and so on.

Flash Cards

A flash card gets its name from a different time in the history of technology. Students who wanted to memorize vocabulary words, math facts, state capitals, and other lists of facts would use index cards for drills. One side of the card would contain the question, like a vocabulary word, and the other would contain the answer, like the definition of that word. This kind of study aid is so effective that it remains in use today and will probably continue to be used for years to come.

These days, technology provides us with more options when it comes to the creation of flash cards. Many of these new options are electronic, allowing us to create drills that can be used on a computer, phone, or tablet. Several different kinds of software, including apps for mobile devices, can be used to do this.

Technology also allows us to use audio recording as a form of flash card. Here the questions and answers are recorded and played back. This method can be an effective study tool when using public transportation.

Get to Work!

After completing the steps described above, you will be aware of the time you have available to study and will be equipped with the material you need to work on. All that remains is to start working the plan and keep working the plan every day.

TEST-TAKING STRATEGY

Whenever you take any kind of exam, whether it is the GED® test or some other test, you must have a strategy. Obviously, you also need to be comfortable with the subject matter on the exam. However, having an effective test-taking strategy can help you make the most of the things you know. When you combine knowledge of a test's subject matter with knowledge of the test itself, you create a recipe for success.

Study the Test

You must always study for the particular test that you plan to take. However, you must also study the test itself. The more you know about a test's structure, organization, and rules, the better prepared you will be to take the test efficiently and effectively. Know the following details about the test:

CONTENT What subject matter will be tested?

FORMAT Is it a paper-and-pencil test or a computer-based test?

STRUCTURE How is the test organized? Is it divided into sections? Do these sections have a specific order?

QUESTION TYPES What kinds of questions are used on the test?

TIMING How much time do you have to take each section? How much time is available per question? Will different question types require you to spend different amounts of time on them?

SEQUENCING Must questions be answered in order or can you skip questions and return to them later?

SCORING How is the test scored? Does each question have the same point value, or do different question types carry different point values?

PASSING What is considered a passing score? How many points must you earn to pass the test? How many questions must you answer correctly to earn those points?

LEAVING BLANKS Is a question with no answer selected scored the same way as a question answered incorrectly?

QUESTION LEVELS Do questions differ in terms of complexity or difficulty? How can I recognize questions at different levels?

Not All Questions Are Created Equal

You must study and become familiar with the various kinds of questions you will face on the exam. Each question you see on the exam will have some characteristics that will help you to make choices. You can use these characteristics to choose whether to answer a question, when to answer a question, and how to answer a question.

QUESTION TYPE Some exams are limited to a small number of different question types. Other exams, like the new 2014 GED® test, use a wide variety of question types. Each type will have its own structure or format and its own rules. Each is designed to test your knowledge and skills in a specific way. The best method of approaching a given question will depend on the question type.

SUBJECT MATTER Each question will focus on a specific subject matter (math, language arts, science, or social studies). On the GED® test, themes, or big ideas, often provide a common thread throughout the subject. The subject area of a given question will help you identify the theme you should focus on in your answer.

COMPLEXITY OR DIFFICULTY Most exams contain a mixture of questions, some that seem easier to the test taker and some that seem harder. This apparent difference is generally based on the number of steps required to answer the question, the number of options to choose from, and the level of knowledge or skill being tested. The ability to recognize different levels of question complexity will help you make strategic choices during the test.

GROUPED QUESTIONS Some of the questions may be based on a shared piece of content. A group of reading questions may be based on a common passage. A group of math questions may be based on a common geometric diagram. Science or social studies questions may be based on a common chart or graph. Grouped questions require you to take a slightly different approach than individual questions.

POINT VALUE On some exams, each question is worth the same number of points so each question counts the same toward the overall exam score. On other exams, like the 2014 GED® test, different questions are worth different numbers of points. Unfortunately, you won't know the point value of any question on the 2014 GED® test, so do your best to rule out any obvious wrong answers and make an educated guess with the remaining ones.

COMFORT LEVEL Most students have both strengths and weaknesses. They prefer certain subject matter areas or question types, and they prefer to avoid others. Your individual strengths and weaknesses will determine how comfortable you are with a given question. A good strategy involves playing to your strengths.

Strategy for the 2014 GED® Test

One feature of the exam that works very much in your favor is related to question sequence. Within one exam section, you may answer the questions in any order you choose. The exam software lets you flag questions for review and then return to them later. This will allow you to work through the section on your terms, earning points by using your strengths and avoiding questions where you are less confident.

To take best advantage of this aspect of the GED® test, plan to move through each section by putting questions into one of three categories.

1. **DO NOW** Some questions test areas where your confidence is high. You're very comfortable with the question type, the content, and the level of complexity. As you've practiced, you've learned that you are usually successful with these questions. By answering these questions immediately, you will keep your point total rising and will feel good about your progress in the section.

2. **DO LATER** For some questions, your confidence level will be somewhere in the middle. You're reasonably comfortable with the question but feel that it may take more time or effort to ensure you answer correctly. Flag these. Return to them once you've reviewed the whole section and answered all the Do Now questions. Go through these Do Later questions in order of preference, working slowly and carefully. Do this until you've answered them all or until you have only 3 minutes left in the section.

3. **TACKLE LAST** Every student has weaknesses, and every exam has questions related to those weak areas. Questions in areas where your confidence is low will likely take a lot of time and effort so save those for last. Try to eliminate wrong choices, then guess.

Levels of Complexity

As we've said before, some questions on the GED® test will seem easier or harder than others. Although we often talk about this in terms of how difficult a question is, the new exam is not actually built around the concept of difficulty. Instead, it is designed around the concept of complexity. Test takers will find questions more or less challenging based on how complex the questions are.

At first, the difference between difficulty and complexity may not seem very large. A deeper look, however, will show that there actually is a large and important difference between these two ways of judging a question. Difficulty is based on the likelihood that a test taker will know the answer. A question can be made more difficult by simply asking about a more obscure fact. The less well-known the fact, the more difficult the question becomes. Complexity, though, is based on the level and kind of reasoning required to answer a question. A less complex question may ask a test taker to repeat a fact. A moderately complex question may ask a test taker to apply some given knowledge to a new situation. A highly complex question may require the test taker not only to provide a detailed answer but also to explain the reasoning supporting the answer. These questions are focused not on what the test taker knows but on how he or she thinks.

The new GED® test is designed to evaluate reasoning. The focus of the exam is on measuring how well test takers solve problems in a logical and reasonable fashion. Although the test taker must know facts in order to succeed on the test, the exam is not focused on testing knowledge of facts. Test takers will be presented with tasks that require multiple steps, questions with more than one possible correct answer, and questions that require students to explain their reasoning rather than simply repeat information. When evaluating a question, decide which of these tasks it requires.

REMEMBER AND REPEAT Some questions will simply ask you to repeat information given in a passage, chart, graph, diagram, or other graphic. These questions are the least complex on the test. You will probably find them to be the easiest. However, few questions will be of this type, and they are usually worth the fewest points.

ANALYZE AND APPLY Some questions will provide you with information and then require you to apply that information in new circumstances. These questions test your ability to compare and contrast different situations and to identify relationships among elements in each situation. Answering this type of question requires you to use a higher level of reasoning than simply repeating given information. Analyze and apply questions may seem a little harder than remember and repeat questions. However, there will be quite a few analyze and apply questions on the exam. They are actually not as complex as other questions you will see. They are also usually worth more points than remember and repeat questions.

EXPLAIN AND EXTEND The most complex questions on the exam will ask you to provide an answer and also to explain your reasoning. Sometimes these questions will require you to write a short answer or an extended response (essay). In these cases, you make a statement and then use evidence to support it. These questions will usually involve a larger number of steps and consume more time than less complex questions. Although skipping all questions at this level may be tempting, remember that they are generally worth the most points.

In general, the more complex a question is, the more time will be required to answer it effectively. High-complexity questions require you to evaluate source material, explain your reasoning, and do a large amount of writing. By comparison, lower-complexity questions will usually require less time and be less labor intensive. When starting a new section, you should actively look for remember and repeat questions to do now. Flag all analyze and apply and also all explain and extend questions for later review. This approach focuses the early minutes of your section on the quicker, lower-value questions, earning you a strong base of points. You can then build on this base by methodically selecting and answering the higher-value questions that are related to your strengths.

UNIT 1

Reasoning Through Language Arts

Pretest

DIRECTIONS: This pretest is intended to cover a broad number of skills and give you an idea of how close you are to being ready to take the actual exam. If you answer 75% or more questions correctly, you're almost there! Earning a score of 50% to 75% is a great start. If you score less than 50%, you've got the right book to help you get to where you need to be!

QUESTIONS 1 AND 2 REFER TO THE FOLLOWING PASSAGE:

Excerpt from *Mr. Pottle and Culture*
by Richard Connell

1   Out of the bathtub, rubicund and rotund, stepped Mr. Ambrose Pottle. He anointed his hair with sweet spirits of lilac and dusted his anatomy with crushed rosebud talcum. He donned a virgin union suit; a pair of socks, silk where it showed; ultra low shoes; white-flannel trousers, warm from the tailor's goose; a creamy silk shirt; an impeccable blue coat; a gala tie, perfect after five tyings; and then went forth into the spring-scented eventide to pay a call on Mrs. Blossom Gallup.

2   He approached her new-art bungalow as one might a shrine, with diffident steps and hesitant heart, but with delicious tinglings radiating from his spinal cord. Only the ballast of a three-pound box of Choc-O-late Nutties under his arm kept him on earth. He was in love.

3   To be in love for the first time at twenty is passably thrilling; but to be in love for the first time at thirty-six is exquisitely excruciating.

4   Mr. Pottle found Mrs. Gallup in her living room, a basket of undarned stockings on her lap. With a pretty show of confusion and many embarrassed murmurings she thrust them behind the piano, he protesting that this intimate domesticity delighted him.

5   She sank back with a little sigh into a gay-chintzed wicker chair, and the rosy light from a tall piano lamp fell gently on her high-piled golden hair, her surprised blue eyes, and the ripe, generous outlines of her figure. To Mr. Pottle she was a dream of loveliness, a poem, an idyl. He would have given worlds, solar systems to have been able to tell her so. But he couldn't. He couldn't find the words, for, like many another sterling character in the barbers' supply business, he was not eloquent; he did not speak

with the fluent ease, the masterful flow that comes, one sees it often said, from twenty-one minutes a day of communion with the great minds of all time. His communings had been largely with boss barbers; with them he was cheery and chatty. But Mrs. Gallup and her intellectual interests were a world removed from things tonsorial; in her presence he was tongue-tied as an oyster.

6   Mr. Pottle's worshiping eye roved from the lady to her library, and his good-hearted face showed tiny furrows of despair; an array of fat crisp books in shiny new bindings stared at him: Twenty-one Minutes' Daily Communion With the Master Minds; Capsule Chats on Poets, Philosophers, Painters, Novelists, Interior Decorators; Culture for the Busy Man, six volumes, half calf; How to Build Up a Background; Talk Tips; YOU, Too, Can Be Interesting; Sixty Square Feet of Self-Culture—and a score more. "Culture"—always that wretched word!

1. From what part of the plot is this excerpt likely taken?
    (A) Exposition
    (B) Rising action
    (C) Falling action
    (D) Conclusion

2. The language used in the fifth paragraph indicates the speaker is:
    (A) Confused
    (B) In love
    (C) Bored
    (D) Upset

QUESTIONS 3 AND 4 REFER TO THE FOLLOWING PASSAGE:

Excerpt from *The Last Mile*
by Sarah Orne Jewett

1   It was night now; it was too late in the year for the chirp of any insects; the moving air, which could hardly be called wind, swept over in slow waves, and a few dry leaves rustled on an old hawthorn tree which grew beside the hollow where a house had been, and a low sound came from the river. The whole country side seemed asleep in the darkness, but the lonely woman felt no lack of companionship; it was well suited to her own mood that the world slept and said nothing to her,—it seemed as if she were the only creature alive.

2   A little this side of the river shore there was an old burial place, a primitive spot enough, where the graves were only marked by rough stones, and the short, sheep-cropped grass was spread over departed generations of the farmers and their wives and children. By day it was in sight of the pine woods and the moving water, and nothing hid it from the great sky overhead, but now it was like a prison walled about by the barriers of night. However eagerly the woman had hurried to this place, and with what

purpose she may have sought the river bank, when she recognized her surroundings she stopped for a moment, swaying and irresolute. "No, no!" sighed the child plaintively, and she shuddered, and started forward; then, as her feet stumbled among the graves, she turned and fled. It no longer seemed solitary, but as if a legion of ghosts which had been wandering under cover of the dark had discovered this intruder, and were chasing her and flocking around her and oppressing her from every side. And as she caught sight of a light in a far-away farmhouse window, a light which had been shining after her all the way down to the river, she tried to hurry toward it. The unnatural strength of terror urged her on; she retraced her steps like some pursued animal; she remembered, one after another, the fearful stories she had known of that ancient neighborhood; the child cried, but she could not answer it. She fell again and again, and at last all her strength seemed to fail her, her feet refused to carry her farther and she crept painfully, a few yards at a time, slowly along the ground. The fear of her superhuman enemies had forsaken her, and her only desire was to reach the light that shone from the looming shadow of the house.

3   At last she was close to it; at last she gave one great sigh, and the child fell from her grasp; at last she clutched the edge of the worn doorstep with both hands, and lay still.

3. Based on the context of the word, what is the best definition of the word "shuddered" in the second paragraph?
    (A) Closed window panels
    (B) Trembled
    (C) Shouted
    (D) Fell

4. Which of the following literary elements is used in the first sentence of the second paragraph?
    (A) Hyperbole
    (B) Simile
    (C) Imagery
    (D) Characterization

QUESTIONS 5 AND 6 REFER TO THE FOLLOWING PASSAGE:

Excerpt from *The Importance of Being Earnest*
by Oscar Wilde

1   Cecily: [Rather shy and confidingly.] Dearest Gwendolen, there is no reason why I should make a secret of it to you. Our little county newspaper is sure to chronicle the fact next week. Mr. Ernest Worthing and I are engaged to be married.

2   Gwendolen: [Quite politely, rising.] My darling Cecily, I think there must be some slight error. Mr. Ernest Worthing is engaged to me. The announcement will appear in the *Morning Post* on Saturday at the latest.

3   Cecily: [Very politely, rising.] I am afraid you must be under some misconception. Ernest proposed to me exactly ten minutes ago. [Shows diary.]

4   Gwendolen: [Examines diary through her lorgnettte carefully.] It is certainly very curious, for he asked me to be his wife yesterday afternoon at 5:30. If you would care to verify the incident, pray do so. [Produces diary of her own.] I never travel without my diary. One should always have something sensational to read in the train. I am so sorry, dear Cecily, if it is any disappointment to you, but I am afraid I have the prior claim.

5   Cecily: It would distress me more than I can tell you, dear Gwendolen, if it caused you any mental or physical anguish, but I feel bound to point out that since Ernest proposed to you he clearly has changed his mind.

6   Gwendolen: [Meditatively.] If the poor fellow has been entrapped into any foolish promise I shall consider it my duty to rescue him at once, and with a firm hand.

7   Cecily: [Thoughtfully and sadly.] Whatever unfortunate entanglement my dear boy may have got into, I will never reproach him with it after we are married.

8   Gwendolen: Do you allude to me, Miss Cardew, as an entanglement? You are presumptuous. On an occasion of this kind it becomes more than a moral duty to speak one's mind. It becomes a pleasure.

9   Cecily: Do you suggest, Miss Fairfax, that I entrapped Ernest into an engagement? How dare you? This is no time for wearing the shallow mask of manners. When I see a spade I call it a spade.

10   Gwendolen: [Satirically.] I am glad to say that I have never seen a spade. It is obvious that our social spheres have been widely different.

11   [Enter Merriman, followed by the footman. He carries a salver, table cloth, and plate stand. Cecily is about to retort. The presence of the servants exercises a restraining influence, under which both girls chafe.]

12   Merriman: Shall I lay tea here as usual, Miss?

13   Cecily: [Sternly, in a calm voice.] Yes, as usual. [Merriman begins to clear table and lay cloth. A long pause. Cecily and Gwendolen glare at each other.]

14   Gwendolen: Are there many interesting walks in the vicinity, Miss Cardew?

15   Cecily: Oh! yes! a great many. From the top of one of the hills quite close one can see five counties.

16   Gwendolen: Five counties! I don't think I should like that; I hate crowds.

17   Cecily: [Sweetly.] I suppose that is why you live in town? [Gwendolen bites her lip, and beats her foot nervously with her parasol.]

18   Gwendolen: [Looking round.] Quite a well-kept garden this is, Miss Cardew.

19   Cecily: So glad you like it, Miss Fairfax.

20   Gwendolen: I had no idea there were any flowers in the country.

21   Cecily: Oh, flowers are as common here, Miss Fairfax, as people are in London.

22   Gwendolen: Personally I cannot understand how anybody manages to exist in the country, if anybody who is anybody does. The country always bores me to death.

23   Cecily: Ah! This is what the newspapers call agricultural depression, is it not? I believe the aristocracy are suffering very much from it just at present. It is almost an epidemic amongst them, I have been told. May I offer you some tea, Miss Fairfax?

24   Gwendolen: [With elaborate politeness.] Thank you. [Aside.] Detestable girl! But I require tea!

25   Cecily: [Sweetly.] Sugar?

26   Gwendolen: [Superciliously.] No, thank you. Sugar is not fashionable any more. [Cecily looks angrily at her, takes up the tongs and puts four lumps of sugar into the cup.]

27   Cecily: [Severely.] Cake or bread and butter?

28   Gwendolen: [In a bored manner.] Bread and butter, please. Cake is rarely seen at the best houses nowadays.

29   Cecily: [Cuts a very large slice of cake, and puts it on the tray.] Hand that to Miss Fairfax.

30   [Merriman does so, and goes out with footman. Gwendolen drinks the tea and makes a grimace. Puts down cup at once, reaches out her hand to the bread and butter, looks at it, and finds it is cake. Rises in indignation.]

31   Gwendolen: You have filled my tea with lumps of sugar, and though I asked most distinctly for bread and butter, you have given me cake. I am known for the gentleness of my disposition, and the extraordinary sweetness of my nature, but I warn you, Miss Cardew, you may go too far.

32   Cecily: [Rising.] To save my poor, innocent, trusting boy from the machinations of any other girl there are no lengths to which I would not go.

33   Gwendolen: From the moment I saw you I distrusted you. I felt that you were false and deceitful. I am never deceived in such matters. My first impressions of people are invariably right.

34   Cecily: It seems to me, Miss Fairfax, that I am trespassing on your valuable time. No doubt you have many other calls of a similar character to make in the neighborhood.

5.   Which of the following happened second?
    (A)   Cecily believes she is taking up Gwendolen's time.
    (B)   Gwendolen says Ernest proposed to her.
    (C)   Cecily says Ernest proposed to her.
    (D)   The wedding announcement will be in the *Morning Post*.

6.   Based on the excerpt, which of the following best characterizes Ernest?
    (A)   Faithful
    (B)   Bashful
    (C)   Forthright
    (D)   Deceptive

Executive Order 10924: Establishment of the Peace Corps. (1961)

The founding of the Peace Corps is one of President John F. Kennedy's most enduring legacies.

7. Choose one.
   (A) Yet it got his start in a fortuitous and unexpected moment. Kennedy, arriving late to speak to students at the University of Michigan on October 14, 1960, found himself thronged by a crowd of 10,000 students at 2 o'clock in the morning.
   (B) Yet it got its start in a fortuitous and unexpected moment. Kennedy, arriving late to speak to students at the University of Michigan on October 14, 1960, found himself thronged by a crowd of 10,000 students at 2 o'clock in the morning.
   (C) Yet it got it's start in a fortuitous and unexpected moment. Kennedy, arriving late to speak to students at the University of Michigan on October 14, 1960, found himself thronged by a crowd of 10,000 students at 2 o'clock in the morning.

Speaking extemporaneously, the Presidential candidate challenged American youth to devote a part of their lives to living and working in Asia, Africa, and Latin America. Would students back his effort to form a Peace Corps? Their response was immediate: Within weeks, students organized a petition drive and gathered 1,000 signatures in support of the idea. Several hundred others pledged to serve. Enthusiastic letters poured into Democratic headquarters. This response was crucial to Kennedy's decision to make the founding of a Peace Corps a priority. Since then, more than 168,000 citizens of all ages and backgrounds have worked in more than 130 countries throughout the world as volunteers in such fields as health, teaching, agriculture, urban planning, skilled trades, forestry, sanitation, and technology.

8. Choose one.
   (A) By 1960. Two bills were introduced in Congress that were the direct forerunners of the Peace Corps.
   (B) By 1960 two bills was introduced in Congress that were the direct forerunners of the Peace Corps.
   (C) By 1960 two bills were introduced in Congress that were the direct forerunners of the Peace Corps.

Representative Henry S. Reuss of Wisconsin proposed that the Government study the idea, and Senator Hubert Humphrey of Minnesota asked for the establishment of a Peace Corps itself. These bills were not likely to pass Congress at the time, but they caught the attention of then-Senator Kennedy for several important reasons. In contrast to previous administrations, Kennedy foresaw a "New Frontier" inspired by Roosevelt's New Deal. The New Frontier envisioned programs to fight poverty, help cities, and expand governmental benefits to a wide array of Americans. In foreign affairs, Kennedy was also more of an activist than his predecessor. He viewed the Presidency as "the vital center of action in our whole scheme of government." Concerned by what was then perceived to be the global threat of communism, Kennedy looked for creative as well as military solutions. He was eager to revitalize our program of economic aid and to counter negative images of the "Ugly American" and Yankee imperialism. He believed that sending idealistic Americans abroad to work at the grass-roots level would spread American goodwill into the Third World and help stem the growth of communism there.

Kennedy lost no time in actualizing his dream for a Peace Corps. Between his election and inauguration, he ordered Sargent Shriver, his brother-in-law, to do a feasibility study. Shriver remembered, "We received more letters from people offering to work in or to volunteer for the Peace Corps, which did not then exist, than for all other existing agencies." Within two months of taking office, Kennedy issued an Executive order establishing the Peace Corps within the State Department, using funds from mutual security appropriations. Shriver, as head of the new agency, assured its success by his fervent idealism and his willingness to improvise and take action. But to have permanency and eventual autonomy, the Peace Corps would have to be approved and funded by Congress. In September 1961, the 87th Congress passed Public Law 87-293 establishing a Peace Corps. By this time, because of Kennedy's Executive order and Shriver's leadership, Peace Corps volunteers were already in the field.

Answers and Explanations

1. **(B)** The passage is not giving a full introduction of the characters but explaining the dynamic of relationships and how characters feel about one another, effectively "setting the stage" for complications, indicating that this is part of the rising action.

2. **(B)** The passage indicates that Mrs. Gallup was a "dream of loveliness" and he (the speaker) was tongue-tied in her presence, which indicates he is in love.

3. **(B)** The subsequent information in the sentence all has to do with physical instability, so *trembled* would be the best answer.

4. **(C)** The first sentence is highly descriptive, and the reader should be able to imagine it.

5. **(B)** Reviewing the sequence of events, Cecily first says Ernest has proposed to her and then Gwendolyn says the same about herself.

6. **(D)** Ernest has made both women feel like he loved them exclusively, making him deceptive.

7. **(B)** Option A lacks agreement between *its* and *his.* Option C incorrectly uses *it's* which is a contraction for *it is.*

8. **(C)** Option A incorrectly has a period after 1960. Option B lacks agreement between *two* and *was.*

Reading

The GED® test evaluates your ability to read, interpret, and respond to a variety of literary and informational texts. The length of the texts will range from 400 to 900 words and have 6 to 8 questions each. Several different question types will be used to evaluate your literacy skills in Reasoning Through Language Arts, Reading:

→ **MULTIPLE CHOICE**
→ **FILL IN THE BLANK**
→ **DRAG AND DROP**
→ **SHORT ANSWER**
→ **EXTENDED RESPONSE**

The following skills will be covered in this unit:

Lesson 1: Identifying Main Ideas and Supporting Details

Lesson 2: Summarizing Details and Ideas

Lesson 3: Drawing Conclusions and Making Generalizations

Lesson 4: Making Inferences and Assumptions

Lesson 5: Analyzing Language

Lesson 6: Identifying Plot Elements

Lesson 7: Analyzing Relationships of Ideas

The 2014 GED® test and the Barron's *How to Prepare for the GED® Test* book are aligned with the Common Core Learning Standards. The adoption of these standards is an attempt to set nationwide standards by grade level so that high school graduates will have skills that will enable them to succeed in college, postsecondary education, and the workplace. These standards are called the College and Career Readiness Anchor Standards.

Here is an excerpt from the Common Core Learning Standards with which the test is aligned.

COLLEGE AND CAREER READINESS ANCHOR STANDARDS FOR READING

KEY IDEAS AND DETAILS

1. Read closely to determine what the text says explicitly and to make logical inferences from it; cite specific textual evidence when writing or speaking to support conclusions drawn from the text.

2. Determine central ideas or themes of a text and analyze their development; summarize the key supporting details and ideas.

3. Analyze how and why individuals, events, and ideas develop and interact over the course of a text.

CRAFT AND STRUCTURE

4. Interpret words and phrases as they are used in a text, including determining technical, connotative, and figurative meanings, and analyze how specific word choices shape meaning or tone.

5. Analyze the structure of texts, including how specific sentences, paragraphs, and larger portions of the text (e.g., a section, chapter, scene, or stanza) relate to each other and the whole.

6. Assess how point of view or purpose shapes the content and style of a text.

INTEGRATION OF KNOWLEDGE AND IDEAS

7. Integrate and evaluate content presented in diverse formats and media, including visually and quantitatively, as well as in words.

8. Delineate and evaluate the argument and specific claims in a text, including the validity of the reasoning as well as the relevance and sufficiency of the evidence.

9. Analyze how two or more texts address similar themes or topics in order to build knowledge or to compare the approaches the authors take.

RANGE OF READING AND LEVEL OF TEXT COMPLEXITY

10. Read and comprehend complex literary and informational texts independently and proficiently.

RESPONDING TO LITERATURE

11. Respond to literature by employing knowledge of literary language, textual features, and forms to read and comprehend, reflect upon, and interpret literary texts from a variety of genres and a wide spectrum of American and world cultures.

LESSON 1: IDENTIFYING MAIN IDEAS AND SUPPORTING DETAILS

Main Idea

When reading literary and informational texts, keep in mind that the author has written the passage for a reason and that each section of the passage has a purpose. In general, the passages you encounter on the GED® test will have a particular idea that the author is trying to convey; this is called the central or main idea.

WHERE IS THE MAIN IDEA LOCATED?

The main idea is very often stated in the first sentence or two of a passage. However, this is not always the case. The main idea can also be stated in the middle of a passage, at the end of the passage, or even not at all, leaving the reader to determine the main idea.

Supporting Details

Authors can make claims and take positions on issues. However, if no evidence is provided to support those positions, their claims become worthless. In order to substantiate the main idea, authors use *supporting details*. A supporting detail is evidence that gives credibility to or proves the main idea.

Inferring the Main Idea

When the author does not specifically state the main idea of a paragraph or passage, the reader must put the stated and unstated pieces together and determine the main idea. This is called *inferring*. To infer the main idea, you must examine the supporting details and what the author implies. Since supporting details are the individual pieces of evidence that support a main idea, looking at what the supporting details have in common can enable you to determine the main idea. For example, an author may write about an individual who went to Costa Rica to go surfing, Montauk Point to go fishing, and Mt. Kilimanjaro to go mountain climbing. What do all these have in common? Each event took place in a very different location and involved some kind of outdoor sport. So we can infer that the main idea is the person likes to travel and enjoys outdoor activities.

 TIP

Be careful not to mistake supporting details for main ideas.

PRACTICE

READ THE FOLLOWING PASSAGE, AND ANSWER THE QUESTIONS THAT FOLLOW.

Excerpt from *Billy Budd, Sailor*
by Herman Melville

1   At sea in the old time, the execution by halter of a military sailor was generally from the fore-yard. In the present instance, for special reasons the main-yard was assigned. Under an arm of that lee-yard the prisoner was presently brought up, the Chaplain attending him. It was noted at the time and remarked upon afterwards, that in this final scene the good man evinced little or nothing of the perfunctory. Brief speech indeed he had with the condemned one, but the genuine Gospel was less on his tongue than in

his aspect and manner towards him. The final preparations personal to the latter being speedily brought to an end by two boatswain's mates, the consummation impended. Billy stood facing aft. At the penultimate moment, his words, his only ones, words wholly unobstructed in the utterance were these—"God bless Captain Vere!" Syllables so unanticipated coming from one with the ignominious hemp about his neck—a conventional felon's benediction directed aft towards the quarters of honor; syllables too delivered in the clear melody of a singing-bird on the point of launching from the twig, had a phenomenal effect, not unenhanced by the rare personal beauty of the young sailor spiritualized now thro' late experiences so poignantly profound.

2   Without volition as it were, as if indeed the ship's populace were but the vehicles of some vocal current electric, with one voice from alow and aloft came a resonant sympathetic echo—"God bless Captain Vere!" And yet at that instant Billy alone must have been in their hearts, even as he was in their eyes.

3   At the pronounced words and the spontaneous echo that voluminously rebounded them, Captain Vere, either thro' stoic self-control or a sort of momentary paralysis induced by emotional shock, stood erectly rigid as a musket in the ship-armorer's rack.

4   The hull deliberately recovering from the periodic roll to leeward was just regaining an even keel, when the last signal, a preconcerted dumb one, was given. At the same moment it chanced that the vapory fleece hanging low in the East, was shot thro' with a soft glory as of the fleece of the Lamb of God seen in mystical vision, and simultaneously therewith, watched by the wedged mass of upturned faces, Billy ascended; and, ascending, took the full rose of the dawn.

5   In the pinioned figure, arrived at the yard-end, to the wonder of all no motion was apparent, none save that created by the ship's motion, in moderate weather so majestic in a great ship ponderously cannoned.

1. What is the main idea of the passage?
    (A) A sailor is being put to death.
    (B) The ship was rocking.
    (C) The people on the ship were the vehicles of some vocal current.
    (D) The shipmates were celebrating.

2. Based on its context, what is the best definition for the word "hull" in the fourth paragraph?
    (A) The outside of a fruit
    (B) To drag something
    (C) The deck
    (D) The main part of a ship

Answers and Explanations

1. **(A)** The entire passage describes the moments leading up to the execution of a sailor.

2. **(D)** This portion of the story takes place on a ship. The passage indicates that the ship regained "even keel," which is a nautical term. No evidence is provided to support options A, B, or C.

QUESTIONS 1 AND 2 REFER TO THE FOLLOWING PASSAGE:

Excerpt from *The Adventures of Tom Sawyer*
by Mark Twain

1   But Tom's energy did not last. He began to think of the fun he had planned for this day, and his sorrows multiplied. Soon the free boys would come tripping along on all sorts of delicious expeditions, and they would make a world of fun of him for having to work—the very thought of it burnt him like fire. He got out his worldly wealth and examined it—bits of toys, marbles, and trash; enough to buy an exchange of WORK, maybe, but not half enough to buy so much as half an hour of pure freedom. So he returned his straitened means to his pocket, and gave up the idea of trying to buy the boys. At this dark and hopeless moment an inspiration burst upon him! Nothing less than a great, magnificent inspiration.

2   He took up his brush and went tranquilly to work. Ben Rogers hove in sight presently—the very boy, of all boys, whose ridicule he had been dreading. Ben's gait was the hop-skip-and-jump—proof enough that his heart was light and his anticipations high. He was eating an apple, and giving a long, melodious whoop, at intervals, followed by a deep-toned ding-dong-dong, ding-dong-dong, for he was personating a steamboat. As he drew near, he slackened speed, took the middle of the street, leaned far over to starboard and rounded to ponderously and with laborious pomp and circumstance—for he was personating the Big Missouri, and considered himself to be drawing nine feet of water. He was boat and captain and engine-bells combined, so he had to imagine himself standing on his own hurricane-deck giving the orders and executing them:

3   "Stop her, sir! Ting-a-ling-ling!" The headway ran almost out, and he drew up slowly toward the sidewalk.

4   "Ship up to back! Ting-a-ling-ling!" His arms straightened and stiffened down his sides.

5   "Set her back on the stabboard! Ting-a-ling-ling! Chow! ch-chow-wow! Chow!" His right hand, mean-time, describing stately circles—for it was representing a forty-foot wheel.

6   "Let her go back on the labboard! Ting-a-ling-ling! Chow-ch-chow-chow!" The left hand began to describe circles.

7   "Stop the stabboard! Ting-a-ling-ling! Stop the labboard! Come ahead on the stabboard! Stop her! Let your outside turn over slow! Ting-a-ling-ling! Chow-ow-ow! Get out that head-line! LIVELY now! Come—out with your spring-line—what's you about there! Take a turn round that stump with the bight of it! Stand by that stage, now—let her go! Done with the engines, sir! Ting-a-ling-ling! SH'T! S'H'T! SH'T!" (trying the gauge-cocks).

8   Tom went on whitewashing—paid no attention to the steamboat. Ben stared a moment and then said: "Hi-YI! YOU'RE up a stump, ain't you!"

9   No answer. Tom surveyed his last touch with the eye of an artist, then he gave his

brush another gentle sweep and surveyed the result, as before. Ben ranged up alongside of him. Tom's mouth watered for the apple, but he stuck to his work. Ben said:

10   "Hello, old chap, you got to work, hey?"

11   Tom wheeled suddenly and said:

12   "Why, it's you, Ben! I warn't noticing."

13   "Say—I'm going in a-swimming, I am. Don't you wish you could? But of course you'd druther WORK—wouldn't you? Course you would!"

14   Tom contemplated the boy a bit, and said:

15   "What do you call work?"

16   "Why, ain't THAT work?"

17   Tom resumed his whitewashing, and answered carelessly:

18   "Well, maybe it is, and maybe it ain't. All I know, is, it suits Tom Sawyer."

1. What literary element is used when Twain writes "Ting-a-ling-ling!"?
   (A) Metaphor
   (B) Onomatopoeia
   (C) Assonance
   (D) Repetition

2. What is the main idea in the first paragraph?
   (A) Tom was determined.
   (B) Tom became less focused.
   (C) Work was not where Tom wanted to be.
   (D) Work made Tom feel productive.

Answers and Explanations

1. **(B)** Onomatopoeia is when a word is meant to sound like the noise it identifies.

2. **(C)** Tom had plans for the day, and they did not including working.

Summarizing

We've all been asked, "What did you do on your vacation?," "What happened in the movie?," or "What was that book about?" When asked these questions, we usually don't reiterate every word that was said and recount every move that was made. Instead, we recount the most important events. This is called summarizing.

WHAT GOES INTO AN EFFECTIVE SUMMARY?

When summarizing, only the most important information should be included. Minor details can be left out. For example, if you were reading an excerpt from a biography about an author, the excerpt may focus on how she was a best-selling author. It may also mention that she was left-handed. Because it was the focus of the the biography, her being a best-selling author is something you would include or look for in a summary. In contrast, being left-handed is likely nonessential and should have been left out of the summary.

The easiest way to summarize what has happened is to act like a detective and ask the following questions:

→ Who?
→ What?
→ When?
→ Where?
→ Why?
→ How?

Answering these questions will help you outline the most important information in the passage as well as help you become a better reader. The summary is defined as a short restatement of the most important ideas in the passage. So if you're able to assemble these answers into a sentence or two, you have just effectively summarized a passage.

PRACTICE

READ THE FOLLOWING PASSAGE, AND ANSWER THE QUESTIONS THAT FOLLOW.

Excerpt from *The Adventures of Sherlock Holmes*
by Sir Arthur Conan Doyle

1   To Sherlock Holmes she is always *the* woman. I have seldom heard him mention her under any other name. In his eyes she eclipses and predominates the whole of her sex. It was not that he felt any emotion akin to love for Irene Adler. All emotions, and that one particularly, were abhorrent to his cold, precise but admirably balanced mind. He was, I take it, the most perfect reasoning and observing machine that the world has seen, but as a lover he would have placed himself in a false position. He never spoke of the softer passions, save with a gibe and a sneer. They were admirable things for the observer—excellent for drawing the veil from men's motives and actions. But for the

TIP

As you read, ask yourself the 5 W's and 1 H.

trained reasoner to admit such intrusions into his own delicate and finely adjusted temperament was to introduce a distracting factor which might throw a doubt upon all his mental results. Grit in a sensitive instrument, or a crack in one of his own high-power lenses, would not be more disturbing than a strong emotion in a nature such as his. And yet there was but one woman to him, and that woman was the late Irene Adler, of dubious and questionable memory.

2   I had seen little of Holmes lately. My marriage had drifted us away from each other. My own complete happiness, and the home-centred interests which rise up around the man who first finds himself master of his own establishment, were sufficient to absorb all my attention, while Holmes, who loathed every form of society with his whole Bohemian soul, remained in our lodgings in Baker Street, buried among his old books, and alternating from week to week between cocaine and ambition, the drowsiness of the drug, and the fierce energy of his own keen nature. He was still, as ever, deeply attracted by the study of crime, and occupied his immense faculties and extraordinary powers of observation in following out those clues, and clearing up those mysteries which had been abandoned as hopeless by the official police. From time to time I heard some vague account of his doings: of his summons to Odessa in the case of the Trepoff murder, of his clearing up of the singular tragedy of the Atkinson brothers at Trincomalee, and finally of the mission which he had accomplished so delicately and successfully for the reigning family of Holland. Beyond these signs of his activity, however, which I merely shared with all the readers of the daily press, I knew little of my former friend and companion.

3   One night—it was on the twentieth of March, 1888—I was returning from a journey to a patient (for I had now returned to civil practice), when my way led me through Baker Street. As I passed the well-remembered door, which must always be associated in my mind with my wooing, and with the dark incidents of the Study in Scarlet, I was seized with a keen desire to see Holmes again, and to know how he was employing his extraordinary powers. His rooms were brilliantly lit, and, even as I looked up, I saw his tall, spare figure pass twice in a dark silhouette against the blind. He was pacing the room swiftly, eagerly, with his head sunk upon his chest and his hands clasped behind him. To me, who knew his every mood and habit, his attitude and manner told their own story. He was at work again. He had risen out of his drug-created dreams and was hot upon the scent of some new problem. I rang the bell and was shown up to the chamber which had formerly been in part my own.

1.   In the space provided, answer the following questions.

Who? _____

What? _____

When? _____

Where? _____

Why? _____

How? _____

2. Using your answers to question 1, write a paragraph summarizing the third paragraph.

_____

_____

_____

_____

READ THE FOLLOWING PASSAGE, AND ANSWER THE QUESTION THAT FOLLOWS.

Excerpt from *Bleak House*
by Charles Dickens

1   The day had brightened very much, and still brightened as we went westward. We went our way through the sunshine and the fresh air, wondering more and more at the extent of the streets, the brilliancy of the shops, the great traffic, and the crowds of people whom the pleasanter weather seemed to have brought out like many-colored flowers. By and by we began to leave the wonderful city and to proceed through suburbs which, of themselves, would have made a pretty large town in my eyes; and at last we got into a real country road again, with windmills, rick-yards, milestones, farmers' waggons, scents of old hay, swinging signs, and horse troughs: trees, fields, and hedge-rows. It was delightful to see the green landscape before us and the immense metropolis behind; and when a waggon with a train of beautiful horses, furnished with red trappings and clear-sounding bells, came by us with its music, I believe we could all three have sung to the bells, so cheerful were the influences around.

2   "The whole road has been reminding me of my namesake Whittington," said Richard, "and that waggon is the finishing touch. Halloa! What's the matter?"

3   We had stopped, and the waggon had stopped too. Its music changed as the horses came to a stand, and subsided to a gentle tinkling, except when a horse tossed his head or shook himself and sprinkled off a little shower of bell-ringing.

4   "Our postilion is looking after the waggoner," said Richard, "and the waggoner is coming back after us. Good day, friend!" The waggoner was at our coach-door. "Why, here's an extraordinary thing!" added Richard, looking closely at the man. "He has got your name, Ada, in his hat!"

5   He had all our names in his hat. Tucked within the band were three small notes—one addressed to Ada, one to Richard, one to me. These the waggoner delivered to each of us respectively, reading the name aloud first. In answer to Richard's inquiry from whom they came, he briefly answered, "Master, sir, if you please"; and putting on his hat again (which was like a soft bowl), cracked his whip, re-awakened his music, and went melodiously away.

3. Write a paragraph summarizing the passage. Make sure you include who, what, when, where, why, and how.

_____

_____

_____

_____

_____

PRACTICE

QUESTIONS 1 AND 2 REFER TO THE FOLLOWING PASSAGE:

Excerpt from "State of the Union Address" (1941)
Franklin Delano Roosevelt

1   Certainly this is no time for any of us to stop thinking about the social and economic problems which are the root cause of the social revolution which is today a supreme factor in the world.

2   For there is nothing mysterious about the foundations of a healthy and strong democracy. The basic things expected by our people of their political and economic systems are simple. They are:

3   Equality of opportunity for youth and for others. Jobs for those who can work. Security for those who need it. The ending of special privilege for the few. The preservation of civil liberties for all.

4   The enjoyment of the fruits of scientific progress in a wider and constantly rising standard of living.

5   These are the simple, basic things that must never be lost sight of in the turmoil and unbelievable complexity of our modern world. The inner and abiding strength of our economic and political systems is dependent upon the degree to which they fulfill these expectations.

6   Many subjects connected with our social economy call for immediate improvement. As examples:

7   We should bring more citizens under the coverage of old-age pensions and unemployment insurance.

8   We should widen the opportunities for adequate medical care.

9   We should plan a better system by which persons deserving or needing gainful employment may obtain it.

10   I have called for personal sacrifice. I am assured of the willingness of almost all Americans to respond to that call.

11   A part of the sacrifice means the payment of more money in taxes. In my Budget Message I shall recommend that a greater portion of this great defense program be paid for from taxation than we are paying today. No person should try, or be allowed, to get rich out of this program; and the principle of tax payments in accordance with ability to pay should be constantly before our eyes to guide our legislation.

12   If the Congress maintains these principles, the voters, putting patriotism ahead of pocketbooks, will give you their applause.

13   In the future days, which we seek to make secure, we look forward to a world founded upon four essential human freedoms.

14   The first is freedom of speech and expression—everywhere in the world.

15   The second is freedom of every person to worship God in his own way—everywhere in the world.

16   The third is freedom from want—which, translated into world terms, means economic understandings which will secure to every nation a healthy peacetime life for its inhabitants—everywhere in the world.

17   The fourth is freedom from fear—which, translated into world terms, means a world-wide reduction of armaments to such a point and in such a thorough fashion that no nation will be in a position to commit an act of physical aggression against any neighbor—anywhere in the world.

18   That is no vision of a distant millennium. It is a definite basis for a kind of world attainable in our own time and generation. That kind of world is the very antithesis of the so-called new order of tyranny which the dictators seek to create with the crash of a bomb.

19   To that new order we oppose the greater conception—the moral order. A good society is able to face schemes of world domination and foreign revolutions alike without fear.

20   Since the beginning of our American history, we have been engaged in change—in a perpetual peaceful revolution—a revolution which goes on steadily, quietly adjusting itself to changing conditions—without the concentration camp or the quick-lime in the ditch. The world order which we seek is the cooperation of free countries, working together in a friendly, civilized society.

21   This nation has placed its destiny in the hands and heads and hearts of its millions of free men and women; and its faith in freedom under the guidance of God. Freedom means the supremacy of human rights everywhere. Our support goes to those who struggle to gain those rights or keep them. Our strength is our unity of purpose. To that high concept there can be no end save victory.

Source: ourdocuments.gov

1. Which of the following summarizes the speech?
   (A) There is much to be done to improve the economy.
   (B) We are enjoying a time of great prosperity.
   (C) A revolution is inevitable.
   (D) Only God can change the country's destiny.

2. All of the following are things that Americans should expect EXCEPT:
   (A) Free medical care
   (B) Old-age insurance
   (C) Unemployment insurance
   (D) The fruits of science

Answers and Explanations

1. **(A)** President Roosevelt outlined the various sacrifices all would have to make.

2. **(A)** President Roosevelt indicated that Americans should expect adequate health care, not free health care.

LESSON 3: DRAWING CONCLUSIONS AND MAKING GENERALIZATIONS

Drawing Conclusions

To draw a conclusion, you must consider the facts provided and then judge or decide what the information means. To keep with the theme of solving a crime, a detective looks for evidence. Once he or she has assembled a good deal of evidence, the detective may be able to come to a conclusion about what happened or who perpetrated the crime.

Making Generalizations

When a broad statement is made about a group, this is called a generalization. A generalization suggests that all group members share a certain common trait or characteristic.

PRACTICE

READ THE FOLLOWING PASSAGE, AND ANSWER THE QUESTION THAT FOLLOWS.

Excerpt from *Metamorphosis*
by Franz Kafka
Translated by David Wyllie

1   One morning, when Gregor Samsa woke from troubled dreams, he found himself transformed in his bed into a horrible vermin. He lay on his armor-like back, and if he lifted his head a little he could see his brown belly, slightly domed and divided by arches into stiff sections. The bedding was hardly able to cover it and seemed ready to slide off any moment. His many legs, pitifully thin compared with the size of the rest of him, waved about helplessly as he looked.

2   "What's happened to me?" he thought. It wasn't a dream. His room, a proper human room although a little too small, lay peacefully between its four familiar walls. A collection of textile samples lay spread out on the table—Samsa was a traveling salesman—and above it there hung a picture that he had recently cut out of an illustrated magazine and housed in a nice, gilded frame. It showed a lady fitted out with a fur hat and fur boa who sat upright, raising a heavy fur muff that covered the whole of her lower arm towards the viewer.

3   Gregor then turned to look out the window at the dull weather. Drops of rain could be heard hitting the pane, which made him feel quite sad. "How about if I sleep a little bit longer and forget all this nonsense", he thought, but that was something he was unable to do because he was used to sleeping on his right, and in his present state couldn't get into that position. However hard he threw himself onto his right, he always rolled back to where he was. He must have tried it a hundred times, shut his eyes so that he wouldn't have to look at the floundering legs, and only stopped when he began to feel a mild, dull pain there that he had never felt before.

1. What conclusion can be drawn from the passage?

_____

_____

_____

_____

_____

Answer and Explanation

Samsa had turned into a turtle or tortoise. The evidence presented, such as "armor-like back" indicate a "vermin" like a turtle.

PRACTICE

QUESTIONS 1 AND 2 REFER TO THE FOLLOWING PASSAGE:

Excerpt from George Washington's "Farewell Address" (1796)

1   Against the insidious wiles of foreign influence (I conjure you to believe me, fellow-citizens) the jealousy of a free people ought to be constantly awake, since history and experience prove that foreign influence is one of the most baneful foes of republican government. But that jealousy to be useful must be impartial; else it becomes the instrument of the very influence to be avoided, instead of a defense against it. Excessive partiality for one foreign nation and excessive dislike of another cause those whom they actuate to see danger only on one side, and serve to veil and even second the arts of influence on the other. Real patriots who may resist the intrigues of the favorite are liable to become suspected and odious, while its tools and dupes usurp the applause and confidence of the people, to surrender their interests.

2   The great rule of conduct for us in regard to foreign nations is in extending our commercial relations, to have with them as little political connection as possible. So far as we have already formed engagements, let them be fulfilled with perfect good faith. Here let us stop. Europe has a set of primary interests, which to us have none; or a very remote relation. Hence she must be engaged in frequent controversies, the causes of which are essentially foreign to our concerns. Hence, therefore, it must be unwise in us to implicate ourselves by artificial ties in the ordinary vicissitudes of her politics, or the ordinary combinations and collisions of her friendships or enmities.

3   Our detached and distant situation invites and enables us to pursue a different course. If we remain one people under an efficient government, the period is not far off when we may defy material injury from external annoyance; when we may take such an attitude as will cause the neutrality we may at any time resolve upon to be scrupulously respected; when belligerent nations, under the impossibility of making acquisitions

upon us, will not lightly hazard the giving us provocation; when we may choose peace or war, as our interest, guided by justice, shall counsel.

4   Why forego the advantages of so peculiar a situation? Why quit our own to stand upon foreign ground? Why, by interweaving our destiny with that of any part of Europe, entangle our peace and prosperity in the toils of European ambition, rivalship, interest, humor or caprice?

5   It is our true policy to steer clear of permanent alliances with any portion of the foreign world; so far, I mean, as we are now at liberty to do it; for let me not be understood as capable of patronizing infidelity to existing engagements. I hold the maxim no less applicable to public than to private affairs, that honesty is always the best policy. I repeat it, therefore, let those engagements be observed in their genuine sense. But, in my opinion, it is unnecessary and would be unwise to extend them.

6   Taking care always to keep ourselves by suitable establishments on a respectable defensive posture, we may safely trust to temporary alliances for extraordinary emergencies.

Source: ourdocuments.gov

1. What can be concluded from the second paragraph?
    (A) America should increase its imports and exports.
    (B) America should align politically with its neighbors.
    (C) We should attempt to quell the controversies in Europe.
    (D) America should subscribe to isolationism.

2. According to the passage, America should be most concerned with _____.

Answers and Explanations

1. **(A)** Washington suggested we expand our commercial relationships, which would be imports and exports.

2. The best word to complete the sentence would be "itself," "America," or another word with a similar meaning.

Inferences

Making an inference involves analyzing the information you are given directly or indirectly and drawing conclusions based on that information. You must often make inferences when an author does not clearly state all of the information directly.

Assumptions

An author does not always need to define everything that he or she is writing about because it is assumed that the reader already knows something about the topic being discussed. For example, if a character in a story traveled to Chihuahua, the author would likely indicate that this is a city in Mexico because the reader may not have heard of that city. However, if a character went to a pet store and bought a Chihuahua, chances are the author would not have to indicate that a Chihuahua is a type of dog because most people would know this. The author assumes the reader knows this and therefore omits the definition.

PRACTICE

READ THE FOLLOWING PASSAGE, AND ANSWER THE QUESTION THAT FOLLOWS.

Excerpt from *Fathers and Children*
by Ivan Turgenev

1 "Well, Piotr, not in sight yet?" was the question asked on May the 20th, 1859, by a gentleman of a little over forty, in a dusty coat and checked trousers, who came out without his hat on to the low steps of the posting station at S——. He was addressing his servant, a chubby young fellow, with whitish down on his chin, and little, lack-luster eyes.

2 The servant, in whom everything—the turquoise ring in his ear, the streaky hair plastered with grease, and the civility of his movements—indicated a man of the new, improved generation, glanced with an air of indulgence along the road, and made answer:

3 "No, sir; not in sight."

4 "Not in sight?" repeated his master.

5 "No, sir," responded the man a second time.

6 His master sighed, and sat down on a little bench. We will introduce him to the reader while he sits, his feet tucked under him, gazing thoughtfully round.

7 His name was Nikolai Petrovitch Kirsanov. He had, twelve miles from the posting station, a fine property of two hundred souls, or, as he expressed it—since he had arranged the division of his land with the peasants, and started "a farm"—of nearly five thousand acres. His father, a general in the army, who served in 1812, a coarse, half-educated, but not ill-natured man, a typical Russian, had been in harness all his life, first in command of a brigade, and then of a division, and lived constantly in the provinces, where, by virtue of his rank, he played a fairly important part. Nikolai

Petrovitch was born in the south of Russia like his elder brother, Pavel, of whom more hereafter. He was educated at home till he was fourteen, surrounded by cheap tutors, free-and-easy but toadying adjutants, and all the usual regimental and staff set. His mother, one of the Kolyazin family, as a girl called Agathe, but as a general's wife Agathokleya Kuzminishna Kirsanov, was one of those military ladies who take their full share of the duties and dignities of office. She wore gorgeous caps and rustling silk dresses; in church she was the first to advance to the cross; she talked a great deal in a loud voice, let her children kiss her hand in the morning, and gave them her blessing at night—in fact, she got everything out of life she could. Nikolai Petrovitch, as a general's son—though so far from being distinguished by courage that he even deserved to be called "a funk"—was intended, like his brother Pavel, to enter the army; but he broke his leg on the very day when the news of his commission came, and, after being two months in bed, retained a slight limp to the end of his days. His father gave him up as a bad job, and let him go into the civil service. He took him to Petersburg directly he was eighteen, and placed him in the university. His brother happened about the same time to be made an officer in the Guards. The young men started living together in one set of rooms, under the remote supervision of a cousin on their mother's side, Ilya Kolyazin, an official of high rank. Their father returned to his division and his wife, and only rarely sent his sons large sheets of grey paper, scrawled over in a bold clerkly hand. At the bottom of these sheets stood in letters, enclosed carefully in scroll-work, the words, "Piotr Kirsanov, General-Major."

1. In the last paragraph, Turgenev wrote, "His father, a general in the army, who served in 1812, a coarse, half-educated, but not ill-natured man, a typical Russian, had been in harness all his life, first in command of a brigade, and then of a division, and lived constantly in the provinces, where, by virtue of his rank, he played a fairly important part."

   What does the author assume the reader understands?
   (A) There was a riff between him and his father.
   (B) There is a connection between military rank and importance.
   (C) His father is half-educated.
   (D) His father was typical.

Answer and Explanation

1. **(B)** Although the author doesn't specifically say that there is a connection between importance and military rank, the proximity of the two statements suggests a connection. Options C and D are incorrect. They are expressly stated in the selection. Option A is incorrect. No evidence is provided in the selection to support this.

PRACTICE

QUESTION 1 REFERS TO THE FOLLOWING PASSAGE:

Excerpt from *The Legend of Sleepy Hollow*
by Washington Irving

1.   In the bosom of one of those spacious coves which indent the eastern shore of the Hudson, at that broad expansion of the river denominated by the ancient Dutch navigators the Tappan Zee, and where they always prudently shortened sail and implored the protection of St. Nicholas when they crossed, there lies a small market town or rural port, which by some is called Greensburgh, but which is more generally and properly known by the name of Tarry Town. This name was given, we are told, in former days, by the good housewives of the adjacent country, from the inveterate propensity of their husbands to linger about the village tavern on market days. Be that as it may, I do not vouch for the fact, but merely advert to it, for the sake of being precise and authentic. Not far from this village, perhaps about two miles, there is a little valley or rather lap of land among high hills, which is one of the quietest places in the whole world. A small brook glides through it, with just murmur enough to lull one to repose; and the occasional whistle of a quail or tapping of a woodpecker is almost the only sound that ever breaks in upon the uniform tranquillity.

2.   I recollect that, when a stripling, my first exploit in squirrel-shooting was in a grove of tall walnut-trees that shades one side of the valley. I had wandered into it at noontime, when all nature is peculiarly quiet, and was startled by the roar of my own gun, as it broke the Sabbath stillness around and was prolonged and reverberated by the angry echoes. If ever I should wish for a retreat whither I might steal from the world and its distractions, and dream quietly away the remnant of a troubled life, I know of none more promising than this little valley.

3.   From the listless repose of the place, and the peculiar character of its inhabitants, who are descendants from the original Dutch settlers, this sequestered glen has long been known by the name of SLEEPY HOLLOW, and its rustic lads are called the Sleepy Hollow Boys throughout all the neighboring country. A drowsy, dreamy influence seems to hang over the land, and to pervade the very atmosphere. Some say that the place was bewitched by a High German doctor, during the early days of the settlement; others, that an old Indian chief, the prophet or wizard of his tribe, held his powwows there before the country was discovered by Master Hendrick Hudson. Certain it is, the place still continues under the sway of some witching power, that holds a spell over the minds of the good people, causing them to walk in a continual reverie. They are given to all kinds of marvellous beliefs, are subject to trances and visions, and frequently see strange sights, and hear music and voices in the air. The whole neighborhood abounds with local tales, haunted spots, and twilight superstitions; stars shoot and meteors glare oftener across the valley than in any other part of the country, and the nightmare, with her whole ninefold, seems to make it the favorite scene of her gambols.

1. What does the author assume the reader knows in the second paragraph?
   - (A) That walnut trees were on one side of the valley
   - (B) Where the story is taking place
   - (C) Greensburgh is also called Tarry Town
   - (D) What the Sabbath is

Answer and Explanation

1. **(D)** The author does not define the Sabbath, so it is assumed the reader knows the meaning of that word.

LESSON 5: ANALYZING LANGUAGE

Style

If we talk about style in terms of the way we dress, we talk about shoes, pants, shirts, and accessories. We can also talk about colors, patterns, and fit of those items. In other words, we're talking about all the elements of how an individual dresses. When we talk about style in terms of literature, we're looking at all the elements of an individual's writing—how he or she writes. Word choice, sentence structure, and length are indicators of style.

EXAMPLES OF STYLE

Formal—This style is not personal, may be complicated, and is used for higher forms of writing such as scholarly journals.

Informal—This style may be personal and is written more for everyday reading. An example of this is a local newspaper reporting on a parade or fair.

Technical—This style is usually used within a field of study for people who are familiar with that field such as doctors reading medical literature or information technology (IT) specialists reading something about a piece of technology.

Simple—This style is straightforward and easy to follow.

Complex—This style is more complicated than simple style and may be more difficult for someone unfamiliar with the content.

Tone

The tone of a work is very similar to tone of voice. Tone involves how something is said. If you saw a mother walking down the street with her son, and she said, "Come over here," her tone of voice would indicate if she was angry or just being cautious. In literature, the author's feelings about the subject—the tone—are conveyed through the style, literary elements, and statements about the topic being discussed.

Point of View and Purpose

The point of view and the purpose go hand in hand. An author's point of view is simply how he or she views the topic. This often comes through in the purpose. The purpose is the author's reason for writing the passage or section of the passage.

EXAMPLES

The author's purpose for writing the piece can vary. The writing can:

Inform—This type of writing is intended to provide the reader with information on a topic. This is characteristic of many newspaper articles.

Entertain—This type of writing is characteristic of fiction. The author wants the reader to gain pleasure from reading the work.

Persuade—This type of writing is intended to make the reader believe what the author is writing. This is characteristic of movie reviews, book reviews, and restaurant reviews.

Literal and Figurative Language

Authors may use both literal and figurative language in their writing. Literal language means that what is stated is actually true. In contrast, figurative language means that what is stated is not actually true. Instead, it is a way of expressing an idea. For example if someone said, "I was so startled that I jumped three feet in the air," a literal interpretation would be that the person actually jumped three feet in the air. The figurative interpretation would be that the person was very surprised.

PRACTICE

READ THE FOLLOWING PASSAGE, AND ANSWER THE QUESTIONS THAT FOLLOW.

Excerpt from *Jane Eyre*
by Charlotte Brontë

1   There was no possibility of taking a walk that day. We had been wandering, indeed, in the leafless shrubbery an hour in the morning; but since dinner (Mrs. Reed, when there was no company, dined early) the cold winter wind had brought with it clouds so [somber], and a rain so penetrating, that further out-door exercise was now out of the question.

2   I was glad of it: I never liked long walks, especially on chilly afternoons: dreadful to me was the coming home in the raw twilight, with nipped fingers and toes, and a heart saddened by the chidings of Bessie, the nurse, and humbled by the consciousness of my physical inferiority to Eliza, John, and Georgiana Reed.

3   The said Eliza, John, and Georgiana were now clustered round their mama in the drawing-room: she lay reclined on a sofa by the fireside, and with her darlings about her (for the time neither quarrelling nor crying) looked perfectly happy. Me, she had dispensed from joining the group; saying, "She regretted to be under the necessity of keeping me at a distance; but that until she heard from Bessie, and could discover by her own observation, that I was endeavoring in good earnest to acquire a more sociable and childlike disposition, a more attractive and sprightly manner—something lighter, franker, more natural, as it were—she really must exclude me from privileges intended only for contented, happy, little children."

4   "What does Bessie say I have done?" I asked.

5   "Jane, I don't like cavillers or questioners; besides, there is something truly forbidding in a child taking up her elders in that manner. Be seated somewhere; and until you can speak pleasantly, remain silent."

6   A breakfast-room adjoined the drawing-room, I slipped in there. It contained a bookcase: I soon possessed myself of a volume, taking care that it should be one stored with pictures. I mounted into the window-seat: gathering up my feet, I sat cross-legged, like a Turk; and, having drawn the red moreen curtain nearly close, I was shrined in double retirement.

7   Folds of scarlet drapery shut in my view to the right hand; to the left were the clear panes of glass, protecting, but not separating me from the drear November day. At intervals, while turning over the leaves of my book, I studied the aspect of that winter

afternoon. Afar, it offered a pale blank of mist and cloud; near a scene of wet lawn and storm-beat shrub, with ceaseless rain sweeping away wildly before a long and lamentable blast.

1. What is the tone of the first paragraph?
    (A) Eager
    (B) Subdued
    (C) Longing
    (D) Angered

2. Which literary element is used in the final paragraph?
    (A) Metaphor
    (B) Personification
    (C) Hyperbole
    (D) Imagery

Answers and Explanations

1. **(B)** She describes the clouds as "somber," indicating that the mood is subdued. Option A is incorrect as she is not excited. Option C is incorrect as she is not missing or wanting something. Option D is incorrect; no evidence suggests that she is mad at something.

2. **(D)** The author uses a detailed description so the reader can picture the scene. Option A is incorrect because no comparison is being made. Option B is incorrect because nothing inanimate is being given human characteristics. Option C is incorrect because nothing is being exaggerated.

PRACTICE

QUESTIONS 1 AND 2 REFER TO THE FOLLOWING PASSAGE:

Excerpt from "The Nose"
by Nikolai Gogol

1   On the 25th March, 18—, a very strange occurrence took place in St. Petersburg. On the Ascension Avenue there lived a barber of the name of Ivan Jakovlevitch. He had lost his family name, and on his sign-board, on which was depicted the head of a gentleman with one cheek soaped, the only inscription to be read was, "Blood-letting done here."

2   On this particular morning he awoke pretty early. Becoming aware of the smell of fresh-baked bread, he sat up a little in bed, and saw his wife, who had a special partiality for coffee, in the act of taking some fresh-baked bread out of the oven.

3   "To-day, Prasskovna Ossipovna," he said, "I do not want any coffee; I should like a fresh loaf with onions."

4   "The blockhead may eat bread only as far as I am concerned," said his wife to herself; "then I shall have a chance of getting some coffee." And she threw a loaf on the table.

5   For the sake of propriety, Ivan Jakovlevitch drew a coat over his shirt, sat down at the table, shook out some salt for himself, prepared two onions, assumed a serious expression, and began to cut the bread. After he had cut the loaf in two halves, he looked, and to his great astonishment saw something whitish sticking in it. He carefully poked round it with his knife, and felt it with his finger.

6   "Quite firmly fixed!" he murmured in his beard. "What can it be?"

7   He put in his finger, and drew out—a nose!

8   Ivan Jakovlevitch at first let his hands fall from sheer astonishment; then he rubbed his eyes and began to feel it. A nose, an actual nose; and, moreover, it seemed to be the nose of an acquaintance! Alarm and terror were depicted in Ivan's face; but these feelings were slight in comparison with the disgust which took possession of his wife.

9   "Whose nose have you cut off, you monster?" she screamed, her face red with anger. "You scoundrel! You tippler! I myself will report you to the police! Such a rascal! Many customers have told me that while you were shaving them, you held them so tight by the nose that they could hardly sit still."

10   But Ivan Jakovlevitch was more dead than alive; he saw at once that this nose could belong to no other than to Kovaloff, a member of the Municipal Committee whom he shaved every Sunday and Wednesday.

11   "Stop, Prasskovna Ossipovna! I will wrap it in a piece of cloth and place it in the corner. There it may remain for the present; later on I will take it away."

12   "No, not there! Shall I endure an amputated nose in my room? You understand nothing except how to strop a razor. You know nothing of the duties and obligations of a respectable man. You vagabond! You good-for-nothing! Am I to undertake all responsibility for you at the police-office? Ah, you soap-smearer! You blockhead! Take it away where you like, but don't let it stay under my eyes!"

1. What is the tone of the excerpt?
    (A) Patronizing
    (B) Disgusted
    (C) Bitter
    (D) Neutral

2. What is the mood of the excerpt?
    (A) Cheerful
    (B) Joyful
    (C) Morbid
    (D) Whimsical

Answers and Explanations

1. **(B)** The author's attitude toward the action is that of disgust. This is evident in the wife's response.

2. **(C)** The mood is morbid and disturbing because a nose has been cut off.

Plot

The plot of a work of literature is the sum of events that occur to create the story. Depending on whom you speak to, a plot has either 5 or 7 distinct components. The following lists the 7 components.

→ **EXPOSITION**
→ **CATALYST**
→ **RISING ACTION**
→ **CLIMAX**
→ **FALLING ACTION**
→ **RESOLUTION**
→ **CONCLUSION**

The *exposition* is the introductory part of the story, where the reader is given information about the setting and various characters. At some point, something occurs that complicates things in the story and sets the plot in motion; this is called the *catalyst*. As the plot progresses, the actions of the characters cause the excitement or tension to build; this is called the *rising action*. Tensions rise as the plot thickens and becomes more complicated. The peak of the plot and turning point of the story are called the *climax*. After the climax, the plot begins to slow down; this is called the *falling action*. Eventually, the conflict is resolved and the story is ended; these are called the *resolution* and *conclusion*.

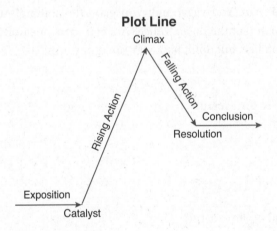

Plot Line

Theme

The theme of a piece of literature is the central idea that the author has woven into the fabric of the work. Sometimes the theme is clearly presented. At other times, the reader must read more deeply into what the author is saying in order to find the theme. For example, an author may write about the struggles a person has had over the course of his lifetime. The author may include a chapter on how he struggled in school, another about how he struggled in love, another chapter about struggling at work, and another about struggling with money. The author describes at the end of each chapter how the person always overcame the struggle.

Each chapter would have a different main idea, but the overall theme would be overcoming obstacles.

Setting

The setting encompasses all the information dealing with *when* and *where*. For example, the setting may indicate the time the story is taking place, such as the day, month, year, season, or time of day. It can also indicate the location, such as the country, state/province, city, or street. Additionally, it may include information about the environment, such as the temperature, condition of the location, sounds, and smells.

Characterization

When we talk about the attributes or characteristics of an individual, we may discuss things like demeanor, personality, and behavior. When asked to characterize someone, these are the elements about which we are being asked.

PRACTICE

READ THE FOLLOWING PASSAGE, AND ANSWER THE QUESTION THAT FOLLOWS.

Excerpt from *Pride and Prejudice*
by Jane Austen

1   Mr. Bingley was good-looking and gentlemanlike; he had a pleasant countenance, and easy, unaffected manners. His sisters were fine women, with an air of decided fashion. His brother-in-law, Mr. Hurst, merely looked the gentleman; but his friend Mr. Darcy soon drew the attention of the room by his fine, tall person, handsome features, noble mien, and the report which was in general circulation within five minutes after his entrance, of his having ten thousand a year. The gentlemen pronounced him to be a fine figure of a man, the ladies declared he was much handsomer than Mr. Bingley, and he was looked at with great admiration for about half the evening, till his manners gave a disgust which turned the tide of his popularity; for he was discovered to be proud; to be above his company, and above being pleased; and not all his large estate in Derbyshire could then save him from having a most forbidding, disagreeable countenance, and being unworthy to be compared with his friend.

2   Mr. Bingley had soon made himself acquainted with all the principal people in the room; he was lively and unreserved, danced every dance, was angry that the ball closed so early, and talked of giving one himself at Netherfield. Such amiable qualities must speak for themselves. What a contrast between him and his friend! Mr. Darcy danced only once with Mrs. Hurst and once with Miss Bingley, declined being introduced to any other lady, and spent the rest of the evening in walking about the room, speaking occasionally to one of his own party. His character was decided. He was the proudest, most disagreeable man in the world, and everybody hoped that he would never come there again. Amongst the most violent against him was Mrs. Bennet, whose dislike of his general behavior was sharpened into particular resentment by his having slighted one of her daughters.

1. How would you characterize Mr. Bingley?

Mr. Bingley is a _____ man.

Answer and Explanation

1. Answers include "social," "attractive," "polite," or any similar word.

PRACTICE

QUESTIONS 1–3 REFER TO THE FOLLOWING PASSAGE:

Excerpt from "The Ransom of Red Chief"
by O. Henry

I waited an hour and then concluded the thing was square. I slid down the tree, got the note, slipped along the fence till I struck the woods, and was back at the cave in another half an hour. I opened the note, got near the lantern and read it to Bill. It was written with a pen in a crabbed hand, and the sum and substance of it was this:

> Two Desperate Men.
>
> Gentlemen: I received your letter to-day by post, in regard to the ransom you ask for the return of my son. I think you are a little high in your demands, and I hereby make you a counter-proposition, which I am inclined to believe you will accept. You bring Johnny home and pay me two hundred and fifty dollars in cash, and I agree to take him off your hands. You had better come at night, for the neighbours believe he is lost, and I couldn't be responsible for what they would do to anybody they saw bringing him back.
>
> Very respectfully,
>
> EBENEZER DORSET.

"Great pirates of Penzance!" says I; "of all the impudent—"

But I glanced at Bill, and hesitated. He had the most appealing look in his eyes I ever saw on the face of a dumb or a talking brute.

"Sam," says he, "what's two hundred and fifty dollars, after all? We've got the money. One more night of this kid will send me to a bed in Bedlam. Besides being a thorough gentleman, I think Mr. Dorset is a spendthrift for making us such a liberal offer. You ain't going to let the chance go, are you?"

"Tell you the truth, Bill," says I, "this little he ewe lamb has somewhat got on my nerves too. We'll take him home, pay the ransom and make our get-away."

We took him home that night. We got him to go by telling him that his father had bought a silver-mounted rifle and a pair of moccasins for him, and we were going to hunt bears the next day.

It was just twelve o'clock when we knocked at Ebenezer's front door. Just at the moment when I should have been abstracting the fifteen hundred dollars from the box under the tree, according to the original proposition. Bill was counting out two hundred and fifty dollars into Dorset's hand.

When the kid found out we were going to leave him at home he started up a howl like a calliope and fastened himself as tight as a leech to Bill's leg. His father peeled him away gradually, like a porous plaster.

"How long can you hold him?" asks Bill.

"I'm not as strong as I used to be," says old Dorset, "but I think I can promise you ten minutes."

"Enough," says Bill. "In ten minutes I shall cross the Central, Southern and Middle Western States, and be legging it trippingly for the Canadian border."

And, as dark as it was, and as fat as Bill was, and as good a runner as I am, he was a good mile and a half out of Summit before I could catch up with him.

1. What is the best definition for the word *impudent* in the line immediately following the note?
   (A) Disrespectful
   (B) Funny
   (C) Tiresome
   (D) Confusing

2. What is the style of this short story?
   (A) Informal
   (B) Technical
   (C) Amusing
   (D) Serious

3. Which of the following aspects from this excerpt illustrates irony? Select all that apply.
   (A) Bill says that in ten minutes they'll be well on their way to Canada.
   (B) The kidnappers have to pay the father to take back the child.
   (C) Dorset is not as strong as he used to be.
   (D) The child who was kidnapped is torturing the kidnappers.
   (E) Mr. Dorset is a spendthrift.
   (F) The kidnappers told the child that his father had a silver-mounted rifle and a pair of moccasins.
   (G) The child held on to Bill's leg when he found out he was being brought home.

Answers and Explanations

1. **(A)** After Sam says "Great pirates of Penzance!" it is clear that he is upset because the father was disrespectful in the letter.

2. **(C)** The idea of a child being so poorly behaved that a father is able to get the kidnappers to pay him to take the child back is an outrageous scenario and is meant to be amusing.

3. **(B, D, G)** Irony is the contrast between what one expects to happen and what actually happens. Because these choices stand in direct contrast to what we would expect to happen in a kidnapping, they represent irony.

Cause and Effect

Cause and effect relationships are common in the various sections of the GED® test. A cause is an action that makes something else happen, while an effect is what happens as a result of that action. These relationships can sometimes be confusing because whether an action is a cause or an effect depends on the context. For example, let's take the scenario that Sue bumped into Chuck, Chuck bumped into the table, and the lamp fell to the floor. Sue bumping into Chuck is what caused Chuck to bump into the table, which is the effect. However, Chuck bumping into the table is what caused the lamp to fall to the floor, which is the effect. Depending on the context, Chuck bumping into the table could be either a cause or an effect.

Comparing and Contrasting

Chances are that at some point during the test, you will be asked to either compare or contrast elements of a reading. These are commonly confused terms. You must understand the difference between them. When you are asked to compare items, you will be looking for ways in which they are similar. When asked to contrast items, you will be looking for ways in which they are different. For example, if comparing apples and oranges, you may indicate that they are both fruits and are both sweet. If contrasting apples and oranges, you may indicate that apples are usually red or green while oranges live up to their name and are usually orange.

> **NOTE**
>
> **Comparing deals with similarities. Contrasting deals with differences.**

PRACTICE

READ THE FOLLOWING PASSAGE, AND ANSWER THE QUESTION THAT FOLLOWS.

Excerpt from *The True Story of My Life*
by Hans Christian Andersen

1   My life is a lovely story, happy and full of incident. If, when I was a boy, and went forth into the world poor and friendless, a good fairy had met me and said, "Choose now thy own course through life, and the object for which thou wilt strive, and then, according to the development of thy mind, and as reason requires, I will guide and defend thee to its attainment," my fate could not, even then, have been directed more happily, more prudently, or better. The history of my life will say to the world what it says to me— There is a loving God, who directs all things for the best.

2   My native land, Denmark, is a poetical land, full of popular traditions, old songs, and an eventful history, which has become bound up with that of Sweden and Norway. The Danish islands are possessed of beautiful beech woods, and corn and clover fields: they resemble gardens on a great scale. Upon one of these green islands, Funen, stands Odense, the place of my birth. Odense is called after the pagan god Odin, who, as tradition states, lived here: this place is the capital of the province, and lies twenty-two Danish miles from Copenhagen.

3   In the year 1805 there lived here, in a small mean room, a young married couple, who were extremely attached to each other; he was a shoemaker, scarcely twenty-two years old, a man of a richly gifted and truly poetical mind. His wife, a few years older than himself, was ignorant of life and of the world, but possessed a heart full of love. The young man had himself made his shoemaking bench, and the bedstead with which he began housekeeping; this bedstead he had made out of the wooden frame which had borne only a short time before the coffin of the deceased Count Trampe, as he lay in state, and the remnants of the black cloth on the wood work kept the fact still in remembrance.

4   Instead of a noble corpse, surrounded by crape and wax-lights, here lay, on the second of April, 1805, a living and weeping child,—that was myself, Hans Christian Andersen. During the first day of my existence my father is said to have sate by the bed and read aloud in Holberg, but I cried all the time. "Wilt thou go to sleep, or listen quietly?" it is reported that my father asked in joke; but I still cried on; and even in the church, when I was taken to be baptized, I cried so loudly that the preacher, who was a passionate man, said, "The young one screams like a cat!" which words my mother never forgot. A poor emigrant, Gomar, who stood as godfather, consoled her in the mean time by saying that the louder I cried as a child, all the more beautifully should I sing when I grew older.

5   Our little room, which was almost filled with the shoemaker's bench, the bed, and my crib, was the abode of my childhood; the walls, however, were covered with pictures, and over the work-bench was a cupboard containing books and songs; the little kitchen was full of shining plates and metal pans, and by means of a ladder it was possible to go out on the roof, where, in the gutters between and the neighbor's house, there stood a great chest filled with soil, my mother's sole garden, and where she grew her vegetables. In my story of the Snow Queen that garden still blooms.

1.   Based on the first paragraph, what caused Hans Christian Andersen to write fairy tales?

_____

_____

_____

_____

_____

Answer and Explanation

1.   He indicates that his life was "a lovely story, happy and full of incident" like a fairy tale.

QUESTIONS 1 AND 2 REFER TO THE FOLLOWING PASSAGE:

Excerpt from *Narrative of the Life of Frederick Douglass, An American Slave*
by Frederick Douglass

1   The plan which I adopted, and the one by which I was most successful, was that of making friends of all the little white boys whom I met in the street. As many of these as I could, I converted into teachers. With their kindly aid, obtained at different times and in different places, I finally succeeded in learning to read. When I was sent of errands, I always took my book with me, and by going through one part of my errand quickly, I found time to get a lesson before my return. I used also to carry bread with me, enough of which was always in the house, and to which I was always welcome; for I was much better off in this regard than many of the poor white children in our neighborhood. This bread I used to bestow upon the hungry little urchins, who, in return, would give me that more valuable bread of knowledge. I am strongly tempted to give the names of two or three of those little boys, as a testimonial of the gratitude and affection I bear them; but prudence forbids;—not that it would injure me, but it might embarrass them; for it is almost an unpardonable offence to teach slaves to read in this Christian country. It is enough to say of the dear little fellows, that they lived on Philpot Street, very near Durgin and Bailey's ship-yard. I used to talk this matter of slavery over with them. I would sometimes say to them, I wished I could be as free as they would be when they got to be men. "You will be free as soon as you are twenty-one, *but I am a slave for life!* Have not I as good a right to be free as you have?" These words used to trouble them; they would express for me the liveliest sympathy, and console me with the hope that something would occur by which I might be free.

2   I was now about twelve years old, and the thought of being *a slave for life* began to bear heavily upon my heart. Just about this time, I got hold of a book entitled "The Columbian Orator." Every opportunity I got, I used to read this book. Among much of other interesting matter, I found in it a dialogue between a master and his slave. The slave was represented as having run away from his master three times. The dialogue represented the conversation which took place between them, when the slave was retaken the third time. In this dialogue, the whole argument in behalf of slavery was brought forward by the master, all of which was disposed of by the slave. The slave was made to say some very smart as well as impressive things in reply to his master— things which had the desired though unexpected effect; for the conversation resulted in the voluntary emancipation of the slave on the part of the master.

3   In the same book, I met with one of Sheridan's mighty speeches on and in behalf of Catholic emancipation. These were choice documents to me. I read them over and over again with unabated interest. They gave tongue to interesting thoughts of my own soul, which had frequently flashed through my mind, and died away for want of utterance. The moral which I gained from the dialogue was the power of truth over the conscience of even a slaveholder. What I got from Sheridan was a bold denunciation of slavery, and a powerful vindication of human rights. The reading of these documents enabled me to utter my thoughts, and to meet the arguments brought forward to sustain slavery; but while they relieved me of one difficulty, they brought on another even more painful

than the one of which I was relieved. The more I read, the more I was led to abhor and detest my enslavers. I could regard them in no other light than a band of successful robbers, who had left their homes, and gone to Africa, and stolen us from our homes, and in a strange land reduced us to slavery. I loathed them as being the meanest as well as the most wicked of men. As I read and contemplated the subject, behold! that very discontentment which Master Hugh had predicted would follow my learning to read had already come, to torment and sting my soul to unutterable anguish. As I writhed under it, I would at times feel that learning to read had been a curse rather than a blessing. It had given me a view of my wretched condition, without the remedy. It opened my eyes to the horrible pit, but to no ladder upon which to get out. In moments of agony, I envied my fellow-slaves for their stupidity. I have often wished myself a beast. I preferred the condition of the meanest reptile to my own. Any thing, no matter what, to get rid of thinking! It was this everlasting thinking of my condition that tormented me. There was no getting rid of it. It was pressed upon me by every object within sight or hearing, animate or inanimate. The silver trump of freedom had roused my soul to eternal wakefulness. Freedom now appeared, to disappear no more forever. It was heard in every sound, and seen in every thing. It was ever present to torment me with a sense of my wretched condition. I saw nothing without seeing it, I heard nothing without hearing it, and felt nothing without feeling it. It looked from every star, it smiled in every calm, breathed in every wind, and moved in every storm.

1. Which of the following is a way in which Frederick Douglass stood in contrast to white boys.
   (A) Initially, they knew how to read and he didn't.
   (B) They were all friends.
   (C) They were all given money for running errands
   (D) None of them had parents.

2. The "little white boys" had a _____ effect on Frederick Douglass.

Answers and Explanations

1. **(A)** The question asks for *contrast* or *difference*; the passage states that Frederick Douglass learned to read with the white boys' help.

2. Possible answers include *positive, beneficial, good.* Douglass indicates that they were friends and he had *gratitude and affection* for them.

Although the GED® test does not have a vocabulary section per se, higher-level vocabulary words will appear in the passages. Questions will ask you to define words in context. Additionally, having a broad vocabulary is absolutely essential for fully understanding the passages you read. For these reasons, we have included a list of key words you should know.

ALLITERATION The repetition of a sound at the beginning of two or more words, such as "She sells sea shells by the sea shore."

ALLUSION A reference to someone or something well-known or commonly known.

ANALOGY An identical relationship or function.

ANTAGONIST The character who goes against the main character.

ANTONYM A word with an opposite meaning.

ASSONANCE Repetition of a vowel sound.

AUTOBIOGRAPHY A work of literature about a person's life, written by that person.

BALLAD A type of narrative poem that is usually sung.

BIOGRAPHY A work of literature about a particular person's life.

CATALYST The point in a story when an event puts the plot in motion.

CHARACTERIZATION The description of a character.

CHRONOLOGICAL ORDER The order of events based on time.

CLIMAX The turning point of the story.

COMPARE To look at similarities between things.

CONCLUSION The closing of a story.

CONFLICT Various types of struggles that characters face.

CONNOTATION The implied or associated meaning of a word.

CONTRAST To look at the difference between things.

DENOTATION The literal, dictionary meaning of a word.

DIALOGUE A coversation between two or more people.

EPIC A story that is narrated in a grand way.

EXPOSITION The introductory part of a plot.

FABLE A story with a moral.

FALLING ACTION The part of the plot when the story begins to conclude.

FATE The idea that life will play out in a certain way and nothing can be done about it.

FICTION In literature, a story that is completely made up.

FIGURATIVE Language that is not to be taken literally but, instead, symbolically.

FIRST PERSON Narration told by a person who is involved in the plot.

FLASHBACK A break in a plot to relive something in the past.

FORESHADOWING An indication of what is to come.

GENRE A particular style of literature.

HARLEM RENAISSANCE A period in the early part of the 1900s when literature, art, music, and culture flourished in Harlem.

HOMONYM A word that sounds the same as another.

HYPERBOLE Figurative language that states that something is more extreme, such as significantly larger or smaller, than it actually is.

IMAGERY Descriptive language that enables the reader to visualize a scene.

INTERNAL CONFLICT A conflict within a character.

IRONY The contrast between what is expected to happen and what actually happens.

LITERAL What actually happens as opposed to what symbolically happens.

METAPHOR A comparison of two unlike things that doesn't use the words "like" or "as."

NARRATOR The teller of a story.

NONFICTION A work of literature that describes something that actually happened.

ONOMATOPOEIA A word that is intended to imitate a sound, such as "bang."

PARABLE A short story with a lesson or moral.

PARODY A writing that is intended to imitate and mock something.

PERSONIFICATION Attributing human characteristics to something nonhuman.

PLOT The complete sequence of events in a story.

POINT OF VIEW The author's perspective.

PROSE Ordinary language.

PROTAGONIST The hero of a story.

RESOLUTION The part of the plot when the conflict is resolved.

RISING ACTION The part of the plot when tension is building.

SETTING The details about where and when something takes place.

SIMILE A comparison of unlike things using the words "like" or "as."

SOLILOQUY A monologue in which the character is speaking to himself/herself.

SYMBOL Something that stands for something else.

SYNONYM Words that have the same meaning.

THEME   The topic about which the author is writing.

THIRD PERSON   Narration told by someone who is not involved in a story.

THIRD PERSON OMNISCIENT   Narration told by someone who is not involved in a story and who can express the thoughts of the characters.

TRAGEDY   A work of literature in which the story ends badly.

TRAGIC FLAW   A character flaw that leads to the demise of the protagonist.

TRAGIC HERO   A protagonist who ultimately falls.

Review Test

DIRECTIONS: This review test contains both fiction and nonfiction passages, which you will need to analyze in order to answer the questions that follow.

QUESTIONS 1 THROUGH 7 ARE BASED ON THE FOLLOWING PASSAGE:

"Second Inaugural Address"
Abraham Lincoln

<u>Fellow Countrymen</u>

1   At this second appearing to take the oath of the presidential office, there is less occasion for an extended address than there was at the first. Then a statement, somewhat in detail, of a course to be pursued, seemed fitting and proper. Now, at the expiration of four years, during which public declarations have been constantly called forth on every point and phase of the great contest which still absorbs the attention,

and engrosses the energies of the nation, little that is new could be presented. The progress of our arms, upon which all else chiefly depends, is as well known to the public as to myself; and it is, I trust, reasonably satisfactory and encouraging to all. With high hope for the future, no prediction in regard to it is ventured.

2   On the occasion corresponding to this four years ago, all thoughts were anxiously directed to an impending civil-war. All dreaded it—all sought to avert it. While the inaugural address was being delivered from this place, devoted altogether to saving the Union without war, insurgent agents were in the city seeking to destroy it without war—seeking to dissolve the Union, and divide effects, by negotiation. Both parties deprecated war; but one of them would make war rather than let the nation survive; and the other would accept war rather than let it perish. And the war came.

3   One eighth of the whole population were colored slaves, not distributed generally over the Union, but localized in the Southern half part of it. These slaves constituted a peculiar and powerful interest. All knew that this interest was, somehow, the cause of the war. To strengthen, perpetuate, and extend this interest was the object for which the insurgents would rend the Union, even by war; while the government claimed no right to do more than to restrict the territorial enlargement of it. Neither party expected for the war, the magnitude, or the duration, which it has already attained. Neither anticipated that the cause of the conflict might cease with, or even before, the conflict itself should cease. Each looked for an easier triumph, and a result less fundamental and astounding. Both read the same Bible, and pray to the same God; and each invokes His aid against the other. It may seem strange that any men should dare to ask a just God's assistance in wringing their bread from the sweat of other men's faces; but let us judge not that we be not judged. The prayers of both could not be answered; that of neither has been answered fully. The Almighty has His own purposes. "Woe unto the world because of offences! for it must needs be that offences come; but woe to that man by whom the offence cometh!" If we shall suppose that American Slavery is one of those offences which, in the providence of God, must needs come, but which, having continued through His appointed time, He now wills to remove, and that He gives to both North and South, this terrible war, as the woe due to those by whom the offence came, shall we discern therein any departure from those divine attributes which the believers in a Living God always ascribe to Him? Fondly do we hope—fervently do we pray—that this mighty scourge of war may speedily pass away. Yet, if God wills that it continue, until all the wealth piled by the bond-man's two hundred and fifty years of unrequited toil shall be sunk, and until every drop of blood drawn with the lash, shall be paid by another drawn with the sword, as was said f[our] three thousand years ago, so still it must be said "the judgments of the Lord, are true and righteous altogether."

4   With malice toward none; with charity for all; with firmness in the right, as God gives us to see the right, let us strive on to finish the work we are in; to bind up the nation's wounds; to care for him who shall have borne the battle, and for his widow, and his orphan—to do all which may achieve and cherish a just, and a lasting peace, among ourselves, and with all nations.

Source: ourdocuments.gov

1. What is the central idea expressed in this passage?

   _____

   _____

   _____

   _____

   _____

2. What is the central idea of the second paragraph?
   (A) One side would enter war to save the country.
   (B) Neither side wanted war; however, both would enter war.
   (C) War was inevitable.
   (D) Both sides hated war.

3. Based on President Lincoln's speech, he can be characterized as _____.

4. In the third paragraph, what can be further inferred about the cause of the war?
   (A) Few Northerners supported the war because all of the slaves were in the South.
   (B) The country was divided in reference to slavery.
   (C) Generally, people in the South supported the abolition of slavery.
   (D) The government had no right to declare war.

5. In the third paragraph, Lincoln indicated that 1/8 of the population was enslaved African Americans. What is his statement suggesting?
   (A) The population was a small minority.
   (B) This constituted a large portion of the population and should be taken into consideration.
   (C) This constituted a majority and could not be ignored.
   (D) There was little that could be done as the population was in the South.

6. Based on its context, which of the following is the best definition of the word "malice" in the fourth paragraph?
   (A) Evil intention
   (B) Indescribable feelings
   (C) Positive intentions
   (D) Mild dislike

7. What does the last paragraph suggest Lincoln valued?
   (A) Peace and perseverance
   (B) Capitalism and a strong military
   (C) Organized religion and personal gain
   (D) Families and adoption

QUESTIONS 8 THROUGH 13 ARE BASED ON THE FOLLOWING PASSAGE:

President John F. Kennedy's Inaugural Address (1961)

1   So let us begin anew—remembering on both sides that civility is not a sign of weakness, and sincerity is always subject to proof. Let us never negotiate out of fear. But let us never fear to negotiate.

2   Let both sides explore what problems unite us instead of belaboring those problems which divide us.

3   Let both sides, for the first time, formulate serious and precise proposals for the inspection and control of arms—and bring the absolute power to destroy other nations under the absolute control of all nations.

4   Let both sides seek to invoke the wonders of science instead of its terrors. Together let us explore the stars, conquer the deserts, eradicate disease, tap the ocean depths and encourage the arts and commerce.

5   Let both sides unite to heed in all corners of the earth the command of Isaiah—to "undo the heavy burdens . . . (and) let the oppressed go free."

6   And if a beachhead of cooperation may push back the jungle of suspicion, let both sides join in creating a new endeavor, not a new balance of power, but a new world of law, where the strong are just and the weak secure and the peace preserved.

7   All this will not be finished in the first one hundred days. Nor will it be finished in the first one thousand days, nor in the life of this Administration, nor even perhaps in our lifetime on this planet. But let us begin.

8   In your hands, my fellow citizens, more than mine, will rest the final success or failure of our course. Since this country was founded, each generation of Americans has been summoned to give testimony to its national loyalty. The graves of young Americans who answered the call to service surround the globe.

9   Now the trumpet summons us again—not as a call to bear arms, though arms we need—not as a call to battle, though embattled we are— but a call to bear the burden of a long twilight struggle, year in and year out, "rejoicing in hope, patient in tribulation"—a struggle against the common enemies of man: tyranny, poverty, disease and war itself.

10   Can we forge against these enemies a grand and global alliance, North and South, East and West, that can assure a more fruitful life for all mankind? Will you join in that historic effort?

11   In the long history of the world, only a few generations have been granted the role of defending freedom in its hour of maximum danger. I do not shrink from this responsibility—I welcome it. I do not believe that any of us would exchange places with any other people or any other generation. The energy, the faith, the devotion which we bring to this endeavor will light our country and all who serve it—and the glow from that fire can truly light the world.

12   And so, my fellow Americans: ask not what your country can do for you—ask what you can do for your country.

13   My fellow citizens of the world: ask not what America will do for you, but what together we can do for the freedom of man.

14   Finally, whether you are citizens of America or citizens of the world, ask of us here the same high standards of strength and sacrifice which we ask of you. With a good conscience our only sure reward, with history the final judge of our deeds, let us go forth to lead the land we love, asking His blessing and His help, but knowing that here on earth God's work must truly be our own.

Source: ourdocuments.gov

8. What is the central idea of President Kennedy's speech?
   - (A) We must all work together to support our country.
   - (B) Few generations have faced such danger.
   - (C) The country should have a fresh start.
   - (D) All must go to battle.

9. What can be inferred by the statement, "In the long history of the world, only a few generations have been granted the role of defending freedom in its hour of maximum danger."
   - (A) Democracy is the best type of government.
   - (B) There have been few generations of people.
   - (C) The history of the world is longer than most people think.
   - (D) If people don't defend freedom, it may be lost.

10. President Kennedy said, "Together let us explore the stars, conquer the deserts, eradicate disease, tap the ocean depths and encourage the arts and commerce." All of the following would fit into those categories except:
    - (A) Funding of programs that assist endangered species
    - (B) Establishing free trade agreements
    - (C) Increasing military funding to support space exploration
    - (D) Offering college scholarships to students in the arts

11. Based on the context of the word, which of the following is the best definition of the word "eradicate" in the fourth paragraph?
    - (A) Lessen
    - (B) Control
    - (C) Develop remedies for
    - (D) Completely eliminate

12. President Kennedy's speech can best be described as _____.

13. The tone of President Kennedy's speech can best be described as:
    - (A) Conciliatory
    - (B) Disciplinary
    - (C) Energizing
    - (D) Apologetic

Excerpt from *Don Quixote*
by Miguel de Cervantes

1   At this point they came in sight of thirty forty windmills that there are on the plain, and as soon as Don Quixote saw them he said to his squire, "Fortune is arranging matters for us better than we could have shaped our desires ourselves, for look there, friend Sancho Panza, where thirty or more monstrous giants present themselves, all of whom I mean to engage in battle and slay, and with whose spoils we shall begin to make our fortunes; for this is righteous warfare, and it is God's good service to sweep so evil a breed from off the face of the earth."

2   "What giants?" said Sancho Panza.

3   "Those thou seest there," answered his master, "with the long arms, and some have them nearly two leagues long."

4   "Look, your worship," said Sancho, "what we see there are not giants but windmills, and what seem to be their arms are the sails that turned by the wind make the millstone go."

5   "It is easy to see," replied Don Quixote, "that thou art not used to this business of adventures; those are giants; and if thou art afraid, away with thee out of this and betake thyself to prayer while I engage them in fierce and unequal combat."

6   So saying, he gave the spur to his steed Rocinante, heedless of the cries his squire Sancho sent after him, warning him that most certainly they were windmills and not giants he was going to attack. He, however, was so positive they were giants that he neither heard the cries of Sancho, nor perceived, near as he was, what they were, but made at them shouting, "Fly not, cowards and vile beings, for a single knight attacks you."

7   A slight breeze at this moment sprang up, and the great sails began to move, seeing which Don Quixote exclaimed, "Though ye flourish more arms than the giant Briareus, ye have to reckon with me."

8   So saying, and commending himself with all his heart to his lady Dulcinea, imploring her to support him in such a peril, with lance in rest and covered by his buckler, he charged at Rocinante's fullest gallop and fell upon the first mill that stood in front of him; but as he drove his lance-point into the sail the wind whirled it round with such force that it shivered the lance to pieces, sweeping with it horse and rider, who went rolling over on the plain, in a sorry condition. Sancho hastened to his assistance as fast as his ass could go, and when he came up found him unable to move, with such a shock had Rocinante fallen with him.

9   "God bless me!" said Sancho, "did I not tell your worship to mind what you were about, for they were only windmills? And no one could have made any mistake about it but one who had something of the same kind in his head."

10   "Hush, friend Sancho," replied Don Quixote, "the fortunes of war more than any other are liable to frequent fluctuations; and moreover I think, and it is the truth, that

that same sage Friston who carried off my study and books, has turned these giants into mills in order to rob me of the glory of vanquishing them, such is the enmity he bears me; but in the end his wicked arts will avail but little against my good sword."

11   "God order it as he may," said Sancho Panza, and helping him to rise got him up again on Rocinante, whose shoulder was half out; and then, discussing the late adventure, they followed the road to Puerto Lapice, for there, said Don Quixote, they could not fail to find adventures in abundance and variety, as it was a great thoroughfare. For all that, he was much grieved at the loss of his lance, and saying so to his squire, he added, "I remember having read how a Spanish knight, Diego Perez de Vargas by name, having broken his sword in battle, tore from an oak a ponderous bough or branch, and with it did such things that day, and pounded so many Moors, that he got the surname of Machuca, and he and his descendants from that day forth were called Vargas y Machuca. I mention this because from the first oak I see I mean to rend such another branch, large and stout like that, with which I am determined and resolved to do such deeds that thou mayest deem thyself very fortunate in being found worthy to come and see them, and be an eyewitness of things that will with difficulty be believed."

12   "Be that as God will," said Sancho, "I believe it all as your worship says it; but straighten yourself a little, for you seem all on one side, may be from the shaking of the fall."

13   "That is the truth," said Don Quixote, "and if I make no complaint of the pain it is because knights-errant are not permitted to complain of any wound, even though their bowels be coming out through it."

14   "If so," said Sancho, "I have nothing to say; but God knows I would rather your worship complained when anything ailed you. For my part, I confess I must complain however small the ache may be; unless this rule about not complaining extends to the squires of knights-errant also."

14.   Sancho can best be characterized as _____.

15.   Initially, how did Don Quixote feel about the loss of his lance?
      (A) Panicked
      (B) Confused
      (C) Relieved
      (D) Upset

16.   Write the following characteristics in the correct boxes to match them with the appropriate character.

      Imaginative   Realistic   Devoted   Bold

Sancho Panza	Don Quixote

17. Based on the passage, what does Don Quixote value?
    (A) Negotiating
    (B) Heroism
    (C) Mediation
    (D) Peace

18. Based on his actions in the passage, what might Sancho Panza do if Don Quixote fell down a hill chasing "giants"?
    (A) Run for help
    (B) Run after the "giants" with Don Quixote
    (C) Warn Don Quixote and then walk away
    (D) Follow Don Quixote and help him up

19. In the fourth paragraph, Sancho Panza refers to Don Quixote as "your worship." What does this suggest about their relationship?
    (A) Panza is a servant of Quixote.
    (B) Quixote is a servant of Panza.
    (C) Quixote is a king.
    (D) Panza forgot Quixote's name.

20. Based on the context of the word, which of the following is the best definition of the word "heedless" in the sixth paragraph?
    (A) Distorted
    (B) Loud
    (C) Inaudible
    (D) Careless disregard

21. Which of the following can be concluded about Quixote?
    (A) He has delusions of grandeur.
    (B) He has always been a great knight.
    (C) He speaks Spanish.
    (D) He prefers business to adventure.

Excerpt from *Little Women*
by Louisa May Alcott

1   "Merry Christmas, little daughters! I'm glad you began at once, and hope you will keep on. But I want to say one word before we sit down. Not far away from here lies a poor woman with a little newborn baby. Six children are huddled into one bed to keep from freezing, for they have no fire. There is nothing to eat over there, and the oldest boy came to tell me they were suffering hunger and cold. My girls, will you give them your breakfast as a Christmas present?"

2   They were all unusually hungry, having waited nearly an hour, and for a minute no one spoke, only a minute, for Jo exclaimed impetuously, "I'm so glad you came before we began!"

3   "May I go and help carry the things to the poor little children?" asked Beth eagerly.

4   "I shall take the cream and the muffings," added Amy, heroically giving up the article she most liked.

5   Meg was already covering the buckwheats, and piling the bread into one big plate.

6   "I thought you'd do it," said Mrs. March, smiling as if satisfied. "You shall all go and help me, and when we come back we will have bread and milk for breakfast, and make it up at dinnertime."

7   They were soon ready, and the procession set out. Fortunately it was early, and they went through back streets, so few people saw them, and no one laughed at the queer party.

8   A poor, bare, miserable room it was, with broken windows, no fire, ragged bedclothes, a sick mother, wailing baby, and a group of pale, hungry children cuddled under one old quilt, trying to keep warm.

9   How the big eyes stared and the blue lips smiled as the girls went in.

10   "Ach, mein Gott! It is good angels come to us!" said the poor woman, crying for joy.

11   "Funny angels in hoods and mittens," said Jo, and set them to laughing.

12   In a few minutes it really did seem as if kind spirits had been at work there. Hannah, who had carried wood, made a fire, and stopped up the broken panes with old hats and her own cloak. Mrs. March gave the mother tea and gruel, and comforted her with promises of help, while she dressed the little baby as tenderly as if it had been her own. The girls meantime spread the table, set the children round the fire, and fed them like so many hungry birds, laughing, talking, and trying to understand the funny broken English.

13   "Das ist gut!" "Die Engel-kinder!" cried the poor things as they ate and warmed their purple hands at the comfortable blaze. The girls had never been called angel children before, and thought it very agreeable, especially Jo, who had been considered a 'Sancho' ever since she was born. That was a very happy breakfast, though they didn't get any of it. And when they went away, leaving comfort behind, I think there were not in all the

city four merrier people than the hungry little girls who gave away their breakfasts and contented themselves with bread and milk on Christmas morning.

14   "That's loving our neighbor better than ourselves, and I like it," said Meg, as they set out their presents while their mother was upstairs collecting clothes for the poor Hummels.

22. Based on its context, what does the word "impetuously" mean in the second paragraph?
     (A) Suddenly
     (B) Sullenly
     (C) Quietly
     (D) Doubtfully

23. Jo's and Hannah's actions can be categorized as all of the following except:
     (A) Thoughtful
     (B) Considerate
     (C) Divisive
     (D) Helpful

24. Put the following events in chronological order.
     (A) Mrs. March collected clothes upstairs.
     (B) Mrs. March gave the mother tea.
     (C) Beth was eager to help the poor children.
     (D) Hannah made a fire.

25. The actions of Jo and Hannah most likely had a _____ effect on the children of the poor woman.

26. What does the pause in the second paragraph suggest?
     (A) The children wanted to help the poor family.
     (B) The children had to weigh their hunger against helping the poor family.
     (C) The family was praying for the poor family.
     (D) The children were shy.

27. Which literary element was the author using when she said, "A poor, bare, miserable room it was, with broken windows, no fire, ragged bedclothes, a sick mother, wailing baby, and a group of pale, hungry children cuddled under one old quilt, trying to keep warm"?
     (A) Metaphor
     (B) Imagery
     (C) Personification
     (D) Hyperbole

28. What can be concluded about Mrs. March?
    (A) Christmas is her favorite holiday.
    (B) She values helping others.
    (C) She works hard each day.
    (D) She is tough on her children.

Answers and Explanations

1. Answers will vary.

2. **(B)** The paragraph indicates that neither side wanted war. For different reasons, though, they would enter war. Options A and D are incorrect; these are supporting details. Option C is incorrect. No evidence supports this answer.

3. "Brave," "confident," or other similar words would be the best answer.

4. **(B)** Paragraph 3 states that slaves were localized in the South.

5. **(B)** Although not a majority, 1/8 is a large portion of the population. Lincoln indicates that African-American slaves constituted a powerful interest. Options A, C, and D are incorrect. No evidence supports these answers. Additionally, option C indicates that 1/8 is a majority, which it is not

6. **(A)** Evil intention is the opposite of charity. Options B, C, and D are incorrect. No information supports these answers.

7. **(A)** Peace and perseverance are aligned with kindness, charity, and rebuilding.

8. **(A)** President Kennedy indicates various ways in which citizens must work together. Option B is incorrect. Although this is mentioned, it is a supporting detail, not the central idea. Options C and D are incorrect.

9. **(D)** The quote clearly indicates that freedom is in danger and therefore could be lost.

10. **(A)** Funding for endangered species does not fit into the categories indicated.

11. **(D)** "Eradicate" means to *completely eliminate*.

12. "Motivational," "inspirational," or any similar word would be the best answer.

13. **(C)** President Kennedy used language that is motivational and was intended to spur people into action.

14. "Loyal," "committed," "steadfast" or any similar word would be the best answer.

15. **(D)** The passage indicates that Don Quixote grieved, so it is logical that he was upset. Options A, B, and C are incorrect. No evidence supports these answers.

16.

Sancho Panza	Don Quixote
Realistic	Imaginative
Devoted	Bold

17. **(B)** Don Quixote says in paragraph 1 that this is "righteous warfare," which indicates heroism.

18. **(D)** It is reasonable to assume Sancho Panza would do the same thing he did when Quixote went after "giants." Answers A, B, and C are incorrect. No information supports these answers.

19. **(A)** The passage clearly highlights Panza's relationship with Quixote as that of sidekick or a servant.

20. **(D)** Quixote ignores Panza's warning.

21. **(A)** Based on his belief that he would face the "giants" alone, Don Quixote believes that he is greater than he actually is.

22. **(A)** The word was exclaimed after a moment of silence.

23. **(C)** The girls could be described as option A, B, or D. However, "divisive" indicates that they have caused division, which they have not.

24. **(C, D, B, A)** First, Beth was eager to help the poor children. Then Hannah made a fire. Next, Mrs. March gave the mother tea. Finally, Mrs. March collected clothes upstairs.

25. "Positive," "good," or any similar word would be the best answer.

26. **(B)** If the children were certain, they would have answered right away. A pause indicates thought.

27. **(B)** The sentence enables one to picture the scene.

28. **(B)** Her actions indicate that Mrs. March values helping those in need.

Language

The GED® test evaluates your ability to edit and understand the use of standard written English in context. The purpose of this unit is to provide you with the skills needed to be successful on the test. These skills will enable you to answer document-based questions effectively. You will also be able to write effective short and extended responses that are generally free of grammatical, syntactical, and mechanical errors.

> **The following topics will be covered in this unit:**
>
> Lesson 1: Parts of Speech
>
> Lesson 2: Parts of the Sentence
>
> Lesson 3: Independent and Subordinate Clauses
>
> Lesson 4: Types of Sentences
>
> Lesson 5: Agreement
>
> Lesson 6: Capitalization
>
> Lesson 7: Punctuation
>
> Lesson 8: Commonly Confused Words
>
> Lesson 9: Editing

COLLEGE AND CAREER READINESS ANCHOR STANDARDS FOR LANGUAGE

Note on range and content of student language use:

To be college and career ready in language, students must have firm control over the conventions of standard English. At the same time, they must come to appreciate that language is as at least as much a matter of craft as of rules and be able to choose words, syntax, and punctuation to express themselves and achieve particular functions and rhetorical effects. They must also have extensive vocabularies, built through reading and study, enabling them to comprehend complex texts and engage in purposeful writing about and conversations around content. They need to become skilled in determining or clarifying the meaning of words and phrases they encounter, choosing flexibly from an array of strategies to aid them. They must learn to see an individual word as part of a network of other words—words, for example, that have similar denotations but different connotations. The inclusion of Language standards in their own strand should not be taken as an indication that skills related to conventions, effective language use, and vocabulary are unimportant to reading, writing, speaking, and listening; indeed, they are inseparable from such contexts.

The grades 6–12 standards on the following pages define what students should understand and be able to do by the end of each grade. They correspond to the College and Career Readiness (CCR) anchor standards below by number. The CCR and grade-specific standards are necessary complements—the former providing broad standards, the latter providing additional specificity—that together define the skills and understandings that all students must demonstrate.

CONVENTIONS OF STANDARD ENGLISH

1. Demonstrate command of the conventions of standard English grammar and usage when writing or speaking.
2. Demonstrate command of the conventions of standard English capitalization, punctuation, and spelling when writing.

KNOWLEDGE OF LANGUAGE

3. Apply knowledge of language to understand how language functions in different contexts, to make effective choices for meaning or style, and to comprehend more fully when reading or listening.

VOCABULARY ACQUISITION AND USE

4. Determine or clarify the meaning of unknown and multiple-meaning words and phrases by using context clues, analyzing meaningful word parts, and consulting general and specialized reference materials, as appropriate.
5. Demonstrate understanding of figurative language, word relationships, and nuances in word meanings.
6. Acquire and use accurately a range of general academic and domain-specific words and phrases sufficient for reading, writing, speaking, and listening at the college and career readiness level; demonstrate independence in gathering vocabulary knowledge when considering a word or phrase important to comprehension or expression.

The English language consists of hundreds of thousands of words. However, these words can be broken up into just a few different categories. These categories are called parts of speech. Although the exam does not specifically ask test takers to identify a word's part of speech, understanding how different parts of speech work with each other will help you better understand grammatical rules.

Nouns

A noun is a person, place, thing, or idea. Nouns are usually things that are tangible. This means they appeal to the five senses so you can see, feel, hear, smell, and/or taste them. Examples of nouns that are tangible are *boy, city,* and *clothing.* A boy is a person. A city is a place. Clothing is a thing. Nouns, however, can also be intangible. Examples of these abstract ideas include:

happiness	sadness
running	walking
kindness	rudeness
love	hate

These are all familiar nouns. However, they cannot be touched or put into your hand.

Pronouns

A pronoun is a word that takes the place of a noun but functions in the same way. Some common pronouns include:

all	it	several
both	me	that
each	mine	them
him	most	us
her	none	we
I	she	you

Verbs

A verb is a word that shows action or a state of being. Examples of action words are *run, jump, work, sit, push, learn,* and *smile.* Each of these words is an action of some sort. However, not all verbs show action. The verb *to be* shows a state of being. Forms of the verb *to be* include:

am	was
are	will be
is	were
am being	have been

Adjectives

An adjective is a descriptive word that gives additional information about nouns and pronouns. Some of the characteristics that adjectives describe are size, shape, color, and quantity. Some examples of adjectives include:

Size	large, medium, small
Shape	round, square, triangular, rectangular
Color	red, orange, yellow, green, blue
Quantity	one, two, three, four, five

EXAMPLES

Size	A **large** car is parked in the street.
	The adjective large *describes the noun* car.
Shape	The **oval** table goes into the dining room.
	The adjective oval *describes the noun* table.
Color	Melissa named the **black** cat Gabriel.
	The adjective black *describes the noun* cat.
Quantity	I've lived here for **seven** years.
	The adjective seven *describes the noun* years.

Note that sometimes nouns can be used as adjectives and that sometimes adjectives can be used as nouns. Although we wouldn't use *large* as a noun, *oval* and *seven* could be nouns.

Adverbs

An adverb is very similar to an adjective because it is a descriptive word. Rather than describing nouns, adverbs describe verbs, adjectives, or adverbs. Additionally, adverbs very often (but not always) end in -ly. Here are some examples:

slowly	fast
happily	very
softly	loudly
internally	externally

EXAMPLES

We drove **slowly**.
The adverb slowly *describes the verb* drove.

She owns a **slightly** larger house than I own.
The adverb slightly *describes the adjective* larger.

The old man moved **quite** slowly.
The adverb quite *describes the adverb* slowly.

Prepositions

Prepositions are words that show the relationship to a noun. Prepositions tell us about the nature of something's time, placement, or direction. Some common prepositions include the following:

about	below	except	inside	over	up
against	between	for	into	through	with
around	by	from	off	toward	without
at	down	in	on	under	
before	during	in between	out	until	

EXAMPLES

I have to go to the doctor **on** Monday because I have an earache.

The preposition on *tells us about the relationship between going to the doctor and Monday. Since we used the preposition* on, *the doctor visit will occur that day. If we had used* before *or* after, *the relationship between the doctor visit and Monday would have been different.*

A beautiful silver necklace sat **in** the display case.

The preposition in *tells us about the relationship between the silver necklace and the display case. Since we used the preposition* in, *the necklace is physically inside of the case. If we had used* on *or* under, *the relationship between the necklace and display case would have been different.*

Conjunctions

Conjunctions are the glue that holds sentences together. When we want to join together items or thoughts, we use conjunctions. We will discuss two types of conjunctions: coordinating and subordinating. Coordinating conjunctions connect similar ideas, contrasting ideas, and related ideas. The following are some common coordinating conjunctions:

or	nor	so	for	yet	but

EXAMPLES

John **and** Andre work at the same store.

The word and *connects John and Andre. It shows similarity because they both work at the store.*

We arrived at the theater early, **but** the tickets were already sold out.

The word but *connects the ideas that we arrived early and the tickets were sold out. It shows contrast, or difference, because you would expect to get a ticket if you show up early.*

Katie didn't want her dessert, **so** Matthew ate her bowl of ice cream.

The word so *connects the two different but related ideas of Katie not wanting dessert and Matthew eating her bowl of ice cream.*

The other type of conjunction is a subordinating conjunction, which we will discuss in Lesson 3 when we cover subordination.

Interjections

An interjection is an interrupting word. It usually shows emotion and is not a complete sentence. Examples of interjections include:

Hey!   Wow!   Ouch!   Hi!   Great!

PRACTICE

For each, indicate the word's part of speech by writing **N** for noun, **PN** for pronoun, **V** for verb, **Adj** for adjective, **Adv** for adverb, **C** for conjunction, and **Prep** for preposition.

1. beach ____N____
2. lightly ____Adv____
3. from ____Prep____
4. throughout ____Prep____
5. him ____PN____
6. team ____N____
7. invest ____V____
8. talk ____V____
9. but ____C____
10. responsible ____Adj____

11. them ____PN____
12. peace ____N____
13. tall ____Adj____
14. forgot ____V____
15. desk ____N____
16. and ____C____
17. hot ____Adj____
18. tightly ____Adv____
19. phone ____N____
20. affordable ____Adj____

Answers

1. N	**6.** N	**11.** PN	**16.** C
2. Adv	**7.** V	**12.** N	**17.** Adj
3. Prep	**8.** V	**13.** Adj	**18.** Adv
4. Prep	**9.** C	**14.** V	**19.** N
5. PN	**10.** Adj	**15.** N	**20.** Adj

In the English language, a sentence has several major components. Some need to be in every sentence, while others do not. The seven sentence parts are *subjects, predicates, direct objects, indirect objects, predicate nouns, predicate adjectives,* and *prepositional phrases.*

Subject

The subject of a sentence is who or what is doing the action. It can be singular or compound. A compound subject is when more than one person or thing does the action, such as *cookies and ice cream* or *John and Jane.*

EXAMPLES

Jennifer went to the store to get some limes for the Mexican food.
In this sentence, Jennifer *is the doer of the action. She went (to the store) so* Jennifer *is the subject.*

Robert and Rick brought a birthday cake to Kelly's surprise party.
In this sentence, Robert and Rick *are the doers of the action. They brought (a birthday cake) so the subject is* Robert and Rick.

Every sentence *must* have a subject. However, the subject is not always stated directly. In the previous two examples, the subjects were explicitly stated. *Jennifer* was the subject in the first, and *Robert and Rick* was the subject in the second. If I were telling either subject to get limes or to bring a cake, the subject may be implied.

EXAMPLES

Go to the store and get limes for the Mexican food.
Bring a birthday cake to Kelly's surprise party.
In these cases, the subjects are assumed to be you, *or the person to whom I'm speaking.*

Predicate

The predicate of a sentence contains the verb and, in some cases, additional information. So the predicate indicates the action or state of being. Just like the subject, the predicate can be singular or compound. A compound predicate is when there is more than one action or state of being, such as *ran and jumped* or *went and bought*.

EXAMPLES

Jennifer **went** to the store to get some limes for the Mexican food.
In this sentence, went *is the verb and shows action. Everything that follows gives additional information.*

Robert and Rick **brought** a birthday cake to Kelly's surprise party.
In this sentence, brought *is the verb and shows action. Everything that follows gives additional information.*

Direct Object

The direct object is a noun and appears in some sentences with action verbs. The direct object is what or who receives the action. The direct object is never the subject.

EXAMPLES

I hit the **ball** out of the park.
In this sentence, ball *is the receiver of the action* hit.

Renaldo read the **passage** aloud.
In this sentence, passage *is the receiver of the action* read.

Indirect Object

The indirect object is a noun and appears in some sentences with a direct object. The indirect object is who or what receives the direct object.

EXAMPLES

I gave the **teacher** my report.
In this sentence, my report *is what is given and* the teacher *receives it.*

Brad threw **Molly** the Frisbee.
In this sentence, the Frisbee *is what is thrown and* Molly *receives it.*

Predicate Noun

A predicate noun is sometimes found in a sentence that uses the verb *to be*. It tells what the subject is.

> **EXAMPLES**
>
> Mike is a **doctor**.
> Mike *is the subject, and* doctor *tells us what Mike is.*
>
> Billy was such a **joker**!
> Billy *is the subject, and* joker *tells us what Billy is.*

Predicate Adjective

A predicate adjective is sometimes found in a sentence that uses the verb *to be*. It tells what the subject is like.

> **EXAMPLES**
>
> My mother was very **sweet** when I was sick.
> My mother *is the subject, and* sweet *is what she was like.*
>
> The soldier was **brave** in the face of danger.
> The soldier *is the subject, and* brave *is what he was like.*

Prepositional Phrase

Prepositional phrases can appear in any type of sentence but are not essential. They provide the reader with additional information. All prepositional phrases begin with a preposition and end with a noun. However, prepositional phrases may include adjectives or adverbs.

> **EXAMPLES**
>
> Keith drove **to the university**.
> *The preposition is* to, *and the noun is* university.
>
> Sheila went home **after work**.
> *The preposition is* after, *and the noun is* work.

PRACTICE

INDICATE WHAT PART OF THE SENTENCE IS BOLDED IN THE SENTENCES BELOW. USE THE FOLLOWING ABBREVIATIONS.

S	Subject
DO	Direct object
IO	Indirect object
PN	Predicate noun
PA	Predicate adjective
PP	Prepositional phrase

1. The audience at the show was **hysterical**.

2. Jose returned the books **to the library**.

3. While at school, **Erin** ran into a friend.

4. Colleen told **the customer service representative** her problem.

5. In almost every case, the student did **the homework**.

6. Sorin would be a great **president**.

Answers

1. PA

2. PP

3. S

4. IO

5. DO

6. PN

Independent Clauses

If someone walks into a room and says, "I went to the movies," you would be content with that information. It is a complete thought. Since it contains both a subject and a predicate, it is a *clause*. It is called an *independent clause* because it can stand on its own two feet. The following are independent clauses:

> **EXAMPLES**
>
> The teacher wrote the assignment on the whiteboard.
> As a favor, I drove my neighbor to work.
> Sonia's friends planned a surprise birthday party for her.

Subordinate Clauses

Although a complete sentence must have both a subject and a predicate, just because both are present does not mean the clause is a complete sentence. For example, if someone walks into a room and says, "When I went to the movies," you would be waiting for the rest of the information. The statement has a subject and a verb, but it is not a complete sentence because it begins with the word *when*. This is what we call a *subordinate clause*. Subordinate clauses, or dependent clauses as they are sometimes referred to, must be joined to an independent clause. All subordinate clauses begin with a subordinating conjunction.

Subordinating Conjunctions

A subordinating conjunction is similar to a regular conjunction in that it is a connecting word. However, a subordinating conjunction changes the clause that follows into a subordinate clause. These are examples of subordinating conjunctions:

after	how	until
although	if	though
because	now that	unless
even if	since	when
even though	unless	while

PRACTICE

IDENTIFY WHICH OF THE FOLLOWING ARE SENTENCE FRAGMENTS AND WHICH ARE COMPLETE SENTENCES.

1. After all that was done to save the community garden.

2. Even if the home team scores another touchdown, it looks like the visiting team will win the game.

3. Unless the airline refunds our money.

4. When Jane was surfing the Internet, she came across an interesting article on genetics.

5. Now that the beach has been reopened.

6. Since both the cars cost the same amount.

7. I will probably stay home and study this weekend even if I study Friday night.

Answers and Explanations

1. Sentence fragment; this is a subordinate clause.

2. Complete sentence; this contains both a subordinate clause and an independent clause.

3. Sentence fragment; this is a subordinate clause.

4. Complete sentence; this contains both a subordinate clause and an independent clause.

5. Sentence fragment; this is a subordinate clause.

6. Sentence fragment; this is a subordinate clause.

7. Complete sentence; this contains both a subordinate clause and an independent clause.

Now that we are familiar with the structure of sentences and the different types of clauses, we can take a look at different types of complete sentences. There are four types of sentences in English: simple, compound, complex, and compound/complex.

Simple Sentences

A simple sentence is one independent clause. It contains either a singular or a compound subject and either a singular or a compound predicate. Examples of simple sentences include:

EXAMPLES

James *worked* on his science project all night.

During the costume party, the **children** *carved* pumpkins.

After the graduation, **Adam's parents** *took* him to a nice restaurant and *bought* him dinner.

Kristen and Rob *took* the dog to the park.

Compound Sentences

A compound sentence consists of *two or more* independent clauses that are joined by a conjunction or a semicolon. Examples of compound sentences include:

EXAMPLES

The sales associate cleaned up the store, **and** the manager counted the money.

Jasmine took her daughters to nursery school, **and** they played with the other children.

Scott and Melissa had planned to meet some friends, **but** they were too tired after the movie.

The play was enjoyable; it was just too long.

Complex Sentences

A complex sentence consists of one independent clause and one or more subordinate clauses. If the subordinate clause occurs at the beginning of the sentence, it is followed by a comma. If it occurs at the end of a sentence, it is not preceded by a comma. Examples of complex sentences include:

EXAMPLES

Even if things are not perfect, life is still pretty good!

Lisa returned the dress to the store *after she noticed there was a tear along the seam.*

Angela took the dog out *because it was whining and scratching at the back door.*

Sue brought her lunch to school with her *so she could eat while she studied.*

Compound/Complex Sentences

A compound/complex sentence consists of two or more independent clauses and one or more subordinate clauses. Examples of compound/complex sentences include:

EXAMPLES

While the turkey was cooking, Mary set the table, **and** Charlie finished making the stuffing.

I would really like to go on vacation this year; however, *if I cannot save up the money,* I can't go.

Roberto forgot about his friend's birthday, **but** *when he remembered,* he sent her a gift.

The trip was exciting, and we bought some souvenirs *when we came across a little boutique.*

PRACTICE

INDICATE IF THE SENTENCE IS SIMPLE, COMPOUND, COMPLEX, OR COMPOUND/
COMPLEX.

_____ 1. When you are working on a computer, you should take breaks and rest your eyes.

_____ 2. The children loved to go see the clowns, elephants, and acrobats at the circus.

_____ 3. Effective immediately, all employees must submit their time sheets to the departmental administrator by 5:00 P.M. each Friday.

_____ 4. Barbara's flight was late, and the airline lost her luggage.

_____ 5. Although cooking in a microwave has become the norm, you probably don't want to cook a turkey in one, but you can certainly heat up vegetables and side dishes.

_____ 6. Dr. Lewiston has many patients to attend to this afternoon, and her assistant has to leave early.

_____ 7. In the past decade, the cost of cell phones and wireless service has come down.

_____ 8. As we get older, it becomes harder to keep off extra weight.

_____ 9. Working out can be very rewarding, especially if it becomes a way of life rather than an intermittent activity.

_____ 10. We finally spoke to the customer service representative after being placed on hold for 20 minutes, but in the end, our money was refunded.

Answers

1. Complex

2. Simple

3. Simple

4. Compound

5. Compound/Complex

6. Compound

7. Simple

8. Complex

9. Complex

10. Compound/Complex

Run-on Sentences

Although you should vary your sentence structure and enhance the quality of your writing by including more robust and dynamic sentences, make sure that the sentences do not become run-ons. A sentence becomes a run-on when multiple sentences are put together without the proper punctuation. For example:

> After sleeping late last Saturday, I went to the café down the block, I saw my friend while I was there, he was out for a bike ride and stopped to get a bottle of water.

This run-on should be broken up into several sentences. An appropriate revision would be:

> After sleeping late last Saturday, I went to the café down the block. I saw my friend while I was there. He was out for a bike ride and stopped to get a bottle of water.

In this revision, periods are used instead of the comma. The different thoughts in the run-on are now separated.

Sentence Fragments

To have a fragment of something is to have a piece, not a whole. Therefore, a sentence fragment is a piece of a sentence and incomplete. When determining whether or not you have a sentence fragment, ask yourself, "What is the action, and who or what is doing the action?"

> This morning went to the airport to pick up his sister.

What is the action? The action is *went*. Who or what is doing the action? There is no doer of the action in this sentence, so we need to add a subject to make this a complete sentence. Appropriate revisions would be:

> This morning, **Chris** went to the airport to pick up his sister.
> This morning, **he** went to the airport to pick up his sister.

The first revision adds the proper noun, *Chris*, who is now the doer of the action, *went*. The second revision uses the pronoun *he* as the subject instead of using a proper noun.

> My favorite kind of cuisine.

What is the action? No action is shown, which indicates this is a fragment. If this contained an action, *my favorite kind of cuisine* would be the subject, or doer, of the action. Appropriate revisions would be:

> My favorite kind of cuisine is Thai food.
> Thai food is my favorite kind of cuisine.

In both revisions, the verb *to be* has been used to show a state of being. The first revision uses *my favorite kind of cuisine* as the subject. The second revision uses it as a predicate noun. However, both sentences include exactly the same information.

PRACTICE

ON THE COMPUTER-BASED EXAM, YOU WILL BE ASKED TO DRAG AND DROP ITEMS IN ORDER TO MATCH THEM APPROPRIATELY. FOR THESE PRACTICE QUESTIONS, DRAW A STAR NEXT TO THE *COMPLETE* SENTENCES:

1. Ran toward the burning house with a fire hose.

2. He left.

3. Jocelyn traveled across the country with her dog.

4. On Friday, Maricel will receive an award for her short story.

5. The best friend a boy could have.

6. A car in front of the house.

7. The group of friends went on a camping trip for the weekend.

Answers and Explanations

1. No star; the subject is missing.

2. ★ This has both a subject and a predicate.

3. ★ This has both a subject and a predicate.

4. ★ This has both a subject and a predicate.

5. No star; the verb is missing.

6. No star; the verb is missing.

7. ★ This has both a subject and a predicate.

The following shows possible ways to turn the sentence fragments in the practice questions into complete sentences:

- *The firefighter* ran toward the burning house with a fire hose.
- *A dog is* the best friend a boy could have.
- A car *has been parked* in front of the house.

PRACTICE

INDICATE IF THE SENTENCE IS COMPLETE OR IS A FRAGMENT. IF IT IS A FRAGMENT, REVISE THE SENTENCE TO MAKE IT COMPLETE.

1. Although the principal, the teachers, and the students arrived at the assembly on time.

2. Justin, while hiking in the Adirondack Mountains, slipped on some gravel and sprained his ankle.

3. Come here!

4. The tallest mountain in the world, which is Mount Everest.

5. Finding a $100 bill in a taxicab.

6. The car repairs, which cost $450, were done in a matter of hours.

7. While studying for the math test, Jenna received a call from her classmate to tell her that tomorrow's class had been canceled.

8. After saving enough money to go on a weeklong vacation to Mexico.

9. Li's favorite class in school was an art history class with Ms. Smith.

10. When Annmarie heard that the radio station was giving away tickets to see her favorite band play.

Answers and Explanations

1. Fragment; the word *although* is a subordinating conjunction, and there is no independent clause attached. A correct revision would be: *Although the principal, the teachers, and the students arrived at the assembly on time, the guest speaker was late.*

2. Complete

3. Complete; although no subject is stated, the implied subject is *you.*

4. Fragment; there is no predicate. A correct revision would be: *The tallest mountain in the world, which is Mount Everest, is in the Himalayas.*

5. Incomplete; there is no predicate. A correct revision would be: *Finding a $100 bill in a taxicab made my day!*

6. Complete

7. Complete

8. Incomplete; the word *after* makes this a subordinate clause. A correct revision would be: *After saving enough money to go on a weeklong vacation to Mexico, Trevor went online and purchased plane tickets.*

9. Complete

10. Incomplete; the word *when* makes this a subordinate clause. A correct revision would be: *When Annmarie heard that the radio station was giving away tickets to see her favorite band play, she grabbed her phone and excitedly called the station.*

Verb Form Agreement

Verbs come in many forms. You must be consistent in your form when writing extended responses. It is also very important to be aware of the different forms when you're editing passages in the language section. This includes tense agreement, subject-verb agreement, and pronoun-antecedent agreement.

Tense Agreement

In English, verbs indicate when something happened, is happening, or will happen; this is called *verb tense.* Most of the time, tense form should be consistent within a sentence. However, there are exceptions to this rule. The following sentence does not have tense agreement:

Jeremy went to the baseball game last week and is sitting in box seats.

In this sentence, the verb *went* is in past tense whereas *is sitting* is in the present. To correct this, one of the tenses must be changed. A proper revision would be:

Jeremy went to the baseball game last week and sat in box seats.

An example of an exception to this rule would be:

Andy is in Las Vegas and will see some shows.

This example purposefully has two different tenses. Andy is currently in Las Vegas. Sometime in the future, he will go to some shows.

Subject-Verb Agreement

A common writing mistake, and one that will be tested in the language section, is making errors in subject-verb agreement. In most cases, if the subject is plural, the verb must also be plural. If the subject is singular, so must be the verb. For example:

Dana attend meetings on Monday mornings with the other managers.

Dana is singular and *attend* is plural. Two possible revisions would be:

Dana **attends** meetings on Monday mornings with the other managers.
Dana and Sorin attend meetings on Monday mornings with the other managers.

Pronoun-Antecedent Agreement

As discussed in Lesson 1, pronouns take the place of nouns. The pronoun must agree with the noun that it replaces, which is called the antecedent. For example, if I were talking about a woman named Chelsea, I could use the pronouns *she* and *her* because they agree with the antecedent *Chelsea.* Pronouns and antecedents must also agree in quantity. If the sentence is discussing Bradley and James, *he* would be an inappropriate pronoun choice because it does not agree in quantity. The pronoun *they* agrees with the antecedent *Bradley and James* because more than one person is being discussed.

Unclear Pronoun Reference

When discussing more than one person or thing, make sure your writing clearly shows who or what the pronoun is referring to. The following is an example of an unclear pronoun reference:

Jan and Alexandra went to the movies, and she bought a tub of popcorn.

In the sentence, it is unclear who the pronoun *she* refers to. Did Jan buy the tub of popcorn or did Alexandra? In this example, it is necessary to use the person's name again instead of a pronoun. A proper revision would be:

Jan and Alexandra went to the movies, and Jan bought a tub of popcorn.

There are many rules regarding the capitalization of letters within sentences. The three most important are beginning of sentences, proper nouns, and proper adjectives.

Beginning of Sentences

The first letter of the first word of every sentence must be capitalized. There are no exceptions to this rule. Keep in mind that you need to conform to standard English. Although you can make some mistakes and still receive full credit, capitalizing the first letter of the first word of each sentence is the most commonly encountered rule and perhaps the easiest mechanical rule to remember.

Proper Nouns

Proper nouns are the names of people, places, things, or ideas. They are always capitalized.

> **EXAMPLES**
>
> Carlos
> Anna Maria
> Statue of Liberty
> United States of America
> Olympics

Proper Adjectives

Proper adjectives are similar to proper nouns in that they refer to the proper name of a person, place, thing, or idea. They are always capitalized.

> **EXAMPLES**
>
> Irish soda bread
> American cheese
> Asian music
> African heritage

PRACTICE

CAPITALIZE THE FOLLOWING WORDS WHERE APPROPRIATE.

squirrel	
romanian	
table	
procession	
greece	
jim	
lift	
internet	

Answers

squirrel	
romanian	Romanian
table	
procession	
greece	Greece
jim	Jim
lift	
internet	Internet

The rules for punctuation can be confusing, but they can be approachable. One of the best ways to improve your punctuation skills is to become familiar with the general rules of punctuation and then see how punctuation is used in a newspaper. Newspapers are written by professional writers and then checked by copy editors. So the vast majority of what you see in a newspaper is going to have proper punctuation. If you compare the punctuation you see in a newspaper to the few rules in this book, you'll begin to see the practical application of those rules.

Periods

Periods, also known as full stops, must be used at the end of each sentence. A period indicates that the sentence has ended. They are also used after an abbreviation, such as Dr., Mrs., Mr., Jr., Sr., Ph.D., or other common titles.

Question Marks

Question marks are used at the end of sentences. They indicate that a question is being asked.

Commas

Commas are commonly misused. Commas are intended to separate, not connect. This means they are used to separate items on a list, independent clauses, and certain phrases. Keep in mind that if you are using a comma to separate independent clauses, you must include a conjunction after the comma.

Semicolons

People often use a comma when they really should use a semicolon. A semicolon separates and connects at the same time. For example, this shows a common mistake:

I went to the store, Katie went to the movies.

This is an improper use of a comma. Correct revisions would be:

I went to the store, and Katie went to the movies.
I went to the store; Katie went to the movies.

Both of these revisions separate the two different ideas but also connect the ideas since they are related.

Possessives and Contractions

Possessives and contractions often look similar because they both use apostrophes. However, they use apostrophes in different ways. In a possessive, the apostrophe is often, but not always, used to show ownership. In a contraction, it is used to show where letters are omitted.

COMMON CONTRACTIONS

are not	aren't	cannot	can't
is not	isn't	would have	would've
was not	wasn't	could have	could've
were not	weren't	should have	should've
have not	haven't	might have	might've
do not	don't	of the clock	o'clock
did not	didn't		

EXAMPLES OF POSSESSIVES

car's engine

president's house

John's dog

Rita's job

television's picture quality

computer's speed

student's score

your house

their parents

our neighborhood

Homonyms

Homonyms are words that sound the same but are spelled differently and have different meanings. All too often, an incorrect homonym is used in writing. So, be careful.

COMMONLY CONFUSED HOMONYMS

ACCEPT, EXCEPT

Accept means to receive something; *except* means something is not included.

AFFECT, EFFECT

Affect means to influence something; *effect* is what happens as a result of an action.

BARE, BEAR

Bare is to be uncovered or naked; *bear* is an animal.

BOARD, BORED

Board is a piece of wood; *bored* is to have nothing to do.

BREAK, BRAKE

Break means to damage or ruin something; *brake* means to slow down or stop doing something.

EMIGRATE, IMMIGRATE

Emigrate means to come *from* somewhere; *immigrate* means to go *to* somewhere.

ENSURE, INSURE

Ensure is to make sure something happens; *insure* means to have a policy that will pay money should something be stolen or damaged.

FEET, FEAT

Feet are body parts; *feat* is an accomplishment.

ITS, IT'S

Its shows possession; *it's* is a contraction meaning "it is."

KNOW, NO

Know is to have knowledge of something; *no* is a negative response.

ONE, WON

One is a number; *won* is past tense for winning something.

PASSED, PAST

Passed is past tense for going by something or passing something along; *past* is what has already happened.

PRINCIPLE, PRINCIPAL

A *principle* is a rule; a *principal* is the leader of a school.

SURE, SHORE

Sure means "certainty"; *shore* means "coastline."

THAN, THEN

Than makes a comparison between two things; *then* indicates a certain time.

THERE, THEIR, THEY'RE

There indicates a location; *their* shows possession; *they're* is a contraction meaning "they are."

TO, TOO, TWO

To is a preposition indicating motion; *too* means "also" or "more than is wanted"; *two* is a number.

WHETHER, WEATHER

Whether indicates a choice; *weather* is temperature, humidity, precipitation, and so on.

WHOLE, HOLE

Whole is something that is complete; *hole* is an empty space.

YOUR, YOU'RE

Your shows possession; you're is a contraction meaning "you are."

In addition to using correct grammar, punctuation, and spelling, make sure you have structured your sentences correctly and have used words efficiently.

Wordiness and Awkward Structure

Wordiness and awkward structure refer to the flow of the sentences. Sometimes when we first write something, the sentence evolves as we are writing. As a result, sometimes we use too many words. This means we could say the same thing using fewer words. On the GED® test, you will be tested on your ability to recognize wordy and awkwardly structured sentences.

Non-Standard and Informal Language

The goal of the language questions on the exam is to test your knowledge of standard English. One way is by giving you answer choices that use non-standard English and informal language. In other words, some answer choices will sound more like they belong in a conversation you're having with a friend rather than in a more formal work of literature. As a rule of thumb, you should always elevate your language when you're writing. Likewise, you should be looking for choices with elevated language that are also grammatically and mechanically correct.

PRACTICE

CHOOSE THE BEST REVISION OF THE SENTENCE.

1. The head chef of the restaurant. Likes to use chipotle in his recipes.
   (A) The head chef of the restaurant, who likes to use chipotle in his recipes.
   (B) The head chef of the restaurant likes to use chipotle in his recipes.
   (C) The head chef of the restaurant, using chipotle in his recipes.
   (D) No revision is necessary.

2. While studying at the library, Juan ran into his classmate, Lisa.
   (A) Juan, while studying at the library, running into his classmate, Lisa.
   (B) While studying at the library and running into his classmate, Lisa.
   (C) Juan and Lisa, while studying at the library.
   (D) No revision is necessary.

3. Even though Nate and Justin both attended the same school, they never met one another.
   (A) Nate and Justin, attending the same school, never met one another.
   (B) Even though Nate and Justin both attended the same school, never meeting one another.
   (C) Although Nate and Justin attended the same school and never meeting one another.
   (D) No revision is necessary.

4. Ambulances, speeding down the highway and rushing to the scene of the accident.
   (A) Ambulances that were speeding down the highway and rushing toward the scene of the accident.
   (B) Ambulances, speeding and rushing toward the accident scene.
   (C) Speeding down the highway, the ambulances that were rushing toward the scene of the accident.
   (D) Ambulances were speeding down the highway and rushing toward the scene of the accident.

5. Because the construction was blocking both lanes of the expressway, and traffic was diverted to the service road.
   (A) Construction, blocking both lanes of the expressway, and traffic was diverted to the service road.
   (B) Because the construction was blocking both lanes of the expressway and traffic, being diverted to the service road.
   (C) Because the construction was blocking both lanes of the expressway, traffic was being diverted to the service road.
   (D) The construction, blocking the service road, traffic was being diverted to the service road.

6. Cannot be at your wedding but wish you all the best!
   (A) We cannot be at your wedding but wish you all the best!
   (B) Cannot be at your wedding but wishing you all the best!
   (C) While we cannot be at your wedding but wish you all the best!
   (D) No revision is necessary.

7. Although, while in high school, Jamal and Steven were inseparable, hadn't seen each other since graduation.
   (A) Although, while in high school, Jamal and Steven were inseparable, they hadn't seen each other since graduation.
   (B) Although, while in high school, Jamal and Steven being inseparable and hadn't seen each other since graduation.
   (C) While in high school, Jamal and Steven were inseparable, having not seen each other since graduation.
   (D) While in high school and inseparable, Jamal and Steven having not seen each other since graduation.

8. When Racine's friend didn't show up to take her to school. She called him.
   (A) When Racine's friend didn't show up. To take her to school, she called him.
   (B) When Racine's friend didn't show up to take her to school, she called him.
   (C) Racine called her friend, not showing up to take her to school.
   (D) When Racine's friend didn't show up to take her to school, called him.

9. The teacher asked the students to put their phones away while in class.
   - (A) The teacher asked the students putting their phones away in class.
   - (B) While in class, the teacher to ask the students to put their phones away while in class.
   - (C) The teacher asked the student put their phones away in class.
   - (D) No revision is necessary.

Answers and Explanations

1. **(B)** This choice combines the two fragments into one complete sentence. Options A and C do not resolve the fragments.

2. **(D)** The sentence is correct as written.

3. **(D)** The sentence is correct as written.

4. **(D)** The incomplete sentence was missing a verb. Option D adds the verb *were*, resolving the conflict. Option C is incorrect because it begins with a dangling participle. In other words, it needs a preposition at the beginning.

5. **(C)** The original did not contain an independent clause. Option C removes the conjunction *and*, making the second half of the question an independent clause to support the subordinate clause.

6. **(A)** The original is missing a subject. Who cannot be at the wedding? Option A adds a subject, correcting the problem.

7. **(A)** In the original, "hadn't seen each other since graduation" is missing a subject. Option A adds the subject *they*, resolving the problem.

8. **(B)** The original is a subordinate clause. Combining the sentences resolves the problem.

9. **(D)** The sentence is correct as written.

Review Test

QUESTIONS 1–5 ARE EMBEDDED IN THE FOLLOWING PASSAGE:

Excerpt from *The Einstein Theory of Relativity*
by Hendrik Antoon Lorentz

The action of the Royal Society at its meeting in London on November 6, in recognizing Dr. Albert Einstein's "theory of relativity" has caused a great stir in scientific circles on both sides of the Atlantic. Dr. Einstein propounded his theory nearly fifteen years ago. The present revival of interest in it is due to the remarkable confirmation which it received in the report of the observations made during the sun's eclipse of last May to determine whether rays of light passing close to the sun are deflected from their course.

The actual deflection of the rays that was discovered by the astronomers was precisely what had been predicted theoretically by Einstein many years since.

1. Choose one.
   (A) This striking confirmation having led certain German scientists to assert that no scientific discovery of such importance has been made since Newton's theory of gravitation was promulgated.
   (B) This confirmation, having been striking to us, has led certain german scientists to assert that no scientific discovery of such importance has been made since Newton's theory of gravitation was promulgated. -
   (C) This striking confirmation has led certain German scientists to assert that no scientific discovery of such importance has been made since Newton's theory of gravitation was promulgated. -

This suggestion, however, was put aside by Dr. Einstein himself when he was interviewed by a correspondent of *The New York Times* at his home in Berlin. To this correspondent he expressed the difference between his conception and the law of gravitation in the following terms:

"Please imagine the earth removed, and in its place suspended a box as big as a room or a whole house, and inside a man naturally floating in the center, there being no force whatever pulling him. Imagine, further, this box being, by a rope or other contrivance, suddenly jerked to one side, which is scientifically termed 'difform motion', as opposed to 'uniform motion.' The person would then naturally reach bottom on the opposite side. The result would consequently be the same as if he obeyed Newton's law of gravitation, while, in fact, there is no gravitation exerted whatever, which proves that difform motion will in every case produce the same effects as gravitation.

"I have applied this new idea to every kind of difform motion and have thus developed mathematical formulas which I am convinced give more precise results than those based on Newton's theory. Newton's formulas, however, are such close approximations that it was difficult to find by observation any obvious disagreement with experience."

2. Choose one.
   (A) Dr. Einstein, it must be remembered, as a physicist and not an astronomer. _
   (B) dr. Einstein, it must be remembered, is a physicist and not an astronomer.
   (C) Dr. Einstein, it must be remembered, is a physicist and not an astronomer.

He developed his theory as a mathematical formula.

3. Choose one.
   (A) The confirmation of it came from the astronomers as he himself says,
       the crucial test was supplied by the last total solar eclipse.
   (B) The confirmation of it came from the astronomers. As he himself says,
       the crucial test by the last total solar eclipse.
   (C) The confirmation of it came from the astronomers. As he himself says,
       the crucial test was supplied by the last total solar eclipse.

Observations then proved that the rays of fixed stars, having to pass close to the sun to reach the earth, were deflected the exact amount demanded by Einstein's formulas. The deflection was also in the direction predicted by him.

The question must have occurred to many, what has all this to do with relativity? When this query was propounded by the *Times* correspondent to Dr. Einstein he replied as follows:

4. Choose one.
   (A) "The term relativity referring to time and space.
   (B) "The term relativity refers to time and space.
   (C) "The term relativity having referred to time and space.

According to Galileo and Newton, time and space were absolute entities, and the moving systems of the universe were dependent on this absolute time and space. On this conception was built the science of mechanics. The resulting formulas sufficed for all motions of a slow nature; it was found, however, that they would not conform to the rapid motions apparent in electrodynamics.

"This led the Dutch professor, Lorentz, and myself to develop the theory of special relativity. Briefly, it discards absolute time and space and makes them in every instance relative to moving systems. By this theory all phenomena in electrodynamics, as well as mechanics, hitherto irreducible by the old formulae—and there are multitudes—were satisfactorily explained.

"Till now it was believed that time and space existed by themselves, even if there was nothing else—no sun, no earth, no stars—while now we know that time and space are not the vessel for the universe, but could not exist at all if there were no contents, namely, no sun, earth and other celestial bodies.

"This special relativity, forming the first part of my theory, relates to all systems moving with uniform motion; that is, moving in a straight line with equal velocity.

"Gradually I was led to the idea, seeming a very paradox in science, that it might apply equally to all moving systems, even of difform motion, and thus I developed the conception of general relativity which forms the second part of my theory."

As summarized by an American astronomer, Professor Henry Norris Russell, of Princeton, in the *Scientific American* for November 29, Einstein's contribution amounts to this:

"The central fact which has been proved—and which is of great interest and importance—is that the natural phenomena involving gravitation and inertia (such as the motions of the planets) and the phenomena involving electricity and magnetism (including the motion of light) are not independent of one another, but are intimately related, so that both sets of phenomena should be regarded as parts of one vast system, embracing all Nature.

5. Choose one.
   (A) The relation of the two is however of such a character that it is perceptible only in a very few instances, and then only to refined observations."
   (B) The relation of the two is, however, of such a character that it is perceptible only in a very few instances, and then only to refined observations."
   (C) The relation of the two, however, of such a character that it is perceptible only in a very few instances, and then only to refined observations."

Already before the war, Einstein had immense fame among physicists, and among all who are interested in the philosophy of science, because of his principle of relativity.

Excerpt from *A Life of William Shakespeare*
by Sidney Lee

William Shakespeare.

The father in municipal office

In July 1564, when William was three months old, the plague raged with unwonted vehemence at Stratford, and his father liberally contributed to the relief of its poverty-stricken victims. Fortune still favored him. On July 4, 1565, he reached the dignity of an alderman. From 1567 onwards he was accorded in the corporation archives the honorable prefix of "Mr." At Michaelmas 1568 he attained the highest office in the corporation gift, that of bailiff, and during his year of office the corporation for the first time entertained actors at Stratford. The Queen's Company and the Earl of Worcester's Company each received from John Shakespeare an official welcome.

6. Choose one.
    (A) On september 5, 1571, he was chief alderman, a post which he retained till september 30 the following year.
    (B) He was chief alderman, a post which he retained till September 30 the following year, but that was on September 5, 1571.
    (C) On September 5, 1571, he was chief alderman, a post which he retained till September 30 the following year.

In 1573 Alexander Webbe, the husband of his wife's sister Agnes, made him overseer of his will; in 1575 he bought two houses in Stratford, one of them doubtless the alleged birthplace in Henley Street; in 1576 he contributed twelve pence to the beadle's salary. But after Michaelmas 1572 he took a less active part in municipal affairs; he grew irregular in his attendance at the council meetings, and signs were soon apparent that his luck had turned. In 1578 he was unable to pay, with his colleagues, either the sum of four pence for the relief of the poor or his contribution "towards the furniture of three pikemen, two bellmen, and one archer" who were sent by the corporation to attend a muster of the trained bands of the county.

Brothers and sisters

7. Choose one.
    (A) Meanwhile his increasing family.
    (B) Meanwhile his family was increasing.
    (C) Meanwhile his family were increasing.

Four children besides the poet—three sons, Gilbert (baptized October 13, 1566), Richard (baptized March 11, 1574), and Edmund (baptized May 3, 1580), with a daughter Joan (baptized April 15, 1569)—reached maturity. A daughter Ann was baptized September 28, 1571, and was buried on April 4, 1579. To meet his growing liabilities, the father borrowed money from his wife's kinsfolk, and he and his wife mortgaged, on November 14, 1578, Asbies, her valuable property at Wilmcote, for £40 to Edmund Lambert of Barton-on-the-Heath, who had married her sister, Joan Arden. Lambert was to receive no interest on his loan, but was to take the "rents and profits" of the estate. Asbies was thereby alienated forever. Next year, on October 15, 1579, John and his wife made over to Robert Webbe, doubtless a relative of Alexander Webbe, for the sum apparently of £40, his wife's property at Snitterfield.

The father's financial difficulties

John Shakespeare obviously chafed under the humiliation of having parted, although as he hoped only temporarily, with his wife's property of Asbies, and in the autumn of 1580 he offered to pay off the mortgage; but his brother-in-law, Lambert, retorted that other sums were owing, and he would accept all or none.

8. Choose one.
    (A) The negotiation, which was the beginning of much litigation, thus proved abortive.
    (B) The Negotiation, which was the beginning of much litigation, thus proved abortive.
    (C) The negotiation which was the beginning of much litigation thus proved abortive.

Through 1585 and 1586 a creditor, John Brown, was embarrassingly importunate, and, after obtaining a writ of distraint, Brown informed the local court that the debtor had no goods on which distraint could be levied. On September 6, 1586, John was deprived of his alderman's gown, on the ground of his long absence from the council meetings.

Education

Happily John Shakespeare was at no expense for the education of his four sons. They were entitled to free tuition at the grammar school of Stratford, which was reconstituted on a [medieval] foundation by Edward VI. The eldest son, William, probably entered the school in 1571, when Walter Roche was master, and perhaps he knew something of Thomas Hunt, who succeeded Roche in 1577.

9. Choose one.
(A) The instruction that he received was mainly confined to the latin language and literature.
(B) Latin language and literature was the instruction that he received and was mainly confined to that.
(C) The instruction that he received was mainly confined to the Latin language and literature.

From the Latin accidence, boys of the period, at schools of the type of that at Stratford, were led, through conversation books like the "Sententiæ Pueriles" and Lily's grammar, to the perusal of such authors as Seneca, Terence, Cicero, Virgil, Plautus, Ovid, and Horace. The eclogues of the popular renaissance poet, Mantuanus, were often preferred to Virgil's for beginners. The rudiments of Greek were occasionally taught in Elizabethan grammar schools to very promising pupils; but such coincidences as have been detected between expressions in Greek plays and in Shakespeare seem due to accident, and not to any study, either at school or elsewhere, of the Athenian drama.

Dr. Farmer enunciated in his "Essay on Shakespeare's Learning" (1767) the theory that Shakespeare knew no language but his own, and owed whatever knowledge he displayed of the classics and of Italian and French literature to English translations. But several of the books in French and Italian whence Shakespeare derived the plots of his dramas—Belleforest's "Histoires Tragiques," Ser Giovanni's "Il Pecorone," and Cinthio's "Hecatommithi," for example—were not accessible to him in English translations; and on more general grounds the theory of his ignorance is adequately confuted.

10. Choose one.
(A) A boy with Shakespeares exceptional alertness of intellect, during whose schooldays a training in Latin classics lay within reach, could hardly lack in future years all means of access to the literature of France and Italy.
(B) A boy with Shakespeare's exceptional alertness of intellect, during whose schooldays a training in Latin classics lay within reach, could hardly lack in future years all means of access to the literature of France and Italy.
(C) A boy with Shakespeare's exceptional alertness of intellect, during whose schooldays a training in Latin classics lay within reach, could hardly lack in future years all means of access to the literature of france and italy.

Excerpt from *My Life and Work*
by Henry Ford

WHAT IS THE IDEA?

We have only started on our development of our country—we have not as yet, with all our talk of wonderful progress, done more than scratch the surface. The progress has been wonderful enough—but when we compare what we have done with what there is to do, then our past accomplishments are as nothing. When we consider that more power is used merely in plowing the soil than is used in all the industrial establishments of the country put together, an inkling comes of how much opportunity there is ahead. And now, with so many countries of the world in ferment and with so much unrest every where, is an excellent time to suggest something of the things that may be done in the light of what has been done.

11. Choose one.
   (A) When one speaks of increasing power, machinery, and industry there comes up a picture of a cold, metallic sort of world in which great factories will drive away the trees, the flowers, the birds, and the green fields.
   (B) When one speaks of increasing power, machinery, and industry. There comes up a picture of a cold, metallic sort of world in which great factories will drive away the trees, the flowers, the birds, and the green fields.
   (C) When one speaks of increasing power, machinery, and industry there coming up a picture of a cold, metallic sort of world in which great factories will drive away the trees, the flowers, the birds, and the green fields.

And that then we shall have a world composed of metal machines and human machines.

12. Choose one.
   (A) With all of that I does not agree.
   (B) With all of that. I do not agree.
   (C) With all of that I do not agree.

I think that unless we know more about machines and their use, unless we better understand the mechanical portion of life, we cannot have the time to enjoy the trees, and the birds, and the flowers, and the green fields.

I think that we have already done too much toward banishing the pleasant things from life by thinking that there is some opposition between living and providing the means of living. We waste so much time and energy that we have little left over in which to enjoy ourselves.

Power and machinery, money and goods, are useful only as they set us free to live. They are but means to an end. For instance, I do not consider the machines which bear my name simply as machines. If that was all there was to it I would do something else. I take them as concrete evidence of the working out of a theory of business, which I hope is something more than a theory of business—a theory that looks toward making this world a better place in which to live. The fact that the commercial success of the Ford Motor Company has been most unusual is important only because it serves to demonstrate, in a way which no one can fail to understand, that the theory to date is right. Considered solely in this light I can criticize the prevailing system of industry and the organization of money and society from the standpoint of one who has not been beaten by them.

13. Choose one.
    (A) As things are now organized, I could, were I thinking only selfishly, ask for no change.
    (B) As things are now organized. I could, were I thinking only selfishly, ask for no change.
    (C) As things are now organized, I could, were thinking only selfishly, ask for no change.

If I merely want money the present system is all right; it gives money in plenty to me. But I am thinking of service. The present system does not permit of the best service because it encourages every kind of waste—it keeps many men from getting the full return from service. And it is going nowhere. It is all a matter of better planning and adjustment.

I have no quarrel with the general attitude of scoffing at new ideas.

14. Choose one.
    (A) Better to be skeptical of all new ideas and to insist upon being shown rather than to rush around in a continuous brainstorm after every new idea.
    (B) It is better to be skeptical of all new ideas and to insist upon being shown rather than to rush around in a continuous brainstorm after every new idea.
    (C) It better to be skeptical of all new ideas and to insist upon being shown rather than to rush around in a continuous brainstorm after every new idea.

Skepticism, if by that we mean cautiousness, is the balance wheel of civilization. Most of the present acute troubles of the world arise out of taking on new ideas without first carefully investigating to discover if they are good ideas. An idea is not necessarily good because it is old, or necessarily bad because it is new, but if an old idea works, then the weight of the evidence is all in its favor. Ideas are of themselves extraordinarily valuable, but an idea is just an idea. Almost any one can think up an idea. The thing that counts is developing it into a practical product.

I am now most interested in fully demonstrating that the ideas we have put into practice are capable of the largest application—that they have nothing peculiarly to do with motor cars or tractors but form something in the nature of a universal code. I am quite certain that it is the natural code and I want to demonstrate it so thoroughly that it will be accepted, not as a new idea, but as a natural code.

The natural thing to do is to work—to recognize that prosperity and happiness can be obtained only through honest effort. Human ills flow largely from attempting to escape from this natural course. I have no suggestion which goes beyond accepting in its fullest this principle of nature. I take it for granted that we must work. All that we have done comes as the result of a certain insistence that since we must work it is better to work intelligently and forehandedly; that the better we do our work the better off we shall be. All of which I conceive to be merely elemental common sense.

15. Choose one.
    (A) I are not a reformer.
    (B) Not being a reformer.
    (C) I am not a reformer.

I think there is entirely too much attempt at reforming in the world and that we pay too much attention to reformers. We have two kinds of reformers. Both are nuisances. The man who calls himself a reformer wants to smash things. He is the sort of man who would tear up a whole shirt because the collar button did not fit the buttonhole. It would never occur to him to enlarge the buttonhole. This sort of reformer never under any circumstances knows what he is doing. Experience and reform do not go together. A reformer cannot keep his zeal at white heat in the presence of a fact. He must discard all facts.

QUESTIONS 16 THROUGH 20 ARE EMBEDDED IN THE FOLLOWING PASSAGE:

Excerpt from *Story of My Life*
by Helen Keller

It is with a kind of fear that I begin to write the history of my life. I have, as it were, a superstitious hesitation in lifting the veil that clings about my childhood like a golden mist. The task of writing an autobiography is a difficult one. When I try to classify my earliest impressions, I find that fact and fancy look alike across the years that link the past with the present. The woman paints the child's experiences in her own fantasy. A few impressions stand out vividly from the first years of my life; but "the shadows of the prison-house are on the rest." Besides, many of the joys and sorrows of childhood have lost their poignancy; and many incidents of vital importance in my early education have been forgotten in the excitement of great discoveries. In order, therefore, not to be tedious I shall try to present in a series of sketches only the episodes that seem to me to be the most interesting and important.

16. Choose one.
    (A) Born on June 27, 1880, in Tuscumbia, a little town of northern Alabama.
    (B) I was born on June 27, 1880, in Tuscumbia, a little town of northern Alabama.
    (C) I was born on June 27, 1880. It was a little town of northern Alabama. It was called Tuscumbia,

The family on my father's side is descended from Caspar Keller, a native of Switzerland, who settled in Maryland. One of my Swiss ancestors was the first teacher of the deaf in Zurich and wrote a book on the subject of their education—rather a singular coincidence; though it is true that there is no king who has not had a slave among his ancestors, and no slave who has not had a king among his.

My grandfather, Caspar Keller's son, "entered" large tracts of land in Alabama and finally settled there. I have been told that once a year he went from Tuscumbia to Philadelphia on horseback to purchase supplies for the plantation, and my aunt has in her possession many of the letters to his family, which give charming and vivid accounts of these trips.

My Grandmother Keller was a daughter of one of Lafayette's aides, Alexander Moore, and granddaughter of Alexander Spotswood, an early Colonial Governor of Virginia. She was also second cousin to Robert E. Lee.

17. Choose one.
    (A) My father, Arthur H. Keller, was a captain in the Confederate Army, and my mother, her name was Kate Adams, was his second wife and many years younger.
    (B) My father, Arthur H. Keller, was a captain in the Confederate Army, and my mother, Kate Adams, was his second wife and many years younger.
    (C) My father, Arthur H. Keller, was a captain in the Confederate Army, and my mother, Kate Adams, his second wife and many years younger.

Her grandfather, Benjamin Adams, married Susanna E. Goodhue, and lived in Newbury, Massachusetts, for many years. Their son, Charles Adams, was born in Newburyport, Massachusetts, and moved to Helena, Arkansas. When the Civil War broke out, he fought on the side of the South and became a brigadier-general. He married Lucy Helen Everett, who belonged to the same family of Everetts as Edward Everett and Dr. Edward Everett Hale. After the war was over the family moved to Memphis, Tennessee.

I lived, up to the time of the illness that deprived me of my sight and hearing, in a tiny house consisting of a large square room and a small one, in which the servant slept. It is a custom in the South to build a small house near the homestead as an annex to be used on occasion. Such a house my father built after the Civil War, and when he married my mother they went to live in it. It was completely covered with vines, climbing roses and honeysuckles. From the garden it looked like an arbor.

18. Choose one.
    (A) The little porch, having been hidden from view by a screen of yellow roses and Southern smilax.
    (B) The little porch was hidden from view by a screen of yellow roses and Southern smilax.
    (C) The little porch was hidden from having been seen by a screen of yellow roses and Southern smilax.

It was the favorite haunt of humming-birds and bees.

The Keller homestead, where the family lived, was a few steps from our little rose-bower. It was called "Ivy Green" because the house and the surrounding trees and fences were covered with beautiful English ivy. Its old-fashioned garden was the paradise of my childhood.

Even in the days before my teacher came, I used to feel along the square stiff boxwood hedges, and, guided by the sense of smell would find the first violets and lilies. There, too, after a fit of temper, I went to find comfort and to hide my hot face in the cool leaves and grass. What joy it was to lose myself in that garden of flowers, to wander happily from spot to spot, until, coming suddenly upon a beautiful vine, I recognized it by its leaves and blossoms, and knew it was the vine which covered the tumble-down summer-house at the farther end of the garden! Here, also, were trailing clematis, drooping jessamine, and some rare sweet flowers called butterfly lilies, because their fragile petals resemble butterflies' wings. But the roses—they were loveliest of all. Never have I found in the greenhouses of the North such heart-satisfying roses as the climbing roses of my southern home. They used to hang in long festoons from our porch, filling the whole air with their fragrance, untainted by any earthy smell; and in the early morning, washed in the dew, they felt so soft, so pure, I could not help wondering if they did not resemble the asphodels of God's garden.

The beginning of my life was simple and much like every other little life. I came, I saw, I conquered, as the first baby in the family always does.

19. Choose one.
    (A) There was the usual amount of discussion as to a name for me.
    (B) Their was the usual amount of discussion as to a name for me.
    (C) They're was the usual amount of discussion as to a name for me.

The first baby in the family was not to be lightly named, every one was emphatic about that. My father suggested the name of Mildred Campbell, an ancestor whom he highly esteemed, and he declined to take any further part in the discussion. My mother solved the problem by giving it as her wish that I should be called after her mother, whose maiden name was Helen Everett. But in the excitement of carrying me to church my father lost the name on the way, very naturally, since it was one in which he had declined to have a part.

20. Choose one.
    (A) When the minister asked him for it, he just remembered that it had been decided to call me after my grandmother, and he gave her name as Helen Adams.
    (B) When the minister asked him for it. He just remembered that it had been decided to call me after my grandmother, and he gave her name as Helen Adams.
    (C) When the minister asked him for it, he just remembered that it had been decided to call me after my grandmother, and he gave her name as Helen adams.

Answers and Explanations

1. **(C)** A is missing a verb. B is too wordy.

2. **(C)** A is missing a verb. B incorrectly has a lowercase letter for "dr."

3. **(C)** A is a run-on sentence. B is missing a verb in the second sentence.

4. **(B)** A and C incorrectly use -ing words.

5. **(B)** A is missing commas before and after "however." C is missing the verb "is."

6. **(C)** A should have a capital "s" for "September." B incorrectly uses the conjunction "but."

7. **(B)** A is missing a "being" verb. C incorrectly uses a plural verb.

8. **(A)** B incorrectly capitalizes "negotiation." C is missing commas before "which" and after "litigation."

9. **(C)** A doesn't capitalize "Latin." B is unnecessarily wordy and its use of "was" is redundant.

10. **(B)** A is missing the apostrophe in "Shakespeare's." C fails to capitalize "France" and "Italy."

11. **(A)** The first sentence in B is actually a sentence fragment. C incorrectly uses the word "coming."

12. **(C)** A does not have subject-verb agreement. The first sentence in B is actually a sentence fragment.

13. **(A)** The first sentence in B is actually a sentence fragment. C should have the word "I" before "thinking."

14. **(B)** A is missing a subject. C is missing a verb.

15. **(C)** A does not have subject-verb agreement. B is a sentence fragment.

16. **(B)** A is missing a subject. C should be combined into one sentence and should end with a period, not a comma.

17. **(B)** A is wordy. Its use of "her name was" is redundant. C is missing a verb in the second independent clause.

18. **(B)** A is a sentence fragment. C is framed awkwardly.

19. **(A)** B incorrectly uses the possessive "their." C incorrectly uses the contraction "they're."

20. **(A)** The first sentence in B is actually a sentence fragment and should be combined with the second sentence. C incorrectly has a lowercase "a" for the proper noun "Adams."

Extended Responses

The extended-response section of the Language Arts subject test gives test takers the chance to express their ideas to an assigned prompt. Test takers must develop their ideas logically and include details to support their assertions. In addition, they must use proper grammar and include varied, precise, and appropriate words.

In layman's terms, you need to elevate your language, make sure there are few errors, and express yourself clearly!

> **The following topics will be covered in this unit:**
>
> **Lesson 1: Format and Planning**
>
> **Lesson 2: Beginning**
>
> **Lesson 3: Middle**
>
> **Lesson 4: End**
>
> **Lesson 5: Planning**
>
> **Lesson 6: Constructing Your Response**

The test evaluators use a fairly complex system of evaluating your writing. However, it can be broken down into three categories:

1. Quality and validity of your argument
2. Organization and level of language
3. Conformity to standard English

So what do you need to be able to do? Here is an excerpt from the Common Core Learning Standards:

COLLEGE AND CAREER READINESS ANCHOR STANDARDS FOR WRITING

Note on range and content of student writing

For students, writing is a key means of asserting and defending claims, showing what they know about a subject, and conveying what they have experienced, imagined, thought, and felt. To be college- and career-ready writers, students must take task, purpose, and audience into careful consideration, choosing words, information, structures, and formats deliberately. They need to know how to combine elements of different kinds of writing—for example, to use narrative strategies within argument and explanation within narrative—to produce complex and nuanced writing. They need to be able to use technology strategically when creating, refining, and collaborating on writing. They have to become adept at gathering information, evaluating sources, and citing material accurately, reporting findings from their research and analysis of sources in a clear and cogent manner. They must have the flexibility, concentration, and fluency to produce high-quality first-draft text under a tight deadline as well as the capacity to revisit and make improvements to a piece of writing over multiple drafts when circumstances encourage or require it.

TEXT TYPES AND PURPOSES

1. Write arguments to support claims in an analysis of substantive topics or texts, using valid reasoning and relevant and sufficient evidence.
2. Write informative/explanatory texts to examine and convey complex ideas and information clearly and accurately through the effective selection, organization, and analysis of content.
3. Write narratives to develop real or imagined experiences or events using effective technique, well-chosen details, and well-structured event sequences.

PRODUCTION AND DISTRIBUTION OF WRITING

4. Produce clear and coherent writing in which the development, organization, and style are appropriate to task, purpose, and audience.
5. Develop and strengthen writing as needed by planning, revising, editing, rewriting, or trying a new approach.
6. Use technology, including the Internet, to produce and publish writing and to interact and collaborate with others.

RESEARCH TO BUILD AND PRESENT KNOWLEDGE

7. Conduct short as well as more sustained research projects based on focused questions, demonstrating understanding of the subject under investigation.
8. Gather relevant information from multiple print and digital sources, assess the credibility and accuracy of each source, and integrate the information while avoiding plagiarism.
9. Draw evidence from literary or informational texts to support analysis, reflection, and research.

RANGE OF WRITING

10. Write routinely over extended time frames (time for research, reflection, and revision) and shorter time frames (a single sitting or a day or two) for a range of tasks, purposes, and audiences.

RESPONDING TO LITERATURE

11. Develop personal, cultural, textual, and thematic connections within and across genres as they respond to texts through written, digital, and oral presentations, employing a variety of media and genres.

Writing can be a daunting task, but it doesn't have to be. If you walk into a kitchen for the first time, you may not know exactly where everything is. However, certain things are usually in certain places. Glasses and plates will probably be in the cabinets, utensils will probably be in one of the drawers, and cleaning supplies will probably be under the sink. Layouts of kitchens are pretty predictable, and so are layouts for the extended responses on the GED® test.

The Structure of an Extended Response

A well-written extended response has three main components:

→ **BEGINNING**
→ **MIDDLE**
→ **END**

This may seem overly simplistic. However, the evaluators are simply looking for your writing to have a clear structure with a logical order. Just like in a kitchen, certain things belong in each of these paragraphs and certain things don't.

We've all heard the expression, "You never get a second chance to make a first impression." First impressions are important because they influence others' expectations and set the tone for the relationships. The same is true in writing. The introductory paragraph is like a first impression. It sets the tone for the rest of the extended response.

The purpose of the introductory paragraph is to let the reader know what you are going to discuss in the body paragraphs. As with the extended response as a whole, certain things should be included in an introductory paragraph:

> → **INTRODUCTORY SENTENCE**
> → **LISTING OF SUPPORTING DETAILS/EXAMPLES**
> → **CONTROLLING IDEA/THESIS STATEMENT**

The Introductory Sentence

The introductory sentence is the very first sentence of the extended response. It should grab the reader's attention and give a sense of the topic. Several types of introductory sentences work well as a "hook":

> → **GENERAL STATEMENT ABOUT THE TOPIC**
> → **QUOTE**
> → **QUESTION**
> → **STATEMENT OF A FACT**

Keep in mind that however you choose to begin your introductory paragraph, it must fit within the context of the extended response as a whole.

List of Supporting Details/Examples

The next sentence should be a list of the details that will be discussed in the body paragraphs to support the thesis statement. You should not elaborate on the details, as that is the purpose of the body of the extended response; simply list the details and examples.

Controlling Idea/Thesis Statement

The thesis statement is the controlling idea of your extended response. It should address the questions:

> *Why are you writing this?*
> *What is your point?*
> *What do you want to prove?*

So . . .

When put together, these three sentences form the beginning or introductory paragraph. Although the introductory sentence should always come first, the list of supporting details and examples may come either before or after the thesis statement.

The body paragraphs make up the majority of the extended response. So they must be complete and properly organized. Much like the introductory paragraph, certain types of sentences go at the beginning, middle, and end of each body paragraph. Each of these paragraphs should discuss one of the details listed in the introductory paragraph and contain the following:

→ **TRANSITIONAL SENTENCE**
→ **TOPIC SENTENCE**
→ **EXAMPLES AND SUPPORTING DETAILS**
→ **CONCLUDING SENTENCE**

Having all of these components in this order in each paragraph will help ensure that the paragraph is organized and complete.

Transitional Sentence

When moving from the introductory paragraph to a body paragraph or from one body paragraph to another, transition smoothly. Use transitional words and phrases.

Topic Sentence

The topic sentence should tell the reader the main idea of the paragraph. It is very similar to the thesis statement in that it should indicate the purpose of the paragraph.

Examples and Supporting Details

Being told that the moon is made of green cheese isn't very persuasive unless you're presented with evidence to support that claim. When taking a position on an issue, you must include an adequate amount of evidence to support that position.

Concluding Sentence

The concluding sentence should tie up any loose ends. More importantly, it should tell the reader how the information in the paragraph relates to the thesis statement.

Depending on the number of body paragraphs and the complexity of the sentences, a good length for a body paragraph is typically 4 to 7 sentences. However, the length is less important than the quality of the information. A well-written, well-supported short paragraph is far better than a poorly written, inadequately supported long paragraph.

Just as a well-written introductory paragraph is important in making a good first impression, the conclusion is important in making a good final impression. In fact, the conclusion contains much of the same information as the introductory paragraph, just in different words. The conclusion should contain the following items:

→ **RESTATEMENT OF THE CONTROLLING IDEA/THESIS STATEMENT**
→ **REITERATION OF THE MOST IMPORTANT DETAILS**
→ **CONCLUDING SENTENCE/CLINCHER**

Restatement of the Controlling Idea/Thesis Statement

Saying the same exact thing twice doesn't strengthen your argument; it just sounds repetitive. So be careful when restating the controlling idea or thesis statement. Make sure that how you phrase the idea in the introductory and concluding paragraphs is different.

Summary of the Most Important Details

Just like with the controlling idea, do not repeat the details from the body paragraphs word for word. Rather than listing the details again, paraphrase your most interesting or important points.

Concluding Sentence/Clincher

Have you ever had a great meal and saved the best bite of food for last? The last bite is the one that stays with you after the meal is over. The concluding sentence has the same effect on the reader. For better or for worse, the concluding sentence will stay with the reader. So be sure it will make a strong impact.

LESSON 5: PLANNING

The GED® test is a timed exam. Keep this in mind, and work quickly. Remember that working quickly does not mean cutting corners! People tend to want to begin writing their essay right away because they don't want to waste time. However, if you take a few minutes to plan your response, you will save time because your thoughts will already be in order.

While writing extended responses in this book, we recommend you use a diagramming technique to plan your essay. Diagramming helps you not only plan your essay, but also helps you visualize the material. This is especially important when you compare and contrast or put events in a logical order.

Below is a Venn diagram that is useful for planning extended responses that ask you to compare and contrast. The far left and far right areas are where you will list the ways in which each is unique. Where the circles overlap in the middle is where you will list the ways in which they are similar.

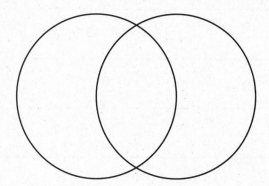

The following is a planning web. This is especially useful when you are listing characteristics of a single item or how multiple things relate to a single item.

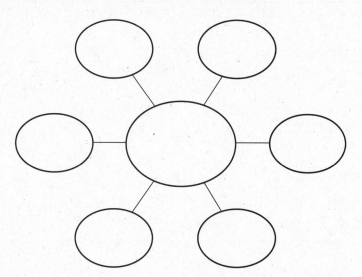

If nothing else, keep it simple and come up with a list!

1.	
2.	
3.	
4.	
5.	
6.	
7.	
8.	
9.	
10.	

Here are 7 steps to follow when constructing an extended response.

STEP 1 Carefully read both the question and the passage.

In order to construct a high-quality response to the prompt, you must understand what the question is asking you as well as the material contained within the passages. Read the prompt first and then the passage. This way, you will know what type of information to look for while reading the passage.

STEP 2 Reread the prompt and identify important words.

Rereading the prompt and extracting the key words will help ensure that you respond to the given prompt. If you write a wonderful response that doesn't address the prompt, you will not receive any credit.

STEP 3 Write a direct response to the question or prompt.

Begin by making sure you have responded to the prompt. If you do so, it is more likely that your response will stay on track and that you will write about what is being asked of you.

STEP 4 Refer back to the passage, and find details that support your position.

A large portion of the score on the extended responses will have to do with your argument. An argument is more effective when you include evidence to back it. So make sure you cite a sufficient amount of evidence from the passage.

STEP 5 Arrange your ideas logically.

Now that you have assembled your supporting details, make sure that the essay is written in a logical order. You can order the ideas by time, size, significance, or some other logical methods.

STEP 6 Write a rough draft.

Write out a preliminary version of the response. Remember that since you are typing your extended response, it will be very easy to go back and change things or to cut out and move entire sections if need be.

STEP 7 Reread and revise your essay.

The goal is for the essay to be as good as possible. So if you can avoid it, don't submit the essay until you've reread and revised it. Ask yourself the following questions:

- Have I responded to the prompt?
- Have I included enough evidence?
- Do my ideas follow a logical order?
- Are any words misspelled?
- Have I confused any homonyms?
- Have I used proper punctuation, including periods, commas, semicolons, and apostrophes?
- Do I need to break up any run-on sentences?
- Can I combine any strings of short, choppy sentences?

After you have asked yourself these questions and made all appropriate changes, read your response one last time. If you are satisfied, submit it.

Review Test

DIRECTIONS: Read and use the passages that follow to construct an extended response to this prompt.

> Over the years, the United States has had varying policies on Native Americans as is suggested in the two passages below. In your extended response, compare and contrast the attitudes toward Native Americans and indicate whether the Treaty of Fort Laramie was beneficial or detrimental to Native Americans.

Cite specific information and examples to support your position. Be sure to develop your answers fully.

President Andrew Jackson's Message to Congress "On Indian Removal" (1830)

1   With the onset of westward expansion and increased contact with Indian tribes, President Jackson set the tone for his position on Indian affairs in his message to Congress on December 6, 1830. Jackson's message justified the removal policy already established by the Indian Removal Act of May 28, 1830.

2   The Indian Removal Act was passed to open up for settlement those lands still held by Indians in states east of the Mississippi River, primarily Georgia, Tennessee, Alabama, Mississippi, North Carolina, and others. Jackson declared that removal would "incalculably strengthen the southwestern frontier." Clearing Alabama and Mississippi of their Indian populations, he said, would "enable those states to advance rapidly in population, wealth, and power."

3   White inhabitants of Georgia were particularly anxious to have the Cherokees removed from the state because gold had been discovered on tribal lands. Violence was commonplace in Georgia, and in all likelihood, a portion of the tribe would have been decimated if they had not been removed.

4   Removal of the Indian tribes continued beyond Jackson's tenure as President. The most infamous of the removals took place in 1838, two years after the end of Jackson's final term, when the Cherokee Indians were forcibly removed by the military. Their journey west became known as the "Trail of Tears," because of the thousands of deaths along the way.

REASONING THROUGH LANGUAGE ARTS 131

UNIT 1: LANGUAGE ARTS

Excerpt from Treaty of Fort Laramie (1868)

1   ARTICLES OF A TREATY MADE AND CONCLUDED BY AND BETWEEN

2   Lieutenant General William T. Sherman, General William S. Harney, General Alfred H. Terry, General O. O. Augur, J. B. Henderson, Nathaniel G. Taylor, John G. Sanborn, and Samuel F. Tappan, duly appointed commissioners on the part of the United States, and the different bands of the Sioux Nation of Indians, by their chiefs and headmen, whose names are hereto subscribed, they being duly authorized to act in the premises.

3   ARTICLE I. From this day forward all war between the parties to this agreement shall for ever cease. The government of the United States desires peace, and its honor is hereby pledged to keep it. The Indians desire peace, and they now pledge their honor to maintain it.

4   If bad men among the whites, or among other people subject to the authority of the United States, shall commit any wrong upon the person or property of the Indians, the United States will, upon proof made to the agent, and forwarded to the Commissioner of Indian Affairs at Washington city, proceed at once to cause the offender to be arrested and punished according to the laws of the United States, and also reimburse the injured person for the loss sustained.

5   If bad men among the Indians shall commit a wrong or depredation upon the person or property of nay one, white, black, or Indian, subject to the authority of the United States, and at peace therewith, the Indians herein named solemnly agree that they will, upon proof made to their agent, and notice by him, deliver up the wrongdoer to the United States, to be tried and punished according to its laws, and, in case they willfully refuse so to do, the person injured shall be reimbursed for his loss from the annuities, or other moneys due or to become due to them under this or other treaties made with the United States; and the President, on advising with the Commissioner of Indian Affairs, shall prescribe such rules and regulations for ascertaining damages under the provisions of this article as in his judgment may be proper, but no one sustaining loss while violating the provisions of this treaty, or the laws of the United States, shall be reimbursed therefor.

6   ARTICLE II. The United States agrees that the following district of country, to wit, viz: commencing on the east bank of the Missouri river where the 46th parallel of north latitude crosses the same, thence along low-water mark down said east bank to a point opposite where the northern line of the State of Nebraska strikes the river, thence west across said river, and along the northern line of Nebraska to the 104th degree of longitude west from Greenwich, thence north on said meridian to a point where the 46th parallel of north latitude intercepts the same, thence due east along said parallel to the place of beginning; and in addition thereto, all existing reservations of the east back of said river, shall be and the same is, set apart for the absolute and undisturbed use and occupation of the Indians herein named, and for such other friendly tribes or individual Indians as from time to time they may be willing, with the consent of the United States, to admit amongst them; and the United States now solemnly agrees that no persons, except those herein designated and authorized so to do, and except such officers, agents, and employees of the government as may be authorized to enter upon Indian reservations in discharge of duties enjoined by law, shall ever be permitted to

pass over, settle upon, or reside in the territory described in this article, or in such territory as may be added to this reservation for the use of said Indians, and henceforth they will and do hereby relinquish all claims or right in and to any portion of the United States or Territories, except such as is embraced within the limits aforesaid, and except as hereinafter provided.

7   ARTICLE III. If it should appear from actual survey or other satisfactory examination of said tract of land that it contains less than 160 acres of tillable land for each person who, at the time, may be authorized to reside on it under the provisions of this treaty, and a very considerable number of such persons hsall be disposed to comence cultivating the soil as farmers, the United States agrees to set apart, for the use of said Indians, as herein provided, such additional quantity of arable land, adjoining to said reservation, or as near to the same as it can be obtained, as may be required to provide the necessary amount.

8   ARTICLE IV. The United States agrees, at its own proper expense, to construct, at some place on the Missouri river, near the centre of said reservation where timber and water may be convenient, the following buildings, to wit, a warehouse, a store-room for the use of the agent in storing goods belonging to the Indians, to cost not less than $2,500; an agency building, for the residence of the agent, to cost not exceeding $3,000; a residence for the physician, to cost not more than $3,000; and five other buildings, for a carpenter, farmer, blacksmith, miller, and engineer—each to cost not exceeding $2,000; also, a school-house, or mission building, so soon as a sufficient number of children can be induced by the agent to attend school, which shall not cost exceeding $5,000.

CONSTRUCTING A RESPONSE

When reviewing your extended response, make sure you have asked yourself the following questions:

- Have I responded to the prompt?
- Do I have enough evidence?
- Do my ideas follow a logical order?
- Are there any misspellings?
- Have I confused any homonyms?
- Have I used proper punctuation, including periods, commas, semicolons, apostrophes, and so forth?
- Do I need to break up any run-on sentences?
- Can I combine any strings of short, choppy sentences?

The prompt asks you to compare and contrast the attitudes toward Native Americans and indicate whether the Treaty of Fort Laramie was beneficial or detrimental to Native Americans. Make sure that you have chosen a side; either the treaty was beneficial or it was not. Make sure you have clearly articulated your position in the introductory part of the response. Following your introduction, compare and contrast the attitudes and cite specific evidence from both of the passages that you feel supports your position. Be sure to explain why. Finally, restate your position in the conclusion.

Homestead Act (1862)

1   The Homestead Act, enacted during the Civil War in 1862, provided that any adult citizen, or intended citizen, who had never borne arms against the U.S. government could claim 160 acres of surveyed government land. Claimants were required to "improve" the plot by building a dwelling and cultivating the land. After 5 years on the land, the original filer was entitled to the property, free and clear, except for a small registration fee. Title could also be acquired after only a 6-month residency and trivial improvements, provided the claimant paid the government $1.25 per acre. After the Civil War, Union soldiers could deduct the time they had served from the residency requirements.

2   Although this act was included in the Republican Party platform of 1860, support for the idea began decades earlier. Even under the Articles of Confederation before 1787, the distribution of government lands generated much interest and discussion.

3   The act, however, proved to be no panacea for poverty. Comparatively few laborers and farmers could afford to build a farm or acquire the necessary tools, seed, and livestock. In the end, most of those who purchased land under the act came from areas quite close to their new homesteads (Iowans moved to Nebraska, Minnesotans to South Dakota, and so on). Unfortunately, the act was framed so ambiguously that it seemed to invite fraud, and early modifications by Congress only compounded the problem. Most of the land went to speculators, cattlemen, miners, lumbermen, and railroads. Of some 500 million acres dispersed by the General Land Office between 1862 and 1904, only 80 million acres went to homesteaders. Indeed, small farmers acquired more land under the Homestead Act in the 20th century than in the 19th.

National Interstate and Defense Highways Act (1956)

1   Popularly known as the National Interstate and Defense Highways Act of 1956, the Federal-Aid Highway Act of 1956 established an interstate highway system in the United States. The movement behind the construction of a transcontinental superhighway started in the 1930s when President Franklin D. Roosevelt expressed interest in the construction of a network of toll superhighways that would provide more jobs for people in need of work during the Great Depression. The resulting legislation was the Federal-Aid Highway Act of 1938, which directed the chief of the Bureau of Public Roads (BPR) to study the feasibility of a six-route toll network. But with America on the verge of joining the war in Europe, the time for a massive highway program had not arrived. At

the end of the war, the Federal-Aid Highway Act of 1944 funded highway improvements and established major new ground by authorizing and designating, in Section 7, the construction of 40,000 miles of a "National System of Interstate Highways."

2   When President Dwight D. Eisenhower took office in January 1953, however, the states had only completed 6,500 miles of the system improvements. Eisenhower had first realized the value of good highways in 1919, when he participated in the U.S. Army's first transcontinental motor convoy from Washington, DC, to San Francisco. Again, during World War II, Eisenhower saw the German advantage that resulted from their autobahn highway network, and he also noted the enhanced mobility of the Allies, on those same highways, when they fought their way into Germany. These experiences significantly shaped Eisenhower's views on highways and their role in national defense. During his State of the Union Address on January 7, 1954, Eisenhower made it clear that he was ready to turn his attention to the nation's highway problems. He considered it important to "protect the vital interest of every citizen in a safe and adequate highway system."

3   Between 1954 and 1956, there were several failed attempts to pass a national highway bill through the Congress. The main controversy over the highway construction was the apportionment of the funding between the Federal Government and the states. Undaunted, the President renewed his call for a "modern, interstate highway system" in his 1956 State of the Union Address. Within a few months, after considerable debate and amendment in the Congress, The Federal-Aid Highway Act of 1956 emerged from the House-Senate conference committee. In the act, the interstate system was expanded to 41,000 miles, and to construct the network, $25 billion was authorized for fiscal years 1957 through 1969. During his recovery from a minor illness, Eisenhower signed the bill into law at Walter Reed Army Medical Center on the 29th of June. Because of the 1956 law, and the subsequent Highway Act of 1958, the pattern of community development in America was fundamentally altered and was henceforth based on the automobile.

CONSTRUCTING A RESPONSE

When reviewing your extended response, make sure you have asked yourself the following questions:

- Have I responded to the prompt?
- Do I have enough evidence?
- Do my ideas follow a logical order?
- Are there any misspellings?
- Have I confused any homonyms?
- Have I used proper punctuation, including periods, commas, semicolons, apostrophes, and so forth?
- Do I need to break up any run-on sentences?
- Can I combine any strings of short, choppy sentences?

The prompt asks you to identify which act, the Homestead Act or the National Interstate and Defense Highways Act, had greater potential to help the American public and why. Make sure that you choose one of the two acts; do not choose both. Make sure you have clearly articulated your position in the introductory part of the response. Following your introduction, cite specific evidence from both of the passages that you feel indicates greater benefit and be sure to explain why. Finally, restate your position in the conclusion.

DIRECTIONS: Read and use the passages that follow to construct an extended response to this prompt.

Climate change has been a national dialogue over the past few decades, but is there enough evidence to suggest that global warming is taking place?

Cite specific information and examples to support your position. Be sure to develop your answers fully.

Climate Change Is Happening

1   Our Earth is warming. Earth's average temperature has risen by 1.4°F over the past century, and is projected to rise another 2 to 11.5°F over the next hundred years. Small changes in the average temperature of the planet can translate to large and potentially dangerous shifts in climate and weather.

2   The evidence is clear. Rising global temperatures have been accompanied by changes in weather and climate. Many places have seen changes in rainfall, resulting in more floods, droughts, or intense rain, as well as more frequent and severe heat waves. The planet's oceans and glaciers have also experienced some big changes—oceans are warming and becoming more acidic, ice caps are melting, and sea levels are rising. As these and other changes become more pronounced in the coming decades, they will likely present challenges to our society and our environment.

Humans are largely responsible for recent climate change

3   Over the past century, human activities have released large amounts of carbon dioxide and other greenhouse gases into the atmosphere. The majority of greenhouse gases come from burning fossil fuels to produce energy, although deforestation, industrial processes, and some agricultural practices also emit gases into the atmosphere.

4   Greenhouse gases act like a blanket around Earth, trapping energy in the atmosphere and causing it to warm. This phenomenon is called the greenhouse effect and is natural and necessary to support life on Earth. However, the buildup of greenhouse gases can change Earth's climate and result in dangerous effects to human health and welfare and to ecosystems.

5   The choices we make today will affect the amount of greenhouse gases we put in the atmosphere in the near future and for years to come.

Climate change affects everyone

6   Our lives are connected to the climate. Human societies have adapted to the relatively stable climate we have enjoyed since the last ice age which ended several thousand years ago. A warming climate will bring changes that can affect our water supplies, agriculture, power and transportation systems, the natural environment, and even our own health and safety.

7   Some changes to the climate are unavoidable. Carbon dioxide can stay in the atmosphere for nearly a century, so Earth will continue to warm in the coming decades. The warmer it gets, the greater the risk for more severe changes to the climate and Earth's system. Although it's difficult to predict the exact impacts of climate change, what's clear is that the climate we are accustomed to is no longer a reliable guide for what to expect in the future.

8   We can reduce the risks we will face from climate change. By making choices that reduce greenhouse gas pollution, and preparing for the changes that are already underway, we can reduce risks from climate change. Our decisions today will shape the world our children and grandchildren will live in.

We can make a difference

9   You can take action. You can take steps at home, on the road, and in your office to reduce greenhouse gas emissions and the risks associated with climate change. Many of these steps can save you money; some, such as walking or biking to work can even improve your health! You can also get involved on a local or state level to support energy efficiency, clean energy programs, or other climate programs.

10   Calculate your carbon footprint and find ways to reduce your emissions through simple everyday actions.

Source: epa.gov

Hurricane Sandy Overview

1   Hurricane Sandy will always be remembered for its devastating effects through several states across the northeastern United States. Although, before Sandy became a historic and tragic reminder of the power of Mother Nature, it wreaked havoc along the southeast Florida coast as it paralleled the coastline on its trek to the north. Although Sandy did not make landfall across south Florida, it did have a significant impact, most notably with regard to the large swells produced by Sandy's large wind field and their impacts on coastal flooding.

2   During the weekend of October 20–21, 2012, an area of disturbed weather just south of Hispaniola began to push to the west and strengthen. By Monday October 22, 2012, this area of convection eventually developed into Tropical Storm Sandy, becoming the 18th named storm of the Atlantic hurricane season. From this point, Tropical Storm Sandy turned and moved northward, making landfall in Jamaica as a category 1 hurricane on October 24th. Sandy then further intensified into a category 2 hurricane over the waters north of Jamaica and slammed into eastern Cuba at strong category 2 intensity. Sandy eventually weakened back down to a category 1 hurricane while tracking across the Bahamas. Sandy then began to take on a slight northwestward motion near the northern Bahamas. It is during this timeframe that the offshore Atlantic waters were heavily impacted by Sandy's passing.

Source: noaa.gov

CONSTRUCTING A RESPONSE

When reviewing your extended response, make sure you have asked yourself the following questions:

- Have I responded to the prompt?
- Do I have enough evidence?
- Do my ideas follow a logical order?
- Are there any misspellings?
- Have I confused any homonyms?
- Have I used proper punctuation, including periods, commas, semicolons, apostrophes, and so forth?
- Do I need to break up any run-on sentences?
- Can I combine any strings of short, choppy sentences?

The prompt asks if there is enough information to suggest that global warming is taking place. Make sure that you have chosen a side; either there is or there isn't. Make sure you have clearly articulated your position in the introductory part of the response. Following your introduction, indicate if the specific evidence is sufficient or insufficient and why. Finally, restate your position in your conclusion.

DIRECTIONS: Read and use the passages that follow to construct an extended response to this prompt.

There have been many great people who have changed the course of history. How did the lives of Charles Darwin and Theodore Roosevelt compare, and what childhood events may have influenced them?

Cite specific information and examples to support your position. Be sure to develop your answers fully.

Excerpt from *The Autobiography of Charles Darwin*

1   A German Editor having written to me for an account of the development of my mind and character with some sketch of my autobiography, I have thought that the attempt would amuse me, and might possibly interest my children or their children. I know that it would have interested me greatly to have read even so short and dull a sketch of the mind of my grandfather, written by himself, and what he thought and did, and how he worked. I have attempted to write the following account of myself, as if I were a dead man in another world looking back at my own life. Nor have I found this difficult, for life is nearly over with me. I have taken no pains about my style of writing.

2   I was born at Shrewsbury on February 12th, 1809, and my earliest recollection goes back only to when I was a few months over four years old, when we went to near Abergele for sea-bathing, and I recollect some events and places there with some little distinctness.

3   My mother died in July 1817, when I was a little over eight years old, and it is odd that I can remember hardly anything about her except her deathbed, her black velvet gown, and her curiously constructed worktable. In the spring of this same year I was sent to a day school in Shrewsbury, where I stayed a year. I have been told that I was much slower in learning than my younger sister Catherine, and I believe that I was in many ways a naughty boy.

4   By the time I went to this day school (Kept by Rev. G. Case, minister of the Unitarian Chapel in the High Street. Mrs. Darwin was a Unitarian and attended Mr. Case's chapel, and my father as a little boy went there with his elder sisters. But both he and his brother were christened and intended to belong to the Church of England; and after his early boyhood he seems usually to have gone to church and not to Mr. Case's. It appears ("St. James' Gazette", Dec. 15, 1883) that a mural tablet has been erected to his memory in the chapel, which is now known as the 'Free Christian Church.') my taste for natural history, and more especially for collecting, was well developed. I tried to make out the names of plants (Rev. W.A. Leighton, who was a schoolfellow of my father's at Mr. Case's school, remembers his bringing a flower to school and saying that his mother had taught him how by looking at the inside of the blossom the name of the plant could be discovered. Mr. Leighton goes on, "This greatly roused my attention and curiosity, and I enquired of him repeatedly how this could be done?"—but his lesson was naturally enough not transmissible.—F.D.), and collected all sorts of things, shells,

seals, franks, coins, and minerals. The passion for collecting which leads a man to be a systematic naturalist, a virtuoso, or a miser, was very strong in me, and was clearly innate, as none of my sisters or brother ever had this taste.

5   One little event during this year has fixed itself very firmly in my mind, and I hope that it has done so from my conscience having been afterwards sorely troubled by it; it is curious as showing that apparently I was interested at this early age in the variability of plants! I told another little boy (I believe it was Leighton, who afterwards became a well-known lichenologist and botanist), that I could produce variously colored polyanthuses and primroses by watering them with certain colored fluids, which was of course a monstrous fable, and had never been tried by me. I may here also confess that as a little boy I was much given to inventing deliberate falsehoods, and this was always done for the sake of causing excitement. For instance, I once gathered much valuable fruit from my father's trees and hid it in the shrubbery, and then ran in breathless haste to spread the news that I had discovered a hoard of stolen fruit.

6   I must have been a very simple little fellow when I first went to the school. A boy of the name of Garnett took me into a cake shop one day, and bought some cakes for which he did not pay, as the shopman trusted him. When we came out I asked him why he did not pay for them, and he instantly answered, "Why, do you not know that my uncle left a great sum of money to the town on condition that every tradesman should give whatever was wanted without payment to any one who wore his old hat and moved [it] in a particular manner?" and he then showed me how it was moved. He then went into another shop where he was trusted, and asked for some small article, moving his hat in the proper manner, and of course obtained it without payment. When we came out he said, "Now if you like to go by yourself into that cake-shop (how well I remember its exact position) I will lend you my hat, and you can get whatever you like if you move the hat on your head properly." I gladly accepted the generous offer, and went in and asked for some cakes, moved the old hat and was walking out of the shop, when the shopman made a rush at me, so I dropped the cakes and ran for dear life, and was astonished by being greeted with shouts of laughter by my false friend Garnett.

Excerpt from *Theodore Roosevelt*
an Autobiography by Theodore Roosevelt

1   My grandfather on my father's side was of almost purely Dutch blood. When he was young he still spoke some Dutch, and Dutch was last used in the services of the Dutch Reformed Church in New York while he was a small boy.

2   About 1644 his ancestor Klaes Martensen van Roosevelt came to New Amsterdam as a "settler"—the euphemistic name for an immigrant who came over in the steerage of a sailing ship in the seventeenth century instead of the steerage of a steamer in the nineteenth century. From that time for the next seven generations from father to son every one of us was born on Manhattan Island.

3   My father's paternal ancestors were of Holland stock; except that there was one named Waldron, a wheelwright, who was one of the Pilgrims who remained in Holland when the others came over to found Massachusetts, and who then accompanied the

Dutch adventurers to New Amsterdam. My father's mother was a Pennsylvanian. Her forebears had come to Pennsylvania with William Penn, some in the same ship with him; they were of the usual type of the immigration of that particular place and time. They included Welsh and English Quakers, an Irishman,—with a Celtic name, and apparently not a Quaker,—and peace-loving Germans, who were among the founders of Germantown, having been driven from their Rhineland homes when the armies of Louis the Fourteenth ravaged the Palatinate; and, in addition, representatives of a by-no-means altogether peaceful people, the Scotch Irish, who came to Pennsylvania a little later, early in the eighteenth century. My grandmother was a woman of singular sweetness and strength, the keystone of the arch in her relations with her husband and sons. Although she was not herself Dutch, it was she who taught me the only Dutch I ever knew, a baby song of which the first line ran, "Trippe troppa tronjes." I always remembered this, and when I was in East Africa it proved a bond of union between me and the Boer settlers, not a few of whom knew it, although at first they always had difficulty in understanding my pronunciation—at which I do not wonder. It was interesting to meet these men whose ancestors had gone to the Cape about the time that mine went to America two centuries and a half previously, and to find that the descendants of the two streams of emigrants still crooned to their children some at least of the same nursery songs.

4   Of my great-grandfather Roosevelt and his family life a century and over ago I know little beyond what is implied in some of his books that have come down to me—the Letters of Junius, a biography of John Paul Jones, Chief Justice Marshall's "Life of Washington." They seem to indicate that his library was less interesting than that of my wife's great-grandfather at the same time, which certainly included such volumes as the original *Edinburgh Review*, for we have them now on our own book-shelves. Of my grandfather Roosevelt my most vivid childish reminiscence is not something I saw, but a tale that was told me concerning him. In *his* boyhood Sunday was as dismal a day for small Calvinistic children of Dutch descent as if they had been of Puritan or Scotch Covenanting or French Huguenot descent—and I speak as one proud of his Holland, Huguenot, and Covenanting ancestors, and proud that the blood of that stark Puritan divine Jonathan Edwards flows in the veins of his children. One summer afternoon, after listening to an unusually long Dutch Reformed sermon for the second time that day, my grandfather, a small boy, running home before the congregation had dispersed, ran into a party of pigs, which then wandered free in New York's streets. He promptly mounted a big boar, which no less promptly bolted and carried him at full speed through the midst of the outraged congregation.

CONSTRUCTING A RESPONSE

When reviewing your extended response, make sure you have asked yourself the following questions:

- Have I responded to the prompt?
- Do I have enough evidence?
- Do my ideas follow a logical order?
- Are there any misspellings?
- Have I confused any homonyms?

- Have I used proper punctuation, including periods, commas, semicolons, apostrophes, and so forth?
- Do I need to break up any run-on sentences?
- Can I combine any strings of short, choppy sentences?

The prompt asks how the lives of Charles Darwin and Theodore Roosevelt compare and what may have influenced them as children. Make sure that you draw comparisons—how they are the same, not different. Make sure you have clearly articulated your position in the introductory part of the response. Following your introduction, cite specific evidence from their childhoods that you feel supports your position and be sure to explain why. Finally, restate your position in the conclusion.

UNIT 2

Mathematical Reasoning

Pretest

1. Which answer is the correct way to write the number 485,555 in words?
   (A) Four thousand hundred, fifty-five
   (B) Forty-eight thousand five hundred, fifty-five
   (C) Four hundred eighty-five thousand, five hundred, fifty-five
   (D) Four hundred, eighty five

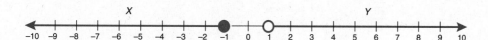

2. Use the number line above to answer the following:

   a. Write the inequality represented by X. -1

   b. Write the inequality represented by Y. $+1$

3. Estimate an answer for each of the following to the nearest hundred:

   a. $860 + 641 + 222 =$ 1,723

   b. $443 \times 31 =$ 13,673

   c. $516 \div 12 =$ 43

4. Find an exact answer for each of the following:

   a. $3,544 - 612 =$ 2932

   b. $112 \times 37 =$ 4,144

   c. $3,542 \div 20 =$ 177.1

5. Find the value of the expression 4($8.25 – $2.00) + ($13.80 ÷ 3).

= 29.6

6. What is the mean price of the shoes listed in the table below?

Shoe	Price
A	$32
B	$18
C	$7

B

7. How is this number read in words: 0.075?

8. Which of the following is the greatest?

(A) $\frac{1}{4}$

(B) 0.75

(C) 50%

(D) 1

9. Choose the proper symbol to compare each of the following pairs of numbers.

=, >, <

a. $\frac{4}{8}$ ___ $\frac{1}{2}$

b. $4\frac{1}{2}$ ___ $\frac{15}{3}$

c. $4\frac{2}{5}$ ___ $4\frac{1}{8}$

10. Solve the following:

a. $3\frac{1}{3} + 2\frac{4}{5} =$

b. $\frac{2}{5} \cdot \frac{1}{3} =$ $\frac{2}{15}$

c. $\frac{1}{2} \div \frac{4}{5} =$ $\frac{5}{8}$

11. Choose the proper symbol to compare each of the following pairs of numbers.

=, >, <

a. 0.74 __>__ 0.095

b. 0.378 __<__ 0.42

c. 2.51 __>__ 2.499

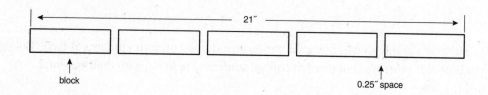

block   0.25″ space

12. Which expression can be used to find the width of each block?

(A) $\dfrac{21-(4\bullet0.25)}{5}$ 4

(B) $\dfrac{21+(5\bullet0.25)}{4}$

(C) $\dfrac{21-(5-4)}{0.25}$

(D) $\dfrac{21+(4\bullet0.25)}{5}$

13. Solve the following:

a. 2.68 − 1.44 = 1.24

b. 5.05 × 0.04 = 0.202

c. 5.144 ÷ 1.6 = 3215

14. The Fix-It Depot is offering a 30% discount on all ceiling fans. If sales tax is 7%, what will Danny pay for a ceiling fan with a normal price of $62?
(A) $18.60
(B) $14.46
(C) $46.44
(D) $54.20

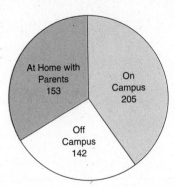

15. The circle graph above shows the various residential options students at Eagle College chose this year. What percent of college students are living with their parents?
    (A) 51%
    (B) 30.6%
    (C) 25.4%
    (D) 34.6%

16. Suppose that next year there is a 20% increase in enrollment at the school. If the ratios stay the same, how many college students will either be living off-campus or be living with their parents?
    (A) 354 students
    (B) 250 students
    (C) 264 students
    (D) 194 students

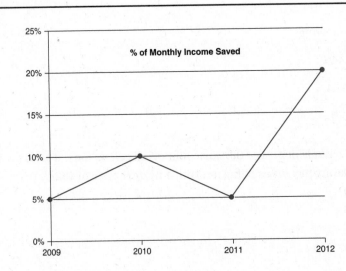

17. Based on the line graph above, what is the ratio of the amount that the Robinson family saved in 2009 to the amount they saved in 2012?
    (A) 1:4
    (B) 2:1
    (C) 4:1
    (D) 4:5

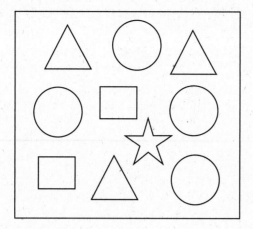

18. If Heather randomly takes a shape out of the box, shown in the diagram above, what is the probability she will grab a triangle?

    (A) $\dfrac{3}{7}$

    (B) $\dfrac{3}{10}$

    (C) $\dfrac{1}{2}$

    (D) $\dfrac{4}{7}$

19. Solve for x: $x - 12 = 8$.
    (A) 4
    (B) 6
    (C) −8
    (D) 20

20. Solve for y: $4y = 48$.
    (A) 24
    (B) 8
    (C) 12
    (D) 9

21. Solve for m: $\dfrac{m}{4} = 12$.

    (A) 32
    (B) 64
    (C) 38
    (D) 48

22. Solve for z: $\dfrac{4}{9} = \dfrac{z}{54}$.

(A) 16

(B) 24

(C) 4

(D) 20

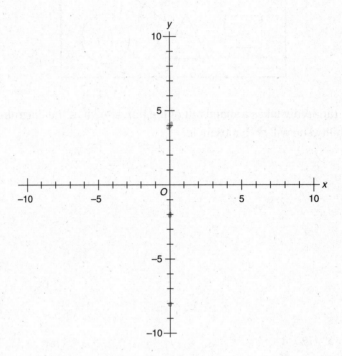

23. Use the coordinate plane shown above to complete the following:

a. Graph the equation $y = 3x + 1$. Plot the three points with x-values of –3, –1, and 1. Then connect the points with an extended line.

b. What is the y-intercept of the line you graphed?

c. What is the slope of the line?

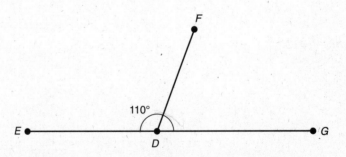

24. Line EG is a straight line. What is the measure of angle FDG? 70

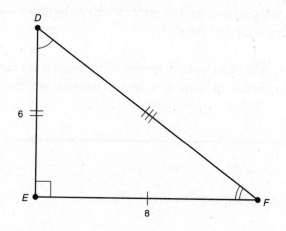

25. Use the Pythagorean theorem to find the length of side *DF* in the triangle shown above.

26. Compare using <, >, or =:

   a. 0.8357 _____ 0.8624

   b. 0.0009 _____ 0.009

27. Add and subtract:

   a. 0.861 + 0.06

   b. 0.09 – 0.004

28. Which of the following is equivalent to $(3.2 \times 10^{16}) \times (1.8 \times 10^{-11})$?
   (A) 5.76×10^5
   (B) 5.76×10^{19}
   (C) 5.76×10^{-5}
   (D) 5.76

29. 182 is what percent of 280?

30. A pair of Italian leather shoes goes on sale. The price is reduced from $280 to $182. By what percentage was the price of the shoes reduced?

31. A pair of Italian leather shoes goes on sale. The price is reduced from $280 to $182. What percentage of the original price is the sale price?

32. A leather laptop bag goes on sale. The price is reduced by 65% from the original price of $280. What is the sale price?

33. Damon is a writer. 45% of his published work is fiction, and the rest is nonfiction. What is the ratio of fiction to nonfiction among Damon's published work?
    (A) 55 to 45
    (B) 11 to 9
    (C) 9 to 11
    (D) 45 to 100

34. How many feet are in 8 meters? (1 meter = 3.28 feet)

35. How many cups are in 4 liters? (1 liter = 1.06 quarts and 1 quart = 4 cups)

Answers and Explanations

1. **(C)**

2. **a.** $x \le -1$ The closed endpoint on the line indicates that the range includes the endpoint (–1). The arrow extends away to the left, showing that the numbers are getting smaller. So x is less than or equal to –1.

   b. $y > 1$ The open endpoint on the line indicates that the range does not include the endpoint (1). The arrow extends away to the right, showing that the numbers are getting larger. So y is greater than 1.

3. **a. 1,700** When estimating to the nearest hundred, look at the digit in the tens place. If that digit is less than 5, the hundreds digit remains unchanged. This is called rounding down. If the digit in the tens place is 5 or greater, the hundreds digit is rounded up by adding 1 to it. Round each number in the equation:

   $$900 + 600 + 200 = 1,700.$$

   b. 12,000 $400 \times 30 = 12,000$

   c. 50 $500 \div 10 = 50$

4. **a. 2,932**

   b. 4,144

   c. 177.1

5. **29.60** Using the order of operations, first complete the operations inside the parentheses: ($8.25 – $2.00 = $6.25) and ($13.80 ÷ 3 = $4.60). The expression is now: 4($6.25) + $4.60. The next step is multiplication: $6.25 × 4 = $25.00. Finally, add $25.00 + $4.60 = $29.60.

6. **19** A mean is an average. This means you should add up the numbers and divide by the number of items:

   $$32 + 18 + 7 = 57 \div 3 = 19.$$

7. **Seventy-five thousandths** The third decimal place is called the "thousandths" place, and the number is read from the first nonzero digit.

8. **(D)** The other three numbers are all quantities between 0 and 1.

9. **a. =** Since 4 is one-half of 8, $\frac{4}{8}$ equals $\frac{1}{2}$.

   b. < $\frac{15}{3} = 5$, and 5 is greater than $4\frac{1}{2}$.

   c. > Since the leading whole number is the same, convert the fractions into decimals to compare: $\frac{2}{5} = 0.4$ and $\frac{1}{8} = 0.125$. So $4\frac{1}{2} = 4.4$ and $4\frac{1}{8} = 4.125$. Since 4.4 is greater than 4.125, use the > symbol.

10. **a.** $6\frac{2}{15}$ $3\frac{1}{3} + 2\frac{4}{5} = \frac{10}{3} + \frac{14}{5} = \frac{50}{15} + \frac{42}{15} = \frac{92}{15} = 6\frac{2}{15}$, or $3\frac{5}{15} + 2\frac{12}{15} = 5\frac{17}{15} = 6\frac{2}{15}$.

b. $\frac{2}{15}$ $\frac{2}{5} \cdot \frac{1}{3} = \frac{2}{15}$

c. $\frac{5}{8}$ $\frac{1}{2} \div \frac{4}{5} = \frac{1}{2} \cdot \frac{5}{4} = \frac{5}{8}$. When dividing fractions, invert the second fraction and multiply. Alternatively, you can cross multiply the numerator of the first fraction with the denominator of the second to form the new numerator. Then cross multiply the denominator of the first fraction with the numerator of the second to form the new denominator. So $1 \times 5 = 5$ is the new numerator and $2 \times 4 = 8$ is the new denominator.

11. a. > Compare the digits from left to right, starting with the first decimal place where at least one number has a nonzero digit. If the digits in that place are equal, move to the right. When one nonzero digit is greater or less than a digit in the same place, stop. 0.74 is greater than 0.095 because 7 is greater than 0.

b. < 0.378 is less than 0.42 because 3 is less than 4.

c. > 2.51 is greater than 2.499 because 5 is greater than 4.

12. (A) The total width given must be reduced by removing the spaces between the blocks: $21 - (4 \times 0.25) = 21 - 1 = 20$. Then the result should be divided by 5 to determine the length of each block:

$$20 \div 5 = 4.$$

13. a. 1.24 $2.68 - 1.44 = 1.24$

b. 2.02 $5.05 \times 0.04 = 0.202$

c. 3.215 $5.144 \div 1.6 = 3.215$

14. (C) The discount must be applied prior to the sales tax: $\$62 \times 0.3 = \$18.60$ off, and $\$62 - \$18.60 = \$43.40$. Then, apply the sales tax to the sales price to get the total $\$43.40 \times 1.07 = \$46.44$. Alternatively, you can find the amount of tax ($43.40 \times 0.07 = \$3.04$) and then add it to the discount price ($\$43.40 + \$3.04 = \$46.44$).

15. (B) First, calculate the total number of students: $205 + 142 + 153 = 500$. Then divide the number of students who live with their parents by the total number of students: $153 \div 500 = 0.306$. Then convert to percent by multiplying the answer by 100:

$$0.306 \times 100 = 30.6\%.$$

16. (A) Increase the original number of students who are living off campus and with their parents by 20%. Use decimals. The 1 in 1.2 represents the original number of students: $142 \times 1.2 = 170.4$ and $153 \times 1.2 = 183.6$. Add the amounts to get the total number of students who are either living off campus or are living with their parents:

$$170.4 + 183.6 = 354 \text{ students.}$$

17. (A) In 2009, the Robinsons saved 5%. In 2012, they saved 20%. This is 5:20, which simplifies to 1:4.

18. (B) There are 3 triangles out of 10 total shapes.

19. **(D)** Add 12 to both sides to isolate x.

20. **(C)** Divide both sides by 4 to isolate y: $\dfrac{4y}{4} = \dfrac{48}{4} \rightarrow y = 12$.

21. **(D)** Multiply both sides by 4 to isolate m.

22. **(B)** First cross multiply, which will result in $9z = 216$. Then divide both sides by 9 to isolate z: $\dfrac{9z}{9} = \dfrac{216}{9}$. This will result in $z = 24$.

23. **a.** The line is shown in the following graph. The points $(-3, -8)$, $(-1, -2)$, and $(1, 4)$ must be indicated.

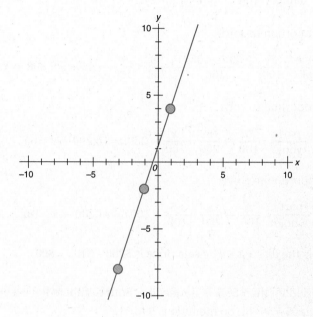

   b. 1 The line crosses the y–axis at $(0, 1)$.

   c. 3 When an equation is in $y = mx + b$ form, m is the slope. Since $y = 3x + 1$, $m = 3$. Instead, you may calculate the rise over run ratio by looking at your line. The result is the slope.

24. **70°** A straight line has 180°. The two angles are supplementary: $180° - 110° = 70°$.

25. **10** Pythagorean theorem says that in a right triangle, $a^2 + b^2 = c^2$. So $(6)(6) + (8)(8) = c^2$. Since $36 + 64 = 100$, that means $c^2 = 100$, and $c = 10$.

26. **a. <** Compare digits from left to right. If both are zero, move to the right. If both are the same, move to the right. If the digits are not the same, compare them. The 8 in the tenths place is the same in both numbers. The 3 in the hundreths place in 0.8357 is less than the 6 in the hundreths place in 0.8624. So 0.8357 < 0.8624.

   b. < The digits in the tenths and hundredths places are the same, 0. The 0 in the thousandths place in 0.0009 is less than the 9 in the thousandths place in 0.009. So 0.0009 < 0.009.

27. a. 0.921 Line up the decimal points, add zeros to the right as needed, and then add the columns: 0.861 + 0.06 = 0.921.

b. 0.086 Line up the decimal points, add zeros to the right as needed, and then subtract the columns: 0.09 − 0.004 = 0.086.

28. (A) Multiply the decimal numbers as normal: 3.2 × 1.8 = 5.76. Since this is multiplication, add the exponents of 10: 16 − 11 = 5. Scientific notation conventionally puts the decimal point next to the units digit, which is where it currently is: 5.76×10^5.

29. 65%. Use a proportion to solve:

$$\frac{\text{part}}{\text{whole}} = \frac{\%}{100} \rightarrow \frac{182}{280} = \frac{x}{100} \rightarrow 280x = 18,200 \rightarrow x = 65.$$

30. 35% Use a proportion to solve.

$$\frac{\text{difference}}{\text{original}} = \frac{\%}{100} \rightarrow \frac{(280 - 182)}{100} \cdot \rightarrow \frac{98}{280} = \frac{x}{100} \rightarrow 280x = 9,800 \rightarrow x = 35.$$

31. 65% Use a proportion to solve:

$$\frac{\text{part}}{\text{whole}} = \frac{\%}{100} \rightarrow \frac{182}{280} = \frac{x}{100} \rightarrow 280x = 18,200 \rightarrow x = 65.$$

32. $98 Use a proportion to solve:

$$\frac{\text{part}}{\text{whole}} = \frac{\%}{100} \rightarrow \frac{x}{280} = \frac{65}{100} \rightarrow 100x = 18,200 \rightarrow x = 182.$$

This represents the discount. The sale price is $280 − $182 = $98.

33. (C) If 45% is fiction, then 55% is nonfiction. Both numbers have a common factor of 5. 45 ÷ 5 = 9 and 55 ÷ 5 = 11. So the ratio is 9 to 11.

34. 26.24 Set up a proportion to solve. Remember to put one unit in each numerator and the other unit in each denominator:

$$\frac{x \text{ feet}}{8 \text{ meters}} = \frac{3.28 \text{ feet}}{1 \text{ meter}} \rightarrow x = (8)(3.28) = 26.24.$$

35. 16.96 Set up two proportions to solve. Remember that for each proportion, put one unit in each numerator and the other unit in each denominator:

$$\frac{x \text{ quarts}}{4 \text{ liters}} = \frac{1.06 \text{ quarts}}{1 \text{ liter}} \rightarrow x = (4)(1.06) = 4.24 \text{ quarts}$$

and

$$\frac{y \text{ cups}}{4.24 \text{ quarts}} = \frac{4 \text{ cups}}{1 \text{ quart}} \rightarrow y = (4)(4.24) = 16.96 \text{ cups}$$

Mathematical Reasoning Overview

The Math subject test measures your math skills in two contexts. The first deals with math in an academic way, focusing on the terms, concepts, and methods that math students learn in school. Problems may involve more formal presentations of math: equations, functions, geometric diagrams, and so on. These are called math world questions because they test math in a formal way.

The Math subject test also measures your math skills in more familiar, real-world settings. These questions are often in the form of word problems involving familiar objects or situations. Your job is to translate the story into mathematical terms and then perform some math operations to find the answer. These are called real-world questions because they test math using real settings.

You'll need to be comfortable in both worlds. However, you must keep your priorities straight. To do well on the Math test, you will need to be very comfortable dealing with math in the real world.

SUBJECT MATTER

The Mathematical Reasoning test covers two areas of content:

1. Quantitative Problem Solving (45%)
2. Algebraic Problem Solving (55%)

Quantitative subjects include:

- Numbers and operations
- Ratios, proportions, and rates
- Word problems
- Geometry
- Statistics

Algebraic subjects include:

- Expressions
- Equations
- The Coordinate Plane
- Functions

Every topic tested on the Math test is covered in the math lessons. Since some topics are emphasized on the test more than others, we've tried to apply a similar emphasis in the lessons. Each topic includes relevant terms and concepts as well as some examples.

Question Types

On the computer-based Mathematical Reasoning test, the following types of questions will appear:

> → **MULTIPLE CHOICE**
>
> → **FILL IN THE BLANK**
>
> → **DROP DOWN**
>
> → **HOT SPOT**
>
> → **DRAG AND DROP**

Note that certain question types, such as drop down, will be modified in this book so you can practice them using pen and paper.

Subject Integration

Some math skills will also be tested in the Science and Social Studies tests. Math questions on these tests will focus on skills used in statistics, like interpreting graphs and charts, calculating averages and other measures of center, and analyzing data.

BIG PICTURE

You can do several things to increase your readiness for math questions, wherever they may appear:

- Practice fundamentals
- Practice making calculations both manually and with a calculator
- Practice data analysis
- Pay attention to your strengths and weaknesses
- Learn to estimate

Practice Fundamentals

In the general introduction of this book, we talked about the importance of preparing for the test every day. One way to build study time into your daily routine is to use portable study tools (like flash cards) to help you memorize important information. Fundamental math skills are perfectly suited to this kind of studying. You can create cards to help you study:

- Multiplication tables
- Factors and multiples
- Number conversions (fraction to decimal to percent)
- Divisibility rules
- Formulas for area and perimeter
- Any other fact-based math you want to memorize.

All math questions will require you to use these fundamentals. Many students struggle with the Math test because they haven't strengthened these skills. As you memorize more of these math facts, you will find that all math questions become easier.

PRACTICE CALCULATION BOTH WAYS

You can make calculations using two different methods: manually or with a calculator. Practice using both methods.

Manual Calculation

Your mental math skills are important. The best way to sharpen them is to do math in your head or on paper. Look for opportunities to make some quick calculations by hand. Double-check sales receipts and recalculate the sales tax, recalculate your utility bills, add up the transactions on bank statements, or create and track a weekly budget and record your expenses. Work on paper, even if you are comfortable doing mental math, so that you can review your calculations later. It will be easier to remember what you did if you write it down.

Using a Calculator

The Exam will provide you with an online scientific calculator. So you should be familiar with the kinds of functions that will be available. Buy or borrow a scientific calculator and learn how to use it. The GED® Testing Service provides an online demonstration of the calculator that they will provide, so you can compare it to whichever calculator you learn on. You'll find the link to the testing service's website in the book's introduction.

PRACTICE DATA ANALYSIS

Certain math skills related to statistics are tested in the Science and Social Studies tests. The integrated subjects include measures of center (mean, median, mode), weighted averages, range, identifying outliers, and similar subjects related to analyzing numerical data. Make these skills a priority since they will help you earn points in three different parts of the test.

Pay Attention to Your Strengths and Weaknesses

Every test taker has strengths and weaknesses. Try to recognize the math subjects you prefer and the subjects you prefer to avoid. For example, in geometry, you may be very comfortable answering questions about triangles, but have difficulty answering questions about solids (three-dimensional shapes). Knowing your strengths and weaknesses will help you in two ways. First, before the test, you can make your studying more efficient by focusing attention on your weaker subjects. Second, during the test, you'll be able to make better choices about which questions to answer and when.

Learn to Estimate

Once your fundamentals and calculation skills are sharp, you'll be able to use them to estimate. Estimation is a very powerful tool when working on math questions. Rounding numbers in a problem before doing the calculation can make the problem noticeably easier. Number conversions like "21% is about 1/5" or "one-eighth is about 12%" can be very useful in estimating parts of wholes.

Numbers and Operations

Success on the Math subject test relies heavily on the fundamental skills covered in this section. Having a solid foundation in the basics, including how to perform all the basic operations (adding, subtracting, multiplying, and dividing), is critical for succeeding on the exam. If these skills are not strong, you can't do more advanced math. Since most students are already fairly familiar with these basic skills, we present them at a summary level along with some practice in case you need to remove the rust.

LESSON 1: DIGITS AND NUMBERS

DIGITS   The symbols we use to construct numbers: 0, 1, 2, 3, 4, 5, 6, 7, 8, and 9.

NUMBERS   Combinations of digits used to represent amounts or values.

INTEGERS   Whole numbers, including all positive and negative whole numbers and zero (zero is neutral).

PRACTICE

Count the digits of the number shown in the "Number" column, and write your answer in the "Digits" column.

	Number	Digits
1.	5,241,916	7
2.	5	1
3.	532	3
4.	59,730	5
5.	52	2
6.	5,916	4
7.	546,287	6
8.	259	3

Answers

1. 7		**3.** 3		**5.** 2		**7.** 6	
2. 1		**4.** 5		**6.** 4		**8.** 3	

The *number line* is a horizontal line with zero in the middle that extends forever in either direction. Along the line, small *tick marks* indicate the location of numbers that are greater or less than zero.

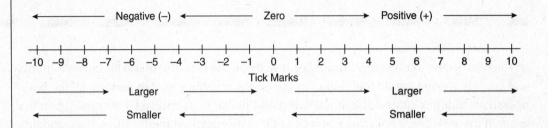

- Numbers to the right of zero are called ***positive*** numbers. They increase in value (get larger) as they move away from zero. Positive numbers are greater than zero.
- Numbers to the left of zero are called ***negative*** numbers. They decrease in value (get smaller) as they move away from zero. Negative numbers are less than zero.
- Zero is called ***neutral***, because it is neither positive nor negative.

Positive numbers are distinguished from negative numbers using symbols called ***signs***. A plus (+) is used to indicate positive numbers, and a minus (–) is used indicate negative numbers. Any number without a sign is assumed to be positive.

The number line can be used to compare and order numbers:

- Positive numbers get larger as they get farther away from 0. 5 is greater than 3.
- Negative numbers get smaller as they get farther away from 0. –5 is less than –3.
- These ideas apply to more than the whole numbers shown on the tick marks. They apply to all of the numbers between the tick marks (fractions, decimals, percentages, and so on). Any of these numbers can be compared and ordered using the number line.

PRACTICE

QUESTIONS 1 AND 2 REFER TO THE FOLLOWING NUMBER LINE:

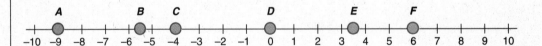

1. List the points that are:

   a. Positive _EF_

   b. Negative _ABC_

   c. Integers _ABCDE_

2. Point X (not shown) is between point B and point C on the number line above. Which of the following could be point X?

(A) -6

(B) $-\dfrac{10}{3}$

(C) $-\dfrac{14}{3}$

(D) -4

Answers and Explanations

1. **a. *E, F*** Positive numbers are greater than 0 (to the right of 0).

   b. *A, B, C* Negative numbers are less than 0 (to the left of 0).

   c. *A, C, D, F* Integers are whole numbers. Points between the tick marks are between whole numbers, so they are not integers themselves.

2. **(C)** Point X must be between and not equal to -4 (point C) and -5.5 (point B). Convert the improper fractions to decimals. Option $B = -3.333\ldots$ and is greater than -4. Option C is $-4.6666\ldots$ and is between -4 and -5.5.

When we use phrases like "greater than" and "less than" to compare and order numbers, we are speaking in terms of *inequalities*. An inequality is a statement about a range of possible values for an unknown number relative to a known number, such as "a number greater than 5." Instead of identifying one specific value for the unknown number, we are identifying numbers that the unknown could equal. We're doing this by talking about numbers that the unknown does not equal. A number greater than 5 is not equal to 5. This is how inequalities got their name.

INCLUSIVE AND EXCLUSIVE INEQUALITIES

Inequalities define a range (or domain) of possible values starting with a specific, known number called an endpoint. An inclusive range includes the endpoint, and an exclusive range does not. Look at the following examples.

Inclusive: A number 4 or smaller.

- It could be 3.99999, 2, 0.4, 0, –1, or any smaller number.
- It could be 4.
- The endpoint is included in the domain of possible values.
- Inclusive inequalities use greater than or equal to (GTE) and less than or equal to (LTE) comparisons.

Exclusive: A number greater than 5.

- It could be 6, 7, 8, or any larger number.
- It could also be 5.1 or 5.2. It could even be 5.00000000001.
- It could not be 5, 4.9999999, or any smaller number.
- The endpoint is excluded from the domain of possible values.
- Exclusive inequalities use greater than (GT) and less than (LT) comparisons.

INEQUALITY SYMBOLS

$\neq$	Not equal to
$>$	Greater than
$<$	Less than
$\geq$	Greater than or equal to
$\leq$	Less than or equal to
•	Inclusive endpoint
o	Exclusive endpoint

SIMPLE AND COMPOUND INEQUALITIES

SIMPLE INEQUALITY   This is an inequality made up of a single comparing statement. An example is "a number less than 7."

COMPOUND INEQUALITY   This is an inequality made up of two comparing statements joined by the word *and* or by the word *or*: One example is "a number greater than 2 **and** less than 8." Another is "a number less than or equal to 3 **or** greater than 6."

PRACTICE

1. Translate the following simple inequalities using the letter y for the unknown number. If needed, reverse the inequality so that y is always on the left side:

   a. y is greater than –2

   b. y is less than 9

   c. y is greater than or equal to 1

   d. y is less than or equal to 2

   e. 5 is greater than y

   f. –3 is less than y

2. Translate the following compound inequalities using the letter y for the unknown number. If needed, reverse the inequality so that the smallest number is always on the left side:

   a. y is less than 4 and greater than –3

   b. y is greater than –2 and less than 7

   c. y is less than or equal to 6 and greater than –4

   d. y is greater than or equal to –5 and less than 3

   e. 8 is greater than y and –1 is less than y

   f. 3 is greater than or equal to y and –7 is less than y

Answers and Explanations

1. **a. $y > -2$** To translate a simple inequality, you may have to rearrange the statement to place the unknown on the left. When rearranging the statement, you will have to reverse the inequality sign.

    b. $y < 9$

    c. $y \geq 1$

    d. $y \leq 2$

    e. $y < 5$

    f. $y > -3$

2. a. $-3 < y < 4$ To translate a compound inequality, you may have to rearrange the order of the statements to place the unknown in the middle. When doing this, you may have to reverse one or more inequality signs.

b. $-2 < y < 7$

c. $-4 < y \leq 6$

d. $-5 \leq y < 3$

e. $-1 < y < 8$

f. $-7 < y \leq 3$

GRAPHING INEQUALITIES

Graphing inequalities on the number line means plotting the endpoint and then using arrows or line segments to describe the domain.

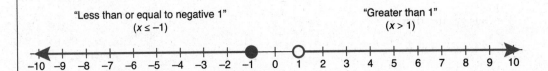

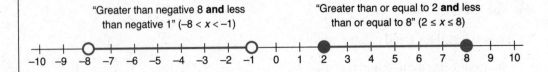

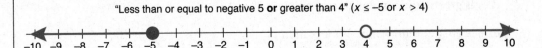

PRACTICE

1. Graph the following simple inequalities:

a. *y* is greater than –2

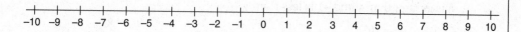

b. *y* is less than 9

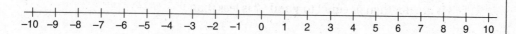

c. *y* is greater than or equal to 1

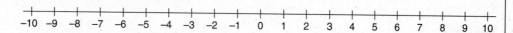

d. *y* is less than or equal to 2

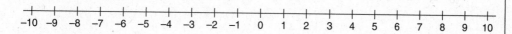

e. 5 is greater than *y*

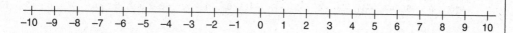

f. –3 is less than *y*

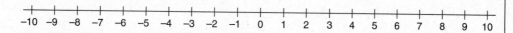

2. Graph the following compound inequalities:

a. *y* is less than 4 and greater than –3

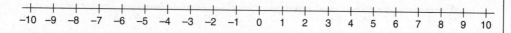

b. *y* is greater than –2 and less than 7

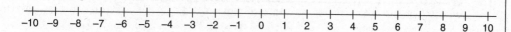

c. *y* is less than or equal to 6 and greater than –4

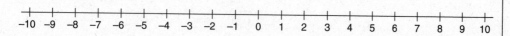

UNIT 2: MATH

d. y is greater than or equal to –5 and less than 3

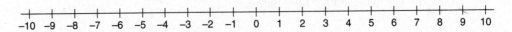

e. 8 is greater than y and –1 is less than y

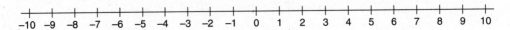

f. 3 is greater than or equal to y and –7 is less than y

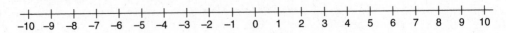

Answers

1. a. $y > -2$

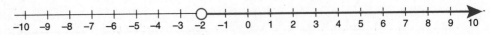

b. $y < 9$

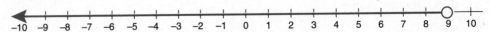

c. $y \geq 1$

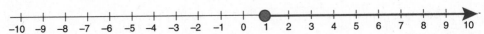

d. $y \leq 2$

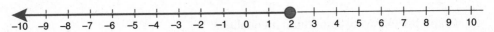

e. $y < 5$

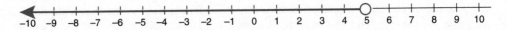

f. $y > -3$

2. **a.** $-3 < y < 4$

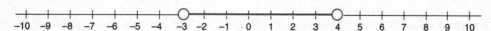

b. $-2 < y < 7$

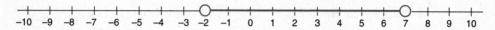

c. $-4 < y \le 6$

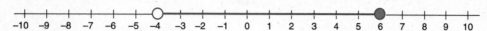

d. $-5 \le y < 3$

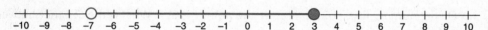

e. $-1 < y < 8$

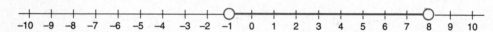

f. $-7 < y \le 3$

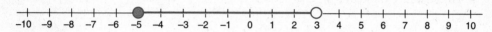

Absolute value is the unit distance on the number line between a number and 0. For all positive and negative numbers absolute value is always positive. Absolute value is symbolized like this with two vertical lines: | |. The absolute value of 0, |0|, is 0.

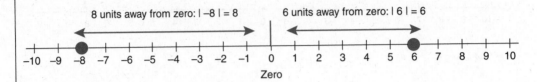

- The absolute value of 6 or |6| is 6.
- The absolute value of –8 or |–8| is 8.
- The absolute value of 0 or |0| is 0.

PRACTICE

QUESTIONS 1 AND 2 REFER TO THE FOLLOWING NUMBER LINE:

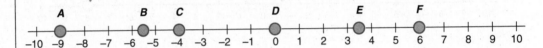

1. On the number line, point C is at –4 and point F is at 6. What is the distance between point C and point F?

2. Organize the points above from least absolute value to greatest absolute value.

Answers and Explanations

1. **10** Point C is 4 units from 0, and point F is 6 units from 0: $4 + 6 = 10$.

2. ***D, E, C, B, F, A*** Make all point values positive. So the absolute values are 0, 3.5, 4, 5.5, 6, 9.

The value of a digit is based on its position in the number. These positions are called places.

- The first whole number place is the **ones place**, located to the left of a starting point called the **decimal point**.
- Whole number places increase in value from right to left by multiples of 10.
- Commas are used to divide periods (groups of three places).

Place	____,	____	____	____,	____	____	____	.
Place name:	Millions	Hundred thousands	Ten thousands	Thousands	Hundreds	Tens	Ones	Decimal Point
Number:	1,000,000	100,000	10,000	1,000	100	10	1	
Prior number × 10:	100,000 × 10	10,000 × 10	1,000 × 10	100 × 10	10 × 10	1 × 10	1	
Exponent:	× 10^6	× 10^5	× 10^4	× 10^3	× 10^2	× 10^1		

The **exponent** row in the table above is used in **scientific notation** and will be discussed later.

The table below illustrates the way that digits in place values become numbers. Each example shows the digits that make up the number and the value of the digit in each place:

Place	Millions	Hundred Thousands	Ten Thousands	Thousands	Hundreds	Tens	Ones	Number
Digit					3	5	8	358
Value					300	50	8	
Digit				9	2	6	3	9,263
Value				9,000	200	60	3	
Digit		1	6	2	7	8	4	162,784
Value		100,000	60,000	2,000	700	80	4	
Digit	8	6	3	9	2	5	0	8,639,250
Value	8,000,000	600,000	30,000	9,000	200	50	0	

UNIT 2: MATH

PRACTICE

1. For each number below, find the number place where the 5 is, and write the place name in the "place" column.

	Number	Place			Number	Place
a.	5,241,916	_____	e.		52	_____
b.	5	_____	f.		5,916	_____
c.	532	_____	g		546,287	_____
d.	59,730	_____	h.		259	_____

2. Write out each number using words as you would say it out loud:

	Number	Word Form
a.	5,241,916	_____
b.	5	_____
c.	532	_____
d.	59,730	_____
e.	52	_____
f.	5,916	_____
g.	546,287	_____
h.	259	_____

Answers

1. **a.** millions

    b. ones

    c. hundreds

    d. ten thousands

    e. tens

    f. thousands

    g. hundred thousands

    h. tens

2. **a.** Five million, two hundred forty-one thousand, nine hundred sixteen

    b. Five

    c. Five hundred thirty-two

    d. Fifty-nine thousand, seven hundred thirty

    e. Fifty-two

    f. Five thousand, nine hundred sixteen

    g. Five hundred forty-six thousand, two hundred eighty-seven

    h. Two hundred fifty-nine.

Round numbers are numbers that end in one or more zeros. They are useful when estimating.

- Numbers are rounded to a specific place. "1,475 rounded to the hundreds place is 1,500."
- The digit in the place to be rounded is called the rounding digit.
- If the digit to the right of the rounding digit is 5 or greater, the rounding digit is rounded up by adding 1.
- If the digit to the right is 4 or smaller, the rounding digit remains unchanged. This is called rounding down.
- All digits to the right of the selected place are replaced with zeros.

Number	1,234	8,765	7,263	3,509
Nearest 10	Round **down** to 1,230	Round **up** to 8,770	Round **down** to 7,260	Round **up** to 3,510
Nearest 100:	Round **down** to 1,200	Round **up** to 8,800	Round **up** to 7,300	Round **down** to 3,500
Nearest 1,000:	Round **down** to 1,000	Round **up** to 9,000	Round **down** to 7,000	Round **up** to 4,000

PRACTICE

1. The average price for a Luxurama sedan is $76,240. Round this amount to the nearest thousand dollars.

2. For each row in the table below, round the number to the place shown in the "round to" column and write the result in the "result" column:

	Number	Round To	Result
a.	5,241,916	Nearest million	_____
b.	5	Nearest ten	_____
c.	532	Nearest hundred	_____
d.	59,730	Nearest thousand	_____
e.	52	Nearest hundred	_____
f.	5,916	Nearest thousand	_____
g.	546,287	Nearest ten thousand	_____
h.	259	Nearest ten	_____

Answers and Explanations

1. **$76,000**

2. **a.** 5,000,000 **c.** 500 **e.** 100 **g.** 550,000
   b. 10 **d.** 60,000 **f.** 6,000 **h.** 260

In the sections below, we've included a lot of the formal vocabulary associated with arithmetic operations. Some of these terms may be familiar (sum, product). Others (subtrahend, multiplicand) are probably not. Don't worry about it. You don't need to know the vocabulary to do well on the test. You just need to have strong calculation skills.

ADDING AND SUBTRACTING

When adding, the numbers being added are the addends and the result is the sum.

When subtracting, the first number is the minuend, the second number is the subtrahend, and the result is the difference.

$$
\begin{array}{r}
\text{addends} \searrow\; 4 \\
+5 \\
\hline
\text{sum} \longrightarrow \; 9
\end{array}
$$

$$
\begin{array}{r}
\text{minuend} \longrightarrow 6 \\
-2 \longleftarrow \text{subtrahend} \\
\hline
\text{difference} \longrightarrow 4
\end{array}
$$

MULTIPLYING

When multiplying, the first number is the multiplicand, the second number is the multiplier, and the result is the product.

The multiplicand and multiplier are factors of the product, and the product is a multiple of both factors.

$$
\begin{array}{r}
\text{multiplicand} \longrightarrow 4 \longleftarrow \text{factors} \\
\times 2 \longleftarrow \text{multiplier} \\
\hline
\text{product} \longrightarrow 8 \longleftarrow \text{multiple}
\end{array}
$$

Multiplication can be expressed using the word "times," the times sign ($\times$), a dot, or parentheses.

Multiplication Symbol	Times $\times$	Dot $\bullet$	Parentheses $()$
	4×2	$4 \bullet 2$	$4(2)$ or $(4)(2)$

Multiplication Table

Each intersection of a row number and a column number shows their product. For example, the following table shows $8 \times 3 = 24$.

x	1	2	3	4	5	6	7	8	9	10	11	12
1	1	2	3	4	5	6	7	8	9	10	11	12
2	2	4	6	8	10	12	14	16	18	20	22	24
3	3	6	9	12	15	18	21	24	27	30	33	36
4	4	8	12	16	20	24	28	32	36	40	44	48
5	5	10	15	20	25	30	35	40	45	50	55	60
6	6	12	18	24	30	36	42	48	54	60	66	72
7	7	14	21	28	35	42	49	56	63	70	77	84
8	8	16	24	32	40	48	56	64	72	80	88	96
9	9	18	27	36	45	54	63	72	81	90	99	108
10	10	20	30	40	50	60	70	80	90	100	110	120
11	11	22	33	44	55	66	77	88	99	110	121	132
12	12	24	36	48	60	72	84	96	108	120	132	144

PRACTICE

COMPLETE THE FOLLOWING SCRAMBLED MULTIPLICATION TABLE.

	2	11	3	10	4	9	5	8	6	7	1	12
12												
5												
11												
4												
10												
3												
9												
2												
8												
1												
7												
6												

UNIT 2: MATH

Answer

	2	11	3	10	4	9	5	8	6	7	1	12
12	24	132	36	120	48	108	60	96	72	84	12	144
5	10	55	15	50	20	45	25	40	30	35	5	60
11	22	121	33	110	44	99	55	88	66	77	11	132
4	8	44	12	40	16	36	20	32	24	28	4	48
10	20	110	30	100	40	90	50	80	60	70	10	120
3	6	33	9	30	12	27	15	24	18	21	3	36
9	18	99	27	90	36	81	45	72	54	63	9	108
2	4	22	6	20	8	18	10	16	12	14	2	24
8	16	88	24	80	32	72	40	64	48	56	8	96
1	2	11	3	10	4	9	5	8	6	7	1	12
7	14	77	21	70	28	63	35	56	42	49	7	84
6	12	66	18	60	24	54	30	48	36	42	6	72

Distributive Property in Multiplication

Several math properties apply to operations like addition and multiplication. However, the most important one on the Math subject test is the *distributive* property in multiplication. This property applies to expressions like the following:

$$3(4 + 5)$$

Order of operations tells us to add inside the parentheses first and then multiply:

$$3(4 + 5) = 3(9) = 27$$

The distributive property says that we will get the same result if we multiply the number outside the parentheses (3) by each of the numbers inside them (4 and 5) and then perform the operation between the inside numbers (+):

$$3(4 + 5) = 3(4) + 3(5) = 12 + 15 = 27$$

In cases that involve only numbers, like the one above, you should follow the order of operations and add inside the parentheses first. The distributive property becomes very important later on in algebra when not everything is a number.

DIVIDING

When dividing, the number being divided is the *dividend*, the other number is the *divisor*, and the result is the *quotient*. The amount left over, if any, is the *remainder*. If there is no remainder, the divisor is a *factor* of the dividend and the dividend is a *multiple* of the divisor.

$$5 \leftarrow \text{quotient}$$
$$\text{divisor} \longrightarrow 3\overline{)15} \leftarrow \text{dividend}$$

Division can be expressed using the division symbol, slash, fraction bar, or long division symbol.

Division Symbol	Division ÷	Slash /	Fraction Bar —	Long Division $\overline{)}$
	$15 \div 3$	15/3	$\dfrac{15}{3}$	$3\overline{)15}$

ADDING

- When adding two positive numbers, the sum is positive: $6 + 3 = 9$.
- When adding two negative numbers, the sum is negative: $-8 + -3 = -11$.
- When adding a positive number and a negative number, first find the difference between them. If the positive number is farther from 0 than the negative number, the result is positive: $5 + -3 = 2$. If the negative number is farther from 0 than the positive number, the result is negative: $5 + -9 = -4$.

SUBTRACTING

Subtracting signed numbers is a little trickier. The examples below illustrate the various cases. They are all based on the first number minus the second number. Remember that in algebra, subtraction means to add the opposite.

When subtracting two positive numbers:

- If the first number is larger, the difference is positive: $7 - 4 = 3$.
- If the second number is larger, the difference is negative: $4 - 7 = -3$.

When subtracting a negative second number:

- First change the subtraction operation to addition.
- Then change the sign of the second number to positive: $6 - (-2) = 6 + 2 = 8$ and $-5 - (-3) = -5 + 3 = -2$.

When subtracting a positive second number from a negative first number:

- First change the subtraction operation to addition.
- Then change the sign of the second number to negative: $-3 - 6 = -3 + -6 = -9$.

MULTIPLYING AND DIVIDING

These two operations are a little simpler.

If the signs are the same, the result is positive:

- $4 \cdot 6 = 24$
- $-3 \cdot -8 = 24$
- $18 \div 3 = 6$
- $-27 \div -3 = 9$

If the signs are not the same, the result is negative:

- $4 \cdot -6 = -24$
- $-3 \cdot 8 = -24$
- $18 \div -3 = -6$
- $-27 \div 3 = -9$

PRACTICE

1. Add and subtract:

   a. $10 + 5$

   b. $12 - (-3)$

   c. $152 - 64$

   d. $-4 - (-8)$

2. Multiply and divide:

   a. 128×14

   b. $16 \div (-4)$

   c. $196 \div 14$

   d. $-49 \div 7$

3. Rebecca went shopping for a dress at Save It Wear It boutique. Rebecca selected a dress that was priced at $24.50. Rebecca had a store discount that saved her $4.25 on any of her purchases. When Rebecca went to pay for the dress, she was given another discount of $2.25 off because it was "Super Tuesday." What did Rebecca ultimately pay for the dress, excluding sales tax?

4. John had $1 in his checking account Thursday morning. That night after the bank closed, he wrote a check for $200 on Thursday night. On Friday, he deposited his $740 paycheck. What was John's balance after he deposited his paycheck and the check he wrote was cashed?

5. Roland purchases 10 cans of paint at $4.75 per can to paint his house. How much change will John receive if he pays with a $50 dollar bill?

Answers and Explanations

1. **a. 15** When subtraction involves negative numbers, remember to change the operations to addition and reverse the sign of the second number.

    b. 15

    c. 88

    d. 4

2. **a. 1,792**

    b. –4 When multiplying or dividing with negative numbers, remember that numbers with the same sign produce positive resuts and numbers with different signs produce different results. Also, for division, it is often useful to know the perfect squares and their square roots.

    c. 14

    d. –7

3. **$18.00** Rebecca's total discount was $4.25 + $2.25 = $6.50 and $24.50 – $6.50 = $18.00.

4. **$541** After making the deposit, his balance was $741. When the check was deducted from John's account, the remaining balance was $741 – $200 = $541.

5. **$2.50** $10 \times \$4.75 = \$47.50$ and $50.00 – $47.50 = $2.50.

Consider the following example: $4 \times 6 = 24$.

- 4 and 6 are *factors* of 24. Factors are numbers that divide evenly into a given number.
- 24 is a *multiple* of both 4 and 6. Multiples are the results when a given number is multiplied by other numbers.
- We sometimes also say that 4 and 6 go into 24, and that 24 is divisible by 4 and 6.

The multiplication table shown previously provides a view of both factors and multiples. For example, by moving in from the edges of the table, we see that 8 and 3 are also factors of 24. If we find another occurrence of 24 in the table, we can move out to the edges of the table to find another pair of factors. (The 24 near the upper right corner of the table leads back to 2 and 12.)

The distributive property of multiplication can be applied in reverse by using factors. Suppose we begin with 28 + 42:

- Both 28 and 42 are multiples of 7. $28 \div 7 = 4$ and $42 \div 7 = 6$.
- So we can reexpress the original expression: $7(4 + 6)$
- This is called the factored form of the expression, because 7 is a factor of both numbers. Dividing out a common factor is called factoring.

PRIME NUMBERS

A number that has no factors other than itself and 1 is a **prime** number. All other numbers are **composite** numbers. The first 10 prime numbers are:

$$2, 3, 5, 7, 11, 13, 17, 19, 23, 29$$

Note that 1 is neither a prime nor a composite number.

PRIME FACTORIZATION

You can factor a composite number into a product of prime numbers. This is called prime factorization. It involves repeatedly dividing composite factors by prime factors until only prime factors are left. The process and result can be presented in a factor tree.

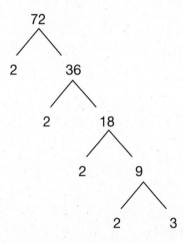

The prime factorization of 72 is expressed as $2 \times 2 \times 2 \times 3 \times 3$.

DIVISIBILITY RULES

Use the rules below when trying to identify factors.

A Number Is Divisible By	When
2	The last digit is 2, 4, 6, 8, or 0. (This means the number is even. Numbers not divisible by 2 are odd.) 32 and 18 are divisible by 2. 37 and 29 are not divisible by 2.
3	The sum of its digits is divisible by 3. 327 is divisible by 3 (3 + 2 + 7 = 12, and 12 is divisible by 3). 241 is not divisible by 3. (2 + 4 + 1 = 7).
4	The last two digits, when taken as a number, are divisible by 4. 1,024 is divisible by 4 because 24 is divisible by 4.
5	The last digit is 0 or 5. 30 and 55 are divisible by 5. 72 and 53 are not divisible by 5.
6	The number is even and the sum of digits is divisible by 3 (rules for 2 and 3 together). 84 is divisible by 6 because it is even and because 8 + 4 = 12 and 12 is divisible by 3.
8	The last three digits, when taken as a number, are divisible by 8. 1,824 is divisible by 8 because 824 is divisible by 8.
9	The sum of digits is divisible by 9. 2,331 is divisible by 9 (2 + 3 + 3 + 1 = 9). 3,124 is not divisible by 9 (3 + 1 + 2 + 4 = 10).
10	The last digit is 0. 380 and 1,250 are divisible by 10. 987 and 3458 are not divisible by 10.

PRACTICE

1. For each number below, make a complete list of its positive factors:

    a. 48

    b. 512

    c. 99

2. For each number below, list the first three positive multiples:

    a. 48

    b. 512

    c. 99

Answers and Explanations

1. **a. 1, 2, 3, 4, 6, 8, 12, 16, 24, 48** When looking for the factors of a number, start with the number itself and 1. Write the 1 to the far left and the number itself to the far right. Then check if the number is divisible by 2. If it divides evenly, list the 2 just to the right of the 1. Also list the result of the division just to the left of the original number. Then check if the number is divisible by 3 and so on. Keep working until your list of numbers meets in the middle.

    b. 1, 2, 4, 8, 16, 32, 64, 128, 256, 512

    c. 1, 3, 9, 11, 33, 99

2. **a. 48, 96, 144** Remember that the first positive multiple of a number is the number itself. Then multiply the number by 2. Then multiply the original number by 3.

    b. 512; 1,024; 1,536

    c. 99, 198, 297

Using exponents allows test takers to multiply the same number repeatedly. It is often referred to as raising a number to a power.

$$\text{base} \longrightarrow 4^3 \longleftarrow \text{exponent}$$

The number is expressed as a combination of a *base*, which is the number to be multiplied, and an *exponent*, or a *power*, which is the number of times to multiply.

SQUARING AND CUBING

In the following example, 5 is the base and 2 is the exponent. Raising a base to the second power is often called squaring. So 5 to the 2nd power can be referred to as "5 squared."

$$5^2 = 5 \bullet 5 = 25$$

Raising a base to the third power is often called cubing. So 2 to the 3rd power can be referred to as "2 cubed."

$$2^3 = 2 \bullet 2 \bullet 2 = 8$$

PRACTICE

Complete the table below and continued on the next page by squaring (raising to the 2nd power) and cubing (raising to the 3rd power) the number in the "Integer" column.

Integer	Square	Cube
1	1	1
2	4	8
3		
4		
5		
6		
7		
8		
9		
10		
11		
12		
13		
14		

Integer	Square	Cube
15		
16		
17		
18		
19		
20		

Answers

Integer	Square	Cube
1	1	1
2	4	8
3	9	27
4	16	64
5	25	125
6	36	216
7	49	343
8	64	512
9	81	729
10	100	1,000
11	121	1,331
12	144	1,728
13	169	2,197
14	196	2,744
15	225	3,375
16	256	4,096
17	289	4,913
18	324	5,832
19	361	6,859
20	400	8,000

RULES FOR OPERATIONS ON EXPONENTS

Certain operations can be performed on exponents with the same base:

- **Multiplication**—Add the exponents: $3^3 \times 3^5 = 3^8$.
- **Division**—Subtract the exponents: $3^5 \div 3^3 = 3^2$.
- **Raising a Power to a power**—Multiply the exponents: $(3^3)^5 = 3^{15}$.
- **Negative exponent**—Equivalent to a fraction with the positive exponent in the denominator: $10^{-4} = \dfrac{1}{10^4}$.

Remember that you cannot perform any of these operations if the numbers have different bases. For example, $2^3 \times 3^5$ is in its simplest exponential form.

PRACTICE

1. Complete the following exponent operations:

   a. $10^{25} \bullet 10^{26}$

   b. $10^{200} \div 10^{189}$

   c. $(10^{15})^{15}$

2. Convert $\dfrac{1}{10^{215}}$ to a negative exponent.

Answers and Explanations

1. **a.** 10^{51} $10^{25} \bullet 10^{26} = 10^{25+26} = 10^{51}$

   b. 10^{11} $10^{200} \div 10^{189} = 10^{200-189} = 10^{11}$

   c. 10^{225} $(10^{15})^{15} = 10^{15 \bullet 15} = 10^{225}$

2. 10^{-215}

A *root* is a special kind of factor of a multiple called the *radicand*. When the root is multiplied by itself a specified number of times, the product is the radicand.

degree
radical $\longrightarrow \sqrt[2]{9} \longleftarrow$ radicand

The symbol for a root ($\sqrt{}$) is called the radical. The expression sometimes includes a degree, which indicates the number of times the root should be multiplied by itself to produce the radicand.

SQUARE ROOTS AND CUBE ROOTS

The *square root* of positive integer x is the positive number that, when squared, yields a product of x. For example, $\sqrt{49} = 7$ because $7 \cdot 7 = 49$. (The degree is not shown for square roots.)

The *cube root* of a positive integer x is the positive number that, when cubed, yields a product of x. For example, $\sqrt[3]{125} = 5$ because $5 \cdot 5 \cdot 5 = 125$.

Perfect Squares and Estimating Square Roots

A perfect square is a number that has an integer (whole number) as a square root. Most numbers are not perfect squares, and their square roots include many decimal places. (For example, the square root of 15, or $\sqrt{15}$, is 3.872983346207417.)

The process for manually calculating the square root of a number that is not a perfect square is complicated. The good news is that you'll never need it. The test provides you with a calculator that has a square root function. You'll often be able to estimate a square root using your knowledge of the perfect squares. The first 20 perfect squares are shown in the following table:

Square	Root
1	1
4	2
9	3
16	4
25	5
36	6
49	7
64	8
81	9
100	10
121	11
144	12
169	13
196	14

UNIT 2: MATH

Square	Root
225	15
256	16
289	17
324	18
361	19
400	20

If the numbers in the perfect squares table look familiar, that's because they also appear in the squaring and cubing practice earlier in the unit. The first 20 integers are the square roots of the first 20 perfect squares. You can use the perfect squares to estimate other square roots.

For example, to estimate the value of $\sqrt{15}$, look for perfect squares that are close to 15. The largest perfect square that is smaller than 15 is 9, and the square root of 9 is 3. The smallest perfect square that is larger than 15 is 16 and the square root of 16 is 4. Since 15 is between 9 and 16, and is much closer to 16, we can estimate that $\sqrt{15}$ is between 3 and 4 and is much closer to 4. (As mentioned earlier, $\sqrt{15}$ = 3.872983346207417, which rounds to 3.9.) You can use this approach for many of the problems you'll see on the Math subject test when the root you need is not the root of a perfect square.

Factoring and Distributing

You can also factor and distribute under the radical:

$$\sqrt{450} = \sqrt{225 \bullet 2} = \sqrt{225} \bullet \sqrt{2} = 15\sqrt{2}$$

This can be useful in estimating as well. Since $\sqrt{2} \approx 1.4$, we know that the root above is close to 21 because 15 × 1.4 equals 21.

Distributing can also be helpful when working with radicals:

$$\sqrt{12} \bullet \sqrt{3} = \sqrt{12 \bullet 3} = \sqrt{36} = 6$$

PRACTICE

1. Estimate the following roots:

    a. The square root of 68 is larger than _____ and smaller than _____.

    b. The square root of 174 is larger than _____ and smaller than _____.

    c. The square root of 99 is larger than _____ and smaller than _____.

2. Factor and simplify:

    a. $\sqrt{432}$

    b. $\sqrt{484}$

    c. $\sqrt{800}$

3. Distribute:

    a. $\sqrt{7} \cdot \sqrt{2} \cdot \sqrt{7}$

    b. $\sqrt{72} \cdot \sqrt{\dfrac{1}{2}}$

Answers and Explanations

1. **a. 8, 9**

   b. 13, 14

   c. 9, 10

2. **a. $12\sqrt{3}$** $432 = 144 \times 3$ and 144 is a perfect square (12^2). So take the root outside the radical: $12\sqrt{3}$.

   b. 22 $484 = 121 \times 4$. Both are perfect squares (11^2 and 2^2). So the result is $11 \times 2 = 22$.

   c. $20\sqrt{2}$ $800 = 2 \times 400$ and 400 is a perfect square (20^2).

3. **a. $7\sqrt{2}$** This becomes $\sqrt{(7 \times 2 \times 7)} = \sqrt{(49 \times 2)}$. Since 49 is a perfect square, the answer is $7\sqrt{2}$.

   b. 6 Combining and multiplying under the radical results in $\sqrt{36}$ (half of 72 is 36). Additionally, 36 is a perfect square (6^2).

The *order of operations*, sometimes called *PEMDAS*, is listed below:

1. **PARENTHESES**   Any operations found inside parentheses should be done first, regardless of the type of operation. This also applies to other grouping symbols, like braces and brackets. A radical is also treated as a grouping symbol.

2. **EXPONENTS**   Any powers should be done next.

3. **MULTIPLICATION AND DIVISION**   All multiplication and division should be done from left to right before doing any addition or subtraction.

4. **ADDITION AND SUBTRACTION**   All addition and subtraction should be done last, from left to right.

Apply the order of operations to the following numerical expression:

$$3(5-2) - 21 \div 3 + 2(7-5)^2$$

1.   **Work inside the parentheses**: $5 - 2 = 3$ and $7 - 5 = 2$.

$$3(3) - 21 \div 3 + 2(2)^2$$

2.   **Calculate the exponents**: $2^2 = 4$.

$$3(3) - 21 \div 3 + 2(4)$$

3.   **Do the multiplication** and **division** from left to right: $3 \bullet 3 = 9$, $21 \div 3 = 7$, and $2 \bullet 4 = 8$.

$$9 - 7 + 8$$

4.   **Do the addition** and **subtraction** from left to right: $9 - 7 = 2$ and $2 + 8 = 10$. So the answer is 10.

UNIT 2: MATH

A fraction expresses a part of a whole: $\frac{3}{5}$ represents "3 of 5 equal parts." The number representing the part is called the *numerator*, and is on the top. The number representing the whole is called the *denominator* and is on the bottom.

EQUIVALENT FRACTIONS AND REDUCING

Equivalent fractions represent the same amount but are expressed in different terms (using different numbers). Two fractions are equivalent if applying a common multiplier to the numerator and denominator of one fraction produces the other fraction. For example, $\frac{3}{5}$ is equivalent to $\frac{6}{10}$ by a factor of 2:

$$\frac{3}{5} = \frac{3 \bullet 2}{5 \bullet 2} = \frac{6}{10}$$

Reducing a fraction to **lowest terms** means finding the equivalent form that uses the smallest numbers. The fraction $\frac{16}{20}$ can be reduced by a factor of 4 because 4 is a factor of both 16 and 20. The numerator 4 goes into 16 four times, and 4 goes into 20 five times:

$$\frac{16}{20} = \frac{16 \div 4}{20 \div 4} = \frac{4}{5}$$

The fraction $\frac{4}{5}$ is an equivalent form of $\frac{16}{20}$. The fraction $\frac{4}{5}$ is in lowest terms because 4 and 5 have no common factor.

COMPARING FRACTIONS

If two fractions have equal numerators, the fraction with the smaller denominator is bigger:

$$\frac{3}{5} > \frac{3}{7}$$

If two fractions have equal denominators, the fraction with the larger numerator is bigger:

$$\frac{3}{5} > \frac{2}{5}$$

If two fractions are completely different, you can compare them by cross multiplying. Alternatively, you can rename the fractions so they have a common denominator. Then compare the fractions.

$$\overset{8}{\underset{}{\frac{2}{3}}} \times \overset{9}{\underset{}{\frac{3}{4}}}$$

The larger product indicates the larger fraction. Since 9 > 8, that means $\frac{2}{3} < \frac{3}{4}$ or $\frac{3}{4} > \frac{2}{3}$.

ADDING AND SUBTRACTING FRACTIONS

Use the *multiplication method*:

- Cross multiply.
- Apply the original operation to the products. If you are supposed to add the fractions, add the products. If you are supposed to subtract the fractions, subtract the products.
- Write the sum or difference as the numerator of a new fraction.
- Multiply the original denominators.
- Write the product as the denominator of your new fraction.
- Reduce if needed.

$$\frac{2}{3} \times \frac{1}{6} = \frac{15}{18} = \frac{5}{6}$$

$$\frac{2}{3} \times \frac{1}{6} = \frac{9}{18} = \frac{1}{2}$$

Alternatively, you can rename the fractions so they have a common denominator. Then add (or subtract) only the numerators. Use the common denominator in your answer.

MULTIPLYING FRACTIONS

Multiply numerator by numerator and denominator by denominator straight across:

$$\frac{2}{3} \times \frac{3}{4} = \frac{2 \times 3}{3 \times 4} = \frac{6}{12} = \frac{1}{2}$$

If common factors exist between numerators and denominators, you may cancel them before multiplying:

$$\frac{5}{11} \times \frac{33}{38} \times \frac{19}{20}$$

$$\downarrow$$

5 is divisible by 5.   20 is divisible by 5.
$5 \div 5 = 1$ $20 \div 5 = 4$

$$\frac{\overset{1}{\cancel{5}}}{11} \times \frac{33}{38} \times \frac{19}{\underset{4}{\cancel{20}}}$$

$$\downarrow$$

33 is divisible by 11.
$33 \div 11 = 3$

$$\frac{1}{\underset{1}{\cancel{11}}} \times \frac{\overset{3}{\cancel{33}}}{38} \times \frac{19}{4}$$

11 is divisible by 11.   19 is divisible by 19.
$11 \div 11 = 1$ $19 \div 19 = 1$

$$\frac{1}{1} \times \frac{3}{38} \times \frac{\overset{1}{\cancel{19}}}{4}$$

38 is divisible by 19. $$\downarrow$$
$38 \div 19 = 2$ $\frac{1}{1} \times \frac{3}{2} \times \frac{1}{4} = \frac{3}{8}$

DIVIDING FRACTIONS

Dividing fractions can be tricky. Just remember the following saying. "When dividing don't ask why, just reverse and multiply." In other words, invert the second fraction in a division problem and then multiply:

$$\frac{1}{4} \div \frac{2}{3} = \frac{1}{4} \times \frac{3}{2} = \frac{1 \times 3}{4 \times 2} = \frac{3}{8}$$

MIXED NUMBERS AND IMPROPER FRACTIONS

Mixed numbers combine a whole number with a fraction. For example, $3\frac{3}{4}$ is a mixed number.

Improper fractions have a numerator that is greater than or equal to the denominator. An example is $\frac{5}{3}$.

Mixed numbers can be converted to improper fractions:

- Multiply the denominator of the fraction by the whole number.
- Add the numerator of the fraction to the product.
- Write the sum as the numerator of a new fraction over the original denominator.

$$3\frac{3}{4} = \frac{12+3}{4} = \frac{15}{4}$$

Improper fractions can be converted to mixed numbers:

- Reduce to lowest terms if needed.
- Divide the numerator by the denominator to get the quotient with remainder.
- Write the quotient as a whole number. Use the remainder as the numerator of a new fraction over the original denominator.

$$\frac{46}{14} = \frac{23}{7} \qquad 23 \div 7 = 3r2 \qquad 3\frac{2}{7}$$

DECIMAL FRACTIONS

Decimal fractions are fractions whose denominators are multiples of 10:

$$\frac{1}{10}, \frac{1}{100}, \frac{1}{1000}, \ldots$$

PRACTICE

1. A gallon container (128 fluid ounces) is filled with 32 fluid ounces of orange juice. What fraction of the container is full? Give the answer in lowest terms.

2. Reduce to lowest terms:

   a. $\dfrac{8}{64}$

   b. $\dfrac{7}{56}$

3. Compare using the symbols >, <, and =:

   a. $\dfrac{4}{9}$ ___ $\dfrac{3}{7}$

   b. $\dfrac{9}{11}$ ___ $\dfrac{13}{14}$

4. Add and subtract:

   a. $\dfrac{4}{9} + \dfrac{3}{7}$

   b. $\dfrac{13}{14} - \dfrac{9}{11}$

5. Multiply and divide. Give the answer in lowest terms:

   a. $\dfrac{3}{8} \bullet \dfrac{2}{3}$

   b. $\dfrac{3}{8} \div \dfrac{2}{3}$

6. Convert $2\dfrac{5}{7}$ to an improper fraction.

7. Convert $\dfrac{15}{9}$ to a mixed number.

Answers and Explanations

1. $\frac{1}{4}$ In a fraction, the part (32) is the numerator and the whole (128) is the denominator.

   $$\frac{32}{128} = \frac{1}{4}$$

2. a. $\frac{1}{8}$

   b. $\frac{1}{8}$

3. a. $>$ Use the multiplication method and compare the products. The bigger product indicates the larger fraction.

   b. $<$

4. a. $\frac{55}{63}$ $\frac{4}{9} + \frac{3}{7} = \frac{28+27}{63} = \frac{55}{63}$

   b. $\frac{17}{154}$ $\frac{13}{14} - \frac{9}{11} = \frac{143-126}{154} = \frac{17}{154}$

5. a. $\frac{1}{4}$ $\frac{3}{8} \cdot \frac{2}{3} = \frac{6}{24} = \frac{1}{4}$

   b. $\frac{9}{16}$ $\frac{3}{8} \div \frac{2}{3} = \frac{3}{8} \times \frac{3}{2} = \frac{9}{16}$

6. $1\frac{9}{7}$ $7 \times 2 = 14$ and $14 + 5 = 19$. Put the result over the original denominator. Reduce if needed.

7. $1\frac{2}{3}$ $15 \div 9 = 1$ r 6. Put the remainder over the original denominator. Reduce if needed.

Decimals use number places called decimal places to express parts of wholes based on decimal fractions.

Place Name	Decimal Point	Tenths	Hundredths	Thousandths	Ten Thousandths
	.	____	____	____	____
Fraction		$\frac{1}{10}$	$\frac{1}{100}$	$\frac{1}{1,000}$	$\frac{1}{10,000}$
Decimal		0.1	0.01	0.001	0.0001
Exponent		$\times 10^{-1}$	$\times 10^{-2}$	$\times 10^{-3}$	$\times 10^{-4}$

(The exponent row in the table above is used in scientific notation, and will be discussed later.)

The table below shows how digits in decimal places become decimals.

Place	.	Tenths	Hundredths	Thousandths	Ten Thousandths	Number
Digit	.				3	
Fractional value					$\frac{3}{10,000}$	0.0003
Decimal value					0.0003	
Digit	.			9	2	
Fractional value				$\frac{9}{1,000}$	$\frac{2}{10,000}$	0.0092
Decimal value				0.009	0.0002	
Digit	.	1	6	2	7	
Fractional value		$\frac{1}{10}$	$\frac{6}{100}$	$\frac{2}{1,000}$	$\frac{7}{10,000}$	0.1627
Decimal value		0.1	0.06	0.002	0.0007	

When saying decimals aloud, people often use the name of the decimal fraction: For example, 0.3 is three tenths, 0.06 is six-hundredths, 0.007 is seven-thousandths. Reciting the digits from left to right is another common method: 0.3 is point three or 0.007 is point zero zero seven.

DECIMAL OPERATIONS

To add and subtract decimals, line up the decimal points, fill in zeros on the end as needed, and add and subtract as usual:

$$
\begin{array}{r} 0.523 \\ + 0.264 \\ \hline 0.787 \end{array}
\qquad\qquad
\begin{array}{r} 0.487 \\ - 0.110 \\ \hline 0.377 \end{array}
$$

To multiply decimals, first multiply as usual. Add up the decimal places in all the factors, and place the decimal point at that spot in the product. For instance, if the first factor has 1 decimal place and the second has 2, the product will have $1 + 2 = 3$ decimal places.

$$
\begin{array}{r} 2.3 \\ \times 0.3 \\ \hline 0.69 \end{array}
\qquad\qquad
\begin{array}{r} 0.25 \\ \times 0.3 \\ \hline 0.075 \end{array}
$$

$$
\begin{array}{r} 0.23 \\ \times 0.3 \\ \hline 0.069 \end{array}
\qquad\qquad
\begin{array}{r} 0.025 \\ \times 0.3 \\ \hline 0.0075 \end{array}
$$

To divide decimals, multiply the divisor by 10 until it becomes an integer. You can do this by moving the decimal point to the right one place for every multiple of 10. Do the same to the dividend and then divide as usual. Make sure to move the decimal point in the dividend the same number of places to the right. You may have to add zeros to the dividend to do this.

$$
2.3\overline{)460.}
$$

$$
\begin{array}{r} 200 \\ 23\overline{)4600.} \\ 46 \\ \hline 000 \end{array}
$$

PRACTICE

1. Compare using the symbols >, <, and =:

    a. 0.5234 _____ 0.5324

    b. 0.0003 _____ 0.003

2. Add and subtract:

    a. 0.531 + 0.03

    b. 0.08 − 0.006

3. Multiply and divide:

    a. 0.12 × 0.12

    b. 0.00121 ÷ 0.011

Answers and Explanations

1. **a. <** Compare digits left to right. If both are zero, move to the right. If both are the same, move to the right. If one of them is not zero and they are not equal, compare.

    b. <

2. **a. 0.561** Line up the decimal points. Add zeros to the right as needed. Then add or subtract the columns.

    b. 0.074

3. **a. 0.0144** Multiply as usual. Then account for all decimal places in both factors by moving the decimal in the product to the left, adding zeros to the left of the answer as needed.

    b. 0.11 Move the decimal point in the divisor to the right until the divisor is an integer. In this case, move it 3 places. Then move the decimal point of the dividend the same number of places (3) to the right. Divide as usual.

LESSON 15: SCIENTIFIC NOTATION

Whole numbers and decimal numbers are very effective ways of representing values. However, even with an effective system, working with numbers that are very large or very small is often difficult:

$$12{,}345{,}678{,}900{,}000{,}000{,}000{,}000$$
$$0.0000000000000000987654321$$

Scientific notation is a standardized way of representing numbers using multiplication by powers of 10. Since both whole numbers and decimal numbers are based on multiples of 10, multiplying by powers of 10 relocates (or shifts) the decimal point without affecting the digits in the number.

- The degree (power) of the exponent in scientific notation indicates the number of places to shift the decimal point. The sign of the exponent indicates the direction of the shift.
- Positive exponents shift the decimal point to the right, and the numbers get larger. So 10^2 shifts the decimal point 2 places to the right and multiplies the decimal number by 100.
- Negative exponents shift the decimal point to the left, and the numbers get smaller. So 10^{-3} shifts the decimal point 3 places to the left and divides the decimal number by 1,000 (multiplies it by $\frac{1}{1{,}000}$).

Place	___	___	___	•	___	___	___	___
Name:	Hundreds	Tens	Ones	Decimal point	Tenths	Hundredths	Thousandths	Ten Thousandths
Number:	100	10	1	•	0.1	0.01	0.001	0.0001
Exponent:	$\times 10^2$	$\times 10^1$	$\times 10^0$	•	$\times 10^{-1}$	$\times 10^{-2}$	$\times 10^{-3}$	$\times 10^{-4}$
Fraction:	$\times \frac{100}{1}$	$\times \frac{10}{1}$	$\times \frac{1}{1}$	•	$\times \frac{1}{10}$	$\times \frac{1}{100}$	$\times \frac{1}{1000}$	$\times \frac{1}{10{,}000}$
Degree (power):	2	1	0	•	−1	−2	−3	−4
Decimal shift:	2 to the right →	1 to the right →	None	•	1 to the left ←	2 to the left ←	3 to the left ←	4 to the left ←
Number size:	← Larger ←			•	→ Smaller →			

To convert a number to scientific notation, place the decimal point so that the first nonzero digit is in the ones place:

- 12,345,678,900,000,000,000,000 becomes 1.2345678900000000000000
- 0.0000000000000000987654321 becomes 9.87654321

After the decimal point has been relocated, powers of 10 are used to show where it originally was.

- We moved the decimal point 22 places to the left to produce 1.2345678900000000000000. So we would write the original number as $1.23456789 \times 10^{22}$. (Note that the zeros on the right end were removed.)
- This tells someone else that they would need to move the decimal 22 places to the right to reproduce the original number, 12,345,678,900,000,000,000,000. (Note that the person would have to restore the zeros that were removed.)
- We moved the decimal point 16 places to the right to produce 9.87654321. So we would write express the original number as $9.87654321 \times 10^{-16}$. (Note that the zeros on the left end were removed.)
- This tells someone else that they would need to move the decimal 16 places to the left to reproduce the original number, 0.0000000000000000987654321. (Note that the person would have to restore the zeros that were removed.)
- The value of the number does not change when it is converted to scientific notation. Only the number of digits that are used to express the number is changed.

PRACTICE

1. Convert the following numbers to scientific notation:

    a. 3,142,536,475,869,708

    b. 0.1029384756

    c. 5,000,000,000,000,000,000,000,000,000

    d. 0.0000000000000000000000000000005

Answers

1. a. $3.142536475869708 \times 10^{15}$

    b. $1.029384756 \times 10^{-1}$

    c. 5×10^{27}

    d. 5×10^{-31}

A percentage expresses a partial quantity (part) out of a total (whole) of 100. The word percent means "out of 100" and is expressed using the percent sign: %. So 30% (thirty percent) is 30 out of 100 and 72% (seventy–two percent) is 72 out of 100.

One way to calculate a percentage is to multiply by the decimal equivalent of the percentage. To get the decimal equivalent of a percentage, move the decimal point two places to the left and delete the percent sign. For example, to take 35% of 60:

- Convert 35% to 0.35.
- Multiply $60 \times 0.35 = 21$

Knowing this method is important. Since it is easy to do with a calculator, you will be able to use this method to solve many questions. You can use a number of other methods to calculate percentages without using a calculator. One is the *proportion method*, which is discussed later.

PRACTICE

1. Calculate the following percentages:

   a. 62% of 150

   b. 38% of 200

   c. 60% of 60

Answers and Explanations

1. **a. 93** $150 \times 0.62 = 93$

   b. 76 $200 \times 0.38 = 76$

   c. 36 $60 \times 0.6 = 36$

FRACTION TO DECIMAL

To convert a fraction to a decimal, divide the numerator by the denominator:

$$\frac{4}{5} = 5\overline{)4.0}^{0.8} = 0.8$$

Although most conversions produce *terminating decimals* that eventually stop producing a remainder, some produce *repeating decimals* that continue to produce a remainder indefinitely. The fraction $\frac{1}{3}$ produces a repeating decimal:

$$\frac{1}{3} = 3\overline{)1.000000000000000\ldots}^{0.333333333333333\ldots} = 0.333\ldots = .33\overline{3} \approx .334$$

- Repeating digits can be symbolized with a bar (—) above a digit that repeats indefinitely.
- Repeating digits can also be rounded (≈ means "almost equal to").

PERCENT TO DECIMAL

To convert a percent to a decimal, divide the percent by 100. Instead, you can move the decimal point 2 places to the left, adding zeros if needed:

- 20% becomes 0.20 (or 0.2)
- 4% becomes 0.04
- 37.5% becomes 0.375

DECIMAL TO PERCENT

To convert a decimal to a percent, multiply the decimal by 100. Instead, you can move the decimal point 2 places to the right, adding zeros if needed:

- 0.25 becomes 25%
- 0.3 becomes 30%
- 0.07 becomes 7%
- 0.125 becomes 12.5%

PRACTICE

1. Complete this table to show equivalent fractions, decimals, and percents:

Fraction	Decimal	Percent
$\frac{1}{4}$	0.25	25%
$\frac{1}{2}$	0.5	50%
		75%
$\frac{1}{3}$	$0.33\ldots = 0.3\overline{3} \approx 0.33$	33% or 33.$\overline{3}$% or 33$\frac{1}{3}$%
	$0.66\ldots = 0.6\overline{6} \approx 0.67$	66%
$\frac{1}{5}$		20%
$\frac{2}{5}$	0.4	
	0.6	60%
$\frac{4}{5}$		80%
$\frac{1}{8}$	0.125	
	0.25	25%
$\frac{3}{8}$		37.5%
$\frac{5}{8}$		62.5%
$\frac{3}{4}$	0.75	
$\frac{7}{8}$	0.875	
$\frac{1}{10}$		10%
	0.5	50%

2. During the basketball season, Dwayne was able to score 56 points or more in 25% of the games he played. Convert this percent to a fraction.

Answers and Explanations

1.

Fraction	Decimal	Percent
$\frac{1}{4}$	0.25	25%
$\frac{1}{2}$	0.5	50%
$\frac{3}{4}$	0.75	75%
$\frac{1}{3}$	$0.33\ldots = 0.3\overline{3} \approx 0.33$	33% or 33.$\overline{3}$% or 33$\frac{1}{3}$ %
$\frac{2}{3}$	$0.66\ldots = 0.6\overline{6} \approx 0.67$	66%
$\frac{1}{5}$	0.2	20%
$\frac{2}{5}$	0.4	40%
$\frac{3}{5}$	0.6	60%
$\frac{4}{5}$	0.8	80%
$\frac{1}{8}$	0.125	12.5%
$\frac{2}{8}$	0.25	25%
$\frac{3}{8}$	0.375	37.5%
$\frac{5}{8}$	0.625	62.5%
$\frac{3}{4}$	0.75	75%
$\frac{7}{8}$	0.875	87.5%
$\frac{1}{10}$	0.1	10%
$\frac{5}{10}$	0.5	50%

2. $\frac{1}{4}$ 25% is 25 out of 100, which reduces to 1 out of 4 or $\frac{1}{4}$.

Ratios, Proportions, and Rates

LESSON 1: RATIOS

A *ratio* describes the relationship between one part and another part. A ratio can be expressed in a number of ways:

- **WORDS**   the ratio of 3 to 5

- **RATIONAL (FRACTION) FORM** $\dfrac{3}{5}$

- **COLON**   3:5

All of these mean that there are 3 of one kind of thing for every 5 of another kind of thing. A class may have 3 male students for every 5 female students, and this is a ratio of 3 to 5.

Ratios can be equivalent to each other. They can be expanded and reduced like fractions.

A ratio of 12:9 $\left(\dfrac{12}{9}\right)$ is equivalent to a ratio of 4:3 $\left(\dfrac{4}{3}\right)$ because 3 is a common factor of both parts of the first ratio (12 ÷ 3 = 4 and 9 ÷ 3 = 3).

Ratios are an extremely important concept on the Math test because other concepts (like fractions, proportions, and rational equations) build on ratios. The following section will illustrate in some more detail how ratios work. It will also provide a useful way for you to work with ratios if you are not already comfortable with them.

THE RATIO BOX

Most ratio questions on the test will ask you to use the ratio of parts in a whole to find the actual numbers. For example:

The ratio of boys to girls in a math club is 2 to 3. If there are 70 students in the club, how many girls are in the club?

Questions such as this can be answered using a very effective tool called the ratio box.

STEP 1   **SET UP A RATIO BOX**

The best way to set up a ratio box is like this:

	Ratio	Multiply By	Actual Number
Boys	2		
Girls	3		
Total			70

As shown here, a ratio box has four columns. The first holds the labels for each part along with a label for the total. The second column is the "Ratio" column. It holds the numbers in the ratio (in this case, 2 and 3). The third column is the "Multiply By" column. It will hold a multiplier that you figure out using the other columns. The fourth column is the "Actual Number" column. It holds the actual numbers for the parts and the whole (in this case, the 70 actual students).

Along with the row for the column labels, the ratio box has rows for each part of the ratio and an additional row for the total. You will always add this "Total" row when setting up a ratio box.

STEP 2 **ADD UP THE PARTS**
The next step in using the ratio box is to add up the numbers representing the parts. Then put the result in the "Total" row of the "Ratio" column.

	Ratio	Multiply By	Actual Number
Boys	2		
Girls	3		
Total	5		70

In this example, the numbers for the parts are 2 and 3. Since 2 + 3 = 5, you would write 5 in the "Total" row of the "Ratio" column.

STEP 3 **FIND THE MULTIPLIER**
The next step is to find the multiplier that is used to go from the ratio numbers to the actual numbers. This multiplier remains constant. In fact, it is the key to working out the answer to the question. Find a row that has a number in both the "Ratio" column and "Actual Number" column.

In this example, the row that contains a value in both columns is the "Total" row. To determine the multiplier, divide the actual number value by the ratio value. Since 70 ÷ 5 = 14, the multiplier is 14.

	Ratio	Multiply By	Actual Number
Boys	2	14	
Girls	3	14	
Total	5	14	70

The multiplier is constant, so it will be the same for each part of the ratio. The multiplier goes into each cell in the "Multiply By" column as shown above.

USE THE MULTIPLIER

The next step is to multiply the ratio numbers by the multiplier for any value not already present in the "Actual Number" column. This gives you the rest of the actual numbers.

	Ratio	Multiply By	Actual Number
Boys	2	14	28
Girls	3	14	42
Total	5	14	70

Since 2 • 14 = 28, 28 goes into the "Boys" row. Since 3 • 14 = 42, 42 goes into the "Girls" row.

You can check that these numbers are correct by adding them together. The problem says that 70 students are in the club. Since 28 + 42 = 70, these numbers are correct because they agree with the information in the problem.

STEP 5 **ANSWER THE QUESTION**

The original question was:

The ratio of boys to girls in a math club is 2 to 3. If there are 70 students in the club, how many girls are in the club?

The completed ratio box looks like this:

	Ratio	Multiply By	Actual Number
Boys	2	14	28
Girls	3	14	42
Total	5	14	70

The ratio box shows that there are 28 boys and 42 girls in the club. The total number of girls is 42.

The ratio box is like a Swiss army knife for working with ratios, proportions, rates, percentages, fractions, and so on. If you're interested in seeing the various ways it can be used, see the "Ratio Box Variations" topic at the end of this lesson.

PRACTICE

1. A 16-fluid-ounce cup is used to create a simple banana milk shake that contains just milk and bananas. The shake requires 12 fluid ounces of milk. In this shake, what is the ratio of bananas to milk?

2. In a certain cooking school, the ratio of French chefs to Italian chefs is 4:7. If there are 33 total chefs in the school, how many of them are Italian chefs?
   (A) 7
   (B) 11
   (C) 12
   (D) 21

3. A train is traveling along a route that includes two stops: Aubreville and Barnesville. of the 140 passengers on the train, 60 are going to Aubreville. What is the ratio of Aubreville passengers to Barnesville passengers?

(A) 60 to 140

(B) 6 to 14

(C) 3 to 4

(D) 2 to 3

4. The graduating class of George Emerson Dawkins University has 300 students in it. The ratio of male students to female students is 2 to 3. What percentage of the graduating class is female?

(A) 60%

(B) 50%

(C) 40%

(D) 30%

5. The ratio of dogs to cats in the window of a pet store is 3:7. What fractional part of the animals in the window are dogs?

(A) $\dfrac{3}{10}$

(B) $\dfrac{3}{7}$

(C) $\dfrac{7}{10}$

(D) $\dfrac{7}{3}$

Answers and Explanations

1. **1 to 3** If the cup holds 16 ounces and 12 ounces are milk, 4 ounces are bananas (16 – 12 = 4). So the ratio of bananas to milk is 4 to 12 = 1 to 3.

2. **22** The smallest group of chefs that could be in a ratio of 4 to 7 is 11 chefs (4 + 7 = 11). This means that the multiplier between the ratio numbers and the actual numbers is 3 (11 × 3 = 33). The ratio number for Italian chefs is 7 and 7 × 3 = 21.

3. **3 to 4** If there are 140 total passengers and 60 are Aubreville passengers, then there are 80 Barnesville passengers (150 – 60 = 80). If we divide both parts by 10, the ratio of 60 to 80 reduces to 6 to 8. Then it reduces again to lowest terms: 3 to 4.

4. **60%** If the ratio of male students to female students is 2 to 3, then 3 students out of 5 are female (2 + 3 = 5). The fraction 3/5 can be enlarged to 6/10 (multiply by 2/2) and then to 60/100 (multiply by 10/10). Since "percent" means out of 100, 60/100 is equivalent to 60%. Another approach to this problem would be to divide: 3 ÷ 5 = 0.6. Converting a decimal to a percent involves moving the decimal point two places to the right, so 0.6 becomes 60%. The number of students in the graduating class does not affect the answer.

5. $\dfrac{3}{10}$ The smallest group of animals that could be in a ratio of 3 to 7 is 10 animals (3 + 7 = 10). Since 3 dogs are in every group of 10 animals, three-tenths $\left(\dfrac{3}{10}\right)$ of the animals in the window are dogs.

A *rate* is a ratio that involves words or phrases like *"per"* (60 miles per hour, $14 per hour) or *"for every"* (1 free coffee for every 3 purchased). Whenever a question asks for an answer involving a unit (like a mile, a minute, an hour, and so on), divide the total amount by the total number of units to calculate the amount per unit. For example, $14 per hour would be 14 dollars ÷ 60 minutes or 23.3 cents per minute.

PRACTICE

1. Luna drove her SUV in the city for a total of 189 miles. She used 9.8 gallons of gas. To the nearest tenth of a mile per gallon, how many miles per gallon was Luna's SUV averaging?

2. Lewis's cellular phone statement shows that he owes $262 for last month's service. The statement also shows that he used 4,750 minutes. To the nearest tenth of a cent, what is Lewis being charged per minute?

Answers and Explanations

1. **19.3** 189 miles ÷ 9.8 gallons = 19.28 . . . = 19.3 miles per gallon.

2. **5.5** $262 = 26,200 cents and 26,200 cents ÷ 4,750 minutes = 5.515 . . . = 5.5 cents per minute.

A *proportion* sets two ratios equal to one another:

$$\frac{1}{4} = \frac{4}{16}$$

Two ratios are proportional when one of them can be converted to the other using the same multiplier for both the numerator and the denominator:

$$\frac{1}{4} \cdot \frac{4}{4} = \frac{4}{16}$$

In a proportion, the cross products of the two ratios are equal:

$$16 = 16$$
$$\frac{1}{4} \diagup\!\!\!\!\diagdown \frac{4}{16}$$

Any combination of the four terms in a proportion that produces the same cross products is an equivalent form of the proportion. In the tale below, the symbols *a*, *b*, *c*, and *d* are used to represent the four parts of the ratios in the proportion. The table shows the cross products of the equivalent proportions in two forms. Then it shows four variations of another proportion, this one containing numbers.

- The first row in the table shows the cross products resulting from multiplying the top left number by the bottom right number and then multiplying the bottom left number by the top right number.
- In the table, the second through fourth shows the cross products in reordered forms to show that the cross products of all four variations are equal.
- The *commutative property of multiplication* allows this reordering. It says that the factors in multiplication can be rearranged without changing the resulting product: $ab = ba$ or $3(4) = 4(3)$.

UNIT 2: MATH

Proportion	Cross Products	Reordered
$\dfrac{a}{b} \diagdown\diagup \dfrac{c}{d}$	$ad = bc$	
$\dfrac{b}{d} = \dfrac{a}{c}$	$bc = da$ →	$ad = bc$
$\dfrac{d}{c} = \dfrac{b}{a}$	$da = cb$ →	$ad = bc$
$\dfrac{b}{a} = \dfrac{d}{c}$	$bc = ad$ →	$ad = bc$
$\dfrac{1}{4} \diagdown\diagup \dfrac{4}{16}$	$1 \cdot 16 = 4 \cdot 4$	
$\dfrac{4}{16} = \dfrac{1}{4}$	$4 \cdot 4 = 16 \cdot 1$ →	$1 \cdot 16 = 4 \cdot 4$
$\dfrac{16}{4} = \dfrac{4}{1}$	$16 \cdot 1 = 4 \cdot 4$ →	$1 \cdot 16 = 4 \cdot 4$
$\dfrac{4}{1} = \dfrac{16}{4}$	$4 \cdot 4 = 1 \cdot 16$ →	$1 \cdot 16 = 4 \cdot 4$

The rule of equal cross products can be used to find a missing term in a proportion if given the other three terms:

- Set up the proportion using a consistent structure.
- Cross multiply two of the known terms.
- Divide the product by the third known term.

Consider the following example:

> The class has a ratio of three males to five females, and there are fifteen female students. How many male students are in the class?

First the two ratios must present the parts in the same order:

- Ratio part: 3 males, 5 females.
- Actual part: 15 female students, unknown number of male students.

$$\frac{3 \text{ males}}{5 \text{ females}} = \frac{x \text{ male students}}{15 \text{ female students}}$$

- In the proportion shown above, males are on the top in both ratios and females are on the bottom. (Note that we use the letter x to represent the number we don't know.)

Now cross multiply. Then divide by the third known term:

$$\frac{3}{5} = \frac{x}{15}$$

- $3 \times 15 = 45$ and $45 \div 5 = 9$. There are nine male students in the class.

To verify this answer, check the cross products:

$$\frac{3}{5} = \frac{9}{15} \rightarrow 3(15) = 5(9) \rightarrow 45 = 45$$

PROPORTION METHOD FOR PERCENTAGES

Proportions give us a very powerful way to calculate percentages manually. Most percentages can be expressed this way:

A part is equal to a percent of a whole, such as "80 is equal to 25% of 320."

In any percentage question, one of these three elements will be missing:

- Missing part: What number is equal to 25% of 320?
- Missing percent: 80 is equal to what percent of 320?
- Missing whole: 80 is equal to 25% of what number?
- The part is always next to the word "is."
- The whole is always next to the word "of."

Percentage questions can be set up as proportions using the following format:

$$\frac{\text{part (is)}}{\text{whole (of)}} = \frac{\text{percent (\%)}}{100}$$

Missing part: What number is equal to 25% of 320?

$$\frac{x \text{ (is)}}{320 \text{ (of)}} = \frac{25}{100} \rightarrow 100x = 8,000 \rightarrow 8,000 \div 100 = 80.$$

Missing percent: 80 is equal to what percent of 320?

$$\frac{80 \text{ (is)}}{320 \text{ (of)}} = \frac{x}{100} \rightarrow \frac{8}{32} = \frac{x}{100} \rightarrow 800 = 32x \rightarrow 800 \div 32 = 25\%.$$

Note that we reduced the ratio on the left by a factor of 10 before we cross multiplied. This is a good way to make the calculation easier. In fact, we could have reduced further:

$$\frac{80 \text{ (is)}}{320 \text{ (of)}} = \frac{8}{32} = \frac{1}{4} = \frac{x}{100} \rightarrow \frac{1}{4} = \frac{x}{100} \rightarrow 100 = 4x \rightarrow 100 \div 4 = 25\%$$

Missing whole: 80 is equal to 25% of what number?

$$\frac{80 \text{ (is)}}{x \text{ (of)}} = \frac{25}{100} \rightarrow \frac{80}{x} = \frac{1}{4} \rightarrow 320 = x = 320$$

Note that this time, we reduced the ratio on the right.

PERCENT CHANGE

Some questions will ask you to work with an increase or a decrease of a number or a percentage. The increase or decrease goes "from" one (original) value "to" another (new) value. An increase makes the new value higher, and a decrease makes it lower.

To answer these questions, you'll need to work with the following proportion:

$$\frac{\text{difference}}{\text{original}} = \frac{\%}{100}$$

The difference is the amount of change from the original value to the new value:

- For increases, the new value will be larger: *difference = new – original.* An increase from 6 to 11 is a difference of $11 - 6 = 5$.
- For decreases, the new value will be smaller: *difference = original – new.* A decrease from 19 to 12 is a difference of $19 - 12 = 7$.

The percent (%) change is the difference represented as a percentage of the original. When given a value for percent change, pay attention to whether the change is an increase or a decrease.

For a *percentage increase*, the new value will be larger than the original. Let's look at a common situation to explain this topic—tipping a server after a meal.

(1) Assume that a meal costs $60 before the tip. This $60 is the original price.
(2) Your server did an excellent job, so you decide to tip 20%. Determine what amount equals 20%.

$$\frac{\text{difference (tip)}}{\text{original}} = \frac{x}{100}$$

$$\frac{\text{difference (tip)}}{\$60} = \frac{20}{100} = \frac{1}{5} \rightarrow \text{difference (tip)} = \frac{(\$60)(20)}{100} = \$12$$

So a 20% tip equals $12.

(3) You actually pay $72 for the meal ($60 + $12 = $72). This $72 is the new price.

You can look at this situation in two ways: either the original price as a percent of the new price or the new price as a percent of the original price.

- Original as a percent of new:

$$\frac{\text{original price}}{\text{new price}} = \frac{x}{100}$$

$$\frac{\$60}{\$72} = \frac{5}{6} = \frac{x}{100} \rightarrow \frac{(100)(5)}{6} = x = 83.33\ldots \approx 83\%$$

So the original price is about 83% of the new price.

- New as percent of original:

$$\frac{\text{new price}}{\text{original price}} = \frac{100}{x}$$

$$\frac{\$72}{\$60} = \frac{6}{5} = \frac{x}{100} \rightarrow \frac{(100)(6)}{5} = x = 120 = 120\%$$

So the new price is 120% of the original price.

Note that although the numbers are all the same—original amount is $60, new amount is $72, and difference is $12—the way you look at the numbers affects the percentage increase.

For a *percentage decrease*, the new value will be smaller than the original. Let's look at a common situation to explain this topic—buying a shirt on sale.

(1) Assume that the shirt originally costs $40. The $40 is the original price.
(2) The sale discounts the original price by 10%. Determine what amount equals 10%.

$$\frac{\text{difference (discount)}}{\text{original}} = \frac{x}{100}$$

$$\frac{\text{difference (discount)}}{\$40} = \frac{10}{100} = \frac{1}{10} \rightarrow \text{difference (discount)} = \frac{(\$40)(10)}{100} = 54$$

So a 10% discount equals $4.

(3) You actually pay $36 for the shirt ($40 − $4 = $36). This $36 is the new price.

You can look at this situation in two ways: either the original price as a percent of the new price or the new price as a percent of the original price.

- Original as a percent of new:

$$\frac{\text{original price}}{\text{new price}} = \frac{x}{100}$$

$$\frac{\$40}{\$36} = \frac{10}{9} = \frac{x}{100} \rightarrow \frac{(100)(10)}{9} = x = 111.11\ldots \approx 111\%$$

So the original price is about 111% of the new price.

- New as percent of original:

$$\frac{\text{new price}}{\text{original price}} = \frac{x}{100}$$

$$\frac{\$36}{\$40} = \frac{9}{10} = \frac{x}{100} \rightarrow \frac{(100)(9)}{10} = x = 90 = 90\%$$

So the new price is 90% of the original price.

Note that although the numbers are all the same—original amount is $40, new amount is $36, and difference is $4—the way you look at the numbers affects the percentage decrease.

In any percent change question, one of these three elements will be missing:

- Missing difference: What number is equal to a 20% change from 250?
- Missing percentage: 50 is equal to what percent change from 250?
- Missing new or original: 80 is equal to 20% change from what number?

Proportions can be used to answer any of these question types:

MISSING DIFFERENCE   Assume the new number is 15% greater than the original, which is 600. What number is equal to 15% of 600?

$$\frac{x}{600} = \frac{15}{100} \rightarrow 9,000 = 100x \rightarrow 9,000 \div 100 = 90$$

The number equal to 15% of 600 is 90. Even though it wasn't asked, you should know that the new number is 600 + 90 = 690.

MISSING PERCENTAGE   Assume the original is 180, and it is reduced by 45. So 45 is equal to what percent of 180?

$$\frac{45}{180} = \frac{x}{100} \rightarrow \frac{1}{4} = \frac{x}{100} \rightarrow 100 = 4x \rightarrow 100 \div 4 = 25$$

The number 45 is 25% of 180.

MISSING NEW   Assume the original was 300 and was reduced by 25%. (Remember that this makes the new number 75% of the original, because 100% − 25% = 75%.) What number is 75% of 300?

$$\frac{x}{300} = \frac{75}{100} \rightarrow \frac{x}{300} = \frac{3}{4} \rightarrow 4x = 900 \rightarrow 900 \div 4 = 225$$

The number 225 is 75% of 300.

MISSING ORIGINAL   Assume the new is 195 after an increase of 30%. (Remember that this makes the new 130% of the original, because 100% + 30% = 130%.) So 195 is 130% of what number?

$$\frac{195}{x} = \frac{130}{100} \rightarrow \frac{195}{x} = \frac{13}{10} \rightarrow 13x = 1,950 \rightarrow 1,950 \div 13 = 150$$

The number 195 is 130% of 150.

RATE CALCULATIONS

Proportions can be used to perform calculations involving rates, like speed in miles per hour. At 60 miles per hour, how far will you travel in 4 hours?

To answer this question: First set up a proportion with the per unit (hours in this case) on the top of the left ratio:

$$\frac{1 \text{ hour}}{60 \text{ miles}} = \frac{4 \text{ hours}}{x \text{ miles}}$$

Solve the proportion:

$$\frac{1}{60} = \frac{4}{x} \rightarrow x = 240$$

So at 60 miles per hour, you will travel 240 miles in 4 hours.

SCALE CONVERSIONS

Proportions can also be used to convert scales, such as the relationship between distances on a map and real distances. Suppose a map has a scale where 1 inch = 5 miles. If a distance on the map is 6 inches, how many miles is the real distance?

$$\frac{1 \text{ inch}}{5 \text{ miles}} = \frac{6 \text{ inches}}{x} \rightarrow x = 30 \text{ miles}$$

The real distance is 30 miles.

PRACTICE

1. If a gallon of gas weighs 2 pounds and is made of 32% crude oil, what portion of the weight, rounded to the nearest ounce, is made of crude oil? (1 pound = 16 ounces)

2. Jonathan earns 12% of the purchase price for every car he sells. What will Jonathan earn if he sells a car for $43,000?

3. To buy a new house, Sharon must make a 10% down payment. If her total down payment is $13,250, what is the price of the house?

4. An architect drafts a building at a scale of 1 inch = 650 feet. To the nearest foot, what is the actual distance of a wall that is $7\frac{3}{4}$ inches on this draft?

Answers and Explanations

1. **10.24 ounces** First use a proportion to convert the pounds to ounces:

$$\frac{x}{2 \text{ pounds}} = \frac{16 \text{ ounces}}{1 \text{ pound}} \rightarrow x = 32 \text{ ounces}.$$

Then use another proportion to find what portion of the weight is crude oil:

$$\frac{y}{32 \text{ ounces}} = \frac{32}{100} \rightarrow y = \frac{(32)(32)}{100} = 10.24 \text{ ounces}.$$

2. **$5,160** Set up a proportion:

$$\frac{x}{\$43,000} = \frac{12}{100} \rightarrow x = \frac{(43,000)(12)}{100} = \$5,160.$$

3. **$132,500** Sharon's down payment of $13,250 is 10% of the total. Use a proportion:

$$\frac{\$13,250}{x} = \frac{10}{100} \rightarrow x = \frac{(13,250)(100)}{10} = \$132,500.$$

4. **5,038 feet** Change the distance on the draft to a decimal:

$$7\frac{3}{4} = 7.75.$$

Now set up a proportion:

$$\frac{x}{7.75 \text{ inches}} = \frac{650 \text{ feet}}{1 \text{ inch}} \rightarrow x = \frac{(7.75)(650)}{1} = 5,037.5 \text{ feet}.$$

Round up to 5,038 feet.

Ratio boxes can be used to solve a variety of question types.

MISSING ACTUAL TOTAL

One type of ratio problem will provide an actual part and ask for the actual total. Here's an example:

A jar contains red and blue marbles in a ratio of 3 red to 5 blue marbles. There are 60 blue marbles in the jar. How many marbles are in the jar altogether?

A ratio box can be set up to solve this problem. In this case, the 60 goes in the "Blue" row "Actual Number" column.

	Ratio	Multiply By	Actual Number
Red	3		
Blue	5		60
Total			

Follow the same ratio box to process described earlier in this lesson to find the multiplier. First, add the ratio numbers to get the total. Then use whichever row contains both a ratio and an actual number to find the multiplier.

	Ratio	Multiply By	Actual Number
Red	3	12	
Blue	5	12	60
Total	8	12	96

Since $3 + 5 = 8$, the total ratio is 8. The "Blue" row contains both a ratio and an actual number, so divide: $60 \div 5 = 12$. The multiplier is constant, so put 12 into each row in the "Multiply By" column. Next multiply $8 \bullet 12$ to get the actual total number of marbles: $8 \times 12 = 96$. So the answer to the question is 96 marbles.

MISSING RATIO

Another question variation will ask for the ratio given some of the actual numbers:

A local parking lot contains only cars and SUVs. There are 36 cars, and the total number of vehicles in the lot is 100. What is the ratio of cars to SUVs in the lot?

	Ratio	Multiply By	Actual Number
Cars			36
SUVs			
Total			100

This question doesn't provide any ratio numbers at all. Instead, it provides an actual total number (100 vehicles) and an actual number for one type (36 cars). Determine the ratio of cars to SUVs by subtracting the number of cars from the total to get the actual number of SUVs: $100 - 36 = 64$.

	Ratio	Multiply By	Actual Number
Cars			36
SUVs			64
Total			100

Usually the goal in using the ratio box is to find a row with both a ratio and an actual number. This is done in order to find the multiplier that goes in the "Multiply By" column. For this problem, though, you don't have a row like that. However, you can still answer the question.

Remember that a ratio can be expressed in a form that is similar to a fraction, where one part is related to another part. The actual numbers of cars and SUVs represent the parts of the actual total. Since the question asks for the "ratio of cars to SUVs," the ratio is set up with the cars on the top and SUVs on the bottom: 36/64.

Now reduce this fraction to lowest terms. The best way to do this with even numbers is to continue dividing both the top and bottom by 2 as many times as you can. Since 36 ÷ 2 = 18 and 64 ÷ 2 = 32, the first reduction would be 18/32. Since 18 ÷ 2 = 9 and 32 ÷ 2 = 16, the next reduction would be 9/16.

Since 9 and 16 do not have a common factor (a number that will divide evenly into both of them), 9/16 is in lowest terms. The answer to the question is 9 to 16, 9:16, or 9/16. All three forms mean the same thing.

	Ratio	Multiply By	Actual Number
Cars	9		36
SUVs	16		64
Total			100

Strictly speaking, a ratio box is not necessary to work out this problem. You can see, though, how it would be helpful. Filling in the actual numbers shows the need to subtract to get the missing actual number of SUVs.

FRACTION AND PERCENT QUESTIONS

The completed ratio box below shows all of the information related to the previous problem:

	Ratio	Multiply By	Actual Number
Cars	9	4	36
SUVs	16	4	64
Total	25	4	100

Other questions could be answered based on the information in this ratio box.

For example, what fraction of the total number of vehicles parked in the lot are cars?

Remember that a fraction is the relationship of a part to a whole (or total). In the completed ratio box, the "Ratio" column shows that the part for cars is 9 and the whole or total is 25. The answer is 9/25.

Another example is SUVs make up what percent of the total number of vehicles in the lot?

This question is very easily answered from the information in the ratio box, especially since the total number of cars in the "Actual Number" column is 100. The actual number of SUVs is 64 out of 100. Since percentages are always based on 100, the answer is 64 percent, or 64%. (In cases where the total number is not so "percent friendly," the answer can be calculated by converting the fraction form to a percent using division.

Measurement and Geometry

7

The topics in this section relate to physical objects and their properties. Measurement deals with ways of quantifying the properties of something. Geometry deals with lines, angles, and shapes in two and three dimensions.

LESSON 1: MEASUREMENT

As we mentioned before, math questions will appear in other subject tests besides the Math test. Material related to measurement will be used in the Science subject test as well as the Math test. Be sure you are comfortable with these topics.

Measurement is a method of describing and comparing things using numerical units. Some of the types of things that are typically measured include:

- Dimensions (lengths, widths, heights, depths)
- Weight or mass
- Time
- Temperature
- Angles (degrees)
- Shapes (perimeter, area, volume)
- Amounts of money
- Data or memory size (gigabytes, megabytes)

All measurements consist of a number and a unit.

- The *number* answers the question "how many." In the measurement 6 grams, the number is 6.
- The *unit* answers the question "of what." In the measurement 40 seconds, the unit is seconds.

SYSTEMS OF MEASUREMENT

A measurement system is a group of standard units used to measure various quantities that represent characteristics of objects. The types of quantities that make up a measurement system include:

- Length
- Weight or mass
- Capacity (volume)
- Temperature

Units in a measurement system can be grouped together into larger units (12 inches in a foot) or broken down into smaller units (3 feet in a yard). Changing units makes it easier to measure things that are very large or very small.

Metric Units

Metric units are sometimes called international units, and they are standard units of measure in the scientific community as well as in many countries around the world. Since metric measurements will be used in all of the material you see on the Science subject test, you must become familiar with them if you aren't already.

The fundamental units in the metric system are the following:

- Length—The meter (m). Length is typically measured with rulers and measuring tapes.
- Mass—The gram (g). Mass is typically measured with scales.
- Capacity—The liter (L). Capacity is typically measured by filling containers with liquids or other substances.
- Temperature—Degrees Celsius (C) or Kelvins (K). Celsius is also called centigrade. Temperature is typically measured using a thermometer.

The metric system is similar to place values for whole and decimal numbers, because the metric system is based on multiples of 10. Each unit that is larger or smaller than the base unit (meter, gram, liter) has a standard prefix (centi-, kilo-, micro-, and so on). On the Math Subject test, you will mostly have to work with the fundamental units and the kilo-, centi-, and milli- prefixes.

- When grouping smaller units into larger units, each larger unit consists of 10 of the next smaller unit. For example, there are 10 millimeters (mm) in 1 centimeter (cm).
- When breaking larger units into smaller units, each larger unit consists of 10 of the next smaller unit. For example, 1 decimeter (dm) is 10 centimeters (cm).

The table below lists these unit relationships. Remember that the relationships don't change for length, mass, or volume.

Metric Prefixes and Their Values

Prefix	Prefix Abbreviation	Exponent	Number
tera	T	10^{12}	1,000,000,000,000
giga	G	10^{9}	1,000,000,000
mega	M	10^{6}	1,000,000
kilo	k	10^{3}	1,000
hecto	h	10^{2}	100
			1
deci	d	10^{-1}	0.1
centi	c	10^{-2}	0.01
milli	m	10^{-3}	0.001
micro	μ	10^{-6}	0.000001
nano	n	10^{-9}	0.000000001

The use of multiples of 10 makes the metric system very compatible with scientific notation since both are based on multiples of 10. For example, 1.2×10^3 centiliters (cL) is equal to 12 liters (L):

$$1cL = 0.01L \rightarrow 1.2cL = 0.012\ L \quad 0.012L \times 10^3 = 12L$$

Customary Units

Customary units are sometimes called imperial units, and they are the standard units of measurement in the United States.

The fundamental units in this system are the following:

- Length – The foot (ft or ′).
- Weight – The pound (lb).
- Capacity – The cup (c).
- Temperature – Degrees Fahrenheit (F).

Conversions Between Customary Units

Length				
1 foot (ft)	=	12 inches (in)		
1 yard (yd)	=	3 feet	=	36 inches
1 mile (mi)	=	1,760 yards	=	5,280 feet
Weight				
1 pound (lb)	=	16 ounces (oz)		
1 ton (T)	=	2,000 pounds		
Capacity				
1 cup (c)	=	8 fluid ounces (fl oz)		
1 pint (pt)	=	2 cups	=	16 fl oz
1 quart (qt)	=	2 pints	=	32 fl oz
1 gallon (gal)	=	4 quarts	=	128 fl oz

Conversions Between Units of Time

1 minute (min)	=	60 seconds (sec)
1 hour (hr)	=	60 minutes
1 day	=	24 hours
1 week (wk)	=	7 days
1 month (mo)		approximately 4 weeks; between 28–31 days
1 year (yr)	=	365 days
1 leap year	=	366 days

Temperature

On the exam, temperatures will be expressed in either degrees Celsius (°C) or degrees Fahrenheit (°F). Both systems use a fundamental unit called a degree (°).

Think of temperature scales as number lines. Temperatures can be positive or negative. One difference between the two systems is the zero point, which is based on the freezing point of a liquid:

- Zero degrees Celsius (0°C)—Freezing point of water.
- Zero degrees Fahrenheit (0°F)—Freezing point of a water-like liquid called brine.

The other significant difference is in the interval between units on the scale (1 degree F is a little less than 2 degrees C). The intervals are different because:

- Celsius has 100 degrees between the freezing and boiling points of water.
- Fahrenheit has 180 degrees between these two points.

Temperatures in Celsius and Fahrenheit

Event	°C	°F
Water boils	100	212
Water freezes	0	32
Brine freezes	–18	0
Temperature is equal on both scales	–40	–40
Absolute zero	–273	–460

CONVERTING BETWEEN SYSTEMS

You can convert between the metric and customary systems.

	Metric	Customary
Length	1 meter	3.28 feet 1.09 yards
Weight	1 gram 1 kilogram	0.035 ounces 2.20 pounds
Capacity	1 liter	1.06 quarts 0.26 gallons
Temperature	1 degree C	1.8 degrees F

Note that some of the conversion rates above have been rounded to two decimal places.

Converting between systems is done using proportions. For example, a 20-degree Celsius change is equivalent to a change of how many degrees Fahrenheit?

$$\frac{1.8°F}{1°C} = \frac{x°F}{20°C} \rightarrow x = 36 \rightarrow 36°F$$

Note that the example above compares number of degrees and not temperatures. If you are asked to convert temperatures, you will be provided with the formula: °F = (1.8)(°C) + 32°. The temperature 20°C is equivalent to 68°F: (1.8)(20) + 32 = 36 + 32 = 68. This formula is required because of the different zero points on the two scales.

PRACTICE

1. Jean's parents asked him to arrange his blocks by their length. The lengths are listed below.

    Block $A = 1\frac{1}{4}$ in.

    Block $B = 1\frac{2}{5}$ in.

    Block $C = 1\frac{11}{23}$ in.

    From shortest to longest, what is the correct order of the blocks?

2. One thousand three hundred twenty yards is what fraction of a mile? (1 mile = 5,280 feet)

3. How many feet are in 7 meters? (1 meter = 3.28 feet)

4. Approximately how many kilograms in a customary ton (T)? (1 kilogram = 2.20 pounds)

5. How many cups are in 3 liters? (1 liter = 1.06 quarts and 1 quart = 4 cups)

6. 10°C is what temperature in Fahrenheit? (°F = 1.8(°C) + 32°)

Answers and Explanations

1. ***A, B, C*** Compare the fractions using the multiplication method. Block *A* is shorter than *B*. Block *B* is shorter than *C*. Block *A* is shorter than *C*.

2. $\frac{3}{4}$ A yard is equal to 3 feet. So 5,280 feet ÷ 3 = 1,760 yards equal 1 mile. So 1,320 ÷ 1,760 = 0.75, which converts to $\frac{3}{4}$.

3. **22.96 feet** Since 1 meter = 3.28 feet, that means 7 meters × 3.28 = 22.96 feet.

4. **909 kg** 1 kilogram = 2.20 pounds and 1 ton = 2,000 pounds. That means 2,000 pounds ÷ 2.2 = 909.0909 . . . ≈ 909 kilograms.

5. **12.72 cups** Since 1 liter = 1.06 quarts, 3 liters × 1.06 = 3.18 quarts. Since 1 quart = 4 cups, 3.18 quarts × 4 = 12.72 cups.

6. **50°F** Use the formula provided: °F = 1.8(10) + 32 → °F = 18 + 32 → °F = 50.

DIMENSIONS   A dimension is a property of shapes. Length, width, and height are all dimensions.

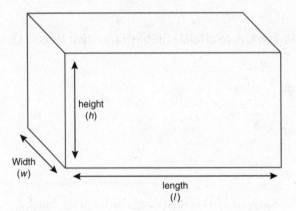

POINTS AND LINES

POINT   A point is a location in space. Points are zero dimensional, which means they have no length, width, or height. Points are usually labeled with a single capital letter: *A*.

ENDPOINT   An endpoint is a point that defines one end of a *ray* or line *segment*.

LINE   A line is a collection of points. Lines are one dimensional, which means they have length but no width or height.

- A line is commonly represented with two points, but these are not the endpoints. Lines extend infinitely in both directions, as shown by the dotted lines above. Lines contain an infinite number of points.
- Lines are labeled with reference to the points that define them. The line above is called $\overleftrightarrow{BC}$ (line *BC*).

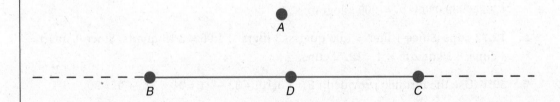

UNIT 2: MATH

COLLINEAR   Points on a common line are collinear. In the figure above, points *B*, *C*, and *D* are collinear.

NONCOLLINEAR   Three or more points that cannot be connected by a single line are noncollinear. In the previous figure, points *A*, *B*, and *C* are noncollinear. Even though two points fall on the line, the third doesn't.

RAY   A ray is a portion of a line that extends infinitely in one direction from a given endpoint. The ray in the figure below is called $\overrightarrow{EF}$ (ray *EF*).

LINE SEGMENT   A line segment is a portion of a line with two endpoints. The segment below is called $\overline{GH}$ (segment *GH*).

MIDPOINT   The midpoint is a point on a line segment that is at an equal distance from both endpoints. It is the middle or halfway point. In the segment below, point *J* is the midpoint of $\overline{GH}$.

PLANES AND SPACE

PLANE   A plane is a two-dimensional surface made up of points. A plane has length and width but no height.

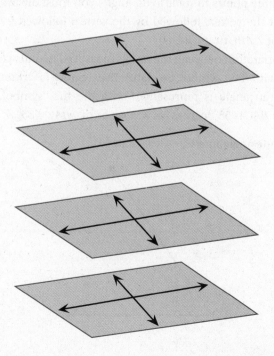

Any three points can define a single plane, as can a line and a single point not on the line. Points and lines can be either coplanar (on the same plane) or noncoplanar (not on the same plane).

SPACE Space is three dimensional. It has length, width, and height. It contains all points, lines, and planes.

ANGLES

INTERSECTION An intersection is a point common to two lines, segments, or rays. It represents a place where they meet or cross.

ANGLE An angle is formed when two rays intersect at a common endpoint, called a *vertex*. Angles are marked with a curved line called an *arc*.

VERTEX A vertex is the point where two rays meet to form an angle.

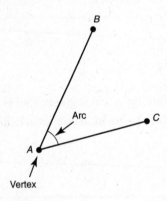

- Angles can be described using only the vertex or using all three points that define the angle. The angle shown above can be named ∠*A*, or "angle *A*." It can also be named ∠*BAC* or ∠*CAB*.
- When using all three points to refer to an angle, you must always start with one of the points that is not the vertex, followed by the vertex, followed by the third point. The angle above is not ∠*ABC* or ∠*CBA*.
- The amount of separation between the rays is measured in units called degrees. Degrees are represented with the ° symbol. So eighty-five degrees is written as 85°.
- The measure of an angle is represented with the m∠ symbol. The sentence "The measure of angle *BAC* is 55 degrees" is written as m∠*BAC* = 55°.

ACUTE ANGLE An acute angle measures less than 90°.

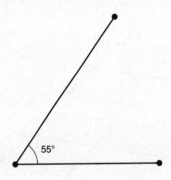

RIGHT ANGLE   A right angle measures exactly 90°. It is marked with a small square symbol.

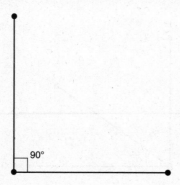

OBTUSE ANGLE   An obtuse angle measures more than 90° but less than 180°.

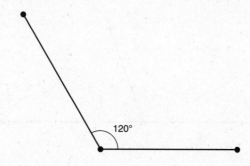

STRAIGHT ANGLE   A straight angle measures exactly 180°. The two rays in a straight angle are called *opposite rays*.

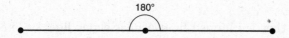

ADJACENT ANGLES   Two angles are adjacent when they share a common side and vertex.

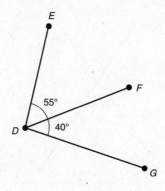

COMPLEMENTARY ANGLES   Two angles are complementary when their measures add to 90°.

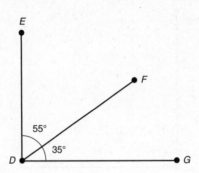

SUPPLEMENTARY ANGLES   Two angles are supplementary when their measures add to 180°.

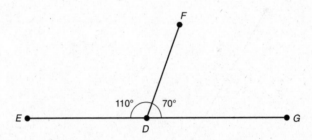

CONGRUENT   When two or more lines or two or more angles have the same measure, they are congruent. Congruency is represented with the ≅ symbol. The sentence "the measure of angle *A* is congruent to the measure of angle *B*" is written as m∠*A* ≅ m∠*B*.

VERTICAL ANGLES   They are formed by two intersecting lines or line segments. Vertical angles are pairs of nonadjacent angles with a common vertex. Vertical angles are congruent.

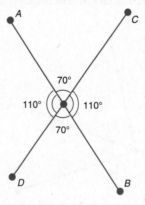

In the figure above, note that each pair of angles is marked with a different number of arcs. This shows that two angles are congruent to each other and that two other angles are congruent to each other. However, an angle in the first set is not congruent to an angle in the second set.

PERPENDICULAR LINES   Two lines are perpendicular if they intersect to form right angles (90°) as shown in the following drawing. The symbol for perpendicular is ⊥, so $\overline{AB} \perp \overline{CD}$ means "segment *AB* is perpendicular to segment *CD*." Note that planes can also be perpendicular.

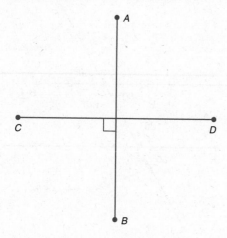

PARALLEL LINES   Two lines are parallel if they never cross (or intersect). Planes can also be parallel. The symbol for parallel is ‖, so $\overline{AB} \parallel \overline{CD}$ means segment *AB* is parallel to segment *CD* in the following drawing.

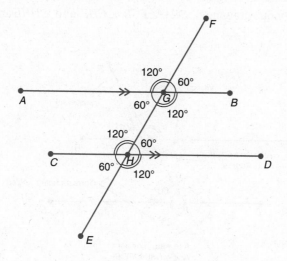

TRANSVERSAL A transversal is a line that intersects or crosses two or more parallel lines. $\overline{EF}$ is a transversal in the above drawing.

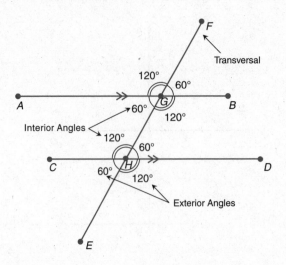

INTERIOR ANGLES Interior angles are formed inside (or between) two parallel lines crossed by a transversal. In the drawing above, $\angle AGH$, $\angle BGH$, $\angle CHG$, and $\angle DHG$ are interior angles.

EXTERIOR ANGLES Exterior angles are formed outside two parallel lines crossed by a transversal. In the previous drawing, $\angle FGA$, $\angle FGB$, $\angle CHE$, and $\angle DHE$ are exterior angles.

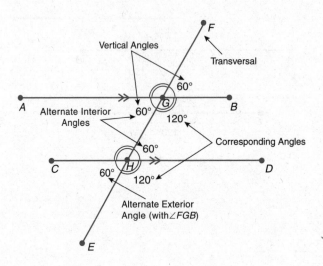

CORRESPONDING ANGLES When two parallel lines are crossed by a transversal as shown in the above diagram, two sets of vertical angle pairs are created. One set of four angles occurs at each point of intersection (one for the top line and one for the bottom line). When an angle in the top set and an angle in the bottom set occupy the same position (upper right, lower left, and so on) in the set, they are called corresponding angles. Corresponding angles are congruent. $\angle BGH$ and $\angle DHE$ are both in the lower right position in their respective sets of angles, so they are corresponding angles.

ALTERNATE ANGLES Congruent angles on opposite sides of the transversal are alternate angles.

ALTERNATE INTERIOR ANGLES Alternate angles inside the parallel lines are alternate interior angles. $\angle AGH$ and $\angle DHG$ are alternate interior angles.

ALTERNATE EXTERIOR ANGLES Alternate angles outside the parallel lines are alternate exterior angles. $\angle CHE$ and $\angle FGB$ are alternate exterior angles.

PRACTICE

1. Which of the following correctly names the angles?

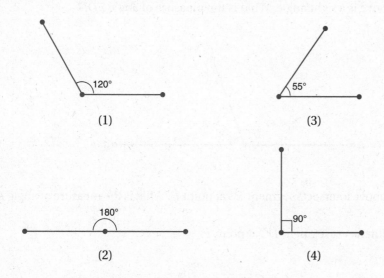

(1)

(3)

(2)

(4)

(A) 1—obtuse; 2—straight; 3—acute; 4—right
(B) 1—acute; 2—obtuse; 3—right; 4—straight
(C) 1—right; 2—acute; 3—straight; 4—obtuse
(D) 1—straight; 2—right; 3—obtuse; 4—acute

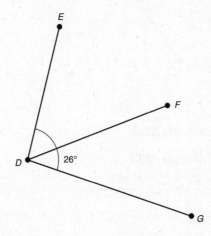

2. The measure of angle *EDG* above is 88°. What is the measure of angle *EDF*?

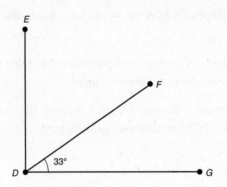

3. Angle *EDG* above is a right angle. What is the measure of angle *EDF*?

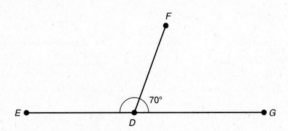

4. Segment *FD* above intersects segment *EG* at point *D*. What is the measure of angle *EDF*?

5. Segment *AB* intersects segment *DC* at point *E*.

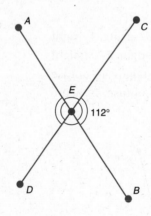

a. What is the measure of angle *AEC*?

b. What is the measure of angle *AED*?

6. Which term best describes these lines?

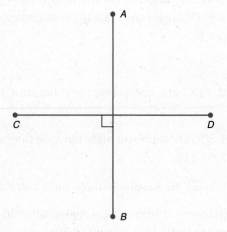

(A) Parallel
(B) Collinear
(C) Vertical
(D) Perpendicular

7. Which term best describes lines *AB* and *CD*?

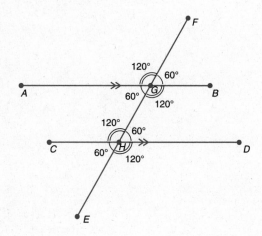

(A) Vertical
(B) Transversal
(C) Parallel
(D) Perpendicular

Answers and Explanations

1. **(A)** Straight angles have 180 degrees. Obtuse angles have less than 180 degrees but more than 90 degrees. Right angles have exactly 90 degrees. Acute angles have less than 90 degrees.

2. **62°** 88° − 26° = 62°.

3. **57°** Angles *EDF* and *FDG* are complementary because they add to 90 degrees: 90° − 33° = 57°.

4. **110°** Angles *EDF* and *FDG* are supplementary because they add to 180 degrees (form a straight line): 180° − 70° = 110°.

5. **a. 68°** Angles *AEC* and *CEB* are supplementary (form a straight line): 180° − 112° = 68°.

   b. 112° Two lines that intersect form vertical angles, which are opposite and congruent. Angle *AED* is congruent to angle *CEB*, so angle *AED* is equal to 112 degrees.

6. **(D)** Two lines that intersect at right angles are perpendicular. The small square angle marker indicates a 90-degree or right angle. The rule of vertical angles means that all four angles measure 90 degrees.

7. **(C)** Two lines that form corresponding sets of vertical angles are parallel and will never cross. The lines have equal slopes. The line crossing both parallel lines is called a transversal.

TWO-DIMENSIONAL FIGURE   A two-dimensional figure is a "flat shape" (occurring in a plane) made up of line segments.

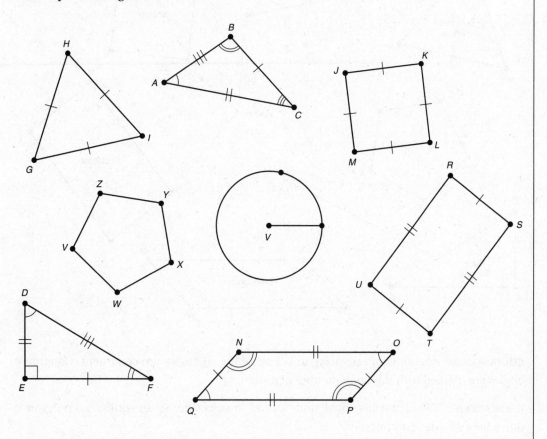

POLYGONS

POLYGON   A two-dimensional figure formed when three or more line segments are joined at their endpoints (or *vertices*) is a polygon. The segments are called *sides*, and the number of sides in a polygon is equal to the number of angles in the polygon.

- "Poly" means "many," and "gon" means angle. So polygons have many (three or more) angles.
- Common polygons include triangles, rectangles, squares, and other shapes with corners. Circles are not polygons because circles have no corners.
- Some polygons have pairs of sides that are parallel.
- Some polygons have pairs of sides that are perpendicular.
- Some polygons have two or more sides that are congruent.

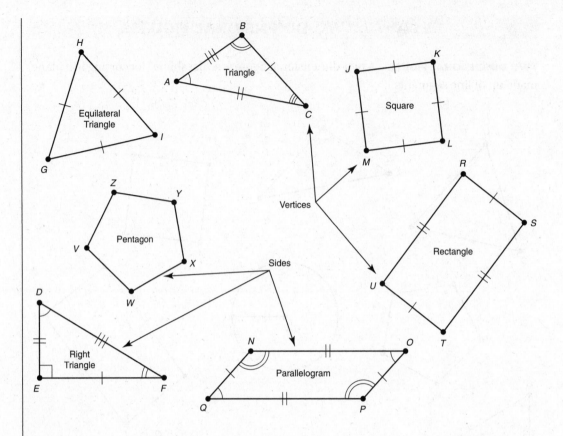

EQUIANGULAR An equiangular polygon is one where all angles are congruent. Congruent angles are marked with the same number of arcs.

EQUILATERAL "Equi" means equal, and "lateral" means side. So an equilateral polygon is one where all sides are congruent.

- Congruent sides are often marked with one or more lines, similar to the way that angles are marked with arcs. Sides having the same number of marks are congruent.
- A shape can be equilateral without being equiangular.

OPPOSITE (SIDE OR ANGLE) The segments that form angles in a polygon sometimes intersect with the endpoints of another side of the polygon. When this happens, the angle and intersecting side are said to be opposite one another.

- There is a consistent relationship between the measures of angles in a polygon and the sides that are formed by those angles (the sides opposite the angles). This relationship allows you to compare the relative sizes of sides and angles in a polygon.
- If two angles are congruent, the sides opposite them must also be congruent. This works in reverse as well.
- The largest angle in a polygon must be opposite the longest side.
- The smallest angle must be opposite the shortest side.

REGULAR POLYGON A regular polygon is both equilateral and equiangular. Squares are the most common regular polygons.

For any regular polygon, the total measure of all interior angles is $180(n - 2)$, where n is the number of sides. Since regular polygons are equiangular, you can divide this total by the number of sides to get the measure of a single angle.

PERIMETER The sum of all the sides of the polygon, or the distance around the outside of the polygon is the perimeter.

AREA OF A POLYGON The area of a polygon is the amount of space inside the polygon. Area is usually measured in square units, as when a floor is measured in square feet. The different types of polygons have different formulas for calculating area. However, all of these formulas involve operations with a *base* and an *altitude* (or height).

BASE (POLYGON) A side serving as the bottom edge of a polygon and used to calculate area is the base of a polygon. Polygons can be rotated. So any side can serve as a base, not just the one that appears to be the bottom in a picture.

ALTITUDE (POLYGON) An altitude is a line extending from the top of the polygon to the base and that is perpendicular to the base.

- In shapes with perpendicular sides (rectangles, squares, right triangles), both the base and the altitude are sides of the polygon.
- In shapes lacking any perpendicular sides (non-right triangles, parallelograms) only the base will be a side. The altitude must always be perpendicular to the base.

QUADRILATERALS

QUADRILATERAL A quadrilateral is any four-sided polygon, including *parallelograms*, *rectangles*, and *squares*. There are several types of quadrilaterals, and their interior angles always add to 360°.

SQUARE A square is a quadrilateral with four congruent sides. The intersecting sides are perpendicular, and the opposite sides are parallel. The length of a side of a square is represented by *s*.

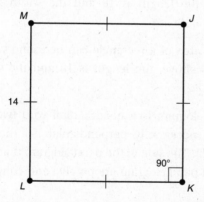

PERIMETER (SQUARE) Perimeter is the sum of all sides of a polygon. In a square, all sides are congruent: $P = s + s + s + s$. As a shortcut, you can also multiply *s* times 4: $P = 4s$. The side of square *LMJK* above is 14, so the perimeter measures $14 \times 4 = 56$.

AREA (SQUARE) In a square, all four sides are congruent. Even though the process of calculating the area of a square involves multiplying a base times an altitude, the formula for area of a square is usually given as side squared. $A = s^2$.

- The side of square *LMJK* above is 14, so the area is $14 \times 14 = 196$.
- Area is represented in *square units*, like square feet (ft^2) and square meters (m^2). This is because each of the two dimensions being multiplied has a number and a unit:

$$14 \text{ cm} \times 14 \text{ cm} = (14 \times 14) (\text{cm} \times \text{cm}) = 14^2 + \text{cm}^2 = 196 \text{ cm}^2$$

RECTANGLE A rectangle is a quadrilateral with two pairs of congruent sides. Intersecting sides are perpendicular. Opposite sides are parallel and congruent.

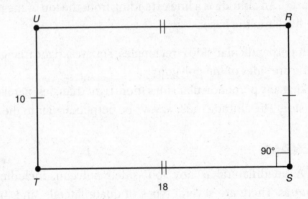

PERIMETER (RECTANGLE) In a rectangle, the base (*b*) is sometimes called the length (*l*) and the height (*h*) is sometimes called the width (*w*). Perimeter is the sum of all sides of a polygon. In a rectangle, there are two pairs of congruent sides (two lengths and two widths): $P = l + w + l + w$. As a shortcut, you can also add *l* times 2 plus *w* times 2: or *P = 2l + 2w*. In rectangle *TURS* above, the length is 18 and the width is 10. So the perimeter is $(2 \times 18) + (2 \times 10) = 36 + 20 = 56$.

AREA (RECTANGLE) The area of a rectangle can be found with the formulas $A = lw$ or $A = bh$. In rectangle *TURS* above, the length is 18 and the width is 10. So the area is $18 \times 10 = 180$.

PARALLELOGRAM A parallelogram is a quadrilateral with two pairs of congruent sides. Intersecting sides are not necessarily perpendicular, so the height (*h*) is an altitude perpendicular to the base (*b*). The side of the parallelogram that is not the base is called the side (*s*). Opposite sides of a parallelogram are parallel and congruent, and opposite angles are also congruent.

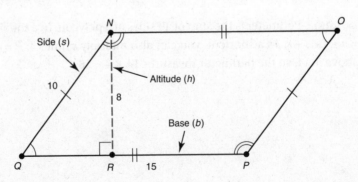

PERIMETER (PARALLELOGRAM) Perimeter is the sum of all sides of a polygon. In a parallelogram, calculating perimeter works the same as in a rectangle, but uses different symbols: $P = 2s + 2b$. The perimeter of parallelogram *QNOP* above is $(2 \times 15) + (2 \times 10) = 30 + 20 = 50$.

AREA (PARALLELOGRAM) In a parallelogram, the altitude (height) is not necessarily a side because intersecting sides are not necessarily perpendicular. Once you have located or determined the height, the formula is the same as that for a rectangle: $A = lw$ or $A = bh$. The area of parallelogram *QNOP* above is $15 \times 8 = 120$.

PRACTICE

1. Quadrilateral *LMJK* is a square.

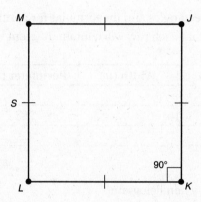

Use the properties of squares and the formulas for perimeter and area to complete the table below. Note that each row will contain different values.

	Side (*s*)	Perimeter (*P*)	Area (*A*)
a.	5		
b.		32	
c.			100

2. Quadrilateral *TURS* is a rectangle.

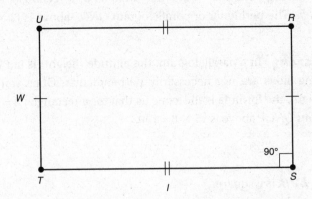

Use the properties of rectangles and the formulas for perimeter and area to complete the table below. Note that each row will contain different values.

	Length (l)	Width (w)	Perimeter (P)	Area (A)
a.	5	3		
b.	6		28	
c.		4		28

3. Quadrilateral *QNOP* is a parallelogram.

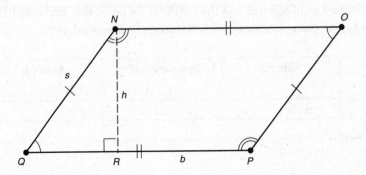

Use the properties of parallelograms and the formulas for perimeter and area to complete the table below. Note that each row will contain different values.

	Base (b)	Height (h)	Side (s)	Perimeter (P)	Area (A)
a.	14	6	8		
b.	12	4		36	
c.	9			26	27

Answers and Explanations

1.

	Side (s)	Perimeter (P)	Area (A)
a.	5	**20**	**25**
b.	**8**	32	**64**
c.	**10**	**40**	100

a. Perimeter = $4s$: $4 \times 5 = 20$. Area = s^2: $5 \times 5 = 25$.

b. Divide the perimeter by 4 to get the length of 1 side: $32 \div 4 = 8$. Area = s^2: $8 \times 8 = 64$.

c. Take the square root of the area to get the length of the side: $\sqrt{100} = 10$. Perimeter = $4s$: $4 \times 10 = 40$.

2.

	Length (l)	Width (w)	Perimeter (P)	Area (A)
a.	5	3	**16**	**15**
b.	6	**8**	28	**48**
c.	**7**	4	**22**	28

a. Perimeter = $2l + 2w$: $2(5) + 2(3) = 10 + 6 = 16$. Area = lw: $5 \times 3 = 15$.

b. Use the perimeter formula in reverse: $28 = 2(6) + 2w = 12 + 2w$; $2w = 28 - 12 = 16$; $w = 8$. Area = lw: $6 \times 8 = 48$.

c. Use the area formula in reverse: $28 = l(4)$; $28 \div 4 = 7$. Perimeter = $2l + 2w$: $2(7) + 2(4) = 14 + 8 = 22$.

3.

	Base (b)	Height (h)	Side (s)	Perimeter (P)	Area (A)
a.	14	6	8	**44**	**84**
b.	12	4	**6**	36	**48**
c.	9	**3**	**4**	26	27

a. Perimeter = $2b + 2s$: $2(14) + 2(8) = 28 + 16 = 44$. Area = bh: $14 \times 6 = 84$.

b. Use the perimeter formula in reverse: $36 = 2(12) + 2(s) = 24 + 2s$; $2s = 36 - 24 = 12$. $s = 6$. Area = bh: $12 \times 4 = 48$.

c. Use the area formula in reverse: $27 = 9h$; $27 \div 9 = h$. $h = 3$. Use the perimeter formula in reverse: $26 = 2(9) + 2(s) = 18 + 2s$; $2s = 26 - 18 = 8$. $s = 4$.

TRIANGLES

TRIANGLE   A triangle is a three-sided polygon. Its interior angles must add to 180°. The longest side is always opposite the largest angle. The shortest side is always opposite the smallest angle. Triangles are named using the three vertices, similar to the way angles are named. The figure below is called triangle *ABC* or △*ABC*.

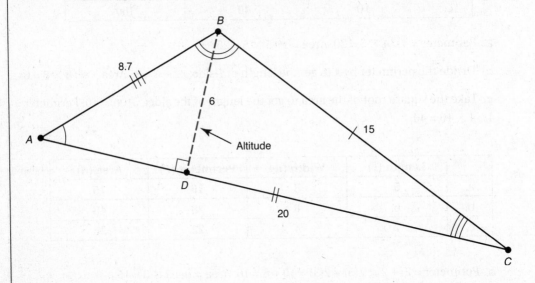

AREA (TRIANGLE)   The formula for the area of a triangle is $A = \frac{1}{2}bh$, where the height (*h*) is an altitude (perpendicular to the base). In all types of triangles except right triangles, the altitude will not be a side of the triangle. The area of triangle *ABC* above is $\frac{1}{2} \cdot 6 \cdot 20 = 60$.

SCALENE TRIANGLE   A scalene triangle has no congruent sides or congruent angles. Each angle measure and each side length is different. Triangle *ABC* above is a scalene triangle.

ISOSCELES TRIANGLE   An isosceles triangle has two congruent sides and two congruent angles. Triangle *BCA* below is an isosceles triangle. Note that the height of an isosceles triangle is not a side. The area of triangle *BCA* below is $\frac{1}{2} \cdot 10 \cdot 12 = 60$.

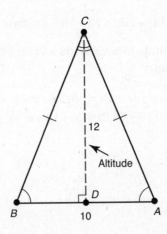

EQUILATERAL TRIANGLE An equilateral triangle has three congruent sides and three congruent angles. Each angle in an equilateral triangle measures 60°. Triangle *DEF* below is an equilateral triangle. Note that the height of an equilateral triangle is not a side.

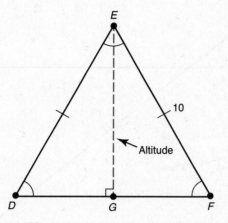

ACUTE TRIANGLE An acute triangle has three angles each measuring less than 90° (three acute angles). Triangle *PQR* below is acute.

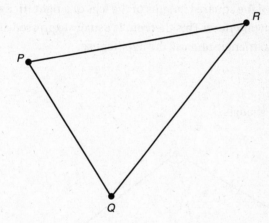

OBTUSE TRIANGLE An obtuse triangle has one angle measuring less than 180°. In an obtuse triangle, like *STU* below, the other two angles must be acute.

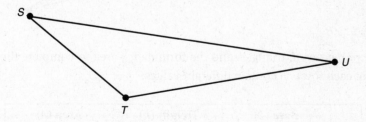

RIGHT TRIANGLE A right triangle has one right angle (90°). In a right triangle, the side opposite the right angle is called the *hypotenuse.* The other two sides are called the *legs,* and the two angles opposite the legs are complementary (must add to 90°). Triangle *DEF* below is a right triangle.

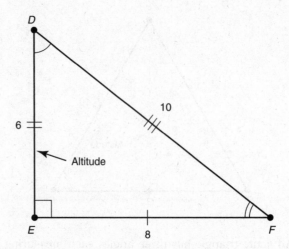

PYTHAGOREAN THEOREM The Pythagorean theorem applies only to right triangles. This rule says that the sum of the squared lengths of the legs of a right triangle will be equal to the squared length of the hypotenuse. This theorem is usually expressed as $a^2 + b^2 = c^2$, where a and b are the legs of the triangle and c is the hypotenuse.

PRACTICE

1. Polygon *ABC* is a triangle.

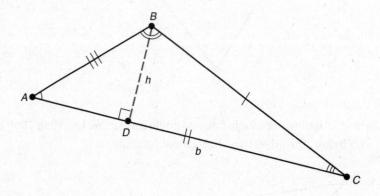

Use the properties of triangles and the formula for area to complete the table below. Note that each row will contain different values:

	Base (*b*)	Height (*h*)	Area (*A*)
a.	15	6	
b.	20		70
c.		6	42

2. This triangle is a right triangle.

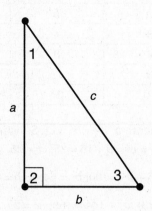

Use the properties of right triangles and the Pythagorean theorem to complete the table below. Note that each row will contain different values.

	a	*b*	*c*
a.	3	4	
b.	6		10
c.		12	13
d.	10		26

Answers and Explanations

1.

	Base (*b*)	**Height (*h*)**	**Area (*A*)**
a.	15	6	**45**
b.	20	**7**	70
c.	**14**	6	42

a. The formula for the area of a triangle is $A = \frac{1}{2}bh$: $A = \frac{1}{2}(15 \times 6) = \frac{1}{2}(90) = 45$.

b. $A = \frac{1}{2}bh$; $70 = \frac{1}{2}(20 \times h)$; $140 = 20 \times h$; $h = 7$.

c. $A = \frac{1}{2}bh$; $42 = \frac{1}{2}(b \times 14)$; $84 = b \times 14$; $b = 6$.

2.

	a	b	c
a.	3	4	**5**
b.	6	**8**	10
c.	**5**	12	13
d.	10	**24**	26

a. Use the Pythagorean theorem: $a^2 + b^2 = c^2$. Substitute the two given sides and solve for the third: $(3)(3) + (4)(4) = c^2 = 9 + 16 = 25$; $c^2 = 25$, so $c = 5$.

b. $(6)(6) + b^2 = (10)(10)$; $36 + b^2 = 100$; $b^2 = 64$, so $b = 8$.

c. $(a)(a) + (12)(12) = (13)(13)$; $a^2 + 144 = 169$; $a^2 = 25$, so $a = 5$.

d. $(10)(10) + (b)(b) = (26)(26)$; $100 + b^2 = 676$; $b^2 = 576$, so $b = 24$.

CIRCLES

CIRCLE A circle is a line through a set of points that are all at an equal distance (or equidistant) from a common point called the center. Circles measure 360°. A circle does not have corners, so it is not considered a polygon. It doesn't have a base or a height. It has dimensions with different names.

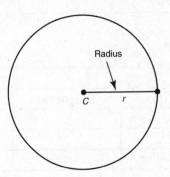

RADIUS The radius is the distance from the center to any point on the circle. The plural of "radius" is "radii" (ray-dee-eye). All radii in the same circle are equal.

DIAMETER A diameter is a line segment passing through the center of the circle whose endpoints are both on the circle. The diameter is equal to twice the radius.

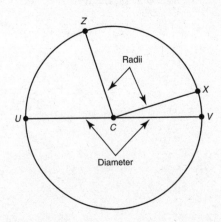

PI (π)   The ratio of a circle's perimeter (called *circumference*) to its diameter is the same in every circle. The value is called pi (π). Its value is equal to 22/7, or approximately 3.14. Pi is a continuing decimal that never establishes a pattern no matter how many decimal places are calculated. In most cases, you will treat pi as a variable, like *x* or *y*. If you need to use π to get a numerical answer, you can probably estimate it to be a little more than 3.

CIRCUMFERENCE (CIRCLE)   The perimeter of a circle is called its circumference. It represents the distance around the outside of the circle. Since the diameter is twice the radius, you can use either one to find circumference: $C = \pi d$ or $C = 2\pi r$. The circumference of circle *C* below is $\pi(2)(8) = 16\pi$.

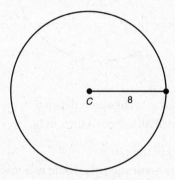

AREA (CIRCLE)   The amount of space inside a circle is the area. The formula for the area of a circle is $A = \pi r^2$. The area of circle *C* above is $\pi(8)(8) = 64\pi$.

CHORD   A chord is any line segment passing through the circle whose endpoints are both on the circle. A diameter is a specific type of chord. In the figure below, $\overline{ST}$ is a chord.

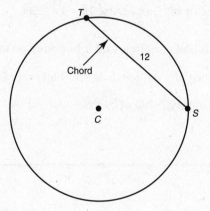

ARC A portion of the circumference defined by two points on the circle is an arc. In the following diagram, the portion containing points *L*, *M*, and *N* is an arc.

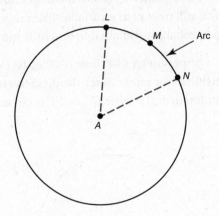

SECTOR A sector is a portion of a circle's area defined by two radii and the arc connecting the endpoints. It can be described as a slice of the circle.

- A sector cuts out a fraction of the circle.
- A sector representing a one-sixth slice of a circle will measure 60° (one-sixth of 360°).
- A sector cutting a one-sixth slice of a circle will contain one-sixth of the area. If circle *A* has a radius of 8, the area of the whole circle is 64π. If angle *A* is a one-sixth slice (60°), then the area of the sector is $10\frac{2}{3}\pi$ because $64 \div 6 = 10.6666\ldots = 10\frac{2}{3}$.

- The arc defining the curved edge of the sector will measure one-sixth of the circumference. If circle *A* has a radius of 8, its circumference is 16π. If angle *A* is a one-sixth slice (60°), then the area of the sector is $2\frac{2}{3}\pi$ because $16 \div 6 = 2.666\ldots = 2\frac{2}{3}$.

SEMICIRCLE A semicircle is half of a circle and is bounded on one side by the diameter. The formula for the circumference of a semicircle is one-half that of a circle: $C = \frac{1}{2}\pi d$ or $C\pi r$. The formula for the area is one-half that of a circle: $A = \frac{1}{2}\pi r^2$.

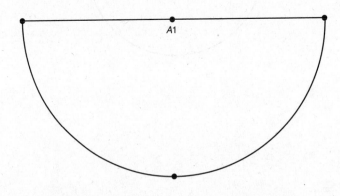

A1

PRACTICE

1. Figure *C* is a circle.

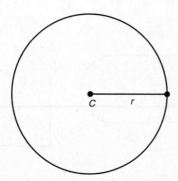

Use the properties of circles and the formulas for circumference and area to complete the table below. Note that each row will contain different values.

	Radius (*r*)	Diameter (*d*)	Circumference (*C*)	Area (*A*)
a.	5			
b.			4π	
c.				36π

Answers and Explanations

1.

	Radius (*r*)	Diameter (*d*)	Circumference (*C*)	Area (*A*)
a.	5	10	10π	25π
b.	2	4	4π	4π
c.	6	12	12π	36π

a. $d = 2r$. Circumference = $2\pi r = \pi d$. Area = πr^2. Diameter: $2 \times 5 = 10$. Circumference: $10 \times \pi = 10\pi$. Area: $(5)(5)\pi = 25\pi$.

b. Use the formula for circumference in reverse and divide by π to get *d*. $4\pi = \pi d$; $d = 4$, so $r = 2$. Area: $(2)(2)\pi = 4\pi$.

c. Use the area formula in reverse, divide by π, and then take the square root of 36. $36\pi = \pi r^2$; $36 = r^2$; $r = 6$, so $d = 12$ and $C = 12\pi$.

COMPOSITE SHAPES

- Composite shapes are nontraditional shapes created by combining traditional shapes.
- Questions will often ask you to find the area or perimeter of composite shapes.
- Break the shapes into traditional shapes using imaginary lines. Then calculate the values for the traditional shapes. Combine your results at the end.

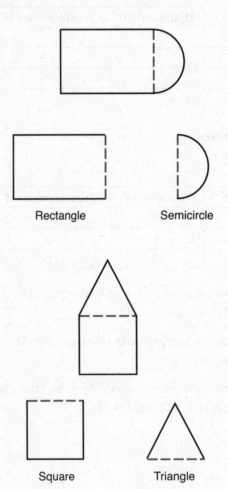

Rectangle   Semicircle

Square   Triangle

When calculating the perimeter of a composite shape be careful not to include any imaginary lines. The dotted lines in the examples above must not be included in perimeter calculations.

THREE-DIMENSIONAL FIGURES   Three-dimensional figures are shapes formed by the intersection of two-dimensional shapes—like squares, rectangles, circles, and triangles—in different planes.

- The two-dimensional shapes are called *faces*, and the lines that make up the two-dimensional faces are called the *edges*.
- The two important dimensions for solids are *surface area* and *volume*.

FACE   The sides of a three-dimensional figure are called the faces. The bottom face is sometimes called the *base*.

EDGE   The line where two faces of a three-dimensional figure touch is the edge.

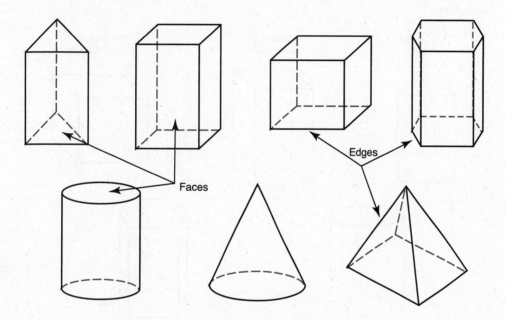

VOLUME   Volume is the total amount of space inside the figure. Volume in three-dimensional figures is similar in concept to area in two-dimensional shapes because it measures the space inside of a shape.

- Volume is often represented in *cubic units* like cubic feet (ft ^{3}) or cubic yards (yd ^{3}). This is because three dimensions are being multiplied, so the units are cubed.
- Volume can also be measured in liters or cups.
- Questions that ask about filling things with liquid (water and so on) are volume questions.

SURFACE AREA   Surface area is the sum of the areas of all faces of the figure. Surface area in three-dimensional figures is similar in concept to perimeter in two-dimensional shapes because it measures the outside of the shape.

PRISMS

PRISM A prism is a solid figure with two opposite, congruent, and parallel faces (triangles, squares, pentagons, and so on). The top face is directly above the bottom face so that a line connecting their centers is perpendicular to both bases. Lines connect the corresponding vertices in the two bases.

- The volume of any prism on the Math subject test is computed using the area of the base (bottom face) multiplied by the height of the prism.
- The surface area of any prism is the sum of the areas of all faces of the prism. First calculate the sum of the areas of the two bases. Then calculate the sum of the areas of the other faces. Finally, add those two sums together.
- One useful shortcut is to use the perimeter of the base (p) times the height of the prism to get the total area of the nonbase faces. Then add this value to 2 times the area of a base (B).

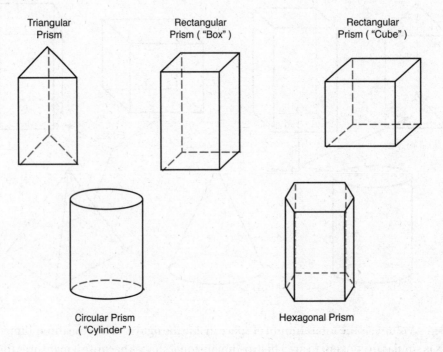

Triangular
Prism

Rectangular
Prism ("Box")

Rectangular
Prism ("Cube")

Circular Prism
("Cylinder")

Hexagonal Prism

RECTANGULAR PRISM (BOX) A rectangular prism is made up of six rectangles and is commonly described as a box. Adjacent faces are perpendicular. The three dimensions of a rectangular prism are called length, width, and height.

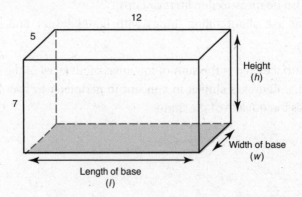

12

5

7

Height
(*h*)

Width of base
(*w*)

Length of base
(*l*)

VOLUME (OF A BOX)   The volume of a box or a rectangular prism equals length times width times height: $V = lwh$. Note that this is the area of the base (bottom face) times the height. The volume of the box above is $12 \times 5 \times 7 = 420$.

SURFACE AREA (OF A BOX)   The formula for the surface area of a box or rectangular prism is $SA = ph + 2B$, where p is the perimeter of a base and B is the area of that base. Calculating the surface area of a box requires three steps. First calculate the area of a base (B) using $A = lw$. Then calculate the perimeter of a base (p). Finally, use the surface area formula. In the box above, $p = (2 \times 5) + (2 \times 12) = 10 + 24 = 34$, $h = 7$, and $B = 12 \times 5 = 60$. The surface area of the box above is $(34 \times 7) + (2 \times 60) = 238 + 120 = 358$.

CUBE   A cube is a rectangular prism made up of six squares (six congruent, square faces).

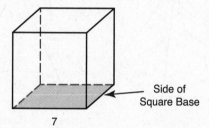

Side of
Square Base

7

VOLUME (OF A CUBE)   Since all faces and edges of a cube are congruent, the length, width, and height are all equal. So volume is often expressed as side cubed: $V = s^3$. The volume of the cube above is $7 \times 7 \times 7 = 343$.

SURFACE AREA (OF A CUBE)   Since all six faces of a cube are congruent squares, the surface area is six times the area of one face: $SA = 6s^2$. The surface area of the cube above is $6 \times 7 \times 7 = 294$.

CYLINDER   A cylinder is a prism with circular bases. It is commonly referred to as a tube.

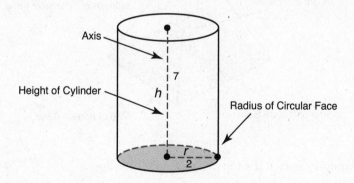

Axis

Height of Cylinder

h

7

Radius of Circular Face

$\frac{r}{2}$

AXIS (OF A CYLINDER)   The axis is a line connecting the bases of a cylinder. On the Math subject test, the axis is always perpendicular to the bases.

VOLUME (OF A CYLINDER)   The volume is equal to the area of the circular base times the height of the cylinder: $V = \pi r^2 h$. The volume of the cylinder above is $\pi(2)(2)(7) = 28\pi$.

SURFACE AREA (OF A CYLINDER)   The surface area is the sum of three areas: the top base, the bottom base, and the curved surface around the outside of the tube: $SA = 2\pi r^2 + 2\pi rh$:

- The formula for surface area of a cylinder is similar to that for a rectangular prism. The length represents the circumference of the circular base. The width represents the height of the cylinder.
- The area of each circle is πr^2, the circumference is $2\pi r$, and the height is h.
- The surface area of the cylinder above is $2\pi(2)(2) + 2\pi(2)(7) = 8\pi + 28\pi = 36\pi$.

PYRAMIDS AND CONES

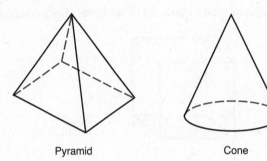

Pyramid   Cone

PYRAMID   On the Math test, the word pyramid refers to a square pyramid. A square pyramid is a solid with a square base and triangular faces that all meet at a common point at the top called the *apex*.

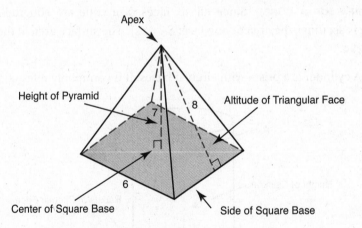

Apex

Height of Pyramid   7   8   Altitude of Triangular Face

6

Center of Square Base   Side of Square Base

APEX   The common vertex at the top of a pyramid is the apex.

VOLUME (OF A PYRAMID)   The formula for the volume of a pyramid is $V = \frac{1}{3}Bh$. This formula uses the area of one base (B). Since the base is a square, B is equal to the square of one side of the base. The volume of the pyramid above is $\frac{1}{3}(6)(6)(7) = 84$.

SURFACE AREA (OF A PYRAMID)   The surface area of a pyramid consists of the area of the square base plus the areas of the four triangular faces. The formula for the surface area of a pyramid is $\frac{1}{2}ps + B$, where p is the perimeter of a base, B is the area of that base, and s is the slant length or altitude of a triangular face.

- Calculating the surface area of a pyramid requires three steps. First calculate the area of the base (B) using $A = s^2$. Then calculate the perimeter of the base (p). Finally, use the surface area formula.
- In the pyramid above, $p = 4 \times 6 = 24$, $s = 8$, and $B = 6 \times 6 = 36$. The surface area of the pyramid is $\frac{1}{2}(24)(8) + 36 = 96 + 36 = 132$.

CONES

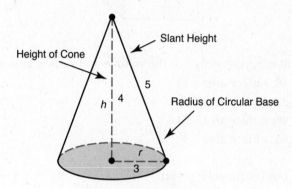

CONE   A cone is similar to a pyramid except that a cone has a circular base.

VOLUME (OF A CONE)   The formula for the volume of a cone is $V = \frac{1}{3}\pi r^2 h$. The volume of the cone above is $\frac{1}{3}\pi(3)(3)(4) = 12\pi$.

SURFACE AREA (OF A CONE)   The surface area of a cone consists of the area of the circular base plus the area of the rest of the cone. The formula for the surface area of a cone is $\pi rs + \pi r^2$, where s is the slant length. The surface area of the cone above is $\pi(3)(5) + \pi(3)(3) = 15\pi + 9\pi = 24\pi$.

SPHERES

SPHERE   A sphere is the three-dimensional version of a circle. It represents all points in space that are an equal distance from the center. The primary dimension in a sphere is the radius.

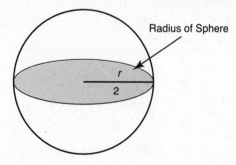

VOLUME (OF A SPHERE)   The formula for the volume of a sphere is $V = \frac{4}{3}\pi r^3$. The volume of the sphere above is $\frac{4}{3}\pi(2)(2)(2) = \frac{32}{3}\pi = 10\frac{2}{3}\pi$.

SURFACE AREA (OF A SPHERE)   The formula for the surface area of a sphere is $SA = 4\pi r^2$. The surface area of the sphere above is $4\pi(2)(2) = 16\pi$.

PRACTICE

1. This figure is a cube.

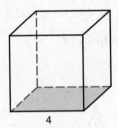

Which of the following correctly lists the volume and surface area of the cube?

(A) Volume = 48; surface area = 12

(B) Volume = 32; surface area = 16 .

(C) Volume = 96; surface area = 64

(D) Volume = 64; surface area = 96

2. This figure is a box (rectangular prism).

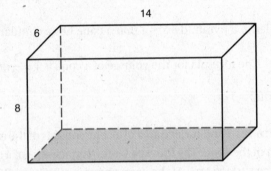

Which of the following correctly lists the volume and surface area of the box?

(A) Volume = 224; surface area = 244

(B) Volume = 672; surface area = 488 .

(C) Volume = 336; surface area = 224

(D) Volume = 488; surface area= 672

3. This figure is a cylinder.

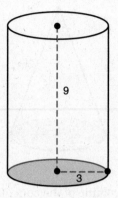

Which of the following is the volume of the cylinder? ($V = \pi r^3 h$)
(A) 81
(B) 243
(C) 81π
(D) 243π

4. This figure is a pyramid.

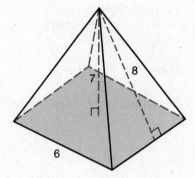

Which of the following is the volume of the pyramid? ($V = \frac{1}{3}Bh$)
(A) 84
(B) 96
(C) 132
(D) 252

5. This figure is a cone.

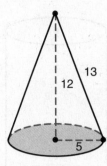

Which of the following is the volume of the cone? ($V = \frac{1}{3}\pi r^3 h$)
(A) 100π
(B) 300
(C) 325
(D) 325π

6. This figure is a sphere.

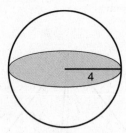

Which of the following is the volume of the sphere to the nearest tenth? ($V = \frac{4}{3}\pi r^3$)
(A) 21.3π
(B) 81.0π
(C) 85.3π
(D) 256.0π

Answers and Explanations

1. **(D)** Use the formula for the volume of a cube: $V = s^3$; $V = 4^3 = 64$. Use the formula for the surface area of a cube: $SA = 6s^2$; $SA = 6 \times 4^2 = 6 \times 16 = 96$.

2. **(B)** Use the formula for the volume of a box: $V = lwh$; $V = 8 \times 6 \times 14 = 672$. Use the formula for the surface area of a box: $SA = ph + 2B$; $SA = (40)(8) + (2)(84) = 320 + 168 = 488$.

3. **(C)** Use the formula for the volume of a cylinder: $V = \pi r^2 h$; $V = \pi \times 3^2 \times 9 = \pi \times 9 \times 9 = 81\pi$.

4. **(A)** Use the formula for the volume of a pyramid:
$$V = \frac{1}{3}Bh; \quad V = \frac{1}{3} \times 6^2 \times 7 = \frac{1}{3} \times 36 \times 7 = 84.$$

5. **(A)** Use the formula for the volume of a cone: $V = \frac{1}{3}\pi r^2 h$; $V = \frac{1}{3} \times \pi \times 5^2 \times 12 = 4 \times \pi \times 25 = 100\pi$.

6. **(C)** Use the formula for the volume of a sphere: $V = \frac{4}{3}\pi r^3$; $V = \frac{4}{3} \times \pi \times 4^3 = \frac{4}{3} \times \pi \times 64 = \frac{256}{3}\pi \approx 85.3\pi$.

Data Analysis

8

The topics in this section discuss how to display, organize, and analyze information. In fact, the word data simply means information. Data presentation deals with ways that information can be represented visually. Statistics (measures of center, probability, and counting methods) deal with different ways of deriving new information from numbers.

DATA Data are quantitative (numbers) or qualitative (words) information.

DATA PRESENTATION Information presented using text, graphics, or both is data presentation.

LESSON 1: INTERPRETING DATA PRESENTATIONS

Information is often presented in textual form (as words). The skills and methods for interpreting text is covered extensively in the RLA unit of this book. In addition to text, formulas and graphics are also used to present information. Numerous examples of formulas can be found throughout Lessons 2 and 3 in this unit. Graphic forms of data presentation include graphs, charts, tables, and diagrams.

GRAPHS

The Math test will use two types of graphs:

- Line graphs
- Scatter plots

A graph shows how a relationship between two things (variables) changes as the values of those things change, like change over time. For example, a graph might be used to plot the changes in temperature over the months of a year.

THE *x*- AND *y*-AXES

A graph is the intersection of two number lines. Each line is called an *axis* (the plural is "axes," pronounced "ak-seez"). One axis is horizontal (moving side to side) and is called the *x*-axis. The other line is vertical (moving up and down) and is called the *y*-axis.

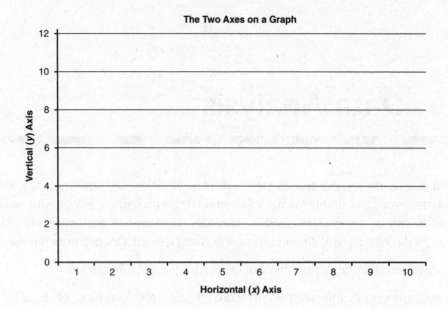

The Two Axes on a Graph

Each axis is numbered at regular intervals (every 2 units, every 5 units, every 10 units, and so on). The numbers are aligned with lines or *tick marks*. These numbers show you the *scale* represented by each axis. For example, in the previous picture, the scale of the *x*-axis goes from 0 to 10 in 1-unit increments, and the scale of the *y*-axis goes from 0 to 12 in 2-unit increments.

POINTS AND COORDINATES

Information on a graph is presented with points, which are markers showing where a location on the *x*-axis intersects with a location on the *y*-axis. In the example below, the point is placed (or *plotted*) at the intersection of 6 on the *x*-axis and 6 on the *y*-axis. These numbers are called *coordinates*. They are usually written in an *ordered pair* in the form (*x,y*). The point shown below is located at (6,6).

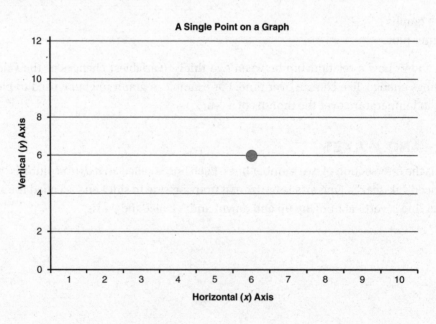

A Single Point on a Graph

Graphs usually contain multiple points, with each point representing a pair of values:

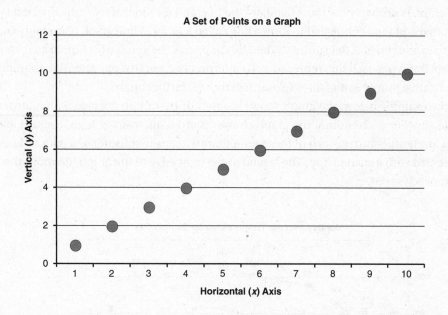

Sometimes these points appear along a clearly defined line, like the ones shown above. So this is called a line graph. In other cases, when the data points appear to be scattered around the graph, the graph is called a scatter plot.

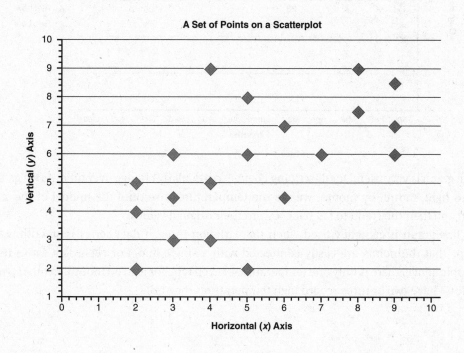

LINE GRAPH

A line graph is probably the most familiar kind of graph for most of us. Individual data points are plotted and then connected to form a line called a *series*. A line graph commonly contains more than one series of data points. When this happens, the graph will contain a *key* or *legend* that explains what each line represents. To interpret line graphs, pay attention to trends and to the relative movement of lines (closer together vs. farther apart).

In the example below, the graph shows the month-by-month average temperatures for a sample city. For each month, the graph shows record high, average high, average low, and record low temperatures. Each of these temperature types is considered a data series, and is represented with a shaded line. The legend at the right edge of the graph identifies the shade used for each series.

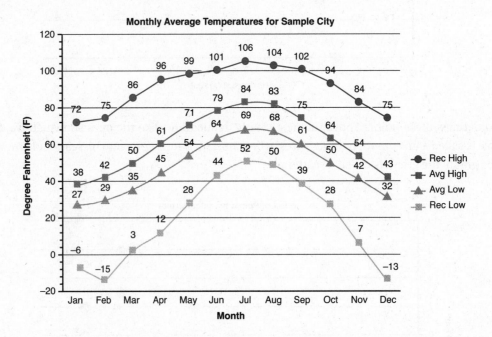

A line graph is very useful for describing change, particularly change over time. As we go from left to right, month by month, we see the temperatures rise until the middle of the *x*-axis (July) and then they tend to fall back toward their original values.

A line graph is generally used when the variation in each data series is smooth, which means that the points are easily connected with a single line. For each data series in the example above, there is only one temperature of each type for a given month. In other words, we don't have two or three record high temperatures for April.

PRACTICE

QUESTIONS 1 THROUGH 3 REFER TO THE GRAPH ON THE PREVIOUS PAGE:

1. Which month had the highest:

    a. Average high

    b. Record high

    c. Average low

    d. Record low

2. Which month had the lowest:

    a. Average high

    b. Record high

    c. Average low

    d. Record low

3. Over the whole year, which temperature series:

    a. changed the least

    b. changed the most

Answers and Explanations

1. **a. July** Make sure you look at the correct data series. Look for the highest point in that series.

    b. July

    c. July

    d. July

2. **a. January** Look for the lowest point in the correct data series.

    b. January

    c. January

    d. February

3. **a. Record high** Subtract the lowest temperature from the highest temperature in each data series to find their ranges.

    b. Record low

SCATTER PLOT

A *scatter plot* is similar to a line graph in that it uses plotted points to represent data points. However, a scatter plot is used where the variation in data is not as smooth as in a line graph. The plot gets its name because the points in the series appear to be scattered around the plot area of the graph.

In the example below, the scatter plot presents the relationship between two variables associated with the eruptions of a geyser (a body of underground water that periodically forces water and steam out of a hole in ground). The wait time in minutes before an eruption occurs is compared with the duration of the eruption in seconds.

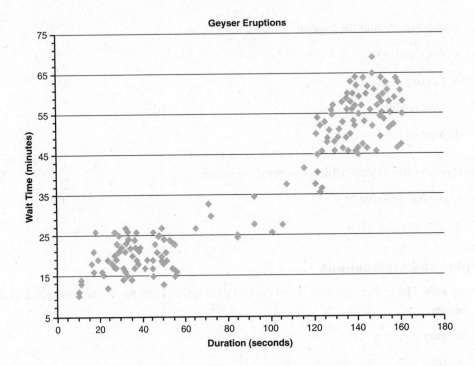

As we can see from the example, the data describing these eruptions is less smooth and orderly than the temperature data in the previous line graph. In some places here, more than one duration is plotted for a given wait time (see 26 minutes). In other places, more than one wait time is plotted for a given duration (see 24 seconds).

Scatter plots are used when the data are distributed in large concentrations of points close together called *clusters*. Those points that are plotted away from the clusters are called *outliers*.

For example, in this example there is a cluster of eruptions that have short wait times (26 minutes or less) and short durations (60 seconds or less). There is another cluster of eruptions that have long wait times (45 minutes or more) and long durations (120 seconds or more). It is not common to have a short wait time with long duration or a long wait time with a short duration. So these few points are considered the outliers.

PRACTICE

QUESTIONS 1 THROUGH 3 REFER TO THE SCATTER PLOT ON THE PREVIOUS PAGE:

1. Which is the most likely duration of an eruption with a wait time between 30 and 35 minutes?
   (A) Between 5 and 15 seconds
   (B) Between 20 and 45 seconds
   (C) Between 50 and 60 seconds
   (D) Between 65 and 80 seconds

2. Is an eruption with a wait time between 30 and 35 minutes an outlier or in a cluster?

3. Which of the following inequalities defines both of the clusters in terms of duration (d):
   (A) $60 < d < 120$
   (B) $d > 160$
   (C) $0 < d < 60; 120 < d < 160$
   (D) $0 > d > 60; 120 > d > 160$

Answers and Explanations

1. **(D)** Wait time is graphed on the y-axis. The points that fall between 30 and 35 minutes on the y-axis are all greater than 65 seconds on the x-axis (duration).

2. **Outlier** That range on the y-axis has relatively few points. The clusters are located elsewhere on the scatter plot.

3. **(C)** Clusters are groupings of data points. Most points occur between 0 and 60 seconds duration and between 120 and 160 seconds duration.

CHARTS

The Math test will use two types of charts:

- Bar charts
- Pie charts (also called circle graphs)

Charts are used to represent relationships between quantities or amounts. In some cases, these amounts are portions of some large total or whole.

Bar Charts

Bar charts are similar to graphs in that they present data using an x-axis and a y-axis. Where they differ is in the way that each data point is presented. On a bar chart, each data point is shown as a shaded bar that extends from one axis to each data point's other coordinate. Bar charts may have either vertical bars that extend from the x-axis or horizontal bars that extend from the y-axis. In the example below, the bars extend from the x-axis to the y-coordinate for each data point.

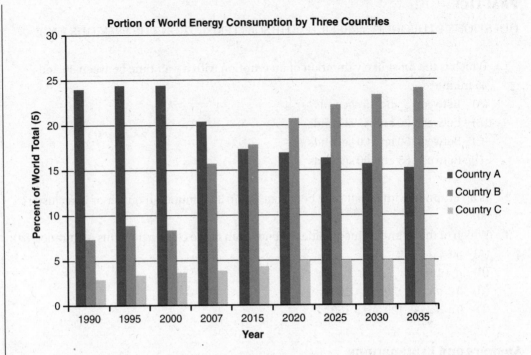

Portion of World Energy Consumption by Three Countries

Bar charts will often have more than one data series (bar) for each coordinate. In the example shown above, each year has a bar for each of the three countries being presented. The use of bars makes it easy to compare relative amounts between bars.

For example, in 1990, energy consumption by Country *A* was much larger than (more than three times) that of Country *B*. In the same year, energy consumption by Country *B* was larger than (more than double) that of Country *C*.

It is, of course, still possible to see change over time in a bar chart. In this example, we see Country *A*'s energy consumption decreasing from 2000 onward but Country *B*'s energy consumption increasing over the same period. Country *C*'s energy consumption increases very gradually during that time period.

PRACTICE

QUESTIONS 1 THROUGH 3 REFER TO THE BAR CHART ABOVE.

Assume global consumption is constant year to year:

1. Which country had the lowest average energy consumption over the period presented on the chart?

2. By approximately what percent did the energy consumption by Country *B* increase from 2000 to 2007?

3. By approximately what percent did the energy consumption by Country *A* decrease over the period presented on the chart?

Answers and Explanations

1. **Country C** The shortest bar in the entire chart is for Country *C* in 1990.

2. **100%** Energy consumption for Country *B* went from 8 in 2000 to 16 in 2007, which is a change of 8. The difference of 8 is 100% of the original value of 8.

3. **33%** Energy consumption for Country *A* went from about 24 in 1990 to about 16 in 2035, which is a change of 8. The difference of 8 is $\frac{1}{3}$ or 33% of the original value of 24.

Pie Charts

Also known as circle graphs, pie charts do not use the *x*- and *y*-axes found in other data presentations. Instead, they represent a total quantity (whole) as a shaded circle. This circle is often divided into portions that represent a part or subset of the total.

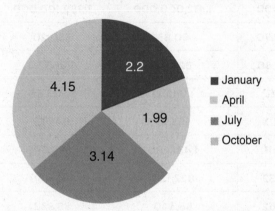

Average Monthly Precipitation (in mm) for Four Months in 2010: Northeast Region U.S.

Pie charts let you easily see the relative composition of a total. The larger sections of the circle represent categories that take up larger portions of the total or whole. In the example above, average monthly precipitation (in millimeters) was measured in January, April, July, and October 2010.

By examining the pie chart, we can see that the second half of the year (July and October) received more precipitation than the first half. We can see that October received the greatest amount of precipitation of the four months measured.

PRACTICE

QUESTIONS 1 THROUGH 3 REFER TO THE PIE CHART ABOVE:

1. What is the average monthly precipitation for all four months shown on the chart?

2. Which months received more than the average precipitation of all four months?

3. Which months got less than the average of all four months?

Answers and Explanations

1. **2.87 mm** Add up all four amounts: 4.15 + 2.2 + 1.99 + 3.14 = 11.48. Then divide by 4: 11.48 ÷ 4 = 2.87.

2. **July, October** These months each received more than the average of 2.87 mm of precipitation.

3. **January, April** These months each received less than the average of 2.87 mm of precipitation.

TABLES

A table is a matrix or grid that organizes information into rows and columns:

Properties of Selected Solar System Objects

Object	Radius (km)	Volume (×10⁹ km³)	Mass (×10²¹ kg)	Density (g/cm³)
Sun	696,000	1,412,000,000	1,989,100,000	1.41
Mercury	2,439.70	60.83	330.20	5.43
Venus	6,051.80	928.43	4,868.50	5.24
Earth	6,371	1,083.21	5,973.60	5.52
Mars	3,390	163.18	641.85	3.94
Jupiter	69,911	1,431,280	1,898,600	1.33
Saturn	58,232	827,130	568,460	0.70
Uranus	25,362	68,340	86,832	1.30
Neptune	24,622	62,540	102,430	1.76
Pluto	1,161	7	13.11	2

Tables make it easy to view and compare information when the data set is simple, when the range of data (from largest to smallest value) is very wide, or when data points contain large numbers of significant digits (large numbers or numbers with many decimal places).

The "Properties of Selected Solar System Objects" table above shows us the vast differences in size, volume, and mass among larger solar system objects (the Sun) and smaller ones (Earth and Mars). Some of the objects with smaller size and volume, like Venus and Earth, still have higher density than objects with larger size and volume, like Jupiter and Saturn.

PRACTICE

QUESTIONS 1 THROUGH 6 REFER TO THE PROPERTIES OF SOLAR SYSTEM
OBJECTS TABLE ON THE PREVIOUS PAGE:

1. Which planet takes up the most space?

2. Which object takes up the least space?

3. Which is the densest planet?

4. Which is the least dense object?

5. Which object has the greatest mass?

6. Which object has the least mass?

Answers and Explanations

1. **Jupiter** Taking up space is defined by volume. The Sun is not a planet. So look for the planet with the largest volume.

2. **Pluto** Taking up space is defined by volume. Look for the object with the smallest volume.

3. **Earth**

4. **Saturn**

5. **Sun**

6. **Pluto**

DIAGRAMS

Diagrams are graphic illustrations of data that are usually nonnumerical. Diagrams are used to present processes and other kinds of information that cannot be easily graphed or charted. The example below shows pedigree information for a genetically inherited trait.

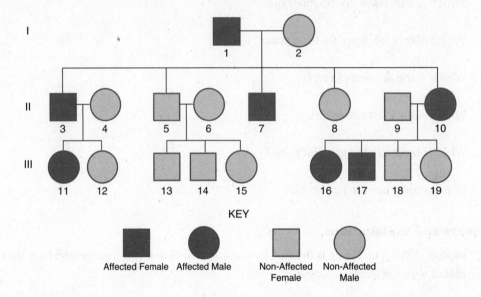

Diagrams are used to represent the most complex kinds of information. However, they are usually easily understood since they are essentially pictures with labels. In this example, shading and shapes that are easy to recognize are used to represent inheritance and gender. We can see the trait being passed from parent to child, from both males and females.

Diagrams are often used to present food webs, chains, and pyramids as well as chemical, biological, or mechanical processes.

PRACTICE

QUESTIONS 1 AND 2 REFER TO THE PEDIGREE CHART ABOVE:

1. How many affected females in all generations are presented on the diagram?

2. How many affected males descended from the affected female parent?

Answers and Explanations

1. **4** Affected females are shown as dark squares.

2. **3** Affected males are shown as dark circles.

UNDERSTANDING DATA REPRESENTATIONS

For questions drawing on any of type of graphics, you need to follow a process before starting to work on the questions. Following the three steps in the process will ensure that you are well prepared to answer any kind of question about graphics that you may find.

1. Examine
2. Analyze
3. Explain

Examine

The first step in the process is to look at and read everything you see: titles, axis labels, axis numbers or words, keys or legends, notes, and so on. Read EVERYTHING. Many wrong answers come from missing an important piece of information in a graphic.

Analyze

The second step is to think about and organize the information you just examined.

- What do the two axes represent?
- What are the numerical scales for each axis? What units do the axes use?
- What does the data series (line or lines, plotted points, bars) represent?
- As it moves from left to right, what is happening to the data series?
- Is the data series increasing, decreasing, or doing both in different places?
- If more than one data series is present, how are they related to each other?
- Are lines getting closer together or farther apart?
- Are bars getting taller or shorter?
- Are there any outliers (dots on the edges away from the other dots) in the scatter plot?

Explain

The third step is the most important one in the process. Before moving to the questions, take time to summarize the results of your analysis in your own words. For example, you may think to yourself, "This line graph shows the average temperature and hours of daylight in New York City for each month in the year. The levels all start out low in January, then they steadily increase to a maximum in early August, and then they steadily decrease to a low in December."

This explanation to yourself is important because the questions that follow will often focus on the elements you have in your explanation. After all, your explanation is like the main idea of the graph or chart. On the exam, the Science test will include short-answer questions that require you to write brief answers. Very often, these questions will ask you to provide a summary of a graph or chart. Your explanation makes you ready to do that.

Statistics is sometimes referred to as "number crunching" because it involves performing calculations on numerical data in order to derive meaning from the data.

MEASURES OF CENTER

SET   A set is a group of numbers sometimes called members, terms, or elements.

MEAN   The mean is the average of a set of numbers. It is calculated by adding the elements and dividing by the number of elements.

MEDIAN   The median is the middle of the set of numbers. As many numbers in the set are larger than the median as are smaller than the median.

- In a set with an odd number of elements, the median is the middle element when the set is arranged in ascending order (smallest to largest).
- In a set with an even number of elements, the median is the average of the middle two elements when the set is arranged in ascending order.

MODE   The mode is the most frequently occurring element in the set.

RANGE   The range is the difference between the smallest element and largest element in the set. It is sometimes called the spread of the data.

WEIGHTED AVERAGE   A weighted average is an average where different elements in the set have different amounts of importance (or weight) in the calculation.

An example of a weighted average would be calculating a student's final grade:

- Suppose the student has a homework average grade of 85, an average of 95 on tests, and a participation grade of 60. A simple average of those three scores would be 80.
- Now suppose homework counts for 25%, tests count for 65%, and participation counts for 10% in the overall grade. To calculate the weighted average, multiply each element by its weight (85×0.25, 95×0.65, 60×0.1) and add the products together.
- The weighted average is 89. The weighted average is higher than the simple average because the test scores make up more than half of the final grade and the participation scores represent a very small portion of the grade.

PRACTICE

QUESTIONS 1 AND 2 REFER TO SET A:

Set A: {7, 2, 5, 1, 4, 9, 8, 3, 6}

1. For set A, find the following measures of center:

   a. Mean

   b. Median

   c. Range

2. Add a number to set A above to make the mode 8. What is the new mean?

QUESTIONS 3 AND 4 REFER TO SET B:

Set B: {13, 14, 17, 18, 16, 15}

3. For set B, find the following measures of center:

   a. Mean

   b. Median

   c. Range

4. Add a number to set A to make the mode 14. What is the new median?

Answers and Explanations

1. **a. 5** A mean is an average. Add up all the elements of the set:

   $$7 + 2 + 5 + 1 + 4 + 9 + 8 + 3 + 6 = 45.$$

   Then divide by the number of elements: $45 \div 9 = 5$.

   b. 5 A median is the middle number in a set when the values are in order from smallest to largest. Since set A has an odd number of elements, the median is the middle element, 5.

   c. 8 Calculate the range by subtracting the smallest element from the largest: $9 - 1 = 8$.

2. **5.3** The new set includes an extra 8. The new sum of elements is 53. Since there are now 10 elements in the set, the new mean is $53 \div 10 = 5.3$.

3. **a. 15.5** A mean is an average. Add up all the elements of the set: $13 + 14 + 17 + 18 + 16 + 15 = 93$. Then divide by the number of elements: $93 \div 6 = 15.5$.

   b. 15.5 A mean is the middle number in a set when the values are in order from smallest to largest. Since set B has an even number of elements, the median is the mean of the middle two elements: $15 + 16 = 31$; $31 \div 2 = 15.5$.

   c. 5 Calculate the range by subtracting the smallest element from the largest: $18 - 13 = 5$.

4. **15** Adding an additional 14 gives the set an odd number of elements. So the middle element, which is the median, is 15.

Probability describes the likelihood that something will occur.

- Something that will definitely happen has a probability of 1.
- Something that will definitely not happen has a probability of 0.
- The probability of anything else is expressed as a value between 0 and 1. It can be expressed as a fraction ($\frac{3}{8}$), a decimal (0.375), or a percentage (37.5%).
- Assume you have some sort of test that you will repeat many times, like flipping a coin with heads and tails or rolling a six-sided die numbered 1 to 6. Each time you repeat the test, you will produce a result called an *outcome*.
- Now assume you want to predict the number of times something will happen (called an *event*), like the number of times you roll an even number (2, 4, 6).
- Outcomes in which the event occurs (rolling a 4) are called positive. Outcomes in which the event does not (rolling a 1) are called negative.
- Probability assumes that all possible results (rolling 1, 2, 3, 4, 5 or 6) are equally likely to occur. It compares the number of ways an event could occur (positive results) and the total number of all possible results (all results).

$$\text{Probability} = \frac{\text{Positive results}}{\text{All positive results}}$$

- There are 6 possible results when rolling the six-sided die, and 3 of those (2, 4, and 6) would be positive results. $P = \frac{3}{6} = \frac{1}{2} = 0.5 = 50\%$.

INDEPENDENT EVENTS   Events whose outcomes do not depend on one another are independent events. On the Math subject test, all events are independent. For example, if you roll a six-sided die twice, the first result will not affect the second. The results do not depend on each other.

COMPOUND EVENTS   Two or more independent events that happen together are compound events. The probability of a compound event is the product of the probabilities of each independent event. For example, rolling two six-sided dice is a compound event.

- To predict the probability of rolling a number greater than 3 (a 4, 5, or 6) with each die, first calculate the probability of getting that result with the first die: $\frac{3}{6} = \frac{1}{2}$.
- Then calculate the probability of getting that result with the second die: $\frac{3}{6} = \frac{1}{2}$.
- The probability of rolling a number greater than 3 on both dice is $\frac{1}{2} \times \frac{1}{2} = \frac{1}{4}$.

Many probability questions on the Math subject test are real-world situations related to selecting from groups of people or objects. Regardless of the context, your job is to:

- Count all possible results.
- Count the event or events that represent positive results.
- Create a fraction: $\text{Probability} = \frac{\text{Positive results}}{\text{All positive results}}$

Some questions may present information or answer choices in decimal or percent form. So you should be able to convert between these forms comfortably (fraction, decimal, and percent).

PRACTICE

1. If you select one shape from the box at random, what is the probability (expressed as a decimal) of selecting each of the following?

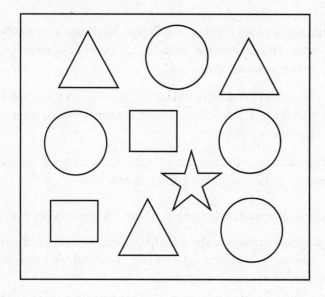

   a. A circle

   b. A star

   c. Not a triangle

   d. A star or a square

Answers

1. **a.** 0.4

   b. 0.1

   c. 0.7

   d. 0.3

COUNTING METHODS There are two different ways of counting the different possible arrangements of a set of elements.

- In some cases, the order of elements does not matter. So 123 and 321 would be considered the same.
- In other cases, order does matter, so 123 and 321 would be considered two distinct arrangements.

FACTORIAL The factorial is the number of different ways that a set of objects or elements can be placed in order. To calculate the factorial, the number of elements is multiplied by each successively smaller number, down to 1.

- The exclamation point (!) is used to symbolize factorial. So 5 factorial is written as 5!
- For example, "5!" = $5 \times 4 \times 3 \times 2 \times 1 = 120$. This means that a set of 5 things can be placed in 120 different orders.

PERMUTATION Permutation is the number of ways that a group of objects selected from a larger group of objects can be placed in a particular order.

- The formula for a permutation is $\dfrac{n!}{(n-k)!}$, where n is the number of elements or objects and k is the number of places or spots we have to fill with selected elements.
- For example, suppose you need to select a 1st-, 2nd-, and 3rd-place winner in a contest with 6 contestants (A, B, C, D, E, and F).
- There are 6 elements (contestants), so n is 6. There are 3 places to fill (1st, 2nd, and 3rd), so k is 3. Apply the formula: $6! = 720$, $n - k = 3$, and $3! = 6$. This becomes $720 \div 6 = 120$.

COMBINATION Combination is the number of different ways that a group of k elements can be formed from a larger group of n elements when order does not matter. The formula is $\dfrac{n!}{(n-k)!k!}$

- For example, suppose you need to choose 3 contest winners from a group of 8 contestants.
- Apply the formula: $8! = 8 \times 7 \times 6 \times 5 \times 4 \times 3 \times 2 \times 1 = 40{,}320$, $n - k = 5$, $5! = 120$, and $3! = 6$.
- This becomes $40{,}320 \div (120 \times 6)$, or $40{,}320 \div 720 = 56$.

Calculating a combination can be simplified using the *cancellation method*. Since many of the same terms appear in both the numerator and denominator, it is possible to cancel out many of the terms and compute the rest manually:

$$\frac{(8)(7)(6)(\cancel{5})(\cancel{4})(\cancel{3})(\cancel{2})(\cancel{1})}{(\cancel{5})(\cancel{4})(\cancel{3})(\cancel{2})(\cancel{1}) \bullet (3)(2)(1)} = \frac{(8)(7)(\cancel{6})}{(\cancel{3})(\cancel{2})(1)} = \frac{(8)(7)}{(1)} = 8(7) = 56$$

PRACTICE

QUESTIONS 1 AND 2 ARE BASED ON THE FOLLOWING INFORMATION:

Karleta, Mario, Kay, Shawn, Lee Ann, Logan, Michael, Anthony, Shaneka, and Chris are the participants in a race-walking competition. First place will receive a blue ribbon. Second place will receive a red ribbon. Third place will receive a white ribbon. Fourth place will receive a green ribbon. After the award ceremony and pie-eating contest, Chris will drive 3 of the others home.

1. How many different groups of prize winners are possible?

2. How many different groups of 3 passengers could Chris drive home? Remember to remove Chris from the total.

Answers and Explanations

1. **5,040** Since the order matters, use the permutation formula:

$$\frac{n!}{(n-k)!} \to = \frac{10 \cdot 9 \cdot 8 \cdot 7 \cdot 6 \cdot 5 \cdot 4 \cdot 3 \cdot 2}{6 \cdot 5 \cdot 4 \cdot 3 \cdot 2} = 9 \cdot 8 \cdot 7 = 5,040.$$

2. **84** Since the order of the passengers does not matter, use the combination forumla:

$$\frac{n!}{(n-k)!k!} \to = \frac{9 \cdot 8 \cdot 7 \cdot 6 \cdot 5 \cdot 4 \cdot 3 \cdot 2}{(6 \cdot 5 \cdot 4 \cdot 3 \cdot 2)(3 \cdot 2)} = \frac{9 \cdot 8 \cdot 7}{6} = \frac{504}{6} = 84.$$

Algebra

9

The topics in this section deal with the algebraic methods of mathematical reasoning. Algebra is a system of mathematical expressions that deals with unknown quantities.

LESSON 1: EXPRESSIONS

Algebra deals with unknown quantities. These are called variables, and are represented with letters such as x, y, z, q, r, and s.

VARIABLE An unknown value is a variable. It is represented by a letter such as x, y, or z.

COEFFICIENT A number placed next to a variable to indicate multiplication is a coefficient.

- For example, $2x$ has a coefficient of 2. This means that the unknown value (x) is being multiplied by 2.
- $5x$ represents 5 times x, $9x$ represents 9 times x, and so on.
- A coefficient of 1 is not usually shown: $1x = x$.

CONSTANT A value that does not change is a constant.

TERM A term is a value expressed with at least one variable, sometimes with a coefficient, and/or sometimes with an exponent. For example, $2x$ is a term and so is x^2.

- Terms can contain large combinations of variables, coefficients, and exponents.
- $2x^2y$ is one term. Each of the parts of the term (2, x^2, and y) are multiplied together so they are *factors* of the term.

BASIC OPERATIONS (IN ALGEBRA) All of the standard rules for basic operations apply to variables:

- **Adding:** $x + x = 2x$, $3x + 5x = 8x$
- **Subtracting:** $3x - 2x = x$, $2x - 3x = -x$
- **Multiplying:** $x \cdot y = xy$, $2y \cdot 4z = 8yz$, $x \cdot x = x^2$

- **Dividing (canceling):** $\dfrac{4x}{2x} = \dfrac{2}{1} = 2$; $\dfrac{9xy}{3xz} = \dfrac{3y}{z}$; $\dfrac{4x^3}{4x^2} = \dfrac{x}{1} = x$

OPERATORS Operators are symbols for arithmetic operations ($+$, $-$, $\cdot$, $/$, x^2, $\sqrt{\ }$). They are used to form expressions.

EXPRESSION   An expression is a group of terms connected by operators, like $2x + 5$.

- The expression above has two terms ($2x$ and 5), one of which has two factors (2 and x).
- Expressions like the one above are often called linear expressions.
- An expression can also be a single term (monomial) with one or more factors, like $3z$.
- Expressions use combinations of symbols to express a value, which is where they got their name.

MONOMIAL   An expression with only one term is a monomial, such as 5, x, $2y$, and z^3.

BINOMIAL   An expression with two terms, connected by addition or subtraction, is a binomial, such as $2x + 3$, $5x - 4$, and $x^2 + x$.

POLYNOMIAL   An expression with more than one term is a polynomial: $2x^2 - 3x + 4$.

- Polynomials include binomials and trinomials. Trinomials have 3 terms, as shown in the expression above.
- Trinomials are usually referred to as polynomials.
- Binomials are sometimes referred to as binomials and sometimes as polynomials.

RATIONAL EXPRESSION   An expression that represents a ratio between two polynomials is a rational expression. It is presented as a fraction made up of two polynomials: $\frac{x^2 + 4}{x + 2}$.

EVALUATING AND SIMPLIFYING EXPRESSIONS

EVALUATING AN EXPRESSION   An expression can be evaluated by substituting numbers for the variables in the expression.

- When $x = 2$, the linear expression $2x + 3$ evaluates to 7.

$$2x + 3 = 2(2) + 3 = 4 + 3 = 7$$

- When $x = 2$, the polynomial expression $2x^2 - 3x + 4$ evaluates to 6.

$$2x^2 - 3x + 4 = 2(2^2) - 3(2) + 4 = 2(4) - 6 + 4 = 8 - 6 + 4 = 2 + 4 = 6.$$

- When $x = 2$, the rational expression $\frac{x^2 + 5}{x + 2}$ evaluates to $\frac{9}{4}$.

$$\frac{x^2 + 5}{x + 2} = \frac{4 + 5}{2 + 2} = \frac{9}{4}$$

SIMPLIFYING   Expressions containing multiple terms that are similar (like terms) can be made simpler by combining the similar terms. For example, the expression

$$2x^2 + 3 - x + 3x^2 + 2x - 1$$

contains several sets of like terms:

- $2x^2$ and $3x^2$ are like terms. So they can be combined to make $5x^2$.
- $2x$ and $-x$ are like terms. So they can be combined to make x (subtracting the coefficients $2 - 1$).
- The numbers 3 and -1 are like terms. So they combine to make 2.
- The simplified expression becomes $5x^2 + x + 2$.

PRACTICE

1. Translate the phrases into algebraic expressions:

   a. 3 more than 5 times x

   b. 7 less than 3 times x

   c. 4 more than 3 times x times x

2. Evaluate these algebraic expressions when $x = 2$.

   a. $6x + 4$

   b. $2x - 9$

   c. $5x^2 + 7$

3. Combine and simplify the following expressions into one algebraic expression:

   $6x + 4$
   $x^2 + 4x - 1$
   $2x - 9$
   $5x^2 + 7$

4. After working 4 days a week, 3 hours each day, Jason earns $244 a week. Because the holidays are quickly approaching, Jason decides to work 6 hours a day throughout this week to earn extra money. For this work, he will work the same number of days and be paid the same hourly pay. If h is Jason's hourly rate, write the expression that represents the amount he will earn this week (w).

Answers and Explanations

1. a. **$5x + 3$**

   b. **$3x - 7$**

   c. **$3x^2 + 4$**

2. a. **14** $6x + 4 \rightarrow (6)(2) + 4 = 12 + 4 = 16$.

   b. **−5** $2x - 9 \rightarrow (2)(2) - 9 = 4 - 9 = -5$.

   c. **27** $5x^2 + 7 \rightarrow (5)(2)(2) + 7 = 20 + 7 = 27$.

3. **$6x^2 + 12x + 1$** Combine like terms: $x^2 + 5x^2 = 6x^2$; $6x + 4x + 2x = 12x$; $4 - 1 - 9 + 7 = 1$.

4. **$w = 24h$** Jason will work 6 hours each day for 4 days for a total of 24 hours: $6 \times 4 = 24$. Since his hourly rate is h, Jason will earn $24h$ this week. So $w = 24h$.

DISTRIBUTING AND FACTORING EXPRESSIONS

DISTRIBUTING When a monomial and a binomial are multiplied, the distributive property of multiplication can be applied. This is sometimes called *expanding* and results in the *distributed form* of the expression:

$$3(x + 2) = 3(x) + 3(2) = 3x + 6$$
$$3(2x - 3) = 3(2x) - 3(3) = 6x - 9$$
$$3x(x + 5) = 3x(x) + 3x(5) = 3x^2 + 15x.$$

FACTORING Polynomial expressions can be factored by using the distributive property in reverse. Look at the following example:

$$8x^2 + 4x + 12$$

The three terms in the above expression have a set of common factors, including 2 and 4. Since 4 is the largest factor that is shared by all terms, it is called the *greatest common factor (GCF)*. Factoring the expression means dividing each term by the GCF:

- The GCF is 4.

- $\dfrac{8x^2}{\cdot 4} = 2x^2$

- $\dfrac{4x}{4} = x$

- $12 \div 4 = 3$
- The *factored form* of the expression is $4(2x^2 + x + 3)$.

PRACTICE

1. Distribute the following expressions:

    a. $2(x + 6)$

    b. $3(2x - 2)$

    c. $x(x + 3)$

2. Factor the following expressions:

    a. $4x + 16$

    b. $3x - 27$

    c. $2x^2 + 6x + 8$

Answers and Explanations

1. **a. $2x + 12$** Multiply the term outside the parentheses by each term inside the parentheses: $(2)(x) + (2)(6) = 2x + 12$.

    b. $6x - 6$ $(3)(2x) + (3)(-2) = 6x - 6$.

    c. $x^2 + 3x$ $(x)(x) + (x)(3) = x^2 + 3x$.

2. a. 4(x + 4) Divide each term by the greatest common factor. Write the factor outside the parentheses. The GCF is 4.

    b. 3(x – 9) The GCF is 3.

    c. 2(x² + 3x + 4) The GCF is 2.

MULTIPLYING BINOMIALS

Multiplying one binomial by another requires distribution. Multiply each term in the first expression by each term in the second, term by term, using a process called FOIL. Look at the following examples:

$$(x + 3)(x + 4)$$

- FOIL stands for First, Outer, Inner, Last. It lists the order in which you should multiply the terms.
- First: This refers to the first term in each binomial: $x \cdot x = x^2$.
- Outer: This refers to the terms on the outside, or the first term in the first binomial and the second term in the second binomial: $x \cdot 4 = 4x$.
- Inner: This refers to the terms on the inside, or the second term in the first binomial and the first term in the second binomial: $3 \cdot x = 3x$.
- Last: This refers to the second term in each binomial: $3 \cdot 4 = 12$.
- Arrange the terms in descending order of exponent values (**degree of the term**):

$$x^2 + 4x + 3x + 12$$

Simplify:

$$x^2 + 7x + 12$$

The rules of signed numbers apply when using FOIL. For example:

$$(x + 5)(x - 4)$$

- First: $x \cdot x = x^2$
- Outer: $x \cdot -4 = -4x$
- Inner: $5 \cdot x = 5x$
- Last: $5 \cdot -4 = -20$

Arrange and simplify:

$$x^2 - 4x + 5x - 20 = x^2 + x - 20$$

FOIL works the same way with coefficients that are negative or are greater than 1. Remember that the rules for multiplying signed numbers apply. For example:

$$(2x + 2)(-3x - 11)$$

- First: $2x \cdot -3x = -6x^2$
- Outer: $2x \cdot -11 = -22x$
- Inner: $2 \cdot -3x = -6x$
- Last: $2 \cdot -11 = -22$

Arrange and simplify:

$$-6x^2 - 22x - 6x - 22 = -6x^2 - 28x - 22$$

This expression can be factored by dividing out the GCF:

$$2(-3x^2 - 14x - 11)$$

Binomials can be multiplied using FOIL even if they don't contain any constants, as in the examples below. Memorize the factored and distributed forms of all three binomials in this table.

Factored Form	FOIL	Distributed Form
$(x + y)(x + y)$	$(x)(x) + (x)(y) + (y)(x) + (y)(y) = x^2 + xy + xy + y^2$	$x^2 + 2xy + y^2$
$(x - y)(x - y)$	$(x)(x) + (x)(-y) + (-y)(x) + (-y)(-y) = x^2 - xy - xy + y^2$	$x^2 - 2xy + y^2$
$(x + y)(x - y)$	$(x)(x) + (x)(-y) + (y)(x) + (y)(-y) = x^2 - xy + xy - y^2$	$x^2 - y^2$

Remember that the rules for exponents can also be involved when multiplying by FOIL:

$$(x^2 + x)(x^3 - x^2)$$

- First: $x^2 \bullet x^3 = x^5$
- Outer: $x^2 \bullet -x^2 = -x^4$
- Inner: $x \bullet x^3 = x^4 \ (x = x^1)$
- Last: $x \bullet -x^2 = -x^3 \ (x = x^1)$

Arrange and simplify:

$$x^5 - x^4 + x^4 - x^3 = x^5 - x^3$$

This expression can also be factored using x^3 as the GCF. Keep the rules for exponents in mind when factoring:

$$x^5 - x^3 = (x^3)(x^2) - (x^3) = x^3(x^2 - 1)$$

PRACTICE

1. Use FOIL to multiply the following expressions:

   a. $(x + 3)(x + 5)$

   b. $(x - 2)(x - 6)$

   c. $(2x + 2)(x - 2)$

2. Factor the following expressions:

   a. $x^2 + 2xy + y^2$

   b. $x^2 - 2xy + y^2$

   c. $x^2 - 49$

Answers and Explanations

1. **a.** $x^2 + 8x + 15$ FOIL stands for First, Outer, Inner, Last. Multiply each term in the first binomial by each term in the second binomial in the order given in FOIL.

   b. $x^2 - 8x + 12$

   c. $2x^2 - 2x - 4$

2. **a.** $(x + y)(x + y)$

   b. $(x - y)(x - y)$

   c. $(x + 7)(x - 7)$

FACTORING POLYNOMIALS

FOIL can be used in reverse to factor a polynomial into the product of two binomials.

- Certain kinds of polynomials take the form $ax^2 + bx + c$.
- The symbols a and b are placeholders for coefficients; b is the coefficient of x.
- The symbol c represents a constant (a number).
- Even though they are letters when in the format $ax^2 + bx + c$, the values for a, b, and c will be numbers in a polynomial expressed using this format.

To factor a polynomial, look for pairs of numbers that are factors of c and add to b. Use the following example:

$$x^2 + 5x + 6$$

- Factor pairs of 6 (c) include (1, 6) and (2, 3). Negative factors are also possible.
- Since $1 + 6$ does not add to 5 (b), this pair is not valid.
- Since $2 + 3$ do add to 5, this pair of factors is valid. They each become a second term in one of the two binomials that will make up the factored form of the polynomial:

$$(x + 2)(x + 3)$$

- To verify that you have factored correctly, FOIL the expression you produced:

$$(x + 2)(x + 3) = x^2 + 3x + 2x + 6 = x^2 + 5x + 6$$

This process can be applied to polynomials with coefficients that are negative and/or greater than 1.

WORKING WITH RATIONAL EXPRESSIONS

A rational expression is an expression involving a ratio between two polynomials. It is presented in a form similar to a fraction, with one polynomial as the numerator and another as the denominator:

$$\frac{x^2 + 4}{x + 2}$$

Simplifying rational expressions or performing operations on rational expressions can involve factoring and distributing polynomials.

PRACTICE

1. Translate the following phrase into an expression, and then evaluate it using $x = 5$.

   "the sum of x and 5 divided by x minus 3"

   a. Expression

   b. Value

Answers and Explanations

1. a. $\dfrac{x+5}{x-3}$

   b. **5** Substitute 5 for each x. Evaluate the numerator first and then evaluate the denominator. Simplify:

   $$\frac{x+5}{x-3} = \frac{5+5}{5-3} = \frac{10}{2} = 5.$$

Simplifying

Rational expressions can often be simplified by canceling terms that appear in both the top and the bottom of the ratio. For example:

$$\frac{x^2-4}{x+2}$$

- By using one of the common factored forms, $(x + y)(x - y) = x^2 + y^2$, we can factor the expression above.
- $x^2 - 4 = (x + 2)(x - 2)$, so the expression becomes:

$$\frac{(x+2)(x-2)}{(x+2)}$$

- Since $(x + 2)$ is in both the top and the bottom of the ratio, it can be canceled out:

$$x - 2$$

In many cases, the simplified form will still be a rational expression:

$$\frac{x^2+x-12}{x^2-9} = \frac{(x+4)(x-3)}{(x+3)(x-3)} = \frac{x+4}{x+3}$$

Multiplying and Dividing

Factoring, canceling, and distributing can help simplify the process of multiplying and dividing rational expressions.

To multiply a rational expression, factor it first:

$$\frac{x+4}{y^2-16} \cdot \frac{y+4}{x^2+5x+4} = \frac{(x+4)}{(y+4)(y-4)} \cdot \frac{(y+4)}{(x+4)(x+1)} = \frac{1}{(y-4)(x-1)}$$

Division of rational expressions can be complicated. Remember to flip the bottom expression and multiply:

$$\frac{\frac{x^2-25}{x+7}}{\frac{x+5}{x^2-49}} = \frac{(x^2-25)}{(x+7)} \bullet \frac{(x^2-49)}{(x+5)} = \frac{(x+5)(x-5)}{(x+7)} \bullet \frac{(x+7)(x-7)}{(x+5)} = \frac{(x-5)}{1} \bullet \frac{(x-7)}{1} = x^2 - 12x + 35$$

Adding and Subtracting

Adding and subtracting rational expressions can be complicated. You must use the rules for operations with fractions, including common denominators.

- When adding or subtracting numerical fractions, we sometimes convert both fractions to a common denominator:

$$\frac{1}{2} + \frac{1}{3} = \frac{3}{6} + \frac{2}{6} = \frac{5}{6}$$

- This same rule applies to rational expressions where the denominators are polynomials. This means that factoring and distributing will often be required:

$$\frac{4x}{x+2} + \frac{x}{x+3}$$

- Get a common denominator by multiplying the top and bottom of each ratio by the denominator of the other:

$$\frac{4x}{(x+2)} \bullet \frac{(x+3)}{(x+3)} = \frac{4x(x+3)}{(x+2)(x+3)} = \frac{4x^2+12x}{x^2+5x+6}$$

$$\frac{x}{(x+3)} \bullet \frac{(x+2)}{(x+2)} = \frac{x(x+2)}{(x+3)(x+2)} = \frac{x^2+2x}{x^2+5x+6}$$

- Add the two numerators, and express the new fraction over the common denominator:

$$\frac{4x^2+12x}{x^2+5x+6} + \frac{x^2+2x}{x^2+5x+6} = \frac{5x^2+14x}{x^2+5x+6}$$

- Factor and simplify if needed:

$$\frac{5x^2+14x}{x^2+5x+6} = \frac{x(5x+14)}{x^2+5x+6}$$

- Depending on the result, you may find additional ways to factor and cancel.

EQUATION An equation is an algebraic expression set equal to a constant or it is an expression set equal to another expression. This is called equating the two sides of the equal sign, which is how equations get their name. The following are equations:

$$5x + 9 = 64$$
$$2x + 15 = 6x - 5$$
$$x^2 + 6x + 5 = 0$$

COMBINING SIMILAR TERMS

Similar terms in an equation can be combined. Start with the equation:

$$2x + 3 + 3x - 4 = 19$$

After combining similar terms, the equation becomes:

$$5x - 1 = 19$$

Similar terms can also be combined across the equal sign. Start with the equation:

$$7x - 2 = 3x + 6$$

- There are multiple sets of similar terms in the equation above: ($7x$, $3x$) and (-2, 6). However, the similar terms are on opposite sides of the equal sign.
- These terms can be combined by moving them across the equal sign using inverse operations.

INVERSE OPERATIONS

Inverse operations are used to move terms across the equal sign by doing the opposite of the operations represented by the terms:

- Keep equations in balance. Always perform inverse operations on both sides of the equation.
- Move positive terms by subtracting them, and move negative terms by adding them:

$$7x - 2 = 3x + 6$$
$$7x - 2 - 3x = 3x + 6 - 3x$$
$$4x - 2 = 6$$
$$4x - 2 + 2 = 6 + 2$$
$$4x = 8$$

Inverse operations can also be used to remove coefficients or denominators:

- Remove coefficients by dividing:

$$3x = 21$$

$$\frac{3x}{3} = \frac{21}{3}$$

$$x = 7$$

- Remove denominators by multiplying:

$$\frac{x}{2} = 4$$

$$\frac{2}{1} \bullet \frac{x}{2} = 4 \bullet 2$$

$$x = 8$$

SOLVING EQUATIONS

When evaluating an expression, you must either be given a value for the variable or you must choose one yourself. When an expression is set equal to something, forming an equation, you can evaluate the variable using inverse operations. This is called manipulating the equation to isolate the variable:

- First combine like terms on each side of the equals sign if necessary.
- Then use inverse operations so the variable terms are on one side of the equals sign and the numerical terms are on the other.
- Then remove coefficients and/or denominators so that the variable is the only term on its side of the equal sign.
- Maintain balance throughout the process by applying inverse operations to both sides of the equation:

$$7x - 2 = 3x + 6$$
$$7x - 2 - 3x = 3x + 6 - 3x$$
$$4x - 2 = 6$$
$$4x - 2 + 2 = 6 + 2$$
$$4x = 8$$
$$\frac{4x}{4} = \frac{8}{4}$$
$$x = 2$$

PRACTICE

1. Solve the following equations:

   a. $5x + 6 = 126$

   b. $-4x - 5 = -29$

   c. $3x + 7 + x - 4 - 2x + 1 = 8$

   d. $-2x + 9 = -3x$

   e. $7x - 4 = 5x + 8$

2. Write the result from cross multiplying the proportion $\frac{2}{3} = \frac{32}{y}$.

3. In the equation $y = 4x - 6$, what is the value of y when $x = 8$?

Answers and Explanations

1. **a.** $x = 24$ Subtract 6 from both sides: $5x = 120$. Divide both sides by 5: $x = 24$.

 b. $x = 6$ Add 5 to both sides. $-4x = -24$. Divide both sides by -4: $x = 6$.

 c. $x = 2$ Combine like terms: $2x + 4 = 8$. Subtract 4 from both sides: $2x = 4$. Divide both sides by 2: $x = 2$.

 d. $x = -9$ Add $3x$ to both sides: $x + 9 = 0$. Subtract 9 from both sides: $x = -9$.

 e. $x = 6$ Subtract $5x$ from both sides: $2x - 4 = 8$. Add 4 to both sides: $2x = 12$. Divide by 2: $x = 6$.

2. $2y = 96$

3. $y = 26$ Substitue 8 for x and solve:

$$y = (4)(8) - 6$$
$$= 32 - 6$$
$$= 26.$$

INEQUALITIES

All of the rules for manipulating equations apply to inequalities as well:

$$2x + 5 > 21$$
$$2x > 16$$
$$x > 8$$

The rules apply for all inequality operators: $>$, $<$, $\geq$, and $\leq$.

One special case that applies only to inequalities relates to negative coefficients and negative denominators. When multiplying or dividing to simplify these sorts of inequalities, you must reverse the inequality sign:

$$-3x < 21$$

$$\frac{-3x}{-3} > \frac{21}{-3}$$

$$x > -7$$

$$\frac{x}{-5} \leq 4$$

$$\frac{-5}{1} \cdot \frac{x}{-5} \geq 4 \cdot -5$$

$$x \geq -20$$

1. Solve the following inequalities:

    a. $5x > 125$

    b. $-6x \leq 54$

    c. $3x + 6 > 27$

Answers and Explanations

1. **a.** $x > 25$ Divide both sides by 5.

    b. $x \geq -9$ Divide both sides by -6. Remember to flip the sign.

    c. $x > 7$ Subtract 6 from both sides: $3x > 21$. Divide both sides by 3: $x > 7$.

MULTIPLE VARIABLES

Equations frequently involve more than one variable:

$$2x + y = 9$$
$$4x + 3y = 6x + y + 2$$

These equations can be evaluated if we're given (or we assume) a value for one of the two variables. Assume that $y = 6$ in the equations below:

$$2x + y = 16$$
$$2x + 6 = 16$$
$$2x = 10$$
$$x = 5$$

$$4x + 3y = 6x + y + 2$$
$$4x + 18 = 6x + 8$$
$$10 = 2x$$
$$x = 5$$

Simultaneous Equations

Multivariable equations are sometimes presented in pairs, called simultaneous equations or systems of equations:

$$4x + 3y = 38$$
$$4x - 3y = 2$$

The values for x and y are the same for each of the equations in the system. One method for solving a system like the one above is to add or subtract one of the equations from the other:

$$
\begin{array}{r}
4x + 3y = 38 \\
+4x - 3y = \ 2 \\
\hline
8x \quad\ \ = 40
\end{array}
$$

$$\frac{8x}{8} = \frac{40}{8}$$

$$x = 5$$

$$
\begin{array}{r}
3x + 3y = 33 \\
-\ x + 3y = 23 \\
\hline
2x \quad\ \ = 10
\end{array}
$$

$$\frac{2x}{2} = \frac{10}{2}$$

$$x = 5$$

PRACTICE

1. Solve the following using $y = 4$:

   a. $2x + 3y = 72$

   b. $4x - 2y = y + 8$

   c. $5x + 3y = -3x + 36$

2. Solve the following systems of equations for x:

   a. $3x + 7y = 32$ and $x - 7y = -8$

   b. $5x + 2y = 23$ and $3x + 2y = 17$

Answers

1. a. $x = 30$

   b. $x = 5$

   c. $x = 3$

2. a. $x = 6$

   b. $x = 3$

Quadratic Equations

A quadratic equation is a polynomial equation in the form $ax^2 + bx + c = 0$. The symbols a and b represent coefficients, and c represents a constant.

The polynomial side of a quadratic equation can be factored:

$$x^2 - 2x - 15 = 0$$
$$(x - 5)(x + 3) = 0$$

The factored form of the equation shows that the product of two terms is equal to 0. This means that one of the two terms must be equal to 0. (If $ab = 0$, then $a = 0$ or $b = 0$.)

- If $x - 5 = 0$, then $x = 5$.
- If $x + 3 = 0$, then $x = -3$.
- This means that there are two possible values of x: (5, –3).
- These two values are called the *roots* of the quadratic equation.

PRACTICE

1. Find the roots of the following:

    a. $x^2 + 14x + 48 = 0$

    b. $x^2 - x - 20 = 0$

    c. $x^2 - 5x + 6 = 0$

Answers and Explanations

1. **a.** **(–6,–8)** After factoring the polynomial, roots are values for x that make one of the two binomials equal to zero. The signs of the roots are the opposite of the signs in the binomials. $x^2 + 14x + 48 = (x + 6)(x + 8) = 0$.

    b. **(5,–4)** $x^2 - x - 20 = (x - 5)(x + 4) = 0$

    c. **(3,2)** $x^2 - 5x + 6 = (x - 3)(x - 2) = 0$.

A *function* is an expression that contains one variable: $3x - 2$. In *function notation* this would be expressed as $f(x) = 3x - 2$.

A given value for the variable x will produce one and only one value for the function $f(x)$:

x	Operation $(3x - 2)$	$f(x)$
0	$3(0) - 2 = -2$	-2
1	$3(1) - 2 = 1$	1
2	$3(2) - 2 = 4$	4
3	$3(3) - 2 = 7$	7
4	$3(4) - 2 = 10$	10
5	$3(5) - 2 = 13$	13

Since the value of the function depends on the value of the variable, the value of the function is called the *dependent variable*. The value of the variable is called the *independent variable*. These concepts play an important role in interpreting and graphing scientific data.

DOMAIN

DOMAIN The set of all allowed values for the variable in a function is the domain. Consider the function below:

$$f(x) = \frac{x + 2}{x}$$

One of the laws of mathematics says that a rational expression may not have zero as a denominator. As a result, the domain of values for the function above is all real numbers except 0: $x \neq 0$.

RANGE The set of possible values of the function, based on using all the values in the domain, is called the range.

Coordinate geometry deals with points and lines in the *coordinate plane*. This plane is sometimes called the **x, y** plane because it is defined by two perpendicular number lines called the *x*-axis and *y*-axis:

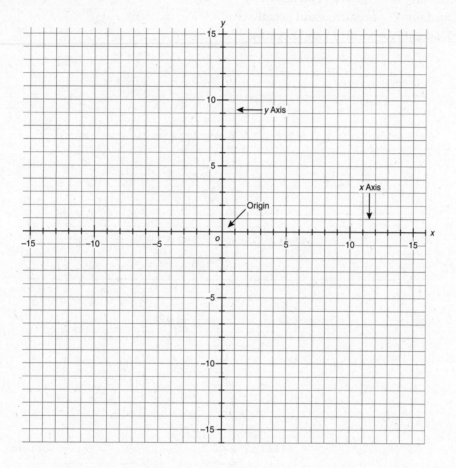

The two number lines (axes) intersect at their zero points, creating the *origin*.

POINTS AND QUADRANTS

As discussed in the section about geometry, a point represents a location in space. The coordinate plane provides a standard method of describing the locations of points using the *x*- and *y*-axes to provide *coordinates* (numerical addresses) for the points. The coordinates of the origin are (0, 0).

ORDERED PAIR   An ordered pair is a pair of numbers in the format (*x*, *y*) representing the coordinates, or location, of a point in the coordinate plane.

QUADRANT A quadrant is a one-quarter portion of the coordinate plane and contains all points with a specific combination of coordinate signs. Quadrants are numbered with roman numerals and go in counterclockwise order:

- Quadrant I – positive *x* and positive *y*
- Quadrant II – negative *x* and positive *y*
- Quadrant III – negative *x* and negative *y*
- Quadrant IV – positive *x* and negative *y*

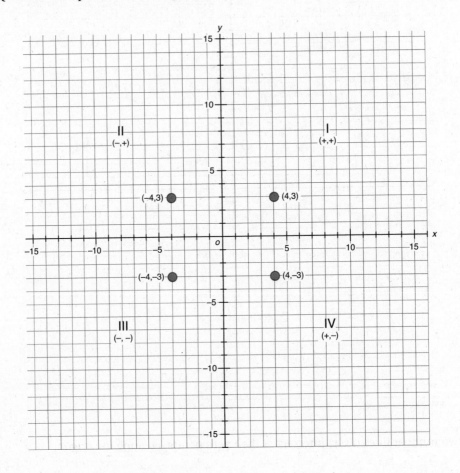

To plot a point using its coordinates:

- Start at the origin (0,0) and move along the *x*-axis according to the *x*-coordinate (right for positive, left for negative).
- From your location on the *x*-axis, move up or down according to the *y*-coordinate (up for positive, down for negative).

To determine the coordinates of a point on a graph:

- Start at the origin and move to the point's location.
- Move along the *x*-axis first, then up or down.
- Note the number of units you move horizontally and vertically.
- The horizontal movement is the *x*-coordinate.
- The vertical movement is the *y*-coordinate.

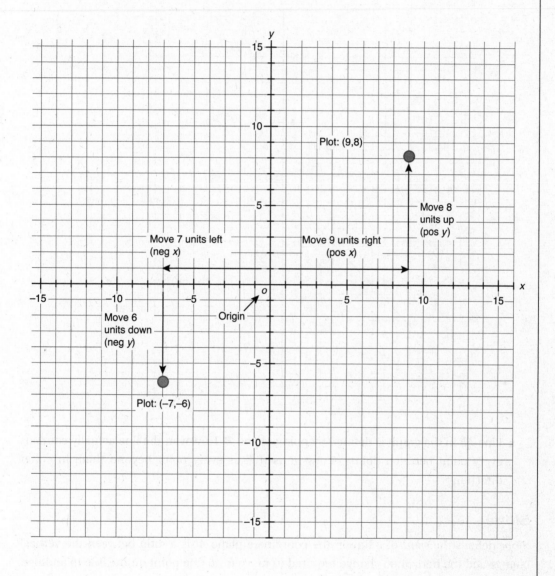

GRAPHING LINES

- Two points on the coordinate plane define a line.
- As discussed in the geometry section, a line extends beyond its endpoints in both directions to connect an infinite number of points.

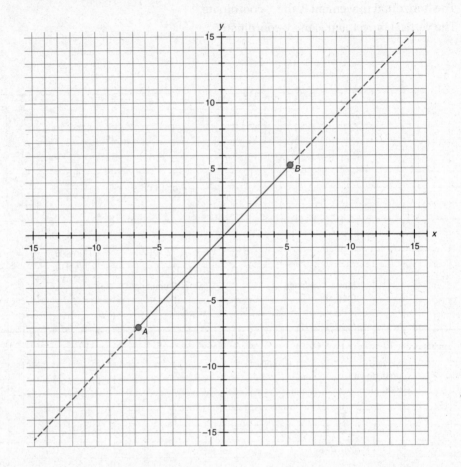

- Line *AB* in the graph is defined by points *A* and *B*. However, the line actually contains every point between points *A* and *B* as well as every point beyond them in either direction.

Slope

Slope defines the slant of a line in the coordinate plane. It is a ratio between the vertical change and the horizontal change required to move from one point on the line to another. This ratio has several names as well as an important formula:

- Rise over run

- Change in *y* over change in *x* or $\dfrac{\Delta y}{\Delta x}$

- Slope formula: $\dfrac{y_2 - y_1}{x_2 - x_1}$

For example, if the points (6,5) and (–5, –6) lie on a line, you can calculate their slope. Make sure you call one set of coordinates (x_1, y_1) and the other $(x_2 - y_2)$.

$$\frac{y_2 - y_1}{x_2 - x_1} = \frac{-6-5}{-5-6} = \frac{-11}{-11} = 1$$

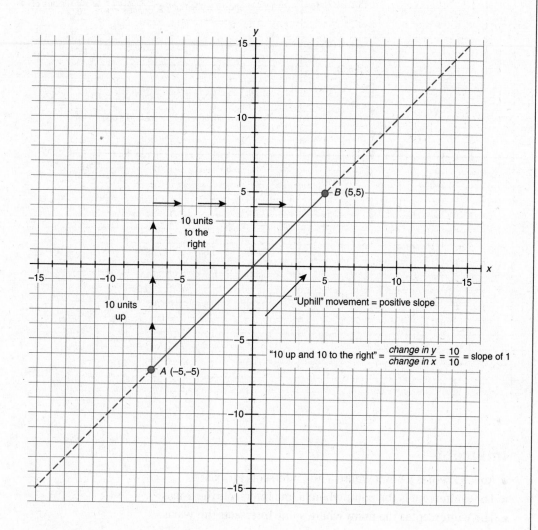

- Slopes can be positive or negative.
- Positive slopes go uphill, and negative slopes go downhill.
- To calculate slope using two given points, substitute the coordinates of your two points into the formula for slope.

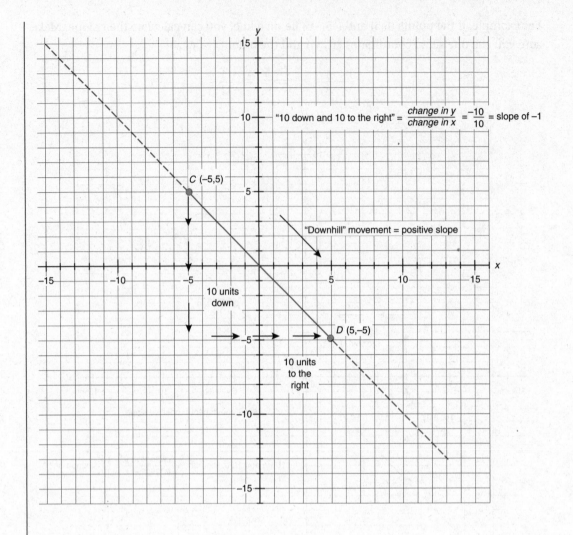

"10 down and 10 to the right" = $\dfrac{change\ in\ y}{change\ in\ x}$ = $\dfrac{-10}{10}$ = slope of −1

C (−5,5)

"Downhill" movement = positive slope

10 units down

D (5,−5)

10 units to the right

y-Intercept

- An intercept is a point where a line intersects an axis.
- The *x*-intercept is the point where a line intersects the *x*-axis.
- The *y*-intercept is the point where a line intersects the *y*-axis.

Slope-Intercept Equation

The equation of a line can be written in several ways. One of the most common methods is the slope-intercept equation:

$$y = mx + b$$

The slope-intercept formula for a line, or $y = mx + b$, includes 4 variables: y, m, x, and b.

- x represents the x-coordinate of a point on the line.
- y represents the y-coordinate of a point on the line.
- m represents the slope of the line and is based on the slope formula.
- b represents the y-intercept.

For example, the line $y = 3x - 2$ has a slope of 3. This line is graphed on the following coordinate plane and crosses the y-axis at (0,–2).

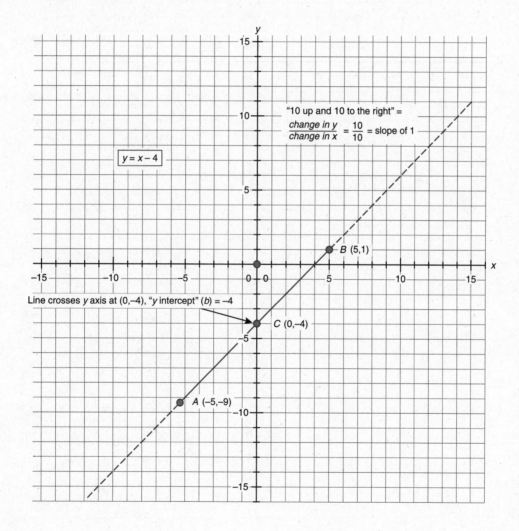

The next graph shows the line $y = -x + 6$. Since $m = -1$, the slope is -1. Since $b = 6$, the y-intercept is $(0,6)$.

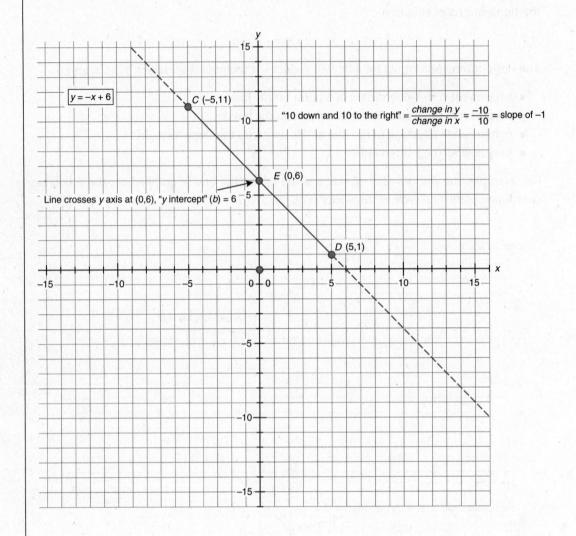

$y = -x + 6$

C $(-5,11)$

"10 down and 10 to the right" $= \dfrac{change\ in\ y}{change\ in\ x} = \dfrac{-10}{10} = $ slope of -1

E $(0,6)$

Line crosses y axis at $(0,6)$, "y intercept" $(b) = 6$

D $(5,1)$

Values for Slope

- Slopes can be greater or less than 1.
- Slopes greater than 1 are expressed as integers or improper fractions.

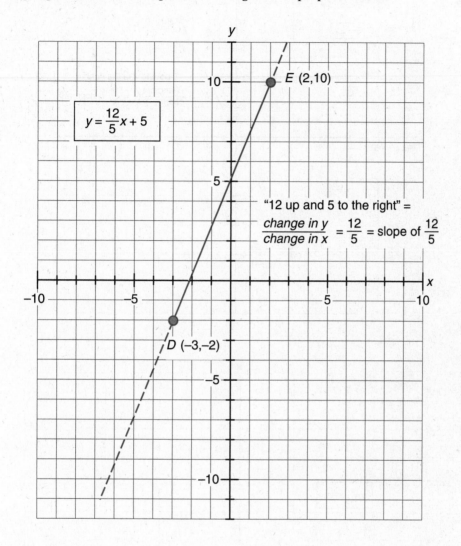

$$y = \frac{12}{5}x + 5$$

E (2,10)

"12 up and 5 to the right" =

$$\frac{change\ in\ y}{change\ in\ x} = \frac{12}{5} = \text{slope of } \frac{12}{5}$$

D (−3,−2)

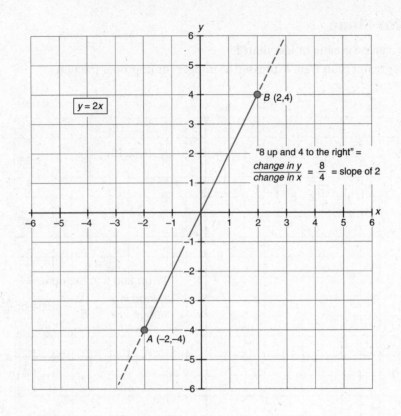

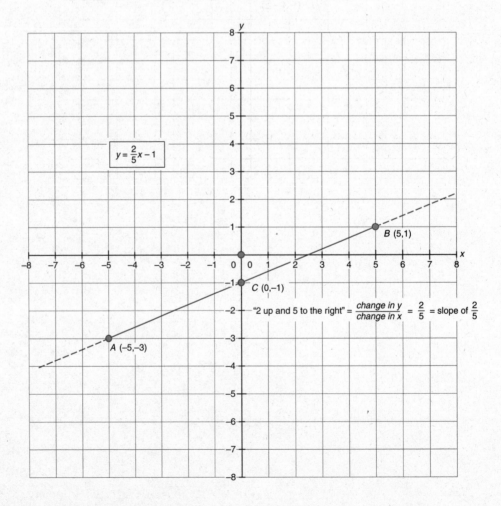

Point-Slope Formula

The equation of a line can be written in point-slope form:

$$y - y_1 = m(x - x_1)$$

When you're given the slope of a line and the coordinates of one point on the line, you can use the point-slope formula to produce a formula in slope-intercept format. Assume a line with a slope of 2 that passes through point (2, 3):

- y_1 is the y-coordinate of the point (2,3), so $y_1 = 3$.
- x_1 is the x-coordinate of the point (2,3), so $x_1 = 2$.
- m is the slope of the line, so $m = 2$.

$$y - 3 = 2(x - 2)$$

- Rearrange the terms

$$y - 3 = 2x - 4 \rightarrow y = 2x - 1$$

Perpendicular Lines

The slopes of perpendicular lines are negative reciprocals (inverted and sign switched).

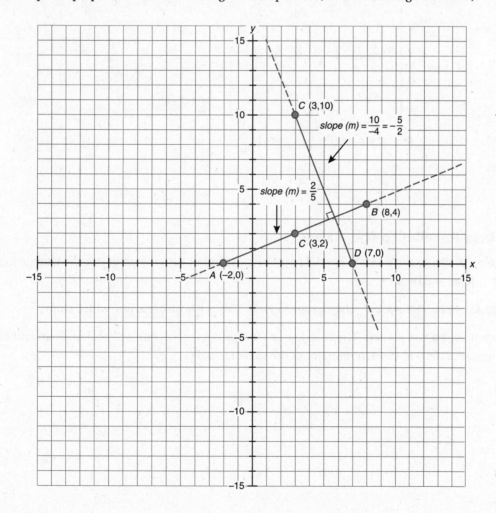

Parallel Lines

The slopes of parallel lines are identical.

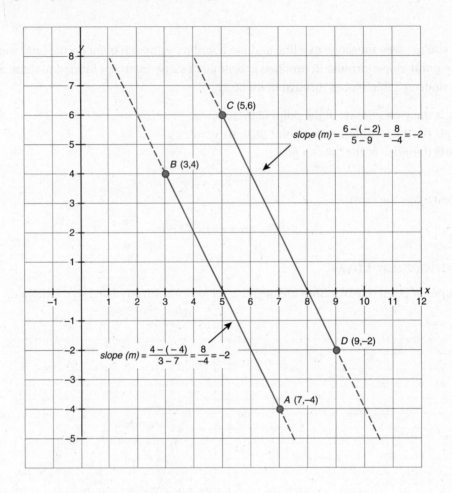

$$slope\ (m) = \frac{6 - (-2)}{5 - 9} = \frac{8}{-4} = -2$$

$$slope\ (m) = \frac{4 - (-4)}{3 - 7} = \frac{8}{-4} = -2$$

Lines Parallel to the Axes

Lines parallel to the axes are special cases because either the change in y or the change in x (the slope) will be zero.

PARALLEL TO THE x-AXIS The change in $y = 0$. This is a horizontal line with 0 slope.

PARALLEL TO THE y-AXIS The change in $x = 0$. This is a vertical line whose slope is undefined because of the 0 in the denominator of the slope formula.

QUESTIONS 1 AND 2 REFER TO THE FOLLOWING GRAPH:

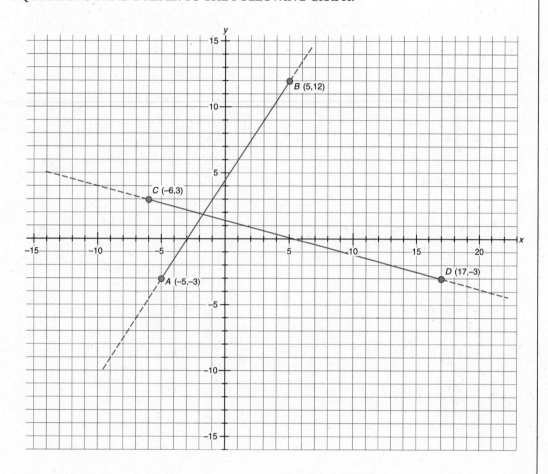

1. For line *AB*, identify the following:

    a. Slope

    b. *y*-intercept

    c. Slope-intercept formula

    d. Formula of a parallel line that has a *y*-intercept of 10

    e. Formula of a perpendicular line with *y*-intercept –2

2. For line *CD*, identify the following:

    a. Slope

    b. *y*-intercept to the nearest tenth

    c. Slope-intercept formula

    d. Formula of a parallel line that has a *y*-intercept of –5

    e. Formula of a perpendicular line that has a *y*-intercept of 1

Answers

1. a. $\dfrac{3}{2}$

   b. 4.5

   c. $y = \dfrac{3}{2}x + 4.5$

   d. $y = \dfrac{3}{2}x + 10$

   e. $y = -\dfrac{2}{3}x - 2$

2. a. $-\dfrac{6}{23}$

   b. 1.4

   c. $y = -\dfrac{6}{23}x + 1.4$

   d. $y = -\dfrac{6}{23}x - 5$

   e. $y = \dfrac{23}{6}x + 1$

Functions can be graphed using x for the x-coordinate and using $f(x)$ for the y-coordinate. This is expressed as $y = f(x)$, and each point has the coordinates $(x, f(x))$. To identify coordinates, perform the operations defined as $f(x)$ on a series of values for x (inputs) and record the resulting values for $f(x)$ (outputs).

- These ordered pairs become the (x, y) coordinates of points on the graph.
- Once the pairs are plotted, a line can be drawn to connect the points.
- Some lines are straight (linear equations), and some are not (quadratics, some functions).

GRAPHS OF FUNCTIONS

The graph below shows the function $y = f(x)$. It shows the values of $f(x)$ for a range of values for x from –3 to 3. The range of x-values graphed is called an *interval*.

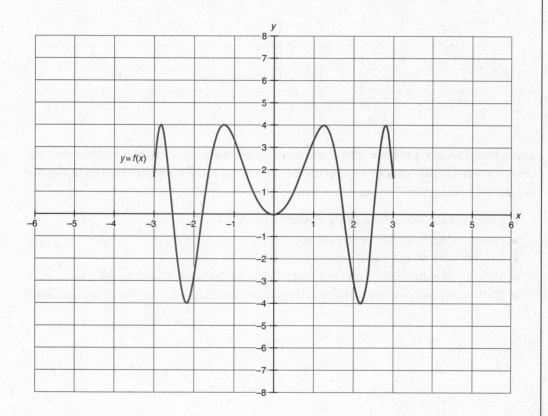

UNIT 2: MATH

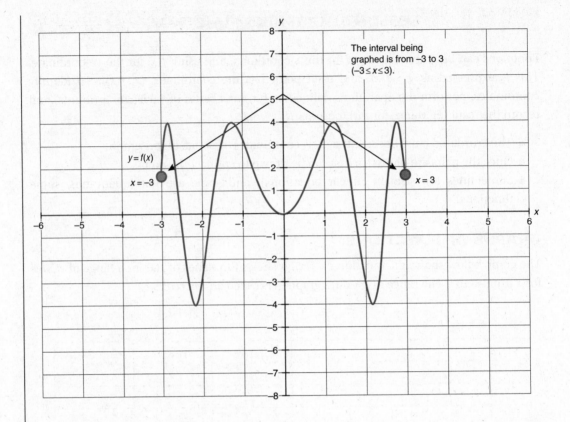

The interval being graphed is from −3 to 3 ($-3 \leq x \leq 3$).

$y = f(x)$

$x = -3$

$x = 3$

Even though we may not know what expression $f(x)$ represents, we can analyze the graph and draw some conclusions about some of the characteristics of the function based on things that we already know about the coordinate plane:

- y-coordinates above the x-axis are positive.
- y-coordinates below the x-axis are negative.
- y-coordinates on the x-axis are equal to zero.
- The highest point reached on the y-axis is the maximum (max) value for the y-coordinate.
- The lowest point reached on the y-axis is the minimum (min) value for the y-coordinate.

By looking at the following graph and remembering that the *y*-coordinate represents the value of $f(x)$, we can say the following:

- The value of the function is positive for four different ranges of values for *x*. Another way to say this is that $f(x)$ is greater than zero over four different intervals.
- The value of $f(x)$ is less than zero over two different intervals.

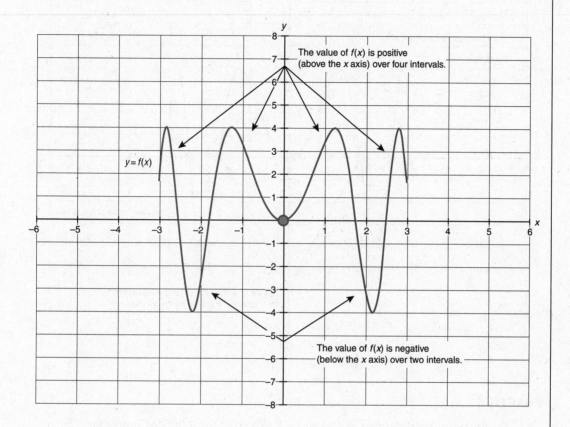

The value of $f(x)$ is positive (above the *x* axis) over four intervals.

$y = f(x)$

The value of $f(x)$ is negative (below the *x* axis) over two intervals.

We can also say that:

- The maximum value for $f(x)$ is 4, and the minimum value is –4.
- There are 5 different values of x where $f(x)$ is equal to zero.

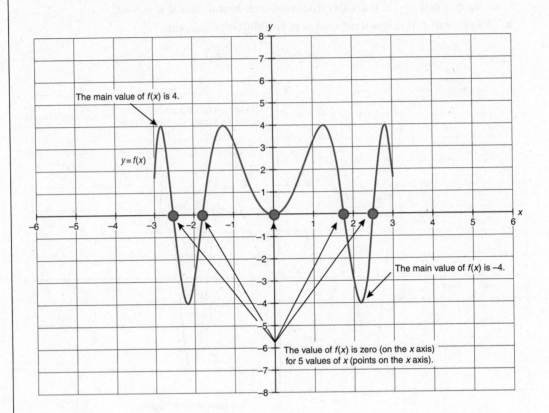

The main value of $f(x)$ is 4.

$y = f(x)$

The main value of $f(x)$ is –4.

The value of $f(x)$ is zero (on the x axis) for 5 values of x (points on the x axis).

PRACTICE

1. The function $f(x)$ is defined as $f(x) = 3x + 1$. Which of the following points lies on the graph of $f(x)$?
   - (A) (1, 5)
   - (B) (2, 7)
   - (C) (3, 8)
   - (D) (4, 12)

2. The y-intercept of $f(x)$ is at (0, 5). Which of the following could be the expression defined by $f(x)$?
   - (A) $f(x) = 2x - 5$
   - (B) $f(x) = x - 5$
   - (C) $f(x) = 2x + 5$
   - (D) $f(x) = x + 3$

1. **(B)** The correct point will produce the *y*-coordinate when the *x*-coordinate is plugged into the expression defined by $f(x)$: $3(2) + 1 = 7$.

2. **(C)** The *y*-intercept of the function is at $(0, 5)$. The correct function will produce 5 when 0 is plugged into the expression for *x*: $2(0) + 5 = 5$.

OPERATIONS ON FUNCTIONS (TRANSFORMATIONS)

The graph below shows $y = f(x)$. A reference point has been added at the center of the graph. Basic arithmetic functions can be applied to functions and/or to the variable within the function. These operations will affect either the curve's position or its shape.

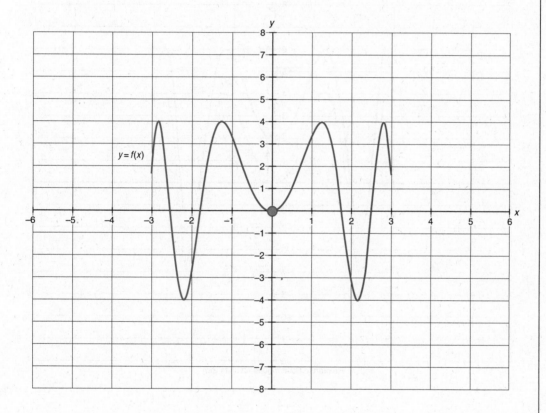

ADDING AND SUBTRACTING

Adding and subtracting affect the position of the function on the graph but leave the shape of the function unchanged. These operations can be performed on the function $f(x)$ or on the variable x.

Operations on the function $f(x)$ are applied outside the parentheses: $y = f(x) + 2$.

- Adding outside the parentheses causes a vertical shift in an upward direction.
- Subtracting outside causes vertical shift in a downward direction.
- The shifts are vertical (along the y-axis), because an operation on $f(x)$ affects the value of the y-coordinate.

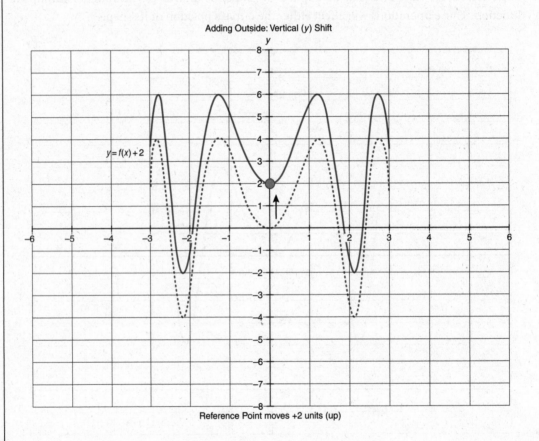

Adding Outside: Vertical (y) Shift

$y = f(x) + 2$

Reference Point moves +2 units (up)

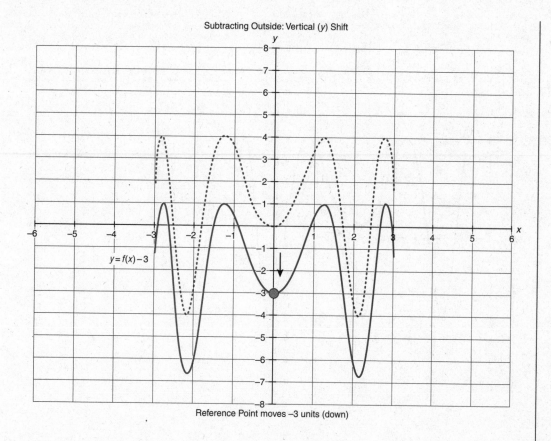

Subtracting Outside: Vertical (*y*) Shift

$y = f(x) - 3$

Reference Point moves −3 units (down)

Operations on the variable *x* are applied inside the parentheses: $y = f(x - 3)$.

- Adding inside the parentheses causes a horizontal shift to the left.
- Subtracting inside the parentheses causes a horizontal shift to the right.
- The shifts are horizontal (along the *x*-axis) because an operation on *x* affects the value of the *x*-coordinate.

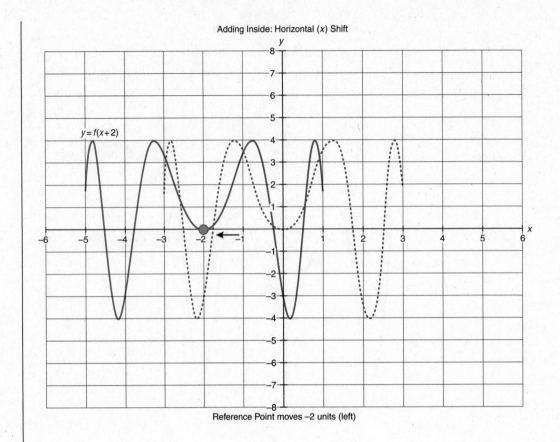

Adding Inside: Horizontal (x) Shift

$y = f(x + 2)$

Reference Point moves −2 units (left)

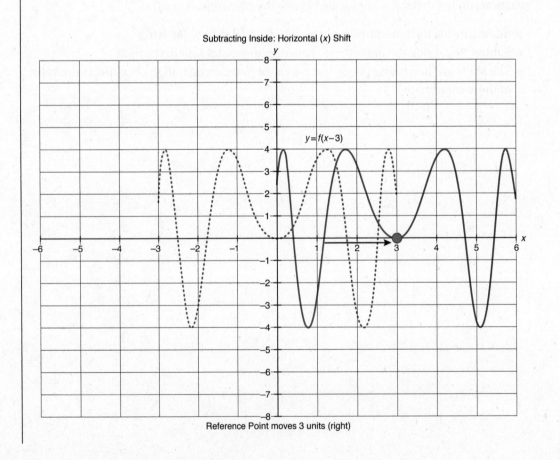

Subtracting Inside: Horizontal (x) Shift

$y = f(x - 3)$

Reference Point moves 3 units (right)

MULTIPLYING AND DIVIDING

Multiplying and dividing affect the shape of the curve without changing the location of the center. Operations on $f(x)$ affect the height (or vertical range) of the curve. Operations on x affect the width of the curve:

- Multiplying outside the function causes vertical stretching.
- Dividing outside the function causes vertical compression.

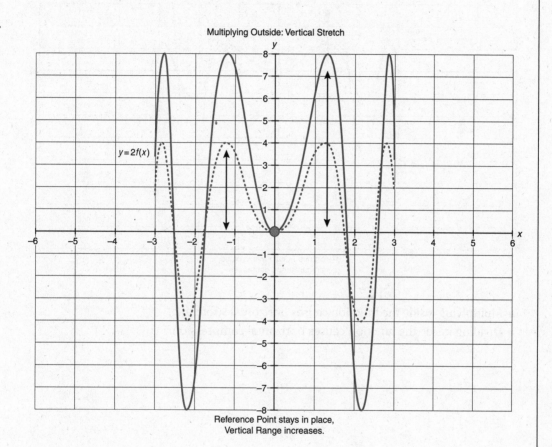

Multiplying Outside: Vertical Stretch

$y = 2f(x)$

Reference Point stays in place,
Vertical Range increases.

UNIT 2: MATH

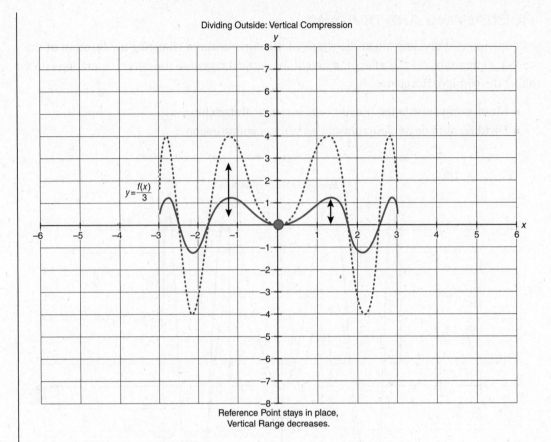

Dividing Outside: Vertical Compression

$y = \dfrac{f(x)}{3}$

Reference Point stays in place,
Vertical Range decreases.

- Multiplying inside the function causes horizontal stretching.
- Dividing inside the function causes horizontal compression.

Multiplying Inside: Horizontal Compression

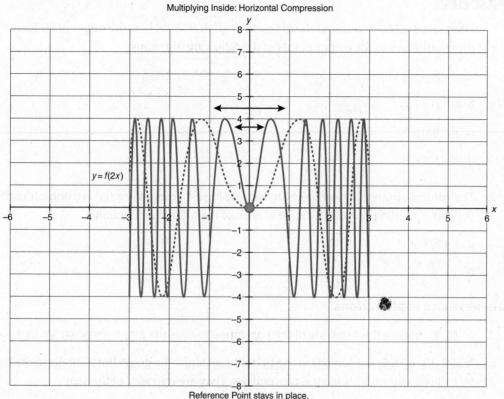

$y = f(2x)$

Reference Point stays in place,
Horizontal Range decreases.

Dividing Inside: Horizontal Stretch

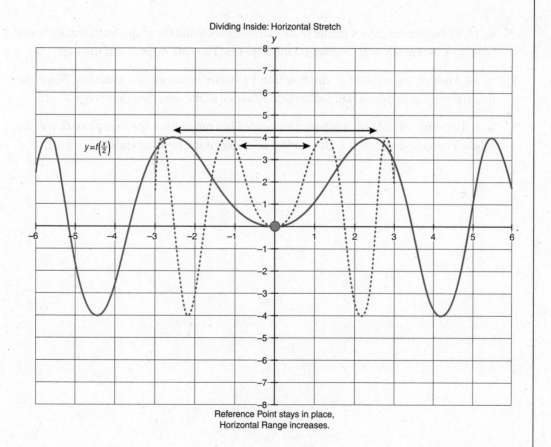

$y = f\left(\dfrac{x}{2}\right)$

Reference Point stays in place,
Horizontal Range increases.

PRACTICE

1. Point A is the center point of the graph of $y = f(x)$. Point A is at the origin $(0,0)$. Identify the coordinates of the center points of the following functions:

   a. $y = f(x) + 4$

   b. $y = f(x + 1)$

   c. $y = f(x) - 2$

   d. $y = f(x - 4)$

2. The vertical distance between the highest and lowest points of $y = f(x)$ is 6 units. Identify the corresponding vertical distance of each of the following functions:

   a. $y = 2f(x)$

   b. $y = \dfrac{f(x)}{3}$

Answers and Explanations

1. **a. (0, 4)** Adding the 4 outside of the parentheses shifts the graph vertically up by 4.

   b. (–1, 0) Adding the 1 inside of the parentheses shifts the graph horizontally to the left by 1. Be careful with horizontal movements. They are opposite of the sign.

   c. (0, –2) Subtracting the 2 outside of the parentheses shifts the graph vertically down by 2.

   d. (4, 0) Subtracting the 4 inside of the parentheses shifts the graph horizontally to the right by 4. Be careful with horizontal movements. They are opposite of the sign.

2. **a. 12** Multiplying outside of the function vertically stretches the function. Since the original vertical distance is 6, the vertical distance of the new function is $6 \times 2 = 12$.

   b. 2 Dividing outside of the function vertically compresses the function. Since the original vertical distance is 6, the vertical distance of the new function is $6 \div 3 = 2$.

ABSOLUTE VALUE The unit distance on the number line between a number and zero. Absolute value is either positive or zero and is symbolized with vertical bars, $|\ \ |$.

ACUTE ANGLE An angle that measures less than 90°.

ACUTE TRIANGLE A triangle with three angles each measuring less than 90° (three acute angles).

ADDEND The name for the numbers that are added together.

ADDITION The operation that combines two quantities.

ADJACENT ANGLES Two angles that share a common side and vertex.

ALTERNATE ANGLES Congruent angles on opposite sides of the transversal.

ALTERNATE INTERIOR ANGLES Alternate angles inside the parallel lines.

ALTITUDE (OF A POLYGON) A line extending from the "top" of the shape to the base and that is perpendicular to the base.

ANGLE An angle is formed when two rays intersect at a common endpoint, called a vertex. Angles are marked with a curved line called an arc.

APEX The common vertex at the top of a pyramid.

ARC A portion of the circumference defined by two points on the circle.

AREA (OF A CIRCLE) The amount of space inside a circle; $A = \pi r^2$.

AREA (OF A PARALLELOGRAM) The amount of space inside a parallelogram; $A = lw$ or $A = bh$.

AREA (OF A POLYGON) The amount of space inside a polygon. Area is usually measured in square units, as when a floor is measured in square feet.

AREA (OF A RECTANGLE) The amount of space inside a rectangle; $A = lw$ or $A = bh$

AREA (OF A SQUARE) The amount of space inside a square; side squared or $A = s^2$.

AREA (OF A TRIANGLE) The amount of space inside a triangle; $A = \frac{1}{2}bh$.

AXIS A line connecting the bases of a cylinder.

BAR CHART A chart in which the relative amounts of things being compared over time, by geography, or by some other grouping factor are represented by the height of vertical bars or the length of horizontal bars.

BASE (OF A POLYGON) A side serving as the bottom edge of a polygon and used to calculate area. Polygons can be rotated, so any side can serve as a base, not just the one that appears at the bottom in a picture.

BINOMIAL An expression with two terms connected by addition or subtraction: $2x + 3$; $5x - 4$; $x^2 + x$.

CELSIUS The metric scale for temperature; another name for Centigrade.

CENTIGRADE   The metric scale for temperature; another name for Celsius.

CHORD   Any line segment with both endpoints on a circle.

CIRCLE   A set of points that are all at an equal distance (or equidistant) from a common point called the center. Circles measure 360°.

CIRCUMFERENCE (CIRCLE)   The perimeter of a circle is called its circumference; $C = \pi d$ or $C = 2\pi r$.

COEFFICIENT   A number placed next to a variable to indicate multiplication.

COLLINEAR   Points on a common line.

COMBINATION   The number of different ways that a group of k elements can be formed from a larger group of n elements when order does not matter; $\dfrac{n!}{(n-k)k!}$.

COMPLEMENTARY ANGLES   Two angles whose measures add to 90°.

COMPOUND EVENTS   Two or more independent events that happen together. The probability of a compound event is the product of the probabilities of each independent event.

COMPOUND INEQUALITY   Two or more inequalities joined together by either "and" or "or." One "and" example is $-3 \le x < 7$. An "or" example is $x < 10$ or $x > 20$. A compound inequality can be graphed.

CONE   A three-dimensional shape similar to a pyramid except that it has a circular base.

CONGRUENT   When two or more lines or two or more angles have the same measure, they are congruent. Congruency is represented with the $\cong$ symbol.

CONSTANT   A value that does not change.

COORDINATE GEOMETRY   Points and lines in the coordinate plane.

COORDINATES   The two numbers in an ordered pair that specify the location of a point; expressed in the form (x, y) where x is the x-coordinate and y is the y-coordinate.

CORRESPONDING ANGLES   Angles that are in the same position but part of two different groups of angles (in parallel lines, in similar triangles, and so on).

COUNTING METHODS   Ways of counting the number of different possible arrangements of a set of elements.

CUBE   A prism made up of six squares; it has six congruent square faces.

CUP   The customary unit of capacity.

CUSTOMARY SYSTEM   A system of measurement used in the U.S.

CYLINDER   A prism with circular bases, commonly referred to as a tube.

DATA   Quantitative (numbers) or qualitative (words) information.

DATA PRESENTATION   Information presented using text, graphics, or both.

DECIMAL   An expression of a partial quantity that uses division by 10 (decimal places) to represent numbers; related to decimal fractions.

DECIMAL FRACTION   A fraction where the denominator is a multiple of 10.

DIAGRAM   A simplified picture or model or a system, process, or concept.

DIAMETER   A line segment passing through the center of the circle whose endpoints are both on the circle. The diameter is equal to twice the radius.

DIFFERENCE   The result of subtraction.

DIGIT   The symbols we use to construct numbers: 0, 1, 2, 3, 4, 5, 6, 7, 8, and 9.

DIMENSIONS   Properties of objects: length, width, height, area, volume, and so on.

DIVIDEND   The number being divided.

DIVISION   The operation that collects numbers into groups: "twenty divided by five" means, separating 20 things into groups of 5.

DIVISOR   The number being divided by.

DOMAIN   The set of all allowed values for the variable in a function.

ENDPOINT   A point at the end of a line on a number line or graph. A point that defines one "end" of a ray or line segment. In inequalities, an endpoint may or may not be included in the range of the inequality.

EQUATIONS   Expressions set equal to each other. Equations can be solved for an unknown value.

EQUIANGULAR   "Equi" means "equal," so an equiangular polygon is one where all angles are congruent.

EQUILATERAL   "Equi" means "equal" and "lateral" means "side," so an equilateral polygon is one where all sides are congruent.

EQUILATERAL TRIANGLE   A triangle with three congruent sides and three congruent angles. Each angle in an equilateral triangle measures 60°.

EVALUATING AN EXPRESSION   A method of substituting numbers for the variables in the expression.

EXCLUSIVE   An inequality that does not include its endpoint(s). Expressed using greater than or less than.

EXPONENT   A symbol for repeated multiplication by the same number.

EXPRESSION   A group of terms connected by operators: $2x + 5$.

EXTERIOR ANGLES   The angles formed outside two parallel lines crossed by a transversal

FACE   Side of a three-dimensional figure. The bottom face is sometimes called the base.

FACTOR   A number that divides evenly into another number. The multiplicand and multiplier are both factors of the product.

FACTORIAL The number of different ways that a set of objects or elements can be placed in order. To calculate the factorial, the number of elements is multiplied by each successively smaller number, down to 1.

FAHRENHEIT The customary scale for temperature.

FOIL The order to multiply the terms in two binomials: First, Outer, Inner, Last.

FOOT The customary unit of length.

FRACTION A ratio that relates a part to a whole. If a pie is cut in four pieces and I have one, I ate 1 piece out of 4, or one-fourth, or $\frac{1}{4}$.

FUNCTION A set of operations defined by a mathematical expression that can be applied to multiple numbers to produce multiple results. A function can be graphed.

GRAM The metric unit of mass.

GRAPH A data presentation using a horizontal (x) axis and a vertical (y) axis to show the locations of points. Points may be joined in a line (line graph) or scattered around the plot area in clusters (scatter plot).

IMPROPER FRACTION A fraction where the numerator is greater than or equal to the denominator, making it greater than or equal to 1.

INCLUSIVE An inequality that includes its endpoint(s). Expressed using greater than or equal to or less than or equal to.

INDEPENDENT EVENTS Events whose outcomes do not depend on one another. On the Math subject test, all events are independent.

INEQUALITY A statement about a value relative to other values: 3 is less than 5, –2 is greater than –4, and so on.

INTEGER Whole numbers, including all positive and negative whole numbers and zero (zero is neutral).

INTERCEPT A point where a line intersects an axis.

INTERIOR ANGLES The angles formed inside (or between) two parallel lines crossed by a transversal.

INTERSECTION A point common to two lines, segments, or rays, representing a place where the two meet or cross.

INVERSE OPERATIONS Operations used to isolate a variable when solving an equation. For example, addition and subtraction, are inverse operations. Multiplication and division are also inverse operations.

ISOSCELES TRIANGLE A triangle with two congruent sides and two congruent angles.

LINE A collection of points. Lines are one-dimensional, which means they have length but no width or height.

LINE GRAPH A graph in which the points are connected by one or more lines.

LINE SEGMENT   A portion of a line; it has two endpoints.

LITER   The metric unit of capacity.

MEAN   The average of a set of numbers. Mean is calculated by adding the elements and dividing by the number of elements.

MEASUREMENT   Using a standard unit to assign a numerical value to a property of a physical object.

MEASURES OF CENTER   Mean, median, mode, weighted average, and range.

MEDIAN   The middle number in a set of numbers that are arranged in ascending order. As many numbers in the set are larger than the median as are smaller than the median. In a set with an odd number of elements, the median is the middle element when the set is arranged in ascending order (smallest to largest). In a set with an even number of elements, the median is the average of the two middle elements when the set is arranged in ascending order.

METER   The metric unit of length.

METRIC SYSTEM   A system of measurement based on standard units grouped into multiples and factors of 10. A kilometer is 1,000 meters. There are 100 centimeters in a meter.

MIDPOINT   A point on a line segment that is at an equal distance from both endpoints; the middle or halfway point.

MINUEND   The number being subtracted from or taken away from.

MIXED NUMBER   A number that consists of an integer (whole number) and a fraction.

MODE   The most frequently occurring element in the set.

MONOMIAL   An expression with only one term: 5, x, $2y$, z^3.

MULTIPLE   A number that results from incremental multiplication. For example, the first few multiples of 2 are $2 \times 1 = 2$, $2 \times 2 = 4$, and $2 \times 3 = 6$.

MULTIPLICAND   The number being multiplied.

MULTIPLICATION   The operation that counts the numbers in groups: "four times five" means 4 groups of 5.

MULTIPLIER   The number being multiplied by.

NEGATIVE NUMBERS   Numbers that are less than zero.

NONCOLLINEAR   Three or more points that cannot be connected by a single line.

NUMBER   Combinations of digits used to represent amounts or values.

NUMBER LINE   A horizontal line with zero in the middle that extends forever in either direction.

OBTUSE ANGLE   An angle that measures more than 90° but less than 180°.

OBTUSE TRIANGLE   A triangle with one angle measuring less than 180°. In an obtuse triangle, the other two angles must be acute.

OPERATORS   Symbols for arithmetic operations $(+, -, \bullet, /, x^2, \sqrt{\ })$; used to form expressions.

ORDER OF OPERATIONS   Specifies the order in which operations should be performed in an expression: parentheses, exponents, multiplication, division, addition, subtraction (PEMDAS).

ORDERED PAIR   A pair of numbers in the format (x, y) representing the coordinates, or location, of a point in the coordinate plane.

PARALLEL LINES   Two lines or planes that never cross (or intersect).

PARALLELOGRAM   A quadrilateral with two pairs of congruent sides. Intersecting sides are not necessarily perpendicular, so the height (h) is an altitude perpendicular to the base (b). The side of the parallelogram that is not the base is called the side (s). Opposite sides are parallel.

PEMDAS   Specifies the order in which operations should be performed in an expression (Order of Operations): Parentheses, Exponents, Multiplication, Division, Addition, Subtraction.

PERCENTAGE   An expression of a partial quantity that relates a part to a whole in terms of 100.

PERIMETER   The sum of all the sides of the polygon; the distance around the outside of the polygon.

PERIMETER (OF A PARALLELOGRAM)   The distance around a parallelogram; $P = 2s + 2b$.

PERIMETER (OF A RECTANGLE)   The distance around a rectangle; $P = l + w + l + w$. As a shortcut, you can also add l times 2 plus w times 2: $P = 2l + 2w$.

PERIMETER (OF A SQUARE)   The distance around a square; $P = s + s + s + s$. As a shortcut, you can also multiply s times 4: $P = 4s$.

PERMUTATION   The number of ways that a group of objects selected from a larger group of objects can be placed in order. The formula for a permutation is $\dfrac{n!}{(n-k)!}$, where n is the number of elements or objects, and k is the number of places or spots that must be filled with selected elements.

PERPENDICULAR LINES   Two lines that intersect to form right angles (90°).

PI (π)   The ratio of a circle's circumference to its diameter; equal to $22 \div 7$ or approximately 3.14. Pi is a continuing decimal that never establishes a pattern no matter how many decimal places are calculated.

PIE CHART   A chart in the shape of a circle, with slices that represent percentages or portions of the total.

PLACE VALUE   One of the number places that are used to express numbers: the ones place, the tens place, the hundreds place, and so on.

PLANE   A two-dimensional surface made up of points. A plane has length and width but no height.

POINT A location in space. Points are zero dimensional, which means they have no length, width, or height.

POLYGON A two-dimensional figure formed when three or more line segments are joined at their endpoints (or vertices). The segments are called sides, and the number of sides in a polygon is equal to the number of angles in the polygon.

POLYNOMIAL An expression with three or more terms: $2x^2 - 3x + 4$.

POSITIVE NUMBERS Numbers that are greater than zero.

POUND The customary unit of weight.

PRIME FACTORIZATION The reduction of a number to a product of its prime factors: $30 = 2 \times 3 \times 5$.

PRIME NUMBER A number that is not divisible by any number other than itself and 1. The number 1 is not prime. The number 2 is the only even prime number.

PRISM A solid figure with two opposite, congruent, and parallel faces (triangles, squares, pentagons, and so on). The top face is directly above the bottom face so that a line connecting their centers is perpendicular to both bases. Lines connect the corresponding vertices in the two bases.

PROBABILITY The likelihood that something (result, event, outcome) will occur.

PRODUCT The result of multiplication.

PROPORTION The setting of two ratios equal to each other, which allows the proportion to be solved for one unknown value.

PYRAMID A solid with a square base and triangular faces that all meet at a common point at the top called the apex. On the Math test, pyramid refers to a square pyramid.

PYTHAGOREAN THEOREM The rule of right triangles that says the sum of the squared lengths of the legs of a right triangle will be equal to the squared length of the hypotenuse. This is usually expressed as $a^2 + b^2 = c^2$, where a and b are the legs of the triangle and c is the hypotenuse.

QUADRANT A one-quarter portion of the coordinate plane containing all points with a specific combination of coordinate signs. Quadrants are numbered with roman numerals and go in counterclockwise order.

QUADRATIC EQUATIONS Polynomial equations in the form $ax^2 + bx + c = 0$. Quadratic equations can be factored to find their roots, which are the numbers that would make the equation true. The signs of the roots are opposite the signs in the binomials that result from factoring.

QUADRILATERAL A four-sided polygon, including parallelograms, rectangles, and squares. There are several types of quadrilaterals, and their interior angles always add to 360°.

QUOTIENT The result of division.

RADIUS The distance from the center to any point on the circle. The plural of "radius" is "radii" (ray-dee-eye), and all radii in a particular circle are equal in length.

RANGE The difference between the smallest element and the largest element in the set. Range is sometimes called the spread of data. Range is also the set of possible values of the function, based on using all the values in the domain.

RATE (UNIT RATE) A ratio between 1 unit of something and a quantity of something else: 36 miles per 1 gallon, 55 miles per 1 hour, 3 sale items per customer, and so on.

RATIO A comparison between one part and another part, like the ratio of men to women in a math class.

RATIONAL EXPRESSION An expression that represents a ratio between two polynomials; presented as a fraction made up of two polynomials.

RAY A portion of a line that extends infinitely in one direction from a given endpoint.

RECTANGLE A quadrilateral with two pairs of congruent sides. Intersecting sides are perpendicular. Opposite sides are parallel and congruent.

RECTANGULAR PRISM (BOX) A prism made up of six rectangles; commonly described as a box. Adjacent faces are perpendicular. The three dimensions of a rectangular prism are length, width, and height.

REDUCING Dividing the top and the bottom of a fraction by a common factor to make them both smaller; can also be done in reverse.

REGULAR POLYGON A polygon that is both equilateral and equiangular.

REMAINDER The whole-number portion left over from division of whole numbers: $15 \div 6 = 2r3$.

RIGHT ANGLE An angle that measures exactly 90°. It is marked with a small square symbol.

RIGHT TRIANGLE A triangle with one right angle (90°). In a right triangle, the side opposite the right angle is called the hypotenuse. The other two sides are called the legs. The two angles opposite the legs are complementary (must add to 90°).

ROOT The root of a number is a number that, when multiplied by itself, produces the original number.

ROUNDING Estimating a number by increasing it or decreasing it to the closest multiple of 10, 100, 1,000, and so on. For example, 1916 rounded to the nearest 100 is 1,900.

SCALENE TRIANGLE A triangle with no congruent sides or angles. Each angle measure and each side length is different.

SCATTER PLOT A graph in which the points are plotted in groups called clusters, with some individual outlier points plotted in areas of relatively low point concentration.

SCIENTIFIC NOTATION A way to express very large or very small numbers. A decimal number greater than or equal to 1 but less than 10 is mulitplied by 10 raised to a positive or negative power. Multiplying by exponents of 10 serves to move the decimal point to the left or right.

SECTOR A portion of a circle's area defined by two radii and the arc connecting the endpoints.

SEMICIRCLE Half of a circle, bounded on one side by the diameter.

SET A group of numbers, sometimes called members, terms, or elements.

SIGNED NUMBER Refers to whether a number is positive, negative, or neutral (zero).

SIMILAR TERMS Terms that can be combined: $3x + 2 + 4x + 3 = 7x + 5$.

SIMPLE INEQUALITY One inequality. One example is $x > 3$. Another example is $x \leq -8$. A simple inequality can be graphed.

SIMPLIFYING AN EXPRESSION Combining similar terms, factoring, and distributing to enable canceling and reducing; taking an expression to its smallest and simplest form.

SIMULTANEOUS EQUATIONS Two or more equations each containing one or more variables in common; used to solve for more than one variable.

SLANT LENGTH The altitude of a triangular face of a pyramid.

SLOPE The slant of a line in the coordinate plane. It is a ratio between the vertical change and horizontal change required to move from one point on the line to another. This ratio has several names as well as an important formula: $\frac{y_2 - y_1}{x_2 - x_1}$.

SLOPE-INTERCEPT EQUATION The equation of a line written in the form $y = mx + b$. The formula includes 4 variables: y, m, x, and b. x represents the x-coordinate of a point on the line. y represents the y-coordinate of a point on the line. m represents the slope of the line, based on the slope formula. b represents the y-intercept. For example, $y = 3x - 2$ has a slope of 3 and crosses the y-axis at $(0, -2)$.

SPACE Space is three dimensional. It has length, width, and height. It contains all points, lines, and planes.

SPHERE The three-dimensional version of a circle. It represents all points in space that are an equal distance from the center. The primary dimension in a sphere is the radius.

SQUARE A quadrilateral with four congruent sides. Intersecting sides are perpendicular. Opposite sides are parallel. The length of a side of a square is represented by s.

STATISTICS Numbers involved in data (measurement) analysis. Measures of center, probabilities, and so on.

STRAIGHT ANGLE An angle that measures exactly 180°. The two rays in a straight angle are called opposite rays.

SUBTRACTION The operation that finds the difference between two quantities by taking one away from the other.

SUBTRAHEND The number being subtracted or taken away.

SUM The result of addition.

SUPPLEMENTARY ANGLES Two angles whose measures add to 180°.

SURFACE AREA The sum of the areas of all faces of the figure. Surface area is similar in concept to perimeter because it measures the outside of the shape.

SURFACE AREA (OF A BOX) The sum of the areas of all the faces; $SA = ph + 2B$, where p is the perimeter of a base and B is the area of that base. Calculating the surface area of a box requires three steps. First calculate the area of a base (B) using $A = lw$. Then calculate the perimeter of a base (p). Finally use the surface area formula.

SURFACE AREA (OF A CONE) The sum of the areas of circular base and the area of the rest of the cone. The formula for the surface area of a pyramid is $\pi rs + \pi r^2$, where s is the slant length.

SURFACE AREA (OF A CUBE) Since all six faces of a cube are congruent squares, the surface area is six times the area of one face; $SA = 6s^2$.

SURFACE AREA (OF A CYLINDER) The sum of the areas of: the top base, the bottom base, and the curved surface around the outside of the tube. $SA = 2\pi r^2 + 2\pi rh$.

SURFACE AREA (OF A PYRAMID) The sum of the areas of the base and of the sides; $\frac{1}{2}ps + B$.

SURFACE AREA (OF A SPHERE) The area along the outside of a sphere; $SA = 4\pi r^2$.

TERM A value expressed with at least one variable, sometimes with a coefficient and/or an exponent. $2x$ is a term, and so is x^2.

TICK MARKS Marks that indicate the location of numbers that are greater than, less than, or equal to zero.

TRANSVERSAL The name given to a line that intersects or crosses two or more parallel lines.

TRIANGLE A three-sided polygon; the interior angles must add to 180°.

TWO-DIMENSIONAL FIGURE A flat shape, occurring in a plane, made up of line segments.

VARIABLE An unknown value; represented by a letter: x, y, z.

VERTEX The point where two rays meet to form an angle.

VERTICAL ANGLES Pairs of nonadjacent angles with a common vertex where two lines or line segments intersect. Vertical angles are congruent.

VOLUME The total amount of space inside a three-dimensional shape. Volume is similar in concept to area, because it measures the space inside of a shape.

VOLUME (OF A BOX) The space inside a box; $V = lwh$.

VOLUME (OF A CONE) The space inside a cone; $V = \frac{1}{3}\pi r^2 h$.

VOLUME (OF A CUBE) The space inside a cube. Since all faces and edges in a cube are congruent, the length, width, and height are all equal; volume is often expressed as side cubed: $V = s^3$.

VOLUME (OF A CYLINDER) The space inside a cylinder; equal to the area of the circular base times the height of the cylinder; $V = \pi r^2 h$.

VOLUME (OF A PYRAMID) The space inside a pyramid; $V = \frac{1}{3}Bh$.

VOLUME (OF A SPHERE) The space inside a sphere; $V = \frac{4}{3}\pi r^3$.

WEIGHTED AVERAGE   An average where different elements in the set have different amounts of importance (or weight) in the calculation.

***X*-INTERCEPT**   The point where a line intersects the *x*-axis.

***Y*-INTERCEPT**   The point where a line intersects the *y*-axis.

ZERO   The number at the center of the number line. Zero is neither positive nor negative. Zero is even.

Review Test

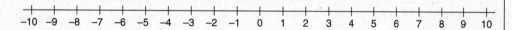

Translate and graph the following simple inequalities using the letter y for the unknown number. If needed, reverse the inequality so that y is always on the left side:

a. y is greater than –4

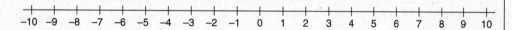

b. y is less than 6

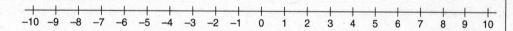

c. y is greater than or equal to 0

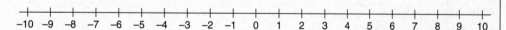

d. y is less than or equal to 3

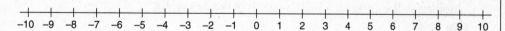

e. 7 is greater than y

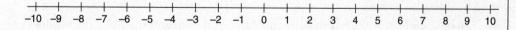

f. –2 is less than y

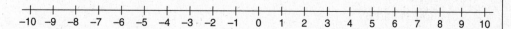

2. Translate the following compound inequalities using the letter *y* for the unknown number. If needed, reverse the inequality so that the smallest number is always on the left side:

a. *y* is less than 5 and greater than –2

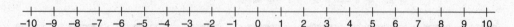

b. *y* is greater than –3 and less than 6

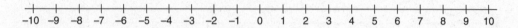

c. *y* is less than or equal to 7 and greater than –2

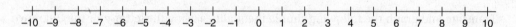

d. *y* is greater than or equal to –7 and less than 2

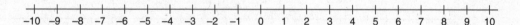

e. 9 is greater than *y* and 0 is less than *y*

f. 4 is greater than or equal to *y* and –6 is less than *y*

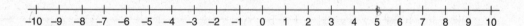

3. In the inequality "*y* is less than or equal to 5 and is greater than or equal to –2," the product of the endpoints will be which of the following?
(A) Odd
(B) Positive
(C) Negative
(D) None of the above

4. In the inequality "*y* is less than or equal to 7 and is greater than –2," the product of all the integer values for *y* will be which of the following?
(A) Even
(B) Zero
(C) Both A and B
(D) None of the above

5. In the inequality "y is greater than or equal to –3 and is less than or equal to 6," the product of the endpoints will be which of the following?
   (A) –18
   (B) –9
   (C) 9
   (D) 18

6. In the inequality "y is greater than or equal to –7 and is less than 2," the sum of the endpoints will be which of the following?
   (A) Positive
   (B) Negative
   (C) Zero
   (D) None of the above

7. Which describes all of the numbers in Set C?

   Set $C = \{2, 3, 5, 7, 11\}$

   (A) Prime
   (B) Even
   (C) Odd
   (D) Negative

QUESTIONS 8 AND 9 REFER TO THE FOLLOWING 3 EQUATIONS:

$$x = q^{11} \qquad y = q^7 \qquad z = q^{-2}$$

8. Which of the following expresses $\left(\dfrac{x}{y}\right)^3$ in terms of q?
   (A) q^{12}
   (B) q^{33}
   (C) q^{54}
   (D) q^{64}

9. Which of the following is equivalent to zx?
   (A) q^{13}
   (B) q^9
   (C) q^{-9}
   (D) q^{-13}

10. $\sqrt{397}$ is between which numbers?
   (A) 18 and 19
   (B) 19 and 20
   (C) 20 and 21
   (D) 21 and 22

11. $\sqrt{3}$ is between which numbers?
   (A) 0 and 1
   (B) 1 and 2
   (C) 2 and 3
   (D) 3 and 4

12. $\sqrt{26}$ is between which numbers?
   (A) 5 and 6
   (B) 6 and 7
   (C) 7 and 8
   (D) 8 and 9

13. $\sqrt{80}$ is equivalent to which of the following?
   (A) $4\sqrt{5}$
   (B) $5\sqrt{4}$
   (C) $2\sqrt{40}$
   (D) 40

14. $\sqrt{392}$ is equivalent to which of the following?
   (A) $2\sqrt{196}$
   (B) $14\sqrt{2}$
   (C) $2\sqrt{14}$
   (D) 14

15. A barrel has a volume of 50 gallons. It $\frac{3}{4}$ filled with water.

   a. What fraction of the container is empty?

   b. How many gallons of water are in the barrel?

16. Reduce to simplest terms:

   a. $\frac{128}{192}$

   b. $\frac{11}{121}$

17. Compare using <, >, or =

    a. $\dfrac{5}{8}$ —— $\dfrac{6}{7}$

    b. $\dfrac{9}{12}$ —— $\dfrac{12}{13}$

18. Solve the following:

    a. $\dfrac{4}{5} + \dfrac{3}{11} =$

    b. $\dfrac{12}{15} - \dfrac{9}{11} =$

19. Simplify the following:

    a. $\dfrac{3}{8} \bullet \dfrac{2}{5} =$

    b. $\dfrac{3}{8} \div \dfrac{2}{5} =$

20. Convert the mixed number to an improper fraction and the improper fraction to a mixed number:

    a. $3\dfrac{1}{6}$

    b. $\dfrac{19}{9}$

21. Simplify the following:

    a. 0.14×0.14

    b. $0.00225 \div 0.015$

22. Which of the following is equivalent to $(2.3 \times 10^{19}) \times (4.8 \times 10^{-14})$?
    (A) 11.04×10^6
    (B) 1.104×10^6
    (C) 71×10^6
    (D) 7.1×10^6

23. What number is 65% of 280?

24. 364 is 65% of what number?

25. What is the percent change from 280 to 182?

26. A leather laptop bag goes on sale. The price is reduced 35% from the original price of $280. What is the amount, in dollars, that the price was reduced?

27. Complete the table below by converting the given numbers into each of the other forms:

Fraction	Decimal	Percent
$\frac{1}{4}$		
$\frac{1}{2}$		
		75%
$\frac{1}{3}$		
		66%
		20%
$\frac{2}{5}$		
	0.6	
		80%
	0.125	
$\frac{3}{8}$		
		62.5%
$\frac{3}{4}$		
$\frac{7}{8}$		
$\frac{1}{10}$		
	0.5	

28. David's networking group has 30 men and 25 women as members. What is the ratio of women to men?

(A) 30 to 25

(B) 6 to 5

(C) 5 to 6

(D) 25 to 55

29. Kevin has a tattoo on his arm. If 65% of the skin on his arm is covered by the tattoo, what is the ratio of covered skin to uncovered skin on Kevin's arm?

(A) 35 to 65

(B) 13 to 7

(C) 7 to 13

(D) 65 to 100

30. Two thousand six hundred forty feet is what fraction of a mile? (1 mile = 5,280 feet)

31. Approximately how many tons are in 1,000 kilograms? (1 kilogram = 2.20 pounds)

32. 6 degrees Celsius is what temperature in degrees Fahrenheit? The conversion formula is °F = 1.8 (°C) + 32°.

Answers and Explanations

1. a. $y > -4$

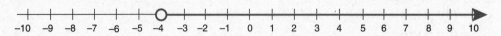

b. $y < 6$

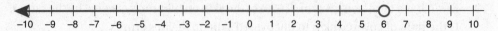

c. $y \geq 0$

d. $y \leq 3$

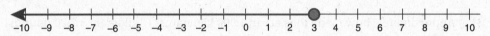

e. $y < 7$

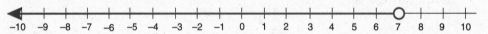

f. $y > -2$

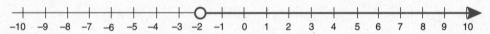

2. a. $-2 < y < 5$

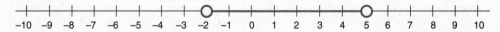

b. $-3 < y < 6$

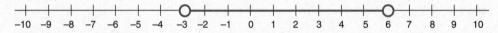

c. $-2 < y \leq 7$

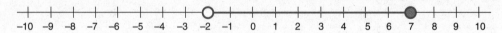

d. $-7 \leq y < 2$

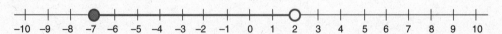

e. $0 < y < 9$

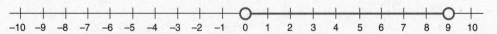

f. $-6 < y \leq 4$

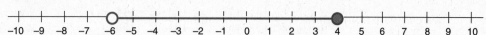

3. **(C)** When multiplying numbers with different signs, the product will be negative: $5 \times -2 = -10$.

4. **(C)** This problem asks for the product of all the integer values. This inequality includes zero. Any multiplication involving zero is equal to zero. Zero is even.

5. **(A)** When multiplying numbers with different signs, the product will be negative: $-3 \times 6 = -18$

6. **(B)** When adding numbers with different signs, subtract and use the sign of the number with the larger absolute value. Remember that 2 is not an endpoint. However $-7 + 1.999\ldots$ will give you a negative result.

7. **(A)** 2 is the only even prime number.

8. **(A)** Remember the rules for exponents with the same base: Multiplication means add the exponents together. Division means subtract the exponents. Raising a power to a power means multiply the exponents: $11 - 7 = 4 \rightarrow 4 \times 3 = 12$. The result is $-q^{12}$.

9. **(B)** Remember the rules for exponents with the same base. Multiplication means add the exponents together. Division means subtract the exponents. Raising a power to a power means multiply the exponents: $11 + (-2) = 9$. The result is q^9.

10. **(B)** 397 is between 361 (19^2) and 400 (20^2).

11. **(B)** 3 is between 1 (1^2) and 4 (2^2).

12. **(A)** 26 is between 25 (5^2) and 36 (6^2).

13. **(A)** $80 = 16 \times 5$. The square root of 16 is 4. $\sqrt{80} = \sqrt{16} \times 5 = 4\sqrt{5}$.

14. **(B)** $392 = 196 \times 2$. The square root of $196 = 14$. $\sqrt{392} = \sqrt{196} \times 2 = 14\sqrt{2}$.

15. **a.** $\dfrac{1}{4}$ The whole container = 1. So the empty portion is $1 - \dfrac{3}{4} = \dfrac{4}{4} - \dfrac{3}{4} = \dfrac{1}{4}$.

   b. 37.5 gallons Convert the fraction to a decimal: $\dfrac{3}{4} = 0.75$. Then multiply: $50 \times 0.75 = 37.5$.

16. **a.** $\dfrac{2}{3}$ $\dfrac{128}{192} = \dfrac{64}{96} = \dfrac{32}{48} = \dfrac{2}{3}$

   b. $\dfrac{1}{11}$ $\dfrac{11}{121} = \dfrac{1}{11}$

17. **a.** $<$ Convert each fraction to an equivalent fraction with a common denominator. Then compare numerators: $\dfrac{5}{8} \times \dfrac{7}{7} = \dfrac{35}{56}$ and $\dfrac{6}{7} \times \dfrac{8}{8} = \dfrac{48}{56}$.

   Since 35 is less than 48, $\dfrac{5}{8} < \dfrac{6}{7}$.

b. < Convert each fraction to an equivalent fraction with a common denominator. Then compare numerators: $\frac{9}{12} \times \frac{13}{13} = \frac{117}{156}$ and $\frac{12}{13} \times \frac{12}{12} = \frac{144}{156}$.

Since 117 is less than 144, $\frac{9}{12} < \frac{12}{13}$.

18. **a.** $1\frac{4}{55}$ $\frac{4}{5} + \frac{3}{11} = \frac{44}{55} + \frac{15}{55} = \frac{44+15}{55} = \frac{59}{55} = 1\frac{4}{55}$

     b. $-\frac{1}{55}$ $\frac{12}{15} - \frac{9}{11} = \frac{132}{165} - \frac{135}{165} = \frac{132-135}{165} = -\frac{3}{165} = -\frac{1}{55}$

19. **a.** $\frac{3}{20}$ $\frac{3}{8} \cdot \frac{2}{5} = \frac{6}{40} = \frac{3}{20}$

     b. $\frac{15}{16}$ $\frac{3}{8} \div \frac{2}{5} = \frac{3}{8} \cdot \frac{5}{2} = \frac{15}{16}$

20. **a.** $\frac{19}{6}$

     b. $2\frac{1}{9}$

21. **a. 0.0196** When multiplying decimals, first multiply as usual. Then account for all decimal places in both factors by moving the decimal in the product to the left, adding zeros to the left end as needed.

     b. 0.15 When dividing, move the decimal point in the divisor to the right until it is an integer. Then move the decimal point of the dividend the same number of places to the right. Divide as usual.

22. **(B)** Multiply the decimals numbers as usual: $2.3 \times 4.8 = 11.04$. Since this is multiplication, add the exponents of 10: $19 - 14 = 5$. Scientific notation conventionally puts the decimal point next to the units digit, which means we need one additional exponent of 10 to move the decimal point one place to the left: $11.04 \times 10^5 = 1.104 \times 10^6$.

23. **182** Use a proportion to solve.

$$\frac{\text{part}}{\text{whole}} = \frac{\%}{100} \rightarrow \frac{x}{280} = \frac{65}{100} \rightarrow 100x = 18,200 \rightarrow x = 182.$$

24. **560** Use a proportion to solve.

$$\frac{\text{part}}{\text{whole}} = \frac{\%}{100} \rightarrow \frac{364}{x} = \frac{65}{100} \rightarrow 65x = 36,400 \rightarrow x = 560.$$

25. **35%** Use a proportion to solve.

$$\frac{\text{difference}}{\text{original}} = \frac{\%}{100} \rightarrow \frac{98}{280} = \frac{x}{100} \rightarrow 280x = 9,800 \rightarrow x = 35.$$

The difference between the original number and the final number is $280 - 182 = 98$.

26. **$98** Use a proportion to solve.

$$\frac{\text{difference}}{\text{original}} = \frac{\%}{100} \rightarrow \frac{x}{280} = \frac{35}{100} \rightarrow 100x = 9{,}800 \rightarrow x = 98.$$

27.

Fraction	Decimal	Percent
$\frac{1}{4}$	0.25	25%
$\frac{1}{2}$	0.5	50%
$\frac{3}{4}$	0.75	75%
$\frac{1}{3}$	$0.33\ldots = 0.3\overline{3} \approx 0.33$	33% or $33.\overline{3}$% or $33\frac{1}{3}$ %
$\frac{2}{3}$	$0.66\ldots = 0.6\overline{6} \approx 0.67$	66%
$\frac{1}{5}$	0.2	20%
$\frac{2}{5}$	0.4	40%
$\frac{3}{5}$	0.6	60%
$\frac{4}{5}$	0.8	80%
$\frac{1}{8}$	0.125	12.5%
$\frac{3}{8}$	0.375	37.5%
$\frac{5}{8}$	0.625	62.5%
$\frac{3}{4}$	0.75	75%
$\frac{7}{8}$	0.875	87.5%
$\frac{1}{10}$	0.1	10%
$\frac{1}{2}$	0.5	50%

28. **(C)** The ratio of women to men is 25 to 30. Both numbers have a common factor of 5. $25 \div 5 = 5$ and $30 \div 5 = 6$. The ratio can be written as 5 to 6.

29. **(B)** If 65% is covered by the tattoo and 35% is not covered, the ratio is 65 to 35. Both numbers have a common factor of 5: $65 \div 5 = 13$ and $35 \div 5 = 7$. So the ratio can be written as 13 to 7.

30. $\frac{1}{2}$ Set up a proportion to solve: $\dfrac{x}{2{,}640 \text{ feet}} = \dfrac{1 \text{ mile}}{5{,}280 \text{ feet}}$.

Cross multiply: $5{,}280x = 2{,}640$. Divide to solve: $x = \dfrac{2{,}640}{5{,}280} = \dfrac{1}{2}$.

31. **1.1** First set up a proportion to solve for the number of pounds:

$$\frac{x}{1{,}000 \text{ kilograms}} = \frac{2.20 \text{ pounds}}{1 \text{ kilogram}}.$$

Cross multiply: $x = 2{,}200$ pounds. The question asks for the number of tons. Remember that 1 ton = 2,000 pounds. Use a proportion to convert into tons:

$$\frac{x}{2{,}200 \text{ pounds}} = \frac{1 \text{ ton}}{2{,}000 \text{ pounds}}$$

Cross multiply: $2{,}000x = 2{,}200$.

Divide to solve: $x = \dfrac{2{,}200}{2{,}000} = 1.1$.

32. **42.8 degrees Fahrenheit** Use the formula provided and substitute 6 for °C:
°F = $(1.8)(6°) + 32° = 10.8° + 32° = 42.8°$.

UNIT 3

Social Studies

Pretest

QUESTIONS 1 THROUGH 3 REFER TO THE FOLLOWING PASSAGE:

General Dwight D. Eisenhower's Order of the Day (1944)

Almost immediately after France fell to the Nazis in 1940, the Allies planned a cross-Channel assault on the German occupying forces. At the Quebec Conference in August 1943, Winston Churchill and Franklin Roosevelt reaffirmed the plan, which was code-named Overlord. Although Churchill acceded begrudgingly to the operation, historians note that the British still harbored persistent doubts about whether Overlord would succeed.

The decision to mount the invasion was cemented at the Teheran Conference held in November and December 1943. Joseph Stalin, on his first trip outside the Soviet Union since 1912, pressed Roosevelt and Churchill for details about the plan, particularly the identity of the supreme commander of Overlord. Churchill and Roosevelt told Stalin that the invasion "would be possible" by August 1, 1944, but that no decision had yet been made to name a supreme commander. To this latter point, Stalin pointedly rejoined, "Then nothing will come of these operations. Who carries the moral and technical responsibility for this operation?" Churchill and Roosevelt acknowledged the need to name the commander without further delay. Shortly after the conference ended, Roosevelt appointed Gen. Dwight David Eisenhower to that position.

By May 1944, 2,876,000 Allied troops were amassed in southern England. While awaiting deployment orders, they prepared for the assault by practicing with live ammunition. The largest armada in history, made up of more than 4,000 American, British, and Canadian ships, lay in wait. More that 1,200 planes stood ready to deliver seasoned airborne troops behind enemy lines, to silence German ground resistance as best they could, and to dominate the skies of the impending battle theater. Against a tense backdrop of uncertain weather forecasts, disagreements in strategy, and related timing dilemmas predicated on the need for optimal tidal conditions, Eisenhower decided before dawn on June 5 to proceed with Overlord. Later that same afternoon, he scribbled a note intended for release, accepting responsibility for the decision to launch the invasion and full blame should the effort to create a beachhead on the Normandy coast fail. Much more polished is his printed Order of the Day for June 6, 1944, which Eisenhower began drafting in February. The order was distributed to the 175,000-member expeditionary force on the eve of the invasion.

Source: ourdocuments.gov

1. Which of the following was the cause of the military action by the Allied powers?
   (A) The attack on Pearl Harbor
   (B) The Teheran Conference
   (C) Troops gathering in England
   (D) The German occupation of France

2. Which of the following can be assumed about the United States and England?
   (A) They were both Allied nations.
   (B) They were both Axis nations.
   (C) England was aligned with Germany.
   (D) Neither was involved in the war.

3. After 1912, when was the next year that Stalin left the Soviet Union?
   (A) 1943
   (B) 1944
   (C) 1945
   (D) 1946

QUESTIONS 4 AND 5 REFER TO THE FOLLOWING PASSAGE:

Official Program for the March on Washington (1963)

The civil rights movement in the United States during the late 1950s and 1960s was the political, legal, and social struggle to gain full citizenship rights for black Americans and to achieve racial equality. Individuals and civil rights organizations challenged segregation and discrimination using a variety of activities, including protest marches, boycotts, and refusal to abide by segregation laws.

On August 28, 1963, more than 250,000 demonstrators descended upon the nation's capital to participate in the "March on Washington for Jobs and Freedom." Not only was it the largest demonstration for human rights in United States history, but it also occasioned a rare display of unity among the various civil rights organizations. The event began with a rally at the Washington Monument featuring several celebrities and musicians. Participants then marched the mile-long National Mall to the Memorial. The three-hour long program at the Lincoln Memorial included speeches from prominent civil rights and religious leaders. The day ended with a meeting between the march leaders and President John F. Kennedy at the White House.

The idea for the 1963 March on Washington was envisioned by A. Philip Randolph, a long-time civil rights activist dedicated to improving the economic condition of black Americans. When Randolph first proposed the march in late 1962, he received little response from other civil rights leaders. He knew that cooperation would be difficult because each had his own agenda for the civil rights movement, and the leaders competed for funding and press coverage. Success of the March on Washington would depend on the involvement of the so-called

"Big Six"—Randolph and the heads of the five major civil rights organizations: Roy Wilkins of the National Association for the Advancement of Colored People (NAACP); Whitney Young, Jr., of the National Urban League; Rev. Martin Luther King, Jr., of the Southern Christian Leadership Conference (SCLC); James Farmer of the Conference of Racial Equality (CORE); and John Lewis of the Student Nonviolent Coordinating Committee (SNCC).

The details and organization of the march were handled by Bayard Rustin, Randolph's trusted associate. Rustin was a veteran activist with extensive experience in putting together mass protest. With only two months to plan, Rustin established his headquarters in Harlem, NY, with a smaller office in Washington. He and his core staff of 200 volunteers quickly put together the largest peaceful demonstration in U.S. history.

Source: ourdocuments.gov

4. Which of the following ideas is exemplified in protest marches?
   (A) Suffrage
   (B) Jim Crow laws
   (C) Natural rights
   (D) Freedom of assembly

5. The "March on Washington for Jobs and Freedom" was the largest demonstration in United States history. What does this suggest about the Civil Rights Movement?
   (A) A large number of Americans believed in the civil rights movement.
   (B) The civil rights movement represented a minority of the population.
   (C) The civil rights movement was not successful.
   (D) The civil rights movement led to equality for all.

Answers

1. **(D)** The first sentence indicates that an Allied assault was the result of the fall of France.
2. **(A)** The entire passage details the cooperation of the United States and England.
3. **(A)** The second paragraph indicates 1943 was the first time since 1912 that Stalin left the Soviet Union.
4. **(D)** Protests are a form of assembly.
5. **(A)** The number of participants indicates a broad belief in the civil rights movement.

Social Studies Skills

10

The GED® test tests your ability to read, interpret, and respond to social studies texts, maps, charts, graphs, and political cartoons. Six different types of items will be used to evaluate your literacy skills in social studies:

→ **MULTIPLE CHOICE**

→ **DROP DOWN**

→ **FILL IN THE BLANK**

→ **DRAG AND DROP**

→ **HOT SPOT**

→ **EXTENDED RESPONSE**

The following skills will be covered in this unit:

Lesson 1: Drawing Conclusions and Making Inferences

Lesson 2: Identifying Central Ideas and Drawing Conclusions

Lesson 3: Analyzing Events and Ideas

Lesson 4: Analyzing Language

Lesson 5: Integrating Content Presented in Different Ways

Lesson 6: Evaluating Reasoning and Evidence

Lesson 7: Writing Analytic Responses to Source Texts

COLLEGE AND CAREER READINESS ANCHOR STANDARDS FOR READING

Note on range and content of student reading:

Reading is critical to building knowledge in history/social studies. . . . College and career ready reading in these fields requires an appreciation of the norms and conventions of each discipline, such as the kinds of evidence used in history and science; an understanding of domain-specific words and phrases; an attention to precise details; and the capacity to evaluate intricate arguments, synthesize complex information, and follow detailed descriptions of events and concepts. In history/social studies, for example, students need to be able to analyze, evaluate, and differentiate primary and secondary sources. . . . Students must be able to read complex informational texts in these fields with independence and confidence because the vast majority of reading in college and workforce training programs will be sophisticated nonfiction. It is important to note that these Reading standards are meant to complement the specific content demands of the disciplines, not replace them.

The grades 6–12 standards on the following pages define what students should understand and be able to do by the end of each grade span. They correspond to the College and Career Readiness (CCR) anchor standards below by number. The CCR and grade-specific standards are necessary complements—the former providing broad standards, the latter providing additional specificity—that together define the skills and understanding that all students must demonstrate.

KEY IDEAS AND DETAILS

1. Read closely to determine what the text says explicitly and to make logical inferences from it; cite specific textual evidence when writing or speaking to support conclusions drawn from the text.
2. Determine central ideas or themes of a text and analyze their development; summarize the key supporting details and ideas.
3. Analyze how and why individuals, events, or ideas develop and interact over the course of a text.

CRAFT AND STRUCTURE

4. Interpret words and phrases as they are used in a text, including determining technical, connotative, and figurative meanings, and analyze how specific word choices shape meaning or tone.
5. Analyze the structure of texts, including how specific sentences, paragraphs, and larger portions of the text (e.g., a section, chapter, scene, or stanza) relate to each other and the whole.
6. Assess how point of view or purpose shapes the content and style of a text.

INTEGRATION OF KNOWLEDGE AND IDEAS

7. Integrate and evaluate content presented in diverse formats and media, including visually and quantitatively, as well as in words.
8. Delineate and evaluate the argument and specific claims in a text, including the validity of the reasoning as well as the relevance and sufficiency of the evidence.
9. Analyze how two or more texts address similar themes or topics in order to build knowledge or to compare the approaches the authors take.

RANGE OF READING AND LEVEL OF TEXT COMPLEXITY

10. Read and comprehend complex literary and informational texts independently and proficiently.

© Copyright 2010. National Governors Association Center for Best Practices and Council of Chief State School Officers. All rights reserved.

LESSON 1: DRAWING CONCLUSIONS AND MAKING INFERENCES

Reading a social studies document is much like reading any other type of document. It requires the reader to be able to identify elements that are stated or implied by the text and to make reasonable assumptions based on the supplied information.

Details

Specific pieces of information in social studies documents, such as dates, locations, incidents, and so on, are known as details. The details are what support the larger idea of the passage. In other words, details are the proof in an argument and the happenings in the larger event.

Summaries

Maybe you don't realize it, but you summarize things all the time. Think about the last time somebody asked you, "What did you do yesterday?" You probably didn't say, "Well, I woke up, got out of bed, walked into the kitchen and over to the refrigerator. When I got to the refrigerator, I opened it and took out the milk." You probably didn't continue to provide an account of every move you made. Instead, what did you say? Your response was a summary.

Another perspective on summarizing and a way to be an active reader is to think like a detective. When a crime takes place, the detective's job is to determine what has happened. While the detective is piecing together what transpired, he or she tries to find answers to the 5W's and 1H. The 5W's and 1H are:

Who?
What?
When?
Where?
Why?
How?

As we discussed in the Reasoning Through Language Arts section, the answers to the above questions will outline the most important information in the passage. A summary is defined as a short restatement of the most important ideas in the passage. So if you're able to assemble these answers into a sentence or two, you have just effectively summarized a passage.

Unstated Assumptions, Implications, and Inferences

Although some answers to questions can be found directly in the passages and excerpts, questions will often require the reader to determine what is suggested by the passage. In other words, you will have to read between the lines to answer these questions. You will have to make assumptions.

If you're reading an article about how the Constitution was adopted in Philadelphia, Pennsylvania, chances are the author is not going to explain that Pennsylvania is a state located on the East Coast of the United States of America. The author is going to assume that you already know this and therefore require no further explanation.

Another way passages convey information without directly stating it is through implication. An implication is when an author uses information to suggest something or indicate a particular belief. The author does not directly state the item or belief.

Although assumptions and implications are more about what the author does with the information at hand, inferences are more about what you as the reader do with the information. Making an inference requires the reader to look at the available information and data and then determine what reasonable conclusion can be made.

Evidence to Support Inference Analyses

When making inferences, you must be able to back up your belief with evidence. In other words, go with your gut but make sure that you have the solid facts to back it.

PRACTICE

TIP

When answering questions or writing reponses, you must provide evidence to support your position.

Pacific Railway Act (1862)

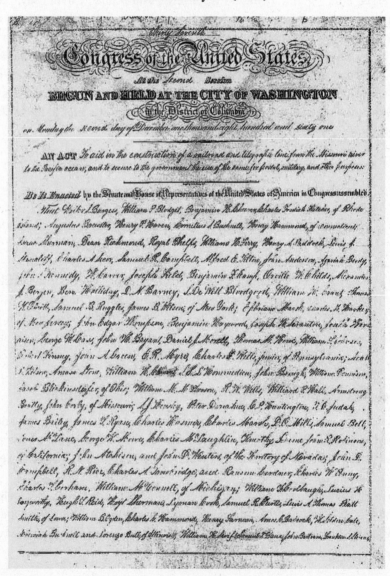

The question of "internal improvements" was constantly before Congress in the 19th century: Should Congress assist in improving the country's transportation system? One such improvement was the dream of constructing a railroad that would cross the entire country. In the 1850s, Congress commissioned several topographical surveys across the West to determine the best route for a railroad, but private corporations were reluctant to undertake the task without Federal assistance. In 1862 Congress passed the Pacific Railway Act, which designated the 32nd parallel as the initial transcontinental route and gave huge grants of lands for rights-of-way. The act was an effort to aid in the construction of a railroad and telegraph line from the Missouri River to the Pacific Ocean and to secure the use of that line to the government.

The legislation authorized two railroad companies, the Union Pacific and the Central Pacific, to construct the lines. Beginning in 1863, the Union Pacific, employing more than 8,000 Irish, German, and Italian immigrants, built west from Omaha, NE; the Central Pacific, whose workforce included over 10,000 Chinese laborers, built eastward from Sacramento, CA. Each company faced unprecedented construction problems—mountains, severe weather, and the hostility of Native Americans. On May 10, 1869, in a ceremony at Promontory, UT, the last rails were laid and the last spike driven. Congress eventually authorized four transcontinental railroads and granted 174 million acres of public lands for rights-of-way.

Source: ourdocuments.gov

1. Which of the following is a conclusion that can be drawn from the passage?
   (A) Irish, German, Italian, and Chinese immigrants put pressure on Congress to pass the Pacific Railway Act.
   (B) The country's railway system needed to be improved.
   (C) Congress was obligated to approve the Pacific Railway Act.
   (D) The Pacific Railway act was the result of people moving west during the gold rush.

Answer and Explanation

1. **(B)** The passage clearly states that the idea of railway improvement was an issue and the Pacific Railway Act was the result. Option A is incorrect. It identifies groups that were hired to build the railways. However, no evidence is provided in the passage to suggest that they put pressure onto Congress. No evidence is in the passage to support either option C or option D.

PRACTICE

QUESTIONS 1 AND 2 ARE BASED ON THE FOLLOWING PASSAGE:

Voting Rights Act (1965)

This "act to enforce the fifteenth amendment to the Constitution" was signed into law 95 years after the amendment was ratified. In those years, African Americans in the South faced tremendous obstacles to voting, including poll taxes, literacy tests, and other bureaucratic restrictions to deny them the right to vote. They also risked harassment, intimidation, economic reprisals, and physical violence when they tried to register or vote. As a result, very few African Americans were registered voters, and they had very little, if any, political power, either locally or nationally.

In 1964, numerous demonstrations were held, and the considerable violence that erupted brought renewed attention to the issue of voting rights. The murder of voting-rights activists in Mississippi and the attack by state troopers on peaceful marchers in Selma, AL, gained national attention and persuaded President Johnson and Congress to initiate meaningful and effective national voting rights legislation. The combination of public revulsion to the violence and Johnson's political skills stimulated Congress to pass the voting rights bill on August 5, 1965.

The legislation, which President Johnson signed into law the next day, outlawed literacy tests and provided for the appointment of Federal examiners (with the power to register qualified citizens to vote) in those jurisdictions that were "covered" according to a formula provided in the statute. In addition, Section 5 of the act required covered jurisdictions to obtain "preclearance" from either the District Court for the District of Columbia or the U.S. Attorney General for any new voting practices and procedures. Section 2, which closely followed the language of the 15th Amendment, applied a nationwide prohibition of the denial or abridgment of the right to vote on account of race or color. The use of poll taxes in national elections had been abolished by the 24th Amendment (1964) to the Constitution; the Voting Rights Act directed the Attorney General to challenge the use of poll taxes in state and local elections. In *Harper v. Virginia State Board of Elections*, 383 U.S. 663 (1966), the Supreme Court held Virginia's poll tax to be unconstitutional under the 14th amendment.

Because the Voting Rights Act of 1965 was the most significant statutory change in the relationship between the Federal and state governments in the area of voting since the Reconstruction Period following the Civil War, it was immediately challenged in the courts. Between 1965 and 1969, the Supreme Court issued several key decisions upholding the constitutionality of Section 5 and affirming the broad range of voting practices for which preclearance was required.

The law had an immediate impact. By the end of 1965, a quarter of a million new black voters had been registered, one-third by Federal examiners. By the end of 1966, only 4 out of the 13 southern states had fewer than 50 percent of African Americans registered to vote. The Voting Rights Act of 1965 was readopted and strengthened in 1970, 1975, and 1982.

Source: ourdocuments.gov

1. Based on the passage, which of the following assumptions can be made?
   (A) Poll taxes in national elections were abolished by the 24th amendment.
   (B) Only white men who owned land were permitted to vote.
   (C) Currently, nearly 99% of all African Americans living in southern states are registered to vote.
   (D) Prior to 1965, less than 50% of the African American population in southern states were typically registered to vote.

2. What is the likely reason that there were a quarter of a million newly registered black voters by the end of 1965?
   (A) African Americans wanted to vote but were unable to previously.
   (B) Prior to 1965, it was difficult to track who was and who wasn't registered to vote.
   (C) Caucasians in southern states came to accept African Americans.
   (D) The number of registered African-American voters was actually miscounted prior to 1965.

Answers and Explanations

1. **(D)** The passage makes a point of saying that by the end of 1966, most of the states had less than 50% of African Americans unregistered. Citing this benchmark indicates that this was not true previously. Option A is incorrect because it is directly stated in the passage. It is not an assumption. Options B and C are incorrect because no evidence supports these claims.

2. **(A)** The passage indicates that African Americans held demonstrations for fair voting legislation prior to 1965. Options B, C, and D are incorrect because no evidence supports these answer choices.

LESSON 2: IDENTIFYING CENTRAL IDEAS AND DRAWING CONCLUSIONS

Central Ideas

The central idea of a social studies passage is the main idea of the paragraph or passage; it is the main point that the author is trying to convey. All the other elements in the passage are known as supporting details. As we discussed in Lesson 1, details are pieces of evidence that support the central idea.

Think of the central idea as the roof of a house and the supporting details as the beams. The central idea covers all the supporting details like a roof covers the beams. The supporting details uphold the central idea like the beams support and hold up the roof.

Where can we find the central idea? As discussed earlier in the Reasoning Through Language Arts section, the main idea can be found in various places. Most of the time, it is located in the first sentence or two. Sometimes it is at the end of the passage. Occasionally, it is not stated at all.

Drawing Conclusions

Drawing a conclusion utilizes many of the components we've already discussed. After you recognize the details and central idea and have asked yourself the 5W's and 1H, you can look at the evidence and ask, "What does this mean?" Like a detective, the evidence is put together to form a conclusion about what the evidence means.

PRACTICE

QUESTIONS 1 AND 2 ARE BASED ON THE FOLLOWING PASSAGE:

Monroe Doctrine (1823)

President James Monroe's 1823 annual message to Congress contained the Monroe Doctrine, which warned European powers not to interfere in the affairs of the Western Hemisphere.

Understandably, the United States has always taken a particular interest in its closest neighbors—the nations of the Western Hemisphere. Equally understandably, expressions of this concern have not always been favorably regarded by other American nations.

The Monroe Doctrine is the best-known U.S. policy toward the Western Hemisphere. Buried in a routine annual message delivered to Congress by President James Monroe in December 1823, the doctrine warns European nations that the United States would not tolerate further colonization or puppet monarchs. The doctrine was conceived to meet major concerns of the moment, but it soon became a watchword of U.S. policy in the Western Hemisphere.

The Monroe Doctrine was invoked in 1865 when the U.S. government exerted diplomatic and military pressure in support of the Mexican President Benito Juárez. This support enabled Juárez to lead a successful revolt against the Emperor Maximilian, who had been placed on the throne by the French government.

Almost 40 years later, in 1904, European creditors of a number of Latin American countries threatened armed intervention to collect debts. President Theodore Roosevelt promptly proclaimed the right of the United States to exercise an "international police power" to curb such "chronic wrongdoing." As a result, U. S. Marines were sent into Santo Domingo in 1904, Nicaragua in 1911, and Haiti in 1915, ostensibly to keep the Europeans out. Other Latin American nations viewed these interventions with misgiving, and relations between the "great Colossus of the North" and its southern neighbors remained strained for many years.

In 1962, the Monroe Doctrine was invoked symbolically when the Soviet Union began to build missile-launching sites in Cuba. With the support of the Organization of American States, President John F. Kennedy threw a naval and air quarantine around the island. After several tense days, the Soviet Union agreed to withdraw the missiles and dismantle the sites. Subsequently, the United States dismantled several of its obsolete air and missile bases in Turkey.

Source: ourdocuments.gov

1. Based on the passage, what was the central idea or purpose of the Monroe Doctrine?

   _____

   _____

   _____

   _____

   _____

2. Cite two details from the passage that support the central idea or purpose of the Monroe Doctrine.

   _____

   _____

   _____

   _____

   _____

Answers and Explanations

1. The first paragraph states that the purpose of the Monroe Doctrine was to warn European powers not to interfere in the affairs of the Western Hemisphere.

2. Details that support the central idea include:

   - In 1823, President Monroe warned European nations about further colonization in the Western Hemisphere.
   - The U.S. supported Mexico in 1865 in a revolt against the French government.
   - Between 1904 and 1915, the U.S. entered Santo Domingo, Nicaragua, and Haiti in order to keep out European creditors.
   - In 1962, the U.S. set up an air and naval quarantine around Cuba in order to keep the Soviet Union from completing their missile-launching sites.

QUESTIONS 1 AND 2 ARE BASED ON THE FOLLOWING PASSAGE:

Excerpt from *Democracy in America*
by Alexis de Tocqueville

The remarks I have made will suffice to display the character of Anglo-American civilization in its true light. It is the result (and this should be constantly present to the mind of two distinct elements), which in other places have been in frequent hostility, but which in America have been admirably incorporated and combined with one another. I allude to the spirit of Religion and the spirit of Liberty.

The settlers of New England were at the same time ardent sectarians and daring innovators. Narrow as the limits of some of their religious opinions were, they were entirely free from political prejudices. Hence arose two tendencies, distinct but not opposite, which are constantly discernible in the manners as well as in the laws of the country.

It might be imagined that men who sacrificed their friends, their family, and their native land to a religious conviction were absorbed in the pursuit of the intellectual advantages which they purchased at so dear a rate. The energy, however, with which they strove for the acquirement of wealth, moral enjoyment, and the comforts as well as liberties of the world, is scarcely inferior to that with which they devoted themselves to Heaven.

Political principles and all human laws and institutions were molded and altered at their pleasure; the barriers of the society in which they were born were broken down before them; the old principles which had governed the world for ages were no more; a path without a turn and a field without an horizon were opened to the exploring and ardent curiosity of man: but at the limits of the political world he checks his researches, he discreetly lays aside the use of his most formidable faculties, he no longer consents to doubt or to innovate, but carefully abstaining from raising the curtain of the sanctuary, he yields with submissive respect to truths which he will not discuss. Thus, in the moral world everything is classed, adapted, decided, and foreseen; in the political world everything is agitated, uncertain, and disputed: in the one is a passive, though a voluntary, obedience; in the other an independence scornful of experience and jealous of authority.

These two tendencies, apparently so discrepant, are far from conflicting; they advance together, and mutually support each other.

Religion perceives that civil liberty affords a noble exercise to the faculties of man, and that the political world is a field prepared by the Creator for the efforts of the intelligence. Contented with the freedom and the power which it enjoys in its own sphere, and with the place which it occupies, the empire of religion is never more surely established than when it reigns in the hearts of men unsupported by aught beside its native strength. Religion is no less the companion of liberty in all its battles and its triumphs; the cradle of its infancy, and the divine source of its claims. The safeguard of morality is religion, and morality is the best security of law and the surest pledge of freedom.

Source: gutenberg.org

1. What was the central idea conveyed in the fourth paragraph?
   (A) Everything in the moral world is classified.
   (B) People changed laws as they wanted.
   (C) Things rarely change.
   (D) Things have changed from how they have been.

2. What can you conclude about the author's view on religion based on the last paragraph?
   (A) Religion supports freedom.
   (B) Religion has no effect on freedom.
   (C) Religion can negatively impact freedom.
   (D) Religion and morality have no connection.

Answers and Explanations

1. **(D)** The numerous supporting details all suggest that things have changed. Option C is incorrect because there is no evidence to support this statement. Options A and B are incorrect. Although they are stated in the passage, they do not encompass the broader idea of the paragraph.

2. **(A)** Since religion safeguards morality and since morality is the best security of law and surest pledge of freedom, religion indirectly supports freedom. Options B and C are incorrect because no information in the passage supports these statements. Option D is incorrect; the opposite is stated in the passage.

The test will sometimes ask you to compare or to contrast various topics. Sometimes it will ask you about the cause or about the effect of a situation. Test takers often confuse what these words mean. You must know and understand what each of these terms mean because all four will likely be on the test.

Compare and Contrast

Comparing and contrasting have different meanings. Very often people say "compare" when they really mean "contrast." When we compare two things, we describe the ways in which they are similar. For example, both a dog and a cat have four legs and fur. When we contrast two things, we describe the ways in which they are different. For example, a dog barks, but a cat purrs. When responding to questions on the Social Studies subject test, make sure you distinguish between questions that are asking you to compare and questions that are asking you to contrast.

Cause and Effect

A cause is an action, and an effect is what happens as a result of that action. Although this may seem simple and straightforward, cause-and-effect relationships can often be confusing because an effect of one action may be the cause of another action.

Chronological Order and Sequence

Chronological order means putting things in time order. Sequence simply means putting things in the order in which they belong. In terms of your ability to read well, understand social studies passages, and write effective responses to passages, you must be able to think sequentially. In order to understand a situation fully, you need to understand the order in which the events took place. In order for you to write an effective response to a prompt, the sentences and paragraphs you write must be in a logical order that is going to make sense and be clear to the reader.

PRACTICE

QUESTIONS 1 AND 2 REFER TO THE FOLLOWING PASSAGE:

Social Security Act (1935)

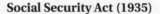

Before the 1930s, support for the elderly was a matter of local, state and family rather than a Federal concern (except for veterans' pensions). However, the widespread suffering caused by the Great Depression brought support for numerous proposals for a national old-age insurance system. On January 17, 1935, President Franklin D. Roosevelt sent a message to Congress asking for "social security" legislation. The same day, Senator Robert Wagner of New York and Representative David Lewis of Maryland introduced bills reflecting the administration's views. The resulting Senate and House bills encountered opposition from those who considered it a governmental invasion of the private sphere and from those who sought exemption from payroll taxes for employers who adopted government-approved pension plans. Eventually the bill passed both houses, and on August 15, 1935, President Roosevelt signed the Social Security Act into law.

The act created a uniquely American solution to the problem of old-age pensions. Unlike many European nations, U.S. social security "insurance" was supported from "contributions" in the form of taxes on individuals' wages and employers' payrolls rather than directly from Government funds. The act also provided funds to assist children, the blind, and the unemployed; to institute vocational training programs; and provide family health programs. As a result, enactment of Social Security brought into existence complex administrative challenges. The Social Security Act authorized the Social Security Board to register citizens for benefits, to administer the contributions received by the Federal Government, and to send payments to recipients. Prior to Social Security, the elderly routinely faced the prospect of poverty upon retirement. For the most part, that fear has now dissipated.

Source: ourdocuments.gov

1. According to the passage, the Social Security Act was a result of what event?

_____

_____

_____

_____

2. Put the following events into chronological order.
   (A) President Roosevelt signed the Social Security Act into law.
   (B) Old-age care was a matter of family support.
   (C) President Roosevelt asked for "social security" legislation.
   (D) The Unites States was faced with administrative difficulties.
   (E) The bill passed both houses.

Answers and Explanations

1. The passage indicates that as a result of the widespread suffering during the Great Depression, there was support for a form of old-age insurance. Since Social Security is old-age insurance, it was obviously a result of the Great Depression.

2. (B, C, E, A, D) The passage clearly indicates that old-age care was a matter of family support. Then President Roosevelt asked for "social security" legislation. The bill passed both houses, and President Roosevelt signed the Social Security Act into law. Finally, the Unites States was faced with administrative difficulties.

PRACTICE

QUESTIONS 1 THROUGH 3 ARE BASED ON THE FOLLOWING PASSAGE:

"The Declaration of Sentiments"
by the Seneca Falls Conference

When, in the course of human events, it becomes necessary for one portion of the family of man to assume among the people of the earth a position different from that which they have hitherto occupied, but one to which the laws of nature and of nature's God entitle them, a decent respect to the opinions of mankind requires that they should declare the causes that impel them to such a course.

We hold these truths to be self-evident: that all men and women are created equal; that they are endowed by their Creator with certain inalienable rights; that among these are life, liberty, and the pursuit of happiness; that to secure these rights governments are instituted, deriving their just powers from the consent of the governed. Whenever any form of government becomes destructive of these ends, it is the right of those who suffer from it to refuse allegiance to it, and to insist upon the institution of a new government, laying its foundation on such principles, and organizing its powers in such form, as to them shall seem most likely to effect their safety and happiness. Prudence, indeed, will dictate that governments long established should not be changed for light and transient causes; and accordingly all experience hath shown that mankind are more disposed to suffer while evils are sufferable, than to right themselves by abolishing the forms to which they are accustomed. But when a long train of abuses and usurpations, pursuing invariably the same object, evinces a design to reduce them under absolute despotism, it is their duty to throw off such government, and to provide new guards for their future security. Such has been the patient sufferance of the women under this government, and such is now the necessity which constrains them to demand the equal station to which they are entitled. The history of mankind is a history of repeated injuries and usurpations on the part of man toward woman, having in direct object the establishment of an absolute tyranny over her. To prove this, let facts be submitted to a candid world.

The history of mankind is a history of repeated injuries and usurpations on the part of man toward woman, having in direct object the establishment of an absolute tyranny over her. To prove this, let facts be submitted to a candid world.

He has never permitted her to exercise her inalienable right to the elective franchise.

He has compelled her to submit to laws, in the formation of which she had no voice.

He has withheld from her rights which are given to the most ignorant and degraded men—both natives and foreigners.

Having deprived her of this first right of a citizen, the elective franchise, thereby leaving her without representation in the halls of legislation, he has oppressed her on all sides.

He has made her, if married, in the eye of the law, civilly dead. He has taken from her all right in property, even to the wages she earns.

He has made her, morally, an irresponsible being, as she can commit many crimes with impunity, provided they be done in the presence of her husband. In the covenant of marriage, she is compelled to promise obedience to her husband, he becoming, to all intents and purposes, her master—the law giving him power to deprive her of her liberty, and to administer chastisement.

He has so framed the laws of divorce, as to what shall be the proper causes, and in case of separation, to whom the guardianship of the children shall be given, as to be wholly regardless of the happiness of women—the law, in all cases, going upon a false supposition of the supremacy of man, and giving all power into his hands.

After depriving her of all rights as a married woman, if single, and the owner of property, he has taxed her to support a government which recognizes her only when her property can be made profitable to it.

He has monopolized nearly all the profitable employments, and from those she is permitted to follow, she receives but a scanty remuneration. He closes against her all the avenues to wealth and distinction which he considers most honorable to himself. As a teacher of theology, medicine, or law, she is not known.

He has denied her the facilities for obtaining a thorough education, all colleges being closed against her.

He allows her in church, as well as state, but a subordinate position, claiming apostolic authority for her exclusion from the ministry, and, with some exceptions, from any public participation in the affairs of the church.

He has created a false public sentiment by giving to the world a different code of morals for men and women, by which moral delinquencies which exclude women from society are not only tolerated, but deemed of little account in man.

He has usurped the prerogative of Jehovah himself, claiming it as his right to assign for her a sphere of action, when that belongs to her conscience and to her God.

He has endeavored, in every way that he could, to destroy her confidence in her own powers, to lessen her self-respect, and to make her willing to lead a dependent and abject life.

Now, in view of this entire disfranchisement of one-half the people of this country, their social and religious degradation—in view of the unjust laws above mentioned, and because women do feel themselves aggrieved, oppressed, and fraudulently deprived of their most sacred rights, we insist that they have immediate admission to all the rights and privileges which belong to them as citizens of the United States.

1. What value is embodied in the second paragraph?
   (A) Communism
   (B) Natural rights philosophy
   (C) Democracy
   (D) States rights

2. Many of the paragraphs begin with "He has. . . ." What does this suggest the author believed about men?
   (A) Men were the head of the household.
   (B) Men had inflicted many offenses upon women.
   (C) Up to that point, men were primarily the ones in office.
   (D) This passage was written by a man.

3. How are men and women contrasted in this passage?
   (A) Both men and women are created equal.
   (B) The author believes that women are oppressed and that men are the oppressors.
   (C) Men and women both should have the right to vote.
   (D) Men and women should adhere to the traditional roles.

Answers and Explanations

1. **(B)** The author cites the Declaration of Independence in the second paragraph, which is rooted in natural rights philosophy. Options A and C are incorrect because the passage is not referring to forms of government. Option D is incorrect because the topic was not a matter of state rights.

2. **(B)** "He has" is followed mostly by negative and limiting words, indicating that these statements are about offenses against women. Options A and C are incorrect because the passage is clearly against traditional roles and privileges. Option D is incorrect because no evidence suggests that the passage was written by man.

3. **(B)** The passage repeatedly shows that men and women are treated differently by society and law. Both option A and option C are incorrect because they indicate how men and women are similar, not different. Option D is incorrect. This argument does not appear in the passage.

Bias and Propaganda

Authors don't always write objectively. Sometimes they want to push an agenda. They try to convince others of something in order to achieve some objective. Bias exists when an author does not give a balanced, objective description of an issue. This may be intentional or unintentional. Propaganda is material that is purposefully misleading. It is usually used to promote a particular political agenda.

Credibility

How do we know if the individual who has authored a passage is credible? Unfortunately, determining an author's credibility is often difficult without doing further research. However, you can look for certain things in the writing to determine the author's credibility:

- Has the author cited facts?
- Has the author avoided using his or her opinion as evidence?
- Has the author given data from a reputable source?
- Is the author affiliated with a reputable organization?

If the answer to all of these questions is "yes," there is a good chance that the material is credible and that the information is likely to be objective.

Meaning of Symbols, Words, and Phrases

Whether in fiction or in nonfiction, symbols, words, and phrases very often have meanings not found in a dictionary. You must analyze these symbols, words, and phrases in order to fully understand the meaning of the text. For example, if the author writes, "That's water under the bridge," he or she is not talking about either water or bridges. That phrase means the topic or subject is over and cannot be changed.

PRACTICE

Senate Resolution 301: Censure of Senator Joseph McCarthy (1954)

The early years of the Cold War saw the United States facing a hostile Soviet Union, the "loss" of China to communism, and war in Korea. In this politically charged atmosphere, fears of Communist influence over American institutions spread easily. On February 9, 1950, Joseph McCarthy, a Republican Senator from Wisconsin, claimed that he had a list of 205 State Department employees who were Communists. While he offered little proof, the claims gained the Senator great notoriety. In June, Senator Margaret Chase Smith of Maine and six fellow Republicans issued a "Declaration of Conscience" asserting that because of McCarthy's tactics, the Senate had been "debased to the level of a forum for hate and character assassination." However, McCarthy took advantage of the Cold War atmosphere of fear and suspicion. With strong support in the opinion polls, McCarthy's attacks and interventions in senatorial elections brought defeat to some of his party's Democratic opponents.

After Republicans took control of the White House and Congress in 1953, McCarthy was named chairman of the Committee on Government Operations and its Subcommittee on Investigations. From these posts, he continued to accuse Government agencies of being "soft" on communism, but he was now attacking a Republican administration. In 1954 McCarthy's investigation of security threats in the U.S. Army was televised. McCarthy's bullying of witnesses turned public opinion against the Senator. On December 2, 1954, the Senate voted to censure him, describing his behavior as "contrary to senatorial traditions."

Republican Senators Ralph Flanders of Vermont, Arthur Watkins of Utah, and Margaret Chase Smith of Maine led the efforts to discipline McCarthy. Flanders introduced two separate resolutions against McCarthy, one removing McCarthy from his chairmanships and the other calling for his censure. The censure resolution moved forward with debate beginning July 30, 1954. The full Senate took up the resolution on November 5. This copy of the resolution catches the debate on November 9 as the Senate refined the wording of its resolution. The substance of the first count, charging McCarthy with failure to cooperate with a Senate subcommittee, remained unchanged in the final resolution. The second count was dropped for a condemnation of McCarthy's attacks on the very members of the committee that considered his censure.

Source: ourdocuments.gov

1. Senator McCarthy's claim that he had a list of 205 State Department workers who were Communists is most like what other event?
   (A) The witch hunts of the 1600s
   (B) The search for Osama Bin Laden
   (C) An effort to find the individual responsible for leaking classified government information
   (D) The investigation into Nixon's involvement in the Watergate scandal.

Answer and Explanation

1. **(A)** In both situations, widespread fear led to false accusations. Option B is incorrect because Osama Bin Laden claimed responsibility for the 9/11 attacks. Option C is incorrect because the individual responsible for leaking classified information actually committed a crime. So that person was not pursued falsely. Option D is incorrect; an investigation is not an accusation.

PRACTICE

QUESTIONS 1 AND 2 ARE BASED ON THE FOLLOWING EXCERPT:

Excerpt from President Franklin Roosevelt's Radio Address
Unveiling the Second Half of the New Deal (1936)

Our vision for the future contains more than promises.

This is our answer to those who, silent about their own plans, ask us to state our objectives.

Of course we will continue to seek to improve working conditions for the workers of America—to reduce hours over-long, to increase wages that spell starvation, to end the labor of children, to wipe out sweatshops. Of course we will continue every effort to end monopoly in business, to support collective bargaining, to stop unfair competition, to abolish dishonorable trade practices. For all these we have only just begun to fight.

Of course we will continue to work for cheaper electricity in the homes and on the farms of America, for better and cheaper transportation, for low interest rates, for sounder home financing, for better banking, for the regulation of security issues, for reciprocal trade among nations, for the wiping out of slums. For all these we have only just begun to fight.

Of course we will continue our efforts in behalf of the farmers of America. With their continued cooperation we will do all in our power to end the piling up of huge surpluses which spelled ruinous prices for their crops. We will persist in successful action for better land use, for reforestation, for the conservation of water all the way from its source to the sea, for drought and flood control, for better marketing facilities for farm commodities, for a definite reduction of farm tenancy, for encouragement of farmer cooperatives, for crop insurance and a stable food supply. For all these we have only just begun to fight.

Of course we will provide useful work for the needy unemployed; we prefer useful work to the pauperism of a dole.

Here and now I want to make myself clear about those who disparage their fellow citizens on the relief rolls. They say that those on relief are not merely jobless—that they are worthless. Their solution for the relief problem is to end relief—to purge the rolls by starvation. To use the language of the stockbroker, our needy unemployed would be cared for when, as, and if some fairy godmother should happen on the scene.

You and I will continue to refuse to accept that estimate of our unemployed fellow Americans. Your Government is still on the same side of the street with the Good Samaritan and not with those who pass by on the other side.

Again—what of our objectives?

Of course we will continue our efforts for young men and women so that they may obtain an education and an opportunity to put it to use. Of course we will continue our help for the crippled, for the blind, for the mothers, our insurance for the unemployed, our security for the aged. Of course we will continue to protect the consumer against unnecessary price spreads, against the costs that are added by monopoly and speculation. We will continue our successful efforts to increase his purchasing power and to keep it constant.

For these things, too, and for a multitude of others like them, we have only just begun to fight.

All this—all these objectives—spell peace at home. All our actions, all our ideals, spell also peace with other nations.

Today there is war and rumor of war. We want none of it. But while we guard our shores against threats of war, we will continue to remove the causes of unrest and antagonism at home which might make our people easier victims to those for whom foreign war is profitable. You know well that those who stand to profit by war are not on our side in this campaign.

"Peace on earth, good will toward men"—democracy must cling to that message. For it is my deep conviction that democracy cannot live without that true religion which gives a nation a sense of justice and of moral purpose. Above our political forums, above our market places stand the altars of our faith—altars on which burn the fires of devotion that maintain all that is best in us and all that is best in our Nation.

We have need of that devotion today. It is that which makes it possible for government to persuade those who are mentally prepared to fight each other to go on instead, to work for and to sacrifice for each other. That is why we need to say with the Prophet: "What doth the Lord require of thee—but to do justly, to love mercy and to walk humbly with thy God." That is why the recovery we seek, the recovery we are winning, is more than economic. In it are included justice and love and humility, not for ourselves as individuals alone, but for our Nation.

That is the road to peace.

Source: ourdocuments.gov

1. What is the central idea of the speech, which indicates President Roosevelt's opinion?
   (A) People without jobs are not contributing their fair share.
   (B) It is not the government's role to provide for the people.
   (C) People should work harder to pull themselves out of poverty.
   (D) The American people deserve programs that would benefit them.

2 What is the central idea of the third paragraph?
   (A) The rights of the workers must be taken into account.
   (B) The rights of business always outweigh the rights of the individual.
   (C) Labor unions have ended child labor problems.
   (D) Unfair trade practices will always be a part of business.

Answers and Explanations

1. **(D)** President Roosevelt outlines various programs to assist the American public. Options A, B, and C are incorrect. No evidence is provided to support these answers.

2. **(A)** The paragraph itemizes what will be done in favor of laborers. Option B is incorrect; the paragraph suggests the opposite. Options C and D are incorrect. No evidence is provided to support these.

Analysis of Maps, Graphic Organizers, Tables, and Charts

When analyzing maps, graphic organizers, tables, and charts, it is important to look at all of the information available. First, look for any headings or titles as they can provide a concise overview of the data. Second, look at any labels. They will indicate the specific type of data being displayed. Third, look to see if there is a key of some type. It will define any symbols you may encounter. Finally, look at the big picture and ask yourself, "What is the central idea of this information?" Following these steps will help you fully analyze and understand what is being displayed.

Trends in Data

The exam is going to test your ability, not only to locate specific pieces of data, but to identify trends as well. The word *trend* simply refers to the direction in which something is moving. So if housing costs are trending upward, this means the costs are increasing.

Maps

When analyzing maps, examine all the information provided. See if there is a title, a legend or key, and labels. Additionally, make sure you read all passages that correspond with the map as they may contain valuable information and help you further analyze the map.

Examine the sample map that follows:

I-95 Population Density Profile, 2010

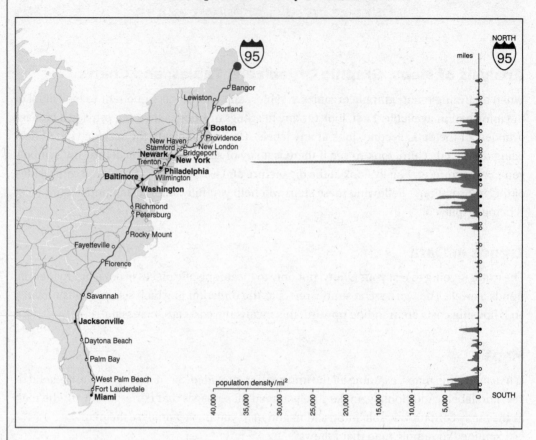

Running from Florida to Maine, I-95 passes through 15 states and several major cities. I-95 serves the most densely populated region of the U.S., the Boston-to-Washington corridor. Peaks and valleys in population density within 5 miles of the interstate show several stretches of continuously built-up area, especially evident from Petersburg, VA to Lewiston, ME. Selected cities along the route are labeled, for reference.

NOTES: Data are from the 2010 Census. The graph is based on average population density within 5 miles of the I-95 route, in 2-mile increments, using 2010 block group centroids.

This map, which also has a graph embedded in it, displays the population density along the I-95 corridor. Both the title and the graph indicate that these refer to population density. The title and graph also mention in three different spots that the corridor is, in fact, I-95. Additionally, notice that some of the cities are in bold and others are not. Can you figure out why? What do the bolded cities have in common? The bolded cities are all large cities or capitals.

SET, MEAN, MEDIAN, MODE, AND RANGE

As discussed in more detail in the Mathematical Reasoning section, mean, median, mode, and range are ways of looking at and analyzing data. These can be applied not only to math questions but to social studies questions as well.

Set

A set is a group of numbers that conveys information in numeric form. An example of a set is 2, 7, 5, 4, 2.

Mean

The mean is the average of a set of numbers. To calculate the mean, add all the elements together and divide by the number of elements. For example, if the set is 2, 7, 5, 4, 2, adding all of these elements together gives $2 + 7 + 5 + 4 + 2 = 20$. Since there are 5 elements, divide 20 by 5 to get 4. The mean is 4.

Median

The median is the middle of a set of numbers when the numbers are in order from smallest to largest. As many numbers in the set are larger than the median as are smaller than the median.

- In a set with an odd number of elements, the median is the middle element when the set is arranged in ascending order (from smallest to largest).
- In a set with an even number of elements, the median is the average of the middle two elements when the set is arranged in ascending order.

For example, if the set is 2, 7, 5, 4, 2, start by placing the values in order: 2, 2, 4, 5, 7. This set has an odd number of elements, and the middle number is 4. So the median is 4. If, instead, the set is 2, 4, 5, 7, 8, 10, it contains an even number of elements. The two middle numbers are 5 and 7. Since their average is 6, the median is 6.

Mode

The mode is the most frequently occurring element in the set. A set of numbers can have more than one mode or can have no mode.

- In the set 2, 7, 5, 4, 2, the 2 occurs the most often. The mode is 2.
- In the set 2, 7, 5, 4, 2, 7, both the 2 and the 7 occur the most often. The mode is 2 and 7.
- In the set 2, 4, 5, 7, 8, 10, all of the numbers occur only once. There is no mode.

Range

The range of a set of numbers is the difference between the smallest element and largest element in the set. Sometimes range is referred to as the spread of data. In the set 2, 7, 5, 4, 2, the smallest number is 2 and the largest is 7. So the range is 7 minus 2, which equals 5. The range is 5.

Tables

Look at the table below. What sort of information is it giving you? Look at the title, the column headings, and the units. If a question asked you to find how many billions of dollars of Chinese imports came into the U.S. in 2004, you would go to the column heading labeled "China Imports" and go down to the year 2004. The table indicates that $44.66 billion in Chinese imports came into the U.S. in 2004.

PRACTICE

QUESTIONS 1 THROUGH 3 REFER TO THE FOLLOWING TABLE:

Table 1: Statistical Discrepancy of Westbound Trade

Year	U.S. Exports	China Imports	Bilateral Discrepancy	Discrepancy in Percentage
2000	16.25	22.36	6.11	27.3%
2004	34.72	44.66	9.94	22.3%
2006	55.22	59.21	3.99	6.7%
2008	71.46	81.36	9.90	12.2%
2009	69.57	77.46	7.89	10.2%
2010	91.88	102.1	10.22	10.0%

Unit: Billions of U.S. Dollars

Source: eoc.gov

1. The total value of U.S. exports in 2009 totaled $_____ billion dollars.

2. The total percent discrepancy in 2006 was _____%.

3. The total discrepancy for 2008 was $_____ billion dollars.

Answers

1. **69.57**

2. **6.7**

3. **9.90**

PRACTICE

QUESTIONS 1 AND 2 ARE BASED ON THE FOLLOWING TABLE:

Table 2: Numbers of Marriages and Divorces by State: ACS (2008) and Vital Statistics (2007)

State	Marriages			Divorces		
	Vital Statistics	ACS		Vital Statistics	ACS	
	Couples	Men	Women	Couples	Men	Women
Total	2,197,000	2,327,018	2,227,084	1,087,920	1,178,915	1,309,921
Alabama	41,622	40,125	40,292	21,255	24,509	26,329
Alaska	5,800	7,822	6,366	2,897	3,710	3,216
Arizona	39,495	46,961	42,762	24,515	28,503	30,434
Arkansas	34,275	28,099	28,749	16,858	12,164	16,607
California	225,920	281,580	259,206	—	119,315	145,281
Colorado	34,160	43,314	40,853	21,177	25,646	22,943
Connecticut	19,502	23,824	22,960	11,194	12,703	12,556
Delaware	4,970	5,309	5,143	3,215	3,720	4,318
District of Columbia	2,418	4,524	4,616	994	2,818	2,241
Florida	155,929	132,171	132,618	84,373	74,045	81,444
Georgia	64,034	75,167	73,496	—	41,601	45,466
Hawaii	27,346	10,078	9,265	—	4,411	4,062
Idaho	14,981	15,687	15,062	7,348	6,048	8,538
Illinois	76,830	87,648	79,645	33,239	43,643	51,272
Indiana	44,441	50,417	47,932	—	30,648	30,620
Iowa	19,895	22,917	24,275	7,622	11,192	12,119
Kansas	19,024	26,904	24,809	9,426	13,768	14,396
Kentucky	33,351	37,164	35,299	19,743	22,018	26,533
Louisiana	32,787	36,583	35,425	—	17,343	19,007
Maine	9,870	8,924	9,324	5,614	6,620	6,744
Maryland	36,618	44,190	43,125	16,662	21,889	23,592
Massachusetts	37,895	38,648	37,089	14,644	20,098	24,329
Michigan	56,996	65,593	64,943	34,502	40,202	40,952
Minnesota	30,070	38,624	38,179	—	19,211	19,613
Mississippi	15,824	23,821	23,023	13,095	15,477	13,909
Missouri	40,405	48,540	46,267	22,223	25,604	27,830
Montana	7,263	7,300	7,287	3,901	3,752	4,062
Nebraska	12,159	17,544	17,109	6,151	8,504	6,993
Nevada	126,354	22,323	21,944	16,593	13,220	11,244
New Hampshire	9,350	9,237	8,663	4,981	5,145	5,059
New Jersey	46,519	59,179	55,511	25,687	23,616	31,466
New Mexico	11,229	17,594	17,487	8,434	7,380	8,224
New York	129,943	130,216	121,435	55,068	53,679	58,514

	Marriages			Divorces		
	Vital Statistics	ACS		Vital Statistics	ACS	
State	Couples	Men	Women	Couples	Men	Women
North Carolina	63,932	75,105	70,200	36,205	33,930	38,293
North Dakota	4,316	6,907	6,265	1,925	2,672	1,583
Ohio	70,632	80,228	78,787	38,884	43,778	47,365
Oklahoma	26,508	34,478	33,983	18,954	19,230	24,471
Oregon	26,664	31,120	30,052	14,499	15,788	17,549
Pennsylvania	71,094	78,722	75,752	35,508	40,128	42,323
Rhode Island	6,786	6,785	6,298	3,006	3,461	3,834
South Carolina	34,908	27,155	28,849	13,194	16,505	18,311
South Dakota	6,170	6,939	5,555	2,442	3,548	2,885
Tennessee	62,149	48,689	47,170	26,501	30,790	33,060
Texas	176,313	205,704	194,389	77,810	101,116	119,569
Utah	25,060	27,783	28,538	9,491	12,145	14,036
Vermont	5,317	3,997	3,911	2,256	2,938	2,688
Virginia	58,289	64,009	59,375	29,516	29,606	36,032
Washington	41,397	58,974	55,971	26,138	30,109	33,311
West Virginia	13,303	14,208	13,461	9,299	7,480	9,873
Wisconsin	32,159	42,301	42,393	16,458	18,996	22,624
Wyoming	4,826	5,887	5,976	2,610	4,493	2,201

Source: American Community Survey, 2008 and Division of Vital Statistics, National Center for Health Statistics, CDC, 2007

1. How many couples were married in Connecticut?
   (A) 19,502
   (B) 23,824
   (C) 20,960
   (D) 11,194

2. About how many more couples got married than divorced?
   (A) 2,200,000
   (B) 1,100,000
   (C) 870,000
   (D) 500,000

Answers and Explanations

1. **(A)** Locate the state, then follow your finger over to the couples number under the marriage column.

2. **(B)** If you subtract the total number of divorces from the total number of marriages, the result is about 1,100,000.

When an author writes about a particular topic, the author often reveals a great deal about himself or herself. The passages that you'll encounter on the Social Studies subject test will be informational texts. However, they may not be objective. The author may shed light on his or her values by using both fact and opinion to make a point.

Fact and Opinion

The differences between a fact and an opinion can be confusing. So you must consider the options carefully when encountering a question that deals with fact and opinion. Remember that a fact has objective truth. In other words, a fact can't be argued about. In contrast, an opinion is how someone feels about a fact. For example, it is a fact that the stock market crashed in 1929. However, it is an opinion that the government should have done something to prevent the crash. One cannot argue that the stock market didn't crash in 1929. However, one could argue that the United States government should not have done more to prevent the crash.

Reasoned Judgment

When a person makes a reasoned judgment, he or she is using both fact and opinion in the argument. Reasoned judgment involves taking one side of an argument by using facts to support that position.

Unsupported Claims and Informed Hypotheses

We've all heard the old adage, "Don't believe everything you hear." This holds true for the passages you will read on the Social Studies subject test. Secondary sources, such as editorials, may take one side or the other on a particular issue and make certain claims. Instead of using reasoned judgment, though, they make a claim and do not provide the needed evidence to support the claim.

In contrast to an unsupported claim, an informed hypothesis is rooted in fact. Sufficient evidence is provided to support the hypothesis.

NOTE

A fact has objective truth, but opinions may vary.

PRACTICE

QUESTIONS 1 AND 2 ARE BASED ON THE FOLLOWING PASSAGE:

Excerpt from Transcript of
President Woodrow Wilson's 14 Points (1918)

All the peoples of the world are in effect partners in this interest, and for our own part we see very clearly that unless justice be done to others it will not be done to us. The programme of the world's peace, therefore, is our programme; and that programme, the only possible programme, as we see it, is this:

I. Open covenants of peace, openly arrived at, after which there shall be no private international understandings of any kind but diplomacy shall proceed always frankly and in the public view.

II. Absolute freedom of navigation upon the seas, outside territorial waters, alike in peace and in war, except as the seas may be closed in whole or in part by international action for the enforcement of international covenants.

III. The removal, so far as possible, of all economic barriers and the establishment of an equality of trade conditions among all the nations consenting to the peace and associating themselves for its maintenance.

IV. Adequate guarantees given and taken that national armaments will be reduced to the lowest point consistent with domestic safety.

V. A free, open-minded, and absolutely impartial adjustment of all colonial claims, based upon a strict observance of the principle that in determining all such questions of sovereignty the interests of the populations concerned must have equal weight with the equitable claims of the government whose title is to be determined.

VI. The evacuation of all Russian territory and such a settlement of all questions affecting Russia as will secure the best and freest cooperation of the other nations of the world in obtaining for her an unhampered and unembarrassed opportunity for the independent determination of her own political development and national policy and assure her of a sincere welcome into the society of free nations under institutions of her own choosing; and, more than a welcome, assistance also of every kind that she may need and may herself desire. The treatment accorded Russia by her sister nations in the months to come will be the acid test of their good will, of their comprehension of her needs as distinguished from their own interests, and of their intelligent and unselfish sympathy.

VII. Belgium, the whole world will agree, must be evacuated and restored, without any attempt to limit the sovereignty which she enjoys in common with all other free nations. No other single act will serve as this will serve to restore confidence among the nations in the laws which they have themselves set and determined for the government of their relations with one another. Without this healing act the whole structure and validity of international law is forever impaired.

VIII. All French territory should be freed and the invaded portions restored, and the wrong done to France by Prussia in 1871 in the matter of Alsace-Lorraine, which has unsettled the peace of the world for nearly fifty years, should be righted, in order that peace may once more be made secure in the interest of all.

IX. A readjustment of the frontiers of Italy should be effected along clearly recognizable lines of nationality.

X. The peoples of Austria-Hungary, whose place among the nations we wish to see safeguarded and assured, should be accorded the freest opportunity to autonomous development.

XI. Rumania, Serbia, and Montenegro should be evacuated; occupied territories restored; Serbia accorded free and secure access to the sea; and the relations of the several Balkan states to one another determined by friendly counsel along historically established lines of allegiance and nationality; and international guarantees of the political and economic independence and territorial integrity of the several Balkan states should be entered into.

XII. The Turkish portion of the present Ottoman Empire should be assured a secure sovereignty, but the other nationalities which are now under Turkish rule should be assured an undoubted security of life and an absolutely unmolested opportunity of autonomous development, and the Dardanelles should be permanently opened as a free passage to the ships and commerce of all nations under international guarantees.

XIII. An independent Polish state should be erected which should include the territories inhabited by indisputably Polish populations, which should be assured a free and secure access to the sea, and whose political and economic independence and territorial integrity should be guaranteed by international covenant.

XIV. A general association of nations must be formed under specific covenants for the purpose of affording mutual guarantees of political independence and territorial integrity to great and small states alike.

In regard to these essential rectifications of wrong and assertions of right we feel ourselves to be intimate partners of all the governments and peoples associated together against the Imperialists. We cannot be separated in interest or divided in purpose. We stand together until the end.

For such arrangements and covenants we are willing to fight and to continue to fight until they are achieved; but only because we wish the right to prevail and desire a just and stable peace such as can be secured only by removing the chief provocations to war, which this program does remove. We have no jealousy of German greatness, and there is nothing in this program that impairs it. We grudge her no achievement or distinction of learning or of pacific enterprise such as have made her record very bright and very enviable. We do not wish to injure her or to block in any way her legitimate influence or power. We do not wish to fight her either with arms or with hostile arrangements of trade if she is willing to associate herself with us and the other peace-loving nations of the world in covenants of justice and law and fair dealing. We wish her only to accept a place of equality among the peoples of the world,—the new world in which we now live,—instead of a place of mastery.

Source: ourdocuments.gov

1. Which of the following is an opinion expressed in the first paragraph?
   - (A) The world should work together.
   - (B) Every country should work independently.
   - (C) World peace is unattainable.
   - (D) Partnering with other countries will be difficult.

2. What did the 14 points have in common?
   - (A) They are absolute truths.
   - (B) They are Woodrow Wilson's opinions on foreign-policy issues.
   - (C) They are mandated by the Constitution.
   - (D) They are mandatory for world peace.

Answers and Explanations

1. **(A)** The passage states that the people of the world are partners, which is an opinion. Options B, C, and D are incorrect; no evidence supports any of these answers.

2. **(B)** The word "should," which is often used in this passage, indicates preference and therefore opinion. Option A is incorrect because no evidence suggests that these are absolute truths. Options C and D are incorrect because no evidence supports these answers.

Constructing a well-written extended response on the Social Studies subject test is very similar to constructing one on the Reasoning Through Language Arts subject test.

Development of Ideas

As a teacher, I've had moments when I have not explained an idea as well as I should have. As a result, my students did not fully understand the concept. The same can happen when writing an extended response. Even if you understand the topic, make sure you explain everything to your audience. Fully explain why each idea is relevant to your argument.

Supporting Evidence

Just like an author must provide evidence to support his or her position, you must provide adequate supporting evidence in your extended response to support your argument. Chances are that enough material is available in the stimulus passages for you to use in your response. However, if you choose to add outside information, make sure that it is relevant to the topic and agrees with your argument.

Clarity and Sequence

Have you ever put together a piece of furniture or built a model airplane? What would happen if you started on the last step of the directions rather than the first? The assembly would probably not go so well. The same is true when writing an extended response. Your extended response must proceed in a logical fashion. This means that the order in which you choose to put your main points and details really does matter. Some common methods include using chronological order, size order, or order of importance.

UNIT 3: SOCIAL STUDIES

The Mayflower Compact
November 11, 1620

In the name of God, Amen. We, whose names are underwritten, the Loyal Subjects of our dread Sovereigne Lord, King James, by the Grace of God, of Great Britaine, France, and Ireland, King, Defender of the Faith, c.

Having undertaken for the Glory of God, and Advancement of the Christian Faith, and the Honour of our King and Country, a Voyage to plant the first colony in the Northerne Parts of Virginia; doe, by these Presents, solemnly and mutually in the Presence of God and one of another, covenant and combine ourselves together into a civill Body Politick, for our better Ordering and Preservation, and Furtherance of the Ends aforesaid; And by Virtue hereof do enact, constitute, and frame, such just and equall Laws, Ordinances, Acts, Constitutions, and Offices, from time to time, as shall be thought most meete and convenient for the Generall Good of the Colonie; unto which we promise all due Submission and Obedience.

In Witness whereof we have hereunto subscribed our names at Cape Cod the eleventh of November, in the Raigne of our Sovereigne Lord, King James of England, France, and Ireland, the eighteenth, and of Scotland, the fiftie-fourth, Anno. Domini, 1620.

Source: gutenberg.org

Transcript of the Constitution of the United States (1787)

We the People of the United States, in Order to form a more perfect Union, establish Justice, insure domestic Tranquility, provide for the common defense, promote the general Welfare, and secure the Blessings of Liberty to ourselves and our Posterity, do ordain and establish this Constitution for the United States of America.

Article. I.

Section. 1.
All legislative Powers herein granted shall be vested in a Congress of the United States, which shall consist of a Senate and House of Representatives.

Section. 2.
The House of Representatives shall be composed of Members chosen every second Year by the People of the several States, and the Electors in each State shall have the Qualifications requisite for Electors of the most numerous Branch of the State Legislature.

No Person shall be a Representative who shall not have attained to the Age of twenty five Years, and been seven Years a Citizen of the United States, and who shall not, when elected, be an Inhabitant of that State in which he shall be chosen.

Representatives and direct Taxes shall be apportioned among the several States which may be included within this Union, according to their respective Numbers, which shall be determined by adding to the whole Number of free Persons, including those bound to Service for a Term of Years, and excluding Indians not taxed, three fifths of all other Persons. The actual Enumeration shall be made within three Years after the first Meeting of the Congress of the United States, and within every subsequent Term of ten Years, in such Manner as they shall by Law direct. The Number of Representatives shall not exceed one for every thirty Thousand, but each State shall have at Least one Representative; and until such enumeration shall be made, the State of New Hampshire shall be entitled to [choose] three, Massachusetts eight, Rhode-Island and Providence Plantations one, Connecticut five, New-York six, New Jersey four, Pennsylvania eight, Delaware one, Maryland six, Virginia ten, North Carolina five, South Carolina five, and Georgia three.

When vacancies happen in the Representation from any State, the Executive Authority thereof shall issue Writs of Election to fill such Vacancies.

The House of Representatives shall [choose] their Speaker and other Officers; and shall have the sole Power of Impeachment.

Source: ourdocuments.gov

1. Compare and contrast the ideas expressed in these two documents.

   _____

   _____

   _____

   _____

   _____

Explanation

Make sure you have discussed the ways in which these documents are similar and the ways in which they are different.

PRACTICE

Excerpt from the Declaration of Independence (1776)

IN CONGRESS, July 4, 1776.

The unanimous Declaration of the thirteen united States of America

When in the Course of human events, it becomes necessary for one people to dissolve the political bands which have connected them with another, and to assume among the powers of the earth, the separate and equal station to which the Laws of Nature and of Nature's God entitle them, a decent respect to the opinions of mankind requires that they should declare the causes which impel them to the separation.

We hold these truths to be self-evident, that all men are created equal, that they are endowed by their Creator with certain unalienable Rights, that among these are Life, Liberty and the pursuit of Happiness.—That to secure these rights, Governments are instituted among Men, deriving their just powers from the consent of the governed, —That whenever any Form of Government becomes destructive of these ends, it is the Right of the People to alter or to abolish it, and to institute new Government, laying its foundation on such principles and organizing its powers in such form, as to them shall seem most likely to effect their Safety and Happiness. Prudence, indeed, will dictate that Governments long established should not be changed for light and transient causes; and accordingly all experience hath shown, that mankind are more disposed to suffer, while evils are sufferable, than to right themselves by abolishing the forms to which they are accustomed. But when a long train of abuses and usurpations, pursuing invariably the same Object evinces a design to reduce them under absolute Despotism, it is their right, it is their duty, to throw off such Government, and to provide new Guards for their future security.—Such has been the patient sufferance of these Colonies; and such is now the necessity which constrains them to alter their former Systems of Government. The history of the present King of Great Britain is a history of repeated injuries and usurpations, all having in direct object the establishment of an absolute Tyranny over these States. . . .

In every stage of these Oppressions We have Petitioned for Redress in the most humble terms: Our repeated Petitions have been answered only by repeated injury. A Prince whose character is thus marked by every act which may define a Tyrant, is unfit to be the ruler of a free people.

Nor have We been wanting in attentions to our British brethren. We have warned them from time to time of attempts by their legislature to extend an unwarrantable jurisdiction over us. We have reminded them of the circumstances of our emigration and settlement here. We have appealed to their native justice and magnanimity, and we have conjured them by the ties of our common kindred to disavow these usurpations, which, would inevitably interrupt our connections and correspondence. They too have been deaf to the voice of justice and of consanguinity. We must, therefore, acquiesce in the necessity, which denounces our Separation, and hold them, as we hold the rest of mankind, Enemies in War, in Peace Friends.

We, therefore, the Representatives of the united States of America, in General Congress, Assembled, appealing to the Supreme Judge of the world for the rectitude of our intentions, do, in the Name, and by Authority of the good People of these Colonies, solemnly publish and declare, That these United Colonies are, and of Right ought to be Free and Independent States; that they are Absolved from all Allegiance to the British Crown, and that all political connection between them and the State of Great Britain, is and ought to be totally dissolved; and that as Free and Independent States, they have full Power to levy War, conclude Peace, contract Alliances, establish Commerce, and to do all other Acts and Things which Independent States may of right do. And for the support of this Declaration, with a firm reliance on the protection of divine Providence, we mutually pledge to each other our Lives, our Fortunes and our sacred Honor.

Source: ourdocuments.gov

1. Describe the reasoning used to explain how people are entitled to certain rights.

    _____

    _____

    _____

    _____

    _____

Explanation

Make sure you explain why the author thinks people are entitled to certain rights and how he argues that point.

Although the GED® test does not include a separate vocabulary section, the passages will contain high-level vocabulary words and questions will ask you to define words in context. Additionally, having a broad vocabulary is absolutely essential for fully understanding the passages you read. For these reasons, we have included this vocabulary section.

ABOLISH   To do away with something completely.

ALLIED POWERS   The nations that were aligned with the United States during World War I and World War II.

AMENDMENT   A change or an addition to a legal document.

ARTICLES OF CONFEDERATION   The original agreement between the 13 colonies; a precursor to the Constitution.

ASSIMILATE   To become like something or someone else.

AXIS POWERS   The nations that were against the United States in World War I and World War II.

BILL OF RIGHTS   A founding document of the United States that outlines basic rights of the individual.

BROWN V. BOARD OF EDUCATION   Landmark Supreme Court case that ended segregation in schools.

CAPITAL   Money or other items of value used in business.

CAPITALISM   An economic system based on free trade.

CHECKS AND BALANCES   System to ensure that no one branch of the government (executive, legislative, or judicial) has too much power.

CIVICS   Relating to the civil government.

COLONIZATION   The establishment of a country's citizens in another territory.

COMMUNISM   An economic system that is wholly run and controlled by the state.

COMPARATIVE ADVANTAGE   The ability of one company or country to produce a good at a lower cost than another company or country.

CONSERVATISM   A political philospohy that subscribes to traditional beliefs and small government.

CONSTITUTION OF THE UNITED STATES   A founding document on which the government of the United States is based.

CONSTITUTIONALISM   A governmental framework where powers are limited and divided among various branches.

CULTURAL DIFFUSION   The spread of ideas among cultures.

CULTURE The set of beliefs, customs, and traditions of a group of people.

DECLARATION OF INDEPENDENCE One of the founding documents that declared the 13 original colonies independent from Great Britain.

DEFLATION An increase in the value of money.

DEMAND The amount of a product that people are willing to buy.

DIASPORA A group of people who live together but outside their home country.

DIRECT DEMOCRACY A type of democracy where people vote on issues directly.

ELECTORAL COLLEGE The group of people who directly elect the president.

EMIGRATION The act of leaving one country to live in another.

ENTREPRENEURSHIP The setting up of a business venture.

EXECUTIVE BRANCH The branch of government of which the president is the head; responsible for carrying out laws.

FASCISM A harsh and authoritarian form of government.

FEDERAL GOVERNMENT The central government of the country.

FISCAL POLICIES Policies dealing with budgets.

GDP The gross domestic product; the value of all goods and services produced within a country.

GREAT MIGRATION The movement of millions of African Americans from the south to the industrialized cities of the north.

HOLOCAUST The period during World War II when 6 million Jews and millions of others were killed in German concentration camps.

HOUSE OF REPRESENTATIVES A portion of the U.S. Congress; the number of representatives elected from each state is determined by the population of that state; part of the legislative branch.

IMMIGRATION The act of moving into a country from another to live in the new country.

INCENTIVES Something that influences a person or people to do something.

INDUSTRIAL REVOLUTION The development and introduction of machinery in industry.

INFLATION The devaluation of money.

INTERDEPENDENCE The mutual dependence of people, businesses, countries, or other entities.

ISOLATIONISM A policy that dictates that a country not become entangled in the affairs of other countries.

JAPANESE-AMERICAN INTERNMENT The imprisonment of over 100,000 Japanese-Americans by the U.S. government after the attack on Pearl Harbor.

JIM CROW LAWS Laws that were put in place in the south to limit the freedoms of African Americans.

JUDICIAL BRANCH The branch of government responsible for deciding the consitutionality of various issues; the Supreme Court.

LEAGUE OF NATIONS The precursor to the United Nations.

LEGISLATIVE BRANCH The Senate and House of Representatives; the Congress; the part of the federal government responsible for making laws.

LIBERALISM A political philosophy that subscribes to progressive beliefs and a strong central government.

MANIFEST DESTINY The idea that the United States would inevitably expand from coast to coast.

MARKETS Exchanges where stocks, commodities, or other things of value are bought, sold, and traded.

MARSHALL PLAN Aid given to European countries after World War II.

MAYFLOWER COMPACT The first governing document of the Plymouth Colony.

MELTING POT The term used to describe the assimilation of immigrants in the United States.

MIGRATION The movement from one place to another.

MILITARISM The idea that a government must maintain a strong military.

MONARCHY A form of government with one ruler, such as a king or an emperor.

MONOPOLIES Companies that have exclusive control over a type of business or product so that no other companies can realistically compete.

NATIONALISM Having great pride in one's country.

NATIONHOOD The condition of being a nation.

NATO North Atlantic Treaty Organization; a group where member nations agreed to mutual defense.

NATURAL RESOURCES The raw materials available in a certain area.

NATURAL RIGHTS Rights that everyone posesses regardless of laws.

NEUTRALITY ACTS Laws passed by Congress to keep the United States neutral.

PARLIAMENTARY DEMOCRACY A two-house form of democracy.

PLESSY V. FERGUSON Landmark Supreme Court case where racial segregation and "separate but equal" were upheld.

PRESIDENTIAL DEMOCRACY A democracy where a president is head of the executive branch of a government.

PRICE The cost of something.

PROFIT Money made after the cost of producing a good has been paid.

RECONSTRUCTION The period of time when the South rebuilt after the Civil War.

REGULATION The act of setting policies and laws.

REPRESENTATIVE DEMOCRACY A democracy where elected officials make decisions for the people.

RURAL Refers to an agricultural area.

SCIENTIFIC REVOLUTION A time of great advances in science and math during the 18th and 19th centuries.

SECTIONALISM Extreme local patriotism.

SEGREGATION The act of separating people by ethnicity.

SENATE A portion of the U.S. Congress; each state elects two senators; part of the legislative branch.

STATEHOOD The condition of being a state.

SUBURBAN Refers to an area that is less populous than a city but is not rural.

SUFFRAGE The right to vote.

SUPPLY The amount of a product available to be sold.

SUSTAINABILITY The ability to maintain something, such as the environment.

TARIFFS Taxes.

TOTALITARIANISM A form of government where the ruler has complete power.

TREATY OF VERSAILLES The post–World War I treaty that demanded repayment from Germany.

TRUMAN DOCTRINE The belief that the United States should provide aid to countries that were threatened by communist forces.

URBAN Relating to a city.

WARREN COURT DECISIONS Refers to decisions made while Earl Warren was Chief Justice of the Supreme Court and that expanded civil rights and liberties.

WARSAW PACT A mutual protection treaty that was the precursor to NATO.

WATERGATE SCANDAL The political scandal that led to the resignation of Richard M. Nixon.

Review Test

DIRECTIONS: This practice exam contains passages, maps, charts, graphs, and political cartoons, which you will need to analyze in order to answer the questions that follow. The first portion of the exam has 33 questions. In the second portion of the exam, you will be asked to write an extended response to multiple stimuli.

QUESTIONS 1 THROUGH 3 ARE BASED ON THE FOLLOWING GRAPH AND PASSAGE:

Press Release Announcing U.S. Recognition of Israel (1948)

In 1917 Chaim Weizmann, scientist, statesperson, and supporter of the effort to establish a state of Israel, persuaded the British government to issue a statement favoring the establishment of a Jewish national home in Palestine. The statement, which became known as the Balfour Declaration, was, in part, payment to the Jews for their support of the British against the Turks during World War I. After the war, the League of Nations ratified the declaration and in 1922 appointed Britain to rule Palestine.

This course of events caused Jews to be optimistic about the eventual establishment of a homeland. Their optimism inspired the immigration to Palestine of Jews from many countries, particularly from Germany when Nazi persecution of Jews began. The arrival of many Jewish immigrants in the 1930s awakened Arab fears that Palestine would become a national homeland for the Jews. By 1936 guerrilla fighting had broken out between the Jews and the Arabs. Unable to maintain peace, Britain issued a white paper in 1939 that restricted Jewish immigration into Palestine. The Jews, feeling betrayed, bitterly opposed the policy and looked to the United States for support.

While President Franklin D. Roosevelt appeared to be sympathetic to the Jewish cause, his assurances to the Arabs that the United States would not intervene without consulting both parties caused public uncertainty about his position. When Harry S. Truman took office, he made clear that his sympathies were with the Jews and accepted the Balfour Declaration, explaining that it was in keeping with former President Woodrow Wilson's principle of "self-determination." Truman initiated several studies of the Palestine situation that supported his belief that, as a result of the Holocaust, Jews were oppressed and also in need of a homeland. Throughout the Roosevelt and Truman administrations, the Departments of War and State, recognizing the possibility of a Soviet-Arab connection and the potential Arab restriction on oil supplies to this country, advised against U.S. intervention on behalf of the Jews.

Britain and the United States, in a joint effort to examine the dilemma, established the "Anglo-American Committee of Inquiry." In April 1946 the committee submitted recommendations that Palestine not be dominated by either Arabs or Jews. It concluded that attempts to establish nationhood or independence would result in civil strife; that a trusteeship agreement aimed at bringing Jews and Arabs together should be established by the United Nations; that full Jewish immigration be allowed into Palestine; and that two autonomous states be established with a strong central government to control Jerusalem, Bethlehem, and the Negev, the southernmost section of Palestine.

British, Arab, and Jewish reactions to the recommendations were not favorable. Britain, anxious to rid itself of the problem, set the United Nations in motion, formally requesting on April 2, 1947, that the UN General Assembly set up the Special Committee on Palestine (UNSCOP). This committee recommended that the British mandate over Palestine be ended and that the territory be partitioned into two states. Jewish reaction was mixed—some wanted control of all of Palestine; others realized that partition spelled hope for their dream of a homeland. The Arabs were not at all agreeable to the UNSCOP plan. In October the Arab League Council directed the governments of its member states to move troops to the Palestine border. Meanwhile, President Truman instructed the State Department to support the UN plan, and it reluctantly did so. On November 29, 1947, the partition plan was passed by the UN General Assembly.

At midnight on May 14, 1948, the Provisional Government of Israel proclaimed a new State of Israel. On that same date, the United States, in the person of President Truman, recognized the provisional Jewish government as de facto authority of the Jewish state (de jure recognition was extended on January 31, 1949). The U.S. delegates to the UN and top-ranking State Department officials were angered that Truman released his recognition statement to the press without notifying them first. On May 15, 1948, the first day of Israeli Independence and exactly one year after UNSCOP was established, Arab armies invaded Israel and the first Arab-Israeli war began.

Source: ourdocuments.gov

1. According to the passage, the establishment of Israel was _____.

2. The passage suggests that the United States supported which of the following?
   (A) The Arabs
   (B) The Jews
   (C) The British
   (D) The Palestinians

3. Which of the following was the initial catalyst for the formation of a Jewish state?
   (A) President Truman's recognition of Israel
   (B) The British government's support of the creation of a Jewish state
   (C) Nazi persecution of Jews
   (D) UNSCOP

President George Washington's First Inaugural Speech (1789)

On April 16, 1789, two days after receiving official notification of his election, George Washington left his home on the Potomac for New York. Accompanied by Charles Thompson, his official escort, and Col. David Humphreys, his aide, he traveled through Alexandria, Baltimore, Wilmington, Philadelphia, Trenton, Princeton, New Brunswick, and Bridgetown (now Rahway, NJ). At these and other places along his route, the artillery roared a salute of honor and the citizens and officials presented him with marks of affection and honor, so that his trip became a triumphal procession. On April 23, he crossed the bay from Bridgetown to New York City in a magnificent barge built especially for the occasion.

Lacking precedents to guide them in their preparations for the first Presidential inaugural, Congress appointed a joint committee to consider the time, place, and manner in which to administer to the President the oath of office required by the Constitution. Certain difficulties in planning and arrangements arose from the fact that Congress was meeting in New York's former City Hall, rechristened Federal Hall, which was in process of renovation under the direction of Pierre L'Enfant. On April 25, Congress adopted the joint committee's recommendation that the inaugural ceremonies be held the following Thursday, April 30, and that the oath of office be administered to the President in the Representatives' Chamber. The final report of the committee slightly revised this plan with its recommendation that the oath be administered in the outer gallery adjoining the Senate Chamber, "to the end that the Oath of Office may be administered to the President in the most public manner, and that the greatest number of people of the United States, and without distinction, may witness the solemnity."

On inauguration day, the city was crowded with townspeople and visitors. At half past noon, Washington rode alone in the state coach from his quarters in Franklin Square to Federal Hall on the corner of Wall and Nassau Streets. Troops of the city, members of Congress appointed to escort the President, and heads of executive departments of the government under the Confederation preceded the President's coach, while to the rear followed ministers of foreign countries and local citizenry.

At Federal Hall, Vice President John Adams, the Senate, and the House of Representatives awaited the President's arrival in the Senate Chamber. After being received by Congress, Washington stepped from the chamber onto the balcony, where he was followed by the Senators and Representatives. Before the assembled crowd of spectators, Robert Livingston, Chancellor of the State of New York, administered the oath of office prescribed by the Constitution: "I do solemnly swear that I will faithfully execute the office of President of the United States, and will, to the best of my ability, preserve, protect, and defend the Constitution of the United States." After repeating this oath, Washington kissed the Bible held for him by the Chancellor, who called out, "Long live George Washington, President of the United States," and a salvo of 13 cannons was discharged. Except for taking the oath, the law required no further inaugural ceremonies. But, upon reentering the Senate Chamber, the President read the address. . . . After this address, he and the members of Congress proceeded to St. Paul's Church for divine service. A brilliant fireworks display in the evening ended the official program for this historic day.

Source: ourdocuments.gov

4. Put the following events into chronological order.
   (A) Washington rode to Federal Hall.
   (B) Washington left for New York.
   (C) The oath of office was administered.
   (D) Washington passed through Bridgetown.
   (E) Washington crossed the bay to New York on a barge.

5. Where did the inauguration take place?
   (A) Washington, DC
   (B) The White House
   (C) Albany, NY
   (D) New York City

6. What is the significance of the 13 cannons?
   (A) They symbolize the authors of the constitution.
   (B) They symbolize the 13 original states.
   (C) They symbolize the number of senators.
   (D) They symbolize "lucky 13."

QUESTIONS 7 THROUGH 9 ARE BASED ON THE FOLLOWING PASSAGE AND CHART:

Sustainability and the EPA

Sustainability is based on a simple principle: Everything that we need for our survival and well-being depends, either directly or indirectly, on our natural environment. Sustainability creates and maintains the conditions under which humans and nature can exist in productive harmony, that permit fulfilling the social, economic and other requirements of present and future generations.

Sustainability is important to making sure that we have and will continue to have, the water, materials, and resources to protect human health and our environment.

Sustainability has emerged as a result of significant concerns about the unintended social, environmental, and economic consequences of rapid population growth, economic growth and consumption of our natural resources. In its early years, EPA acted primarily as the nation's environmental watchdog, striving to ensure that industries met legal requirements to control pollution. In subsequent years, EPA began to develop theory, tools, and practices that enabled it to move from controlling pollution to preventing it.

Today EPA aims to make sustainability the next level of environmental protection by drawing on advances in science and technology to protect human health and the environment, and promoting innovative green business practices.

Energy Efficiency	Reduce energy intensity 30 percent by 2015, compared to an FY 2003 baseline.
Greenhouse Gases	Reduce greenhouse gas emissions through reduction of energy intensity 30 percent by 2015, compared to an FY 2003 baseline.
Renewable Power	At least 50 percent of current renewable energy purchases must come from new renewable sources (in service after January 1, 1999).
Building Performance	Construct or renovate buildings in accordance with sustainability strategies, including resource conservation, reduction, and use; siting; and indoor environmental quality.
Water Conservation	Reduce water consumption intensity 16 percent by 2015, compared to an FY 2007 baseline.
Vehicles	Increase purchase of alternative fuel, hybrid, and plug-in hybrid vehicles when commercially available.
Petroleum Conservation	Reduce petroleum consumption in fleet vehicles by 2 percent annually through 2015, compared to an FY 2005 baseline.
Alternative Fuel	Increase use of alternative fuel consumption by at least 10 percent annually, compared to an FY 2005 baseline.
Pollution Prevention	Reduce use of chemicals and toxic materials and purchase lower risk chemicals and toxic materials.
Procurement	Expand purchases of environmentally sound goods and services, including biobased products.
Electronics Management	Annually, 95 percent of electronic products purchased must meet Electronic Product Environmental Assessment Tool standards where applicable; enable Energy Star® features on 100 percent of computers and monitors; and reuse, donate, sell, or recycle 100 percent of electronic products using environmentally sound management practices.

Source: epa.gov

7. Indoor environmental quality relates to which point?
   (A) Procurement
   (B) Vehicles
   (C) Building performance
   (D) Energy efficiency

8. Which of the following does not have to do with oil conservation?
   (A) Water conservation
   (B) Alternative fuel
   (C) Electronics management
   (D) Renewable Power

9. Sustainability has to do with the protection of the _____.

Excerpt from *The Truman Doctrine* (1947)

I am fully aware of the broad implications involved if the United States extends assistance to Greece and Turkey, and I shall discuss these implications with you at this time.

One of the primary objectives of the foreign policy of the United States is the creation of conditions in which we and other nations will be able to work out a way of life free from coercion. This was a fundamental issue in the war with Germany and Japan. Our victory was won over countries which sought to impose their will, and their way of life, upon other nations.

To ensure the peaceful development of nations, free from coercion, the United States has taken a leading part in establishing the United Nations. The United Nations is designed to make possible lasting freedom and independence for all its members. We shall not realize our objectives, however, unless we are willing to help free peoples to maintain their free institutions and their national integrity against aggressive movements that seek to impose upon them totalitarian regimes. This is no more than a frank recognition that totalitarian regimes imposed on free peoples, by direct or indirect aggression, undermine the foundations of international peace and hence the security of the United States.

The peoples of a number of countries of the world have recently had totalitarian regimes forced upon them against their will. The Government of the United States has made frequent protests against coercion and intimidation, in violation of the Yalta agreement, in Poland, Rumania, and Bulgaria. I must also state that in a number of other countries there have been similar developments.

At the present moment in world history nearly every nation must choose between alternative ways of life. The choice is too often not a free one.

One way of life is based upon the will of the majority, and is distinguished by free institutions, representative government, free elections, guarantees of individual liberty, freedom of speech and religion, and freedom from political oppression.

The second way of life is based upon the will of a minority forcibly imposed upon the majority. It relies upon terror and oppression, a controlled press and radio; fixed elections, and the suppression of personal freedoms.

I believe that it must be the policy of the United States to support free peoples who are resisting attempted subjugation by armed minorities or by outside pressures.

I believe that we must assist free peoples to work out their own destinies in their own way.

I believe that our help should be primarily through economic and financial aid which is essential to economic stability and orderly political processes.

Source: ourdocuments.gov

10. What is the main goal of the United Nations?
    (A) To ensure lasting peace
    (B) To remain aligned with the United States
    (C) To prevent the spread of communism
    (D) To ensure all people of the world have the same rights

11. President Truman states, "One way of life is based upon the will of the majority, and is distinguished by free institutions, representative government, free elections, guarantees of individual liberty, freedom of speech and religion, and freedom from political oppression." Which of the following is a philosophy not expressed in this statement?

(A) Democracy

(B) Natural rights

(C) Totalitarianism

(D) Majority rule, minority rights

QUESTION 12 IS BASED ON THE FOLLOWING POLITICAL POSTER:

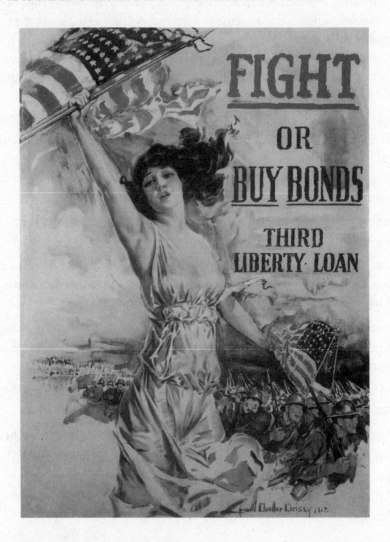

12. This poster suggests that everyone must

(A) Enlist in the army

(B) Buy bonds

(C) Do their part for the war effort

(D) Take out a third-party loan

QUESTIONS 13 THROUGH 15 ARE BASED ON THE FOLLOWING PASSAGE:

Excerpt from the *Transcript of United Nations Charter* (1945)

WE THE PEOPLES OF THE UNITED NATIONS DETERMINED to save succeeding generations from the scourge of war, which twice in our lifetime has brought untold sorrow to mankind, and to reaffirm faith in fundamental human rights, in the dignity and worth of the human person, in the equal rights of men and women and of nations large and small, and to establish conditions under which justice and respect for the obligations arising from treaties and other sources of international law can be maintained, and to promote social progress and better standards of life in larger freedom, AND FOR THESE ENDS to practice tolerance and live together in peace with one another as good neighbors, and to unite our strength to maintain international peace and security, and to ensure, by the acceptance of principles and the institution of methods, that armed force shall not be used, save in the common interest, and to employ international machinery for the promotion of the economic and social advancement of all peoples, HAVE RESOLVED TO COMBINE OUR EFFORTS TO ACCOMPLISH THESE AIMS. Accordingly, our respective Governments, through representatives assembled in the city of San Francisco, who have exhibited their full powers found to be in good and due form, have agreed to the present Charter of the United Nations and do hereby establish an international organization to be known as the United Nations.

CHAPTER I
PURPOSES AND PRINCIPLES
Article 1
The Purposes of the United Nations are:

1. To maintain international peace and security, and to that end: to take effective collective measures for the prevention and removal of threats to the peace, and for the suppression of acts of aggression or other breaches of the peace, and to bring about by peaceful means, and in conformity with the principles of justice and international law, adjustment or settlement of international disputes or situations which might lead to a breach of the peace;

2. To develop friendly relations among nations based on respect for the principle of equal rights and self-determination of peoples, and to take other appropriate measures to strengthen universal peace;

3. To achieve international co-operation in solving international problems of an economic, social, cultural, or humanitarian character, and in promoting and encouraging respect for human rights and for fundamental freedoms for all without distinction as to race, sex, language, or religion; and

4. To be a centre for harmonizing the actions of nations in the attainment of these common ends.

Source: ourdocuments.gov

13. According to the charter, which of the following problems will the United Nations not address?
    (A) Election problems
    (B) Social problems
    (C) Economic problems
    (D) Cultural problems

14. What is the central idea of the first paragraph?
    (A) The goal of the United Nations is to avoid war and to maintain peace.
    (B) The goal of the United Nations is to contain conflicts.
    (C) The goal of the United Nations is to use force when necessary.
    (D) The goal of the United Nations is to establish various international organizations.

15. What value is not expressed in the charter?
    (A) Teamwork
    (B) Tolerance
    (C) Isolationism
    (D) Cooperation

QUESTIONS 16 AND 17 ARE BASED ON THE FOLLOWING DIAGRAM AND PASSAGE:

Changing Ranks of States by Congressional Representation

	1789	1790	1800	1900	2000	2010
1	VA	VA	VA	NY	CA	CA
2	MA/PA	MA	PA	PA	TX	TX
3		PA	NY/MA	IL	NY	NY/FL
4	NY/MD	NY/NC		OH	FL	
5			NC	TX/MO	PA/IL	PA/IL
6	NC/SC/CT	MD	MD			
7		CT	SC	MA	OH	OH

The number of representatives given to each state as a result of apportionment has shifted over time. Shifts in political representation are due to changes in state population relative to other states, the admission of new states to the union, and increases to the total number of memberships in the U.S. House of Representatives instituted by Congress over the decades. The seven states with the largest number of representatives in a given year are included in the graph, beginning with the Continental Congress in 1789 (prior to the first decennial census) and following each decennial census from 1790 through 2010.

Source: census.gov

16. According to the chart and the passage, which of the following states had the greatest number of representatives in 1800?
    (A) California
    (B) Kentucky
    (C) Virginia
    (D) New York

17. According to the chart, which of the following states currently has the fourth-largest population?
    (A) Florida
    (B) Pennsylvania
    (C) California
    (D) None

QUESTIONS 18 AND 19 ARE BASED ON THE FOLLOWING MAP, GRAPH, AND PASSAGE:

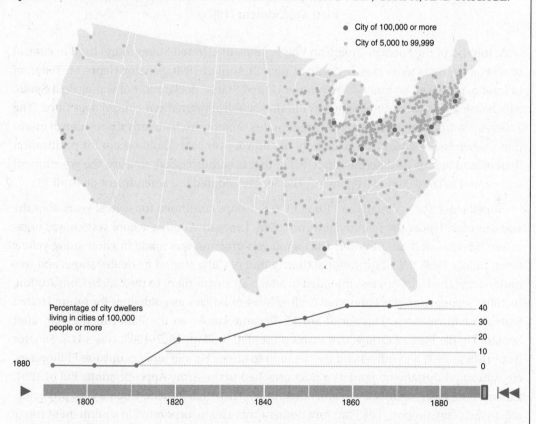

The number and size of cities increased dramatically between 1790 and 1890 as the country's population grew and became increasingly urban. By 1890, people living in cities of 100,000 or more made up a larger proportion of all urban dwellers. This reflected a shift from a rural, agrarian society to one focused on industrial production, especially in the Northeast and around the Great Lakes.

Source: census.gov

18. According to the map, graph, and passage, during which period of time did the nation see the greatest increase in urban population?

(A) 1810–1820

(B) 1830–1840

(C) 1850–1860

(D) 1870–1880

19. According to the map, which area of the country has the most cities?

(A) South

(B) West

(C) Midwest

(D) Northeast

QUESTIONS 20 THROUGH 22 ARE BASED ON THE FOLLOWING PASSAGE:

Platt Amendment (1903)

At the end of the Spanish-American War in 1898, the United States found itself in control of several overseas territories, including Cuba. In April of 1898, Senator Henry M. Teller, of Colorado, proposed an amendment to the United States' declaration of war against Spain, which stated that the United States would not establish permanent control over Cuba. The Teller Amendment asserted that the United States "hereby disclaims any disposition of intention to exercise sovereignty, jurisdiction, or control over said island except for pacification thereof, and asserts its determination, when that is accomplished, to leave the government and control of the island to its people." The Senate adopted the amendment on April 19.

Nonetheless, the occupation of Cuba by U.S. troops continued for several years after the war was over. Under the military governor, Gen. Leonard Wood, a school system was organized, finances were set in order, and significant progress was made in eliminating yellow fever. In July 1900, the Constitutional Convention of Cuba started its deliberations and was notified that the U.S. Congress intended to attach an amendment to the Cuban Constitution. In 1901, Secretary of War Elihu Root drafted a set of articles as guidelines for future United States–Cuban relations. This set of articles became known as the Platt Amendment, after Senator Orville Platt of Connecticut, who presented it. Platt, 1827–1905, was a U.S. Senator from 1879 to 1905 and influenced the decision to annex Hawaii and occupy the Philippines. He sponsored this amendment as a rider attached to the Army Appropriations Bill of 1901. Cubans reluctantly included the amendment, which virtually made Cuba a U.S. protectorate, in their constitution. The Platt Amendment was also incorporated in a permanent treaty between the United States and Cuba.

The Platt Amendment stipulated the conditions for U.S. intervention in Cuban affairs and permitted the United States to lease or buy lands for the purpose of the establishing naval bases (the main one was Guantánamo Bay) and coaling stations in Cuba. It barred Cuba from making a treaty that gave another nation power over its affairs, going into debt, or stopping the United States from imposing a sanitation program on the island. Specifically, Article III required that the government of Cuba consent to the right of the United States to intervene in Cuban affairs for "the preservation of Cuban independence, the maintenance of a government adequate for the protection of life, property, and individual liberty, and for discharging the obligations with respect to Cuba imposed by the Treaty of Paris on the United States, now to be assumed and undertaken by the Government of Cuba." The Platt Amendment supplied the terms under which the United States intervened in Cuban affairs in 1906, 1912, 1917, and 1920. By 1934, rising Cuban nationalism and widespread criticism of the Platt Amendment resulted in its repeal as part of Franklin D. Roosevelt's Good Neighbor policy toward Latin America. The United States, however, retained its lease on Guantánamo Bay, where a naval base was established.

Source: ourdocuments.gov

20. What provision in the Platt Amendment enabled the United States to set up a naval base at Guantánamo Bay?
    (A) The amendment provided for a Cuban naval base in the United States.
    (B) The amendment provided for lands to be leased or purchased by the United States to set up naval bases.
    (C) The amendment provided for military protection for Cuba.
    (D) The amendment provided for the acquisition of Cuba.

21. Based on the statement, "Rising Cuban nationalism and widespread criticism of the Platt Amendment," what is the best definition of the word "nationalism"?
    (A) Great feeling of pride in one's country
    (B) Hatred of European countries
    (C) Love of rural areas
    (D) Desire to join another nation

22. At the end of the Spanish-American War, the United States had _____ over Cuba and other territories.

QUESTIONS 23 AND 24 ARE BASED ON THE FOLLOWING GRAPHS AND PASSAGE:

Population Distribution by Region, 1790 to 2010

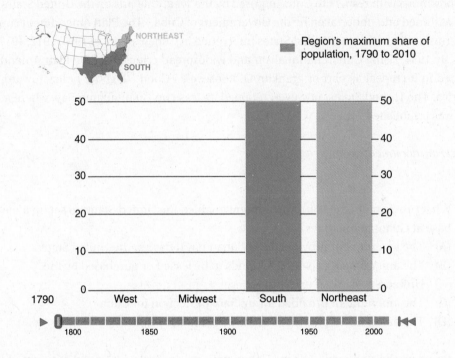

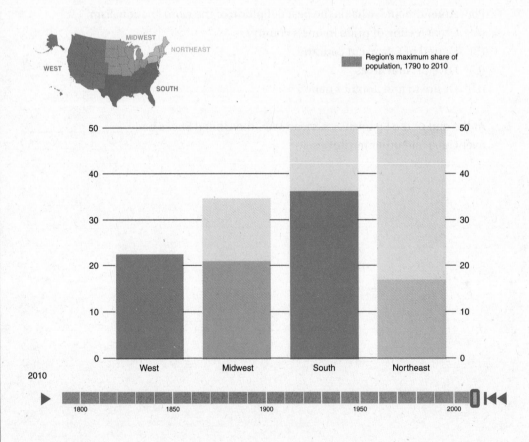

The Northeast and South each held about half of the U.S. population in 1790. As the Midwest opened to settlement, it gained an increasingly large share of the population due to migration from the Northeast and South, as well as international migration. By 1890, the Midwest held its largest share of the population. The 20th century saw continued declines in the shares of the population living in the Northeast and Midwest alongside gains in the South and West.

Source: census.gov

23. About what percent of the population was held in the West and Midwest in 2010?
    (A) 22%
    (B) 45%
    (C) 57%
    (D) 63%

24. What was the greatest percentage of the population held in the South and Northeast combined?
    (A) 50%
    (B) 53%
    (C) 75%
    (D) 100%

QUESTIONS 25 THROUGH 27 ARE BASED ON THE FOLLOWING PASSAGE:

16th Amendment to the U.S. Constitution:
Federal Income Tax (1913)

Far-reaching in its social as well as its economic impact, the income tax amendment became part of the Constitution by a curious series of events culminating in a bit of political maneuvering that went awry.

The financial requirements of the Civil War prompted the first American income tax in 1861. At first, Congress placed a flat 3-percent tax on all incomes over $800 and later modified this principle to include a graduated tax. Congress repealed the income tax in 1872, but the concept did not disappear.

After the Civil War, the growing industrial and financial markets of the eastern United States generally prospered. But the farmers of the south and west suffered from low prices for their farm products, while they were forced to pay high prices for manufactured goods. Throughout the 1860s, 1870s, and 1880s, farmers formed such political organizations as the Grange, the Greenback Party, the National Farmers' Alliance, and the People's (Populist) Party. All of these groups advocated many reforms considered radical for the times, including a graduated income tax.

In 1894, as part of a high tariff bill, Congress enacted a 2-percent tax on income over $4,000. The tax was almost immediately struck down by a five-to-four decision of the Supreme Court, even though the Court had upheld the constitutionality of the Civil War tax as recently as 1881. Although farm organizations denounced the Court's decision as a prime example of the alliance of government and business against the farmer, a general return of prosperity around the turn of the century softened the demand for reform. Democratic Party Platforms under the leadership of three-time Presidential candidate William Jennings Bryan, however, consistently included an income tax plank, and the progressive wing of the Republican Party also espoused the concept.

In 1909 progressives in Congress again attached a provision for an income tax to a tariff bill. Conservatives, hoping to kill the idea for good, proposed a constitutional amendment enacting such a tax; they believed an amendment would never receive ratification by three-fourths of the states. Much to their surprise, the amendment was ratified by one state legislature after another, and on February 25, 1913, with the certification by Secretary of State Philander C. Knox, the 16th amendment took effect. Yet in 1913, due to generous exemptions and deductions, less than 1 percent of the population paid income taxes at the rate of only 1 percent of net income.

This document settled the constitutional question of how to tax income and, by so doing, effected dramatic changes in the American way of life.

Source: ourdocuments.gov

25. Which of the following first prompted the United States government to enact an income tax?
    (A) The need to build highways
    (B) The cost of the Civil War
    (C) A Supreme Court ruling
    (D) The need for farm organizations

26. Originally there was a flat tax of 3% on incomes over $800, but this was later changed to a graduated tax. What is the best definition of "graduated tax"?
    (A) It is an all-inclusive tax.
    (B) Those who make more money pay less in taxes.
    (C) The amount paid in taxes goes up as income increases.
    (D) It is another term for sales tax.

27. In 1894, what was the tax on a $5,000 income?
    (A) $80
    (B) $100
    (C) $400
    (D) $500

28. What opinion is being expressed in the political cartoon above?
    (A) Income tax reform has made filing confusing.
    (B) You need to work with many numbers when filing your taxes.
    (C) Some people will owe as much as $6 billion.
    (D) There are few provisions for income taxes.

Consumer Price Index—Average Price Data

Original Data Value

Series Id: APU000074712

Area: U.S. city average

Item: Gasoline, leaded regular (cost per gallon/3.8 liters)

Years: 1981 to 1991

Year	Jan	Feb	Mar	Apr	May	Jun	Jul	Aug	Sep	Oct	Nov	Dec
1981	1.238	1.321	1.352	1.344	1.333	1.324	1.315	1.310	1.305	1.299	1.297	1.293
1982	1.285	1.260	1.206	1.148	1.166	1.242	1.263	1.254	1.236	1.219	1.207	1.181
1983	1.150	1.099	1.064	1.131	1.177	1.197	1.207	1.203	1.189	1.172	1.156	1.146
1984	1.131	1.125	1.125	1.145	1.154	1.147	1.129	1.116	1.120	1.127	1.124	1.109
1985	1.060	1.041	1.071	1.119	1.144	1.153	1.154	1.143	1.129	1.117	1.123	1.123
1986	1.107	1.034	0.894	0.815	0.852	0.885	0.822	0.778	0.797	0.771	0.762	0.764
1987	0.806	0.848	0.856	0.879	0.888	0.906	0.921	0.946	0.940	0.931	0.928	0.912
1988	0.881	0.859	0.850	0.883	0.911	0.910	0.923	0.945	0.933	0.910	0.904	0.885
1989	0.876	0.886	0.907	1.047	1.098	1.093	1.075	1.034	1.007	1.001	0.975	0.961
1990	1.006	1.011	0.999	1.027	1.044	1.077	1.089	1.198	1.297	1.354	1.351	1.335
1991	1.246	1.137	1.047	1.062								

29. From 1982 to 1986, gas prices were relatively _____.

30. What was the average price per gallon for regular gasoline in July 1989?
    (A) $1.075
    (B) $1.089
    (C) $1.062
    (D) $0.961

QUESTIONS 31 THROUGH 33 ARE BASED ON THE FOLLOWING PASSAGES:

Excerpt from "Check for the Purchase of Alaska" (1868)

In 1866 the Russian government offered to sell the territory of Alaska to the United States. Secretary of State William H. Seward, enthusiastic about the prospects of American Expansion, negotiated the deal for the Americans. Edouard de Stoeckl, Russian minister to the United States, negotiated for the Russians. On March 30, 1867, the two parties agreed that the United States would pay Russia $7.2 million for the territory of Alaska.

For less that 2 cents an acre, the United States acquired nearly 600,000 square miles. Opponents of the Alaska Purchase persisted in calling it "Seward's Folly" or "Seward's Icebox" until 1896, when the great Klondike Gold Strike convinced even the harshest critics that Alaska was a valuable addition to American territory.

The check for $7.2 million was made payable to the Russian Minister to the United States Edouard de Stoeckl, who negotiated the deal for the Russians. . . . [T]he Treaty of Cession, signed by Tzar Alexander II, . . . formally concluded the agreement for the purchase of Alaska from Russia.

Source: ourdocuments.gov

Excerpt from "Joint Resolution to Provide for Annexing the Hawaiian Islands to the United States" (1898)

In the 1890s, the efforts of the Hawaiian people to preserve their national sovereignty and native heritage ran headlong into the unstoppable force of American expansionism. Throughout the 19th century, westerners—particularly Americans—came to dominate Hawaii's economy and politics. When Queen Liliuokalani assumed the throne in 1891 and tried to reassert the power of the throne and the will of Native Hawaiians, she was deposed by a small group of American businessmen, with the support of the American diplomats and the U.S. Navy.

Although even President Cleveland challenged the legitimacy of this takeover, it did stand. To a nation poised to take its place as a world power, the control of Hawaii, strategically located to serve as a mid-Pacific naval installation, seemed crucial. In 1898, with a naval base firmly established at Pearl Harbor, the United States officially annexed Hawaii.

Source: ourdocuments.gov

31. Which of the following is a benefit of the purchase of Alaska that Seward could not have foreseen?
    (A) During the Cold War, the United States had territory strategically close to the Soviet Union.
    (B) Many organizations would protest drilling for oil in the arctic.
    (C) Ice manufacturers would relocate to Alaska.
    (D) Many species of animal indigenous to Alaska would become endangered.

32. How did the acquisition of Alaska differ from the acquisition of the Hawaiian Islands?
    (A) Alaska was purchased, whereas Hawaii was taken by force.
    (B) Sums of money were paid for both.
    (C) In both cases, the United States doubled its total area.
    (D) Alaska was acquired through war, whereas Hawaii was purchased.

33. What do Alaska and Hawaii have in common?
    (A) They both have abundant natural resources.
    (B) They are both strategically located.
    (C) Both acquisitions represent American entrepreneurship.
    (D) Both are composed of hundreds of islands.

> **DIRECTIONS:** Read the following passages. In your response, explain how the Truman Doctrine and the Marshall Plan worked together to achieve the same goal. Make sure you cite specific examples to support your position. Develop your answer fully. You have 25 minutes to complete this section.

Truman Doctrine (1947)

On Friday, February 21, 1947, the British Embassy informed the U.S. State Department officials that Great Britain could no longer provide financial aid to the governments of Greece and Turkey. American policymakers had been monitoring Greece's crumbling economic and political conditions, especially the rise of the Communist-led insurgency known as the National Liberation Front, or the EAM/ELAS. The United States had also been following events in Turkey, where a weak government faced Soviet pressure to share control of the strategic Dardanelle Straits. When Britain announced that it would withdraw aid to Greece and Turkey, the responsibility was passed on to the United States.

In a meeting between Congressmen and State Department officials, Undersecretary of State Dean Acheson articulated what would later become known as the domino theory. He stated that more was at stake than Greece and Turkey, for if those two key states should fall, communism would likely spread south to Iran and as far east as India. Acheson concluded that not since the days of Rome and Carthage had such a polarization of power existed. The stunned legislators agreed to endorse the program on the condition that President Truman stress the severity of the crisis in an address to Congress and in a radio broadcast to the American people.

Addressing a joint session of Congress on March 12, 1947, President Harry S. Truman asked for $400 million in military and economic assistance for Greece and Turkey and established a doctrine, aptly characterized as the Truman Doctrine, that would guide U.S. diplomacy for the next 40 years. President Truman declared, "It must be the policy of the United States to support free peoples who are resisting attempted subjugation by armed minorities or by outside pressures." The sanction of aid to Greece and Turkey by a Republican Congress indicated the beginning of a long and enduring bipartisan cold war foreign policy.

Source: ourdocuments.gov

Marshall Plan (1948)

When World War II ended in 1945, Europe lay in ruins: its cities were shattered; its economies were devastated; its people faced famine. In the two years after the war, the Soviet Union's control of Eastern Europe and the vulnerability of Western European countries to Soviet expansionism heightened the sense of crisis. To meet this emergency, Secretary of State George Marshall proposed in a speech at Harvard University on June 5, 1947, that European nations create a plan for their economic reconstruction and that the United States provide economic assistance. On December 19, 1947, President Harry Truman sent Congress a message that followed Marshall's ideas to provide economic aid to Europe. Congress overwhelmingly passed the Economic Cooperation Act of 1948, and on April 3, 1948, President Truman signed the act that became known as the Marshall Plan.

Over the next four years, Congress appropriated $13.3 billion for European recovery. This aid provided much needed capital and materials that enabled Europeans to rebuild the continent's economy. For the United States, the Marshall Plan provided markets for American goods, created reliable trading partners, and supported the development of stable democratic governments in Western Europe. Congress's approval of the Marshall Plan signaled an extension of the bipartisanship of World War II into the postwar years.

Source: ourdocuments.gov

Answers and Explanations

1. "Controversial" or any similar word would be the best answer.

2. **(B)** According to the passage, several presidents supported the Jews. Options A, C, and D are incorrect. While the passage mentions all of these groups, it does not indicate that the United States supported them.

3. **(B)** The first paragraph states that Chaim Weizmann was able to persuade the British government to favor the creation of a Jewish state. Options A, C, and D are incorrect because no evidence is provided to support these answers.

4. **(B, D, E, A, C)** First Washington left for New York. Then he passed through Bridgetown. Next Washington crossed the bay to New York on a barge. He then rode to Federal Hall. Finally, the oath of office was administered.

5. **(D)** The passage indicates that the inauguration took place in New York City. Options A, B, and C are incorrect.

6. **(B)** At the time of Washington's inauguration, there were only 13 states. The 13 cannons likely signified the 13 states.

7. **(C)** The chart indicates that building performance has to do with, among other things, indoor environmental quality. Option A is incorrect because procurement has to do with purchasing. Option B is incorrect because vehicles have to do with the way cars are built. Option D is incorrect because energy efficiency has to do with the overall performance of machinery.

8. **(A)** Water conservation is not directly part of oil conservation. Options B, C, and D all are directly involved with oil conservation.

9. "Environment" or any similar word would be the best answer.

10. **(A)** The third paragraph indicates the main goal of the United Nations. Options B, C, and D are incorrect because these are not the main goals of the United Nations.

11. **(C)** Totalitarianism is complete control by a ruler. That philosophy is not expressed in President Truman's statement. Options A, B, and D are incorrect because they are all expressed in the statement.

12. **(C)** The poster suggests that people should either enlist in the army or buy bonds. So the general message is that people should do their part for the war effort. Option D is incorrect.

13. **(A)** The charter does not state that the United Nations will address election problems. Options B, C, and D are incorrect because these are clearly mentioned in the charter.

14. **(A)** The charter clearly states that the goal of the United Nations is to maintain international peace and security. Options B, C, and D are incorrect. No evidence is provided to support these answers.

15. **(C)** The charter clearly expresses the need for nations to work together; no evidence suggests that nations should isolate themselves. Options A, B, and D are incorrect.

16. **(C)** In 1800, Virginia was ranked number one.

17. **(D)** According to the chart, New York and Florida are tied for third place, so no state is ranked in fourth place.

18. **(A)** The steepest part of the graph is from 1810 to 1820, indicating the most rapid growth. Options B, C, and D are incorrect.

19. **(D)** The highest concentration of dots, which indicates cities, is in the Northeast.

20. **(B)** The passage indicates that the United States was able to buy or lease lands in order to set up naval bases in Cuba. Option A is incorrect because the opposite is indicated in the passage. Options C and D are incorrect. No evidence is provided to support these answers.

21. **(A)** Nationalism has to do with feelings of patriotism.

22. "Control" or any similar word would be the best answer.

23. **(B)** According to the 2010 graph, the West and the Midwest each hold about 22% to 23% of the entire population. When combined, these two geographic areas hold about 45% of the U.S. population.

24. **(D)** According to the 1790 graph, the South held 50% of the population and the Northeast held 50% of the population. When combined, these two areas held 100% of the U.S. population.

25. **(B)** The passage indicates that the Civil War was the catalyst for implementing an income tax. Options A, C, and D are incorrect because no evidence supports these answers.

26. **(C)** Something "graduated" is scaled, so it is logical that taxes paid go up as income increases.

27. **(B)** In 1894, all incomes over $4,000 were taxed at a rate of 2%, and 2% of $5,000 is $100.

28. **(B)** The swirling numbers and pieces of scrap paper indicate that people have to work with many numbers when filing their taxes. Options A, C, and D are incorrect because no evidence supports these answers.

29. "Stable" or any similar word would be acceptable.

30. **(A)** According to the table, regular gasoline averaged $1.075 per gallon in July 1989.

31. **(A)** During the Cold War, the proximity of Alaska to the Soviet Union was advantageous for the United States. Option B is incorrect. Protesters are not advantageous. Options C and D are incorrect because no evidence supports these answers.

32. **(A)** The first passage states the amount that the United States paid for Alaska. The second passage says that American diplomats and the U.S. Navy deposed Queen Liliuokalani. Options B, C, and D are not supported by both passages.

33. **(B)** Alaska is positioned by Northeast Asia, and Hawaii is positioned in the mid-Pacific. Options A, C, and D are not supported by both passages.

Extended Response Review Test

Answers will vary.

When reviewing your extended response, make sure you have asked yourself the following questions:

- Have I responded to the prompt?
- Do I have enough evidence?
- Do my ideas follow a logical order?
- Are there any misspellings?
- Have I confused any homonyms?
- Have I used proper punctuation, including periods, commas, semicolons, apostrophes, and so forth?
- Do I need to break up any run-on sentences?
- Can I combine any strings of short, choppy sentences?

The prompt asks how the Truman Doctrine and the Marshall Plan worked together to achieve the same goal. Make sure that you have discussed the most important ways in which they worked toward the same goal, not how they worked toward different goals. Make sure you have clearly articulated your position in the introductory part of the response. Following your introduction, discuss the aspects of the Truman Doctrine followed by the aspects from the Marshall Plan (or vice versa). Be sure to cite specific evidence from both of the passages that you feel supports your position. Be sure to explain how these aspects worked to achieve the same goal. Finally, make sure you have restated your position in your conclusion.

UNIT 4

Science

Pretest

1. Which of the following is a unit in the metric system?
   (A) Inch
   (B) Liter
   (C) Pound
   (D) Fluid ounce

2. Which of the following is a unit in the customary system?
   (A) Inch
   (B) Liter
   (C) Gram
   (D) Meter

3. Which of the following is NOT a unit of length?
   (A) Foot
   (B) Kilometer
   (C) Gram
   (D) Mile

4. Which of the following organizes the units from smallest to largest?
   (A) Kilogram, milligram, gram, microgram
   (B) Kilogram, gram, milligram, microgram
   (C) Milligram, microgram, gram, kilogram
   (D) Microgram, milligram, gram, kilogram

QUESTIONS 5 TO 8 REFER TO THE FOLLOWING DATA PRESENTATIONS:

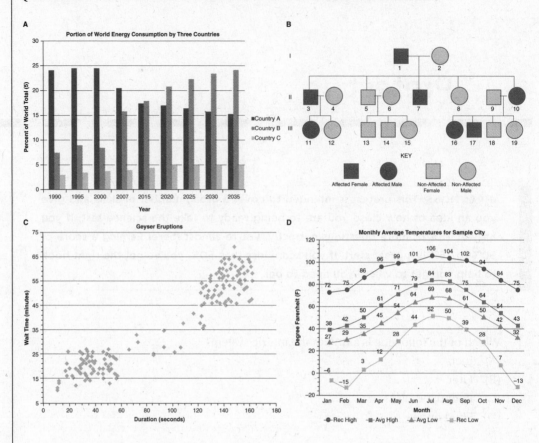

5. Which of the above is a scatter plot?
   (A) Presentation *A*
   (B) Presentation *B*
   (C) Presentation *C*
   (D) Presentation *D*

6. Which of the above is a bar chart?
   (A) Presentation *A*
   (B) Presentation *B*
   (C) Presentation *C*
   (D) Presentation *D*

7. Which of the above is a diagram?
   (A) Presentation *A*
   (B) Presentation *B*
   (C) Presentation *C*
   (D) Presentation *D*

8. Which of the above is a line graph?
    (A) Presentation A
    (B) Presentation B
    (C) Presentation C
    (D) Presentation D

---

9. Which of the following correctly identifies the atoms in the following compounds?
    (A) CO has 1 chlorine atom and 1 oxygen atom.
    (B) CH_4 has 4 carbon atoms and 1 hydrogen atom.
    (C) $C_6H_{12}O_6$ has 6 carbon atoms, 12 helium atoms, and 6 oxygen atoms.
    (D) H_2O has 2 hydrogen atoms and 1 oxygen atom.

10. Which of the following is correct?
    (A) Correlation refers to two things that happen together and may be related.
    (B) If two items are correlated, a causation always exists between them.
    (C) Causation is an inferred cause-and-effect relationship. A causation cannot be proved.
    (D) Two items that are correlated must always increase or must always decrease together.

11. A scientist wants to determine whether the quantity of soil affects the number of earthworms found in the soil. So the scientist measures out 10 samples, each with a different volume. Then the scientist counts the number of earthworms found in each sample. Finally, the scientist plots the data. Which of the following is true about the experiment and the data plot?
    (A) The independent variable is the number of earthworms, which is plotted on the x-axis.
    (B) The dependent variable is the number of earthworms, which is plotted on the y-axis.
    (C) The dependent variable is the volume of soil, which is plotted on the x-axis.
    (D) The independent variable is the volume of soil, which is plotted on the y-axis.

12. On a scatter plot, what is the difference between clusters and outliers?

_____

_____

_____

_____

_____

13. Which of the following correctly defines the mean and the median of a set of numbers?
    (A) The mean is the average of all the numbers. The median is the most commonly occurring number.
    (B) The mean is the difference between the highest and the lowest numbers. The median is the average of all the numbers.
    (C) The mean is the most commonly occurring number. The median is the middle number when a set of numbers is arranged in ascending order.
    (D) The mean is the average of all the numbers. The median is the middle number when the set of numbers is arranged in ascending order.

14. What is a mode?
    (A) A mode is the difference between the highest and the lowest value in a set of numbers.
    (B) A mode is the most common element in a set of numbers.
    (C) A mode is the average of a set of numbers.
    (D) A mode is the middle element when a set of numbers is arranged in ascending order.

15. Which of the following definitions is correct?
    (A) When calculating the simple average, add each element in the set and then divide by 2.
    (B) When calculating the simple average, add each element in the set except for the highest and lowest values. Then divide by the number of elements in that set.
    (C) When calculating the weighted average, add each element in the set and divide by the number of elements in that set.
    (D) When calculating the weighted average, those elements with more weight have a greater effect on the final outcome than those elements with less weight.

QUESTIONS 16 TO 18 REFER TO THE FOLLOWING SET:

Set *A*: {3, 6, 9, 12, 15, 18, 21}

16. What is the arithmetic mean (average) of set *A*?
    (A) 12
    (B) 14
    (C) 18
    (D) 84

17. What is the median of set *A*?
    (A) 12
    (B) 14
    (C) 18
    (D) 84

18. What is the range of set *A*?
    (A) 12
    (B) 14
    (C) 18
    (D) 84

QUESTIONS 19 TO 21 REFER TO THE FOLLOWING SET:

Set *B*: {4, 4, 6, 6, 8, 8, 8}

19. What is the mode in set *B*?
    (A) 4
    (B) 6
    (C) 8
    (D) No mode

20. What is the simple average of the members of set *B* (rounded to the nearest tenth)?
    (A) 6.0
    (B) 6.2
    (C) 6.3
    (D) 14.7

21. If the numbers equal to the mode of set *B* are weighted 50% and all other numbers combined are weighted 50%, what is the weighted average of set *B*?
    (A) 5.0
    (B) 5.6
    (C) 6.3
    (D) 6.5

QUESTIONS 22 TO 25 REFER TO THE FOLLOWING DEFINITIONS
OF SCIENTIFIC THEORIES:

Theory *A*: The theory that the sun is the center of the solar system and that the planets orbit around it

Theory *B*: The theory that all complex organisms are composed of small, fundamental, living units

Theory *C*: The theory that all physical material (matter) is made up of extremely small, fundamental particles

Theory *D*: The theory that natural selection is responsible for adaptation (adjusting to the environment) and speciation (the development of species)

22. Which is the best description of cell theory?
     (A) Theory *A*
     (B) Theory *B*
     (C) Theory *C*
     (D) Theory *D*

23. Which is the best description of the theory of evolution?
     (A) Theory *A*
     (B) Theory *B*
     (C) Theory *C*
     (D) Theory *D*

24. Which is the best description of the heliocentric model of the solar system?
     (A) Theory *A*
     (B) Theory *B*
     (C) Theory *C*
     (D) Theory *D*

25. Which is the best description of atomic theory?
     (A) Theory *A*
     (B) Theory *B*
     (C) Theory *C*
     (D) Theory *D*

26. Which of the following definitions is correct?
    (A) A theory is an educated guess that cannot be tested.
    (B) A hypothesis is an educated guess that can be tested.
    (C) A theory is a narrowly defined fact that can never be questioned or changed.
    (D) A hypothesis is a broad, comprehensive statement that is based on numerous facts that have been repeatedly tested and confirmed.

27. Which of the following definitions is correct?
    (A) An inference is an educated guess but is unverified.
    (B) An inference is an educated guess based on facts.
    (C) A conclusion is made as soon as the scientist forms a hypothesis.
    (D) A conclusion always proves the original hypothesis.

28. Researchers want to study the effects of medication X on patients with high blood pressure. Which of the following experimental setups is correct?
    (A) The control group consists of 100 patients. In this group, 50 have high blood pressure and 50 have normal blood pressure. In the control group, 25 patients receive medication X and 75 receive a placebo (fake pill). The experimental group consists of 5 patients, all with high blood pressure. All people in the experimental group receive medication X.
    (B) The control group consists of 100 patients, all with high blood pressure. In this group, 50 patients receive medication X and 50 receive a placebo (fake pill). The experimental group consists of 100 patients, all with low blood pressure. In this group, 50 patients receive medication X and 50 receive a placebo (fake pill).
    (C) The control group consists of 100 patients, all with high blood pressure. Every member of the control group receives a placebo (fake pill). The experimental group consists of 5 patients, all with high blood pressure. Every member of the experimental group receives medication X.
    (D) The control group consists of 100 patients, all with high blood pressure. Every member of the control group receives a placebo (fake pill). The experimental group consists of 100 patients, all with high blood pressure. Every member of the experimental group receives medication X.

Answers and Explanations

1. **(B)** The liter is a metric unit of capacity or volume. The inch is a customary unit of length. The pound is a customary unit of weight. The fluid ounce is a customary unit of capacity or volume.

2. **(A)** The inch is a customary unit of length. The liter is a metric unit of capacity or volume. The gram is a customary unit of mass. The meter is a metric unit of length.

3. **(C)** The gram is a metric unit of mass. The foot and mile are customary units of length. The kilometer is a metric unit of length.

4. **(D)** A microgram is 10^{-9} grams. A milligram is 10^{-6} grams. A kilogram is 10^3 grams. A complete list of metric prefixes and their values appears in the appendix.

5. **(C)** A scatter plot is a data presentation using points plotted on the *x*- and *y*-axes. The points often appear scattered across the plot area, with many points collected into clusters and a few points (outliers) scattered farther away.

6. **(A)** A bar chart is a presentation with solid columns, often of different colors or shades. The heights of the columns represent the relative amounts.

7. **(B)** A diagram can take many forms and have many different components but is still essentially a picture (or model) of a system or an idea. Diagram *B* is specifically a genetic pedigree chart.

8. **(D)** A line graph is one of the most familiar forms of data presentation. Individual points are plotted on the *x*- and *y*-axes and then connected with a line. More than one set of points, or data series, may be plotted on a single line graph.

9. **(D)** H stands for hydrogen, and O stands for oxygen. The small 2 to the right of the H means there are 2 hydrogen atoms. Option A is incorrect because CO consists of 1 carbon atom, not 1 chlorine atom, and of 1 oxygen atom. Option B is incorrect; CH_4 has 1 carbon atom and 4 hydrogen atoms. Option C is incorrect because $C_6H_{12}O_6$ is made of 6 carbon atoms, 12 hydrogen atoms, not helium atoms, and 6 oxygen atoms.

10. **(A)** This is the definition of a correlation. Option B is incorrect. Just because two items are correlated does not mean that causation exists between them. Remember that correlation is not causation. Option C is incorrect because a causation is a proven cause-and-effect relationship, not an inferred one. Option D is incorrect. If two items are correlated, one can increase while the other decreases. This is called a negative correlation.

11. **(B)** In an experiment, the independent variable is the one that scientists believe to be the cause in a cause-and-effect relationship. The dependent variable is believed to be the effect. In this experiment, the volume of soil is the independent variable and the number of earthworms is the dependent variable. The dependent variable gets its name because its value depends on the value of the independent variable. The independent variable gets its name because its value does not depend on another variable in the experiment. Data presentations in science often graph or plot the independent variable on the *x*-axis and the dependent variable on the *y*-axis.

12. On a scatter plot, each cluster is a densely organized group of points and each outlier is a single point plotted away from any cluster. A cluster represents a large group of results within a small range of values. Outliers represent a small group of results distributed across a wide range of values.

13. **(D)** The mean is the simple average. It is calculated by adding up all of the elements in a set and dividing by the number of elements. The median is the middle number when a set of odd-numbered elements is arranged in ascending order. If the set has an even number of elements, the median is the average of the two middle numbers when the elements are arranged in ascending order.

14. **(B)** A mode is the most commonly occurring element in a set. A set can have more than one mode when two different elements occur the same number of times. A set can also have no mode. Option A is incorrect because this is the definition of range. Option C is incorrect because this is the definition of mean. Option D is incorrect because this is the definition of median.

15. **(D)** To calculate the simple average, add all the elements in a set and divide by the number of elements. To calculate the weighted average, divide the elements into groups based on the elements' relative weight (often based on percentages). Then take the average of the groups while taking each group's weight into consideration.

16. **(A)** The sum of the elements in the set is 84, and there are 7 elements in the set. So the arithmetic mean is $84 \div 7 = 12$. Also, in any odd-numbered set with equally spaced elements, the mean will be the middle number (median) in the set. To use this method, though, the elements must first be organized in ascending order.

17. **(A)** In a set with an odd number of elements, the median is the middle number when the elements are arranged in ascending order. In an even-numbered set, the median is the average of the two middle numbers when the elements are arranged in ascending order.

18. **(C)** The range of a set is the difference between the highest value and the lowest value: $21 - 3 = 18$.

19. **(C)** The mode is the element that appears the most often. There are more 8s in the set than any other element, so the mode is 8.

20. **(C)** The sum of the elements in the set is 44, and there are 7 elements in the set. So the average is $44 \div 7 = 6.285714$. Round up because 8 is greater than 5. So the answer is 6.3.

21. **(D)** The mode is 8. The average of the group of 8s is $24 \div 3 = 8$. The average of the rest of the elements is $20 \div 4 = 5$. Taking the average of 8 and 5 gives a 50% weight to the mode and a 50% weight to the rest of the elements: $13 \div 2 = 6.5$.

22. **(B)** The small, fundamental living units that make up all complex living things are called cells.

23. **(D)** Natural selection is the mechanism that underlies Darwin's theory of evolution.

24. **(A)** "Helio" means "sun, and "centric" means "center." The currently accepted model of the solar system is the heliocentric model.

25. **(C)** The extremely small, fundamenal units of matter are called atoms.

26. **(B)** A theory is a broad, comprehensive statement about a wide range of related subjects. It is based on numerous facts that have been repeatedly tested and confirmed. A hypothesis is an educated guess. It is a very narrowly defined and specific statement that can be tested and shown to be either true or false.

27. **(A)** An inference is an educated guess but is unverified. Option B is incorrect because an inference is not based on either data or facts. Options C and D are incorrect because a conclusion is based on experimental and observational evidence (facts). A conclusion is not found immediately after forming a hypothesis. In addition, it can disprove the original hypothesis.

28. **(D)** The control group is similar to the experimental group in every way except the one variable being tested. The use of a control group and of an experimental group allows scientists to isolate the variable being tested and to measure the variable's effects. In medical testing, the control group is not given the medication being tested. It is given a placebo (fake pill). In medical testing, the experimental group is given the medication being tested. Options A and B are incorrect because the control and experimental groups vary in several ways, not just one. Option C is incorrect because the control and experimental groups contain different numbers of individuals.

Science Overview

11

As we've already said a number of times in this book, the GED® test is an assessment of reasoning skills. It values your ability to explain your reasoning much more than it values your ability to repeat recalled (remembered) information. In other words, the test is much more about how you think than which facts you know. The test will provide source materials for you to review and will ask you questions based on them. You'll answer the questions and support your answers using evidence (facts) from the source materials.

→ **MULTIPLE CHOICE**

→ **FILL IN THE BLANK**

→ **DROP DOWN**

→ **HOT SPOT**

→ **DRAG AND DROP**

→ **SHORT ANSWER**

The following skills will be covered in this unit:

Lesson 1: Scientific Theories

Lesson 2: Reading and Interpreting Scientific Findings

Lesson 3: Planning and Conducting Investigations

Lesson 4: Reasoning from Evidence

Lesson 5: Communicating and Evaluating Scientific Findings

SCIENTIFIC REASONING: THINK LIKE A SCIENTIST

The Science test measures scientific reasoning. This means that the materials and questions will be related to subjects in science. To do well on the Science test, you'll need to use science-related source materials to answer questions the way a scientist would. So the lessons in this science unit of the book will help you learn to think like a scientist.

Remember that you will not have to learn four years' worth of science facts in order to be ready for the exam. Keep this point in mind when you're looking over the subject matter lists later in this chapter. You are expected to have a *general* understanding of science topics, not a detailed understanding. So always focus on the big picture. You just need to be familiar enough with the concepts that you can use when they are presented on the exam.

One portion of this unit provides you with an overview of the important concepts in science that are likely to be tested. Review this material to get a sense of your strengths and weaknesses in science.

Be Analytical

Analytical skills are critically important on the Science test. "Analysis" is a formal word that describes a process of careful examination. It answers the question "What does this information tell me?" To analyze something means to:

- Look at it closely and break it down into its components (parts)
- Identify the relationships among the parts, such as cause and effect
- Compare multiple items and identify relationships, similarities, and differences

One good example of analysis is the way we broke down the information on photosynthesis on pages 10–11. If you haven't read these pages yet or don't remember, read or review them now.

Scientists analyze everything. They analyze measurements and other observations, looking for structures, patterns, trends, and other relationships. They use this analysis to help them develop questions, answers, and experiments. They analyze work done by other scientists, including the data and experimental design. They do all this to see if the data could be useful in their own work and to see if they agree with the other scientists' conclusions.

In many cases, analysis requires scientists to work with information from more than one source. So scientists must compare these sources to identify relationships, similarities, and differences. The comparison may be between the findings of two different scientists, the results from two different experiments, or the design of experiments themselves. The ability to compare and contrast information from multiple sources is an important analytical skill.

Since different forms of analysis play such a large role in science, analytical skills make up a large part of the skills tested on the Science subject test. This is actually very good news for students, because analytical skills are quite easy to build. You simply have to remember to look closely at the details whenever you are working with new information. Try to break down the information into parts. Look for relationships among the parts. Does one thing seem to cause or to be caused by another thing? When working with multiple sources, look for similarities and differences among them. Do they generally agree or disagree?

As we progress through the individual lessons in the Science test section, we'll periodically point out the roles that analytical skills play in many different aspects of science.

SUBJECT MATTER

The Science test will include source materials from three areas of science:

- Life Science (40%)
- Physical Science (40%)
- Earth and Space Science (20%)

Life science includes biology and related subjects. It focuses on the study of living things, from simple, single-celled organisms to mammals and other more complex forms of life. The life science questions test the following topics:

- Human body and health
- Structure and function of life
- Genetics, heredity, and evolution
- Energy flows in living bodies and ecosystems

Physical science includes chemistry and related subjects. It focuses on the physical materials (sometimes called "matter"). Physical science questions test the following topics:

- Chemistry in human systems
- Physical flow, conservation, and transformation of energy
- Work, motion, and forces

Earth and space science includes geology and related subjects. It focuses on the study of our planet, our solar system, and the galaxy and universe beyond. Earth and space science questions test the following topics:

- Interactions between living things and the earth
- The composition and systems of the earth
- The composition and systems of space and the universe

Major Themes

Throughout the Science test, questions will be related to two major themes:

- Human life/living things
- Energy systems

When examining source information, questions, or answer choices, pay attention to any references to these themes. Information related to how living things interact or how energy is transferred within systems will usually be contained in the correct answer.

COLLEGE AND CAREER READINESS ANCHOR STANDARDS FOR READING

Reading is critical to building knowledge . . . in science and technical subjects. College and career ready reading in these fields requires an appreciation of the norms and conventions of each discipline, such as the kinds of evidence used in history and science; an understanding of domain-specific words and phrases; an attention to precise details; and the capacity to evaluate intricate arguments, synthesize complex information, and follow detailed descriptions of events and concepts. When reading scientific and technical texts, students need to be able to gain knowledge from challenging texts that often make extensive use of elaborate diagrams and data to convey information and illustrate concepts. Students must be able to read complex informational texts in these fields with independence and confidence because the vast majority of reading in college and workforce training programs will be sophisticated nonfiction. It is important to note that these Reading standards are meant to complement the specific content demands of the disciplines, not replace them.

The grades 6–12 standards on the following pages define what students should understand and be able to do by the end of each grade span. They correspond to the College and Career Readiness (CCR) anchor standards number. The CCR and grade-specific standards are necessary complements—the former providing broad standards, the latter providing additional specificity—that together define the skills and understandings that all students must demonstrate.

KEY IDEAS AND DETAILS

1. Read closely to determine what the text says explicitly and to make logical inferences from it; cite specific textual evidence when writing or speaking to support conclusions drawn from the text.
2. Determine central ideas or themes of a text and analyze their development; summarize the key supporting details and ideas.
3. Analyze how and why individuals, events, or ideas develop and interact over the course of a text.

CRAFT AND STRUCTURE

4. Interpret words and phrases as they are used in a text, including determining technical, connotative, and figurative meanings, and analyze how specific word choices shape meaning or tone.
5. Analyze the structure of texts, including how specific sentences, paragraphs, and larger portions of the text (e.g., a section, chapter, scene, or stanza) relate to each other and the whole.
6. Assess how point of view or purpose shapes the content and style of a text.

INTEGRATION OF KNOWLEDGE AND IDEAS

7. Integrate and evaluate content presented in diverse formats and media, including visually and quantitatively, as well as in words.
8. Delineate and evaluate the argument and specific claims in a text, including the validity of the reasoning as well as the relevance and sufficiency of the evidence.
9. Analyze how two or more texts address similar themes or topics in order to build knowledge or to compare the approaches the authors take.

RANGE OF READING AND LEVEL OF TEXT COMPLEXITY

10. Read and comprehend complex literary and informational texts independently and proficiently.

Integrated Math and Writing

Some questions on the Science test will require math skills and calculations, like interpreting graphs and charts, calculating averages and other measures of center (median, mode), and working with scientific notation and units of measurement. For most of these questions, a calculator will be provided. The test will also include some short-answer questions that require you to write a short response to explain your answer.

UNIT 4: SCIENCE

Fundamental Concepts

12

This section contains a more detailed list of the science topics and subtopics covered on the Science test. It provides you with the fundamentals you'll need in some important areas. Remember that you should focus on the big picture when studying science. Get familiar with the fundamental ideas as opposed to all of the technical details.

The Science test puts emphasis on the student having a broad understanding of certain fundamental topics in science. Although this book cannot discuss all the details in the tested subject areas, we've assembled some reviews of fundamental concepts in each area. Read these summaries to get familiar with some of the terms and concepts that are central to modern science. Your goal is not to memorize this information, merely to grasp the big picture so that you will recognize the information when it is presented again. We've selected and emphasized certain topics because they carry more significance on the exam. We've also presented only those aspects of the topics that relate to the test. In some cases, we've simplified the definitions to provide a good fit with what students need to know. Many of the technical details are not required for the test.

TIP

Online encyclopedias like Wikipedia provide comprehensive and detailed content about every area of science. You won't need that level of detail for the test. However, if you're curious, that's a great place to start.

LIFE SCIENCE TOPICS
Human Body and Health

- Body systems and functions
- Homeostasis and the effects of the environment on living things
- Nutrition
- Disease

Life Functions and Energy Intake

- Processes that provide energy to life functions (photosynthesis, respiration)

Energy Flows in Ecosystems

- Energy in ecosystems
- Movement of matter in ecosystems
- Carrying capacity and effects of change on carrying capacity
- Symbiosis and predator/prey relationships
- Disruption of ecosystems and extinction

Structure and Function of Life

- Life functions and supporting cellular components
- Cells
- Mitosis and meiosis

Genetics and Heredity

- Molecular biology, inheritance, chromosomes
- Genotypes, phenotypes, and probability of inheritance in close relatives
- Alleles, environmental alteration of traits, expression of traits

Evolution

- Common ancestry
- Selection and the requirements for selection
- Adaptation, selection pressure, and speciation

PHYSICAL SCIENCE TOPICS
Conservation, Transformation, and Flow of Energy

- Conduction and convection
- Endothermic and exothermic reactions
- Types and transformations of energy
- Sources of energy
- Waves and electromagnetic radiation

Work, Motion, and Forces

- Momentum
- Force, gravitation, mass, and weight
- Work, simple machines, and power

Chemical Properties and Reactions Related to Living Systems

- Structure of matter
- Physical and chemical properties, state changes, and density
- Chemical equations
- Solutions, solubility, and saturation

EARTH AND SPACE SCIENCE TOPICS
Interactions Between Earth's Systems and Living Things

- Cycles of matter and fossil fuels
- Natural hazards
- Resources and sustainability

Earth and Its System Components and Interactions

- The atmosphere
- The oceans
- System interactions (wind, weathering)
- Structure of Earth

Structures and Organization of the Cosmos

- The universe and stars
- Suns, planets, moons, and Earth
- Earth's age

Life Science

13

Living things are called **organisms**. There are many different types of organisms. Some are very large and complex (like humans), and some are smaller and simpler (like bacteria). What makes something alive? For purposes of the Science test, something is alive if it meets all of the following requirements.

- It maintains a balanced internal environment. This is called **homeostasis**, and humans do it when we sweat to maintain a steady body temperature.
- It has an **organized structure** consisting of one or more **cells**. Human bodies have many different kinds of **organs** and **tissues** with different kinds of cells. Bacteria, though, consist of simply one cell.
- It can **transform energy** into a form it can use to sustain itself. Plants do this when they convert sunlight to nutrients during **photosynthesis**. Humans do this when we eat and **digest** food.
- It **grows**, meaning that its systems and individual parts increase in size. Plants grow.
- It can respond to changes in its external environment. This is often indicated by the ability to move. Plants turn to face the sun. Humans react to things we see, hear, feel, taste, or touch. Changes in the external environment are called **stimuli**.
- It can produce new organisms and pass on genetic material through a **replication** (copying) process called **reproduction**. In some cases, reproduction involves a single parent. That is called **asexual** reproduction. For example, bacteria reproduce asexually. In other cases, reproduction involves two parents who both contribute genetic material to the **offspring**. That is called **sexual** reproduction. Humans reproduce sexually.
- It can **adapt** to its external environment by changing over time. The **theory of evolution** states that humans and all other living things have done this over very long periods of time.
- Unfortunately, a living thing can also die, proof that something is an organism.

CELLS

All organisms are made up of fundamental units (or building blocks) called **cells**. Cells are living things because they carry out all or most of the functions listed earlier. Cells maintain homeostasis. They have an organized structure consisting of parts called **organelles** and **membranes**. They break down food and use its energy to sustain themselves through **photosynthesis** and **respiration**. They grow, reproduce through **mitosis** and **meiosis**, and respond to stimuli. Cells can adapt over time.

Cells are self-contained, meaning that they are surrounded by some form of outer shell, like a capsule, **cell wall**, or other **membrane**. These are intended to act as barriers that can regulate the flow of material (food, oxygen, waste products) into and out of the cell. Membranes allow necessary materials to flow in while preventing any unneeded or harmful mate-

TIP

Important terms appear in bold type.

TIP

The word "stimulus" on the exam means you need to respond to the information presented to you, the same way that an organism responds to a change in its environment.

UNIT 4: SCIENCE

rials from entering the cell. They also allow waste products to flow out. (This process is called **excretion**.) For example, plant cells use a process called **osmosis** to maintain a balance of water between their internal environment and the external environment.

Virtually all living things are made up of cells. Some are **unicellular** (one cell). Some—like humans, animals, and plants—are **multicellular** (more than one cell, many cells). Some cells have a fairly simple organization. They have several surrounding layers (capsule, cell wall, and cell membrane) that protect a loosely packed mixture of genetic material and other cellular components. These cells are called **prokaryotes**. Other cells, called **eukaryotes**, have a more complex organization. Humans are made of eukaryotic cells. These cells have an external cell membrane that regulates the flow of materials in and out. However, they also have a number of internal components, called **organelles**, that are surrounded by their own membranes.

Organelles

Organelles are responsible for the more complex cellular functions required by many highly complex forms of life. The most important organelle is the **nucleus**, which is a central membrane-bound container of the cell's **genetic material** (called **chromatin**). This material is made up of the cell's **chromosomes** as well as supporting **proteins**. The chromosomes carry the cell's **DNA**. Other organelles are involved in breaking down food to produce energy and transporting energy and other materials within or out of the cell.

Chromosomes

A cell's genetic material is contained in chromosomes. In humans and many other living things, chromosomes exist in **homologous pairs**. Each pair contains all the genetic information for a **trait** or characteristic of the organism. For example, most human cells have 46 chromosomes, organized into 23 pairs that determine various physical characteristics (height, weight, complexion, eye color, hair color, and so on). Cells with pairs of homologous chromosomes are called **diploid**. Humans are diploid organisms because almost of our cells have pairs of chromosomes. One specialized type of cell, called a **gamete**, carries only one-half of each homologous pair. These are called **haploid** cells. Haploid gametes are a very important part of sexual reproduction and of the science of **genetics**, which studies the inheritance of traits from parents to **offspring**.

Cell Division

Cells reproduce through **cell division**. In this process, a **parent** cell splits into two or more **daughter** cells. The genetic material and other components in the parent cell are shared equally between the daughter cells. A process called **cytokinesis** physically separates the halves into two membrane-bound individuals by pinching or closing off the middle of the cell.

In prokaryotic cells, the process of cell division is called **binary fission** and results in two identical offspring. The cell's DNA is replicated (copied). The resulting duplicate chromosomes are separated within the cell. Then the cell membrane closes off one-half of the cell from the other.

For most eukaryotic cells, cell division includes a process called **mitosis**. The membrane-bound nucleus of the cell separates into two identical **nuclei** (plural of nucleus). This requires the replication of the cell's DNA, followed by the separation of the chromosomes into two identical sets, followed by the closing of the **nuclear membrane** to form separate nuclei. This duplication of the nucleus must happen before the cell itself can complete dividing its organelles and physically separating. Mitosis occurs in several phases in which the cell prepares itself, replicates important genetic information, divides up organelles and chromosomes, and then physically separates in half.

Gametes and Sexual Reproduction

Gametes are specialized cells involved in sexual reproduction. In humans, each gamete carries half of the homologous pairs required for human cells to grow and sustain life. When a **sperm** cell from a male parent and an **egg** cell from a female parent are combined, the resulting **zygote** (new diploid cell or offspring) contains homologous pairs of chromosomes. Half of the chromosomes are from one parent and half from the other. In humans, this means that 23 of the chromosomes are from the mother and 23 are from the father.

Gametes are created from diploid cells through a process called **meiosis**. During meiosis, homologous pairs of chromosomes exchange **genes**, which define human traits. As a result the **gene sequences** in each chromosome are different from the sequences in each parent's chromosome. Virtually all genes from the parent are still present, but they are combined into new sequences. The parent cell then divides, creating two diploid cells whose chromosomes are different from those in the parent's other cells. The new chromosome pairs in the daughter cells then separate. The daughter cells divide again, each receiving one-half of each new pair. This creates 4 haploid cells, each with half a pair of chromosomes that represents a new combination of the parent's genetic code.

Meiosis

Meiosis allows the offspring of humans, other animals, and plants to inherit physical characteristics from their parents without being identical copies of their parents. These new combinations of inherited traits lead to the family resemblance we see among members of a family. For example, fair-skinned parents usually have fair-skinned offspring. These same combinations can also determine whether or not a child has a genetic ability or disability.

ENERGY AND RESPIRATION

All living things, including cells, require **energy** to sustain them. This energy comes from some external source. One characteristic of a living thing is the ability to transform energy from an external form into one that can be used to support life. One method that cells use is called **cellular respiration**. In eukaryotic cells, specialized organelles called **mitochondria** are able to convert a substance called **pyruvate** into **ATP**. ATP is a form of chemical energy that can be transported around the cell and used to power the various cellular life functions. ATP can be extracted from simple sugars (like **glucose**) and other basic **nutrients** in food.

Several types of respiration occur. However, the one most common type among humans, animals, and plants requires oxygen and is called **aerobic respiration**. Cells use a series of chemical reactions called **glycolysis** to break glucose down into pyruvate, the pyruvate then enters the mitochondria, and additional chemical reactions extract the ATP for use by the cell. The overall process requires the presence of **oxygen**, and it produces waste in the form of **carbon dioxide** and **water**. The basic cellular process of aerobic respiration is closely related to important systems in the human body.

- **Respiratory system**—Lungs, nasal cavity, etc. The respiratory system takes in oxygen needed for aerobic respiration and releases carbon dioxide and water vapor.
- **Digestive system**—Mouth, esophagus, stomach, intestines, etc. The digestive system takes in food and breaks it down, until it is in a form simple enough for cells to use in aerobic respiration. The digestive system also filters waste products from food and the blood, releasing the waste from the body through **excretion**.
- **Circulatory system**—Heart, blood, blood vessels, etc. The circulatory system takes oxygen from the lungs to the cells for use in aerobic respiration. It also takes carbon dioxide from the cells to the lungs to be exhaled. This movement of oxygen and carbon dioxide is called a **cardiovascular** process. The circulatory system also takes glucose and other simple nutrients from the digestive system to individual cells for use in aerobic respiration. It also transports the solid waste products from cellular functions to the digestive system so the waste can be expelled from the body.

The human body consists of a number of other systems, including the **nervous system** (brain, nerves), **musculoskeletal system** (bones, joints, muscles), and several others. For the Science test, you must understand the relationship among the respiratory, digestive, and circulatory systems and the underlying process of aerobic respiration.

Aerobic Respiration

Aerobic respiration requires glucose and oxygen. Glucose is a simple sugar that is ideally suited for ATP extraction, and it is contained in the food a human or animal eats. Our digestive system takes in food from a variety of sources and breaks down the food into its basic nutrients (like glucose). Digestion allows the cells to use the glucose for energy and also eliminates waste products. The circulatory system moves glucose from digestive organs to cells. It also removes the waste products from the cells and moves it to the digestive tract for excretion. Our respiratory system brings into the body the oxygen that our cells need to live and also releases the carbon dioxide and water that our cells produce. Put another way: we need food, water, and oxygen because our cells need food, water, and air. Most of our body systems exist to deliver these vital items to our cells and to release the waste products we produce.

> **KNOW THIS**
>
> **Herbivores:** animals that eat plants
>
> **Carnivores:** animals that eat other animals
>
> **Omnivores:** animals (like humans) that can eat either plants or animals

Energy stored in the cells of a plant or an animal is digested and used when that plant or animal is eaten. So some animals get their energy by eating other animals. Some animals get their energy from eating plants. Where, then, do plants get their energy? What do plants eat?

PHOTOSYNTHESIS

The answer is that plants don't really eat. They "eat" sunlight using a process called **photosynthesis**. Plant cells have specialized organelles called **chloroplasts**. Sunlight shines onto chloroplasts, which convert the sunlight into chemical energy that can be stored by the plant's cells. Photosynthesis produces glucose. The plant can then use aerobic respiration to extract energy from the glucose to sustain itself. This glucose also provides the energy consumed by herbivores when they eat plants, which is transferred again when the herbivore is eaten by a carnivore.

Some living things are able to acquire and transform energy through a process that does not require oxygen. This process is called **anaerobic respiration**; **fermentation** is an example. Even so, the purpose of fermentation is to extract ATP by breaking down substances like pyruvate, which is often produced by glycolysis.

ECOSYSTEM AND THE FOOD CHAIN

An **ecosystem** is a collection of living things that occupy a common environment and interact with each other as part of a system in which nutrients and energy flow from producers to consumers. Energy usually enters the system as sunlight, which is converted and captured by plants using photosynthesis. The plants are then eaten by herbivores (primary consumers), many of whom are then eaten by carnivores (secondary consumers). Some organisms (tertiary consumers) eat the secondary consumers. Still others (omnivores like humans) often get food from multiple levels of this **food chain**.

Food chains from producers to consumers are often interconnected into more complex **food webs** in which a number of different plants provide a variety of food sources to a group of consumers, who in turn provide variety to other consumers, and so on. This ensures that each type of consumer has diverse food sources in order to survive.

All energy and matter (physical material) that an organism uses to live and grow comes from its food sources. All of the energy in an ecosystem originates with the producers. No new energy is created as it is transferred from consumer to consumer. In fact, each time a plant or an animal is consumed, an average of only 10% of its energy is transferred to the consumer. The rest is dissipated when it is used to sustain life in the animal that was eaten.

This steady reduction in the amount of energy available at different levels of a food chain is called the **pyramid of energy**. It dictates that only a small fraction of the total energy captured from sunlight will reach secondary or tertiary consumers. This leads to some similar phenomena like the **pyramid of numbers** and **pyramid of biomass (matter)**. As we move from the lowest level of a food chain, which consists of the producers (plants), to the higher levels, we can observe the population getting smaller and the individual size of the organisms getting larger. In other words, there are many more plants than animals. Plus most carnivores are larger than most herbivores.

Predators and Prey

The relationship between levels in a food chain is sometimes classified in terms of **predators** and **prey**. Predators hunt and eat other animals; animals that are eaten are called **prey**. (Plants are not really considered prey, nor are herbivores really considered predators. In general, prey is food you have to chase, and predators do the chasing.)

In some cases, one organism feeds off of another one without killing it or without killing it immediately. Organisms that feed this way are called **parasites**, and the animals they feed on are called **hosts**. Most parasites eventually harm or kill their hosts. However, some animals can form relationships with their hosts that are mutually beneficial, where each provides some benefit to the other. These are called **symbiotic** relationships.

The **carrying capacity** of an ecosystem is the overall population that it can sustain in terms of energy and habitat without its resources becoming exhausted. Changes in the amount of available food, water, or land as well as changes in temperature or other climatic elements

KNOW THIS

Plants are called **producers**.

All animals are called **consumers**.

Herbivores are **primary consumers** because they eat producers (plants).

Carnivores are called **secondary** or **tertiary consumers**.

can all affect an ecosystem's carrying capacity. For example, if warmer temperatures melt ice, more land might be exposed for plants to grow, increasing the system's ability to sustain herbivores and the carnivores that eat them. If an ecosystem is disrupted by a large or sudden change, it may no longer be able to sustain some or all of its organisms. In some cases, groups of similar organisms (called **species**) are able to respond to changes in an ecosystem through adaptation, which can often lead to the eventual development of a new species. The development of a new species based on an adaptation to a new environment or ecosystem is called **speciation**. When an organism no longer exists anywhere, it is considered **extinct**.

SPECIES

A species is the lowest and most specific grouping of living things. Organisms within a single species are able to breed together and produce viable offspring that are themselves capable of reproduction. Individuals within a species may have considerable variation in their physical characteristics (or **characters**). For examples, all dogs are a single species. However, different dogs vary greatly in their shape, size, and color. These are **inheritable variations** within a species, and each variation is called a **trait**.

Inherited Traits

Many of the traits present in a species are **inherited**, meaning that they are passed from parent to offspring through sexual reproduction. The combinations of genes that are present in each parent's gametes determine these traits. Since the gametes contain gene combinations that are different from those in the parents, the offspring can **manifest** (show) traits other than those seen in their parents. For example, two parents with brown hair may have a child with red hair.

The combination of parental traits in offspring has been recognized for thousands and thousands of years, long before a science called **genetics** was developed. For most of that time, the common belief was that these traits were blending in a way similar to the way that paint colors blend when they are mixed. In the mid-19th century, however, a monk and scientist named Gregor Mendel found that traits are passed on in a very structured way. In the process, he changed the way that we understand the inheritance of traits. This revolutionary discovery, along with all the subsequent understanding of chromosomes, genes, and DNA that would follow, took its first steps in a garden full of simple pea plants.

Mendel started his life on a farm and grew up with a good understanding of agriculture. Later in his life, he studied physics and chemistry before going to live and work at a monastery. While there, he spent a great deal of time cultivating many varieties of pea plants in the monastery garden. He became increasingly interested in the various traits that pea plants have and how these traits were passed on from generation to generation. The garden setting gave Mendel a lot of control over the breeding process. So he began to experiment with controlled breeding to try to learn more about the way traits are inherited.

Pea Plant Experiment

One trait that Mendel worked with is the trait for the color of the flower that grows on the pea plant. Some pea plants grow purple flowers, and some grow white flowers. Mendel began by breeding plants with the same colors over many generations. If offspring of the other color were produced, they were removed. Over time, these plants produced offspring with flowers of only the parent color. These were called **true-breeding** plants. Mendel then crossed a true-breeding purple-flowered plant with a true-breeding white-flowered plant. These parent plants were members of the **parent generation (P)**. All of the offspring that resulted from crossing the parent generation produced only purple flowers. The offspring were called the **F1 generation**. The plants in the F1 generation were then bred together. The colors of the flowers in the next generation (called the **F2 generation**) were analyzed. In the F2 generation, 75% of the plants produced purple flowers, but 25% produced white flowers.

The presence of white flowers in the F2 generation suggested that the trait for white flowers was preserved in the F1 generation and passed to the F2 generation, even though none of the members of the F1 generation manifested the trait. It also suggested that the purple trait was somehow stronger than the white trait since a cross between true purple and true white always produced purple. This recognition that traits could be preserved as they moved from generation to generation set the stage for the science of genetics.

Traits

Mendel went on to identify many other traits that behaved in a similar way in both pea plants and other organisms. Over time, he developed the concept of Medelian inheritance, which in turn became our modern science of genetics. When we talk about inheritance, we talk about traits that are passed from parent to offspring. These traits are transmitted through **genes** and **alleles**. Many traits are defined by a single pair of alleles, and offspring receive one allele from each parent during reproduction. Traits (and alleles) are either **dominant** or **recessive**. These terms refer to how the traits appear in a group of offspring. When both parents pass on the dominant trait, the offspring shows the dominant trait. When both parents pass on the recessive trait, the offspring shows the recessive trait. When one parent passes on the dominant trait and the other passes on the recessive trait, the offspring will show the dominant trait.

Pea plant flowers can be either purple (dominant) or white (recessive). Mendel observed that when a true-breeding purple-flowered plant is crossed with a true-breeding white-flowered plant, the offspring will always produce purple flowers. The physical appearance of a trait is called the **phenotype**. Mendel also observed that some of the offspring of the F1 generation, the F2 generation, would produce white flowers. This means that at least some of the F1 purple-flowered plants carried the alleles for white flowers even though they themselves produced only purple flowers. The set of actual genes or alleles present in an individual's genetic material is called the **genotype**. As Mendel observed, identifying an organism's genotype based on its phenotype is not always easy. Some purple-flowering pea plants carry no alleles for white flowers and will always produce purple-flowering offspring. Other purple-flowering pea plants carry alleles for white flowers and will produce some white-flowering offspring. Both kinds of plants produce purple flowers (same phenotype) but they don't have the same alleles (different genotypes).

Inheritance and Probability

As it turns out, probability plays a role in determining how many offspring in the F2 generation will manifest a recessive trait. Consider another pea plant trait that follows the rules of inheritance: seed color. Pea plant seeds are either yellow (dominant) or green (recessive). Since genotypes are defined by pairs of alleles, one way to symbolize this genotype is *Yg*. (Dominant alleles are typically capital letters, and recessive alleles are lowercase.) A true-breeding yellow-seeded plant will have a *YY* genotype, and a true-breeding green-seeded plant will have a *gg* genotype. When each parent produces gametes, each gamete will contain a single allele. The *YY* parent will produce only gametes that contain *Y* for this trait. The *gg* parent will produce only gametes that contain *g* for this trait. These single alleles will combine in the offspring generation, resulting in three possible combinations: *YY*, *Yg*, and *gg*. In our seed color example, both parents are homozygous (*YY* and *gg*). Any cross among their gametes must produce a *Yg* combination of alleles. This means that 100% of the offspring in the F1 generation will produce only yellow seeds but will also be heterozygous.

When the plants in the F1 generation breed, their gametes could combine to produce either homozygous offspring or heterozygous offspring. A gamete containing *Y* could combine with either a gamete containing *Y* or one containing *g*, producing either *YY* or *Yg* offspring. A gamete containing *g* could combine with either a gamete containing *Y* or one containing *g*, producing either *Yg* or *gg* offspring. The key here is that each of the homozygous possibilities is different (*YY* and gg), but the two heterozygous possibilities are the same (*Yg* and *Yg*). This makes the *Yg* variety twice as likely as either the *YY* or the *Yg* varieties in the F2 generation.

Probability says, then, that in a group of four offspring in the F2 generation, 1 will be *YY*, 2 will be *Yg*, and 1 will be *gg*. This means that 75% of the offspring will have yellow seeds and 25% will have green seeds, which agrees with Mendel. Of the 75% that produce yellow seeds, one-third will be homozygous dominant (*YY*) and two-thirds will be heterozygous (*Yg*). All of the green-seeded plants will be homozygous recessive (*gg*).

Not all traits are determined by single pairs of alleles. Some, Mendel found, are determined by two pairs, and some are determined by more than two pairs. In general, however, the broad concept of inheritance provides an explanation for the way that varieties of traits appear in and are passed down among generations within a species.

To help organize and present these ideas, a scientist named Reginald Punnett developed a visual model for Mendelian inheritance called the Punnett square.

THEORY OF EVOLUTION

This concept of variation within a species plays a very important role in another central idea in the life sciences: the theory of evolution by natural selection. This theory deals with the way that changes in the environment or ecosystem will affect the relative chances of survival among the varieties within a species. If these relative chances of survival change, a species may display an adaptation (change). If the species is divided by environmental change, the two groups may eventually become distinct species. These ideas were famously collected and expressed by Charles Darwin. Although it is not clear how much Mendel's ideas influenced Darwin, the two men were both pioneers in developing our understanding of this science of heredity.

Darwin

As part of a survey expedition to South America, Charles Darwin collected fossils and live specimens of plants and animals from many places, including from each of the Galapagos Islands. He documented their various characteristics. Among the animal species he documented were several species of finches (birds) that seemed to have descended from a common species. The common ancestor was the species of finch that had first arrived on the islands from the mainland. All of the finch species were related to this single ancestor, but each was different in some observable ways from both the common ancestor and from one another. The different species had beaks with different shapes (long, short, pointed, blunt, large, small) and different food sources. In general, Darwin observed that the differences were beneficial to the species because they gave the finches access to a local source of food.

For example, some new species had larger, stronger beaks well suited to cracking nuts. These species lived in an area where nuts were plentiful. The original ancestor did not have a beak suited for cracking nuts. Another new species had a long, narrow beak well suited for digging into cactus fruit. This species lived in an area where cactus fruit was available. Darwin imagined that the ancestor species had likely included some individuals that were born with unusual beak shapes but that these shapes were probably not suited to the sources of food in the original environment. Without access to food, the individuals would likely not survive to reproduce. The traits for these unusual beak shapes would remain rare in the population.

Darwin then imagined the effect of migration to the new environment in the Galapagos. Different ecosystems presented different sources of food, and the original beak shapes might not have been well suited to any of them. Instead, he reasoned, the unusual shapes that had been a disadvantage before might provide an advantage in the new environment, as in the case of the nut-cracking and cactus-eating beaks. In this new setting, the individuals with unusual beak shapes would have sources of food for which there was little competition, greatly increasing their survival rates. Further, if the individuals with the original beak shapes weren't able to find a viable food source, the trait for those beak shapes might eventually be reduced or eliminated in that community of finches. The natural environment, by providing various sources of food and other challenges to survival, would select the individuals with the traits that were best suited for survival. Over time, those traits would become the dominant traits within that species.

This realization provided the basis for an understanding of the fossil record, which showed clear evidence of adaptation and speciation over long periods of time. It also agreed with the ideas that Mendel and others were developing. In the years that followed, scientists would find a great deal of additional evidence to support and extend the ideas in these central theories. One of the most important of these findings was the work done by Watson, Crick, and other scientists to develop our knowledge of the existence and function of a molecule called DNA.

DNA

Deoxyribonucleic acid (**DNA**) is the vehicle that carries our genetic information. It is responsible for the development of all of our physical traits. It is the foundation for genetic inheritance and also for adaptation and speciation resulting from natural selection. More information about matter, chemical elements, and molecules is coming later in the review of physical science. However, before we turn to those topics, we should spend a little time on this unique and fascinating molecule. For the purposes of this review, we'll focus mainly on the cells of organisms like humans, animals, and plants.

DNA resides in the chromosomes contained in the nucleus of each cell. When cells divide, each cell receives a complete set of DNA from the parent cell. The exception to this is in gametes (sperm and egg cells), which contain half as many chromosomes as other kinds of human cells. DNA is organized in a very complex **double helix** structure. However, it can be more easily visualized as having a shape similar to a ladder. An even better analogy is the zipper that is used to seal various kinds of clothing. Both a ladder and a zipper are organized with two parallel vertical sides that are joined in the middle. In the case of the ladder, the sides are joined by rungs. In the case of the zipper, the two sides are joined by a connection between the teeth on each side.

A DNA molecule is composed of two vertical **strands** joined at regular intervals by pairs of bases. The sequences of these paired bases make up the genes and alleles responsible for the development of new cells and for the genetic inheritance of traits. The bases are like the teeth in the zipper. At times, they are connected. At other times, they can separate and then reconnect.

DNA Bases

There are four types of bases in DNA:

adenine (A)
cytosine (C)
guanine (G)
thymine (T)

DNA strands are joined when the bases attached to one strand pair up with the bases on the other strand to form **bonds**. There are two categories of bases: **purines** and **pyrimidines**. These different categories of bases differ in size. The bases also differ in terms of the hydrogen bonds that they can form with other bases. The bonds that can be formed are determined by the number of locations that a base has available to form hydrogen bonds with another base. Some bases have 2 bond locations, and some have 3.

Bases can appear along one strand in any sequence, but they form pairs according to certain rules.

1. First, each pair must contain both a purine and a pyrimidine.
2. Second, a base can pair only with a base that has the same number of available bond locations.
3. Third, a base cannot pair with itself (for example, adenine cannot pair with another adenine).

The table below shows information about these DNA bases.

Base	Type	Number of Bond Locations	Base It Bonds With
Adenine (A)	Purine	2	Thymine (T)
Cytosine (C)	Pyrimidine	3	Guanine (G)
Guanine (G)	Purine	3	Cytosine (C)
Thymine (T)	Pyrimidine	2	Adenine (A)

The effect of these pairing restrictions is that adenine will always be paired with thymine, and cytosine will always be paired with guanine. No matter how the bases are sequenced on the many strands that make up the many chromosomes in the human genome, they will always pair with one and only one companion base. This provides endless variation in terms of the combinations of genes that can be expressed along the DNA strands. However, base-pairing rules also provide a strict control mechanism that supports effective replication (copying) of DNA molecules.

Replication

When DNA replicates, the two strands in the original molecule first separate. Then two new strands are created, base by base, along each of the original strands. Each new strand joins its companion original strand, which results in two complete molecules, each a copy of the original. This sets the stage for the division of the cell nucleus and the eventual division of the entire cell. For example, a strand can contain bases in a seemingly random sequence:

ACTCGATCAGATCCGGATAC

During replication, there is only one possible strand it can pair with:

TGAGCTAGTCTAGGCCTATG

This ensures that DNA replication will result in nearly identical molecules.

Bases are also involved in the recombination of genetic material during meiosis. When gametes are created, an exchange of bases among chromosomes prior to separation makes the new chromosomes different from those in the parents, enabling new combinations of traits to manifest themselves in the offspring.

PRACTICE

1. Which of the following statements is NOT true?
   (A) An elephant is alive because it can transform energy into a form that it can use to sustain itself.
   (B) Plants are considered to be alive even though they cannot respond to changes in their external environment.
   (C) Puppies are alive because they grow.
   (D) A man who never fathers a child is considered to be alive even though he never reproduces.

2. Which of the following is an organelle?
   (A) Lung
   (B) Heart
   (C) Kidney
   (D) Nucleus

3. Which of these sequences will pair with the following DNA strand during replication?

AATTAACGGACGTG

(A) TTAATTGCCTGCAC
(B) AATTAACGGACGTG
(C) CCGGCCATTCATGT
(D) UUAAUUGCCUGCAC

Answers and Explanations:

1. **(B)** Plants do respond to changes in their external environment, which is one reason that they are alive. For example, plants turn to face the sun as it moves. The ability to transform energy into a usable form and the ability to grow are both common to all living things. Even if one individual of a species chooses not to reproduce, that individual is part of a species that does reproduce. This explains why a childless man is considered to be alive.

2. **(D)** The nucleus is an internal component of the cell. It is surrounded by its own membrane. All internal cellular components surrounded by membranes are called organelles. Options A, B, and C are wrong because the lungs, heart, and kidneys are all organs. Each one is made of millions of different cells.

3. **(A)** In DNA, adenine (A) pairs only with thymine (T), and cytosine (C) pairs only with guanine (G).

Physical Science

14

Cell theory tells us that all living things are made up of cells and that cells transform energy, reproduce, and pass on their DNA to their offspring. Cells are the building blocks of life. However, what building blocks are used to make up cells and the nutrients and other materials cells need to live?

THE ATOM

The fundamental unit of all the material in our physical world, including all living things and nonliving objects and substance, is called an **atom**. Atoms make up all forms of **matter**, including solids, liquids, gases, and plasma. Atoms are made up of three types of components called **particles: protons**, **neutrons**, and **electrons**. Atoms are identified by the number of protons and neutrons they have. The number of protons determines the **chemical element** (hydrogen, carbon, oxygen, and so on). The number of neutrons determines the specific variation of the element, called the **isotope**.

Atoms have an internal structure that organizes the particles. Protons and neutrons make up the **nucleus** (or center) of the atom. The electrons move around the nucleus in regions called **shells**. Some atomic particles carry an **electrical charge**. Protons have a positive electrical charge. Neutrons have no electrical charge. Electrons have a negative electrical charge. If an atom has the same number of protons and electrons, it is neutrally charged. If it has more protons than electrons, it has a net positive charge. If it has more electrons than protons, it has a net negative charge.

Over time, a system has been developed for describing and organizing the various chemical elements according to their properties. This has led to a shorthand language of abbreviations and numbers that condense the information into a form that is useful to scientists.

One category of properties of atoms deals with the numbers of the different particles that are present in the atoms of a given element. As discussed earlier, elements differ in the number of protons present in the nucleus. Each element has an **atomic number** that indicates the number of protons present in the nucleus of an atom of that element. The atomic number is sometimes called the **proton number**. Some elements have very few protons, like **hydrogen (H)**, which has only 1. Others have many protons, like **gold (Au)**, which has 79.

Since the number of protons is related to the number of electrons, a larger number of protons has an effect on the number of electron shells present in atoms of a given element. The first electron shell can hold up to 2 electrons. Atoms with 2 or fewer electrons have only one shell. Only hydrogen and helium (He) have a single electron shell. Each shell between the first and outermost shells can hold an increasing number of electrons. The outermost electron shell can hold a maximum of 8 electrons. Electrons in the outer shell of an atom are called **valence electrons**.

Periodic Table of Elements

Group →	1	2	3	4	5	6	7	8	9	10	11	12	13	14	15	16	17	18
Period 1	1 H																	2 He
2	3 Li	4 Be											5 B	6 C	7 N	8 O	9 F	10 Ne
3	11 Na	12 Mg											13 Al	14 Si	15 P	16 S	17 Cl	18 Ar
4	19 K	20 Ca	21 Sc	22 Ti	23 V	24 Cr	25 Mn	26 Fe	27 Co	28 Ni	29 Cu	30 Zn	31 Ga	32 Ge	33 As	34 Se	35 Br	36 Kr
5	37 Rb	38 Sr	39 Y	40 Zr	41 Nb	42 Mo	43 Tc	44 Ru	45 Rh	46 Pd	47 Ag	48 Cd	49 In	50 Sn	51 Sb	52 Te	53 I	54 Xe
6	55 Cs	56 Ba		72 Hf	73 Ta	74 W	75 Re	76 Os	77 Ir	78 Pt	79 Au	80 Hg	81 Tl	82 Pb	83 Bi	84 Po	85 At	86 Rn
7	87 Fr	88 Ra		104 Rf	105 Db	106 Sg	107 Bh	108 Hs	109 Mt	110 Ds	111 Rg	112 UUb	113 Uut	114 Uuq	115 Uup	116 Uuh	117 Uus	118 Uuo

Lanthanides	57 La	58 Ce	59 Pr	60 Nd	61 Pm	62 Sm	63 Eu	64 Gd	65 Tb	66 Dy	67 Ho	68 Er	69 Tm	70 Yb	71 Lu
Actinides	89 Ac	90 Th	91 Pa	92 U	93 Np	94 Pu	95 Am	96 Cm	97 Bk	98 Cf	99 Es	100 Fm	101 Md	102 No	103 Lr

THE PERIODIC TABLE

The **Periodic Table of Elements** (shown above) organizes the elements into rows of increasing atomic number, with a new row (or **period**) for each collection of elements with the same number of electron shells. The table currently contains elements with up to 7 shells. Each column (or **group**) in the table represents a collection of elements with the same number of valence electrons in their outer shells, increasing from left to right. For example, nitrogen (N) and oxygen (O) both have two electron shells. However, oxygen has 6 valence electrons but nitrogen has only 5. Oxygen and sulfur (S) both have 6 valence electrons. However, sulfur has 3 electron shells while oxygen has only 2.

Atoms are also described using a **mass number**, which is the total number of particles in the nucleus (protons and neutrons) since those particles contribute the most to an atom's mass. Subtracting the atomic number from the mass number will yield the number of neutrons in an atom, which is called the neutron number. Different isotopes of the same element are often distinguished using their mass numbers since the number of neutrons determines the particular isotope of an element.

Elements can form connections, or **bonds**, with one another. When elements of different types bond together, they form **compounds** (or **molecules**). Many of the more familiar substances in our world are compounds made up of bonded elements. Water is a combination of atoms of hydrogen and oxygen. Carbon dioxide is a combination of carbon and oxygen. Glucose (a sugar) is made up of carbon, hydrogen, and oxygen. In our earlier discussion of DNA, we learned that DNA strands are joined by bonds between the chemical bases that define our genetic code. The ability of elements to form bonds and, in turn, to become part of more complex compounds enables the fundamental building blocks of matter to support the broad diversity that exists in the world of natural substances and materials. The most common types of bonds are covalent bonds and ionic bonds.

UNIT 4: SCIENCE

Common Bonds

Covalent bonds are formed when two atoms share a pair of valence electrons. Covalent bonds can be single (one shared pair), double (two shared pairs), or triple (three shared pairs). The more unpaired electrons in the valence shell, the greater the number of different bonds it can form with other atoms. Covalent bonds tend to form between elements with similar numbers of electrons.

Ionic bonds form between atoms with larger differences in the numbers of their electrons. The number of electrons in an atom has an impact on its **electronegativity,** which describes how powerfully an atom pulls on shared electrons. Some atoms actually pull electrons from other atoms into their own shells, increasing their negative charge. The other atom's charge is made more positive by the loss of the electron. Since opposite charges attract, the two atoms are bonded through the differences in their charges.

Molecules are represented using a combination of letters and numbers indicating which elements it contains and how many of each atom. For example, water is symbolized as H_2O, which means it has 2 atoms of hydrogen (H) and 1 atom of oxygen (O). Carbon monoxide (CO) consists of 1 atom of carbon (C) and 1 of oxygen (O). Carbon dioxide (CO_2) has 1 atom of carbon and 2 of oxygen. Glucose, which is an important sugar for the processes that support life in cells, is symbolized as $C_6H_{12}O_6$ because it has 6 atoms of carbon, 12 atoms of hydrogen, and 6 atoms of oxygen.

Just as bonds can form between atoms, bonds between atoms can also be broken. Once the existing bonds have been broken, new bonds can form between the newly separated atoms. In general, the breaking of bonds requires the presence of some other element. The process of breaking bonds between atoms and then forming new compounds is called a **chemical reaction**.

Chemical Reactions

One commonly used example of a chemical reaction is that for cellular respiration. In this process, chemical energy is extracted from glucose:

$$C_6H_{12}O_6 + 6O_2 \rightarrow 6CO_2 + 6H_2O + \text{energy}$$

This is an example of a **chemical equation** being used to describe a chemical reaction. The arrow represents the reaction itself and acts like an equal sign in an algebraic equation. The numbers to the left of the molecules ($6O_2$, $6CO_2$) indicate the number of each molecule in the reaction. The equation above shows us that 1 molecule of glucose and 6 molecules of oxygen react to produce 6 molecules of carbon dioxide and 6 molecules of water. Some energy in the form of heat is also produced when the bonds between the atoms are broken.

Chemical equations must be kept in balance. This means that the number of each type of atom going into a reaction should equal the number coming out. For example, 18 atoms of oxygen enter the respiration reaction (6 in the glucose and 2 in each of 6 molecules of oxygen for a total of 18). There are also 6 atoms of carbon and 12 of hydrogen. Coming out of the reaction are 18 atoms of oxygen (2 each in 6 atoms of carbon dioxide and 1 in each of 6 atoms of water for a total of 18) as well as 6 carbon and 12 hydrogen atoms.

Photosynthesis is another well-known example of a balanced chemical reaction:

$$6CO_2 + 6H_2O + \text{light energy} \rightarrow C_6H_{12}O_6 + 6O_2$$

As compared with photosynthesis, this process is reversed. Energy in the form of sunlight is put into a reaction along with carbon dioxide and water. The result is glucose and oxygen. In most chemical reactions, a balance is preserved among the atoms going in and coming out. The process either stores energy or releases it.

Reactions that convert chemical bond energy to heat (or light) energy are called **exothermic**. Reactions that convert heat (or light) energy to chemical bond energy are called **endothermic**.

Potential and Kinetic Energy

Chemical bond energy and heat energy are good examples of two categories of energy: **potential energy** and **kinetic energy**. Potential energy, like chemical energy, is a form of stored energy. Kinetic energy, like heat, is energy related to the motion of a physical object. Heat is related to the motion of the particles in a substance.

Consider a pendulum at rest. The pendulum hangs at the end of the string, not moving. No energy is in this system. Now if we pull the pendulum up to one side, we have introduced potential energy into the system. By holding the pendulum against the weight of gravity, we have positioned the pendulum so that it has the potential to move.

When we release the pendulum, the potential energy is converted to kinetic energy as the pendulum begins to swing. The amount of potential energy begins to decrease as the speed of the swing increases. However, as the pendulum starts to swing upward, the speed of the swing slows. This decreases the amount of kinetic energy. As the swing takes the pendulum farther away from the pull of gravity, the potential energy related to its position begins to increase again. When the swing stops and reverses, the cycle repeats itself. Each time the conversion occurs, a small amount of the energy is lost, causing each swing to get progressively slower. Eventually, the swing stops altogether as the energy in the system returns to zero.

Motion

Motion, as demonstrated by the swing of the pendulum, can be defined as a change in an object's position or location. Motion has several properties that can be described quantitatively. One familiar property is called **speed**. Speed indicates the rate of change in an object's position without describing the direction of motion. When you say that a car is traveling at 55 miles per hour, you are discussing its speed. You are describing the rate of change in position but not describing the direction of that change. The description of motion that includes both the **magnitude** (amount) of the change and the **direction** of the change is called **velocity**. If you say that a car is traveling north at 55 miles per hour, you are discussing the car's velocity.

A change in velocity is called **acceleration**. Even though we typically associate that word with something that makes an object move faster (like the accelerator in a car), acceleration can cause an object to slow down as well as speed up. It can also make an object start moving from a stationary position (or **at rest**). Instead, acceleration can stop a moving object and cause it to become stationary. Slowing down or stopping is sometimes called **deceleration**. Acceleration can also act to change an object's direction as opposed to changing its speed.

Force

Acceleration is an example of the result of **force** acting on an object. Anything that can cause a change in an object's shape/structure, direction, or movement is considered a force. There are several different kinds of force, but they can all be classified as either push or pull. Push forces **repel** another object. Pull forces **attract** another object. Gravity, which is a force that pulls all objects near Earth toward Earth's core, is an example of a force that pulls on objects.

When a force is applied in the direction of motion, the moving object accelerates. When a force is applied in the direction opposite the direction of motion, the moving object decelerates (accelerates in reverse). When a force is applied at an angle to the direction of motion, the object's direction changes (accelerates in a different direction). If all the forces applied to an object are balanced in opposite directions, the object's motion stops. This is because there is no **net force** or **unbalanced force** working on the object. When we jump off a chair, gravity causes us to move until we encounter the floor. The floor essentially acts like a force because it provides support against the pull of gravity. The floor balances the pull of gravity because it is strong enough to do so. If the floor were made from cardboard, gravity would be a **net force** on us and we would continue moving through the floor.

THE LAWS OF MOTION

Sir Isaac Newton studied motion extensively and articulated three laws of motion as part of the science of mechanics, which is now known as classical mechanics. Learn Newton's three laws of motion:

First law: "An object at rest will tend to stay at rest, and an object in motion will tend to stay in motion." If no unbalanced force acts on an object, that object's velocity will remain constant. If the object is moving, it will continue to move in the same direction at the same rate (same velocity). If it is not moving, it will continue to not move.

Second law: "The force required to accelerate an object is directly proportional to the object's mass. The amount of acceleration a force can produce in an object is inversely proportional to the object's mass." This is usually expressed as $F = ma$, where F is the force, m is the mass, and a is the acceleration. This law also states that acceleration occurs in the direction of the force applied.

Third law: "For every action, there is an equal and opposite reaction." Forces are balanced. When one object applies force to another, that second object applies an equal force to the first object in the opposite direction. This can be understood in terms of standing on the floor. Most of us know that when we stand on a floor, our weight applies force to the floor. What Newton's third law explains is that the floor also applies a force of equal strength to us but in the opposite direction. While we're pushing down on the floor, it's pushing up on us. Think about how it feels to ride an elevator when the car speeds up and slows down. As the speed of the car changes, the force pushing up on us changes, and we feel the floor shift under our feet.

GRAVITY

One of the largest challenges for Newton and the other scientists of his time was the question of **gravity** or **gravitation**, which refers to the force that large objects exert on one another. It was clear from all the work done in classical mechanics that some fundamental attracting force existed because its effects were visible in the various experiments and observations being conducted. This force could be measured. However, the mechanism by which it operated was still a puzzle. Only much later would Einstein suggest that objects with enough mass can actually cause the fabric of space to curve, causing what appears to be an attraction between bodies.

The question of gravitation arose from investigations into how and why the planets in our solar system moved in elliptical orbits around the sun. Planets are very large objects, arranged at increasingly large distances from the sun. They are in constant motion. This motion of the planets is curved. Newton's laws tell us that some force must be acting on the planets to move them in their curved paths or **orbits**. That force was identified as the gravitational force. Newton deduced that there was a relationship among gravity, mass, and distance. The greater the mass an object has, the greater the gravitational force it will exert on objects around it. The closer an object is to another object, the stronger the effect of gravitational pull.

Since the sun is so much larger than the planets in orbit around it, the motion of the planets is determined by the gravitational pull exerted on them by the sun. The planets continually try to move along a straight line and are continually accelerated along a curved path by the pull of gravity toward the center of their orbits. This same balance of forces causes Earth's moon to follow an elliptical path around Earth. Since Earth is so much more massive than our bodies, Newton's theory of gravity also explains why we experience gravity as a force that pulls us toward the planet.

PRACTICE

1. Which of the following is true about a covalent bond?
   (A) One atom donates a valence electron, and the other atom accepts a valence electron.
   (B) It keeps planets in orbit around the sun.
   (C) Two atoms can form a quadruple covalent bond when they share four pairs of valence electrons.
   (D) Two atoms share a pair of valence electrons.

2. Which of the following is correct?
   (A) CO_2 is made of 2 atoms of carbon and 1 atom of oxygen.
   (B) CH_4 is made of 4 groups bound together, each containing 1 atom of carbon and 1 atom of hydrogen.
   (C) Carbon has an atomic number of 6 because it is made of 2 protons plus 2 neutrons plus 2 electrons.
   (D) Oxygen, which has an atomic number of 8, has 2 more protons than carbon, which has an atomic number of 6.

3. Which of the following is NOT one of Newton's three laws of motion?
   (A) For every action, there is an equal and opposite reaction.
   (B) Velocity is the rate at which an object moves in a specific direction.
   (C) An object at rest will tend to stay at rest. An object in motion will tend to stay in motion.
   (D) The force to accelerate an object is directly proportional to the object's mass, $F = ma$.

Answers and Explanations

1. **(D)** The definition of a covalent bond is when atoms share valence electrons. Option A is incorrect because it is the definition of an ionic bond. Option B is incorrect because it is describing the gravitational force. Option C is incorrect because quadruple covalent bonds never form. Covalent bonds can be single (1 pair of electrons), double (2 pairs of electrons), or triple (3 pairs of electrons).

2. **(D)** The atomic number indicates the number of protons present in the nucleus of an atom. Since oxygen has an atomic number of 8 and carbon has an atomic number of 6, oxygen must have $8 - 6 = 2$ more protons than carbon. Option A is incorrect because CO_2 is made of 1 atom of carbon and 2 atoms of oxygen. Option B is incorrect because CH_4 is made of 1 atom of carbon and 4 atoms of hydrogen. Option C is incorrect. Since carbon has an atomic number of 6, it contains 6 protons in its nucleus. Carbon also contains 6 neutrons in its nucleus. A neutral atom of carbon contains 6 electrons in orbit around the nucleus.

3. **(B)** Although this is an accurate definition of velocity, it is not one of Newton's three laws of motion. Option A is Newton's third law of motion. Option C is Newton's first law of motion. Option D is Newton's second law of motion.

Earth and Space Science

15

Although Newton made major contributions to our understanding of the movement of objects in our solar system and the cosmos beyond it, he was far from the first person to try to understand the **celestial bodies** present in the universe. People have been fascinated with astronomy for thousands of years. **Astronomy** is a science devoted to investigating the things we can observe in space, including **planets**, **stars**, and **galaxies**.

A **star** is a large ball of **plasma** (a form of matter) held together by gravity. The matter in stars undergoes constant chemical reactions in which hydrogen is converted to helium, releasing large amounts of energy across a broad radioactive spectrum (heat, light, other forms of radiation, and so on). The **sun** is a star. The energy it releases is so intense that even after that energy travels over long distances to reach Earth, it is still able to provide all the energy present in all of our food sources. That energy is also sometimes intense enough to melt, burn, or otherwise damage physical objects.

Stars, including the sun, are very dense. This means that stars are very massive and exert a strong gravitational pull. Over time, this pull can attract planets and keep them in orbit around the star.

A **galaxy** is a large concentration of stars grouped together by the attraction of their mutual gravitational forces. Our solar system is part of a galaxy called the **Milky Way**.

THE SOLAR SYSTEM

The **solar system** consists of a star called the **sun** and the planets (including **Earth**) and other objects that orbit the sun and the planets. **Planets** are large, round objects that travel in elliptical paths around the sun. The planets in a solar system are arranged in concentric rings with the sun near the center. Some planets have their own objects (**satellites**) that orbit them, like the moon orbits Earth.

There are many different kinds of planets in the Solar System, representing a wide range of sizes, temperatures, and compositions. Even the planets that are somewhat similar to Earth (like Venus and Mars) are still very different from our home planet. Earth has a number of systems and structural elements that help it provide the home that humanity has needed since time began.

EARTH

Earth is a dense, solid planet consisting mostly of rock, iron, and similar materials. The core of Earth is made up of iron, which makes the planet have a very great mass, as well as a number of radioactive elements that produce a great deal of heat. Temperatures at the center of the planet are measured in many thousands of degrees. Surrounding this core is a layer (or **mantle**) consisting of **magma** (melted rock and metal). As the layers move farther away from Earth's core, temperatures begin to cool. The magma eventually becomes a solid layer referred to as Earth's **crust**. This crust is approximately 18.6 miles (30 km) deep. It is the layer of the planet on which all life resides. The crust is organized in large shelves called **tectonic plates**, which shift and move in response to pressure created at Earth's core. The movements of Earth's tectonic plates have been described in the theory of **continental drift**.

The surface of the planet is surrounded by layers of oxygen and other elements in gaseous form. These layers form Earth's atmosphere. They provide the air we breathe, insulation from the cold temperatures of space, and protection from harmful and powerful solar radiation.

Earth's surface and atmosphere support all the various ecosystems that sustain the diversity of life. The health of Earth's planetary systems and the health of living things on the planet are very closely connected. The effects of human population growth on the surface of the planet and on the atmosphere could cause changes that would make Earth much less hospitable to human life. One of the main themes of the Science test is the close relationship among all living things and all physical matter no matter the size, whether microscopic, planetary, or somewhere in between. The core building blocks of matter influence the behavior of cells and the formation of our planet, which in turn provide the basis for human life to exist and propagate. The same rules and forces that affect the natural world at the level of atoms and cells affect the world at the level of stars, planets, and galaxies.

PRACTICE

1. Which of the following is correct about Earth?
   (A) Earth's crust is made mostly of iron and radioactive elements.
   (B) Tectonic plates are large pieces of the planet's crust that shift and move.
   (C) The core of the planet is very cold because it is insulated from the sun's warmth by the crust.
   (D) Magma consists of solid rock and metal.

Answer and Explanation

1. **(B)** The crust is organized in large shelves called tectonic plates. These plates shift and move in response to pressure created at Earth's core. Option A is incorrect because the crust is made primarily of rock. Option C is incorrect because the core of the planet is extremely hot due to the pressure inside the planet. Option D is incorrect because magna consists of melted rock and metal.

Understanding Science

16

Science comes from curiosity about the natural world. Scientists, like most people, want to know how things work in the world around them, from the microscopically small (atoms and cells) to the life sized (humans and other living things) to the astronomically large (planets, planetary systems, stars, galaxies, and universe). From the very beginning, scientists have observed the natural world, thought about the things and events they observed, and asked questions:

- Why does this happen?
- How does this happen?
- What would happen if . . . ?

Asking these kinds of questions and looking for answers is at the heart of all science. Scientists take great care to ensure that their answers are reliable (or **valid**). In fact, the word "science" comes from a Latin word that means "to know." It describes a very specific way of knowing that an answer is true. In science, knowledge cannot be based on opinions, assumptions, or guesses. It can be based on only facts (or **data**). These facts must be observed in the natural world. If put another way, seeing is believing. Science is not about what scientists think is true. It is only about what the evidence suggests is true. Science is knowledge about the natural world that is based on reliable facts.

So what do scientists do? For the purposes of the Science test, scientists:

- Construct scientific theories to answer questions
- Read and interpret scientific findings
- Plan and conduct investigations
- Conduct quantitative data analysis
- Reason from evidence and draw conclusions
- Communicate their findings
- Evaluate the findings of other scientists

Each of these is a specific reasoning skill tested in context on the Science test. The lessons in this section will provide you with an overview of these skills as well as more detailed coverage of some of the more fundamental skills.

Most of the knowledge developed by scientists is organized into **theories**. Theories offer proposed answers or explanations for the questions scientists ask. In everyday life, when we say "that's just a theory," we usually mean that a given idea is just an unproven opinion. However, that definition doesn't apply to science. In science, a theory is a strongly supported and reliable idea that is accepted as fact.

Examples of well-known scientific theories include:

- **Heliocentric model of the solar system**—This theory states that the sun is the center of the **solar system** and that the planets move in orbit around it.
- **Cell theory**—This theory states that all living things are composed of **cells**.
- **Atomic theory**—This theory states that all physical material (matter) is made up of particles called atoms.
- **Theory of evolution**—This theory states that natural selection is responsible for adaptation (adjustment to the environment) and speciation (the development of species).

From the statements each theory makes, it is possible to identify the question that it answers. For example, the theory of evolution answers the question "How did the various species come into existence?"

Characteristics of a Scientific Theory

For a theory to be accepted as a theory, it has to have certain characteristics:

- It is able to predict future events accurately across many areas of scientific investigation.
- It is supported by a large body of evidence originating from multiple independent sources rather than from a single source. This is called **independent verification**.
- It agrees with preexisting theories and data.
- It can be adjusted to account for new information without becoming inconsistent.
- It is simple. A simple theory is sometimes called "elegant."

Theory Development

By the time they are accepted as theories, scientific ideas have been thoroughly investigated and tested over a long period of time. However, many theories begin with intuition or an **inference**. Think of an inference as an explanation for something that isn't well supported yet with evidence.

According to history, the mathematician and scientist Archimedes made a sudden and famous inference while taking a bath. He had spent a lot of time thinking about how to measure the volume of irregular objects, which was a very challenging task. Typically, the volume of a regular solid, like a cube or a pyramid, is calculated by measuring an object's straight-line dimensions and then multiplying those dimensions based on a particular formula.

The problem with irregular objects is that they lack those easily measured dimensions. It's easy to measure the dimensions of a box or a barrel, but how would you work out the volume of a statue or a metal ornament? Irregular shapes have so many angles, curves, and spaces that measuring dimensions is not a practical way to determine volume.

As the story goes, Archimedes stepped into his bathtub and noticed that the level of water in the tub rose. In a flash, he realized that his body was pushing (**displacing**) some of the water in the tub and was causing the water level to rise. He further realized that the amount of increase in the water level was equivalent to the volume of his body, which was an irregular object (no disrespect to Archimedes). In response to the sudden realization, he yelled, "I have found it!," which in ancient Greek is expressed using the word "eureka." "Eureka" is an exclamation we use in English today to indicate that we've had an idea or a realization. Most scientific theories start with or involve these intuitive moments of realization or inference.

INFERENCES AND EVIDENCE

An inference represents the start of a process of scientific discovery, not the end. Inferences are carefully tested and retested before they become part of accepted theory. Even so, scientists have to be careful to keep their inferences cautious. Every inference involves an intuitive leap from data to explanation. In science, though, it is important not to jump too far. Even an inference must be based on some evidence, and it must use the evidence in a reasonable way.

Suppose scientists were examining soil samples taken by a probe on a mission to Mars. After analyzing the samples, they determine that some of the samples are virtually identical in their composition to soil that can be found in locations on Earth. They know that on Earth, this soil is capable of supporting microbial (very small) life-forms. Now consider the following statements:

Statement *A*: "It may be possible for soil taken from Mars to sustain microbial life-forms."
Statement *B*: "Microbial life-forms may have existed or may exist in the soil on Mars."
Statement *C*: "Microbial life exists in the soil on Mars."

Statement *A* is a reasonable and well-supported inference:

- It says that something "may be" possible, not that it definitely is possible.
- It uses the fact that microbial life-forms live in very similar soil on Earth to conclude that these life-forms may be able to continue living if they were placed into soil from Mars. This is a reasonable use of the available evidence.

Statement *B* goes just slightly too far:

- It talks about things that might be true on Mars as a whole as opposed to things that might be true about an actual, specific soil sample.
- It assumes without proof that the soil sample would sustain microbial life. This idea would have to be proven true before this statement could be reasonable.

Statement *C* goes to an unreasonable extreme. Even when classified as an inference, this statement cannot be supported by the available evidence. A statement like this is called **speculation**.

A good inference is cautious and is supported by evidence. On the Science subject test, you will be asked to do the following:

- Cite evidence to support a given inference or generalization.
- Verify claims based on given evidence.

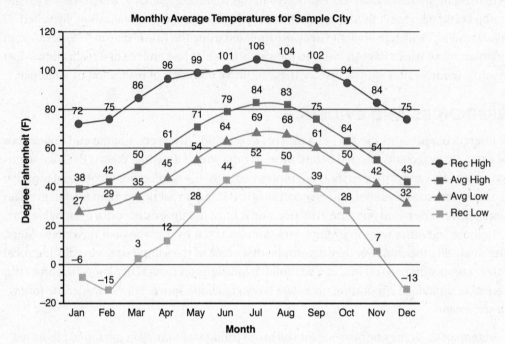

Monthly Average Temperatures for Sample City

1. Select the word or phrase in each bracket that correctly completes the sentence. Based on the data in the graph, we can project that next year's [record high, average high, record low, average low] in May will be [between 52 and 58 degrees, 54 degrees] and the average low in [Jan, Mar, Jul, Nov] will be higher than the [record high, average high] in December.

Answer and Explanation

1. **average low, between 52 and 58 degrees, Jul, average high** Remember to use the key on the right to determine which line means record high, which means average high, and so on. To find the temperature values for each month, first read the horizontal axis on the bottom to find the particular month. Then read up vertically to find all the values for that month. Since this question is about what we think may happen next year, we can't be certain. To be cautious, we should use average temperatures instead of record temperatures, since records are rarely set. We should also not try to predict an exact temperature, but rather a range that seems reasonable.

The following are some important aspects of an accepted scientific theory:

- The theory must provide an explanation for existing, relevant information (prior findings). This is described as being **consistent** with preexisting data.
- The theory must be supported by multiple, independent sources of evidence, ideally generated by different groups of scientists.

In order for these aspects to be addressed, scientists must share their information with and examine information from other scientists. In other words, scientists need to check one another's work. This enables them to apply their theories to preexisting data. This process also allows other scientists to verify results and provide independent sources of evidence. Information sharing is crucial to making progress in the development of scientific theories. Scientists take great care in organizing and presenting their information in "packages" called **findings**.

The ability to read and understand scientific findings is one of the most critical skills in science. It is also one of the most important skills you should develop to do well on the Science test. The majority of questions will refer to scientific information presented in various forms. You will have to read, understand, and apply that information when answering the questions. On the Science subject test, you will need to do the following:

- Interpret information presented as text.
- Interpret information presented in symbolic form (equations and formulas).
- Interpret information presented in graphic form (graphs, charts, and diagrams).
- Relate and integrate information from different sources.

Symbols and Terms

Scientists have adopted a large number of specialized ideas, words, and symbols over the years. These form the basis for a specialized "language" used to express scientific information. The Science test will measure your ability to work with scientific ideas, words, and symbols as they appear in source material. Keep in mind that working with this kind of information is not the same as remembering this information. You will never be asked to define a specialized science term without the test first providing supporting source material that contains the term's meaning. Instead, you may need to work out the meaning of a word or symbol based on other information in a source, or you might be asked to apply a given definition or formula to a new situation.

You will be asked to do the following on the test:

- Determine the meaning of symbols and terms in context.
- Apply scientific terms, concepts, and formulas.

Again, remember that you will not need to memorize symbols, terms, concepts, or formulas in order to do well on the test. Any specialized information needed to answer a question will be defined somewhere in the source material. It will be your job to find that information and apply it.

PRACTICE

QUESTIONS 1 THROUGH 3 ARE BASED ON THE FOLLOWING INFORMATION:

A chemical element's atomic number indicates the number of protons found in the nucleus of an atom of that element. An atom with a neutral charge will have the same number of electrons as protons. An isotope is a variant of an element that has the same number of protons but a different number of neutrons. The number of neutrons in an atom is called the neutron number, and the total of protons and neutrons in a nucleus is called the mass number.

One common method of notation for isotopes is to show the symbol for the element with the atomic number as a subscript and the mass number as a superscript. For example, the element helium (He) has an atomic number of 2. The isotope helium-3 is expressed as ^3_2He. Since the atomic number equals the number of protons and the mass number equals the number of protons and neutrons combined, subtracting the atomic number from the mass number yields the neutron number. From the notation, we can determine that helium-3 has 2 protons, 1 neutron, and 2 electrons.

Individual atoms can join together by forming bonds. When atoms form bonds, they create compounds. For example, carbon (C) and oxygen (O) can bond together to form various compounds, including carbon monoxide (CO) and carbon dioxide (CO_2). Carbon monoxide consists of one carbon atom and one oxygen atom, while carbon dioxide consists of one carbon atom and two oxygen atoms. The prefixes "mono-" (1) and "di-" (2) are used to indicate how many atoms of an element are present in the compound. Other prefixes include "tri-" (3) and "tetra-" (4).

1. Carbon-13 is an isotope of carbon with a neutral charge, and it is represented by the symbol $^{13}_6\text{C}$. Which of the following is an accurate list of the number of protons, neutrons, and electrons in carbon-13?
   (A) 13 protons, 6 neutrons, 13 electrons
   (B) 6 protons, 6 neutrons, 13 electrons
   (C) 13 protons, 7 neutrons, 6 electrons
   (D) 6 protons, 7 neutrons, 6 electrons

2. Fluorocarbons are compounds made up only of fluorine (Fl) and carbon (C). Which of the following is NOT a fluorocarbon?
   (A) $C_{10}F_{18}$
   (B) C_6F_{14}
   (C) CO_2
   (D) C_2F_4

3. How many fluorine atoms are in tetrafluoroethylene?
   (A) 2
   (B) 3
   (C) 4
   (D) 5

Answers and Explanations

1. **(D)** The subscript number (the number on the bottom) indicates the number of protons, which is equal to the number of electrons in a neutral compound. Subtracting the subscript from the superscript (the number on the top) gives the number of neutrons.

2. **(C)** CO_2 contains oxygen (O).

3. **(C)** "Tetra-" means "4."

INTERPRETING GRAPHIC DATA PRESENTATIONS AND MODELS
Analyzing Structure

Think of structure in terms of familiar physical things like buildings and machines. Structure refers to the way something (like an apartment building) is constructed or the way that a process (like pedaling a bicycle) works. When analyzing structure in source material, whether it is presented as text or in a graphic form, try to break down the things being described into parts. These parts may be ideas, terms, or actual components. Whatever form they take, though, the next step is to identify the relationships among the parts. Does one part cause another? If one part is changed, how might another part change?

When analyzing the structure of a building, you might break it down into the foundation, frame, walls, and roof. Then you need to determine how these components are related to each other. When analyzing the process of pedaling a bicycle, you might identify the physical parts (pedals, gears, chain, and wheels). Then you will work out how pushing down on a pedal leads to the turning of a wheel. Regardless of the subject, your goal is always the same. First identify the parts. Then work out the relationships.

On the Science test, you will be asked to do the following:

- **Analyze** the relationships among concepts and elements in given information, including relationships among key terms.
- **Explain** how a change in one variable produces a change in another variable in a given data presentation. A **data presentation** usually takes the form of a table, graph, or chart that shows a relationship between **independent** and **dependent** variables.
- **Predict** the results of additional tests in an **experiment** and predict the future state of a model or system based on given information.

Models

In science, a **model** is a simplified representation of an environment or a process. A **model** is an attempt to describe or simulate a system or process and can take many forms: scatter plot, diagram, formula, equation, and so on. All of the graphic data presentations in this book are examples of models. In particular, diagrams are frequently used to model complex processes. For example, this diagram from the introduction is a simplified model for photosynthesis:

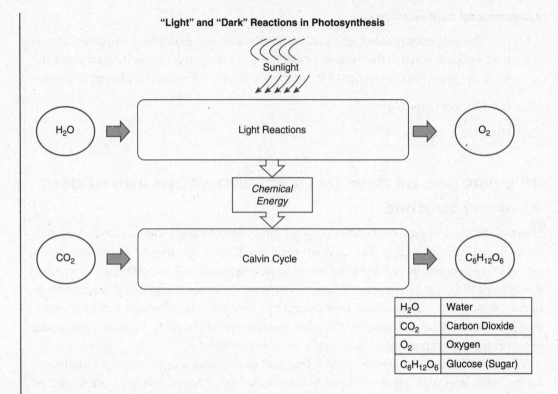

"Light" and "Dark" Reactions in Photosynthesis

H_2O	Water
CO_2	Carbon Dioxide
O_2	Oxygen
$C_6H_{12}O_6$	Glucose (Sugar)

Multiple Content Types

As we've seen, scientific data can be presented in many ways. It can be described in words or formulas. These words will very often be accompanied by graphic representations of data such as tables, charts, graphs, diagrams, and other models. In order to understand fully the information presented, scientists usually have to relate information presented in one form with information presented in another form. To mimic this skill on the Science subject test, you will be asked to do the following:

- Relate information expressed in words to information expressed visually.
- Convert information from words to visual representations and vice versa.
- Use numbers to describe and compare scientific processes and results.
- Record and organize information in tables or graphs to identify patterns and trends.

Key Interpretation Concepts

DEPENDENT AND INDEPENDENT VARIABLES

A lot of the data being presented is quantitative data, often laid out in tables or graphs. A key point in understanding these data is the relationship between the **independent variable** (*x*-axis on a graph) and the **dependent variable** (*y*-axis on a graph). Focus on how a change in the independent variable affects the dependent variable.

CLUSTERS

When data are presented in scatter plots or tables, you must identify intervals of the independent variable where there is a relatively high and dense concentration of dependent variable values. These areas are called **clusters**.

OUTLIERS

When data are presented in scatter plots or tables, you must also identify intervals of the independent variable where there is a relatively low and sparse concentration of dependent variable values. These areas are called **outliers**.

CORRELATION

Scatter plots and graphs can also help model the way that variables are **associated** (or **correlated**). Correlation means the way that a change in the dependent variable relates to a change in the independent variable. If the variables are **strongly correlated**, which means there is a clear relationship between them, the variables may have a cause-and-effect relationship. The key word is "may." Remember that strongly correlated values do not necessarily have a cause-and-effect relationship.

Sometimes, though, the data show no correlation between the variables:

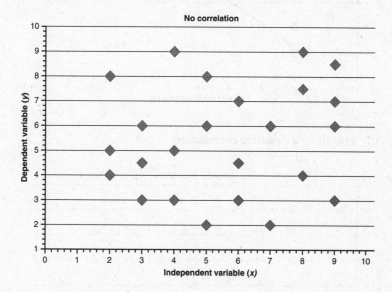

In the scatter plot above, the distribution of points shows no clear pattern.

Sometimes the data show a **positive correlation**:

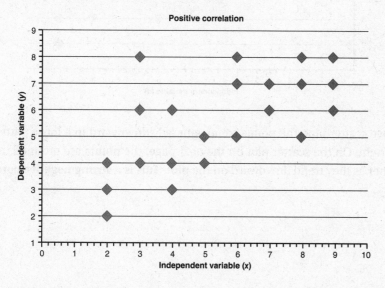

In the scatter plot above, the points trend generally upward as they move to the right. However, they are loosely distributed. The points in the next scatter plot are grouped much more closely together as they trend upward. The black **trendline** shows the average of the points on the plot, and it also indicates a **strong positive correlation**.

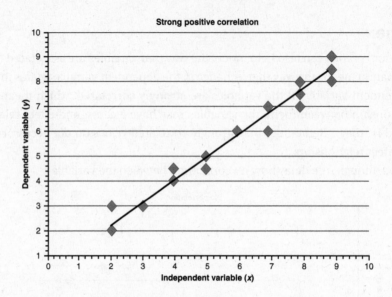

Sometimes the data show a **negative correlation**:

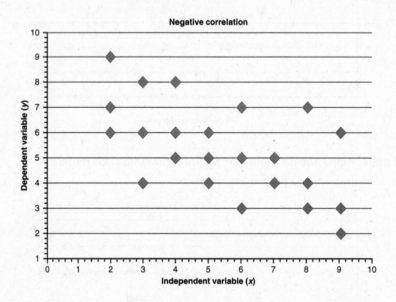

In the above scatter plot, the points trend generally downward in a loose pattern as they move to the right. On the scatter plot on the next page, the points are grouped much more closely together as they trend downward on the plot. This is a **strong negative correlation**.

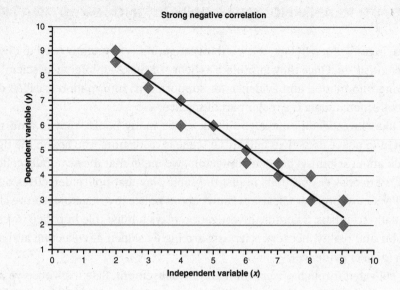

Strong negative correlation

CORRELATION AND CAUSATION

It is important to remember that even if two things are **correlated** (happen together), you don't always know that one of them **caused** the other. A familiar phrase says that correlation is not causation. This means that you can't assume cause and effect just because two things occur together. In fact, scientists often have to conduct **investigations** and design **experiments** in order to demonstrate cause and effect reliably.

Scientists are investigators. In fact, the word **investigation** is frequently used to describe the work that scientists do. Once they formulate a theory or make an inference, scientists get to work gathering information and evidence for support. This information is called **data,** and the careful collection of data is a major part of science.

If words like "investigator" make you think of the many books, movies, and television shows devoted to police detectives and crime scene investigators, you are on the right track. When we talk about scientists being investigators, we mean that they carefully collect information and try to answer questions in just the same way that police detectives do. In fact, many of today's most popular television shows about police investigators feature characters that are actually scientists. Scientific investigation plays a huge role in police investigation, both in fiction and reality, because scientists are highly skilled at collecting and analyzing information (data or **evidence**).

Data are collected through **observation** and **measurement**. Scientists observe and measure objects and events. Then they record those observations and measurements. Since supporting data are required for a theory to be accepted, their measurements and observations must be taken precisely and recorded carefully in order to avoid error. Data that have been collected carefully are described as being **valid** or reliable.

Qualitative and Quantitative Data

Qualitative data describes the characteristics or qualities that scientists observe in a group or environment. Examples of qualitative data include a list of the eye and hair color for each member of the family or photographs of color patterns in the feathers of different groups of birds. Information that describes characteristics or attributes (including shapes, colors, and textures) without using numbers is qualitative data.

Quantitative data are made up of numbers or quantities. These numbers usually represent measurements. Examples of quantitative data include a list of the average recorded temperatures for a certain area or a list of the heights and weights of members of a certain group. Information that uses numbers to present or summarize observations or measurements is quantitative data.

In many cases, both qualitative and quantitative data are collected during scientific observation. In fact, the two types of data are often related. For example, after photographing each member of a very large, extended family and recording the hair and eye color of each member, a scientist may count the number of family members who have each combination of hair and eye color and present the counts in a chart or table. The pictures and list describing the hair and eye color combinations are qualitative data. The counts of each combination are quantitative data and might show which combinations appear more frequently and which appear less frequently.

Precise Measurements

Both qualitative and quantitative data play critical roles in science. So scientists must be careful and precise when collecting any kind of data. From our previous example, the choices for eye color would have to be defined specifically and used consistently to avoid confusion in the recorded data. Without this kind of precision, observers could use the words "brownish," "greenish," and "green-brown" to describe the eye color of three different people whose eyes were, in fact, the same color. Numbers should also be precise. If 6 people out of 20 have blue eyes and 12 people out of 20 have brown eyes, then those specific numbers should be reported. It would not be acceptable to say that there were "roughly 10 of each color" because this presentation of the numbers would not be precise enough for a group this small.

Scientists use a number of instruments and measurement systems to help them be precise when collecting measurements. The most common measurement system used by scientists is the metric system. However, other nonmetric systems are also sometimes used. Each system is made up of different **units** that are used to measure different physical properties. For example, in the metric system, length is measured with a unit called a **meter**, and mass is measured with the **gram**. In the customary system, a **foot** is used to measure length, and a **pound** is used to measure weight. (Weight and mass are very similar concepts.) Some of the instruments used to take measurements include rulers and measuring tapes for length, scales for weight and mass, and thermometers for temperature.

The units that make up a system can often be divided into smaller units or grouped into larger units. For example, a meter is made up of smaller units called **centimeters**, and meters can be grouped into larger units called **kilometers**. This is similar to the customary system, where feet are made up of **inches** and feet can be grouped into **miles**. Part of taking precise measurements is the use of appropriate units. For example, it wouldn't make sense to measure the distance between a person's eyes using meters or kilometers because these units are too large. Centimeters would be a more appropriate unit of measure.

More details on measurement systems, units, and measurement conversions can be found in the math section of this book.

Experimentation

A lot of scientific observation takes place in the field, which means that they are taken in the natural world. For example, the theory of evolution is based on observations of animals in their natural habitats. Darwin collected his data on the Galapagos Islands.

In some cases, however, the information scientists need cannot be easily obtained through field observation alone. In order to observe or measure certain things, scientists must sometimes recreate (or **simulate**) the conditions or environment in a controlled setting called a **laboratory**. A laboratory is usually used when a specific event is difficult to observe in nature, either because it is unusual or because it only occurs in an environment where observation is difficult. This test performed in a simulated environment is called an **experiment**.

For example, it is difficult to measure the temperature at which alcohol (ethanol) freezes in a natural setting because ethanol freezes at temperatures that are too cold for humans to tolerate. It is possible, however, to simulate those temperatures in a laboratory and then take the measurement safely.

A laboratory approach is also used extensively in physical science where scientists are investigating the origin of the universe and an event called the **big bang**. Since scientists cannot yet travel back in time and space to the moment of the huge explosion that created the universe, they must simulate those conditions in a laboratory with the help of complex equipment like **particle accelerators** and **colliders**. These machines accelerate tiny atomic particles up to incredibly high speeds and then smash them together. These collisions cause the particles to fly apart, revealing a lot of information about their structure and their behavior in explosive conditions. Most of modern physics is based on experimental evidence gathered in a laboratory setting like this.

An Hypothesis

The goal of an experiment is to generate evidence in support of a given theory by testing something called an **hypothesis**. A theory is a broad and general statement about the natural world that answers a broad and general question. An hypothesis, in contrast, is a much more specific statement that answers a specific question about an element of the theory. An hypothesis is sometimes called an educated guess. An experiment is then designed to create conditions where the hypothesis can be either confirmed or disproven.

Proving or disproving an hypothesis is part of a chain of "if . . . then . . . therefore" reasoning. This reasoning process starts with making a **prediction**:

If *A* then *B*.

The letter *A* represents the hypothesis, and the letter *B* represents an event that can be tested or measured. The prediction says that if statement *A* is true, statement *B* is also true. If put another way, the prediction means that if the hypothesis is true, the predicted event will occur.

The next step in this reasoning process is the **test** or **experiment**. This step focuses on determining whether the prediction is true or false. The test is performed. The results are recorded. Then the data are analyzed to determine what they say about the prediction. In other words, is the prediction true or false? The answer to this question is then extended to the hypothesis:

- If the experiment shows the prediction to be **true**, the evidence **confirms** the hypothesis.
- If the experiment shows the prediction to be **false**, the evidence **contradicts** the hypothesis.

Applying the experimental results to the hypothesis is called **drawing a conclusion**. This conclusion is the "therefore" step in the chain of reasoning:

- **Confirmation**: If the hypothesis is true, then the predicted event will occur. The event did occur. Therefore, the hypothesis is true.
- **Contradiction**: If the hypothesis is true, then the predicted event will occur. The event did not occur. Therefore, the hypothesis is false.

The outcome of the experiment dictates what will happen next:

- If the experiment contradicted the hypothesis, the next step may be to look for a reason that the experimental results may be wrong. This is called looking for sources of **error** or **bias**.
- If none is found, another hypothesis for the same question may be stated and tested.
- If the hypothesis was **confirmed**, the next step may be to repeat the experiment to see if it produces the same results. This is done to **verify the result**. The more often a given result can be reproduced, the more reliable it is.
- After the result has been verified, another question may be asked and an hypothesis for that question may then be stated and tested.

Imagine that you want to watch television. However, when you pick up the remote control and press the power button, nothing happens. The television does not come on. You might then begin to think of reasons why this is happening:

- The power in your home may be out.
- The television may be unplugged.
- The remote may need to be recharged.

Each of these is an example of an hypothesis. Think of each of these as a possible answer to a specific question: "Why does the television not come on when I press the power button on the remote control?"

Your next step would probably be to test these hypotheses, one by one, to see which one is correct. How could you test the hypothesis that the problem is a power outage? One possibility would be to check other electrical items in your home (microwave, light, hair dryer) to see whether or not they are working properly. If they are, then your home's electricity is probably on. This is an example of prediction, experiment, and result. You predicted that other devices would not work if the power was out. You tried other devices, and they came on. This result would probably lead you to conclude that the power outage hypothesis is not correct.

To test the hypothesis that the television is unplugged, you would probably rely on some more observation and look at the power cord. If it is plugged into the wall, this hypothesis would be contradicted.

Finally, to test the hypothesis that the remote control needs to be recharged, you would probably recharge the remote. If after recharging the remote control you pressed the power button and the television turned on, you would have confirmed this hypothesis. If the television did not turn on, you would then make a new hypothesis, perhaps that the remote is broken. Then you would look for a way to test that new hypothesis, perhaps by predicting that pressing the power button on the television will work and then pressing the button.

This simple example illustrates the process that scientists go through when attempting to answer questions. Because it is simple, the example also shows that this kind of scientific reasoning from tests and evidence doesn't apply only to laboratories and "formal" science. You can apply this kind of reasoning in everyday life as well. The Science subject test will ask you questions about real-world situations that involve this kind of thinking.

Designing Controlled Experiments

An experiment is intended to simulate an environment or a process that occurs somewhere in nature. Scientists perform experiments to confirm or contradict hypotheses. These hypotheses often involve a **cause-and-effect** relationship between two things. An experiment is often intended to determine whether one thing causes another. In more formal terms, an experiment tests for a **causal** (cause-and-effect) relationship between two **variables** (things):

- The **cause** is called the **independent variable**.
- The **effect** is called the **dependent** variable because it depends on (or is caused by) the independent variable.

In order to measure a cause-and-effect relationship properly, it is necessary to eliminate any other possible causes or at least minimize their impact. If more than one potential cause exists for a measured effect, then it is not possible to determine the true cause. Creating an environment where the effect of the independent variable can be reliably measured is called **designing a controlled experiment**.

One familiar example of a controlled experiment is the testing of a new drug. In order to be sure that they are measuring the effect of the drug, scientists create two groups of test subjects: a **control group** and an **experimental group**:

- The members of both groups are as similar as possible in terms age, gender, diet, and other factors that could affect the test.
- The number of people in each group is as similar as possible, preferably identical.
- The experimental group is given the medication to be tested.
- The control group is not given the medication. Instead, its members are given something that appears to be medication but is, in fact, a harmless substance. This is called a **placebo** and is sometimes referred to as a sugar pill.

The goal of this approach is to create a situation where the only significant difference between the two groups is whether they received the medication or the placebo. This way, if there is a measurable difference between the two groups, it can safely be said that the medication caused the difference.

Consider the following situation:

The owner of a greenhouse maintains 30 tomato plants in 6 beds of 5 plants each. The owner determined that the average height of the plants is approximately 140 cm. The owner wants to increase the height of the tomato plants using a new kind of plant food. The owner plans to test two different forms of plant food from a single manufacturer to measure their effectiveness for increasing plant height.

The first form of plant food is a plug, which is a small, solid spike of water-soluble plant food. Plugs are inserted into the ground around the base of plants. As the plants are watered over the course of a growing season, the plugs slowly dissolve, feeding nutrients to the roots of the plant.

The second form of plant food is liquid. It is mixed with water, and that mixture is used to water plants during the growing season. The plants absorb nutrients as they absorb the water into their root system.

This is another scenario in which control and experimental groups can be used to control the variables being tested. Since two different types of plant food are being considered, the experiment would involve two experimental groups, one for each type of plant food, as well as one control group.

Experimental design:

- There are a total of 30 plants in 6 beds of 5 plants each. Each group will contain 10 plants in 2 beds of 5 each.
- All plants will be taken from the same group of parent plants.
- All plants will be grown in soil with the same composition.
- All plants will receive the same amount of light and water.
- All plants will be grown at the same temperature.
- The first experimental group (group *A*) will receive the plug form of the plant food.
- The second experimental group (group *B*) will receive the liquid form of the plant food mixed into its water. Note that the amount of water that this group receives will be identical to the amount of water that each of the other groups receives.
- The control group (group *C*) will receive no plant food.
- Using all of these conditions will ensure that the only factor that is different between the groups is plant food. The plant food is the independent variable in the experiment.

- The height of the plants in each of the three groups is the dependent variable.
- The height of each plant is measured. The results are averaged for each group and are recorded in a table.

	Group A (Receives plug form of food)	Group B (Receives liquid form of food)	Group C (Control Group)
Average height at planting	5 cm	5 cm	5 cm
Average height at end of growing cycle	155 cm	165 cm	140 cm

From the data recorded in the table above, the owner of the greenhouse can conclude that plant food does appear to cause an increase in plant height and that the liquid form appears to be more effective than the plug form.

Verification, Error, and Bias

One way to ensure that the results of an experiment are reliable is to repeat the experiment many times to **verify** the original results. This means the experiment is repeated to see if the new results are similar to the original ones. If the results are similar, they provide additional evidence in support of the conclusion. If the results are not similar, it is possible that some of the data were affected by **error** or **bias**.

For example, suppose the plant food experiment is repeated but this time the results are different:

	Group A (Receives plug form of food)	Group B (Receives liquid form of food)	Group C (Control Group)
Average height at planting	5 cm	5 cm	5 cm
Average height at end of growing cycle	185 cm	165 cm	140 cm

These results seem to show that the plug form of the plant food caused the plants to grow much taller than did the liquid plant food. Since the two sets of results contradict each other, both of them can't be equally valid. There must be a problem somewhere. Looking for this problem is called **identifying sources of error**.

For example, suppose that the controls on the watering process were not followed properly in the second experiment and both experimental groups were watered with liquid plant food. This would mean that group *A* received twice the amount of plant food (both the liquid and the plug) that group *B* received, which would explain the results of the second experiment.

Another possibility is that the results were affected by **bias**, or accidental discrimination between test subjects. For example, the design of the experiment called for all plants to be taken from the same group of parent plants as opposed to a single parent plant. To do this, branches would be cut off of parent plants and then placed into soil and allowed to grow. These cuttings would form roots and begin to grow on their own. The greenhouse owner would use these cuttings in the experiment.

Within a group of plants, there will always be some variation in height. This is why we compare average heights. If the experimenter took cuttings group by group and unconsciously started by choosing the tallest plants in the parent group, all of the cuttings from the tallest plants would be in group A. All of the cuttings in group B would come from shorter parents, which would introduce a new variable (called an **uncontrolled variable**) into the experiment. This new variable could account for the unexpected results if the offspring of the tall parents were taller than the offspring of the shorter parents.

In both scenarios—the watering error and the cutting bias—a third experiment should be conducted. This time, the experimenter should pay stricter attention to the controls. The results of that third experiment might help confirm that the error or bias was eliminated.

PRACTICE

QUESTIONS 1 THROUGH 4 REFER TO THE FOLLOWING INFORMATION:

A pharmaceutical company conducted a trial for a new drug intended to lower cholesterol levels in heart disease patients. They assembled two groups. Group A was made up of 100 women between the ages of 40 and 60 years of age. Group B was made up of 100 men between the ages of 40 and 60 years of age. The members of both groups were very similar in terms of general health, diet, and lifestyle. All of the trial's participants had heart disease. Group A was given the experimental medication, and Group B was given a placebo (a fake or sugar pill).

1. Based on the information provided, which of the following is true?
   (A) Group A was the control group, and group B was the experimental group.
   (B) Group A was the experimental group, and group B was the control group.
   (C) Both groups were experimental groups.
   (D) Both groups were control groups.

2. Which of the following is a possible source of error in this experiment?
   (A) All the participants in the trial had heart disease.
   (B) There was no control group.
   (C) The experimental and control groups were not similar enough.
   (D) One of the groups was not given real medication.

3. Which of the following would eliminate a likely source of error?
   (A) Giving the medication to both groups
   (B) Switching the groups so that group A is all men and group B is all women
   (C) Choose one gender (either male or female) and populate both groups with only that gender
   (D) Look more closely at small differences in diet among group members

4. If the results of the trial showed no change in cholesterol level in members of either group, which of the following is a valid statement?
   (A) The drug lowers cholesterol in men.
   (B) The drug does not lower cholesterol in women.
   (C) The drug could lower cholesterol in men.
   (D) The drug does not lower cholesterol in either men or women.

Answers and Explanations

1. **(B)** The control group is not exposed to the factor being tested. In this case, that factor is the medication.

2. **(C)** The groups were made up exclusively of members of different genders. Since gender is a factor that could affect the outcome of the test, this is a soure of error. A drug that is effective in males may not be effective in females or vice versa.

3. **(C)** To address the source of error, make the two groups similar in terms of gender. Group *A* would still be the experimental group, and group *B* would still be the control group.

4. **(C)** No men were given the medication, so it is still possible that the drug could be effective in men. It's not safe to say that the drug definitely does lower cholesterol for men, only that it could. Since this is only one experiment with only 100 women, it is not safe to say that the drug does not lower cholesterol in women. More experiments would have to be conducted before reaching this conclusion.

Conduct Quantitative Data Analysis

Analyzing quantitative data means applying mathematical skills in a science setting. It is an example of integrated content that is tested on the exam. Scientists must be able to take accurate and appropriate measurements and then correctly make calculations with those measurements. These skills are crucial parts of observation and analysis. To put it more simply, you can't be a scientist if you're not good at math. Analyzing quantitative data includes the following topics:

- Measurements and measurement systems
- Unit conversions
- Scientific notation
- Equations and formulas
- Statistical analysis
- Counting methods (combinations and permutations)
- Probability

The math unit of this book contains detailed coverage of these topics and provides practice problems that use science content. If you have not already completed or reviewed these topics, you should do so before proceeding with the rest of the material in this science unit. You'll also get more chances to practice these skills in this unit's review test and in the practice tests.

After collecting evidence and analyzing it, scientists must do the following:

- Distinguish among data, inferences, and conclusions.
- Determine if the data support a given conclusion.
- Draw a reasonable conclusion based on existing data.
- Reevaluate a conclusion given new data.

Determine Central Ideas, Hypotheses, and Conclusions

To show you understand the experimental method, you will be asked to do the following:

- Summarize given information and determine the central idea or conclusion.
- Identify the hypothesis, data, and/or conclusion in a scientific finding.
- Verify evidence and data plus use new data to corroborate or challenge a conclusion.
- Construct valid questions, determine whether questions are valid, and refine hypotheses.

PRACTICE

QUESTIONS 1 AND 2 REFER TO THE FOLLOWING STATEMENTS:

Statement 1: "Why does water appear blue?"

Statement 2: "Water splits visible light into different colors and absorbs different amounts of these various colors of light. Water reflects more blue light than other colors of light."

Statement 3: "If water absorbs less blue light than any other color in the visible spectrum, a reflection of blue light will be brighter than a reflection of any other visible color."

Statement 4: "Lights of different colors were reflected off of water and onto a light-sensitive panel. The intensity (strength) of each color's reflection was measured."

Statement 5: "All visible-light colors were tested, and the strongest reflection was produced by blue light."

Statement 6: "Water appears blue because it reflects blue light more than it reflects other colors of light."

1. Which of the statements above is a hypothesis?
   - (A) Statement 2
   - (B) Statement 3
   - (C) Statement 5
   - (D) Statement 6

2. Which of the statements shown describes a conclusion?
   (A) Statement 2
   (B) Statement 3
   (C) Statement 5
   (D) Statement 6

Answers and Explanations

1. **(A)** Statement 2 offers a possible explanation for the phenomenon. This statement could be tested and shown to be either true or false.

2. **(D)** Statement 6 is offered as a likely answer to the question based on the results of the experiment.

After all of the work involved in designing an experiment and collecting data, scientists need to evaluate their findings. They also must communicate their findings to other scientists. In order to accomplish these tasks, they must do the following:

- Create charts, graphs, diagrams, or other models to present the information.
- State their conclusions and provide supporting evidence.
- Describe the methods and details of their investigation.
- Evaluate the validity of their data and reasoning based on the findings of other scientists.

Analyze Evidence from Different Sources

Science never sleeps. At any given moment, 24 hours a day, scientists around the world are working to explore new areas, collect new data, conduct new experiments, and report new findings. A conclusion that was once considered valid might be challenged by the results of a new experiment. Imagine that two scientists conduct similar research. Their findings might agree, or their findings might disagree.

A very central part of the work done by all scientists involves carefully analyzing the work done by others. Was the work done carefully? Are the data reliable? Do I agree with the other scientist's conclusions? Were the experiments designed well? How does this new information affect other scientists' findings? Does it support them or weaken them?

All of these questions can be answered using the skills and knowledge you've gained throughout the science portion of this book. By now, you should be able to interpret scientific data (whether in text or graphic form) and determine whether they are reliable. You should be able to recognize whether evidence supports a given conclusion. You should understand how experiments work and should also know what goes into a well-designed experiment. On the test, you will be asked to do the following when comparing one source with another:

- Compare multiple scientific findings, and determine whether they support or contradict each another.
- Compare and contrast models or experiments, identifying their strengths and weaknesses.
- Determine whether new data or evidence support or weaken a previous experiment's findings.

ACCELERATION   The change in velocity resulting from a net force being applied to an object.

ADAPTATION   The response to environmental change by a species; the physical change in a species over time in ways that make survival more likely in a given environment.

AEROBIC   Reactions or organisms that require oxygen.

ALLELE   Individual units of genetic information that define the inheritance of traits.

ANAEROBIC   Reactions or organisms that do not require oxygen.

ASSOCIATION   Another word for correlation. Describes the relationship between two variables in a data set.

ATOM   The fundamental unit that makes up the physical material (called matter) in our natural world. Atoms are made of three particles: protons, neutrons, and electrons. Protons and neutrons make up the nucleus of the atom, and the electrons orbit the nucleus in rings called shells. Protons have a positive electrical charge. Neutrons have no electrical charge. Electrons have a negative electrical charge.

ATOMIC NUMBER   The number of protons in an atom's nucleus.

ATP   A form of chemical energy used in cellular functions.

BASE   A component of DNA whose sequence on a strand defines the genetic code of an organism. Bases provide the mechanism for two DNA strands to join together.

BIAS   Accidental discrimination in experimental design that affects the quality of the results.

BIG BANG   A theoretical giant explosion thought to have created the universe.

BONDS   Connections between atoms, used to form compounds and molecules.

CARBON   A chemical element. The symbol for carbon is C.

CARBON DIOXIDE   A molecule consisting of 1 carbon and 2 oxygen atoms; a very important factor in global warming.

CARBON MONOXIDE   A molecule consisting of 1 carbon atom and 1 oxygen atom.

CARNIVORE   An animal that eats meat (other animals); often called a predator.

CAUSE AND EFFECT   A relationship between two things in which one causes the other.

CELL   The basic unit supporting the structure and function of all living organisms. Some organisms consist of a single cell. Other organisms, like humans, animals, and plants, consist of many cells. Some cells (eukaryotic cells) have a well-defined central container (nucleus) of genetic material. Other cells (prokaryotic cells) do not have a nucleus.

CELL DIVISION   The process that produces two cells from one parent cell.

CELLULAR RESPIRATION   A chemical reaction that takes place in the cell to release chemical energy from food.

CHEMICAL ELEMENT A substance that cannot be divided into simpler substances; a substance consisting of only one kind of atom.

CHEMICAL REACTION A process that tranforms energy from one form to another; for example, chemical bond energy becomes heat, or light becomes chemical bond energy. Chemical reactions must be balanced in terms of the number of atoms that enter and come out of the reaction.

CHLOROPLAST An organelle in plant cells that enables photosynthesis.

CHROMATIN The material in the nucleus that contains the chromosomes.

CHROMOSOME A set of DNA molecules that define an organism's traits; the blueprint for the development of a new, viable cell.

CIRCULATORY SYSTEM The system that includes the heart and blood vessels. It carries food, water, and oxygen to the cells and removes the waste products from cellular functions.

CLUSTER A group of points plotted close together on a scatter plot; indicates high probability.

CONSUMER An animal that eats plants (herbivores).

CONTINENTAL DRIFT The movement of Earth's tectonic plates over long periods of time; responsible for the continents appearing like pieces of a puzzle.

CONTROL GROUP The group in an experiment that is not exposed to the factor being tested.

CONTROLLED EXPERIMENT An experiment with a control group and other design elements intended to reduce error and isolate the variable being tested.

CORE The inner portion of Earth; the planet's center.

CORRELATION A relationship between two variables in a data set.

COVALENT BOND A molecular bond in which two atoms share a pair of valence electrons.

CRUST The outer "skin" of Earth.

CUP The customary unit of volume or capacity.

DATA Information gathered through observation and measurement; can be quantitiative (numbers) or qualitative (characteristics).

DAUGHTER CELL A cell that results from cell division.

DEPENDENT VARIABLE The element in an experiment or observation that is caused by or affected by the independent variable.

DIGESTIVE SYSTEM The system that includes the stomach, intestines, and related organs; breaks food down into forms that cells can use and cycles out the waste products.

DIPLOID A cell with 2 copies of each chromosome; most cells are diploid.

DIRECTION The change in position.

DNA The molecule that contains the genetic code.

DOMINANT A trait that will manifest when paired with a recessive allele.

ECOSYSTEM A system made up of a physical environment and groups of living things called producers and consumers that are organized into food chains and food webs.

EGG The gamete produced by a female.

ELECTRON An atomic particle with a negative charge; orbits an atom's nucleus in an electron shell.

ELECTRON SHELL A ring of electrons around the nucleus of an atom.

ELECTRONEGATIVITY The relative amount of pull one atom has on the electrons of another atom; relevant for ionic bonds.

ENDOTHERMIC A chemical reaction that absorbs heat.

EUKARYOTES Organisms made up of cells with a well-formed nucleus.

EXCRETION The process of eliminating waste products from the body.

EXOTHERMIC A chemical reaction that releases heat.

EXPERIMENT A carefully constructed test of a scientific hypothesis.

EXPERIMENTAL GROUP The group in an experiment that is exposed to the factor being tested.

EXTINCT A species of organism that no longer exists.

FINDINGS The results of scientific investigation or experimentation.

FOOD CHAIN A hierarchy of producers and consumers with a relationship based on sources of food and energy.

FOOD WEB An interconnected set of food chains that more realistically models the patterns of food sources in an ecosystem than does a single food chain.

FOOT The customary unit of length.

FORCE Anything capable of affecting an object's shape/structure, movement, or direction.

FORMULA An expression of a rule, idea, or relationship using mathematical symbols.

GALAXY A collection of stars bound together by their mututal gravitation.

GAMETE A haploid cell involved in sexual reproduction.

GENES The components of heredity; located in the cell's DNA; provide the blueprint for growth and development.

GENETIC MATERIAL The various chemical componds involved in heredity.

GENETICS The study of genes and heredity.

GENOTYPE An organism's genetic makeup.

GLUCOSE A simple sugar that is very important for cellular functions.

GLYCOLYSIS A process that breaks glucose down into pyruvate.

GRAM   The metric unit of mass.

GRAVITATION   The force that causes objects to attract each other; apparent between large masses such as planets.

HAPLOID   A cell with one copy of each chromosome; a gamete is haploid.

HELIOCENTRIC   A model of the solar system with the sun at the center and the planets orbiting around the sun; "helio" means "sun" and "centric" means "at the center."

HERBIVORE   An organism that eats plants (consumers).

HETEROZYGOUS   A genotype consisting of two different alleles.

HOMEOSTASIS   A process by which an organism maintains a beneficial balance in terms of temperature, fluid composition, and so on.

HOMOLOGOUS PAIR   A pair of related chromosomes that contain the genes defining a given set of traits.

HOMOZYGOUS   A genotype consisting of two similar alleles.

HOST   The organism on which a parasite feeds.

HYPOTHESIS   A specific and testable proposal to answer a question related to a scientific investigation; the basis for an experiment; an educated guess.

INDEPENDENT VARIABLE   A variable in a data set that is not affected by other variables.

INDEPENDENT VERIFICATION   The reproduction of scientific findings by a third party.

INFERENCE   An intuitive realization based on observable data.

INHERITANCE   The process by which traits are passed from parents to offspring.

INQUIRY   Another name for scientific investigation.

INVESTIGATION   A process of seeking scientific knowledge by asking questions and gathering evidence.

IONIC BOND   A bond between two atoms based on the attraction of opposing electrical charges.

ISOTOPE   A variation of a chemical element that has a different neutron number.

KINETIC ENERGY   Energy related to an object's motion.

LABORATORY   A specialized environment with scientific equipment and other characteristics that enable experimentation.

LITER   The metric unit of capacity or volume.

MAGMA   Melted rock and metal.

MAGNITUDE   Another word for amount or quantity.

MANTLE   A layer of Earth separating the core from the crust.

MASS NUMBER   The number of particles in an atom's nucleus (protons and neutrons).

MATTER The name given to all the material that makes up our natural world. Matter can be divided into four categories (solid, liquid, gas, and plasma), but all matter is made up of atoms.

MEIOSIS A process of chromosome division specific to gametes.

METER The metric unit of length.

MICROSCOPE An instrument used to magnify and observe very small objects.

MILKY WAY The name of the galaxy that contains our sun and solar system.

MITOCHONDRIA Organelles that can produce chemical energy from pyruvate.

MITOSIS The process of chromosomal replication and separation that supports cell division.

MODEL A simplified version of a natural phenomenon; a diagram.

MOLECULE A group of atoms connected by bonds.

MONO Means "one."

MOON A natural satellite orbiting Earth.

MULTICELLULAR An organism consisting of more than one cell.

MUSCULOSKELETAL SYSTEM The system consisting of the skeleton, muscles, and connective tissue; enables locomotion.

NATURAL SELECTION A mechanism for adaptation and speciation based on the enviromental pressure to survive.

NERVOUS SYSTEM The system consisting of the brain and nerves; responsible for transmitting thoughts into actions and movements, delivering sensory information to the brain, and so on.

NET FORCE A force that is not balanced; the cause of acceleration.

NEUTRAL Having no electrical charge.

NEUTRON An atomic particle in the atom's nucleus. Neutrons have no electrical charge.

NEUTRON NUMBER The number of neutrons in the nucleus of an atom.

NUCLEAR MEMBRANE The membrane surrounding the nucleus of a eukaryotic cell.

NUCLEUS An organelle in eukaryotic cells that contains the genetic material.

NUTRIENTS Elements that provide sustenance and energy to the entire body and to the individual cells.

OBSERVATION A part of the scientific method; involves watching with the eyes or perceiving using an instrument; can occur in the field or in the laboratory.

OFFSPRING The new organisms produced by reproduction.

ORBIT In our solar system, an elliptical (oval) path that a planet takes around the sun or that a satellite (like Earth's moon) takes around a planet.

ORGANELLE A specialized component of a cell.

ORGANISMS Living things. Organisms can grow, reproduce, react to stimuli, adapt to their environment, transform energy, and die.

OUTLIER A point plotted in an area of a scatter plot containing very few points; indicates low probability.

OXYGEN A chemical element. The symbol for oxygen is O.

PARASITE An organism that feeds on and ultimately harms or kills another organism.

PARENT An organism that reproduces and creates offspring.

PHENOTYPE The physical appearance of a trait; may not indicate genotype.

PHOTOSYNTHESIS The process by which producers (green plants) capture sunlight and convert this energy into glucose.

PLACEBO A harmless sugar pill used for control groups in medical experiments.

PLANET In our solar system, an object that is in orbit around the sun, that is made round by its own gravity, and that is the dominant object in its orbit. A planet may have moons or other objects orbiting it. Any object that shares its orbital path with other large objects not in orbit around it is not considered to be a planet. This definition caused Pluto to be reclassified from planet to dwarf planet.

POTENTIAL ENERGY Energy related to an object's position.

POUND The customary unit of weight.

PREDATOR An animal that hunts and eats other animals.

PREDICTION An "if . . . then" statement related to an experimental hypothesis. If the hypothesis is correct, the predicted event will occur.

PREY An animal that is hunted and eaten by another animal.

PRODUCER A plant. It is called a producer because it produces the chemical (food) energy found in an ecosystem.

PROKARYOTES Organisms made up of a single cell without a well-formed nucleus.

PROTON An atomic particle with a positive charge; resides in the nucleus of an atom.

PROTON NUMBER Another name for atomic number.

PYRAMID OF ENERGY Describes the progressive decrease in the amount of energy transferred between tiers in a food chain.

PYRUVATE The substance produced from glucose during glycolysis; enters the mitochondrion for extraction of chemical energy during respiration.

QUALITATIVE Data based on qualities or characteristics of something; nonnumerical information.

QUANTITATIVE Data based on quantities; numerical information.

RECESSIVE A trait that will be hidden or masked when paired with a dominant allele.

REPLICATION Copying, as when cells divide or DNA molecules are copied.

REPRODUCTION A process of creating new individuals from an organism's genetic material.

RESPIRATORY SYSTEM The system including the lungs and diaphragm; circulates air into the body and releases waste products.

SATELLITE An object that orbits a planet; the moon is a naturally occurring satellite.

SCATTER PLOT A data presentation that plots points on a graph in groups called clusters.

SOLAR SYSTEM A group of planets orbiting around a central star. Earth is part of a solar system with the sun as the central star.

SPECIATION The development of new, distinct species of organisms as a result of adaptation and natural section.

SPECIES A group of organisms of the same specific type that are able to breed and produce fertile offspring.

SPEED The rate of change in an object's position.

SPERM The gamete produced by a male.

STIMULI Things in the external environment that cause an organism to react.

STRAND A sequence of bases on a DNA molecule.

SUN The star at the center of our solar system.

SYMBIOTIC A relationship where two organisms provide benefits to one another.

THEORY A strongly supported explanation for a natural phenomenon, such as Charles Darwin's theory of evolution by natural selection. A theory is able to predict future findings accurately. It is supported by large bodies of evidence. A theory can be reconciled with preexisting ideas and observations. It can flexibly account for new information without becoming inconsistent. In addition, a theory is as simple as possible.

UNCONTROLLED VARIABLE A variable affecting experimental data that was not intended to be a factor; a source of experimental error.

UNICELLULAR An organism with only one cell.

VALENCE SHELL The outer electron shell of an atom.

VELOCITY A measurement of an object's speed and direction.

ZYGOTE The cell that results from fertilization, which is the process that combines gametes into a new organism.

Review Test

1. Which of the following is a unit in the metric system?
   (A) Pound
   (B) Centigram
   (C) Ton
   (D) Cup

2. Which of the following is a unit in the customary system?
   (A) Mile
   (B) Centiliter
   (C) Gram
   (D) Meter

3. Which of the following is NOT a unit of weight or mass?
   (A) Ounce
   (B) Kilometer
   (C) Gram
   (D) Ton

4. Which of the following organizes these units from smallest to largest?
   (A) Centiliter, milliliter, liter, deciliter
   (B) Centiliter, deciliter, liter, milliliter
   (C) Liter, deciliter, centiliter, milliliter
   (D) Milliliter, centiliter, deciliter, liter

QUESTIONS 5 TO 9 REFER TO THE FOLLOWING DATA PRESENTATIONS:

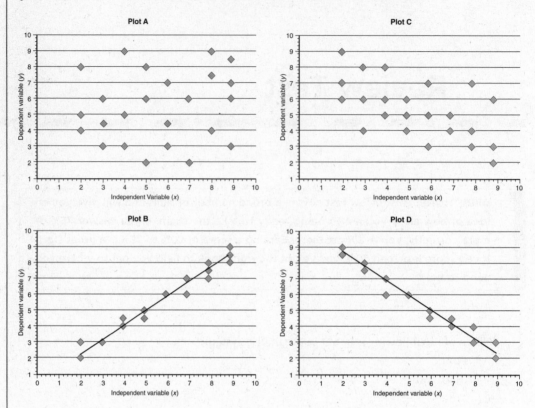

5. Which plot shows no correlation between variables?
    (A) Plot *A*
    (B) Plot *B*
    (C) Plot *C*
    (D) Plot *D*

6. Which plot shows strong positive correlation between variables?
    (A) Plot *A*
    (B) Plot *B*
    (C) Plot *C*
    (D) Plot *D*

7. Which plot shows strong negative correlation between variables?
    (A) Plot *A*
    (B) Plot *B*
    (C) Plot *C*
    (D) Plot *D*

8. What kind of correlation does plot *C* show?
    (A) No correlation
    (B) Incomplete correlation
    (C) Weak negative correlation
    (D) Median correlation

9. Which of the plots provides evidence of causation?
    (A) Plot *A*
    (B) Plot *C*
    (C) Plots *B* and *D*
    (D) None of the plots

---

10. What is the name of the compound with the formula CO?
    (A) Carbon dioxide
    (B) Carbon tetraoxide
    (C) Carbon monoxide
    (D) Carbon oxygen

11. What is the name of the compound with the formula H_2O?
    (A) Water
    (B) Dihydrogen dioxide
    (C) Methane
    (D) Glucose

12. What is the name of the compound with the formula CO_2?
    (A) Water
    (B) Dicarbon monoxide
    (C) Methane
    (D) Carbon dioxide

13. What is the name of the compound with the formula $C_6H_{12}O_6$?
    (A) Methane
    (B) Glucose
    (C) 6-carbon dihydroxide
    (D) Carbon hydroxide

14. What is the name of the compound with the formula CH_4?
    (A) Glucose
    (B) Carbon monoxide
    (C) Carbon tetrachloride
    (D) Methane

15. How many hydrogen atoms in total are in $C_6H_{12}O_6$ and H_2O?
    (A) 2
    (B) 6
    (C) 12
    (D) 14

16. How many oxygen atoms in total are in CH_4 and CO_2?
    (A) 0
    (B) 2
    (C) 4
    (D) 6

17. How many carbon atoms in total are in CO and CO_2?
    (A) 1
    (B) 2
    (C) 3
    (D) 4

QUESTIONS 18 TO 20 REFER TO THE FOLLOWING SET:

Set A: {4, 8, 12, 16, 20, 22}

18. What is the arithmetic mean (average) of set A (rounded to the nearest tenth)?
    (A) 13.6
    (B) 13.7
    (C) 14.0
    (D) 16.4

19. What is the median of set A?
    (A) 12
    (B) 14
    (C) 16
    (D) 12 and 16

20. What is the range of set A?
    (A) 4
    (B) 18
    (C) 22
    (D) 82

Set *B*: {3, 3, 6, 6, 9, 9, 9}

21. What is the mode in set *B*?
    (A) 3
    (B) 6
    (C) 6.4
    (D) 9

22. What is the simple average of the members of set *B* (rounded to the nearest tenth)?
    (A) 6.4
    (B) 7.5
    (C) 15.0
    (D) 45.0

23. If the numbers equal to the mode of set *B* are weighted 75% and all other numbers combined are weighted 25%, what is the weighted average of set *B* (rounded to the nearest tenth)?
    (A) 3.9
    (B) 5.6
    (C) 6.4
    (D) 7.9

24. Which of the following is a brief definition of cell theory?
    (A) The theory that the sun is the center of the solar system and that the planets orbit around it
    (B) The theory that all complex organisms are composed of small, fundamental, living units
    (C) The theory that all physical material (matter) is made up of extremely small, fundamental particles
    (D) The theory that natural selection is responsible for adaptation (adjusting to the environment) and speciation (the development of species)

25. Which of the following is a brief definition of the theory of evolution?
    (A) The theory that the sun is the center of the solar system and that the planets orbit around it
    (B) The theory that all complex organisms are composed of small, fundamental, living units
    (C) The theory that all physical material (matter) is made up of extremely small, fundamental particles
    (D) The theory that natural selection is responsible for adaptation (adjusting to the environment) and speciation (the development of species)

26. Which of the following is a brief definition of the heliocentric model of the solar system?
   (A) The theory that the sun is the center of the solar system and that the planets orbit around it
   (B) The theory that all complex organisms are composed of small, fundamental, living units
   (C) The theory that all physical material (matter) is made up of extremely small, fundamental particles
   (D) The theory that natural selection is responsible for adaptation (adjusting to the environment) and speciation (the development of species)

27. Which of the following is a brief definition of atomic theory?
   (A) The theory that the sun is the center of the solar system and that the planets orbit around it
   (B) The theory that all complex organisms are composed of small, fundamental, living units
   (C) The theory that all physical material (matter) is made up of extremely small, fundamental particles
   (D) The theory that natural selection is responsible for adaptation (adjusting to the environment) and speciation (the development of species)

28. Match the statements below with the role they play in the experimental process using the following vocabulary words:

   question   hypothesis   prediction   test   analysis   conclusion

   a. "If water absorbs less blue light than any other color in the visible spectrum, a reflection of blue light will be brighter than a reflection of any other visible color."
   b. "Water splits visible light into different colors and absorbs different amounts of these various colors of light. Water reflects more blue light than other colors of light."
   c. "Why does water appear blue?"
   d. "All visible-light colors were tested, and the strongest reflection was produced by blue light."
   e. "Water appears blue because it reflects blue light more than it reflects other colors of light."
   f. "Lights of different colors were reflected off of water and onto a light-sensitive panel. The intensity (strength) of each color's reflection was measured."

Answers and Explanations

1. **(B)** The centigram is a metric unit of mass. Option A is incorrect because the pound is a customary unit of weight. Option C is incorrect because the ton is a customary unit of weight. Option D is incorrect because the cup is a customary unit of capacity or volume.

2. **(A)** The mile is a customary unit of length. Option B is incorrect because a centiliter is a metric unit of capacity or volume. Option C is incorrect because the gram is a metric unit of mass. Option D is incorrect because the meter is a metric unit of length.

3. **(B)** The kilometer is a metric unit of length. The ounce and the ton are both customary units of weight. The gram is a metric unit of mass.

4. **(D)** A milliliter is 10^{-3} liters. A centiliter is 10^{-2} liters. A deciliter is 10^{-1} liters. A complete list of metric prefixes and their values appears in the appendix.

5. **(A)** The points in plot A show no directional trend as the independent variable (x-value) increases. Option B is incorrect because plot B shows a strong positive correlation. Option C is incorrect because plot C shows a weak negative correlation. Option D is incorrect because plot D shows a strong negative correlation.

6. **(B)** The points in plot B show a clear postive (upward) trend as the independent variable (x-value) increases. This shows that the dependent variable increases in proportion with the independent variable and suggests the possibility of cause and effect. Option A is incorrect because plot A shows no correlation. Option C is incorrect because plot C shows a weak negative correlation. Option D is incorrect because plot D shows a strong negative correlation.

7. **(D)** The points in plot D show a clear negative (downward) trend as the independent variable (x-value) increases. This shows that the dependent variable decreases in proportion with the independent variable and suggests the possibility of cause and effect. Option A is incorrect because plot A shows no correlation. Option B is incorrect because plot B shows a strong positive correlation. Option C is incorrect because plot C shows a weak negative correlation.

8. **(C)** Plot C shows a negative (downward) trend, but the organization of the points is too loose to be considered a strong correlation. Option A is incorrect because the plot shows no correlation. Options B and D are incorrect because there is no such thing as either an incomplete or a median correlation.

9. **(D)** Correlation refers to two things that happen together and that may be related. Causation, however, refers to a provable cause-and-effect relationship between two things. In causation, one thing clearly and definitely causes the other. Remember, just because two things are correlated does not mean that causation exists between them. Correlation is not causation.

10. **(C)** CO is the chemical formula for carbon monoxide. Option A is incorrect because the formula for carbon dioxide is CO_2. Option B is incorrect because there is no compound called carbon tetraoxide. If it existed, though, its formula would be CO_4. Option D is incorrect because this simply lists the names of the two elements found in CO; it doesn't list the name of the compound.

11. **(A)** H_2O is the chemical formula for water. Option B is incorrect because dihydrogen dioxide is written as H_2O_2 and is commonly called hydrogen peroxide. Option C is incorrect because the formula for methane is CH_4. Option D is incorrect because the formula for glucose is $C_6H_{12}O_6$.

12. **(D)** CO_2 is the chemical formula for carbon dioxide. Option A is incorrect because the formula for water is H_2O. Option B is incorrect because there is no compound called dicarbon monoxide. If it existed, though, its formula would be C_2O. Option C is incorrect because the formula for methane is CH_4.

13. **(B)** $C_6H_{12}O_6$ is the chemical formula for glucose. Option A is incorrect because the formula for methane is CH_4. Option C is incorrect because there is no compound called 6-carbon dihydroxide. If it existed, though, its formula would be something like $C_6(OH)_2$. Option D is incorrect because there is no compound called carbon hydroxide. If it existed, though, its formula would be COH.

14. **(D)** CH_4 is the chemical formula for methane. Option A is incorrect because the formula for glucose is $C_6H_{12}O_6$. Option B is incorrect because the formula for carbon monoxide is CO. Option C is incorrect because the formula for carbon tetrachloride is CCl_4.

15. **(D)** The subscript numbers in a chemical formula indicate the number of atoms of that element present in the compound. When no subscript is present, a 1 is implied. Add the occurrences of H atoms based on the subscripts: $12 + 2 = 14$.

16. **(B)** The subscript numbers in a chemical formula indicate the number of atoms of that element present in the compound. When no subscript is present, a 1 is implied. Add the occurrences of O atoms based on the subscripts: $0 + 2 = 2$.

17. **(B)** The subscript numbers in a chemical formula indicate the number of atoms of that element present in the compound. When no subscript is present, a 1 is implied. Add the occurrences of C atoms based on the subscripts: $1 + 1 = 2$.

18. **(B)** The sum of the elements in the set is 82, and there are 6 elements in the set. So the arithmetic mean (average) is $82 \div 6 = 13.666667$. Round up because 6 is greater than 5. So the answer is 13.7.

19. **(B)** The median is the middle number when a set of odd-numbered elements is arranged in ascending order. If the set has an even number of elements, the median is the average of the two middle numbers when the elements are arranged in ascending order. Since this set has 6 elements, round the two middle numbers: $12 + 16 = 28$ and $28 \div 2 = 14$.

20. **(B)** The range of a set is the difference between the highest value and the lowest value: $22 - 4 = 18$.

21. **(D)** The mode is the element that appears the most often. There are more 9s in the set than any other element, so the mode is 9.

22. **(A)** The sum of the elements in the set is 45, and there are 7 elements in the set. So the arithmetic mean (average) is $45 \div 7 = 6.428571$. Round down because 2 is less than 5. So the answer is 6.4.

23. (D) The mode is 9. The average of the group of 9s is $27 \div 3 = 9$. Multiply 9 by 0.75 to give this average a weight of 75%: $9 \times 0.75 = 6.75$. The average of the rest of the elements is 4.5. Multiply 4.5 by 0.25 to give this average a weight of 25%: $4.5 \times 0.25 = 1.125$. To find the weighted average, add the $6.75 + 1.125 = 7.875$. Round up since 7 is greater than 5. The answer is 7.9.

24. (B) Cell theory states that all complex organisms are composed of small, fundamental, living units.

25. (D) The theory of evolution states that natural selection is responsible for adaptation (adjustment to the environment) and speciation (the development of species).

26. (A) The heliocentric theory states that the sun is the center of the solar system and that the planets orbit around it.

27. (C) The atomic theory states that all physical material (matter) is made up of extremely small, fundamental particles.

28.
    a. Prediction
    b. Hypothesis
    c. Question
    d. Analysis
    e. Conclusion
    f. Test

MODEL
Tests

ANSWER SHEET
Model Test 1

REASONING THROUGH LANGUAGE ARTS EXAM

1. Ⓐ Ⓑ Ⓒ Ⓓ

2. _____

3. Ⓐ Ⓑ Ⓒ Ⓓ

4. Ⓐ Ⓑ Ⓒ Ⓓ

5. Ⓐ Ⓑ Ⓒ Ⓓ

6. Ⓐ Ⓑ Ⓒ Ⓓ

7. Use lines below for your answer.

8. Ⓐ Ⓑ Ⓒ Ⓓ

9. Ⓐ Ⓑ Ⓒ Ⓓ

10. Ⓐ Ⓑ Ⓒ Ⓓ

11. Ⓐ Ⓑ Ⓒ Ⓓ

12. Ⓐ Ⓑ Ⓒ Ⓓ

13. Ⓐ Ⓑ Ⓒ Ⓓ

14. Ⓐ Ⓑ Ⓒ Ⓓ

15. Ⓐ Ⓑ Ⓒ Ⓓ

16. Ⓐ Ⓑ Ⓒ Ⓓ

17. _____

18. Ⓐ Ⓑ Ⓒ Ⓓ

19. Ⓐ Ⓑ Ⓒ Ⓓ

20. Ⓐ Ⓑ Ⓒ Ⓓ

21. Ⓐ Ⓑ Ⓒ Ⓓ

22. Ⓐ Ⓑ Ⓒ Ⓓ

23. Ⓐ Ⓑ Ⓒ Ⓓ

24. ___ , ___ , ___ , ___ , ___

25. _____

26. Ⓐ Ⓑ Ⓒ Ⓓ

27. Ⓐ Ⓑ Ⓒ Ⓓ

28. _____

29. Ⓐ Ⓑ Ⓒ

30. Ⓐ Ⓑ Ⓒ

31. Ⓐ Ⓑ Ⓒ

32. Ⓐ Ⓑ Ⓒ

33. Ⓐ Ⓑ Ⓒ

34. Ⓐ Ⓑ Ⓒ

35. Ⓐ Ⓑ Ⓒ

36. Ⓐ Ⓑ Ⓒ

37. Ⓐ Ⓑ Ⓒ

38. Ⓐ Ⓑ Ⓒ

39. Ⓐ Ⓑ Ⓒ Ⓓ

40. Ⓐ Ⓑ Ⓒ Ⓓ

41. Ⓐ Ⓑ Ⓒ Ⓓ

42. Ⓐ Ⓑ Ⓒ Ⓓ

43. Ⓐ Ⓑ Ⓒ Ⓓ

44. Ⓐ Ⓑ Ⓒ Ⓓ

45. Ⓐ Ⓑ Ⓒ Ⓓ

46. Ⓐ Ⓑ Ⓒ Ⓓ

47. Ⓐ Ⓑ Ⓒ Ⓓ

48. Ⓐ Ⓑ Ⓒ Ⓓ

49. Ⓐ Ⓑ Ⓒ Ⓓ

50. Ⓐ Ⓑ Ⓒ Ⓓ

7. _____

_____

_____

_____

_____

Extended Response

_____

_____

_____

_____

_____

_____

_____

_____

_____

_____

_____

_____

_____

_____

_____

_____

_____

_____

_____

> **DIRECTIONS:** This practice exam contains both fiction and nonfiction passages, which you will need to analyze in order to answer the questions that follow. The first portion of the exam has 50 questions. You will have 2 hours to answer those questions. In the second portion of the exam, you will write an extended response to multiple stimuli. You will have 45 minutes to complete the second portion of the exam.

QUESTIONS 1 THROUGH 7 ARE BASED ON THE FOLLOWING PASSAGE:

Excerpt from "Gift of the Magi"
by O. Henry

1   Jim was never late. Della doubled the fob chain in her hand and sat on the corner of the table near the door that he always entered. Then she heard his step on the stair away down on the first flight, and she turned white for just a moment. She had a habit of saying a little silent prayer about the simplest everyday things, and now she whispered: "Please God, make him think I am still pretty."

2   The door opened and Jim stepped in and closed it. He looked thin and very serious. Poor fellow, he was only twenty-two—and to be burdened with a family! He needed a new overcoat and he was without gloves.

3   Jim stopped inside the door, as immovable as a setter at the scent of quail. His eyes were fixed upon Della, and there was an expression in them that she could not read, and it terrified her. It was not anger, nor surprise, nor disapproval, nor horror, nor any of the sentiments that she had been prepared for. He simply stared at her fixedly with that peculiar expression on his face.

4   Della wriggled off the table and went for him.

5   "Jim, darling," she cried, "don't look at me that way. I had my hair cut off and sold because I couldn't have lived through Christmas without giving you a present. It'll grow out again—you won't mind, will you? I just had to do it. My hair grows awfully fast. Say 'Merry Christmas!' Jim, and let's be happy. You don't know what a nice—what a beautiful, nice gift I've got for you."

6   "You've cut off your hair?" asked Jim, laboriously, as if he had not arrived at that patent fact yet even after the hardest mental labor.

7   "Cut it off and sold it," said Della. "Don't you like me just as well, anyhow? I'm me without my hair, ain't I?"

8   Jim looked about the room curiously.

9   "You say your hair is gone?" he said, with an air almost of idiocy.

10   "You needn't look for it," said Della. "It's sold, I tell you—sold and gone, too. It's Christmas Eve, boy. Be good to me, for it went for you. Maybe the hairs of my head were numbered," she went on with sudden serious sweetness, "but nobody could ever count my love for you. Shall I put the chops on, Jim?"

11 Out of his trance Jim seemed quickly to wake. He enfolded his Della. For ten seconds let us regard with discreet scrutiny some inconsequential object in the other direction. Eight dollars a week or a million a year—what is the difference? A mathematician or a wit would give you the wrong answer. The magi brought valuable gifts, but that was not among them. This dark assertion will be illuminated later on.

12 Jim drew a package from his overcoat pocket and threw it upon the table.

13 "Don't make any mistake, Dell," he said, "about me. I don't think there's anything in the way of a haircut or a shave or a shampoo that could make me like my girl any less. But if you'll unwrap that package you may see why you had me going a while at first."

14 White fingers and nimble tore at the string and paper. And then an ecstatic scream of joy; and then, alas! a quick feminine change to hysterical tears and wails, necessitating the immediate employment of all the comforting powers of the lord of the flat.

15 For there lay The Combs—the set of combs, side and back, that Della had worshipped long in a Broadway window. Beautiful combs, pure tortoise shell, with jeweled rims— just the shade to wear in the beautiful vanished hair. They were expensive combs, she knew, and her heart had simply craved and yearned over them without the least hope of possession. And now, they were hers, but the tresses that should have adorned the coveted adornments were gone.

16 But she hugged them to her bosom, and at length she was able to look up with dim eyes and a smile and say: "My hair grows so fast, Jim!"

17 And then Della leaped up like a little singed cat and cried, "Oh, oh!"

18 Jim had not yet seen his beautiful present. She held it out to him eagerly upon her open palm. The dull precious metal seemed to flash with a reflection of her bright and ardent spirit.

19 "Isn't it a dandy, Jim? I hunted all over town to find it. You'll have to look at the time a hundred times a day now. Give me your watch. I want to see how it looks on it."

20 Instead of obeying, Jim tumbled down on the couch and put his hands under the back of his head and smiled.

21 "Dell," said he, "let's put our Christmas presents away and keep 'em a while. They're too nice to use just at present. I sold the watch to get the money to buy your combs. And now suppose you put the chops on."

22 The magi, as you know, were wise men—wonderfully wise men—who brought gifts to the Babe in the manger. They invented the art of giving Christmas presents. Being wise, their gifts were no doubt wise ones, possibly bearing the privilege of exchange in case of duplication. And here I have lamely related to you the uneventful chronicle of two foolish children in a flat who most unwisely sacrificed for each other the greatest treasures of their house. But in a last word to the wise of these days let it be said that of all who give gifts these two were the wisest. Of all who give and receive gifts, such as they are wisest. Everywhere they are wisest. They are the magi.

Source: gutenberg.org

1. What is the best meaning of the word "scrutiny" in paragraph 11?
   (A) Investigation
   (B) Scolding
   (C) Meaning
   (D) Fault

2. Della can best be described as _____ that Jim won't like her hair.

3. Which of the following is the best characterization of Della?
   (A) Self-centered
   (B) Devoted
   (C) Skeptical
   (D) Naive

4. Which of the following literary terms describes the loss of both the hair and the watch?
   (A) Simile
   (B) Hyperbole
   (C) Metaphor
   (D) Irony

5. What wakes Jim from his trance?
   (A) Della tells him that she loves him.
   (B) Della tells him that she cut her hair.
   (C) Della tells him that she has a gift for him.
   (D) Della tells him that she is upset about her hair.

6. Based on the passage, how would Della and Jim likely react if faced with a challenge?
   (A) Calmly
   (B) Frantically
   (C) Wisely
   (D) Eccentrically

7. Did Jim react to the loss of his wife's long hair in an appropriate manner? Briefly explain and support your answer.

Excerpt from *Common Sense*
by Thomas Paine

1   A government of our own is our natural right: And when a man seriously reflects on the precariousness of human affairs, he will become convinced, that it is infinitely wiser and safer, to form a constitution of our own in a cool deliberate manner, while we have it in our power, than to trust such an interesting event to time and chance. If we omit it now, some, Massanello[1] may hereafter arise, who laying hold of popular disquietudes, may collect together the desperate and discontented, and by assuming to themselves the powers of government, may sweep away the liberties of the continent like a deluge. Should the government of America return again into the hands of Britain, the tottering situation of things, will be a temptation for some desperate adventurer to try his fortune; and in such a case, what relief can Britain give? Ere she could hear the news, the fatal business might be done; and ourselves suffering like the wretched Britons under the oppression of the Conqueror. Ye that oppose independence now, ye know not what ye do; ye are opening a door to eternal tyranny, by keeping vacant the seat of government. There are thousands, and tens of thousands, who would think it glorious to expel from the continent, that barbarous and hellish power, which hath stirred up the Indians and Negroes to destroy us, the cruelty hath a double guilt, it is dealing brutally by us, and treacherously by them.

2   To talk of friendship with those in whom our reason forbids us to have faith, and our affections wounded through a thousand pores instruct us to detest, is madness and folly. Every day wears out the little remains of kindred between us and them, and can there be any reason to hope, that as the relationship expires, the affection will increase, or that we shall agree better, when we have ten times more and greater concerns to quarrel over than ever?

3   Ye that tell us of harmony and reconciliation, can ye restore to us the time that is past? Can ye give to prostitution its former innocence? Neither can ye reconcile Britain and America. The last cord now is broken, the people of England are presenting addresses against us. There are injuries which nature cannot forgive; she would cease to be nature if she did. As well can the lover forgive the ravisher of his mistress, as the continent forgive the murders of Britain. The Almighty hath implanted in us these unextinguishable feelings for good and wise purposes. They are the guardians of his image in our hearts. They distinguish us from the herd of common animals. The social compact would dissolve, and justice be extirpated from the earth, or have only a casual existence were we callous to the touches of affection. The robber, and the murderer, would often escape unpunished, did not the injuries which our tempers sustain, provoke us into justice.

[1] *Thomas Anello, otherwise Massanello, a fisherman of Naples, who after spiriting up his countrymen in the public market place, against the oppression of the Spaniards, to whom the place was then subject, prompted them to revolt, and in the space of a day became king.*

4   O ye that love mankind! Ye that dare oppose, not only the tyranny, but the tyrant, stand forth! Every spot of the old world is overrun with oppression. Freedom hath been hunted round the globe. Asia, and Africa, have long expelled her. Europe regards her like a stranger, and England hath given her warning to depart. O! receive the fugitive, and prepare in time an asylum for mankind.

Source: gutenberg.org

8. What is the central idea of the first paragraph?
    (A) America should be returned to Britain.
    (B) The doors to eternal tyranny must be opened.
    (C) Having a government for the people is a natural right.
    (D) Writing a constitution must be done in a deliberate manner.

9. Who was Massanello?
    (A) A fisherman
    (B) A pundit
    (C) A philosopher
    (D) A doctor

10. What was the most likely purpose of this writing?
    (A) To call people into action
    (B) To calm an agitated group of people
    (C) To make claims about the benefits of tyranny
    (D) To describe liberty

11. What is the best definition for the word "unextinguishable" in the third paragraph?
    (A) Unintentional
    (B) Thought out
    (C) Intense
    (D) Unable to quell

12. Based on the third paragraph, how does the author feel about the prospect of returning to an earlier time?
    (A) It is attainable.
    (B) It is impossible.
    (C) There are difficulties associated with it.
    (D) It is the best option.

13. What was the likely catalyst for the author writing this passage?
    (A) An oppressive government
    (B) A desire to move in an unexplored direction
    (C) Patriotism
    (D) Curiosity

Excerpt from *Walden*
by Henry David Thoreau

1   I went to the woods because I wished to live deliberately, to front only the essential facts of life, and see if I could not learn what it had to teach, and not, when I came to die, discover that I had not lived. I did not wish to live what was not life, living is so dear; nor did I wish to practice resignation, unless it was quite necessary. I wanted to live deep and suck out all the marrow of life, to live so sturdily and Spartan-like as to put to rout all that was not life, to cut a broad swath and shave close, to drive life into a corner, and reduce it to its lowest terms, and, if it proved to be mean, why then to get the whole and genuine meanness of it, and publish its meanness to the world; or if it were sublime, to know it by experience, and be able to give a true account of it in my next excursion. For most men, it appears to me, are in a strange uncertainty about it, whether it is of the devil or of God, and have somewhat hastily concluded that it is the chief end of man here to "glorify God and enjoy him forever."

2   Still we live meanly, like ants; though the fable tells us that we were long ago changed into men; like pygmies we fight with cranes; it is error upon error, and clout upon clout, and our best virtue has for its occasion a superfluous and evitable wretchedness. Our life is frittered away by detail. An honest man has hardly need to count more than his ten fingers, or in extreme cases he may add his ten toes, and lump the rest. Simplicity, simplicity, simplicity! I say, let your affairs be as two or three, and not a hundred or a thousand; instead of a million count half a dozen, and keep your accounts on your thumb-nail. In the midst of this chopping sea of civilized life, such are the clouds and storms and quicksands and thousand-and-one items to be allowed for, that a man has to live, if he would not founder and go to the bottom and not make his port at all, by dead reckoning, and he must be a great calculator indeed who succeeds. Simplify, simplify. Instead of three meals a day, if it be necessary eat but one; instead of a hundred dishes, five; and reduce other things in proportion. Our life is like a German Confederacy, made up of petty states, with its boundary forever fluctuating, so that even a German cannot tell you how it is bounded at any moment. The nation itself, with all its so-called internal improvements, which, by the way are all external and superficial, is just such an unwieldy and overgrown establishment, cluttered with furniture and tripped up by its own traps, ruined by luxury and heedless expense, by want of calculation and a worthy aim, as the million households in the land; and the only cure for it, as for them, is in a rigid economy, a stern and more than Spartan simplicity of life and elevation of purpose. It lives too fast. Men think that it is essential that the Nation have commerce, and export ice, and talk through a telegraph, and ride thirty miles an hour, without a doubt, whether they do or not; but whether we should live like baboons or like men, is a little uncertain. If we do not get out sleepers, and forge rails, and devote days and nights to the work, but go to tinkering upon our lives to improve them, who will build railroads? And if railroads are not built, how shall we get to heaven in season? But if we stay at home and mind our business, who will want railroads? We do not ride on the railroad; it rides upon us. Did you ever think what those sleepers are that underlie the railroad? Each one is a man, an Irishman, or a Yankee man. The rails are laid on them, and they are covered with sand, and the cars run smoothly over them. They are

NOTE

Question 20 on page 510 refers to the highlighted word.

sound sleepers, I assure you. And every few years a new lot is laid down and run over; so that, if some have the pleasure of riding on a rail, others have the misfortune to be ridden upon. And when they run over a man that is walking in his sleep, a supernumerary sleeper in the wrong position, and wake him up, they suddenly stop the cars, and make a hue and cry about it, as if this were an exception. I am glad to know that it takes a gang of men for every five miles to keep the sleepers down and level in their beds as it is, for this is a sign that they may sometime get up again.

Source: gutenberg.org

14. At the beginning of the second paragraph, Thoreau writes, "Still we live meanly, like ants." What literary device does he use here?
    (A) Analogy
    (B) Personification
    (C) Juxtaposition
    (D) Simile

15. What was the narrator's purpose for going to the woods?
    (A) To face only life
    (B) To seek adventure
    (C) To live like God
    (D) To teach those who lived in the wild

16. Which of the following sums up the author's message?
    (A) Attain luxury.
    (B) Simplify.
    (C) Live meanly.
    (D) Go on excursions.

17. The narrator would most likely _____ living in a city near a park.

18. What does the author mean by, "We do not ride on the railroad; it rides upon us"?
    (A) The railroad crosses many towns.
    (B) Technology has encroached upon us.
    (C) Traveling by railroad is uncomfortable.
    (D) It took many people to build the railroad.

19. Which of the following, in general, does the author find most problematic?
    (A) The pace of life
    (B) The telegraph
    (C) Economic principals
    (D) Gangs

20. What is the best definition of the word "unwieldy" in the second paragraph?
    (A) Difficult to carry
    (B) Unorganized
    (C) Unmade
    (D) Displeasing

QUESTIONS 21 THROUGH 28 ARE BASED ON THE FOLLOWING PASSAGE:

Excerpt from *Anne of Green Gables*
by L. M. Montgomery

1   Marilla came briskly forward as Matthew opened the door. But when her eyes fell of the odd little figure in the stiff, ugly dress, with the long braids of red hair and the eager, luminous eyes, she stopped short in amazement.

2   "Matthew Cuthbert, who's that?" . . . "Where is the boy?"

3   "There wasn't any boy," said Matthew wretchedly. "There was only HER."

4   He nodded at the child, remembering that he had never even asked her name.

5   "No boy! But there MUST have been a boy," insisted Marilla. "We sent word to Mrs. Spencer to bring a boy."

6   "Well, she didn't. She brought HER. I asked the station-master. And I had to bring her home. She couldn't be left there, no matter where the mistake had come in."

7   "Well, this is a pretty piece of business!" . . .

8   During this dialogue the child had remained silent, her eyes roving from one to the other, all the animation fading out of her face. Suddenly she seemed to grasp the full meaning of what had been said. Dropping her precious carpet-bag she sprang forward a step and clasped her hands.

9   "You don't want me!" she cried. "You don't want me because I'm not a boy! I might have expected it. Nobody ever did want me. I might have known it was all too beautiful to last. I might have known nobody really did want me. Oh, what shall I do? I'm going to burst into tears!"

10   Burst into tears she did. Sitting down on a chair by the table, flinging her arms out upon it, and burying her face in them, she proceeded to cry stormily. Marilla and Matthew looked at each other deprecatingly across the stove. Neither of them knew what to say or do. Finally Marilla stepped lamely into the breach.

11   "Well, well, there's no need to cry so about it."

12   "Yes, there IS need!" The child raised her head quickly, revealing a tear-stained face and trembling lips. "YOU would cry, too, if you were an orphan and had come to a place you thought was going to be home and found that they didn't want you because you weren't a boy. Oh, this is the most TRAGICAL thing that ever happened to me!"

13   Something like a reluctant smile, rather rusty from long disuse, mellowed Marilla's grim expression.

14   "Well, don't cry any more. We're not going to turn you out-of-doors to-night. You'll have to stay here until we investigate this affair. What's your name?"

15   The child hesitated for a moment.

16   "Will you please call me Cordelia?" she said eagerly.

17   "CALL you Cordelia? Is that your name?"

18   "No-o-o, it's not exactly my name, but I would love to be called Cordelia. It's such a perfectly elegant name."

19   "I don't know what on earth you mean. If Cordelia isn't your name, what is?"

20   "Anne Shirley," reluctantly faltered forth the owner of that name, "but, oh, please do call me Cordelia. It can't matter much to you what you call me if I'm only going to be here a little while, can it? And Anne is such an unromantic name."

21   "Unromantic fiddlesticks!" said the unsympathetic Marilla. "Anne is a real good plain sensible name. You've no need to be ashamed of it."

22   "Oh, I'm not ashamed of it," explained Anne, "only I like Cordelia better. I've always imagined that my name was Cordelia—at least, I always have of late years. When I was young I used to imagine it was Geraldine, but I like Cordelia better now. But if you call me Anne please call me Anne spelled with an E."

23   "What difference does it make how it's spelled?" asked Marilla with another rusty smile as she picked up the teapot.

24   "Oh, it makes SUCH a difference. It LOOKS so much nicer. . . ."

Source: gutenberg.org

21. Which of the following best characterizes Anne?
    (A) Content
    (B) Unsympathetic
    (C) Discontented
    (D) Cunning

22. In the 12th paragraph, the child uses the word "tragical." Which of the following words would be the best replacement for "tragical" ?
    (A) Pleasant
    (B) Funny
    (C) Devastating
    (D) Magical

23. Which of the following characters originally indicated that "Anne" was a good name?
    (A) Cordelia
    (B) Matthew
    (C) The Child
    (D) Marilla

24. Arrange the following events into chronological order, beginning with the first thing that happened.
    a. Anne begins crying.
    b. Marilla is surprised by the arrival of a girl.
    c. Anne believes she is unwanted.
    d. Matthew opens the door.
    e. Anne wants to be called "Anne spelled with an E."

25. Anne's behavior can best be described as _____.

26. Based on the evidence in the passage, how might Anne react if she did not like her outfit?
    (A) She would tolerate it until she was able to change.
    (B) She would reject it and propose other outfits.
    (C) She would go home.
    (D) She would make the best of it.

27. Based on the evidence in the passage, which of the following best describes Marilla?
    (A) Tender
    (B) No-nonsense
    (C) Cruel
    (D) Tyrannical

28. The effect that Marilla has on Anne can best be described as _____.

QUESTIONS 29 THROUGH 33 ARE EMBEDDED IN THE FOLLOWING PASSAGE:

Excerpt from *Great Astronomers: Isaac Newton*
by Robert Stawell Ball

It was just a year after the death of Galileo, that an infant came into the world who was christened Isaac Newton. Even the great fame of Galileo himself must be relegated to a second place in comparison with that of the philosopher who first expounded the true theory of the universe.

Isaac Newton was born on the 25th of December (old style), 1642, at Woolsthorpe, in Lincolnshire, about a half-mile from Colsterworth, and eight miles south of Grantham. His father, Mr. Isaac Newton, had died a few months after his marriage to Harriet Ayscough, the daughter of Mr. James Ayscough, of Market Overton, in Rutlandshire. The little Isaac was at first so excessively frail and weakly that his life was despaired of. The watchful mother, however, tended her delicate child with such success that he seems to have thriven better than might have been expected from the circumstances of his infancy, and he ultimately acquired a frame strong enough to outlast the ordinary span of human life.

29. Choose one.
   (A) For three years they continue to live at Woolsthorpe, the widow's means of livelihood being supplemented by the income from another small estate at Sewstern, in a neighboring part of Leicestershire.
   (B) For three years they continued to live at Woolsthorpe, the widow's means of livelihood was being supplementing by the income from another small estate at Sewstern, in a neighboring part of Leicestershire.
   (C) For three years they continued to live at woolsthorpe, the widow's means of livelihood being supplemented by the income from another small estate at sewstern, in a neighboring part of leicestershire.

In 1645, Mrs. Newton took as a second husband the Rev. Barnabas Smith, and on moving to her new home, about a mile from Woolsthorpe, she entrusted little Isaac to her mother, Mrs. Ayscough. In due time we find that the boy was sent to the public school at Grantham, the name of the master being Stokes. For the purpose of being near his work, the embryo philosopher was boarded at the house of Mr. Clark, an apothecary at Grantham. We learn from Newton himself that at first he had a very low place in the class lists of the school, and was by no means one of those model school-boys who find favor in the eyes of the school-master by attention to Latin grammar. Isaac's first incentive to diligent study seems to have been derived from the circumstance that he was severely kicked by one of the boys who was above him in the class. This indignity had the effect of stimulating young Newton's activity to such an extent that he not only attained the desired object of passing over the head of the boy who had maltreated him, but continued to rise until he became the head of the school.

The play-hours of the great philosopher were devoted to pursuits very different from those of most school-boys. His chief amusement was found in making mechanical toys and various ingenious contrivances. He watched day by day with great interest the workmen engaged in constructing a windmill in the neighborhood of the school, the result of which was that the boy made a working model of the windmill and of its machinery, which seems to have been much admired, as indicating his aptitude for mechanics.

30. Choose one.
    (A) We is told that Isaac also indulged in somewhat higher flights of mechanical enterprise.
    (B) We are told that Isaac also indulged in somewhat higher flights of mechanical enterprise.
    (C) We have also been telling that Isaac also indulged in somewhat higher flights of mechanical enterprise.

He constructed a carriage, the wheels of which were to be driven by the hands of the occupant, while the first philosophical instrument he made was a clock, which was actuated by water.

31. Choose one.
    (A) He also devoted much attention to the construction of paper kites, and his skill in this respect was highly appreciated by his school-fellows.
    (B) he also devoted much attention to the construction of paper kites, and his skill in this respect was highly appreciated by his school-fellows.
    (C) He also devoted much attention to the construction of paper kites and his skill in this respect was highly appreciated by his school-fellows.

32. Choose one.
    (A) Like a true philosopher, even at this stage he experimented on the best methods of attaching the string, and on the proportions, which the tail ought to have.
    (B) Like a true philosopher, even at this stage he experimented on the best methods of attaching the string, and on the proportions which the tail ought to have.
    (C) Like a true philosopher, even at this stage he experimented on the best methods of attaching the string, and on the proportions who the tail ought to have.

He also made lanthorns of paper to provide himself with light as he walked to school in the dark winter mornings.

The only love affair in Newton's life appears to have commenced while he was still of tender years. The incidents are thus described in Brewster's "Life of Newton," a work to which I am much indebted in this chapter.

"In the house where he lodged there were some female inmates, in whose company he appears to have taken much pleasure. One of these, a Miss Storey, sister to Dr. Storey, a physician at Buckminster, near Colsterworth, was two or three years younger than Newton, and to great personal attractions she seems to have added more than the usual allotment of female talent. The society of this young lady and her companions was always preferred to that of his own schoolfellows, and it was one of his most agreeable occupations to construct for them little tables and cupboards, and other utensils for holding their dolls and their trinkets.

33. Choose one.
    (A) He had lived nearly six years in the same house with Miss Storey, and there is reasons to believe that their youthful friendship gradually rose to a higher passion;
    (B) He had lived nearly six years in the same house with Miss Storey, and there is reason to believe that there youthful friendship gradually rose to a higher passion;
    (C) He had lived nearly six years in the same house with Miss Storey, and there is reason to believe that their youthful friendship gradually rose to a higher passion;

but the smallness of her portion, and the inadequacy of his own fortune, appear to have prevented the consummation of their happiness. Miss Storey was afterwards twice married, and under the name of Mrs. Vincent, Dr. Stukeley visited her at Grantham in 1727, at the age of eighty-two, and obtained from her many particulars respecting the early history of our author. Newton's esteem for her continued unabated during his life. He regularly visited her when he went to Lincolnshire, and never failed to relieve her from little pecuniary difficulties which seem to have beset her family."

Source: gutenberg.org

QUESTIONS 34 THROUGH 38 ARE EMBEDDED IN THE FOLLOWING PASSAGE:

Presidential Memorandum—Transforming our Nation's Electric Grid Through Improved Siting, Permitting, and Review

MEMORANDUM FOR THE HEADS OF EXECUTIVE DEPARTMENTS AND AGENCIES

SUBJECT: Transforming our Nation's Electric Grid Through Improved Siting, Permitting, and Review

34. Choose one.
    (A) Our Nations electric transmission grid is the backbone of our economy, a key factor in future economic growth, and a critical component of our energy security.
    (B) Our Nation's electric transmission grid is the backbone of our economy, a key factor in future economic growth and a critical component of our energy security.
    (C) Our Nation's electric transmission grid is the backbone of our economy, a key factor in future economic growth, and a critical component of our energy security.

Countries that harness the power of clean, renewable energy will be best positioned to thrive in the global economy while protecting the environment and increasing prosperity.

35. Choose one.
    (A) In order to ensure the growth of America's clean energy economy and improve energy security, we must modernize and expand our electric transmission grid.
    (B) In order to ensures the growth of America's clean energy economy and improve energy security, we must modernize and expand our electric transmission grid.
    (C) in order to ensure the growth of America's clean energy economy and improve energy security, we must modernize and expand our electric transmission grid.

Modernizing our grid will improve energy reliability and resiliency, allowing us to minimize power outages and manage cyber-security threats.

36. Choose one.
    (A) By diversifying power sources and reducing congestion. A modernized grid will also create cost savings for consumers and spur economic growth.
    (B) By diversifying power sources and reducing congestion, a modernized grid will also create cost savings for consumers and spur economic growth.
    (C) By diversifying power sources, and reducing congestion, a modernized grid will also create cost savings for consumers and spur economic growth.

Modernizing our Nation's electric transmission grid requires improvements in how transmission lines are sited, permitted, and reviewed.

As part of our efforts to improve the performance of Federal siting, permitting, and review processes for infrastructure development, my Administration created a Rapid Response Team for Transmission (RRTT), a collaborative effort involving nine different executive departments and agencies (agencies), which is working to improve the efficiency and effectiveness of transmission siting, permitting, and review, increase interagency coordination and transparency, and increase the predictability of the siting, permitting, and review processes. In furtherance of Executive Order 13604 of March 22, 2012 (Improving Performance of Federal Permitting and Review of Infrastructure Projects), this memorandum builds upon the work of the RRTT to improve the Federal siting, permitting, and review processes for transmission projects.

37. Choose one.
    (A) Because a single projects may cross multiple governmental jurisdictions over hundreds of miles, robust collaboration among Federal, State, local, and tribal governments must be a critical component of this effort.
    (B) Because a single project may cross multiple governmental jurisdictions over hundreds of miles robust collaboration among Federal State local and tribal governments must be a critical component of this effort.
    (C) Because a single project may cross multiple governmental jurisdictions over hundreds of miles, robust collaboration among Federal, State, local, and tribal governments must be a critical component of this effort.

An important avenue to improve these processes is the designation of energy right-of-way corridors (energy corridors) on Federal lands. Section 368 of the Energy Policy Act of 2005 (the "Act") (42 U.S.C. 15926), requires the Secretaries of Agriculture, Commerce, Defense, Energy, and the Interior (Secretaries) to undertake a continued effort to identify and designate such energy corridors. Energy corridors include areas on Federal lands that are most suitable for siting transmission projects because the chosen areas minimize regulatory conflicts and impacts on environmental and cultural resources, and also address concerns of local communities. Designated energy corridors provide an opportunity to co-locate projects and share environmental and cultural resource impact data to reduce overall impacts on environmental and cultural resources and reduce the need for land use plan amendments in support of the authorization of transmission rights-of-way.

38. Choose one.
    (A) The designation of energy corridors can help expedite the siting, permitting, and review processes for projects within such corridors, as well as improve the predictability and transparency of these process.
    (B) the designation of energy corridors can help expedite the siting, permitting, and review processes for projects within such corridors, as well as improve the predictability and transparency of these processes.
    (C) The designation of energy corridors can help expedite the siting, permitting, and review processes for projects within such corridors, as well as improve the predictability and transparency of these processes.

Pursuant to the Act, in 2009, the Secretaries of the Interior and Agriculture each designated energy corridors for the 11 contiguous Western States, as defined in section 368 of the Act. Energy corridors have not yet been designated in States other than those identified as Western States. It is important that agencies build on their existing efforts in a coordinated manner.

Source: whitehouse.gov

Excerpt from *Les Misérables*

by Victor Hugo

1   MY GOOD MADAM: Not a day passes without our speaking of you. It is our established custom; but there is another reason besides. Just imagine, while washing and dusting the ceilings and walls, Madam Magloire has made some discoveries; now our two chambers hung with antique paper whitewashed over, would not discredit a chateau in the style of yours. Madam Magloire has pulled off all the paper. There were things beneath. My drawing-room, which contains no furniture, and which we use for spreading out the linen after washing, is fifteen feet in height, eighteen square, with a ceiling which was formerly painted and gilded, and with beams, as in yours. This was covered with a cloth while this was the hospital. And the woodwork was of the era of our grandmothers. But my room is the one you ought to see. Madam Magloire has discovered, under at least ten thicknesses of paper pasted on top, some paintings, which without being good are very tolerable. The subject is Telemachus being knighted by Minerva in some gardens, the name of which escapes me. In short, where the Roman ladies repaired on one single night. What shall I say to you? I have Romans, and Roman ladies, and the whole train. Madam Magloire has cleaned it all off; this summer she is going to have some small injuries repaired, and the whole revarnished, and my chamber will be a regular museum. She has also found in a corner of the attic two wooden pier-tables of ancient fashion. They asked us two crowns of six francs each to regild them, but it is much better to give the money to the poor; and they are very ugly besides, and I should much prefer a round table of mahogany.

2   I am always very happy. My brother is so good. He gives all he has to the poor and sick. We are very much cramped. The country is trying in the winter, and we really must do something for those who are in need. We are almost comfortably lighted and warmed. You see that these are great treats.

3   My brother has ways of his own. When he talks, he says that a bishop ought to be so. Just imagine! the door of our house is never fastened. Whoever chooses to enter finds himself at once in my brother's room. He fears nothing, even at night. That is his sort of bravery, he says.

4   He does not wish me or Madame Magloire feel any fear for him. He exposes himself to all sorts of dangers, and he does not like to have us even seem to notice it. One must know how to understand him.

5   He goes out in the rain, he walks in the water, he travels in winter. He fears neither suspicious roads nor dangerous encounters, nor night.

6   Last year he went quite alone into a country of robbers. He would not take us. He was absent for a fortnight. On his return nothing had happened to him; he was thought to be dead, but was perfectly well, and said, "This is the way I have been robbed!" And then he opened a trunk full of jewels, all the jewels of the cathedral of Embrun, which the thieves had given him.

7   When he returned on that occasion, I could not refrain from scolding him a little, taking care, however, not to speak except when the carriage was making a noise, so that no one might hear me.

8   At first I used to say to myself, "There are no dangers which will stop him; he is terrible." Now I have ended by getting used to it. I make a sign to Madam Magloire that she is not to oppose him. He risks himself as he sees fit. I carry off Madam Magloire, I enter my chamber, I pray for him and fall asleep. I am at ease, because I know that if anything were to happen to him, it would be the end of me. I should go to the good God with my brother and my bishop. It has cost Madam Magloire more trouble than it did me to accustom herself to what she terms his imprudences. But now the habit has been acquired. We pray together, we tremble together, and we fall asleep. If the devil were to enter this house, he would be allowed to do so. After all, what is there for us to fear in this house? There is always some one with us who is stronger than we. The devil may pass through it, but the good God dwells here.

9   This suffices me. My brother has no longer any need of saying a word to me. I understand him without his speaking, and we abandon ourselves to the care of Providence. That is the way one has to do with a man who possesses grandeur of soul.

10   I have interrogated my brother with regard to the information which you desire on the subject of the Faux family. You are aware that he knows everything, and that he has memories, because he is still a very good royalist. They really are a very ancient Norman family of the generalship of Caen. Five hundred years ago there was a Raoul de Faux, a Jean de Faux, and a Thomas de Faux, who were gentlemen, and one of whom was a seigneur de Rochefort. The last was Guy-Etienne Alexandre, and was commander of a regiment, and something in the light horse of Bretagne. His daughter, Marie-Louise, married Adrien-Charles de Gramont, son of the Duke Louis de Gramont, peer of France, colonel of the French guards, and lieutenant-general of the army. It is written Faux, Fauq, and Faoucq.

11   Good Madame, recommend us to the prayers of your sainted relative, Monsieur the Cardinal. As for your dear Sylvanie, she has done well in not wasting the few moments which she passes with you in writing to me. She is well, works as you would wish, and loves me.

12   That is all that I desire. The souvenir which she sent through you reached me safely, and it makes me very happy. My health is not so very bad, and yet I grow thinner every day. Farewell; my paper is at an end, and this forces me to leave you. A thousand good wishes.

BAPTISTINE.

13   P.S. Your grand nephew is charming. Do you know that he will soon be five years old? Yesterday he saw some one riding by on horseback who had on knee-caps, and he said, "What has he got on his knees?" He is a charming child! His little brother is dragging an old broom about the room, like a carriage, and saying, "Hu!"

Source: gutenberg.org

39. The reference to Telemachus in the first paragraph is an example of which of the following?
    (A) Metaphor
    (B) Allusion
    (C) Apostrophe
    (D) Characterization

40. Which of the following characterizes the speaker's brother?
    (A) Crazy
    (B) Aloof
    (C) Giving
    (D) Self-deprecating

41. In the sentence, "They asked us two crowns of six francs each to regild them, but it is much better to give the money to the poor," what is the best definition of the word "crowns"?
    (A) The top of a head
    (B) A slap on the head
    (C) A hat that adorns a king
    (D) Money

42. Which of the following emotions does the speaker display? You may choose one or more than one answer.
    (A) Anger
    (B) Curiosity
    (C) Concern
    (D) Happiness

43. What effect does the postscript (P.S.) have on the letter?
    (A) It makes the letter insincere.
    (B) It makes the letter more personal.
    (C) It makes the letter lengthy.
    (D) It makes the letter more complicated.

44. The speaker states, "We abandon ourselves to the care of Providence." In this context, to what is "Providence" referring?
    (A) God
    (B) Providence, Rhode Island
    (C) Any given state
    (D) Prudence

Excerpt from *Dracula*
by Bram Stoker

1   3 May. Bistritz.—Left Munich at 8:35 P.M., on 1st May, arriving at Vienna early next morning; should have arrived at 6:46, but train was an hour late. Buda-Pesth seems a wonderful place, from the glimpse which I got of it from the train and the little I could walk through the streets. I feared to go very far from the station, as we had arrived late and would start as near the correct time as possible.

2   The impression I had was that we were leaving the West and entering the East; the most western of splendid bridges over the Danube, which is here of noble width and depth, took us among the traditions of Turkish rule.

3   We left in pretty good time, and came after nightfall to Klausenburgh. Here I stopped for the night at the Hotel Royale. I had for dinner, or rather supper, a chicken done up some way with red pepper, which was very good but thirsty. (Mem. get recipe for Mina.) I asked the waiter, and he said it was called "paprika hendl," and that, as it was a national dish, I should be able to get it anywhere along the Carpathians.

4   I found my smattering of German very useful here, indeed, I don't know how I should be able to get on without it.

5   Having had some time at my disposal when in London, I had visited the British Museum, and made search among the books and maps in the library regarding Transylvania; it had struck me that some foreknowledge of the country could hardly fail to have some importance in dealing with a nobleman of that country.

6   I find that the district he named is in the extreme east of the country, just on the borders of three states, Transylvania, Moldavia, and Bukovina, in the midst of the Carpathian mountains; one of the wildest and least known portions of Europe.

7   I was not able to light on any map or work giving the exact locality of the Castle Dracula, as there are no maps of this country as yet to compare with our own Ordnance Survey Maps; but I found that Bistritz, the post town named by Count Dracula, is a fairly well-known place. I shall enter here some of my notes, as they may refresh my memory when I talk over my travels with Mina.

8   In the population of Transylvania there are four distinct nationalities: Saxons in the South, and mixed with them the Wallachs, who are the descendants of the Dacians; Magyars in the West, and Szekelys in the East and North. I am going among the latter, who claim to be descended from Attila and the Huns. This may be so, for when the Magyars conquered the country in the eleventh century they found the Huns settled in it.

9   I read that every known superstition in the world is gathered into the horseshoe of the Carpathians, as if it were the centre of some sort of imaginative whirlpool; if so my stay may be very interesting. (Mem., I must ask the Count all about them.)

10   I did not sleep well, though my bed was comfortable enough, for I had all sorts of queer dreams. There was a dog howling all night under my window, which may have had something to do with it; or it may have been the paprika, for I had to drink up all the

water in my carafe, and was still thirsty. Towards morning I slept and was wakened by the continuous knocking at my door, so I guess I must have been sleeping soundly then.

11   I had for breakfast more paprika, and a sort of porridge of maize flour which they said was "mamaliga", and eggplant stuffed with forcemeat, a very excellent dish, which they call "impletata". (Mem., get recipe for this also.)

12   I had to hurry breakfast, for the train started a little before eight, or rather it ought to have done so, for after rushing to the station at 7:30 I had to sit in the carriage for more than an hour before we began to move.

13   It seems to me that the further east you go the more unpunctual are the trains. What ought they to be in China?

14   All day long we seemed to dawdle through a country which was full of beauty of every kind. Sometimes we saw little towns or castles on the top of steep hills such as we see in old missals; sometimes we ran by rivers and streams which seemed from the wide stony margin on each side of them to be subject to great floods. It takes a lot of water, and running strong, to sweep the outside edge of a river clear.

15   At every station there were groups of people, sometimes crowds, and in all sorts of attire. Some of them were just like the peasants at home or those I saw coming through France and Germany, with short jackets, and round hats, and home-made trousers; but others were very picturesque.

16   The women looked pretty, except when you got near them, but they were very clumsy about the waist. They had all full white sleeves of some kind or other, and most of them had big belts with a lot of strips of something fluttering from them like the dresses in a ballet, but of course there were petticoats under them.

17   The strangest figures we saw were the Slovaks, who were more barbarian than the rest, with their big cow-boy hats, great baggy dirty-white trousers, white linen shirts, and enormous heavy leather belts, nearly a foot wide, all studded over with brass nails. They wore high boots, with their trousers tucked into them, and had long black hair and heavy black moustaches. They are very picturesque, but do not look prepossessing. On the stage they would be set down at once as some old Oriental band of brigands. They are, however, I am told, very harmless and rather wanting in natural self-assertion.

18   It was on the dark side of twilight when we got to Bistritz, which is a very interesting old place. Being practically on the frontier—for the Borgo Pass leads from it into Bukovina—it has had a very stormy existence, and it certainly shows marks of it. Fifty years ago a series of great fires took place, which made terrible havoc on five separate occasions. At the very beginning of the seventeenth century it underwent a siege of three weeks and lost 13,000 people, the casualties of war proper being assisted by famine and disease.

19   Count Dracula had directed me to go to the Golden Krone Hotel, which I found, to my great delight, to be thoroughly old-fashioned, for of course I wanted to see all I could of the ways of the country.

20   I was evidently expected, for when I got near the door I faced a cheery-looking elderly woman in the usual peasant dress—white undergarment with a long double apron, front, and back, of colored stuff fitting almost too tight for modesty. When I came close she bowed and said, "The Herr Englishman?"

21   "Yes," I said, "Jonathan Harker."

22   She smiled, and gave some message to an elderly man in white shirtsleeves, who had followed her to the door.

23   He went, but immediately returned with a letter:

24   "My friend.—Welcome to the Carpathians. I am anxiously expecting you. Sleep well tonight. At three tomorrow the diligence will start for Bukovina; a place on it is kept for you. At the Borgo Pass my carriage will await you and will bring you to me.

Source: gutenberg.org

45. In the sentence, "It seems to me that the further east you go the more unpunctual are the trains," what is the best definition of the word "unpunctual"?
     (A) Not on time
     (B) Not punctured
     (C) Disrespectful
     (D) Precise

46. The first paragraph implies that the speaker is doing which of the following?
     (A) Researching Vienna
     (B) Working for the train company
     (C) Traveling
     (D) Interviewing people

47. In paragraph 20, the speaker says, "I was evidently expected, for when I got near the door I faced a cheery-looking elderly woman in the usual peasant dress—white undergarment with a long double apron, front, and back, of colored stuff fitting almost too tight for modesty. When I came close she bowed and said, 'The Herr Englishman?'" Why did the woman bow?
     (A) Because the speaker is royalty
     (B) To show respect
     (C) To indicate she had lost
     (D) So the speaker could see the top of her head

48. Which quote has a welcoming tone?
     (A) "All day long we seemed to dawdle through a country which was full of beauty of every kind."
     (B) "I feared to go very far from the station, as we had arrived late and would start as near the correct time as possible."
     (C) "My friend.—Welcome to the Carpathians. I am anxiously expecting you. Sleep well tonight."
     (D) "I had to hurry breakfast, for the train started a little before eight, or rather it ought to have done so, for after rushing to the station at 7:30 I had to sit in the carriage for more than an hour before we began to move."

49. What language did the locals speak in Klausenburgh?
    (A) German
    (B) Turkish
    (C) English
    (D) Romanian

50. Who is the speaker?
    (A) Count Dracula
    (B) Jonathan Harker
    (C) Bram Stoker
    (D) The elderly man in white shirtsleeves

Extended Response

DIRECTIONS: Read and utilize the following passages to construct an extended response to the following prompt:

Do laws such as the Clean Air Act address the specific issues relating to air quality? Cite specific information and examples to support your position and be sure to develop your answers fully. You have 45 minutes to complete this section.

Ecosystems and Air Quality

Research has linked air pollution to many effects on ecosystems. Studies have shown that air pollutants such as sulfur can lead to excess amounts of acid in lakes and streams and damage trees and forest soils. Nitrogen in the atmosphere has been found to harm fish and other aquatic life when deposited on surface waters.

Research has helped to understand ozone pollution's ability to damage tree leaves and negatively affect scenic vistas in protected natural areas. Mercury and other heavy metal compounds that are emitted into the air from combustion of fuel and deposited have been found to accumulate in plants and animals, some of which are consumed by people.

Research is conducted to understand the ecological impacts of air pollutants and to support the secondary National Ambient Air Quality Standards (NAAQS), which provide public welfare protection, including protection against decreased visibility and damage to animals, crops, vegetation, and buildings. Deposition modeling tools are developed, air pollution emissions and precursor pollutants (e.g., ammonia) are measured and pollutant deposition on ecosystems is measured and quantified, among other research activities.

Source: epa.gov

A Brief History of the Clean Air Act

In October 1948, a thick cloud of air pollution formed above the industrial town of Donora, Pennsylvania. The cloud, which lingered for five days, killed 20 people and caused sickness in 6,000 of the town's 14,000 people. In 1952, over 3,000 people died in what became known as London's "Killer Fog." The smog was so thick that buses could not run without guides walking ahead of them carrying lanterns.

Events like these alerted us to the dangers that air pollution poses to public health. Several federal and state laws were passed, including the original Clean Air Act of 1963, which established funding for the study and the cleanup of air pollution. But there was no comprehensive federal response to address air pollution until Congress passed a much stronger Clean Air Act in 1970. That same year Congress created the EPA and gave it the primary role in carrying out the law. Since 1970, EPA has been responsible for a variety of Clean Air Act programs to reduce air pollution nationwide.

In 1990, Congress dramatically revised and expanded the Clean Air Act, providing EPA even broader authority to implement and enforce regulations reducing air pollutant emissions. The 1990 Amendments also placed an increased emphasis on more cost-effective approaches to reduce air pollution.

Clean Air Act Roles and Responsibilities

The Clean Air Act is a federal law covering the entire country. However, states, tribes and local governments do a lot of the work to meet the Act's requirements. For example, representatives from these agencies work with companies to reduce air pollution. They also review and approve permit applications for industries or chemical processes.

EPA's Role

Under the Clean Air Act, EPA sets limits on certain air pollutants, including setting limits on how much can be in the air anywhere in the United States. This helps to ensure basic health and environmental protection from air pollution for all Americans. The Clean Air Act also gives EPA the authority to limit emissions of air pollutants coming from sources like chemical plants, utilities, and steel mills. Individual states or tribes may have stronger air pollution laws, but they may not have weaker pollution limits than those set by EPA.

EPA must approve state, tribal, and local agency plans for reducing air pollution. If a plan does not meet the necessary requirements, EPA can issue sanctions against the state and, if necessary, take over enforcing the Clean Air Act in that area.

EPA assists state, tribal, and local agencies by providing research, expert studies, engineering designs, and funding to support clean air progress. Since 1970, Congress and the EPA have provided several billion dollars to the states, local agencies, and tribal nations to accomplish this.

State and Local Governments' Role

It makes sense for state and local air pollution agencies to take the lead in carrying out the Clean Air Act. They are able to develop solutions for pollution problems that require special understanding of local industries, geography, housing, and travel patterns, as well as other factors.

State, local, and tribal governments also monitor air quality, inspect facilities under their jurisdictions and enforce Clean Air Act regulations.

States have to develop State Implementation Plans (SIPs) that outline how each state will control air pollution under the Clean Air Act. A SIP is a collection of the regulations, programs and policies that a state will use to clean up polluted areas. The states must involve the public and industries through hearings and opportunities to comment on the development of each state plan.

Tribal Nations' Role

In its 1990 revision of the Clean Air Act, Congress recognized that Indian Tribes have the authority to implement air pollution control programs.

EPA's Tribal Authority Rule gives Tribes the ability to develop air quality management programs, write rules to reduce air pollution and implement and enforce their rules in Indian Country. While state and local agencies are responsible for all Clean Air Act requirements, Tribes may develop and implement only those parts of the Clean Air Act that are appropriate for their lands.

Source: epa.gov

ANSWER KEY
Model Test 1

REASONING THROUGH LANGUAGE ARTS EXAM

1. A
2. concerned, worried, nervous, or similar word.
3. B
4. D
5. A
6. A
7. Answers will vary.
8. C
9. A
10. A
11. D
12. B
13. A
14. D
15. A
16. B
17. dislike, or similar word
18. B
19. A
20. B
21. C
22. C
23. D
24. d, b, c, a, e
25. erratic, inconsistent, emotional, or similar word
26. B

27. B
28. calming, disarming, soothing, or similar word
29. A
30. B
31. A
32. A
33. C
34. C
35. A
36. B
37. C
38. C
39. B
40. C
41. D
42. B, C, D
43. B
44. A
45. A
46. C
47. B
48. C
49. A
50. B

EXTENDED RESPONSE

Answers will vary.

REASONING THROUGH LANGUAGE ARTS EXAM
ANSWER EXPLANATIONS

1. **(A)** To scrutinize something means to examine or investigate it.

2. Words that would effectively complete the sentence include "concerned," "worried," and "nervous." Any similar word would also work.

3. **(B)** The gesture of Della selling her hair to pay for a Christmas present indicates that she is devoted to Jim. Option A is incorrect because Della's actions suggest the opposite of being self-centered. Options C and D are incorrect because no evidence supports these answers.

4. **(D)** Irony is the contrast between what is expected to happen and what actually happens. Options A and C are incorrect. These literary terms are concerned with comparing unlike things. Option B is incorrect because a hyperbole is an extreme exaggeration.

5. **(A)** When Della tells Jim she loves him, he wakes from his trance. Option B is incorrect because Jim already knew that Della had cut her hair. Options C and D are incorrect.

6. **(A)** At the end, they both calmly moved forward.

7. Answers will vary but need to be supported by details from the story.

8. **(C)** The central idea is stated in the first sentence. Options A and B are incorrect because the passage indicates the opposite. Option D is incorrect. Although the passage mentions the writing of the Constitution, this is not the central idea.

9. **(A)** The footnote indicates that Massanello was a fisherman. Options B, C, and D are incorrect. No evidence supports any of these answers.

10. **(A)** The language used in the passage is aggressive and lends itself to motivating people. Option B is incorrect because the author does not use calming language. Option C is incorrect. The author is making the opposite claim. Option D is incorrect. Although there is some description of liberty, this is not the main purpose of the writing.

11. **(D)** If something is unextinguishable, it cannot be put out or quelled.

12. **(B)** The author clearly states in the third paragraph that it is impossible to go back to an earlier time. Options A, C, and D are incorrect because nowhere in the passage are any of these options stated.

13. **(A)** The author is speaking out against an oppressive government, so this is the most logical catalyst for writing this passage. Option C is incorrect because the author is feeling the opposite of patriotism toward Britain. Options B and D are incorrect because no evidence supports these answers.

14. **(D)** A simile is a comparison of two unlike things using the words "like" or "as." Option A is incorrect. The author is not inferring that people and ants are similar in numerous respects. Option B is incorrect. Personification means that an animal is given human characteristics. Option C is incorrect. The author is not putting together two contrasting things.

15. **(A)** The author indicates that he went into the woods so he would have to deal with only the essentials of life. Options B, C, and D are incorrect because no evidence supports any of these answers.

16. **(B)** The author indicates in several ways that people should simplify. Options A and C are incorrect. Although these words do appear in the passage, they do not sum up the author's message. Option D is incorrect because no evidence supports this answer.

17. The word that would best complete the sentence is "dislike," although similar words would be accepted.

18. **(B)** The idea that a railroad rides upon us suggests that technology has encroached upon us. Options A and D are incorrect because these interpretations are too literal. Option C is incorrect because no evidence supports this answer.

19. **(A)** The author indicates problems with several things that relate to the pace of life. Option B is incorrect. Although the author mentions that the telegraph is a contributing factor, it is not the most problematic. Options C and D are incorrect. Although these words are used within the passage, the author does not indicate that these are great problems.

20. **(B)** The word "overgrown" suggests that "unorganized" is the best definition. Although option A is a definition of "unwieldy," it does not fit in the context of the sentence. Options C and D are incorrect.

21. **(C)** Several pieces of evidence, including Anne's dissatisfaction with her name, indicate that Anne is discontented. Option A is incorrect; the passage suggests the opposite. Options B and D are incorrect; there is no evidence to support these answers.

22. **(C)** Anne likely wanted to say "tragic," which is similar in meaning to "devastating." Option D is incorrect. It is unlikely that she said "tragical" instead of "magical." Options A and B are incorrect because no evidence supports these answers.

23. **(D)** Marilla says that "Anne is a real good plain sensible name." Options A and C are incorrect because they both refer to Anne. Option B is incorrect. Matthew does not say anything about Anne's name.

24. **(d, b, c, a, e)** First Matthew opens the door, but Marilla is surprised by the arrival of a girl. Then Anne believes she is unwanted, so Anne begins crying. Finally, Anne wants to be called "Anne spelled with an E."

25. The word that best completes the sentence could be "erratic," "inconsistent," or "emotional." Other words with similar meanings would be accepted.

26. **(B)** Since Anne rejected her name and proposed a new one, it is logical that she would do the same with an outfit she did not like.

27. **(B)** Marilla is no-nonsense. Describing her as either cruel or tyrannical would be too extreme.

28. The word that would best complete the sentence includes "calming," "disarming," and "soothing." Other words with similar meanings would be accepted.

29. **(A)** Option B is incorrect for two reasons. First, the verb "being" has an extra verb. Second, the verb "supplementing" is the wrong form of the word. Option C is incorrect because the proper nouns are not capitalized.

30. **(B)** Option A is incorrect because the verb "is" does not agree with the subject "we." Option C is incorrect because it is too wordy.

31. **(A)** Option B is incorrect because the first word is not capitalized. Option C is incorrect. It needs a comma before the conjunction to connect the independent clauses.

32. **(A)** Option B is incorrect because the comma before the word "which" has been omitted. Option C is incorrect because the use of the pronoun "who" is inappropriate.

33. **(C)** Option A is incorrect because the plural subject "reasons" does not agree with the singular verb "is." Option B is incorrect. The "there" is inappropriate and should be replaced with the homonym "their."

34. **(C)** Option A lacks an apostrophe for "Nation's." Option B is missing a comma before "and."

35. **(A)** Option B uses the wrong form of "ensure." Option C is missing a capital letter at the beginning of the sentence.

36. **(B)** Option A begins with a sentence fragment, not a full sentence. Option C has an unnecessary comma after "sources."

37. **(C)** Option A incorrectly uses the plural "projects." Option B lacks commas.

38. **(C)** Option A incorrectly pairs "these" and "process." Option B lacks a capital letter at the beginning of the sentence.

39. **(B)** The author is alluding or making reference to a well-known character from Greek mythology.

40. **(C)** The speaker states, "My brother is so good. He gives all he has to the poor and sick." Therefore, the brother is giving.

41. **(D)** The same sentence also says, "It is much better to give the money to the poor."

42. **(B, C, D)** The speaker displays curiosity, concern, and happiness.

43. **(B)** The postscript mentions "your grand nephew," thereby making a personal connection with the intended reader.

44. **(A)** God is the only choice that fits this context.

45. **(A)** The previous paragraph states, "I had to sit in the carriage for more than an hour before we began to move," indicating that the train is not running on time.

46. **(C)** The author mentions the train and comments on how Buda-Pesth "seems" like a wonderful place, meaning he is not familiar with it.

47. **(B)** The woman's outfit suggests that she works at the hotel. So she is bowing to show the guest respect.

48. **(C)** This quote indicates that the writer is excited to see his friend and has a welcoming tone.

49. **(A)** The speaker says that his "smattering of German [was] very useful here," indicating that the people spoke German.

50. **(B)** At the end of the passage, the speaker indicates that his name is Jonathan Harker.

Extended Response

Answers will vary.

When reviewing your extended response, make sure you have asked yourself the following questions:

- Have I responded to the prompt?
- Do I have enough evidence?
- Do my ideas follow a logical order?
- Are there any misspellings?
- Have I confused any homonyms?
- Have I used proper punctuation, including periods, commas, semicolons, apostrophes, and so forth?
- Do I need to break up any run-on sentences?
- Can I combine any strings of short, choppy sentences?

The prompt asks if laws, such as the Clean Air Act, address the specific issues relating to air quality. Make sure that you have chosen a side; either these laws do or do not. Make sure you have clearly articulated your position in the introductory part of the response. Following your introduction, cite specific evidence from both of the passages that you feel supports your position and be sure to explain why. Finally, restate your position in the conclusion.

ANSWER SHEET
Model Test 1

MATHEMATICAL REASONING EXAM

1. Ⓐ Ⓑ Ⓒ Ⓓ
2. Ⓐ Ⓑ Ⓒ Ⓓ
3. Ⓐ Ⓑ Ⓒ Ⓓ
4. Ⓐ Ⓑ Ⓒ Ⓓ
5. Ⓐ Ⓑ Ⓒ Ⓓ
6. Ⓐ Ⓑ Ⓒ Ⓓ
7. Ⓐ Ⓑ Ⓒ Ⓓ
8. Ⓐ Ⓑ Ⓒ Ⓓ
9. Ⓐ Ⓑ Ⓒ Ⓓ
10. Ⓐ Ⓑ Ⓒ Ⓓ
11. Ⓐ Ⓑ Ⓒ Ⓓ
12. Ⓐ Ⓑ Ⓒ Ⓓ
13. Ⓐ Ⓑ Ⓒ Ⓓ
14. Ⓐ Ⓑ Ⓒ Ⓓ
15. Ⓐ Ⓑ Ⓒ Ⓓ
16. Ⓐ Ⓑ Ⓒ Ⓓ
17. Ⓐ Ⓑ Ⓒ Ⓓ

18. Ⓐ Ⓑ Ⓒ Ⓓ
19. _____
20. Ⓐ Ⓑ Ⓒ Ⓓ
21. Ⓐ Ⓑ Ⓒ Ⓓ
22. Ⓐ Ⓑ Ⓒ Ⓓ
23. Ⓐ Ⓑ Ⓒ Ⓓ
24. Ⓐ Ⓑ Ⓒ Ⓓ
25. Ⓐ Ⓑ Ⓒ Ⓓ
26. Ⓐ Ⓑ Ⓒ Ⓓ
27. Ⓐ Ⓑ Ⓒ Ⓓ
28. Ⓐ Ⓑ Ⓒ Ⓓ
29. Ⓐ Ⓑ Ⓒ Ⓓ
30. Ⓐ Ⓑ Ⓒ Ⓓ
31. (A) _____
    (B) _____
    (C) _____
32. Ⓐ Ⓑ Ⓒ Ⓓ

33. Ⓐ Ⓑ Ⓒ Ⓓ
34. Ⓐ Ⓑ Ⓒ Ⓓ
35. Ⓐ Ⓑ Ⓒ Ⓓ
36. _____
    _____
    _____
37. _____
    _____
    _____
38. (A) _____
    (B) _____
    (C) _____
    (D) _____
39. Ⓐ Ⓑ Ⓒ Ⓓ
40. _____
41. Ⓐ Ⓑ Ⓒ Ⓓ
42. Ⓐ Ⓑ Ⓒ Ⓓ

DIRECTIONS: This practice exam contains mathematical problems. You will have 90 minutes to complete the 42 questions in this portion of the exam. You may use a calculator during this test.

1. Find the best estimate, to the nearest dollar, for the following order at a restaurant: 2 hamburgers at \$3.49 each, 7 garden salads at \$5.47 each, 10 regular drinks at \$2.25 each, and 1 fish platter for \$6.37.
   - (A) \$67
   - (B) \$50
   - (C) \$22
   - (D) \$47

2. What is the correct way of writing "b is greater than or equal to –5 but less than 2"?
   - (A) $-5 \geq b > 2$
   - (B) $2 < b \leq -5$
   - (C) $-5 \leq b < 2$
   - (D) $-5 \geq b < 2$

3. The average monthly pay for a factory worker at Jambo Industries is \$3,472. What is the average monthly salary if you round to the nearest hundred dollars?
   - (A) \$3,400
   - (B) \$3,470
   - (C) \$3,500
   - (D) \$4,000

4. One thousand three hundred twenty yards is what fraction of a mile? (1 mile = 1,760 yards)
   - (A) $\dfrac{1}{2}$
   - (B) $\dfrac{3}{4}$
   - (C) $\dfrac{2}{5}$
   - (D) $\dfrac{4}{9}$

5. The first four sprinters to finish in the 200-meter event had the following times:

Sprinter	Time (seconds)
Jay	22.032
Monroe	22.811
Gregory	23.544
Henry	22.524

Which sprinter finished in second place?
(A) Jay
(B) Monroe
(C) Gregory
(D) Henry

6. A seamstress had four pieces of yarn that were the following lengths:

Yarn	Length (feet)
A	$2\frac{3}{4}$
B	$2\frac{1}{4}$
C	$2\frac{3}{8}$
D	$2\frac{11}{16}$

Which piece of yarn is the longest?
(A) Yarn A
(B) Yarn B
(C) Yarn C
(D) Yarn D

7. The teacher told her class that $\frac{1}{4}$ of the class received an "A" grade on the last test. What percentage of the class received an "A"?
(A) 75%
(B) 30%
(C) 45%
(D) 25%

8. A bus has 20 people on board, and 5 of them are women. What is the ratio of men to women?
(A) 3:1
(B) 1:3
(C) 4:5
(D) 1:2

9. In a recent survey, 3 out of 8 people reported that they drink coffee in the morning. If 480 people were surveyed, how many said that they drink coffee in the morning?

   (A) 210

   (B) 475

   (C) 180

   (D) 206

10. Gasoline cost the following over a period of four weeks:

    Week 1: $2.92 per gallon

    Week 2: $3.04 per gallon

    Week 3: $3.16 per gallon

    Week 4: $3.28 per gallon

    If the trend continues, what will the price be in week 5?

    (A) $3.40

    (B) $4.70

    (C) $3.50

    (D) $5.75

11. A family drove 422 miles on 32.5 gallons of gas. To the nearest tenth, how many miles were driven on one gallon of gas?

    (A) 13.0

    (B) 28.3

    (C) 14.7

    (D) 20.8

QUESTIONS 12 AND 13 REFER TO THE FOLLOWING PICTURE:

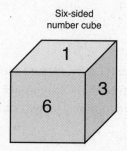

Six-sided
number cube

12. The numbered cube above has six sides, each marked with a different integer from 1 to 6. Suppose you roll the cube above 24 times. How many times are you likely to roll a 1?

    (A) 3

    (B) 16

    (C) 24

    (D) 4

13. What is the probability you will roll a 3 on two successive rolls?

(A) $\frac{1}{9}$

(B) $\frac{1}{36}$

(C) $\frac{1}{64}$

(D) $\frac{1}{2}$

_____

14. Which equation is the result of subtracting 14 from each side of this equation:

$\frac{1}{4}x + 16 = 20$?

(A) $\frac{1}{4}x + 2 = 6$

(B) $\frac{1}{4}x + 30 = 34$

(C) $\frac{1}{4}x - 2 = -4$

(D) $\frac{1}{4}x - 2 = -6$

15. A used car lot announces that all of its cars are on sale for 55% of the original price. If the discounted price of a car is $4,400, what was the original price of the car?
(A) $8,542
(B) $4,000
(C) $7,500
(D) $8,000

16. Two business partners, John and Cathy, formed a joint business that cost a total of $980 to start. The partners agreed that Cathy would pay $350 more than John because John earns less. How much did John pay to help start the joint business?
(A) $265
(B) $155
(C) $315
(D) $255

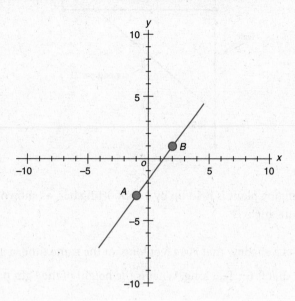

17. What are the coordinates of point *B*?
    (A) (–2, 1)
    (B) (–1, 2)
    (C) (2, –1)
    (D) (2, 1)

18. What is the slope of line *AB*?

    (A) $\dfrac{4}{3}$

    (B) $\dfrac{3}{4}$

    (C) $\dfrac{4}{5}$

    (D) $\dfrac{5}{4}$

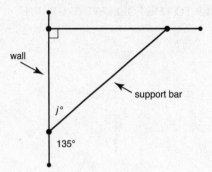

19. A hook for a hanging plant is held up by a supporting bar, as shown above. What is the value of the acute angle *j*?

20. A light pole casts a shadow that is 44 feet long. At the same time, a 3-foot-tall mailbox casts a shadow that is $6\frac{1}{2}$ feet long. What is the height of the light pole? Round to the nearest foot.
    (A) 37 feet
    (B) 20 feet
    (C) 45 feet
    (D) 12 feet

21. The hypotenuse of a right triangle is 9 inches and one of the sides is 6 inches. What is the length of the other side to the nearest inch?
    (A) 9
    (B) 7
    (C) 6
    (D) 8

22. A cylindrical can has a radius of 3 inches. The can has a height of 8 inches. What is the volume of the can in cubic inches? Volume of a cylinder: $V = \pi r^2 h$ (use 3.14 for π).
    (A) 230.08 cubic inches
    (B) 245.11 cubic inches
    (C) 345.18 cubic inches
    (D) 226.08 cubic inches

23. What is the measure of an angle whose vertex is at the center of a circle if the two lines that form the angle border an area that is one-eighth of the area of the circle?
    (A) 45 degrees
    (B) 65 degrees
    (C) 90 degrees
    (D) 30 degrees

QUESTIONS 24 THROUGH 26 REFER TO THE FOLLOWING NUMBER LINE:

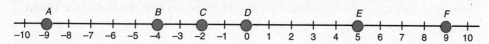

24. What is the value of B minus C?
    (A) –6
    (B) –2
    (C) 2
    (D) 6

25. What is the product of A times E?
    (A) –45
    (B) –14
    (C) –4
    (D) 45

26. Which of the following is true?
    (A) $|A| > |F|$
    (B) $|B| > |E|$
    (C) $-|E| < B$
    (D) $|C| = |D|$

27. If $x = q^5$, $y = q^3$, and $z = q^{-2}$, which of the following expresses $\left(\dfrac{x}{y}\right)^3$ in terms of q?
    (A) q^{24}
    (B) q^{11}
    (C) q^8
    (D) q^6

28. If $x^2 + 5x = 6$, which of these is a possible value of x?
    (A) –1
    (B) 5
    (C) –6
    (D) 11

29. $x^2 + 2xy + y^2$ is equivalent to which of the following?
    (A) $(x + y)(x + y)$
    (B) $(x + y)(x - y)$
    (C) $(x - y)(x - y)$
    (D) $(x + x)(y + y)$

30. The vertex is the point in the center of a parabolic function. Function $z(x)$ is a parabolic function with its vertex at $(0, 0)$. What are the coordinates of the vertex of $z(x) + 3$?

(A) (0, 3)

(B) (3, 0)

(C) (–3, 0)

(D) (0, –3)

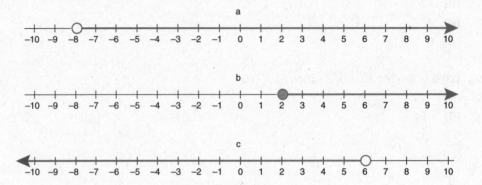

31. Based on the above number lines, provide in the blank the label of the number line that correctly completes the sentence.

(A) "y is less than 6" is represented by number line _____.

(B) "y is greater than –8" is represented by number line _____.

(C) "y is greater than or equal to 2" is represented by number line _____.

32. $\sqrt{156}$ is between which numbers?

(A)   9 and 10

(B)   10 and 11

(C)   11 and 12

(D)   12 and 13

33. $\sqrt{265}$ is between which numbers?

(A)   13 and 14

(B)   14 and 15

(C)   15 and 16

(D)   16 and 17

34. $\sqrt{128}$ is equivalent to which of the following?

(A) $2\sqrt{64}$

(B) $8\sqrt{2}$

(C) $4\sqrt{32}$

(D) 16

35. Which of the following is equivalent to $(2.3 \times 10^{17}) \times (4.8 \times 10^{-12})$?
(A) 11.04×10^6
(B) 1.104×10^6
(C) 0.71×10^6
(D) 7.1×10^6

QUESTIONS 36 AND 37 REFER TO THE FOLLOWING DRAWING:

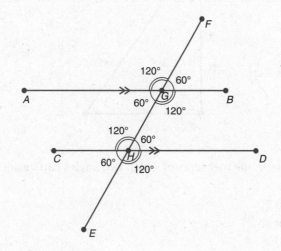

36. Select the word or phrase in each bracket that correctly completes each sentence:

Angle *FGB* is an [obtuse, acute, interior] angle and is [supplementary to, congruent to, complementary to] angle *AGF*. Angles *AGF* and *FGB*, along with angles *CHE* and *EHD*, are [exterior, vertical, right] angles.

37. Select the word or phrase in each bracket that correctly completes each sentence:

Lines *AB* and *CD* are [parallel, perpendicular, intersecting] lines. Line *EF* is a [bisector, ray, transversal], and it intersects lines *AB* and *CD* to form [right, corresponding, complementary] angles.

38. Choose the correct answer from the options below to fill in the blanks in the following sentences.

(A) _____ angles are 180 degrees.

(B) _____ angles are less than 90 degrees.

(C) _____ angles are more than 90 degrees and less than 180 degrees.

(D) _____ angles are exactly 90 degrees.

Acute   Right

Obtuse   Straight

TIP

On the computerized test, a question like this would have you drag and drop the answers into the appropriate space.

QUESTIONS 39 AND 40 REFER TO THE FOLLOWING DRAWING:

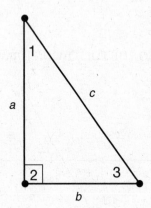

39. In the triangle above, the measures of which two angles can be added together to total 90 degrees?

(A) Angles 1 and 2

(B) Angles 2 and 3

(C) Angles 1 and 3

(D) No two angles can be added together to total 90 degrees

TIP

On the computerized test, a question like this would have you click on the angles to indicate your choices. This would be a hot-spot question.

40. Write the name of the side of the triangle above that is opposite the largest angle.

(1)

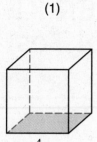

(2)

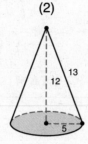

(3)

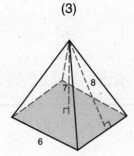

(4)

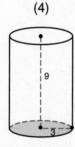

(5)

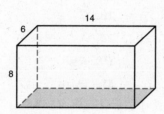

(6)

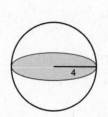

41. Which of the pairs listed below include only solids that require the use of π (pi) to calculate their volumes?
    (A) 2 and 3
    (B) 3 and 4
    (C) 4 and 6
    (D) 5 and 6

42. All of the following are true about the cube (#1) shown above EXCEPT:
    (A) The cube's volume is equal to 64. ($V = s^3$)
    (B) The cube's surface area is 96.
    (C) The cube's edge is equal in length to the sphere's (#6) radius.
    (D) The cube's volume is greater than the sphere's volume.

    (Volume of sphere: $\frac{4}{3}\pi r^3$)

ANSWER KEY
Model Test 1

MATHEMATICAL REASONING EXAM

1. A
2. C
3. C
4. B
5. D
6. A
7. D
8. A
9. C
10. A
11. A
12. D
13. B
14. A
15. D
16. C
17. D
18. A
19. 45°
20. B
21. B
22. D
23. A

24. B
25. A
26. C
27. D
28. C
29. A
30. A
31. (A) c
    (B) a
    (C) b
32. D
33. D
34. B
35. B
36. acute, supplementary to, exterior
37. parallel, transversal, corresponding
38. (A) straight
    (B) acute
    (C) obtuse
    (D) right
39. C
40. hypotenuse or c
41. C
42. D

MATHEMATICAL REASONING EXAM ANSWER EXPLANATIONS

1. **(A)** Round before you calculate: $(2 \times 3) + (7 \times 5) + (10 \times 2) + 6 = 6 + 35 + 20 + 6 = 67$.

2. **(C)** The correct answer is $-5 \leq b < 2$.

3. **(C)** The correct answer is $3,500.

4. **(B)** $1,320 \div 1,760 = \dfrac{3}{4}$

5. **(D)** Compare digit by digit from left to right. Jay had the fastest time at 22.032 seconds. Henry has the second fastest time at 22.524 seconds.

6. **(A)** Since all lengths are between 2 and 3 feet, compare the fractions. Convert the denominators of each fraction to 16, and then compare the numerators:

   $\dfrac{3}{4} = \dfrac{12}{16}$; $\dfrac{1}{4} = \dfrac{4}{16}$; and $\dfrac{3}{8} = \dfrac{6}{16}$.

   Since 12 is the largest numerator, $2\dfrac{3}{4}$ is the largest number.

7. **(D)** $\dfrac{1}{4} = 1 \div 4 = 0.25$ and $0.25 = 25\%$.

8. **(A)** Find the number of men on the bus (20 − 5 women = 15 men). The ratio of men to women is 15:5, which simplifies to 3:1.

9. **(C)** Set up a proportion: $\dfrac{3}{8} = \dfrac{x}{480}$. Cross multiply: $8x = (3)(480) = 1,440$. Divide both sides by 8 to isolate x: $1,440 \div 8$. So $x = 180$.

10. **(A)** The gas price is increasing by $0.12 every week: $0.12 + $3.28 = $3.40.

11. **(A)** First find the miles per gallon (422 miles ÷ 32.5 gallons = 12.98 miles per gallon). Then round to the nearest tenth: 13.0.

12. **(D)** Your chance of rolling a 1 on each roll is 1 out of 6. Since you roll 24 times, divide $24 \div 6 = 4$.

13. **(B)** Your chance of rolling a 3 on the first roll is 1 out of 6. Your chance of rolling a 3 on the second roll is also 1 out of 6. To combine these chances, multiply: $\dfrac{1}{6} \times \dfrac{1}{6} = \dfrac{1}{36}$.

14. **(A)** Subtract 14 from both sides of the equation: 16 − 14 = 2 and 20 − 14 = 6.

15. **(D)** Calculate the original price by dividing the new price by the discount. Remember that 55% is 0.55: $4,400 ÷ 0.55 = $8,000.

16. **(C)** Let c equal what Cathy paid, and let j equal what John paid. Set up your equations: $980 = c + j$ and $c = j + 350$. Substitute $j + 350$ for c in the first equation: $980 = j + 350 + j$. Subtract 350 from each side: $630 = 2j$. Then divide both sides by 2: $j = 315$.

17. **(D)** The correct answer is (2, 1).

18. **(A)** Use the points $(-1, -3)$ and $(2, 1)$ in the slope formula: $\frac{1-(-3)}{2-(-1)} = \frac{4}{3}$.

19. **45°** The two angles where the support meets the wall are supplementary, which means their sum is 180°. Subtract the known angle from 180° to find angle j: $180° - 135° = 45°$.

20. **(B)** Set up the problem as a proportion. Remember to have the actual heights (in feet) in the numerators and the shadow lengths (in feet) in the denominators:

    $\frac{x}{44} = \frac{3}{6.5}$.

    Cross multiply: $6.5x = (3)(44) = 132$. Then divide both sides by 6.5 to get $x = 20.31$. Round to the nearest foot: $x = 20$ feet.

21. **(B)** Use the Pythagorean theorem: $c^2 = a^2 + b^2$. So $(9)(9) = (6)(6) + b^2$ becomes $b^2 = 45$. Take the square root of both sides with your calculator to isolate b: $b = 6.708$. Round to the nearest inch: $b = 7$. You could also approximate. Since 45 is close to 49 and 49 is a perfect square, $(7)(7) = 49$, the answer is about 7.

22. **(D)** Use the volume formula $V = \pi r^2 h$ and use 3.14 for π: $(3.14)(3)(3)(8) = 226.08$.

23. **(A)** Every circle measures 360°. Since the angle has its vertex at the center, the portion of the circumference that the radii cut equals the portion of 360° cut by the angle. So divide 360° by 8 to solve: $360° \div 8 = 45°$.

24. **(B)** When subtracting a negative, change the operation to addition and change the sign of the second number: $-4 - (-2) = -4 + 2 = -2$.

25. **(A)** When the signs are not the same, the product is negative: $(-9)(5) = -45$.

26. **(C)** Absolute value makes a number positive. A negative sign outside the absolute value bars makes the absolute value negative: $-5 < -4$.

27. **(D)** Remember the rules for exponents with the same base. Multiplication means add the exponents together. Division means subtract one exponent from the other. Raising a power to a power means multiply the exponents: $5 - 3 = 2$ and $(2)(3) = 6$. The new exponent is 6, so the answer is q^6.

28. **(C)** Subtracting 6 from both sides makes this a quadratic equation: $x^2 + 5x - 6 = 0$. Factoring the equation gives $(x + 6)(x - 1) = 0$. Set each factor equal to 0 to find the possible values of x: $x + 6 = 0$ and $x - 1 = 0$. Therefore $x = -6$ and $x = 1$. The only choice given is $x = -6$.

29. **(A)** This is a very common polynomial. Memorize both the factored and FOIL forms of this polynomial.

30. **(A)** Adding outside the parentheses moves the curve up. Adding 3 to the original function to form the new function moves up the original function by 3. Moving up involves the y-coordinate.

31. **(c, a, b)** Number line c shows y is less than 6. Number line a shows y is greater than -8. Number line b shows y is greater than or equal to 2.

32. **(D)** 156 is between 144 and 169. Since $(12)(12) = 144$ and $(13)(13) = 169$, $\sqrt{156}$ must be between 12 and 13.

33. **(D)** 265 is between 256 and 289. Since $(16)(16) = 256$ and $(17)(17) = 289$, $\sqrt{265}$ must be between 16 and 17.

34. **(B)** Since $128 = (2)(64)$ and $\sqrt{64} = 8$, $\sqrt{128} = 8\sqrt{2}$.

35. **(B)** Multiply the decimal numbers as normal: $2.3 \times 4.8 = 11.04$. Since this is multiplication, add the exponents of 10: $(17 - 12 = 5)$. Scientific notation puts the decimal point next to the units digit. To move the decimal point one place to the left, we need one additional exponent of 10: $5 + 1 = 6$. So the answer is 1.104×10^6.

36. **Acute, Supplementary to, Exterior** Since angle *FBG* measures 60°, it is acute because acute angles measure less than 90°. Two angles whose sum is 180° are supplementary, like angle *FBG* and angle *AGF*. Exterior angles are outside of the parallel lines.

37. **Parallel, Transversal, Corresponding** The arrow symbols on lines *AB* and *CD* indicate that these lines are parallel. A transversal is a line that intersects two parallel lines. Corresponding angles are in the same position but are part of different groups of angles, like angle *FGB* and angle *GHD*.

38. **(A)** straight
    (B) acute
    (C) obtuse
    (D) right

39. **(C)** The measures of the two acute angles in a right triangle must add up to 90 degrees.

40. **Hypotenuse** or *c* The longest side of a right triangle is called the hypotenuse, and it is labeled *c* on the diagram. The hypotenuse is opposite the 90° angle.

41. **(C)** To calculate the volume of a cone, cylinder, or sphere, π (pi) must be used.

42. **(D)** The volume of the cube is $s^3 = (4)(4)(4) = 64$. The volume of the sphere is

$$\frac{4}{3}\pi r^3 = \frac{4}{3}(3.14)(4)(4)(4) = 267.95.$$

ANSWER SHEET
Model Test 1

SOCIAL STUDIES EXAM

1. Ⓐ Ⓑ Ⓒ Ⓓ
2. Ⓐ Ⓑ Ⓒ Ⓓ
3. Ⓐ Ⓑ Ⓒ Ⓓ
4. Ⓐ Ⓑ Ⓒ Ⓓ
5. Ⓐ Ⓑ Ⓒ Ⓓ
6. Ⓐ Ⓑ Ⓒ Ⓓ
7. _____
8. Ⓐ Ⓑ Ⓒ Ⓓ
9. Ⓐ Ⓑ Ⓒ Ⓓ
10. Ⓐ Ⓑ Ⓒ Ⓓ
11. Ⓐ Ⓑ Ⓒ Ⓓ

12. Ⓐ Ⓑ Ⓒ Ⓓ
13. Ⓐ Ⓑ Ⓒ Ⓓ
14. Ⓐ Ⓑ Ⓒ Ⓓ
15. _____
16. Ⓐ Ⓑ Ⓒ Ⓓ
17. Ⓐ Ⓑ Ⓒ Ⓓ
18. Ⓐ Ⓑ Ⓒ Ⓓ
19. Ⓐ Ⓑ Ⓒ Ⓓ
20. Ⓐ Ⓑ Ⓒ Ⓓ
21. Ⓐ Ⓑ Ⓒ Ⓓ
22. Ⓐ Ⓑ Ⓒ Ⓓ

23. Ⓐ Ⓑ Ⓒ Ⓓ
24. Ⓐ Ⓑ Ⓒ Ⓓ
25. Ⓐ Ⓑ Ⓒ Ⓓ
26. Ⓐ Ⓑ Ⓒ Ⓓ
27. Ⓐ Ⓑ Ⓒ Ⓓ
28. Ⓐ Ⓑ Ⓒ Ⓓ
29. _____
30. Ⓐ Ⓑ Ⓒ Ⓓ
31. Ⓐ Ⓑ Ⓒ Ⓓ
32. Ⓐ Ⓑ Ⓒ Ⓓ
33. Ⓐ Ⓑ Ⓒ Ⓓ

Extended Response

SOCIAL STUDIES EXAM

QUESTIONS 1 THROUGH 3 ARE BASED ON THE FOLLOWING PASSAGE:

President Dwight D. Eisenhower's Farewell Address (1961)

In a speech of less than 10 minutes, on January 17, 1961, President Dwight Eisenhower delivered his political farewell to the American people on national television from the Oval Office of the White House. Those who expected the military leader and hero of World War II to depart his Presidency with a nostalgic, "old soldier" speech like Gen. Douglas MacArthur's, were surprised at his strong warnings about the dangers of the "military-industrial complex." As President of the United States for two terms, Eisenhower had slowed the push for increased defense spending despite pressure to build more military equipment during the Cold War's arms race. Nonetheless, the American military services and the defense industry had expanded a great deal in the 1950s. Eisenhower thought this growth was needed to counter the Soviet Union, but it confounded him. Through he did not say so explicitly, his standing as a military leader helped give him the credibility to stand up to the pressures of this new, powerful interest group. He eventually described it as a necessary evil.

A vital element in keeping the peace is our military establishment. Our arms must be might, ready for instant action, so that no potential aggressor may be tempted to risk his own destruction. . . . American makers of plowshares could, with time and as required, make swords as well. But now we can no longer risk emergency improvisation of national defense; we have been compelled to create a permanent armaments industry of vast proportions. . . . This conjunction of an immense military establishment and a large arms industry is new in the American experience. . . . Yet we must not fail to comprehend its grave implications. . . . In the councils of government, we must guard against the acquisition of unwarranted influence, whether sought or unsought, by the military-industrial complex. The potential for the disastrous rise of misplaced power exists and will persist.

The end of Eisenhower's term as President not only marked the end of the 1950s but also the end of an era in government. A new, younger generation was rising to national power that would set a more youthful, vigorous course. His farewell address was a warning to his successors of one of the many things they would have to be wary of in the coming years.

Source: ourdocuments.gov

1. What did President Eisenhower believe was essential in keeping peace?
   (A) Remaining allies with as many countries as possible
   (B) Maintaining capitalism
   (C) Equal rights for all
   (D) A strong military

2. Based on the passage, which of the following would President Eisenhower most likely support today?
   (A) An increase in educational funding
   (B) An increase in defense spending
   (C) An expansion of the size of the armed forces
   (D) A decrease in worldwide nuclear arsenals

3. Which of the following best describes the tone of President Eisenhower's speech?
   (A) Optimistic
   (B) Nostalgic
   (C) Cautionary
   (D) Pessimistic

Without a High School Education

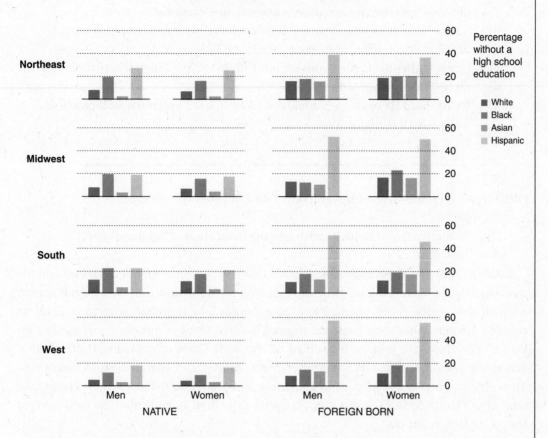

This graph explores variation in high school education attainment within selected race and Hispanic origin groups by sex and nativity between regions. Attainment of a high school diploma (or equivalent level of education) is generally very high in the U.S., so this graph focuses on the percentage of the population 25 and older who do not have that level of education. There are notable differences between foreign-born and native population among many groups. For example, in the West, 57 percent of Hispanic foreign-born males had less than a high school education compared with 19 percent of Hispanic native-born males. Nineteen percent of Asian foreign-born females had less than a high school diploma compared with 5 percent of Asian native-born females.

4. In which area do native-born black men have the highest graduation rate?
    (A) Northeast
    (B) Midwest
    (C) South
    (D) West

5. Based on the information in the graph, which of the following conclusions can be drawn?
   (A) Foreign-born white women in the Northeast are more likely to have a high school diploma than native-born white women in the Northeast.
   (B) Native-born black women in the West are more likely to have a high school diploma than foreign-born Asian men in the West.
   (C) Native-born men in the South are more likely to have a high school diploma than native-born women in the South.
   (D) Native-born Hispanic men are just as likely to have a high school diploma as foreign-born Hispanic men.

QUESTIONS 6 THROUGH 8 ARE BASED ON THE FOLLOWING PASSAGE:

Executive Order 9066: Resulting in the Relocation of Japanese (1942)

Between 1861 and 1940, approximately 275,000 Japanese immigrated to Hawaii and the mainland United States, the majority arriving between 1898 and 1924, when quotas were adopted that ended Asian immigration. Many worked in Hawaiian sugarcane fields as contract laborers. After their contracts expired, a small number remained and opened up shops. Other Japanese immigrants settled on the West Coast of mainland United States, cultivating marginal farmlands and fruit orchards, fishing, and operating small businesses. Their efforts yielded impressive results. Japanese Americans controlled less than 4 percent of California's farmland in 1940, but they produced more than 10 percent of the total value of the state's farm resources.

As was the case with other immigrant groups, Japanese Americans settled in ethnic neighborhoods and established their own schools, houses of worship, and economic and cultural institutions. Ethnic concentration was further increased by real estate agents who would not sell properties to Japanese Americans outside of existing Japanese enclaves and by a 1913 act passed by the California Assembly restricting land ownership to those eligible to be citizens. In 1922 the U.S. Supreme Court, in *Ozawa v. United States*, upheld the government's right to deny U.S. citizenship to Japanese immigrants.

Envy over economic success combined with distrust over cultural separateness and long-standing anti-Asian racism turned into disaster when the Empire of Japan attacked Pearl Harbor on December 7, 1941. Lobbyists from western states, many representing competing economic interests or nativist groups, pressured Congress and the President to remove persons of Japanese descent from the west coast, both foreign born (*issei*— meaning "first generation" of Japanese in the U.S.) and American citizens (*nisei*— the second generation of Japanese in America, U.S. citizens by birthright). During Congressional committee hearings, Department of Justice representatives raised constitutional and ethical objections to the proposal, so the U.S. Army carried out the task instead. The West Coast was divided into military zones, and on February 19, 1942, President Franklin D. Roosevelt issued Executive Order 9066 authorizing exclusion. Congress then implemented the order on March 21, 1942, by passing Public Law 503.

After encouraging voluntary evacuation of the areas, the Western Defense Command began involuntary removal and detention of West Coast residents of Japanese ancestry. In the next 6 months, approximately 122,000 men, women, and children were moved to assembly centers. They were then evacuated to and confined in isolated, fenced, and guarded relocation centers, known as internment camps. The 10 relocation sites were in remote areas in 6 western states and Arkansas: Heart Mountain in Wyoming, Tule Lake and Manzanar in California, Topaz in Utah, Poston and Gila River in Arizona, Granada in Colorado, Minidoka in Idaho, and Jerome and Rowher in Arkansas.

Nearly 70,000 of the evacuees were American citizens. The government made no charges against them, nor could they appeal their incarceration. All lost personal liberties; most lost homes and property as well. Although several Japanese Americans challenged the government's actions in court cases, the Supreme Court upheld their legality. *Nisei* were nevertheless encouraged to serve in the armed forces, and some were also drafted. Altogether, more than 30,000 Japanese Americans served with distinction during World War II in segregated units.

For many years after the war, various individuals and groups sought compensation for the internees. The speed of the evacuation forced many homeowners and businessmen to sell out quickly; total property loss is estimated at $1.3 billion, and net income loss at $2.7 billion (calculated in 1983 dollars based on the Commission investigation . . .). The Japanese American Evacuation Claims Act of 1948, with amendments in 1951 and 1965, provided token payments for some property losses. More serious efforts to make amends took place in the early 1980s, when the congressionally established Commission on Wartime Relocation and Internment of Civilians held investigations and made recommendations. As a result, several bills were introduced in Congress from 1984 until 1988, when Public Law 100-383, which acknowledged the injustice of the internment, apologized for it, and provided for restitution, was passed.

Source: ourdocuments.gov

6. The relocation of Japanese Americans during World War II is most similar to which of the following?
   (A) Relocation of individuals in the path of a hurricane
   (B) Enslavement of African Americans during the 1700s and 1800s
   (C) Imprisonment of someone who has not been charged with nor committed any crime
   (D) Internment of Jews in concentration camps during the 1930s and 1940s

7. In the 1980s, Public Law 100-383 was passed, which provided Japanese Americans with _____.

8. What was the total amount of income and property lost by Japanese Americans?
   (A) $1.3 billion
   (B) $2.7 billion
   (C) $4 billion
   (D) $122,000

9. What does the political cartoon above depict?

(A) There is conflict within the Republican Party.

(B) There is conflict between the Democratic and Republican Parties.

(C) The Democrats oppose the Atlantic Pact.

(D) There is bipartisan agreement on the Atlantic Pact.

Louisiana Purchase Treaty (1803)

Robert Livingston and James Monroe closed on the sweetest real estate deal of the millennium when they signed the Louisiana Purchase Treaty in Paris on April 30, 1803. They were authorized to pay France up to $10 million for the port of New Orleans and the Floridas. When offered the entire territory of Louisiana—an area larger than Great Britain, France, Germany, Italy, Spain and Portugal combined—the American negotiators swiftly agreed to a price of $15 million.

Although President Thomas Jefferson was a strict interpreter of the Constitution who wondered if the U.S. Government was authorized to acquire new territory, he was also a visionary who dreamed of an "empire for liberty" that would stretch across the entire continent. As Napoleon threatened to take back the offer, Jefferson squelched whatever doubts he had and prepared to occupy a land of unimaginable riches.

The Louisiana Purchase Agreement is made up of the Treaty of Cession and the two conventions regarding the financial aspects of the transaction.

Source: ourdocuments.gov

10. What opportunities did the Louisiana Purchase provide for the United States?
    (A) It enabled the United States to expand westward.
    (B) It enabled the United States to be closer to her enemies.
    (C) It enabled the United States to sell the land for more than they paid.
    (D) It enabled the United States Government to search for buried riches.

11. Despite President Jefferson's doubts, what does the execution of the Louisiana Purchase assume?
    (A) Napoleon would take back the land.
    (B) The United States did not have the right to acquire these lands.
    (C) The United States had the right to acquire these lands.
    (D) The United States needed the approval of Great Britain, France, Germany, Italy, Spain, and Portugal to purchase the land.

12. The Louisiana Purchase is most similar to which other acquisition by the United States?
    (A) The capture of Guam during the Spanish-American War
    (B) The United States declaring independence from Great Britain
    (C) The changing of the name New Amsterdam to New York
    (D) The purchase of Alaska for $7.2 million

QUESTIONS 13 AND 14 ARE BASED ON THE FOLLOWING MAPS AND PASSAGE:

Population Change by Decade

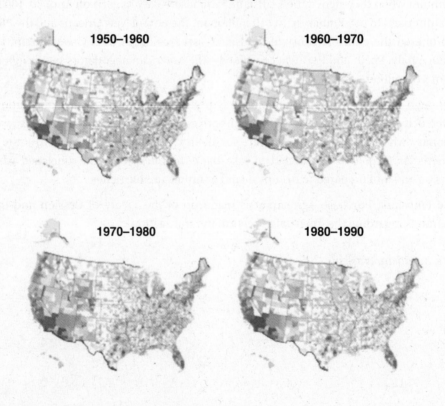

1950–1960

1960–1970

1970–1980

1980–1990

Decade-to-decade population change by county has varied greatly in the last century in many parts of the United States. For example, in the 1930s, 1940s, and 1950s, much of eastern Texas saw population decline (signified on the maps by light [blue] shading), but those areas have seen strong population growth since then (signified by dark [blue] shading). Much of Appalachia, including parts of West Virginia, has seen cycles of population increase and decrease as well.

13. According to the maps, which period of time saw the greatest increase in population for the Southwest?
    (A) 1950–1960
    (B) 1960–1970
    (C) 1970–1980
    (D) 1980–1990

14. During which of the following years is it likely that Texas saw a decrease in its population?
    (A) 1912
    (B) 1927
    (C) 1949
    (D) 1972

QUESTIONS 15 THROUGH 17 ARE BASED ON THE FOLLOWING PASSAGE:

War Department General Order 143:
Creation of the U.S. Colored Troops (1863)

The issues of emancipation and military service were intertwined from the onset of the Civil War. News from Fort Sumter set off a rush by free black men to enlist in U.S. military units. They were turned away, however, because a Federal law dating from 1792 barred Negroes from bearing arms for the U.S. Army. In Boston disappointed would-be volunteers met and passed a resolution requesting that the Government modify its laws to permit their enlistment.

The Lincoln administration wrestled with the idea of authorizing the recruitment of black troops, concerned that such a move would prompt the border states to secede. When Gen. John C. Frémont in Missouri and Gen. David Hunter in South Carolina issued proclamations that emancipated slaves in their military regions and permitted them to enlist, their superiors sternly revoked their orders. By mid-1862, however, the escalating number of former slaves (contrabands), the declining number of white volunteers, and the pressing personnel needs of the Union Army pushed the Government into reconsidering the ban.

As a result, on July 17, 1862, Congress passed the Second Confiscation and Militia Act, freeing slaves who had masters in the Confederate Army. Two days later, slavery was abolished in the territories of the United States, and on July 22 President Lincoln presented the preliminary draft of the Emancipation Proclamation to his Cabinet. After the Union Army turned back Lee's first invasion of the North at Antietam, MD, and the Emancipation

Proclamation was subsequently announced, black recruitment was pursued in earnest. Volunteers from South Carolina, Tennessee, and Massachusetts filled the first authorized black regiments. Recruitment was slow until black leaders such as Frederick Douglass encouraged black men to become soldiers to ensure eventual full citizenship. (Two of Douglass's own sons contributed to the war effort.) Volunteers began to respond, and in May 1863 the Government established the Bureau of Colored Troops to manage the burgeoning numbers of black soldiers.

Nearly 40,000 black soldiers died over the course of the war—30,000 of infection or disease. Black soldiers served in artillery and infantry and performed all noncombat support functions that sustain an army as well. Black carpenters, chaplains, cooks, guards, laborers, nurses, scouts, spies, steamboat pilots, surgeons, and teamsters also contributed to the war cause. There were nearly 80 black commissioned officers. Black women, who could not formally join the Army, nonetheless served as nurses, spies, and scouts, the most famous being Harriet Tubman, who scouted for the 2nd South Carolina Volunteers.

Source: ourdocuments.gov

15. Creation of the U.S. Colored Troops most likely _____ the North in their fights against the Confederate states of the South.

16. What percentage of African-American soldiers died due to infection or disease?
    (A) 40%
    (B) 50%
    (C) 75%
    (D) 85%

17. Why would border states consider seceding if African Americans were permitted to join the armed forces?
    (A) Many people who lived in the border states sided with the South.
    (B) The border states were for the freedom of African Americans but only if African Americans didn't serve in the armed forces.
    (C) The border states were being forced to stay in the Union.
    (D) The border states were staunchly against slavery.

18. What is the central idea of the political cartoon above?
    (A) There are too many guns in Washington, DC.
    (B) The Second Amendment enables the United States to maintain peace with other countries.
    (C) An increase in arms will help the United States maintain peace.
    (D) Peace is in jeopardy.

Lend-Lease Act (1941)

In July 1940, after Britain had sustained the loss of 11 destroyers to the German Navy over a 10-day period, newly elected British Prime Minister Winston Churchill requested help from President Roosevelt. Roosevelt responded by exchanging 50 destroyers for 99-year leases on British bases in the Caribbean and Newfoundland. As a result, a major foreign policy debate erupted over whether the United States should aid Great Britain or maintain strict neutrality.

In the 1940 Presidential election campaign, Roosevelt promised to keep America out of the war. He stated, "I have said this before, but I shall say it again and again and again; your boys are not going to be sent into any foreign wars." Nevertheless, FDR wanted to support Britain and believed the United States should serve as a "great arsenal of democracy." Churchill pleaded, "Give us the tools and we'll finish the job." In January 1941, following up on his campaign pledge and the prime minister's appeal for arms, Roosevelt proposed to Congress a new military aid bill.

The plan proposed by FDR was to "lend-lease or otherwise dispose of arms" and other supplies needed by any country whose security was vital to the defense of the United States. In support of the bill, Secretary of War Henry L. Stimson told the Senate Foreign Relations Committee during the debate over lend-lease, "We are buying . . . not lending. We are buying our own security while we prepare. By our delay during the past six years, while Germany was preparing, we find ourselves unprepared and unarmed, facing a thoroughly prepared and armed potential enemy." Following two months of debate, Congress passed the Lend-Lease Act, meeting Great Britain's deep need for supplies and allowing the United States to prepare for war while remaining officially neutral.

Source: ourdocuments.gov

19. What was the greater purpose of the Lend-Lease Act?
    (A) To provide Britain with destroyers
    (B) To gain leases on British bases
    (C) To support democracy
    (D) To align the United States with Britain

20. What argument for the bill does Secretary of War Henry L. Stimson make?
    (A) The United States is being proactive by making strategic moves.
    (B) The bill is inaccurate because the United States is buying, not lending.
    (C) Congress should be wary about passing the bill because Germany is a potential enemy.
    (D) The bill will enable the United States to continue to remain neutral and avoid war.

21. What did the United States stand to gain from the Lend-Lease Act?
    (A) Destroyers
    (B) Acquisition of lands in England
    (C) Future military support
    (D) A place to dispose of obsolete arms

QUESTIONS 22 AND 23 ARE BASED ON THE FOLLOWING GRAPH:

Population Growth in the District of Columbia

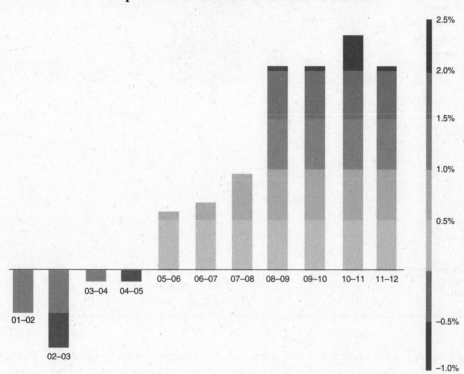

22. According to the graph, which period of time saw the greatest increase in population?
    (A) 2010–2011
    (B) 2007–2008
    (C) 2004–2005
    (D) 2002–2003

23. Which of the following periods would have likely had the least need for an increase of educational funding?
    (A) 2010–2011
    (B) 2007–2008
    (C) 2004–2005
    (D) 2002–2003

State-to-State Migration

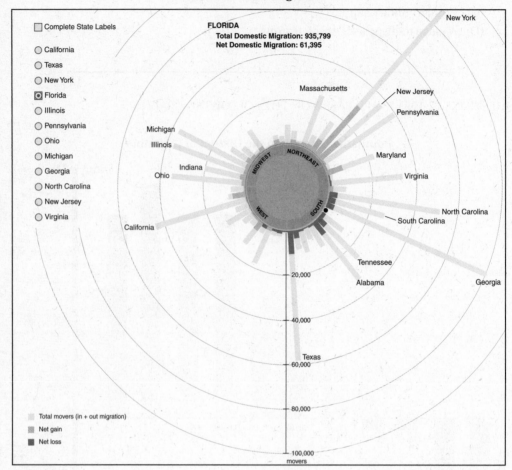

This graphic, using data from the American Community Survey, illustrates the total number of movers between states for the 12 most populous states, based on 2010 population. While there is considerable gross domestic migration (total number of movers) between states each year, the number of movers in and the number of movers out are similar, resulting in relatively small net gains or losses.

24. According to the graph, to which state did Florida lose the most people?
    (A) Michigan
    (B) New York
    (C) Georgia
    (D) Texas

25. According to the graph, which region saw the greatest singular state-to-state migration?
    (A) Northeast
    (B) South
    (C) Midwest
    (D) West

Chinese Exclusion Act (1882)

In the spring of 1882, the Chinese Exclusion Act was passed by Congress and signed by President Chester A. Arthur. This act provided an absolute 10-year moratorium on Chinese labor immigration. For the first time, Federal law proscribed entry of an ethnic working group on the premise that it endangered the good order of certain localities.

The Chinese Exclusion Act required the few non-laborers who sought entry to obtain certification from the Chinese government that they were qualified to immigrate. But this group found it increasingly difficult to prove that they were not laborers because the 1882 act defined excludables as "skilled and unskilled laborers and Chinese employed in mining." Thus very few Chinese could enter the country under the 1882 law.

The 1882 exclusion act also placed new requirements on Chinese who had already entered the country. If they left the United States, they had to obtain certifications to re-enter. Congress, moreover, refused State and Federal courts the right to grant citizenship to Chinese resident aliens, although these courts could still deport them.

When the exclusion act expired in 1892, Congress extended it for 10 years in the form of the Geary Act. This extension, made permanent in 1902, added restrictions by requiring each Chinese resident to register and obtain a certificate of residence. Without a certificate, she or he faced deportation.

The Geary Act regulated Chinese immigration until the 1920s. With increased postwar immigration, Congress adopted new means for regulation: quotas and requirements pertaining to national origin. By this time, anti-Chinese agitation had quieted. In 1943 Congress repealed all the exclusion acts, leaving a yearly limit of 105 Chinese and gave foreign-born Chinese the right to seek naturalization. The so-called national origin system, with various modifications, lasted until Congress passed the Immigration Act of 1965. Effective July 1, 1968, a limit of 170,000 immigrants from outside the Western Hemisphere could enter the United States, with a maximum of 20,000 from any one country. Skill and the need for political asylum determined admission. The Immigration Act of 1990 provided the most comprehensive change in legal immigration since 1965. The act established a "flexible" worldwide cap on family-based, employment-based, and diversity immigrant visas. The act further provides that visas for any single foreign state in these categories may not exceed 7 percent of the total available.

Source: ourdocuments.gov

26. What was the likely catalyst for the Chinese Exclusion Act of 1882?
    (A) The Geary Act
    (B) Lack of jobs for natural-born citizens
    (C) Fear of overcrowding
    (D) Anti-Chinese sentiment

27. After 1968, which of the following would be a legal number of Chinese immigrants?
    (A) 18,744
    (B) 20,482
    (C) 68,002
    (D) 75,000

28. What was the purpose of the Geary Act?
    (A) To extend the regulations in the Chinese Exclusion Act
    (B) To enhance the ability of Chinese to immigrate to the United States
    (C) To grant equal immigration rights to all
    (D) To freeze all immigration

QUESTIONS 29 AND 30 ARE BASED ON THE FOLLOWING TABLE:

Percent of Men and Women with First Marriages by Age

Age	Men			Women		
	1970	1988	2009	1970	1988	2009
Under 20	18.4	6.9	3.6	41.8	17.7	6.9
20–24	57.0	38.7	23.5	46.0	43.3	31.5
25–29	16.2	33.9	34.3	7.7	26.1	32.9
30–34	4.1	13.6	19.5	2.0	8.5	15.3
35–39	1.8	4.4	9.0	0.9	2.8	6.3
40–44	1.0	1.4	4.3	0.6	0.8	2.9
45–49	0.6	0.5	2.8	0.4	0.3	1.9
50–54	0.3	0.3	1.4	0.2	0.2	1.0
55–59	0.2	0.2	0.9	0.1	0.1	0.6
60–64	0.1	0.1	0.3	0.1	0.1	0.4
65 and over	0.1	0.1	0.4	0.1	0.1	0.2

Source: U.S. Census Bureau, American Community Survey, 2009; National Center for Health Statistics, 1970, 1988.

29. About _____% of 50 to 54 year-old women entered into their first marriage in 1988.

30. What does the trend in data suggest?
    (A) People are getting married earlier in life.
    (B) People are getting married later in life.
    (C) People are getting married at about the same age as they always have.
    (D) Women are getting married earlier, while men are getting married later.

Joint Address to Congress Leading to a Declaration of War Against Japan (1941)

On December 7, 1941, the U.S. naval base on the island of Oahu, Hawaii, was subject to an attack that was one of the greatest military surprises in the history of warfare. In less than 2 hours, the U.S. Pacific Fleet was devastated, and more than 3,500 Americans were killed or wounded. The Japanese attack on Pearl Harbor catapulted the United States into World War II.

The American people were outraged. Though diplomatic relations between the United States and Japan were deteriorating, they had not yet broken off at the time of the attack. Instantly, the incident united the American people in a massive mobilization for war and strengthened American resolve to guard against any future lapse of military alertness.

Early in the afternoon of December 7, 1941, President Franklin D. Roosevelt and his chief foreign policy aide, Harry Hopkins, were interrupted by a telephone call from Secretary of War Henry Stimson and told that the Japanese had attacked Pearl Harbor. At about 5 p.m., following meetings with his military advisers, the President calmly and decisively dictated to his secretary, Grace Tully, a request to Congress for a declaration of war. He had composed the speech in his head after deciding on a brief, uncomplicated appeal to the people of the United States rather than a thorough recitation of Japanese treachery, as Secretary of State Cordell Hull had urged.

President Roosevelt then revised the typed draft—marking it up, updating military information, and selecting alternative wordings that strengthened the tone of the speech. He made the most significant change in the critical first line, which originally read, "a date which will live in world history." Grace Tully then prepared the final reading copy, which Roosevelt subsequently altered in three more places.

On December 8, at 12:30 p.m., Roosevelt addressed a joint session of Congress and, via radio, the nation. The Senate responded with a unanimous vote in support of war; only Montana pacifist Jeanette Rankin dissented in the House. At 4 p.m. that same afternoon, President Roosevelt signed the declaration of war.

Roosevelt misplaced his reading copy immediately following the speech; it remained missing for 43 years. Instead of bringing the reading copy back to the White House for Grace Tully to file, the President evidently left it in the House chamber, where he had given the address. A Senate clerk took charge of it, endorsed it "Dec 8, 1941, Read in joint session," and filed it. In March 1984 an archivist located the reading copy among the Records of the U.S. Senate, Record Group 46, located in the National Archives building, where it remains today.

Source: ourdocuments.gov

Surrender of Japan (1945)

On September 2, 1945, Japanese representatives signed the official Instrument of Surrender, prepared by the War Department and approved by President Harry S. Truman. It set out in eight short paragraphs the complete capitulation of Japan. The opening words, "We, acting by command of and in behalf of the Emperor of Japan," signified the importance attached to the Emperor's role by the Americans who drafted the document. The short second paragraph went straight to the heart of the matter: "We hereby proclaim the unconditional surrender to the Allied Powers of the Japanese Imperial General Headquarters and of all Japanese armed forces and all armed forces under Japanese control wherever situated."

That morning, on the deck of the USS *Missouri* in Tokyo Bay, the Japanese envoys Foreign Minister Mamoru Shigemitsu and Gen. Yoshijiro Umezu signed their names on the Instrument of Surrender. The time was recorded as 4 minutes past 9 o'clock. Afterward, Gen. Douglas MacArthur, Commander in the Southwest Pacific and Supreme Commander for the Allied Powers, also signed. He accepted the Japanese surrender "for the United States, Republic of China, United Kingdom, and the Union of Soviet Socialist Republics, and in the interests of the other United Nations at war with Japan."

On September 6, Col. Bernard Thielen brought the surrender document and a second imperial rescript back to Washington, DC. The following day, Thielen presented the documents to President Truman in a formal White House ceremony. The documents were then exhibited at the National Archives after a dignified ceremony led by Gen. Jonathan Wainwright. Finally, on October 1, 1945, they were formally received (accessioned) into the holdings of the National Archives.

Source: ourdocuments.gov

31. Which of the following is an opinion about World War II?
    (A) Dropping the atomic bombs saved American lives.
    (B) The attack on Pearl Harbor caused the United States to enter World War II.
    (C) The Japanese surrendered on September 2, 1945.
    (D) On December 8, 1941, the United States declared war on Japan.

32. Of the following people, who signed the Instrument of Surrender? Select all that apply.
    (A) Foreign Minister Mamoru Shigemitsu
    (B) General Yoshijiro Umezu
    (C) General Douglas MacArthur
    (D) President Truman

33. What caused the United States to enter World War II?
    (A) The signing of a surrender document
    (B) The dropping of the atomic bomb
    (C) The attack on Pearl Harbor
    (D) President Roosevelt's address to Congress

Extended Response

Dred Scott and the 14th Amendment

Dred Scott v. Sanford (1857)

In 1846 a slave named Dred Scott and his wife, Harriet, sued for their freedom in a St. Louis city court. The odds were in their favor. They had lived with their owner, an army surgeon, at Fort Snelling, then in the free Territory of Wisconsin. The Scotts' freedom could be established on the grounds that they had been held in bondage for extended periods in a free territory and were then returned to a slave state. Courts had ruled this way in the past. However, what appeared to be a straightforward lawsuit between two private parties became an 11-year legal struggle that culminated in one of the most notorious decisions ever issued by the United States Supreme Court.

On its way to the Supreme Court, the Dred Scott case grew in scope and significance as slavery became the single most explosive issue in American politics. By the time the case reached the high court, it had come to have enormous political implications for the entire nation.

On March 6, 1857, Chief Justice Roger B. Taney read the majority opinion of the Court, which stated that slaves were not citizens of the United States and, therefore, could not expect any protection from the Federal Government or the courts. The opinion also stated that Congress had no authority to ban slavery from a Federal territory. This decision moved the nation a step closer to Civil War.

The decision of *Scott v. Sanford*, considered by legal scholars to be the worst ever rendered by the Supreme Court, was overturned by the 13th and 14th amendments to the Constitution, which abolished slavery and declared all persons born in the United States to be citizens of the United States.

Source: ourdocuments.gov

14th Amendment to the U.S. Constitution: Civil Rights (1868)

Following the Civil War, Congress submitted to the states three amendments as part of its Reconstruction program to guarantee equal civil and legal rights to black citizens. The major provision of the 14th amendment was to grant citizenship to "All persons born or naturalized in the United States," thereby granting citizenship to former slaves. Another equally important provision was the statement that "nor shall any state deprive any person of life, liberty, or property, without due process of law; nor deny to any person within its jurisdiction the equal protection of the laws." The right to due process of law and equal protection of the law now applied to both the Federal and state governments. On June 16, 1866, the House Joint Resolution proposing the 14th amendment to the Constitution was submitted to the states. On July 28, 1868, the 14th amendment was declared, in a certificate of the Secretary of State, ratified by the necessary 28 of the 37 States, and became part of the supreme law of the land.

Congressman John A. Bingham of Ohio, the primary author of the first section of the 14th amendment, intended that the amendment also nationalize the Federal Bill of Rights by making it binding upon the states. Senator Jacob Howard of Michigan, introducing the amendment, specifically stated that the privileges and immunities clause would extend to the states "the personal rights guaranteed and secured by the first eight amendments." Historians disagree on how widely Bingham's and Howard's views were shared at the time in the Congress, or across the country in general. No one in Congress explicitly contradicted their view of the Amendment, but only a few members said anything at all about its meaning on this issue. For many years, the Supreme Court ruled that the Amendment did not extend the Bill of Rights to the states.

Not only did the 14th amendment fail to extend the Bill of Rights to the states; it also failed to protect the rights of black citizens. One legacy of Reconstruction was the determined struggle of black and white citizens to make the promise of the 14th amendment a reality. Citizens petitioned and initiated court cases, Congress enacted legislation, and the executive branch attempted to enforce measures that would guard all citizens' rights. While these citizens did not succeed in empowering the 14th amendment during the Reconstruction, they effectively articulated arguments and offered dissenting opinions that would be the basis for change in the 20th century.

Source: ourdocuments.gov

ANSWER KEY
Model Test 1

SOCIAL STUDIES EXAM

1. D
2. D
3. C
4. D
5. B
6. C
7. restitution, reparations, money, or similar words
8. C
9. A
10. A
11. C
12. D
13. D
14. C
15. helped, aided, assisted, or similar words
16. C
17. A
18. D
19. C
20. A
21. C
22. A
23. D
24. D
25. A
26. D
27. A
28. A
29. 0.2
30. B
31. A
32. A, B, C
33. C

EXTENDED RESPONSE

Answers will vary.

SOCIAL STUDIES EXAM ANSWERS EXPLAINED

1. **(D)** The passage states in several ways that keeping the peace required maintaining a strong military. Options A, B, and C are incorrect. The passage does not indicate that these were peacekeeping factors in which Eisenhower believed.

2. **(D)** The passage makes clear that President Eisenhower recognized the dangers of an arms race but also considered it to be necessary at the time. It also states that Eisenhower was conflicted with the necessity of building up the military. These factors suggest that he would have supported a worldwide decrease in nuclear arsenals. Option A is incorrect. Although Eisenhower may have supported an increase in educational funding, there is no evidence in the passage to support this answer. Options B and C are incorrect. The passage indicates that although increased military spending and expanding the armed forces were necessary during Eisenhower's presidency, he would probably not support them today.

3. **(C)** The passage indicates that President Eisenhower was warning future generations. Options A, B, and D are incorrect because they don't describe the tone of the speech.

4. **(D)** According to the key, the graphs indicate the percentage of people *without* a high school education so look for the smallest percentage, not the highest percentage. Options A, B, and C are incorrect.

5. **(B)** When comparing the two bar graphs, it is clear that a smaller percentage of native-born black women in the West are without a high school education than foreign-born Asian men in the West.

6. **(C)** The Japanese Americans who were placed into internment camps had not committed any crimes nor had they been charged with any. Option A is incorrect. Individuals who are relocated because of a hurricane are being moved for their own protection. They are free to return to their homes after the danger has passed. Option B is incorrect. Although slavery can be considered to be a form of imprisonment, the Japanese Americans were not forced to work. Option D is incorrect because the Japanese Americans in the internment camps were not put to death.

7. The words that best complete the sentence include "restitution," "reparations," and "money." Other words with similar meanings would be accepted.

8. **(C)** Since the question asks for the total amount of income and property lost, it means you have to add $1.3 billion + $2.7 billion = $4 billion. Option A is incorrect because it is the total property loss. Option B is incorrect because it is the net income loss. Option D is incorrect.

9. **(A)** Taft and Dulles are arguing, and Vandenberg comments that it's "purely an argument between two Republicans." Option B is incorrect because the Democrats are not involved in the argument. Option C is incorrect because no evidence suggests the Democrats oppose the Atlantic Pact. Option D is incorrect. No evidence shows how the Democrats feel about the Atlantic Pact, only that there is bipartisan agreement on foreign policy.

10. **(A)** The Louisiana Purchase included much of the land west of the Mississippi and enabled the United States to expand westward. Option B is incorrect because no evi-

dence suggest that the purchase was a strategic move to be closer to enemies of the United States. Option C is incorrect because no evidence suggests that the purpose was to resell the land. Option D is incorrect. Although the passage refers to the riches of the land, it does not refer to "buried riches."

11. **(C)** Despite President Jefferson's personal reservations based on his interpretation of the Constitution, the execution of the purchase assumes the United States determined that it had the right to acquire these lands. Option B is incorrect; the fact that the United States did acquire these lands indicates the opposite. Options A and D are incorrect because no evidence supports these answers.

12. **(D)** The Louisiana Purchase and the purchase of Alaska were both cash transactions for land. Option A is incorrect because Guam was captured during a war. Options B and C are incorrect because neither one has to do with the acquisition of land.

13. **(D)** The map from 1980 to 1990 shows the darkest shading for the Southwest, indicating the greatest population increase. Options A, B, and C are incorrect.

14. **(C)** The passage indicates that Texas saw a decrease in population during the 1930s, 1940s, and 1950s. Options A, B, and D are incorrect because they do not fall within any of those time periods.

15. "Helped," "aided," or "assisted" best completes the sentence. Other words with similar meanings would be acceptable.

16. **(C)** According to the passage, of the 40,000 African Americans who died, 30,000 died from infection or disease. This constitutes 75% of the African-American soldiers who died. Options A, B, and D are incorrect.

17. **(A)** If the concern was that the border states would secede, obviously many people who lived in those states sided with the South. Options B, C, and D are incorrect. No evidence supports any of these answers.

18. **(D)** The depiction of a hand, labeled "peace," that is grabbing for Uncle Sam's coattails while Uncle Sam runs away with a rifle indicates that peace is in jeopardy. Options A, B, and C are incorrect. Although the political cartoon contains elements from each of these answer choices, none of these choices is fully supported.

19. **(C)** The third paragraph indicates that President Roosevelt suggested the federal government support any country whose security is vital to the defense of the United States. Options A and B are incorrect. Although these were effects, neither was the greater purpose of the Lend-Lease Act.

20. **(A)** The passage indicates that passing the Lend-Lease Act would enable the United States to "[buy] our own security while we prepare." Options B, C, and D are incorrect because no evidence supports these answers.

21. **(C)** Giving Great Britain the support it needed at the time would create a relationship where Great Britain could reciprocate in the future. Option A is incorrect because the United States gave destroyers to Great Britain, not the other way around. Option B is incorrect. The United States was not acquiring lands in England; it was leasing land at British bases. Option D is incorrect because it misinterprets the phrase "dispose of arms."

22. **(A)** The bar aligned with the highest percentage is the one that corresponds with 2010 to 2011. Options B, C, and D are incorrect.

23. **(D)** If the population decreases, there is less need to increase educational funding. The years 2002 to 2003 saw the greatest decrease in population growth. Options A, B, and C are incorrect.

24. **(D)** The black shading indicates net loss, and the bar corresponding to Texas has the largest amount of black shading. Options A, B, and C are incorrect.

25. **(A)** New York had the greatest singular state-to-state migration, and New York is in the Northeast. Options B, C, and D are incorrect.

26. **(D)** The last paragraph states that "anti-Chinese agitation had quieted," indicating that there was, at one time, anti-Chinese sentiment. Option A is incorrect because the Geary Act was a subsequent law. Options B and C are incorrect. No evidence supports these answers.

27. **(A)** The last paragraph states that a maximum of 20,000 people could enter the United States from any one country. Options B, C, and D are incorrect; they are all over 20,000.

28. **(A)** The passage clearly indicates that the Geary Act was intended to extend the provisions of the Chinese Exclusion Act. Options B and D are incorrect. The Geary Act did not enhance or freeze immigration completely. Option C is incorrect because the Geary Act limited immigration rights.

29. **0.2** According to the table, 0.2% of women age 50–54 entered into their first marriage in 1988.

30. **(B)** The chart indicates that fewer people are getting married early in life, while the number of people getting married later has increased. Option A is incorrect because the table suggests the opposite. Option C is incorrect because the table suggests there is a great change in the age when people marry. Option D is incorrect. Although men are, in fact, getting married later, so are women.

31. **(A)** It is hypothesized that dropping the atomic bombs saved lives, but this cannot be proven. Options B, C, and D are incorrect because all of them are factual and can be proven.

32. **(A, B, C)** The second passage indicates that Foreign Minister Shigemitsu and General Umezu signed the Instrument of Surrender for Japan and that General MacArthur signed for the Allies.

33. **(C)** The first passage indicates that once the U.S. naval base on Pearl Harbor was attacked, the United States declared war. Options A and B are incorrect because they happened at the end of the war. Option D is incorrect because President Roosevelt's address didn't cause the United States to enter World War II.

Extended Response

Answers will vary.

When reviewing your extended response, make sure you have asked yourself the following questions:

- Have I responded to the prompt?
- Do I have enough evidence?
- Do my ideas follow a logical order?
- Are there any misspellings?
- Have I confused any homonyms?
- Have I used proper punctuation, including periods, commas, semicolons, apostrophes, and so forth?
- Do I need to break up any run-on sentences?
- Can I combine any strings of short, choppy sentences?

The prompt asks you to discuss both the negative and positive impacts of *Dred Scott v. Sanford* and the 14th Amendment on African Americans. Make sure that you have discussed the most important positive and negative effects. Following your introduction, you may discuss the negative effects of each and the positive effects of each, or you may discuss the positive and negatives of *Dred Scott v. Sanford* and then the positives and negatives of the 14th Amendment. But don't jump around—follow a format. Be sure to cite specific evidence from both of the passages that you feel supports your position. Finally, make sure you have restated your position in the conclusion.

ANSWER SHEET
Model Test 1

SCIENCE EXAM

1. (A) (B) (C) (D)

2. _____
   _____
   _____
   _____

3. _____
   _____
   _____
   _____
   _____

4. (A) (B) (C) (D)

5. (A) (B) (C) (D)

6. (A) (B) (C) (D)

7. Use lines below for your answer.

8. (A) (B) (C) (D)

9. (A) (B) (C) (D)

10. (A) (B) (C) (D)

11. (A) (B) (C) (D)

12. (A) (B) (C) (D)

13. (A) (B) (C) (D)

14. (A) (B) (C) (D)

15. (A) (B) (C) (D)

16. (A) (B) (C) (D)

17. (A) (B) (C) (D)

18. (A) (B) (C) (D)

19. (A) (B) (C) (D)

20. (A) (B) (C) (D)

21. (A) (B) (C) (D)

22. (A) (B) (C) (D)

23. (A) (B) (C) (D)

24. (A) (B) (C) (D)

25. (A) (B) (C) (D)

26. (A) (B) (C) (D)

27. (A) (B) (C) (D)

28. (A) (B) (C) (D)

29. (A) (B) (C) (D)

30. (A) (B) (C) (D)

31. (A) (B) (C) (D)

32. (A) (B) (C) (D)

33. _____
    _____
    _____

34. _____

35. (A) (B) (C) (D)

7. _____
   _____
   _____
   _____
   _____

DIRECTIONS: This practice exam contains various stimuli, which you will need to analyze in order to answer the questions that follow. This exam has 35 questions. You will have 75 minutes to answer the questions.

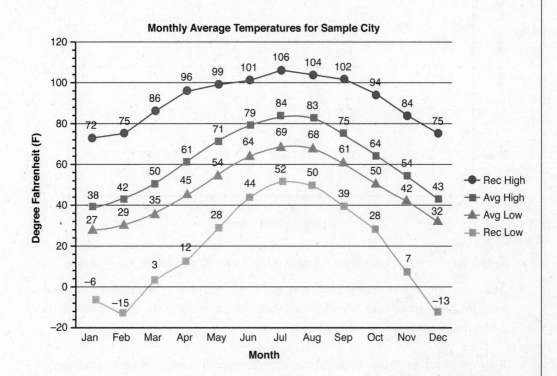

The graph above reflects temperature data gathered over a 10-year period. The "average high" and "average low" temperatures give a single 10-year average for each month. The "record high" and "record low" temperatures are the highest and lowest temperatures recorded for each month during the 10-year period.

1. Which month has the greatest range between record low and record high temperatures?
    (A) January
    (B) February
    (C) November
    (D) December

QUESTIONS 2 AND 3 REFER TO THE FOLLOWING SCATTER PLOT:

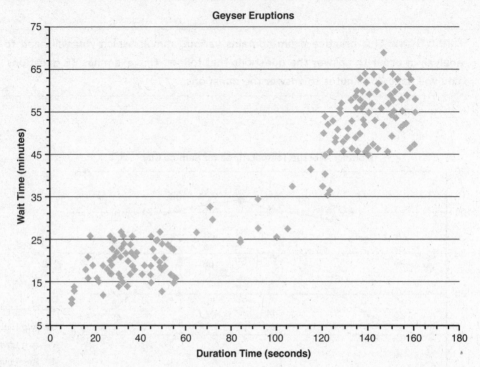

2. Select the word or phrase in each bracket that correctly completes the sentence:

Most eruptions occur with either [short, both long and short] durations after [short, long, long and short] wait times or [long, both long and short] durations after [short, long, long and short] wait times.

3. Select the word or phrase in each bracket that correctly completes each sentence:

Short eruptions tend to last [less than, between, more than] 20 seconds but [less than, between, more than] 60 seconds. Long eruptions tend to last [less than, between, more than] 160 seconds but [less than, between, more than] 120 seconds. Very few eruptions last [less than, between, more than] 60 and 120 seconds.

The temperature of the Earth is regulated by a relationship between the Sun, the surface of the Earth, and the Earth's atmosphere. Energy in the form of solar radiation (sunlight) travels from the Sun to the Earth. A portion of this energy is reflected away, either by the Earth's atmosphere or surface, but roughly half of this energy is absorbed by the surface of the Earth and converted to infrared (heat) energy. This heat is then released back into the atmosphere.

A large portion of the infrared energy emitted passes through the atmosphere and into space. A smaller portion of this energy is absorbed by chemicals in the atmosphere known as "greenhouse gases." As these gases absorb heat, they cause an increase in atmospheric temperature. Without greenhouse gases, the Earth would be significantly colder and unable to support many of its current forms of life, including human life. Greenhouse gases include water vapor (H_2O), carbon dioxide (CO_2), methane (CH_4), and ozone (O_3).

The most significant greenhouse gas in terms of warming effect is water vapor (H_2O). Water vapor absorbs the majority of the global heat emissions absorbed by the atmosphere. Research data suggest that the absorption capacity of water vapor in the atmosphere increases as atmospheric temperature increases. The second most significant greenhouse gas in terms of warming effect is carbon dioxide (CO_2). As the average concentration of atmospheric carbon dioxide increases, it absorbs increasing amounts of heat, contributing to an increase in atmospheric temperature.

The carbon cycle is a process by which carbon in the atmosphere is absorbed, stored, and released by the biosphere (land, oceans, and living things). On land, plants absorb carbon for use in photosynthesis, and most of this carbon is converted to biomass (leaves, stems, and roots) or transmitted into the soil. Living plants return unconverted carbon into the atmosphere during respiration. Biomass carbon is returned to the atmosphere during decomposition. Carbon in the soil is released during the respiration of microbes and other living things in the soil.

A small amount of carbon absorbed and stored by the biosphere is not released back into the atmosphere. Instead, it is retained in the soil. This retention of carbon is called *biosequestration*. The highest levels of carbon biosequestration in soil are found in regions at high latitudes with colder climates. For example, large amounts of carbon are stored in the *permafrost* (frozen soil) found in cold climates like *tundra* and *boreal forests*. Most of the carbon captured in permafrost remains sequestered unless the permafrost melts or is otherwise affected by increasing temperatures.

4. According to the passage, which of the following is NOT a greenhouse gas?
   (A) Carbon dioxide
   (B) Water vapor
   (C) Carbon monoxide
   (D) Ozone

5. Based on the passage, all of the following are true EXCEPT:
   (A) Water vapor is a more significant factor in warming than carbon dioxide.
   (B) Methane is a less significant factor in warming than carbon dioxide.
   (C) Carbon dioxide is a more significant factor in warming than ozone.
   (D) Methane is a more significant factor in warming than ozone.

6. What is the most likely effect of an increase in the concentration of CO_2 in the atmosphere?
   (A) An increase in the concentration of water vapor in the atmosphere
   (B) An increase in the concentration of methane in the atmosphere
   (C) An increase in the absorption capacity of water vapor in the atmosphere
   (D) An increase in the absorption capacity of ozone in the atmosphere

7. In recent decades, global temperatures have been trending higher, with greater rates of change near the North and South Poles. Explain how warming could interfere with carbon biosequestration in soil, including both the cause of the interference and the potential effect on the atmosphere. Include multiple pieces of evidence from the passage to support your answer. (This could take approximately 10 minutes to complete.)

QUESTIONS 8 THROUGH 11 REFER TO THE FOLLOWING INFORMATION:

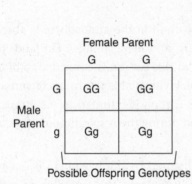

G	Dominant Allele
g	Recessive Allele
GG	Homozygous (shows dominant trait)
Gg	Heterozygous (shows dominant trait)
gg	Homozygous (shows recessive trait)

8. The Punnett square shows a genetic cross. If the cross produces 20 offspring, how many will likely be homozygous?
   (A) 0
   (B) 5
   (C) 10
   (D) 20

9. According to the diagram, what is the probability that an offspring will show the recessive trait (g)?
   (A) 100%
   (B) 50%
   (C) 25%
   (D) 0%

10. Which of the following is the most likely distribution of offspring from a cross between a *Gg* parent and a *Gg* parent?
    (A) All will be heterozygous.
    (B) All will be homozygous.
    (C) Half will be heterozygous, and half will be homozygous.
    (D) One-quarter will be heterozygous, and three-quarters will be homozygous.

11. Based on the information in the passage, if the dominant allele *G* carries the trait for yellow color in pea plants, what percentage of the offspring from a *GG* × *gg* cross will display the yellow phenotype?
    (A) 0%
    (B) 25%
    (C) 50%
    (D) 100%

12. Look at the list of genotypes and the Punnett square shown below. Which genotype belongs in each quadrant? Note that in the answer choices, quadrant 1 is identified as Q1, quadrant 2 as Q2, and so on.

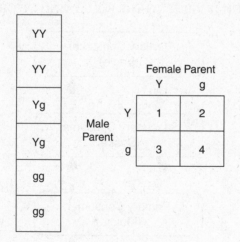

    (A) Q1 = *YY*; Q2 = *Yg*; Q3 = *gg*; Q4 = *gg*
    (B) Q1 = *YY*; Q2 = *Yg*; Q3 = *Yg*; Q4 = *YY*
    (C) Q1 = *YY*; Q2 = *Yg*; Q3 = *Yg*; Q4 = *gg*
    (D) Q1 = *Yg*; Q2 = *Yg*; Q3 = *gg*; Q4 = *gg*

TIP

On the computerized test, a question like this would have you drag and drop the genotypes onto the correct quadrant in the Punnett square.

13. When a new species becomes established in an ecosystem, it can often disrupt the existing relationships between predators and their prey (animals that predators eat). A new species may outcompete an existing predator for food sources and habitat, or an existing predator can become prey for the new species. One of the most well-documented ecological impacts of a species invasion was that of the sea lamprey in the Great Lakes, which devastated the lake trout fishery during the 1940s and 1950s. As the native predator became prey to the invasive sea lampreys, populations of prey fish like the alewife multiplied out of control.

According to the information above, what happened in the Great Lakes during the 1940s and 1950s?

(A) Lake trout began to feed on sea lampreys instead of alewives. This reduced the sea lamprey population, and the alewife population grew as a result.

(B) Alewives began to feed on sea lampreys. This reduced the sea lamprey population, and the lake trout population grew as a result.

(C) Sea lampreys began to feed on lake trout. This reduced the population of lake trout, and the alewife population grew as a result.

(D) Alewives began to feed on lake trout. This reduced the lake trout population, and the sea lamprey population grew as a result.

QUESTIONS 14 THROUGH 18 REFER TO THE FOLLOWING INFORMATION:

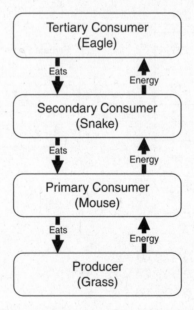

All living things require energy to survive, and this energy is usually contained in the food that a living thing eats. The simple food chain above shows the relationship between producers and consumers as well as the flow of energy between different members of the chain. Light energy from the sun is captured by plants through photosynthesis and is transferred up the chain: primary consumers eat producers, secondary consumers eat primary consumers, and tertiary consumers eat secondary consumers. Consumers are often referred to as "predators" and producers as "prey," although some predators (secondary consumers) are prey for (eaten by) other predators (tertiary consumers).

Since the size of a population is closely related to the size of its food supply, the relationships between the levels in a food chain serve to keep the populations of each group in balance. For example, an increase in the population of mice would reduce the amount of grass since more mice will need to eat more grass to survive. That same increase in the mouse population would likely lead to an increase in the population of snakes since more mice means more food for more snakes. By comparison, a decrease in the population of mice would probably have the opposite effect. There would be more grass since fewer mice exist to eat it and also fewer snakes since they would have less food available.

The top predator in a food chain refers to the consumer that has no natural predator. In the example above, the eagle is the top predator. An invasive species is a species that enters an ecosystem and competes for food with the species that are already present, disrupting the existing food chains. Invasive species are often new top predators because they have no natural predators in the new ecosystem. This can have a negative effect on the existing top predators since competition for their sources of food will increase. For example, if a new species of bird was introduced that fed primarily on snakes, the population of eagles would likely decrease as the eagles faced new competition for their food source (snakes). In some cases, the formerly top predator becomes prey to the new predator, which will also reduce the population of the previous top predator.

14. Which of the following would most negatively affect the total population of all groups in the food chain above?
   (A) A disease that kills grass and other edible green plants
   (B) A disease that paralyzes mice
   (C) A disease that prevents snakes from digesting meat
   (D) A disease that causes blindness in eagles

15. Which invasive species would be the least disruptive to the food chain above?
   (A) A nonnative rodent that eats grass
   (B) A nonnative owl that eats mice
   (C) A nonnative weasel that eats snakes
   (D) A nonnative bird of prey that eats eagles

16. Herbivores are animals that eat plants. Carnivores are animals that eat other animals. Based on the information above, which of the following is true?
   (A) All consumers are carnivores.
   (B) Some consumers are carnivores, and some are plants.
   (C) Some producers are plants, and some are carnivores.
   (D) Some consumers are herbivores, and some are carnivores.

17. The energy that flows up through a food chain begins with producers (plants). According to the information above, how does the producer acquire the energy it supplies to this food chain?
   (A) The grass absorbs fossil fuels in the soil through its roots.
   (B) The grass absorbs heat in the air through its blades (leaves).
   (C) The grass creates energy in its cells through asexual reproduction.
   (D) The grass blades (leaves) absorb light from the sun.

18. Many people argue that humans are the top predator in virtually all food chains. Based on the information in the previous paragraphs, which of the following statements best supports this view?
    (A) Some predators, like bears, wolves, and sharks, eat humans.
    (B) Technology enables humans to use almost any existing top predator as a food source.
    (C) Humans consume large amounts of grains, fruits, and vegetables.
    (D) Humans raise animals like cows and chickens to provide food like eggs and milk.

QUESTIONS 19 AND 20 REFER TO THE FOLLOWING INFORMATION:

Diporeia is a native shrimp-like organism about the size of your smallest fingernail that Great Lakes fish once relied on for food. Researchers [have] documented a dramatic decline in *Diporeia* populations in Lake Michigan at the same time invasive quagga mussel populations were expanding. In just 15 years, *Diporeia* densities declined from an average of 5,200 per square meter to only 82 per square meter. Although exact reasons are unclear, scientists believe it is related to the introduction and expansion of invasive mussels.

Source: NOAA, GLERL

19. According to the passage, which of the following is true?
    (A) Scientists have concluded that the expansion of the quagga mussel population has caused a decrease in the population of *Diporeia*.
    (B) Scientists have hypothesized that the expansion of the quagga mussel population has caused a decrease in the population of *Diporeia*.
    (C) Scientists have observed that the expansion of the quagga mussel population has caused a decrease in the population of *Diporeia*.
    (D) Scientists have inferred that the expansion of the quagga mussel population has caused a decrease in the population of *Diporeia*.

20. According to the passage, by approximately how much has the *Diporeia* population decreased?
    (A) A total of 65% overall
    (B) An average of 6.5% per year
    (C) An average of 2% per year
    (D) A total of 2% overall

QUESTIONS 21 THROUGH 26 REFER TO THE FOLLOWING INFORMATION:

Month	Day of Month	Avg Daily Sunlight (kJ/m²)	Avg Daily Precipitation (mm)
April	1	7390.33	8.62
April	2	22834.31	0.5
April	3	23344.83	0
April	4	5846.87	22.11
April	5	13870.4	2
April	6	15799.67	0.2
April	7	18173.74	0
April	8	23357.81	0
April	9	20661.87	0
April	10	22936.32	0.91
April	11	10553.78	1.32
April	12	16167.93	9.09
April	13	11822.81	0.54
April	14	20765.47	0
April	15	25218.16	0

Source: North America Land Data Assimilation System (NLDAS)

21. What was the mean daily precipitation for the entire 15-day period? (Round to the nearest mm.)
    (A) 3
    (B) 4
    (C) 5
    (D) 6

22. What was the median daily precipitation for the entire 15-day period? (Round to the nearest mm.)
    (A) 0.2
    (B) 0.5
    (C) 0.91
    (D) 1.32

23. What is the mode of the set of 15 daily precipitation measurements?
    (A) 0
    (B) 0.5
    (C) 2
    (D) 22.11

24. What is the approximate range of the set of 15 daily sunlight measurements?
    (A) 25,000
    (B) 22,000
    (C) 20,000
    (D) 19,000

25. Which of the following best describes the correlation between daily precipitation and daily sunlight?
    (A) Positive correlation
    (B) Negative correlation
    (C) No correlation
    (D) Variable correlation

26. A kilojoule (kJ) is equal to 1,000 joules. Which of the following correctly represents the average daily sunlight on April 5 in joules?
    (A) 1.579967×10^7
    (B) 1.38704×10^7
    (C) 1.579967×10^4
    (D) 1.38704×10^4

Excerpt from *The Einstein Theory of Relativity*
by H. A. Lorentz

As summarized by an American astronomer, Professor Henry Norris Russell, of Princeton, in the *Scientific American* for November 29, Einstein's contribution amounts to this:

"The central fact which has been proved—and which is of great interest and importance—is that the natural phenomena involving gravitation and inertia (such as the motions of the planets) and the phenomena involving electricity and magnetism (including the motion of light) are not independent of one another, but are intimately related, so that both sets of phenomena should be regarded as parts of one vast system, embracing all Nature. The relation of the two is, however, of such a character that it is perceptible only in a very few instances, and then only to refined observations."

Source: gutenberg.org

27. Which characteristic of a scientific theory is demonstrated by Einstein's theory as described in the passage above?
    (A) It predicted and explained scientific findings that took place after the theory was first expressed.
    (B) It identified a relation that is very difficult to perceive.
    (C) It involved a lot of refined observation.
    (D) It provided a broad explanation that applies to many large subjects related to the natural world.

Nitro-Glycerin

Professor Doremus of this city was called as a witness at the inquest upon the bodies of the unfortunate persons killed by the recent explosion at Bergen, N.J. The Professor having previously analyzed some of the explosive mixture, testified as follows:—"I have subjected it to chemical analysis, and find it to correspond to the formula C_6, H_3, O_3, and NO_5; it is well made nitro-glycerin; the substance freezes at about 46; it is made to decompose in a very peculiar way; on moistening paper with it, it burns with rapidity; it does not explode when red-hot copper is placed in it; we tried it with the most intense heat—we can produce with a galvanic battery with two hundred cells holding a gallon and a half each; some nitro-glycerin was placed in a cup and connected with one of the poles of the battery; through a pencil of gas carbon the other poles of the battery were connected with the glycerin, no explosion ensued; but when the point touched the britannia vessel the nitro-glycerin took fire, a portion burning and the rest scattering about; this is as severe a test as we can submit it to in the way of heat under the pressure of the air; we therefore would conclude that nitro-glycerin carried about exposed cannot explode, even if you drop a coal of fire into it; if the liquid is confined, or is under pressure, then an explosion will ensue; if paper be moistened with it and put on an anvil and a smart blow given with a hammer, a sharp detonation ensues; if gunpowder or the fulminates of mercury, silver or gun-cotton be ignited in a vacuum by a galvanic battery, none of them will explode; if any gas be introduced so as to produce a gentle pressure during the decomposition, then a rapid evolution of gases will result; the results of decomposition in a vacuum differ from those under atmospheric pressure or when they are burnt in a pistol, musket, a cannon, or in a mine; where we have little or no pressure it is difficult to get these substances to burn rapidly; nitro-glycerin is more difficult to explode than powder; in many respects it resembles gun-cotton which is made in a similar way; if gun-cotton be immersed in the proto-chloride of iron it turns into common cotton; the same experiment was tried with nitro-glycerin by mixing it with proto-chloride of iron, and it reverted into common glycerin; there are four well known varieties of gun-cotton made by employing acids of different strengths; they differ in chemical composition and properties, as well as in their explosive qualities; the late Minister of War in Austria in 1862 stated to me that he had ordered four hundred cannon for gun-cotton, and six months after he stated that he had ordered all the cannon to be changed and adapted to powder, in consequence of spontaneous combustions; much less is known of nitro-glycerin than of gun-cotton, and probably several varieties of this article may be formed as of gun cotton; this would explain cases of spontaneous explosion; if the nitro-glycerin is not carefully washed to get rid of the acid, a gradual decomposition will ensue, producing gases, which, if the vessel be closed, will explode; my opinion is that nitro-glycerin should be used in the most careful hands; do not think I would put it in the hands of a common laborer for blasting purposes; it is less dangerous in a frozen than a liquid state; I think concussion would explode frozen nitro-glycerin.

Source: Scientific American, *Vol. 17, No. 26 December 28, 1867*

28. Which of the following is NOT a characteristic of a scientist as demonstrated by Professor Doremus in his statements on the previous page?
    (A) He shares the design and results of his experiments.
    (B) He conducts tests using control groups with substances other than the one being investigated.
    (C) He offers his conclusion as an opinion rather than as an absolute fact.
    (D) He questions the validity of the experiments of other scientists.

29. What role does the statement "nitro-glycerin should be used in the most careful hands; [I] do not think I would put it in the hands of a common laborer for blasting purposes" play in the passage as a whole?
    (A) It is a conclusion that has been drawn from evidence.
    (B) It is a hypothesis to be tested.
    (C) It is an inference based on intuition rather than data.
    (D) It is a prediction to be verified with an experiment.

30. What method does Professor Doremus use to explain the formation of explosive gases in closed vessels?
    (A) He makes an inference based on comparing the behavior of the nitro-glycerin to the behavior of a similar substance.
    (B) He tries to freeze the liquid to make it less explosive.
    (C) He hits the substance with a hammer.
    (D) He exposes the substance to electrical heat.

QUESTIONS 31 THROUGH 35 REFER TO THE FOLLOWING TABLE AND INFORMATION:

Number of Valence Electrons

		1	2	3	4	5	6	7	8
	1	1 H Hydrogen	2 ← Atomic Number He ← Symbol and Helium Element Name						
Periods	2	3 Li Lithium	4 Be Beryllium	5 B Boron	6 C Carbon	7 N Nitrogen	8 O Oxygen	9 F Fluorine	10 Ne Neon
	3	11 Na Sodium	12 Mg Magnesium	13 Al Aluminum	14 Si Silicon	15 P Phosphorous	16 S Sulphur	17 Cl Chlorine	18 Ar Argon
		S1	S2	P1	P2	P3	P4	P5	P6
		S-Block		P-Block					

Position in Electron Configuration

In the table above, selected information is presented from the Periodic Table of the Elements. Valence electrons are electrons in an atom's outermost electron shell, called a valence shell. Periods refer to the number of electron shells present in an atom of a given type. The first electron shell in an atom can hold a maximum of 2 electrons. For atoms with more than one electron shell, the valence shell can hold a maximum of 8 electrons. All information shown assumes that the elements are neutral, meaning that the number of electrons in each element equals its atomic number.

31. All of the following statements about boron (B) are true EXCEPT:
    (A) Boron's first electron shell can hold a maximum of 2 electrons.
    (B) Boron's atomic number is less than 18.
    (C) Boron has 5 electrons.
    (D) Boron has 3 electron shells.

32. Which of the following is true about phosphorous (P)?
    (A) It has 5 electrons.
    (B) It has fewer valence electrons than does chlorine.
    (C) It has more electron shells than does chlorine.
    (D) It has 2 electron shells.

33. Select the word or phrase in each bracket that correctly completes each sentence. Silicon has a(n) [greater, lesser, equal] number of electron shells than oxygen and a(n) [greater, lesser, equal] number of valence electrons than sulfur. Hydrogen and helium have an equal number of [electron shells, valence electrons, electrons].

34. Write the name of the element that has 2 electron shells and 4 valence electrons.

35. An element's atomic number describes the number of protons in the atomic nucleus of the element. The number of particles in the nucleus of an atom is positively correlated to its atomic weight. A portion of the Periodic Table of the Elements is shown here.

Atomic number →	7	8	9	10
Symbol →	N	O	F	Ne
Element name →	Nitrogen	Oxygen	Fluorine	Neon
	15	16	17	18
	P	S	Cl	Ar
	Phosphorous	Sulphur	Chlorine	Argon

Which element has the smallest atomic weight?
(A) Nitrogen
(B) Neon
(C) Phosphorous
(D) Argon

TIP

On the computerized test, a question like this would have you fill in the blank.

ANSWER KEY
Model Test 1

SCIENCE EXAM

1. B
2. short, short, long, long
3. more than, less than, less than, more than, between
4. C
5. D
6. C
7. Answers will vary (see Answers Explained).
8. C
9. D
10. C
11. D
12. C
13. C
14. A
15. D
16. D
17. D
18. B
19. D
20. B
21. A
22. B
23. A
24. D
25. B
26. B
27. D
28. D
29. A
30. A
31. D
32. B
33. greater, lesser, electron shells
34. carbon
35. A

SCIENCE EXAM ANSWER EXPLANATIONS

1. **(B)** Range is the difference between the highest and lowest values. The range for January is $72 - (-6) = 78$. The range for February is $75 - (-15) = 90$. The range for November is $84 - 7 = 77$. The range for December is $75 - (-13) = 88$.

2. **Short, Short, Long, Long** The clusters on the scatter plot are in areas of short duration and short wait time or of long duration and long wait time. The outliers are dispersed between 60 and 120 seconds' duration and 25 to 45 minutes' wait time.

3. **More than, Less than, Less than, More than, Between** The clusters on the scatter plot are in areas of short duration and short wait time or of long duration and long wait time. The outliers are dispersed between 60 and 120 seconds' duration and 25 to 45 minutes' wait time.

4. **(C)** Paragraph 2 of the passage says, "Greenhouse gases include water vapor (H_2O), carbon dioxide (CO_2), methane (CH_4), and ozone (O_3)."

5. **(D)** The passage says that water vapor is the most significant factor and that carbon dioxide is the second most significant factor in warming. This means that each of these is more significant than methane or ozone. The passage does not indicate whether methane is more or less significant than ozone.

6. **(C)** The passage says, "Research data suggest that the absorption capacity of water vapor in the atmosphere increases as atmospheric temperature increases." It also states, "As the average concentration of atmospheric carbon dioxide increases, it absorbs increasing amounts of heat, contributing to an increase in atmospheric temperature." This means that more concentrated carbon dioxide leads to warmer air, which increases the capacity of water vapor to absorb more heat.

7. A 3-point response to this question might include the following:
    Cause of interference: Warming could interfere with biosequestration of carbon in soil by melting permafrost and reducing the amount of carbon that the soil can hold.
    Potential effect: The effect would be an increase of carbon in the atmosphere.
    Relevant evidence:

    - Most carbon capture in soil happens in cold climates, where carbon is captured in permafrost.
    - Cold climates are in higher latitudes, near the poles.
    - Warming melts permafrost and returns captured carbon to the atmosphere.
    - A reduction in permafrost reduces the soil's ability to capture carbon and increases the amount of carbon returned to the atmosphere.

    Scoring Guide
    3-Point Response
    Provides an explanation of how warming could interfere with biosequestration and supports the explanation with at least two relevant pieces of specific evidence from the supporting material.

2-Point Response

Provides an explanation of how warming could interfere with biosequestration and supports the explanation with at least one relevant piece of specific evidence from the supporting material.

1-Point Response

Provides an explanation of how warming could interfere with biosequestration but provides inaccurate, irrelevant, or no specific supporting evidence.

0-Point Response

Provides no explanation or an inaccurate explanation of how warming could interfere with biosequestration or provides specific evidence without an identifiable explanation.

8. **(C)** The Punnett square shows that 2 out of 4 offspring will be homozygous (*GG*), which represents 50% of the offspring. Half of 20 is 10.

9. **(D)** The Punnett square shows that none of the offspring will have the genotype *gg*, which is the only genotype that would show the recessive trait. The *Gg* offspring have the recessive gene but will show the dominant trait.

10. **(C)** Crossing *Gg* and *Gg* produces 1 *GG* (homozygous) offspring, 2 *Gg* (heterozygous) offspring, and 1 *gg* (homozygous) offspring. So 2 out of 4 offspring are homozygous and 2 out of 4 are heterozygous.

11. **(D)** A phenotype refers to the outward manifestation of a trait. In order for a recessive trait to appear, the offspring's genotype must be homozygous recessive (*gg*). None of the pairings from the cross will produce an offspring with *gg* since the *GG* parent will never contribute a *g* allele to a pairing.

12. **(C)** A *Yg* × *Yg* cross produces 1 *YY* offspring (quadrant 1), 2 *Yg* offspring (quadrants 2 and 3), and 1 *gg* offspring (quadrant 4).

13. **(C)** The sea lampreys invaded the ecosystem and fed on the lake trout. This led to fewer lake trout ("devastated the lake trout fishery"). Since lake trout were predators of prey fish like the alewife, the drop in predator population meant fewer alewives were eaten by trout. This led to a sharp increase in the alewife population.

14. **(A)** All consumers depend on the producer population. A disease that kills plants and grass eliminates food for primary consumers, which leads to a reduced food supply all the way up the food chain. In other words, if there was no grass, the mice wouldn't have food. So the mice would die. If the mice died, the snakes wouldn't have food. So the snakes would die. If the snakes died, the eagles wouldn't have food. So the eagles would die.

15. **(D)** Although option D is definitely not good news for eagles, it primarily affects only the top of the existing chain. A reduction in the eagle population would lead to more snakes. This, in turn, would shrink the mouse population but not as much as the introduction of a new mouse predator in addition to the existing snakes. A new competitor for grass would also have a significant impact on mice, which would lead to fewer snakes and therefore fewer eagles. A weasel competing with snakes would reduce both snakes and eagles.

16. **(D)** Primary consumers eat plants, which means that primary consumers are herbivores. Secondary and tertiary consumers eat other consumers, which means that these consumers are carnivores. All green plants are producers because they make food from sunlight. Green plants don't eat animals or other plants.

17. **(D)** Plants blades (leaves) capture light from the sun and convert that light energy to chemical (food) energy by photosythesis.

18. **(B)** A top predator has no natural predator in any ecosystem and can use other predators as food.

19. **(D)** The passage says that scientists believe there is a relationship between the population densities but that the exact reasons are unclear. This means that the scientists lack sufficient evidence to draw a supportable conclusion. This is an inference.

20. **(B)** The total percent change from 5,200 to 82 per square meter is approximately 98%. This decrease occurred in 15 years. So the average decrease is approximately 6.5% per year ($98 \div 15 = 6.5$).

21. **(A)** Add the precipitation amounts and divide by 15. Then round 3.019 down to 3.

22. **(B)** After ordering the values from smallest to largest, the middle value (the 8th value) is 0.5.

23. **(A)** The most commonly appearing value is 0.

24. **(D)** The difference between the highest and lowest values is approximately 19,371, which is closest to 19,000.

25. **(B)** On days when the precipitation is high, the sunlight is low. On days when the precipitation is low, the sunlight is high.

26. **(B)** A kilojoule is 1,000 joules = 10^3 joules. The average daily sunlight on April 15 in joules $13,870.4 \times 1,000 = 13,870,400$. Converting to scientific notation moves the decimal point 7 places to the left, making the product 1.38704×10^7.

27. **(D)** Theories are expected to provide fundamental explanations for a wide range of different observable aspects of the natural world.

28. **(D)** Professor Doremus doesn't explicitly question the validity of any other scientist's experiments. He does list all of the tests he performed along with his results. He compares the behavior of the substance to that of gunpowder and other substances. He doesn't state that his opinion is fact. He just offers it as an opinion based on his observations.

29. **(A)** This statement is the professor's conclusion and is drawn from all the evidence that he carefully gathered. It is not a hypothesis, as he has concluded his testing. It is not an inference, as ample data are available. It is not a prediction because it is a statement based on experimental results.

30. **(A)** Professor Doremus describes a phenomenon that occurs in gun-cotton. He suggests that nitro-glycerin might have similar properties and behavior.

31. **(D)** Boron's atomic number is 5. This means it has a total of 5 electrons. Boron is in the second period, which means that it has two electron shells. This is because the first electron shell of any element can hold a maximum of two electrons, so an additional shell is needed to hold the other 3 electrons.

32. **(B)** Phosphorus' atomic number is 15, which means it has a total of 15 electrons, not 5. It has 5 valence electrons, which refers to the number of electrons in the outermost electron shell. Chlorine has 7 valence electrons. Both phosphorus and chlorine are in the third period, which means that they both have 3 electron shells.

33. **Greater, Lesser, Electron shells** Silicon is in the third period, which means it has 3 electron shells, while oxygen is in the second period, which means it has 2 electron shells. Silicon has 4 valence electrons, compared to sulphur's 6 valence electrons. Hydrogen and helium are in the first period, which means that they both have 1 electron shell. Hydrogen has 1 electron and 1 valence electron, while helium has 2 electrons and 2 valence electrons.

34. **Carbon** Carbon is in the second period, which means it has two electron shells, and it has 4 valence electrons.

35. **(A)** Nitrogen has the smallest atomic number of the elements shown in the table. Atomic weight is positively correlated to atomic number, so nitrogen has the smallest atomic weight as well.

ANSWER SHEET
Model Test 2

REASONING THROUGH LANGUAGE ARTS EXAM

1. (A) (B) (C) (D)
2. (A) (B) (C) (D)
3. _____
4. ___ , ___ , ___ , ___
5. Use lines below for your answer.
6. (A) (B) (C) (D)
7. (A) (B) (C) (D)
8. (A) (B) (C) (D)
9. (A) (B) (C) (D)
10. _____
11. _____
12. (A) (B) (C) (D)
13. (A) (B) (C) (D)
14. (A) (B) (C) (D)
15. Use lines below for your answer.
16. (A) (B) (C) (D)
17. (A) (B) (C) (D)

18. (A) (B) (C) (D)
19. _____
20. (A) (B) (C) (D)
21. (A) (B) (C) (D)
22. (A) (B) (C) (D)
23. (A) (B) (C) (D)
24. (A) (B) (C) (D)
25. (A) (B) (C) (D)
26. (A) (B) (C) (D)
27. (A) (B) (C) (D)
28. _____
29. (A) (B) (C)
30. (A) (B) (C)
31. (A) (B) (C)
32. (A) (B) (C)
33. (A) (B) (C)
34. (A) (B) (C)

35. (A) (B) (C)
36. (A) (B) (C)
37. (A) (B) (C)
38. (A) (B) (C)
39. (A) (B) (C) (D)
40. (A) (B) (C) (D)
41. ___ , ___ , ___ , ___ , ___
42. _____
_____
43. (A) (B) (C) (D)
44. (A) (B) (C) (D)
45. (A) (B) (C) (D)
46. (A) (B) (C) (D)
47. (A) (B) (C) (D)
48. (A) (B) (C) (D)
49. (A) (B) (C) (D)
50. (A) (B) (C) (D)

5. _____
_____
_____
_____
_____

15. _____
_____
_____
_____
_____

Extended Response

> **DIRECTIONS:** This practice exam contains both fiction and nonfiction passages, which you will need to analyze in order to answer the questions that follow. The first portion of the exam has 50 questions. You will have 2 hours to answer those questions. In the second portion of the exam, you will write an extended response to multiple stimuli. You will have 45 minutes to complete the second portion of the exam.

QUESTIONS 1 THROUGH 7 ARE BASED ON THE FOLLOWING PASSAGE:

Excerpt from *Pride and Prejudice*
by Jane Austen

1   It is a truth universally acknowledged, that a single man in possession of a good fortune, must be in want of a wife.

2   However little known the feelings or views of such a man may be on his first entering a neighborhood, this truth is so well fixed in the minds of the surrounding families, that he is considered the rightful property of some one or other of their daughters.

3   "My dear Mr. Bennet," said his lady to him one day, "have you heard that Netherfield Park is let at last?"

4   Mr. Bennet replied that he had not.

5   "But it is," returned she; "for Mrs. Long has just been here, and she told me all about it."

6   Mr. Bennet made no answer.

7   "Do you not want to know who has taken it?" cried his wife impatiently.

8   "*You* want to tell me, and I have no objection to hearing it."

9   This was invitation enough.

10   "Why, my dear, you must know, Mrs. Long says that Netherfield is taken by a young man of large fortune from the north of England; that he came down on Monday in a chaise and four to see the place, and was so much delighted with it, that he agreed with Mr. Morris immediately; that he is to take possession before Michaelmas, and some of his servants are to be in the house by the end of next week."

11   "What is his name?"

12   "Bingley."

13   "Is he married or single?"

14   "Oh! Single, my dear, to be sure! A single man of large fortune; four or five thousand a year. What a fine thing for our girls!"

15   "How so? How can it affect them?"

16   "My dear Mr. Bennet," replied his wife, "how can you be so tiresome! You must know that I am thinking of his marrying one of them."

17   "Is that his design in settling here?"

18   "Design! Nonsense, how can you talk so! But it is very likely that he *may* fall in love with one of them, and therefore you must visit him as soon as he comes."

19   "I see no occasion for that. You and the girls may go, or you may send them by themselves, which perhaps will be still better, for as you are as handsome as any of them, Mr. Bingley may like you the best of the party."

20   "My dear, you flatter me. I certainly *have* had my share of beauty, but I do not pretend to be anything extraordinary now. When a woman has five grown-up daughters, she ought to give over thinking of her own beauty."

21   "In such cases, a woman has not often much beauty to think of."

22   "But, my dear, you must indeed go and see Mr. Bingley when he comes into the neighborhood."

23   "It is more than I engage for, I assure you."

24   "But consider your daughters. Only think what an establishment it would be for one of them. Sir William and Lady Lucas are determined to go, merely on that account, for in general, you know, they visit no newcomers. Indeed you must go, for it will be impossible for *us* to visit him if you do not."

25   "You are over-scrupulous, surely. I dare say Mr. Bingley will be very glad to see you; and I will send a few lines by you to assure him of my hearty consent to his marrying whichever he chooses of the girls; though I must throw in a good word for my little Lizzy."

26   "I desire you will do no such thing. Lizzy is not a bit better than the others; and I am sure she is not half so handsome as Jane, nor half so good-humored as Lydia. But you are always giving *her* the preference."

27   "They have none of them much to recommend them," replied he; "they are all silly and ignorant like other girls; but Lizzy has something more of quickness than her sisters."

28   "Mr. Bennet, how *can* you abuse your own children in such a way? You take delight in vexing me. You have no compassion for my poor nerves."

29   "You mistake me, my dear. I have a high respect for your nerves. They are my old friends. I have heard you mention them with consideration these last twenty years at least."

30   "Ah, you do not know what I suffer."

31   "But I hope you will get over it, and live to see many young men of four thousand a year come into the neighborhood."

32   "It will be no use to us, if twenty such should come, since you will not visit them."

33   "Depend upon it, my dear, that when there are twenty, I will visit them all."

34   Mr. Bennet was so odd a mixture of quick parts, sarcastic humor, reserve, and caprice, that the experience of three-and-twenty years had been insufficient to make his wife understand his character. *Her* mind was less difficult to develop. She was a

woman of mean understanding, little information, and uncertain temper. When she was discontented, she fancied herself nervous. The business of her life was to get her daughters married; its solace was visiting and news.

Source: gutenberg.org

1. Which of the following best characterizes Mr. Bennet?
   (A) Odd
   (B) Complex
   (C) Funny
   (D) Bland

2. In the sentences "Mr. Bennet, how *can* you abuse your own children in such a way? You take delight in vexing me. You have no compassion for my poor nerves," what is the best definition of the word "vexing"?
   (A) Annoying
   (B) Calming
   (C) Soothing
   (D) Finding

3. The interaction in this conversation can best be described as _____.

4. Arrange the following events into chronological order, beginning with the first thing that happened.
   a. Mr. Bennet's character is described.
   b. Lydia and Lizzy are compared.
   c. It is suggested that Sir William and Lady Lucas are determined to go.
   d. We find out that Mr. Bingley is single.

5. During what time period does this story likely take place and how do you know? Cite specific examples from the passage in your short response.

6. How is Jane described?
   (A) She is better looking than Lizzy.
   (B) She is not as good looking as Lizzy.
   (C) She is as good looking as Lady Lucas.
   (D) She is unattractive.

7. What role does Mr. Bingley fill?
   (A) Father
   (B) Friend
   (C) Uncle
   (D) Suitor

Excerpt from *On the Duty of Civil Disobedience*
by Henry David Thoreau

1   I heartily accept the motto, "That government is best which governs least"; and I should like to see it acted up to more rapidly and systematically. Carried out, it finally amounts to this, which also I believe—"That government is best which governs not at all"; and when men are prepared for it, that will be the kind of government which they will have. Government is at best but an expedient; but most governments are usually, and all governments are sometimes, inexpedient. The objections which have been brought against a standing army, and they are many and weighty, and deserve to prevail, may also at last be brought against a standing government. The standing army is only an arm of the standing government. The government itself, which is only the mode which the people have chosen to execute their will, is equally liable to be abused and perverted before the people can act through it. Witness the present Mexican war, the work of comparatively a few individuals using the standing government as their tool; for in the outset, the people would not have consented to this measure.

2   This American government—what is it but a tradition, though a recent one, endeavoring to transmit itself unimpaired to posterity, but each instant losing some of its integrity? It has not the vitality and force of a single living man; for a single man can bend it to his will. It is a sort of wooden gun to the people themselves. But it is not the less necessary for this; for the people must have some complicated machinery or other, and hear its din, to satisfy that idea of government which they have. Governments show thus how successfully men can be imposed upon, even impose on themselves, for their own advantage. It is excellent, we must all allow. Yet this government never of itself furthered any enterprise, but by the alacrity with which it got out of its way. *It* does not keep the country free. *It* does not settle the West. *It* does not educate. The character inherent in the American people has done all that has been accomplished; and it would have done somewhat more, if the government had not sometimes got in its way. For government is an expedient, by which men would fain succeed in letting one another alone; and, as has been said, when it is most expedient, the governed are most let alone by it. Trade and commerce, if they were not made of India-rubber, would never manage to bounce over obstacles which legislators are continually putting in their way; and if one were to judge these men wholly by the effects of their actions and not partly by their intentions, they would deserve to be classed and punished with those mischievious persons who put obstructions on the railroads.

3   But, to speak practically and as a citizen, unlike those who call themselves no-government men, I ask for, not *at once* no government, but at once a better government. Let every man make known what kind of government would command his respect, and that will be one step toward obtaining it.

8. What is the central idea of the first paragraph?
    (A) Strong governments function best.
    (B) Small government is the best option.
    (C) A militant government stands strong.
    (D) War is sometimes necessary to fix a broken governmental system.

9. In the second paragraph, Thoreau writes, "Is it but a tradition, though a recent one, endeavoring to transmit itself unimpaired to posterity." What is the best definition of the word "posterity?"
    (A) Peers
    (B) Descendants
    (C) Parents
    (D) Colleagues

10. Based on the passage, one can conclude that the author _____ of the current government.

11. Based on the passage, Thoreau likely holds government officials in _____ regard.

12. To which of the following governments is Thoreau referring throughout the passage?
    (A) The American Government
    (B) The British Government
    (C) The Indian Government
    (D) The French Government

13. What reasonable expectation does the author have for the near future?
    (A) No government
    (B) A government like India
    (C) A better government
    (D) A totalitarian government

**Transcript of Jefferson's Secret Message to Congress
Regarding the Lewis & Clark Expedition (1803)**

Confidential

1   Gentlemen of the Senate, and of the House of Representatives:

2   As the continuance of the act for establishing trading houses with the Indian tribes will be under the consideration of the Legislature at its present session, I think it my duty to communicate the views which have guided me in the execution of that act, in order that you may decide on the policy of continuing it, in the present or any other form, or discontinue it altogether, if that shall, on the whole, seem most for the public good.

3   The Indian tribes residing within the limits of the United States, have, for a considerable time, been growing more and more uneasy at the constant diminution of the territory they occupy, although effected by their own voluntary sales: and the policy has long been gaining strength with them, of refusing absolutely all further sale, on any conditions; insomuch that, at this time, it hazards their friendship, and excites dangerous jealousies and perturbations in their minds to make any overture for the purchase of the smallest portions of their land. A very few tribes only are not yet obstinately in these dispositions. In order peaceably to counteract this policy of theirs, and to provide an extension of territory which the rapid increase of our numbers will call for, two measures are deemed expedient. First: to encourage them to abandon hunting, to apply to the raising stock, to agriculture and domestic manufacture, and thereby prove to themselves that less land and labor will maintain them in this, better than in their former mode of living. The extensive forests necessary in the hunting life, will then become useless, and they will see advantage in exchanging them for the means of improving their farms, and of increasing their domestic comforts. Secondly: to multiply trading houses among them, and place within their reach those things which will contribute more to their domestic comfort, than the possession of extensive, but uncultivated wilds. Experience and reflection will develop to them the wisdom of exchanging what they can spare and we want, for what we can spare and they want. In leading them to agriculture, to manufactures, and civilization; in bringing together their and our settlements, and in preparing them ultimately to participate in the benefits of our governments, I trust and believe we are acting for their greatest good. At these trading houses we have pursued the principles of the act of Congress, which directs that the commerce shall be carried on liberally, and requires only that the capital stock shall not be diminished. We consequently undersell private traders, foreign and domestic, drive them from the competition; and thus, with the good will of the Indians, rid ourselves of a description of men who are constantly endeavoring to excite in the Indian mind suspicions, fears, and irritations towards us. A letter now enclosed, shows the effect of our competition on the operations of the traders, while the Indians, perceiving the advantage of purchasing from us, are soliciting generally, our establishment of trading houses among them. In one quarter this is particularly interesting. The Legislature, reflecting on the late occurrences on the Mississippi,

must be sensible how desirable it is to possess a respectable breadth of country on that river, from our Southern limit to the Illinois at least; so that we may present as firm a front on that as on our Eastern border. We possess what is below the Yazoo, and can probably acquire a certain breadth from the Illinois and Wabash to the Ohio; but between the Ohio and Yazoo, the country all belongs to the Chickasaws, the most friendly tribe within our limits, but the most decided against the alienation of lands. The portion of their country most important for us is exactly that which they do not inhabit. Their settlements are not on the Mississippi, but in the interior country. They have lately shown a desire to become agricultural; and this leads to the desire of buying implements and comforts. In the strengthening and gratifying of these wants, I see the only prospect of planting on the Mississippi itself, the means of its own safety. Duty has required me to submit these views to the judgment of the Legislature; but as their disclosure might embarrass and defeat their effect, they are committed to the special confidence of the two Houses.

Source: ourdocuments.gov

14. According to the message, what did Jefferson want to do to the Native-American population?
    (A) Engage in war with them
    (B) Employ them
    (C) Relocate them
    (D) Assimilate them

15. Summarize Jefferson's message using specific details from the passage.

16. According to Jefferson, which of the following areas was most important?
    (A) The land inhabited by Native Americans
    (B) The land uninhabited by Native Americans
    (C) The west coast, which had large deposits of gold
    (D) The north, which had large deposits of oil

17. Based on the passage and on your knowledge of social studies, what was the most likely outcome of this message?
    (A) The Native Americans met the Americans with opposition
    (B) The Native Americans complied with the requests of the Americans
    (C) The Americans went to war with the Native Americans
    (D) The Native Americans relocated themselves

18. Jefferson states, "A letter now enclosed, shows the effect of our competition on the operations of the traders, while the Indians, perceiving the advantage of purchasing from us, are soliciting generally, our establishment of trading houses among them." What tactic was Jefferson using?
    (A) Appeasement
    (B) Deception
    (C) Entrepreneurship
    (D) Bribery

19. The implications of Jefferson's plan would likely affect the Native Americans in a
    _____ way.

20. In the second paragraph, Jefferson writes, "In order peaceably to counteract this policy of theirs." What is the best definition of the word "counteract"?
    (A) To set aside
    (B) To place on a counter
    (C) To work against
    (D) To further

QUESTIONS 21 THROUGH 28 ARE BASED ON THE FOLLOWING PASSAGE:

Excerpt from *A Dog's Tale*
by Mark Twain

1   My father was a St. Bernard, my mother was a collie, but I am a Presbyterian. This is what my mother told me, I do not know these nice distinctions myself. To me they are only fine large words meaning nothing. My mother had a fondness for such; she liked to say them, and see other dogs look surprised and envious, as wondering how she got so much education. But, indeed, it was not real education; it was only show: she got the words by listening in the dining-room and drawing-room when there was company, and by going with the children to Sunday-school and listening there; and whenever she heard a large word she said it over to herself many times, and so was able to keep it until there was a dogmatic gathering in the neighborhood, then she would get it off, and surprise and distress them all, from pocket-pup to mastiff, which rewarded her for all her trouble. If there was a stranger he was nearly sure to be suspicious, and when he got his breath again he would ask her what it meant. And she always told him. He was never expecting this but thought he would catch her; so when she told him, he was the one that looked ashamed, whereas he had thought it was going to be she. The others were always waiting for this, and glad of it and proud of her, for they knew what was going to happen, because they had had experience. When she told the meaning of a big word they were all so taken up with admiration that it never occurred to any dog to doubt if it was the right one; and that was natural, because, for one thing, she answered up so promptly that it seemed like a dictionary speaking, and for another thing, where could

they find out whether it was right or not? for she was the only cultivated dog there was. By and by, when I was older, she brought home the word Unintellectual, one time, and worked it pretty hard all the week at different gatherings, making much unhappiness and despondency; and it was at this time that I noticed that during that week she was asked for the meaning at eight different assemblages, and flashed out a fresh definition every time, which showed me that she had more presence of mind than culture, though I said nothing, of course. She had one word which she always kept on hand, and ready, like a life-preserver, a kind of emergency word to strap on when she was likely to get washed overboard in a sudden way—that was the word Synonymous. When she happened to fetch out a long word which had had its day weeks before and its prepared meanings gone to her dump-pile, if there was a stranger there of course it knocked him groggy for a couple of minutes, then he would come to, and by that time she would be away down wind on another tack, and not expecting anything; so when he'd hail and ask her to cash in, I (the only dog on the inside of her game) could see her canvas flicker a moment—but only just a moment—then it would belly out taut and full, and she would say, as calm as a summer's day, "It's synonymous with supererogation," or some godless long reptile of a word like that, and go placidly about and skim away on the next tack, perfectly comfortable, you know, and leave that stranger looking profane and embarrassed, and the initiated slatting the floor with their tails in unison and their faces transfigured with a holy joy.

Source: gutenberg.org

21. Twain wrote, "When I was older, she brought home the word Unintellectual, one time, and worked it pretty hard all the week at different gatherings, making much unhappiness and despondency." What is the best definition for the word "despondency"?
    (A) Depression
    (B) Boredom
    (C) Aspiration
    (D) Dedication

22. Which of the following best describes the style of writing?
    (A) Technical
    (B) Humorous
    (C) Serious
    (D) Scholarly

23. What literary element is employed in this passage?
    (A) Allusion
    (B) Onomatopoeia
    (C) Personification
    (D) Simile

24. From which part of the story is this passage likely excerpted?
    (A) The exposition
    (B) The climax
    (C) The falling action
    (D) The conclusion

25. How did the narrator's mother feel about education?
    (A) She avoided it.
    (B) She enjoyed it.
    (C) She believed it was unnecessary.
    (D) She believed it was just about big words, nothing else.

26. What is the passage mostly concerned with?
    (A) The care of dogs
    (B) Words
    (C) Presbyterians
    (D) Sunday school

27. The dogs in the passage perceive words like which of the following?
    (A) A toddler
    (B) A teenager
    (C) An adult
    (D) A senior citizen

28. The narrator's attitude toward words can be best described as _____.

QUESTIONS 29 THROUGH 33 ARE EMBEDDED IN THE FOLLOWING PASSAGE:

January 30, 2013
MEMORANDUM FOR THE HEADS OF EXECUTIVE DEPARTMENTS AND AGENCIES

SUBJECT: Coordination of Policies and Programs to Promote Gender Equality and Empower Women and Girls Globally

Promoting gender equality and advancing the status of all women and girls around the world remains one of the greatest unmet challenges of our time, and one that is vital to achieving our overall foreign policy objectives. Ensuring that women and girls, including those most marginalized, are able to participate fully in public life, are free from violence, and have equal access to education, economic opportunity, and health care increases broader economic prosperity, as well as political stability and security.

29. Choose one.
   (A) During my Administration. The United States has made promoting gender equality and advancing the status of women and girls a central element of our foreign policy, including by leading through example at home.
   (B) During my Administration, the United States has made promoting gender equality and advancing the status of women and girls a central element of our foreign policy, including by leading through example at home.
   (C) During my Administration, the united states has made promoting gender equality and advancing the status of women and girls a central element of our foreign policy, including by leading through example at home.

Executive Order 13506 of March 11, 2009, established the White House Council on Women and Girls to coordinate Federal policy on issues, both domestic and international, that particularly impact the lives of women and girls.

30. Choose one.
   (A) This commitments to promoting gender equality are also reflected in the National Security Strategy of the United States, the Presidential Policy Directive on Global Development, and the 2010 U.S. Quadrennial Diplomacy and Development Review.
   (B) Those commitment to promoting gender equality is also reflected in the National Security Strategy of the United States, the Presidential Policy Directive on Global Development, and the 2010 U.S. Quadrennial Diplomacy and Development Review.
   (C) This commitment to promoting gender equality is also reflected in the National Security Strategy of the United States, the Presidential Policy Directive on Global Development, and the 2010 U.S. Quadrennial Diplomacy and Development Review.

To elevate and integrate this strategic focus on the promotion of gender equality and the advancement of women and girls around the world, executive departments and agencies (agencies) have issued policy and operational guidance. For example, in March 2012, the Secretary of State issued *Policy Guidance on Promoting Gender Equality to Achieve our National Security and Foreign Policy Objectives*, and the United States Agency for International Development (USAID) Administrator released *Gender Equality and Female Empowerment Policy*.

31. Choose one.
    (A) The Millennium Challenge Corporation issues Gender Integration Guidelines in March 2011 to ensure its existing gender policy is fully realized.
    (B) The millennium challenge corporation issued Gender Integration Guidelines in March 2011 to ensure its existing gender policy is fully realized.
    (C) The Millennium Challenge Corporation issued Gender Integration Guidelines in March 2011 to ensure its existing gender policy is fully realized.

My Administration has also developed a National Action Plan on Women, Peace, and Security, created pursuant to Executive Order 13595 of December 19, 2011, to strengthen conflict resolution and peace processes through the inclusion of women, and a Strategy to Prevent and Respond to Gender-based Violence Globally, implemented pursuant to Executive Order 13623 of August 10, 2012, to combat gender-based violence around the world.

32. Choose one.
    (A) Improving interagency coordination and information sharing, and strengthening agency capacity and accountability. Will help ensure the effective implementation of these and other Government efforts to promote gender equality and advance the status of women and girls globally.
    (B) Improving interagency coordination and information sharing, and strengthening agency capacity and accountability will help ensure the effective implementation of these and other Government efforts to promote gender equality and advance the status of women and girls globally.
    (C) Improving interagency coordination and information sharing, and is strengthening agency capacity and accountability will help ensure the effective implementation of these and other Government efforts to promote gender equality and advance the status of women and girls globally.

By the authority vested in me as President by the Constitution and the laws of the United States of America, and in order to further strengthen the capacity of the Federal Government to ensure that U.S. diplomacy and foreign assistance promote gender equality and advance the status of women and girls worldwide, I hereby direct the following:

<u>Section 1. Strengthening Capacity and Coordination to Promote Gender Equality and Advance the Status of Women and Girls Internationally</u>. (a) Enhancing U.S. global leadership on gender equality requires dedicated resources, personnel with appropriate expertise in advancing the status of women and girls worldwide, and commitment from senior leadership, as exemplified by the critical and historic role played by the Office of Global Women's Issues

at the Department of State. To assure maximum coordination of efforts to promote gender equality and advance the status of women and girls, the Secretary of State (Secretary) shall designate a coordinator (Coordinator), who will normally also be appointed by the President as an Ambassador at Large (Ambassador at Large) subject to the advice and consent of the Senate. The Ambassador at Large, who shall report directly to the Secretary of State, shall lead the Office of Global Women's Issues at the Department of State and provide advice and assistance on issues related to promoting gender equality and advancing the status of women and girls internationally.

(b) The Ambassador at Large shall, to the extent the Secretary may direct and consistent with applicable law, provide guidance and coordination with respect to global policies and programs for women and girls, and shall lead efforts to promote an international focus on gender equality more broadly, including through diplomatic initiatives with other countries and partnerships and enhanced coordination with international and nongovernmental organizations and the private sector. To this end, the Ambassador at Large shall also, to the extent the Secretary may direct, assist in:

(i) implementing existing and developing new policies, strategies, and action plans for the promotion of gender equality and advancement of the status of women and girls internationally, and coordinating such actions with USAID and other agencies carrying out related international activities, as appropriate; and

(ii) coordinating such initiatives with other countries and international organizations, as well as with nongovernmental organizations.

(c) Recognizing the vital link between diplomacy and development, and the importance of gender equality as both a goal in itself and as a vital means to achieving the broader aims of U.S. development assistance, the Senior Coordinator for Gender Equality and Women's Empowerment at USAID shall provide guidance to the USAID Administrator in identifying, developing, and advancing key priorities for U.S. development assistance, coordinating, as appropriate, with other agencies.

(d) The Assistant to the President for National Security Affairs (or designee), in close collaboration with the Chair of the White House Council on Women and Girls (or designee) and the Ambassador at Large (or designee), shall chair an interagency working group to develop and coordinate Government-wide implementation of policies to promote gender equality and advance the status of women and girls internationally.

33. Choose one.
    (A) the Working Group shall consist of senior representatives from the Departments of State, the Treasury, Defense, Justice, Agriculture, Commerce, Labor, Health and Human Services, Education, and Homeland Security;
    (B) The Working Group shall consists of senior representatives from the Departments of State, the Treasury, Defense, Justice, Agriculture, Commerce, Labor, Health and Human Services, Education, and Homeland Security;
    (C) The Working Group shall consist of senior representatives from the Departments of State, the Treasury, Defense, Justice, Agriculture, Commerce, Labor, Health and Human Services, Education, and Homeland Security;

the Intelligence Community, as determined by the Director of National Intelligence; the United States Agency for International Development; the Millennium Challenge Corporation; the Peace Corps; the U.S. Mission to the United Nations; the Office of the United States Trade Representative; the Office of Management and Budget; the Office of the Vice President; the National Economic Council; and such other agencies and offices as the President may designate.

BARACK OBAMA
Source: whitehouse.gov

QUESTIONS 34 THROUGH 38 ARE EMBEDDED IN THE FOLLOWING PASSAGE:

34. Choose one.
    (A) Over the past couple of month, the Department circulated several "save the date" messages in this newsletter and email messages about regional trainings to be held throughout the state during June & July.
    (B) Over the past couple of months, the Department circulated several "save the date" messages in this newsletter and email messages about regional trainings to be held throughout the state during June & July.
    (C) Over the past couple of months, the Department circulated several "save the date" messages in this newsletter and email messages about regional trainings to be held throughout the state during june & july.

The feedback received from stakeholders and site eligibility partners was a strong preference for the ACA, COHBE and PEAK trainings to be presented in a coordinated and collaborative fashion in order to minimize the disruption to eligibility operations.

35. Choose one.
    (A) We also heard that these trainings should be held closer to october 1st for better retention.
    (B) We also heard that these trainings should be held closer to October 1st. For better retention.
    (C) We also heard that these trainings should be held closer to October 1st for better retention.

With that very clear feedback, those previously announced ACA regional trainings have been postponed until late summer/early fall.

It was also determined that a Non-MAGI training needed to be held, but separate from the combined ACA, COHBE and PEAK trainings. Non-MAGI includes Long-Term Care, Aged, Blind and Disabled, Medicare Savings Program, and Low- Income Subsidy Medical Assistance Programs. To minimize impact on daily operations, many of our partners requested that the Non-MAGI training be conducted using a "train the trainer" model so 1 or 2 people could attend the training, and then train their co-workers when they returned.

36. Choose one.
    (A) The Non-MAGI training will run 3 1⁄2 days Denver metro area from June 25–28.
    (B) The Non-MAGI training will run 3 1⁄2 days in the Denver metro area from June 25–28.
    (C) The Non-MAGI training. Will run 3 1⁄2 days in the Denver metro area from June 25–28.

The Department is finalizing details with the hotel and will announce that location soon.

37. Choose one.
    (A) This training is geared towards county and medical assistance site eligibility workers and/or trainers who are experienced in determining eligibility in CBMS for Medical Programs.
    (B) This training geared towards county and medical assistance site eligibility workers and/or trainers who are experienced in determining eligibility in CBMS for Medical Programs.
    (C) This training is geared towards county and medical assistance site eligibility workers and/or trainers whom are experienced in determining eligibility in CBMS for Medical Programs.

A maximum of 2 representatives from each eligibility site who know the CBMS system well; Have basic health and health policy background and can commit to spending 3 1⁄2 days in Denver; Has the ability to learn and retain the information and train their co-workers to ensure their respective site and its co-workers are ready for day 1 operations.

Meals and lodging will be paid by the Department.

38. Choose one.
    (A) Mileage will be reimbursed for those who travel to the training location exceeds 50 miles one-way.
    (B) Mileage will be reimbursed for those whose travel to the training location exceeds 50 miles one-way.
    (C) Mileage will be reimburse for those whose travel to the training location exceeds 50 miles one-way.

This will be considered a certified training with the expectation that these individuals will return to their site, train their staff and ensure colleagues are ready to implement the upcoming changes on October 1st.

Source: colorado.gov

Excerpt from *The Count of Monte Cristo*
by Alexandre Dumas

1   The sun had nearly reached the meridian, and his scorching rays fell full on the rocks, which seemed themselves sensible of the heat. Thousands of grasshoppers, hidden in the bushes, chirped with a monotonous and dull note; the leaves of the myrtle and olive trees waved and rustled in the wind. At every step that Edmond took he disturbed the lizards glittering with the hues of the emerald; afar off he saw the wild goats bounding from crag to crag. In a word, the island was inhabited, yet Edmond felt himself alone, guided by the hand of God. He felt an indescribable sensation somewhat akin to dread— that dread of the daylight which even in the desert makes us fear we are watched and observed. This feeling was so strong that at the moment when Edmond was about to begin his labor, he stopped, laid down his pickaxe, seized his gun, mounted to the summit of the highest rock, and from thence gazed round in every direction.

2   But it was not upon Corsica, the very houses of which he could distinguish; or on Sardinia; or on the Island of Elba, with its historical associations; or upon the almost imperceptible line that to the experienced eye of a sailor alone revealed the coast of Genoa the proud, and Leghorn the commercial, that he gazed. It was at the brigantine that had left in the morning, and the tartan that had just set sail, that Edmond fixed his eyes. The first was just disappearing in the straits of Bonifacio; the other, following an opposite direction, was about to round the Island of Corsica. This sight reassured him. He then looked at the objects near him. He saw that he was on the highest point of the island,—a statue on this vast pedestal of granite, nothing human appearing in sight, while the blue ocean beat against the base of the island, and covered it with a fringe of foam. Then he descended with cautious and slow step, for he dreaded lest an accident similar to that he had so adroitly feigned should happen in reality.

3   Dantes, as we have said, had traced the marks along the rocks, and he had noticed that they led to a small creek, which was hidden like the bath of some ancient nymph. This creek was sufficiently wide at its mouth, and deep in the centre, to admit of the entrance of a small vessel of the lugger class, which would be perfectly concealed from observation.

4   Then following the clew that, in the hands of the Abbe Faria, had been so skilfully used to guide him through the Daedalian labyrinth of probabilities, he thought that the Cardinal Spada, anxious not to be watched, had entered the creek, concealed his little barque, followed the line marked by the notches in the rock, and at the end of it had buried his treasure. It was this idea that had brought Dantes back to the circular rock. One thing only perplexed Edmond, and destroyed his theory. How could this rock, which weighed several tons, have been lifted to this spot, without the aid of many men? Suddenly an idea flashed across his mind. Instead of raising it, thought he, they have lowered it. And he sprang from the rock in order to inspect the base on which it had formerly stood. He soon perceived that a slope had been formed, and the rock had slid along this until it stopped at the spot it now occupied. A large stone had served as a wedge; flints and pebbles had been inserted around it, so as to conceal the orifice; this

species of masonry had been covered with earth, and grass and weeds had grown there, moss had clung to the stones, myrtle-bushes had taken root, and the old rock seemed fixed to the earth.

5   Dantes dug away the earth carefully, and detected, or fancied he detected, the ingenious artifice. He attacked this wall, cemented by the hand of time, with his pickaxe. After ten minutes' labor the wall gave way, and a hole large enough to insert the arm was opened. Dantes went and cut the strongest olive-tree he could find, stripped off its branches, inserted it in the hole, and used it as a lever. But the rock was too heavy, and too firmly wedged, to be moved by any one man, were he Hercules himself. Dantes saw that he must attack the wedge. But how? He cast his eyes around, and saw the horn full of powder which his friend Jacopo had left him. He smiled; the infernal invention would serve him for this purpose. With the aid of his pickaxe, Dantes, after the manner of a labor-saving pioneer, dug a mine between the upper rock and the one that supported it, filled it with powder, then made a match by rolling his handkerchief in saltpetre. He lighted it and retired. The explosion soon followed; the upper rock was lifted from its base by the terrific force of the powder; the lower one flew into pieces; thousands of insects escaped from the aperture Dantes had previously formed, and a huge snake, like the guardian demon of the treasure, rolled himself along in darkening coils, and disappeared.

Source: gutenberg.org

39. Identify the literary device used in the sentence, "The sun had nearly reached the meridian, and his scorching rays fell full on the rocks, which seemed themselves sensible of the heat."
    (A) Metaphor
    (B) Simile
    (C) Animation
    (D) Alliteration

40. What feeling is conveyed in the second paragraph?
    (A) Acceptance
    (B) Isolation
    (C) Camaraderie
    (D) Elation

41. Arrange the following events into chronological order, beginning with the first thing that happened.

    a. Dantes came upon a creek.
    b. Dantes saw wild goats.
    c. Dantes began digging.
    d. Dantes felt the dread of daylight.
    e. Dantes reached the highest point on the island.

42. The overall tone of the excerpt could be described as _____ or
    _____.

43. In the second paragraph, the speaker states, "Upon the almost imperceptible line that to the experienced eye of a sailor alone revealed the coast of Genoa the proud." What does this mean?

    (A) Most sailors are inexperienced.
    (B) The coast of Genoa is invisible to the naked eye.
    (C) Sailors can never see the coast.
    (D) The coast of Genoa is difficult to see.

44. Why does the author state that the lizards were "glittering with the hues of the emerald?"

    (A) To suggest that the speaker is hallucinating
    (B) To suggest that the lizards are as valuable as emeralds
    (C) To indicate that the lizards were encrusted were emeralds
    (D) To create an image of the lizard in the reader's mind

Excerpt from *2 B R 0 2 B*
by Kurt Vonnegut, Jr.

1   Everything was perfectly swell.

2   There were no prisons, no slums, no insane asylums, no cripples, no poverty, no wars.

3   All diseases were conquered. So was old age.

4   Death, barring accidents, was an adventure for volunteers.

5   The population of the United States was stabilized at forty-million souls.

6   One bright morning in the Chicago Lying-in Hospital, a man named Edward K. Wehling, Jr., waited for his wife to give birth. He was the only man waiting. Not many people were born a day any more.

7   Wehling was fifty-six, a mere stripling in a population whose average age was one hundred and twenty-nine.

8   X-rays had revealed that his wife was going to have triplets. The children would be his first.

9   Young Wehling was hunched in his chair, his head in his hand. He was so rumpled, so still and colorless as to be virtually invisible. His camouflage was perfect, since the waiting room had a disorderly and demoralized air, too. Chairs and ashtrays had been moved away from the walls. The floor was paved with spattered dropcloths.

10   The room was being redecorated. It was being redecorated as a memorial to a man who had volunteered to die.

11   A sardonic old man, about two hundred years old, sat on a stepladder, painting a mural he did not like. Back in the days when people aged visibly, his age would have been guessed at thirty-five or so. Aging had touched him that much before the cure for aging was found.

12   The mural he was working on depicted a very neat garden. Men and women in white, doctors and nurses, turned the soil, planted seedlings, sprayed bugs, spread fertilizer.

13   Men and women in purple uniforms pulled up weeds, cut down plants that were old and sickly, raked leaves, carried refuse to trash-burners.

14   Never, never, never—not even in medieval Holland nor old Japan—had a garden been more formal, been better tended. Every plant had all the loam, light, water, air and nourishment it could use.

15   A hospital orderly came down the corridor, singing under his breath a popular song:

> If you don't like my kisses, honey,
> Here's what I will do:
> I'll go see a girl in purple,
> Kiss this sad world toodle-oo.
> If you don't want my lovin',
> Why should I take up all this space?
> I'll get off this old planet,
> Let some sweet baby have my place.

16   The orderly looked in at the mural and the muralist. "Looks so real," he said, "I can practically imagine I'm standing in the middle of it."

17   "What makes you think you're not in it?" said the painter. He gave a satiric smile. "It's called 'The Happy Garden of Life,' you know."

18   "That's good of Dr. Hitz," said the orderly.

19   He was referring to one of the male figures in white, whose head was a portrait of Dr. Benjamin Hitz, the hospital's Chief Obstetrician. Hitz was a blindingly handsome man.

20   "Lot of faces still to fill in," said the orderly. He meant that the faces of many of the figures in the mural were still blank. All blanks were to be filled with portraits of important people on either the hospital staff or from the Chicago Office of the Federal Bureau of Termination.

21   "Must be nice to be able to make pictures that look like something," said the orderly.

22   The painter's face curdled with scorn. "You think I'm proud of this daub?" he said. "You think this is my idea of what life really looks like?"

23   "What's your idea of what life looks like?" said the orderly.

24   The painter gestured at a foul dropcloth. "There's a good picture of it," he said. "Frame that, and you'll have a picture a damn sight more honest than this one."

25   "You're a gloomy old duck, aren't you?" said the orderly.

26   "Is that a crime?" said the painter.

27   The orderly shrugged. "If you don't like it here, Grandpa—" he said, and he finished the thought with the trick telephone number that people who didn't want to live any more were supposed to call. The zero in the telephone number he pronounced "naught."

28   The number was: "2 B R 0 2 B."

29   It was the telephone number of an institution whose fanciful sobriquets included: "Automat," "Birdland," "Cannery," "Catbox," "De-louser," "Easy-go," "Good-by, Mother," "Happy Hooligan," "Kiss-me-quick," "Lucky Pierre," "Sheepdip," "Waring Blendor," "Weep-no-more" and "Why Worry?"

30   "To be or not to be" was the telephone number of the municipal gas chambers of the Federal Bureau of Termination.

Source: gutenberg.org

45. Which of the following quotes contrasts with the purpose of 2 B R 0 2 B?
    (A) "Everything was perfectly swell."
    (B) "The zero in the telephone number he pronounced 'naught.'"
    (C) "'You're a gloomy old duck, aren't you?' said the orderly."
    (D) "The room was being redecorated. It was being redecorated as a memorial to a man who had volunteered to die."

46. In the sentence, "His camouflage was perfect, since the waiting room had a disorderly and demoralized air, too," what is the best definition for the word "demoralized"?
    (A) Prompted
    (B) Disheartened
    (C) Encouraged
    (D) Engaged

47. The orderly was singing when he entered the room. What does this indicate about how he felt?
    (A) He wanted to be at a concert.
    (B) He didn't like the music they were playing.
    (C) He doesn't take his job seriously.
    (D) He is in a good mood.

48. Which of the following is not an effect of conquering old age and disease?
    (A) Things that were typically done earlier in life are being done later.
    (B) People choose when they die.
    (C) People no longer have any fear.
    (D) The average age has increased.

49. Grandpa's mood can be described as all EXCEPT:
    (A) Chipper
    (B) Gloomy
    (C) Depressed
    (D) Down

50. In the mural, "Men and women in purple uniforms pulled up weeds, cut down plants that were old and sickly, raked leaves, carried refuse to trash-burners." What is this mural a metaphor for?
    (A) The orderlies
    (B) The doctors
    (C) The Federal Bureau of Termination
    (D) Police officers

Extended Response

DIRECTIONS: Read and utilize the following passages to construct an extended response to the following prompt:

Are the central ideas in these two excerpts essentially the same or do they differ greatly? Cite specific information and examples to support your position and be sure to develop your answers fully. You have 45 minutes to complete this section.

Excerpt from *Second Treatise of Government*
by John Locke

Man being born, as has been proved, with a title to perfect freedom, and an [uncontrolled] enjoyment of all the rights and privileges of the law of nature, equally with any other man, or number of men in the world, hath by nature a power, not only to preserve his property, that is, his life, liberty and estate, against the injuries and attempts of other men; but to judge of, and punish the breaches of that law in others, as he is persuaded the offence deserves, even with death itself, in crimes where the heinousness of the fact, in his opinion, requires it. But because no political society can be, nor subsist, without having in itself the power to preserve the property, and in order thereunto, punish the offences of all those of that society; there, and there only is political society, where every one of the members hath quitted this natural power, resigned it up into the hands of the community in all cases that exclude him not from appealing for protection to the law established by it. And thus all private judgment of every particular member being excluded, the community comes to be umpire, by settled standing rules, indifferent, and the same to all parties; and by men having authority from the community, for the execution of those rules, decides all the differences that may happen between any members of that society concerning any matter of right; and punishes those offences which any member hath committed against the society, with such penalties as the law has established: whereby it is easy to discern, who are, and who are not, in political society together. Those who are united into one body, and have a common established law and judicature to appeal to, with authority to decide controversies between them, and punish offenders, are in civil society one with another: but those who have no such common appeal, I mean on earth, are still in the state of nature, each being, where there is no other, judge for himself, and executioner; which is, as I have before shewed it, the perfect state of nature.

And thus the commonwealth comes by a power to set down what punishment shall belong to the several transgressions which they think worthy of it, committed amongst the members of that society, (which is the power of making laws) as well as it has the power to punish any injury done unto any of its members, by any one that is not of it, (which is the power of war and peace;) and all this for the preservation of the property of all the members of that society, as far as is possible. But though every man who has entered into civil society, and is become a member of any commonwealth, has thereby quitted his power to punish offences, against the law of nature, in prosecution of his own private judgment, yet with the judgment of offences, which he has given up to the legislative in all cases, where he can appeal to the magistrate, he has given a right to the commonwealth to employ his force, for the execution of the judgments of the commonwealth, whenever he shall be called to it; which indeed are his own judgments, they being made by himself, or his representative. And herein we have the original of the legislative and executive power of civil society, which is to judge by standing laws, how far offences are to be punished, when committed within the commonwealth; and also to determine, by occasional judgments founded on the present circumstances of the fact, how far injuries from without are to be vindicated; and in both these to employ all the force of all the members, when there shall be need.

Source: gutenberg.org

The Bill of Rights (1791)

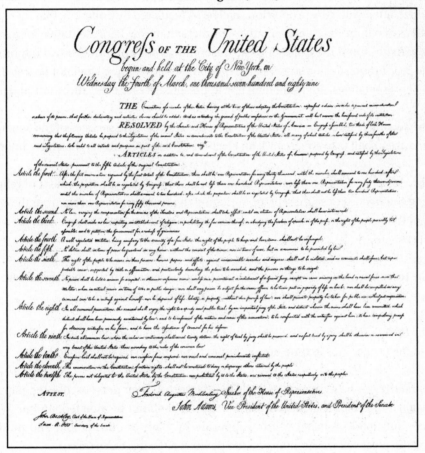

Congress of the United States begun and held at the City of New-York, on Wednesday the fourth of March, one thousand seven hundred and eighty nine.

THE Conventions of a number of the States, having at the time of their adopting the Constitution, expressed a desire, in order to prevent misconstruction or abuse of its powers, that further declaratory and restrictive clauses should be added: And as extending the ground of public confidence in the Government, will best ensure the beneficent ends of its institution.

RESOLVED by the Senate and House of Representatives of the United States of America, in Congress assembled, two thirds of both Houses concurring, that the following Articles be proposed to the Legislatures of the several States, as amendments to the Constitution of the United States, all, or any of which Articles, when ratified by three fourths of the said Legislatures, to be valid to all intents and purposes, as part of the said Constitution; viz.

ARTICLES in addition to, and Amendment of the Constitution of the United States of America, proposed by Congress, and ratified by the Legislatures of the several States, pursuant to the fifth Article of the original Constitution.

Article the first . . . After the first enumeration required by the first article of the Constitution, there shall be one Representative for every thirty thousand, until the number shall amount to one hundred, after which the proportion shall be so regulated by Congress, that there shall be not less than one hundred Representatives, nor less than one Representative for every forty thousand persons, until the number of Representatives shall amount to two hundred; after which the proportion shall be so regulated by Congress, that there shall not be less than two hundred Representatives, nor more than one Representative for every fifty thousand persons.

Article the second . . . No law, varying the compensation for the services of the Senators and Representatives, shall take effect, until an election of Representatives shall have intervened.

Article the third . . . Congress shall make no law respecting an establishment of religion, or prohibiting the free exercise thereof; or abridging the freedom of speech, or of the press; or the right of the people peaceably to assemble, and to petition the Government for a redress of grievances.

Article the fourth . . . A well regulated Militia, being necessary to the security of a free State, the right of the people to keep and bear Arms, shall not be infringed.

Article the fifth . . . No Soldier shall, in time of peace be quartered in any house, without the consent of the Owner, nor in time of war, but in a manner to be prescribed by law.

Article the sixth . . . The right of the people to be secure in their persons, houses, papers, and effects, against unreasonable searches and seizures, shall not be violated, and no Warrants shall issue, but upon probable cause, supported by Oath or affirmation, and particularly describing the place to be searched, and the persons or things to be seized.

Article the seventh . . . No person shall be held to answer for a capital, or otherwise infamous crime, unless on a presentment or indictment of a Grand Jury, except in cases arising in the land or naval forces, or in the Militia, when in actual service in time of War or public danger; nor shall any person be subject for the same offence to be twice put in jeopardy of life or limb; nor shall be compelled in any criminal case to be a witness against himself, nor be deprived of life, liberty, or property, without due process of law; nor shall private property be taken for public use, without just compensation.

Article the eighth . . . In all criminal prosecutions, the accused shall enjoy the right to a speedy and public trial, by an impartial jury of the State and district wherein the crime shall have been committed, which district shall have been previously ascertained by law, and to be informed of the nature and cause of the accusation; to be confronted with the witnesses against him; to have compulsory process for obtaining witnesses in his favor, and to have the Assistance of Counsel for his defence.

Article the ninth . . . In Suits at common law, where the value in controversy shall exceed twenty dollars, the right of trial by jury shall be preserved, and no fact tried by a jury, shall be otherwise re-examined in any Court of the United States, than according to the rules of the common law.

Article the tenth . . . Excessive bail shall not be required, nor excessive fines imposed, nor cruel and unusual punishments inflicted.

Article the eleventh . . . The enumeration in the Constitution, of certain rights, shall not be construed to deny or disparage others retained by the people.

Article the twelfth . . . The powers not delegated to the United States by the Constitution, nor prohibited by it to the States, are reserved to the States respectively, or to the people.

Source: ourdocuments.gov

REASONING THROUGH LANGUAGE ARTS EXAM

1. B
2. A
3. friendly, amicable, playful, or similar word
4. d, c, b, a
5. In the past. See Answer Explanations.
6. A
7. D
8. B
9. B
10. disapproves, or similar word
11. low, or similar word
12. A
13. C
14. D
15. Answers will vary.
16. B
17. A
18. B
19. negative, or similar word
20. C
21. A
22. B
23. C
24. A
25. B

26. B
27. A
28. indifferent, or similar word
29. B
30. C
31. C
32. B
33. C
34. B
35. C
36. B
37. A
38. B
39. C
40. B
41. b, d, e, a, c
42. ominous, dark, desolate, dreadful, or similar word
43. D
44. D
45. A
46. B
47. D
48. C
49. A
50. C

EXTENDED RESPONSE

Answers will vary.

REASONING THROUGH LANGUAGE ARTS EXAM
ANSWER EXPLANATIONS

1. **(B)** The passage indicates that Mr. Bennet was an odd mixture of various characteristics, indicating that he was complex. Option A is incorrect. Although the passage says he was an odd mixture, it doesn't say that he was odd. Option C is incorrect. The passage indicates that he had a sarcastic sense of humor, but it doesn't indicate that Mr. Bennet was funny. Option D is incorrect because no evidence suggests that he was bland.

2. **(A)** The context suggests that what Mr. Bennet was doing was unpleasant. Options B, C, and D are incorrect because no evidence supports these answers.

3. Acceptable answers would include "friendly," "amicable," "playful," or another related word.

4. **(d, c, b, a)** First we find out that Mr. Bingley is single. Then it is suggested that Sir William and Lady Lucas are determined to go. Next Lydia and Lizzy are compared. Finally, Mr. Bennet's character is described.

5. This passage may take place sometime in the past. This is suggested not only by the language used but also by the way in which the girls may be courted.

6. **(A)** The passage states that Lizzy "is not half so handsome as Jane," which means that Lizzy is not as good-looking as Jane. Therefore, Jane is better-looking than Lizzy.

7. **(D)** Mr. Bingley is seen as a potential husband. Options A, B, and C are incorrect because no evidence supports these answers.

8. **(B)** The first sentence states, "That government is best which governs least." Options A and C are incorrect because no evidence supports these answers. Option D is incorrect. Although war is mentioned, it is not the central idea of the first paragraph.

9. **(B)** Traditions are typically passed down, or transmitted, from generation to generation. Options A, C, and D are incorrect because no evidence supports these answers.

10. "Disapproves" or a similar word would be the best answer. The passage clearly indicates that Thoreau would prefer having no government at all.

11. "Low" or a similar word would be the best answer. Thoreau clearly does not approve of government officials and does not hold them in high regard.

12. **(A)** The American government is referenced in the second paragraph. Options B and D are incorrect because no evidence supports these answers. Option C is incorrect. India-rubber is referenced, not the Indian government.

13. **(C)** Although no government would be ideal, the author indicates that a better government is a reasonable goal. Options A, B, and D are incorrect.

14. **(D)** The second paragraph indicates ways in which the Native Americans can give up their traditional ways of life. Options A and C are incorrect because no evidence suggests that Jefferson wants to engage in war with or relocate Native Americans. Option B is incorrect. Although the passage talks about various professions, it does not indicate that Jefferson wants to employ any Native Americans.

15. Answers will vary.

16. **(B)** The passage indicates that the most valuable piece of land that belonged to the Chickasaws was the portion on which they did not live. Option A is incorrect; the passage states the opposite. Options C and D are incorrect because no evidence in the passage supports these answers.

17. **(A)** Although no evidence suggests that a large-scale war occurred, it is likely that the Native Americans were not going to change their way of life willingly. Options B, C, and D are incorrect because no evidence supports these answers.

18. **(B)** The passage clearly states that the Native Americans would be perceiving one thing (an economic benefit) while the U.S. Government would be gaining something else (the removal of those who were encouraging the Native Americans not to trust the government).

19. "Negative" or a similar word would be acceptable.

20. **(C)** To counteract something is to make it ineffective or to neutralize it. Remember, the prefix "counter-" means "opposing."

21. **(A)** Unhappiness and depression are related words. Options B, C, and D are incorrect because no evidence supports these answers.

22. **(B)** Writing from the perspective of the dog plus including several funny parts indicate a humorous style of writing. Options A, C, and D are incorrect.

23. **(C)** Personification is the act of giving human qualities to nonhuman things, which is what Twain has done in this passage. Option A is incorrect; the author is not alluding to anything. Option B is incorrect; onomatopoeia is when a word sounds like its meaning. Option D is incorrect because no comparison is being made.

24. **(A)** Characters are being introduced, indicating the passage is from the beginning of the story. Options B, C, and D are incorrect because no evidence supports these answers.

25. **(B)** The first passage indicates that his mother enjoyed learning things. Options A and C are incorrect because no evidence supports these answers. Option D is incorrect. This choice describes how the speaker felt.

26. **(B)** The passage centers around the learning of words. Option A is incorrect. Although the characters are dogs, the passage does not deal with the care of dogs. Options C and D are incorrect. Although Presbyterians and Sunday school are mentioned, these are not central ideas.

27. **(A)** Although the dogs understand some words, they do not have a complete vocabulary, just like a toddler. Options B, C, and D are incorrect. People of these ages would have well-developed vocabularies, unlike the dogs.

28. "Indifferent" or a related word would be the best answer.

29. **(B)** Option A starts with a sentence fragment. Option C does not capitalize "United States."

30. **(C)** Options A and B both have problems with agreement.

31. **(C)** Option A has problems with tense. Option B does not capitalize the corporation's full name.

32. **(B)** Option A begins with a sentence fragment. Option C incorrectly inserts the word "is" before "strengthening."

33. **(C)** Option A incorrectly begins with a lowercase letter. Option B has problems with agreement.

34. **(B)** In Option A, "couple" and "month" don't agree. Option C lacks capital letters for "June" and "July."

35. **(C)** Option A lacks a capital letter for "October." Option B ends with a sentence fragment.

36. **(B)** Option A is missing the words "in the" before "Denver." Option C begins with a sentence fragment.

37. **(A)** Option B is missing "is" before "geared." Option C incorrectly uses "whom."

38. **(B)** Option A incorrectly uses "who." Option C uses the wrong form of "reimburse."

39. **(C)** The author describes the sun as if it has been brought to life. Option A is incorrect. A metaphor compares objects without using the words "like" or "as." Option B is incorrect because a simile compares objects by using either "like" or "as." Option D is incorrect because alliteration is a repeating sound or letter at the beginning of several words.

40. **(B)** Other than the narrator, there is no human life on the island.

41. **(b, d, e, a, c)** First Dantes saw wild goats. Then Dantes felt the dread of daylight. Next Dantes reached the highest point on the island. Then Dantes came upon a creek. Finally, Dantes began digging.

42. "Ominous," "dark," "desolate," or "dreadful" would all be acceptable answers in either space.

43. **(D)** "Imperceptible" means "difficult to see."

44. **(D)** This is a vivid description that enables the reader to picture the lizard.

45. **(A)** 2 B R 0 2 B is the number people call when they are ready to die. This contrasts with "Everything was perfectly swell."

46. **(B)** "Disorderly" is a negative word. So the context of "demoralized" indicates that "disheartened," the only negative word in the list of answer choices, is the best answer.

47. **(D)** Singing to oneself is often an indication of being in a good mood.

48. **(C)** No evidence suggests that people had stopped feeling fear.

49. **(A)** The passage states that Grandpa is "gloomy." No evidence suggests that he's chipper.

50. (C) The Federal Bureau of Termination is responsible for cutting down people that are old and sickly. The plants in the mural symbolize people.

Extended Response

Answers will vary.

When reviewing your extended response, make sure you have asked yourself the following questions:

- Have I responded to the prompt?
- Do I have enough evidence?
- Do my ideas follow a logical order?
- Are there any misspellings?
- Have I confused any homonyms?
- Have I used proper punctuation, including periods, commas, semicolons, apostrophes, and so forth?
- Do I need to break up any run-on sentences?
- Can I combine any strings of short, choppy sentences?

The prompt asks if the central ideas in the two excerpts are essentially the same or if they differ greatly. Make sure that you have chosen a side; either they differ or do not. Make sure you have clearly articulated your position in the introductory part of the response. Following your introduction, you will need to state the central idea of each passage and cite specific evidence. Then compare and contrast. Finally, restate your position in the conclusion.

MATHEMATICAL REASONING EXAM

1. (A) (B) (C) (D)
2. (A) (B) (C) (D)
3. (A) (B) (C) (D)
4. (A) (B) (C) (D)
5. (A) (B) (C) (D)
6. (A) (B) (C) (D)
7. (A) (B) (C) (D)
8. (A) (B) (C) (D)
9. (A) (B) (C) (D)
10. (A) (B) (C) (D)
11. (A) (B) (C) (D)
12. (A) (B) (C) (D)
13. _____
14. (A) (B) (C) (D)
15. (A) (B) (C) (D)
16. (A) (B) (C) (D)
17. (A) (B) (C) (D)

18. (A) (B) (C) (D)
19. (A) (B) (C) (D)
20. (A) (B) (C) (D)
21. (A) (B) (C) (D)
22. (A) (B) (C) (D)
23. (A) (B) (C) (D)
24. (A) (B) (C) (D)
25. (A) (B) (C) (D)
26. (A) (B) (C) (D)
27. (A) (B) (C) (D)
28. (A) (B) (C) (D)
29. (A) (B) (C) (D)
30. (A) (B) (C) (D)
31. (A) _____
    (B) _____
    (C) _____
32. (A) (B) (C) (D)

33. (A) (B) (C) (D)
34. (A) (B) (C) (D)
35. (A) (B) (C) (D)
36. (A) (B) (C) (D)
37. _____
_____
_____
_____
38. (A) (B) (C) (D)
39. _____
40. _____
_____
_____
_____
41. (A) (B) (C) (D)
42. (A) (B) (C) (D)

DIRECTIONS: This practice exam contains mathematical problems. You will have 90 minutes to complete the 42 questions in this portion of the exam. You may use a calculator during this test.

1. Using the information from the chart, estimate to the nearest hundred the total number of tickets sold at the movie theater.

Movie	Number of Tickets Sold
Movie A	625
Movie B	875
Movie C	233
Movie D	452

   (A) 2,500
   (B) 3,230
   (C) 2,200
   (D) 2,000

2. Jane bought a bag of mixed nuts and separated the different types of nuts. The bag contained 10 pecans, 30 peanuts, 8 pistachios, and 12 cashews. What fraction of the nuts were peanuts? (Reduce to lowest terms.)

   (A) $\frac{6}{11}$

   (B) $\frac{1}{2}$

   (C) $\frac{3}{4}$

   (D) $\frac{1}{8}$

3. A brick manufacturing company bills their client $1,750 for 15,000 bricks. To the nearest cent, what is the cost per brick?
   (A) $1.10
   (B) $0.22
   (C) $0.10
   (D) $0.12

4. What is the value of y in the following equation?

$$\frac{1}{2} = \frac{y}{24}$$

   (A) 36
   (B) 12
   (C) 24
   (D) 32

5. In a tire manufacturing company, defective tires account for 1 out of 25 tires produced. At that rate, how many of the next 2,750 tires will be defective?
   (A) 25
   (B) 110
   (C) 75
   (D) 155

6. A drawing of a sculpture has a scale of 1-inch equals 100 feet. On the drawing, one edge of the sculpture is drawn 3.45 inches long. What is the actual length of the sculpture's edge?
   (A) 345 feet long
   (B) 145 feet long
   (C) 248 feet long
   (D) 355 feet long

QUESTIONS 7 THROUGH 9 REFER TO THE FOLLOWING INFORMATION:

After giving a survey asking people which color is their favorite, the survey team lost some of their data. They know that 380 people chose blue, 297 chose pink, and 428 chose black. Some people chose red, but the number of people who made this choice was lost. Based on a partial analysis before the data were lost, blue represented 32% of the total and pink represented 25% of the total. Percentages for the other two colors were not calculated.

7. What is the total number of people who participated in the survey?
   (A) 354
   (B) 1,188
   (C) 1,207
   (D) 1,364

8. If the number of people who chose red was $\frac{1}{4}$ the number of those who chose blue, what percentage of the total number of people chose red? Round to the nearest whole percent.
   (A) 5%
   (B) 10%
   (C) 8%
   (D) 7%

9. What percentage of people chose either blue or black as their favorite color? Round to nearest whole percent.
   (A) 64%
   (B) 68%
   (C) 57%
   (D) 77%

---

10. Henry has a bag of candy with four pieces left: an orange one, a yellow one, a clear one, and a green one. His favorite flavor is orange, so he wants to save it for last. He reaches into the bag without looking and takes one out, but it's the orange one. So he puts the orange one back in. He takes one out again without looking, but it is once again the orange one. So he again returns it to the bag. He takes one out a third time without looking, and it is yet again the orange one. Henry decides that this is a sign he should eat the orange one now, and he eats it. What was the probability of Henry drawing the orange piece of candy on three consecutive draws?
    (A) 1 out of 64
    (B) 1 out of 12
    (C) 1 out of 4
    (D) 1 out of 3

11. Main Street runs east to west straight across town. Roosevelt Avenue intersects Main Street from the north. The angle at the northwest corner of Roosevelt and Main measures 30 degrees. What is the measure of the angle at the northeast corner?
    (A) 90 degrees
    (B) 60 degrees
    (C) 20 degrees
    (D) 150 degrees

12. For a line whose equation is $y = 3x - 2$, the y-coordinate of a point on the line is 4. What is the value of the corresponding x-coordinate?
    (A) −2
    (B) 2
    (C) 5
    (D) 4

13. Solve the following equation for x: $2x - 7 = 11$.

QUESTIONS 14 THROUGH 18 REFER TO THE FOLLOWING NUMBER LINE:

```
         A              B  C         D         E              F
  +--+---●--+--+--+--+--●--●--+--+---●--+--+--●--+--+--+--●--+--+--+
 -10 -9 -8 -7 -6 -5 -4 -3 -2 -1  0  1  2  3  4  5  6  7  8  9 10
```

14. What is the value of *A* minus *F*?
    (A) −15
    (B) −9
    (C) 0
    (D) 15

15. The product of *D* and *F* will be which of the following?
    (A) Negative
    (B) Positive
    (C) Odd
    (D) None of the above

16. Which of the following is true?
    (A) $|A| > |F|$
    (B) $|B| < |E|$
    (C) $-|E| < B$
    (D) $|C| = |D|$

17. I(*C* + *E*)I is equal to which of the following?
    (A) *B*
    (B) *C*
    (C) *D*
    (D) *E*

18. Which of the following inequalities contains all points less than or equal to *E* but greater than *C*?
    (A) $-3 < x \leq 3$
    (B) $-3 > x \geq 3$
    (C) $-3 > x \leq 3$
    (D) $-3 < x \geq 3$

QUESTIONS 19 THROUGH 21 REFER TO THE FOLLOWING INFORMATION:

$$x = q^8 \quad y = q^4 \quad z = q^{-3}$$

19. Which of the following expresses $\left(\dfrac{x}{y}\right)^3$ in terms of q?

    (A) q^{36}

    (B) q^{24}

    (C) q^{12}

    (D) q^6

20. Which of the following is equivalent to yz?

    (A) q

    (B) x

    (C) y

    (D) z

21. Which of the following is equivalent to xyz?

    (A) q^{-96}

    (B) q^{-36}

    (C) q^9

    (D) q^{96}

---

22. If $x^2 = 9$, which of these is true?

    (A) $x > 3$

    (B) $x < 3$

    (C) $|x| > 3$

    (D) $|x| = 3$

23. $x^2 - 2xy + y^2$ is equivalent to which of the following?

    (A) $(x + y)(x + y)$

    (B) $(x + y)(x - y)$

    (C) $(x - y)(x - y)$

    (D) $(x + x)(y + y)$

QUESTIONS 24 AND 25 REFER TO THE FOLLOWING INFORMATION:

The vertex is the point in the center of a parabolic function.
Function $z(x)$ is a parabolic function with its vertex at $(0, 0)$.

24. What are the coordinates of the vertex of $z(x) - 4$?
    (A) $(0, 4)$
    (B) $(4, 0)$
    (C) $(-4, 0)$
    (D) $(0, -4)$

25. What are the coordinates of the vertex of $z(x + 3)$?
    (A) $(0, 3)$
    (B) $(3, 0)$
    (C) $(-3, 0)$
    (D) $(0, -3)$

_____

QUESTIONS 26 AND 27 REFER TO THE FOLLOWING INFORMATION:

$$f(x) = 6x + 2$$

26. What is the value of $f(x)$ when x is 3?
    (A) 11
    (B) 18
    (C) 20
    (D) 30

27. What is the value of $3f(x)$ when x is 6?
    (A) 38
    (B) 76
    (C) 104
    (D) 114

_____

28. Jim and Rosalie go to the state fair. For lunch, they order 2 hamburgers at $5.49 each, 1 garden salad for $3.35, 2 root beers at $3.50 each, and 1 hot fudge sundae for $4.00. Approximately what did they pay, before tax, for their lunch?
    (A) $60
    (B) $43
    (C) $25
    (D) $14

29. Which is the correct way of writing "b is less than or equal to 5 but greater than –2"?

    (A) $-5 \geq b > -2$

    (B) $-2 < b \leq 5$

    (C) $-5 \leq b < -2$

    (D) $-5 \geq b < -2$

30. After graduating from college, Jessica's starting salary was $28,000 per year before taxes, not including benefits. What was her pretax monthly income?

    (A) $2,333.33

    (B) $2,800.00

    (C) $3,333.33

    (D) $4,000.00

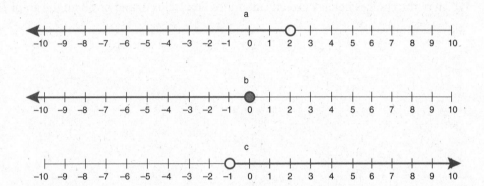

31. Based on the above number lines, choose the correct answer from the options below to fill in the blanks in the following sentences.

    (A) "y is less than 2" is represented by number line _____.

    (B) "y is less than or equal to 0" is represented by number line _____.

    (C) "–1 is less than y" is represented by number line _____.

32. $\sqrt{48}$ is between which numbers?

    (A) 9 and 10

    (B) 8 and 9

    (C) 7 and 8

    (D) 6 and 7

33. $\sqrt{84}$ is between which numbers?

    (A) 9 and 10

    (B) 8 and 9

    (C) 7 and 8

    (D) 6 and 7

34. $\sqrt{162}$ is equivalent to which of the following?

(A) $2\sqrt{86}$

(B) $9\sqrt{2}$

(C) $86\sqrt{2}$

(D) 86

35. Which of the following is equivalent to $(3.2 \times 10^{14}) \times (1.8 \times 10^{-9})$?

(A) 5.76×10^{5}

(B) 5.76×10^{19}

(C) 5.76×10^{-5}

(D) 5.76

36. Which of the choices below correctly identifies box 1, box 2, and box 3 on the graph?

TIP

On the computerized test, a question like this would have you drag and drop the answers onto the graph.

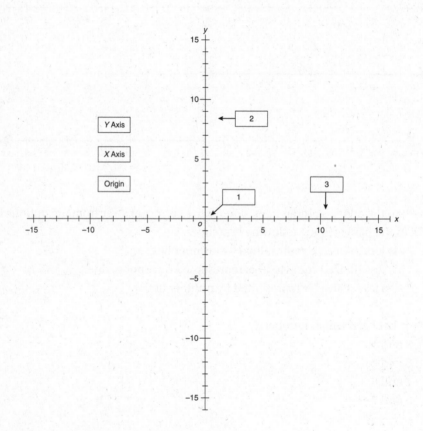

(A) Box 1: y-axis; box 2: x-axis; box 3: origin

(B) Box 1: origin; box 2: y-axis; box 3: x-axis

(C) Box 1: origin; box 2: x-axis; box 3: y-axis

(D) Box 1: x-axis; box 2: origin; box 3: y-axis

37. Select the word or phrase in each bracket that correctly completes each sentence.

Two lines that never intersect are called [parallel, perpendicular, congruent], and their slopes are [consecutive, equal, negative reciprocals]. Two lines that intersect to form 90-degree angles are called [parallel, perpendicular, congruent], and their slopes are [consecutive, equal, negative reciprocals].

TIP

On the computerized test, questions like 37 (and 40) would have you choose from among a column of drop-down choices.

38. Identify the three numbers in the following table that have equivalent values.

One-half	0.375	30%	0.5
One-third	50%	Three-quarters	0.125

(A) One-third, 0.375, 30%
(B) Three-quarters, 0.375, 50%
(C) One-half, 0.125, 30%
(D) One-half, 0.5, 50%

TIP

On the computerized test, questions like 38 (and 41) would have you click on the boxes in the table to indicate your choices. This would be a hot-spot question.

39. Write the decimal equivalent of $\frac{5}{8}$.

40. Select the word or phrase in each bracket that correctly completes each sentence.

Lines that are parallel to the [x-axis, y-axis, the origin] have slopes that are [undefined, positive, negative]. Lines that are parallel to the [x-axis, y-axis, the origin] have slopes that are [negative, positive, equal to zero].

41. Identify which numbers in the following table are perfect squares.

10	12	16	24
36	49	54	67

(A) 16, 24, 36
(B) 12, 49, 54
(C) 16, 36, 49
(D) 10, 54, 67

42. All of the following are true about the number 2 EXCEPT:
(A) It is even.
(B) It is prime.
(C) It is a factor of 21.
(D) It is a factor of 42.

MATHEMATICAL REASONING EXAM

1. C
2. B
3. D
4. B
5. B
6. A
7. B
8. C
9. B
10. A
11. D
12. B
13. 9
14. A
15. D
16. A
17. C
18. A
19. C
20. A
21. C
22. D
23. C

24. D
25. C
26. C
27. D
28. C
29. B
30. A
31. (A) *a*
    (B) *b*
    (C) *c*
32. D
33. A
34. B
35. A
36. B
37. parallel, equal, perpendicular, negative reciprocals
38. D
39. 0.625
40. *y*-axis, undefined, *x*-axis, equal to zero
41. C
42. C

MATHEMATICAL REASONING EXAM ANSWER EXPLANATIONS

1. **(C)** First add the numbers together. Then round to the nearest hundred. Since 8 is greater than 8, round up the hundreds digit: $625 + 875 + 233 + 452 = 2,185$.

2. **(B)** Find the total number of nuts ($10 + 30 + 8 + 12 = 60$). Divide the number of peanuts by the total number of nuts: $\frac{30}{60} = \frac{1}{2}$.

3. **(D)** First find the average cost per brick ($\$1,750 \div \$15,000 = \$0.116$). Round to the nearest cent. Since 6 is greater than 5, round up to $\$0.12$.

4. **(B)** First multiply both sides by 24 to isolate y. This results in $y = 12$. You could also cross multiply to get the same result.

5. **(B)** Set up the problem as a proportion: $\frac{1}{25} = \frac{x}{2,750}$. Then cross multiply: $25x = 2,750$. Divide both sides by 25 to isolate x: $x = 110$.

6. **(A)** Set up the problem as a proportion: $\frac{100}{1} = \frac{y}{3.45}$. Then cross multiply: $y = 345$.

7. **(B)** Set up a proportion using either the data for blue or the data for pink:
$\frac{380}{b} = \frac{32}{100}$ or $\frac{297}{p} = \frac{25}{100}$.
Then cross multiply: $32b = (100)(380)$ or $25p = (100)(297)$. Solve for either p or b. The result is the same: 1,188.

8. **(C)** Since the number of people who chose red is $\frac{1}{4}$ of the people who chose blue, simply divide the percentage of people who chose blue by 4: $32\% \div 4 = 8\%$.

9. **(B)** First calculate the percentage of participants who chose black: $428 \div 1,188 = 0.3602$. Convert to a percent: $0.3602 \times 100 = 36.02\%$. Round to the nearest whole percent: $36.02\% = 36\%$. Add the percentages for black and blue: $36\% + 32\% = 68\%$.

10. **(A)** The probability of Henry drawing the orange piece is 1 out of 4 each time. The probability of consecutive events with replacement is the product of the individual probabilities: $\frac{1}{4} \times \frac{1}{4} \times \frac{1}{4} = \frac{1}{64}$

11. **(D)** Main Street is straight, which means it represents 180 degrees. Roosevelt Avenue intersects to form two supplementary angles, the northwest and northeast corners. One of the angles is 30 degrees. Subtract to find the measure of the other angle: 180 degrees – 30 degrees = 150 degrees.

12. **(B)** Plug $y = 4$ into the equation to solve for x: $4 = 3x - 2 \rightarrow 6 = 3x \rightarrow x = 2$.

13. **9** First add 7 to both sides: $2x - 7 + 7 = 11 + 7$. This will result in $2x = 18$. Then divide both sides by 2 to isolate x: $x = 9$.

14. **(A)** When subtracting a positive from negative, change the operation to addition and change the sign of the second number: $-8 - 7 = -8 + -7 = -15$.

15. **(D)** When multiplying by 0, the product is always 0: $(7)(0) = 0$. Zero is neutral (neither positive nor negative) and is even.

16. **(A)** Absolute value makes everything within the vertical bars positive: $8 > 7$.

17. **(C)** First add $C + E$: $-3 + 3 = 0$. The absolute value of 0 is 0.

18. **(A)** Reorder the three terms from smallest (-3) to largest (3), with x in the middle. All symbols point to the left. The inequality includes 3 but does not include -3.

19. **(C)** Remember the rules for exponents with the same base. Multiplication means add the exponents together. Division means subtract one exponent from the other. Power to a power means multiply the exponents: $8 - 4 = 4$ and $4 \times 3 = 12$. The new exponent is 12.

20. **(A)** Remember the rules for exponents with the same base. Multiplication means add the exponents together. Division means subtract one exponent from the other. Power to a power means multiply the exponents: $4 + (-3) = 1$. The result is q^1, which is equal to q.

21. **(C)** Remember the rules for exponents with the same base. Multiplication means add the exponents together. Division means subtract one exponent from the other. Power to a power means multiply the exponents: $8 + 4 + (-3) = 9$. The new exponent is 9.

22. **(D)** Subtracting 9 from both sides makes this a quadratic equation. Factoring the equation gives $(x + 3)(x - 3) = 0$, which makes the roots 3 and -3. The signs of the roots are opposite the signs in the binomials. Absolute value makes everything positive.

23. **(C)** This is a very common polynomial. Memorize the factored and FOIL forms of this polynomial.

24. **(D)** Subtracting outside the parentheses moves the curve down. Subtracting 4 from the original function to form the new function moves the original function down by 4. Moving either up or down involves the y-coordinate.

25. **(C)** Adding inside the parentheses moves the curve to the left. (Careful, it's the opposite of what you expect.) Adding 3 to the original function to form the new function moves the original function to the left by 3. Moving either left or right involves the x-coordinate.

26. **(C)** Plug $x = 3$ into the function: $6(3) + 2 = 18 + 2 = 20$.

27. **(D)** Plug $x = 6$ into the function: $3[6(6) + 2] = 3(36 + 2) = 3(38) = 114$.

28. **(C)** Add up the prices for each part of the meal and round to the nearest dollar: $\$5.49 + \$5.49 + \$3.35 + \$3.50 + \$3.50 + \$4.00 = \$25.33$. Since 3 is less than 5, round down: $\$25$.

29. **(B)** Reorder the three terms from smallest (-2) to largest (5), with x in the middle. All symbols point to the left. The inequality includes 5 but does not include -2.

30. **(A)** Divide by 12 to find the monthly amount: $\$28,000 \div 12 = \$2,333.33$.

31. **(*a*, *b*, *c*)** Number line a shows y is less than 2. Number line b shows y is less than or equal to 0. Number line c shows -1 is less than y.

32. **(D)** 48 is between 36 and 49. Since $(6)(6) = 36$ and $(7)(7) = 49$, $\sqrt{48}$ must be between 6 and 7.

33. **(A)** 84 is between 81 and 100. Since $(9)(9) = 81$ and $(10)(10) = 100$, $\sqrt{84}$ must be between 9 and 10.

34. **(B)** Since $162 = (2)(81)$ and $\sqrt{81} = 9$, $\sqrt{162} = 9\sqrt{2}$.

35. **(A)** Multiply the decimal numbers as normal: $3.2 \times 1.8 = 5.76$. Since this is multiplication, add the exponents of 10: $(14 - 9 = 5)$. Scientific notation conventionally puts the decimal point next to the units digit, which is where it currently is: 5.76×10^5.

36. **(B)** The origin is the point $(0, 0)$. The y-axis is vertical. The x-axis is horizontal.

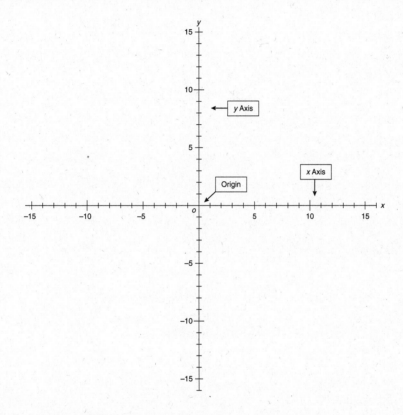

37. **Parallel, Equal, Perpendicular, Negative reciprocals** Parallel lines never meet and have the same slope. Perpendicular lines form a 90-degree angle, and their slopes are negative reciprocals of each other.

38. **(D)** One-half, 0.5, and 50% are all equivalent.

39. **0.625** Divide the numerator by the denominator to find the decimal equivalent: $5 \div 8 = 0.625$.

40. **y-axis, Undefined, x-axis, Equal to zero** Remember that all lines parallel to the y-axis, including the y-axis itself, have an undefined slope. Remember that all lines parallel to the x-axis, including the x-axis itself, have a slope equal to zero.

41. **(C)** 16, 36, and 49 are all perfect squares: $(4)(4) = 16$; $(6)(6) = 36$; and $(7)(7) = 49$.

42. **(C)** The number 21 cannot be evenly divided by 2, so 2 is not a factor of 21.

ANSWER SHEET
Model Test 2

SOCIAL STUDIES EXAM

1. Ⓐ Ⓑ Ⓒ Ⓓ
2. Ⓐ Ⓑ Ⓒ Ⓓ
3. Ⓐ Ⓑ Ⓒ Ⓓ
4. Ⓐ Ⓑ Ⓒ Ⓓ
5. Ⓐ Ⓑ Ⓒ Ⓓ
6. Ⓐ Ⓑ Ⓒ Ⓓ
7. Ⓐ Ⓑ Ⓒ Ⓓ
8. Ⓐ Ⓑ Ⓒ Ⓓ
9. Ⓐ Ⓑ Ⓒ Ⓓ
10. Ⓐ Ⓑ Ⓒ Ⓓ
11. _____

12. Ⓐ Ⓑ Ⓒ Ⓓ
13. Ⓐ Ⓑ Ⓒ Ⓓ
14. Ⓐ Ⓑ Ⓒ Ⓓ
15. _____
16. Ⓐ Ⓑ Ⓒ Ⓓ
17. Ⓐ Ⓑ Ⓒ Ⓓ
18. ___ , ___ , ___ , ___ , ___
19. Ⓐ Ⓑ Ⓒ Ⓓ
20. Ⓐ Ⓑ Ⓒ Ⓓ
21. Ⓐ Ⓑ Ⓒ Ⓓ
22. _____

23. Ⓐ Ⓑ Ⓒ Ⓓ
24. Ⓐ Ⓑ Ⓒ Ⓓ
25. Ⓐ Ⓑ Ⓒ Ⓓ
26. Ⓐ Ⓑ Ⓒ Ⓓ
27. Ⓐ Ⓑ Ⓒ Ⓓ
28. Ⓐ Ⓑ Ⓒ Ⓓ
29. Ⓐ Ⓑ Ⓒ Ⓓ
30. Ⓐ Ⓑ Ⓒ Ⓓ
31. Ⓐ Ⓑ Ⓒ Ⓓ
32. Ⓐ Ⓑ Ⓒ Ⓓ
33. _____

Extended Response

DIRECTIONS: This practice exam contains passages, maps, charts, graphs, and political cartoons, which you will need to analyze in order to answer the questions that follow. The first portion of the exam has 33 questions. You will have 45 minutes to answer those questions. In the second portion of the exam, you will write an extended response to multiple stimuli. You will have 25 minutes to complete the second portion of the exam.

QUESTIONS 1 THROUGH 3 ARE BASED ON THE FOLLOWING PASSAGE:

National Industrial Recovery Act (1933)

The National Industrial Recovery Act (NIRA) was enacted by Congress in June 1933 and was one of the measures by which President Franklin D. Roosevelt sought to assist the nation's economic recovery during the Great Depression. The passage of NIRA ushered in a unique experiment in U.S. economic history—the NIRA sanctioned, supported, and in some cases, enforced an alliance of industries. Antitrust laws were suspended, and companies were required to write industry-wide "codes of fair competition" that effectively fixed prices and wages, established production quotas, and imposed restrictions on entry of other companies into the alliances. The act further called for industrial self-regulation and declared that codes of fair competition—for the protection of consumers, competitors, and employers—were to be drafted for the various industries of the country and were to be subject to public hearings. Employees were given the right to organize and bargain collectively and could not be required, as a condition of employment, to join or refrain from joining a labor organization.

The National Recovery Administration (NRA), created by a separate executive order, was put into operation soon after the final approval of the act. President Roosevelt appointed Hugh S. Johnson as administrator for industrial recovery. The administration was empowered to make voluntary agreements dealing with hours of work, rates of pay, and the fixing of prices. Until March 1934, the NRA was engaged chiefly in drawing up these industrial codes for all industries to adopt. More than 500 codes of fair practice were adopted for the various industries. Patriotic appeals were made to the public, and firms were asked to display the Blue Eagle, an emblem signifying NRA participation.

From the beginning, the NRA reflected divergent goals and suffered from widespread criticism. The businessmen who dominated the code drafting wanted guaranteed profits and insisted on security for their renewed investment and future production. Congressional critics insisted on continued open pricing and saw the NRA codes as a necessary means of making it fair and orderly. A few intellectuals wanted an even more extensive government role in the form of central economic planning. Finally, unhappy labor union representatives fought with little success for the collective bargaining promised by the NIRA. The codes did little to help recovery, and by raising prices, they actually made the economic situation worse.

Though under criticism from all sides, the NRA did not last long enough to fully implement its policies. In May 1935, in the case of *Schechter Poultry Corp. v. United States*, the U.S. Supreme Court invalidated the compulsory-code system on the grounds that the NIRA improperly delegated legislative powers to the executive and that the provisions of the poultry code (in the case in question) did not constitute a regulation of interstate commerce. In a lengthy and unanimous opinion, the Court seemed to demonstrate a complete unwillingness to endorse Roosevelt's argument that the national crisis of economic depression demanded radical innovation. Later, FDR would use this Court opinion as evidence that the Court was living in the "horse and buggy" era and needed to be reformed.

Source: ourdocuments.gov

1. What was the main purpose of the National Industrial Recovery Act (NIRA)?
    (A) Ensure guaranteed return profits for businessmen who participated in drafting the code
    (B) Creation of laws for all industries to adopt
    (C) Suspension of certain laws and regulations to give businesses an advantage over consumers
    (D) Temporary suspension of select laws and regulations pertaining to industry in order to assist in economic recovery

2. In what way are the National Recovery Administration (NRA) and the National Industrial Recovery Act (NIRA) similar?
    (A) Both enacted laws.
    (B) Both dealt with recovery from an industrial standpoint.
    (C) The NRA wrote industrial codes, while NIRA required companies to write "codes of fair competition."
    (D) NIRA was enacted in 1993, and NRA was enacted in 1934.

3. What kind of reception did the National Recovery Administration (NRA) get from the American public?
    (A) Overall acceptance
    (B) Ambivalence
    (C) Sharp criticism
    (D) Mixed reaction

4. During which war was this poster likely issued?

   (A) U.S. Civil War

   (B) Spanish-American War

   (C) World War I

   (D) World War II

QUESTIONS 5 THROUGH 7 ARE BASED ON THE FOLLOWING PASSAGE:

The 14th Amendment

Section 1.

All persons born or naturalized in the United States, and subject to the jurisdiction thereof, are citizens of the United States and of the State wherein they reside. No State shall make or enforce any law which shall abridge the privileges or immunities of citizens of the United States; nor shall any State deprive any person of life, liberty, or property, without due process of law; nor deny to any person within its jurisdiction the equal protection of the laws.

Section 2.

Representatives shall be apportioned among the several States according to their respective numbers, counting the whole number of persons in each State, excluding Indians not taxed. But when the right to vote at any election for the choice of electors for President and Vice-President of the United States, Representatives in Congress, the Executive and Judicial officers of a State, or the members of the Legislature thereof, is denied to any of the male inhabitants of such State, being twenty-one years of age, and citizens of the United States, or in any way abridged, except for participation in rebellion, or other crime, the basis of representation therein shall be reduced in the proportion which the number of such male citizens shall bear to the whole number of male citizens twenty-one years of age in such State.

Section 3.

No person shall be a Senator or Representative in Congress, or elector of President and Vice-President, or hold any office, civil or military, under the United States, or under any State, who, having previously taken an oath, as a member of Congress, or as an officer of the United States, or as a member of any State legislature, or as an executive or judicial officer of any State, to support the Constitution of the United States, shall have engaged in insurrection or rebellion against the same, or given aid or comfort to the enemies thereof. But Congress may by a vote of two-thirds of each House, remove such disability.

Section 4.

The validity of the public debt of the United States, authorized by law, including debts incurred for payment of pensions and bounties for services in suppressing insurrection or rebellion, shall not be questioned. But neither the United States nor any State shall assume or pay any debt or obligation incurred in aid of insurrection or rebellion against the United States, or any claim for the loss or emancipation of any slave; but all such debts, obligations and claims shall be held illegal and void.

Section 5.

The Congress shall have the power to enforce, by appropriate legislation, the provisions of this article.

Source: ourdocuments.gov

5. What is the central idea of Section 2?
   (A) All males age 21 and older have the right to vote.
   (B) Men who commit crimes may not vote.
   (C) Men 18 and older may vote.
   (D) With a few exceptions, males 21 and older have the right to vote.

6. Which group most likely benefited most from this amendment?
   (A) White men
   (B) Men under 21 years of age
   (C) White women
   (D) African-American men

7. What is the central idea of Section 3?
   (A) Certain criminals may not be elected to office.
   (B) There are many types of elected officials.
   (C) A certain process must be followed to become an elected official.
   (D) Congress may enforce this legislation.

Components of Metro Area Change 2010–2011

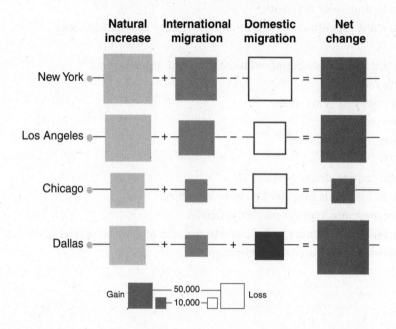

Population change can be attributed to several different processes: natural increase (births minus deaths), net domestic migration, and international migration. Many of the largest metro areas lost population through domestic migration. In most cases, those losses were balanced by gains from natural increase and net international migration.

8. According to the chart, which city saw the greatest gain from domestic migration?
   (A) New York
   (B) Los Angeles
   (C) Chicago
   (D) Dallas

9. According to the chart, which city saw the greatest increase in its immigrant population?
   (A) New York
   (B) Los Angeles
   (C) Chicago
   (D) Dallas

Dawes Act (1887)

Federal Indian policy during the period from 1870 to 1900 marked a departure from earlier policies that were dominated by removal, treaties, reservations, and even war. The new policy focused specifically on breaking up reservations by granting land allotments to individual Native Americans. Very sincere individuals reasoned that if a person adopted white clothing and ways, and was responsible for his own farm, he would gradually drop his Indian-ness and be assimilated into the population. It would then no longer be necessary for the government to oversee Indian welfare in the paternalistic way it had been obligated to do, or provide meager annuities that seemed to keep the Indian in a subservient and poverty-stricken position.

On February 8, 1887, Congress passed the Dawes Act, named for its author, Senator Henry Dawes of Massachusetts. Also known as the General Allotment Act, the law allowed for the President to break up reservation land, which was held in common by the members of a tribe, into small allotments to be parceled out to individuals. Thus, Native Americans registering on a tribal "roll" were granted allotments of reservation land. "To each head of a family, one-quarter of a section; To each single person over eighteen years of age, one-eighth of a section; To each orphan child under eighteen years of age, one-eighth of a section; and To each other single person under eighteen years now living, or who may be born prior to the date of the order of the President directing an allotment of the lands embraced in any reservation, one-sixteenth of a section. . . ."

Section 8 of the act specified groups that were to be exempt from the law. It stated that "the provisions of this act shall not extend to the territory occupied by the Cherokees, Creeks, Choctaws, Chickasaws, Seminoles, and Osage, Miamies and Peorias, and Sacs and Foxes, in the Indian Territory, nor to any of the reservations of the Seneca Nation of New York Indians in the State of New York, nor to that strip of territory in the State of Nebraska adjoining the Sioux Nation on the south."

Subsequent events, however, extended the act's provisions to these groups as well. In 1893 President Grover Cleveland appointed the Dawes Commission to negotiate with the Cherokees, Creeks, Choctaws, Chickasaws, and Seminoles, who were known as the Five Civilized Tribes. As a result of these negotiations, several acts were passed that allotted a share of common property to members of the Five Civilized Tribes in exchange for abolishing their tribal governments and recognizing state and Federal laws. In order to receive the allotted land, members were to enroll with the Bureau of Indian Affairs. Once enrolled, the individual's name went on the "Dawes rolls." This process assisted the BIA and the Secretary of the Interior in determining the eligibility of individual members for land distribution.

The purpose of the Dawes Act and the subsequent acts that extended its initial provisions was purportedly to protect Indian property rights, particularly during the land rushes of the 1890s, but in many instances the results were vastly different. The land allotted to the Indians included desert or near-desert lands unsuitable for farming. In addition, the techniques of self-sufficient farming were much different from their tribal way of life. Many Indians did not want to take up agriculture, and those who did want to farm could not afford the tools, animals, seed, and other supplies necessary to get started. There were also problems with inheritance. Often young children inherited allotments that they could not farm because they had been sent away to boarding schools. Multiple heirs also caused a problem; when several people inherited an allotment, the size of the holdings became too small for efficient farming.

Source: ourdocuments.gov

10. Which of the following groups of Native Americans were unaffected by the Dawes Act?
    (A) Cherokees
    (B) Seminoles
    (C) Creek
    (D) None of the above

11. Initially, the Dawes Act was meant to protect Native Americans' _____ rights; however, the results were quite different.

12. The Dawes Act provided for which of the following?
    (A) Breaking up reservation lands into parcels
    (B) Sale of reservation lands to the United States Government
    (C) Relocation of reservation lands
    (D) Conversion of reservation lands to purely agricultural lands

---

QUESTIONS 13 THROUGH 15 ARE BASED ON THE FOLLOWING PASSAGE:

Treaty of Guadalupe Hidalgo (1848)

The Treaty of Guadalupe Hidalgo, which brought an official end to the Mexican-American War (1846–48), was signed on February 2, 1848, at Guadalupe Hidalgo, a city to which the Mexican government had fled with the advance of U.S. forces.

With the defeat of its army and the fall of the capital, Mexico City, in September 1847, the Mexican government surrendered to the United States and entered into negotiations to end the war. The peace talks were negotiated by Nicholas Trist, chief clerk of the State Department, who had accompanied General Winfield Scott as a diplomat and President Polk's representative. Trist and General Scott, after two previous unsuccessful attempts to negotiate a treaty with President Santa Anna, determined that the only way to deal with Mexico was as a conquered enemy. Nicholas Trist negotiated with a special commission representing the collapsed government led by Don Bernardo Couto, Don Miguel Atristain, and Don Luis Gonzaga Cuevas.

President Polk had recalled Trist under the belief that negotiations would be carried out with a Mexican delegation in Washington. In the six weeks it took to deliver Polk's message, Trist had received word that the Mexican government had named its special commission to negotiate. Trist determined that Washington did not understand the situation in Mexico and negotiated the peace treaty in defiance of the President.

In a December 4, 1847, letter to his wife, he wrote, "Knowing it to be the very last chance and impressed with the dreadful consequences to our country which cannot fail to attend the loss of that chance, I decided today at noon to attempt to make a treaty; the decision is altogether my own."

Source: ourdocuments.gov

13. According to the passage, the Treaty of Guadalupe Hidalgo was signed:
    (A) Against the President's wishes
    (B) As a result of years of planning
    (C) By President Polk
    (D) By the Secretary of State

14. Which of the following led to the end of the Mexican-American War?
    (A) The fall of Mexico City
    (B) Treaty negotiations
    (C) General Winfield Scott's diplomatic efforts
    (D) The removal of Don Miguel Atristain from office

15. According to the passage, Trist _____ negotiated the treaty, despite the message.

QUESTIONS 16 AND 17 ARE BASED ON THE FOLLOWING CHART:

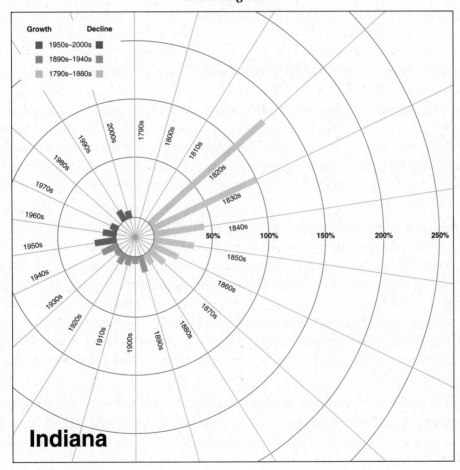

Blooming States

Population growth in successive decades has followed different trends for states across the country. While many states had early, substantial growth in percentage terms most of that population growth was quite small in numeric terms. In contrast, states with high percentage growth in more recent decades also gained very large numbers of people.

16. According to the chart, during which decade did Indiana's population grow by about 45%?
    (A) 1820s
    (B) 1830s
    (C) 1840s
    (D) 1850s

17. According to the chart, during which decade did Indiana's population grow the most?
    (A) 1820s
    (B) 1830s
    (C) 1840s
    (D) 1850s

QUESTIONS 18 THROUGH 20 ARE BASED ON THE FOLLOWING PASSAGE:

19th Amendment to the U.S. Constitution: Women's Right to Vote (1920)

The 19th amendment guarantees all American women the right to vote. Achieving this milestone required a lengthy and difficult struggle; victory took decades of agitation and protest. Beginning in the mid-19th century, several generations of woman suffrage supporters lectured, wrote, marched, lobbied, and practiced civil disobedience to achieve what many Americans considered a radical change of the Constitution. Few early supporters lived to see final victory in 1920.

Beginning in the 1800s, women organized, petitioned, and picketed to win the right to vote, but it took them decades to accomplish their purpose. Between 1878, when the amendment was first introduced in Congress, and August 18, 1920, when it was ratified, champions of voting rights for women worked tirelessly, but strategies for achieving their goal varied. Some pursued a strategy of passing suffrage acts in each state—nine western states adopted woman suffrage legislation by 1912. Others challenged male-only voting laws in the courts. Militant suffragists used tactics such as parades, silent vigils, and hunger strikes. Often supporters met fierce resistance. Opponents heckled, jailed, and sometimes physically abused them.

By 1916, almost all of the major suffrage organizations were united behind the goal of a constitutional amendment. When New York adopted woman suffrage in 1917 and President Wilson changed his position to support an amendment in 1918, the political balance began to shift.

On May 21, 1919, the House of Representatives passed the amendment, and 2 weeks later, the Senate followed. When Tennessee became the 36th state to ratify the amendment on August 18, 1920, the amendment passed its final hurdle of obtaining the agreement of three-fourths of the states. Secretary of State Bainbridge Colby certified the ratification on August 26, 1920, changing the face of the American electorate forever.

Source: ourdocuments.gov

18. Arrange the following events into chronological order, beginning with the first thing that happened.
    a. Most suffrage organizations backed the goal of an amendment.
    b. Women began to organize and picket for the right to vote.
    c. The Senate passed the amendment.
    d. The House passed the amendment.
    e. Nine western states had women's suffrage.

19. Which of the following is most closely aligned with women's actions in the early 1800s?
    (A) Freedom of association
    (B) Freedom of press
    (C) Freedom of religion
    (D) The right to bear arms

20. Based on the passage, how many states were there in 1920?
    (A) 52
    (B) 50
    (C) 48
    (D) 46

21. What is this 1940s political cartoon suggesting about Henry Wallace?

    (A) Wallace is a flip-flopper.

    (B) Times change and so must politicians.

    (C) Wallace believes war is an illusion.

    (D) Wallace believed that change was not possible.

MODEL TEST 2

Federal Judiciary Act (1789)

The founders of the new nation believed that the establishment of a national judiciary was one of their most important tasks. Yet Article III of the Constitution of the United States, the provision that deals with the judiciary branch of government, is markedly smaller than Articles I and II, which created the legislative and executive branches.

The generality of Article III of the Constitution raised questions that Congress had to address in the Judiciary Act of 1789. These questions had no easy answers, and the solutions to them were achieved politically. The First Congress decided that it could regulate the jurisdiction of all Federal courts, and in the Judiciary Act of 1789, Congress established with great particularity a limited jurisdiction for the district and circuit courts, gave the Supreme Court the original jurisdiction provided for in the Constitution, and granted the Court appellate jurisdiction in cases from the Federal circuit courts and from the state courts where those courts rulings had rejected Federal claims. The decision to grant Federal courts a jurisdiction more restrictive than that allowed by the Constitution represented a recognition by the Congress that the people of the United States would not find a full-blown Federal court system palatable at that time.

For nearly all of the next century the judicial system remained essentially as established by the Judiciary Act of 1789. Only after the country had expanded across a continent and had been torn apart by civil war were major changes made. A separate tier of appellate circuit courts created in 1891 removed the burden of circuit riding from the shoulders of the Supreme Court justices, but otherwise left intact the judicial structure.

With minor adjustments, it is the same system we have today. Congress has continued to build on the interpretation of the drafters of the first judiciary act in exercising a discretionary power to expand or restrict Federal court jurisdiction. While opinions as to what constitutes the proper balance of Federal and state concerns vary no less today than they did two centuries ago, the fact that today's Federal court system closely resembles the one created in 1789 suggests that the First Congress performed its job admirably.

Source: ourdocuments.gov

22. The Federal Judiciary Act (or any similar legislation) was needed because the Constitution had to be _____.

23. Which of the articles of the Constitution discuss the judicial branch?
    (A) Article I
    (B) Article II
    (C) Article III
    (D) None of the above

24. According to the first Congress, what authority did it have?
    (A) Authority to regulate circuit courts
    (B) Authority to regulate civil courts
    (C) Authority to regulate federal courts
    (D) Authority to regulate state courts

QUESTIONS 25 AND 26 ARE BASED ON THE FOLLOWING MAP AND PASSAGE:

Urbanized Cities

25 Largest Urbanized Areas

Comparisons of urbanized and metropolitan areas, in spatial extent as well as in population terms, show differences between the 25 largest urbanized areas in the country. Urbanized area extents are defined by the Census Bureau based on population density and other characteristics of the built environment. Metro areas consist of one or more whole counties, and include the counties containing the core urban area (a Census Bureau defined urbanized area), as well as any adjacent counties that have a high degree of social and economic integration (as measured by commuting to work) with the urban core. Metro areas may contain both urban and rural territory and population.

25. According to the map, which of the following cities is in the top 25% of the largest urbanized areas?
    (A) San Antonio
    (B) Portland
    (C) San Diego
    (D) Miami

26. Of the following cities, which is the least urbanized?
    (A) Denver
    (B) Miami
    (C) San Antonio
    (D) Baltimore

Coastline County Populations

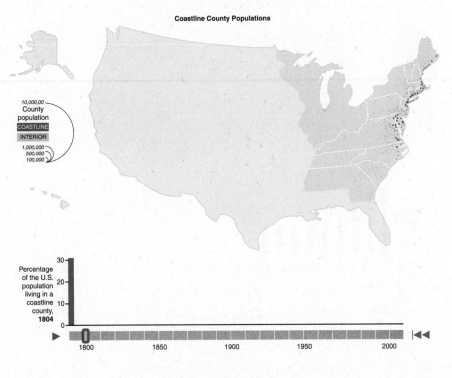

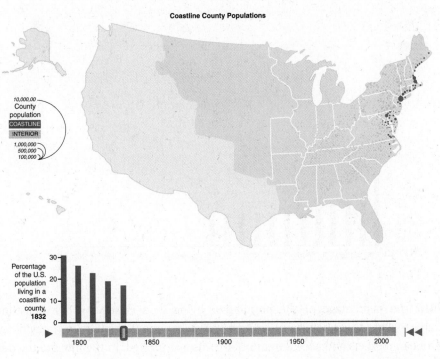

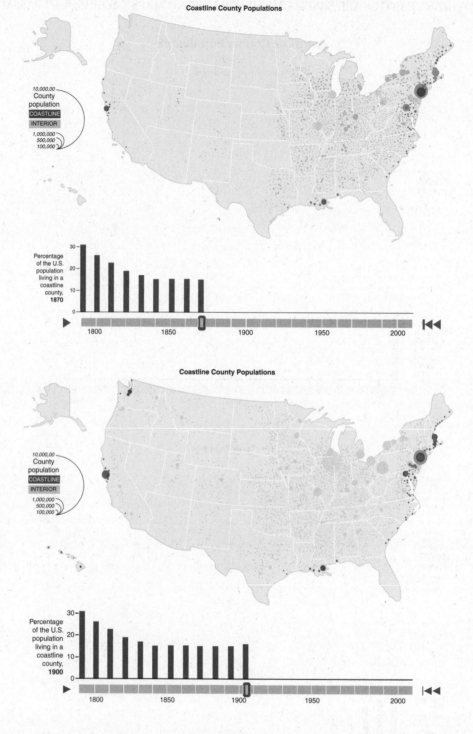

In 2010, the percentage of the population living in a county with a coastline was comparable to what it was between 1790 and 1800, when the U.S. still relied heavily on trade with European markets and access to interior lands was limited. In the intervening decades, the percentage of the population living in coastline counties decreased to an all-time low in 1880. A steady increase led to a recent peak in 1990, and a slight decrease since then has led to 2010's level.

27. According to the previous maps and graphs, which of the following years recorded the greatest percentage of coastal population?
   (A) 1800
   (B) 1832
   (C) 1870
   (D) 1900

28. Which of the following is the correct interpretation of the data in the chart?
   (A) The percentage of people living on the coast initially declined but eventually increased.
   (B) The percentage of people living on the coast initially increased but eventually decreased.
   (C) The percentage of people living on the coast has increased over time.
   (D) The percentage of people living on the coast has decreased over time.

QUESTIONS 29 AND 30 ARE BASED ON THE FOLLOWING TABLE:

Unemployment Rate 2003–2013

Year	Jan	Feb	Mar	Apr	May	Jun	Jul	Aug	Sep	Oct	Nov	Dec	Annual
2003	5.8	5.9	5.9	6.0	6.1	6.3	6.2	6.1	6.1	6.0	5.8	5.7	6.0
2004	5.7	5.6	5.8	5.6	5.6	5.6	5.5	5.4	5.4	5.5	5.4	5.4	5.5
2005	5.3	5.4	5.2	5.2	5.1	5.0	5.0	4.9	5.0	5.0	5.0	4.9	5.1
2006	4.7	4.8	4.7	4.7	4.6	4.6	4.7	4.7	4.5	4.4	4.5	4.4	4.6
2007	4.6	4.5	4.4	4.5	4.4	4.6	4.7	4.6	4.7	4.7	4.7	5.0	4.6
2008	5.0	4.9	5.1	5.0	5.4	5.6	5.8	6.1	6.1	6.5	6.8	7.3	5.8
2009	7.8	8.3	8.7	9.0	9.4	9.5	9.5	9.6	9.8	10.0	9.9	9.9	9.3
2010	9.8	9.8	9.9	9.9	9.6	9.4	9.5	9.5	9.5	9.5	9.8	9.3	9.6
2011	9.1	9.0	8.9	9.0	9.0	9.1	9.0	9.0	9.0	8.9	8.6	8.5	8.9
2012	8.3	8.3	8.2	8.1	8.2	8.2	8.2	8.1	7.8	7.9	7.8	7.8	8.1
2013	7.9												

29. According to the data in the table, what was the average unemployment rate for 2006, 2007, and 2008?
   (A) 5.0
   (B) 4.6
   (C) 9.2
   (D) 15.0

30. According to the data in the table, what is the range of average unemployment from 2006 to 2010?
   (A) 9.6
   (B) 7.2
   (C) 5.0
   (D) 4.6

Test Ban Treaty (1963)

In August of 1945, when the United States dropped two atomic bombs on Japan, World War II came to a conclusion.

Continued testing of atomic and then hydrogen devices led to a rising concern about the effects of radioactive fallout. As knowledge of the nature and effects of fallout increased, and as it became apparent that no region in the world was untouched by radioactive debris, the issue of continued nuclear tests drew widened and intensified public attention. Apprehension was expressed about the possibility of a cumulative contamination of the environment and of resultant genetic damage.

Efforts to negotiate an international agreement to end nuclear tests began in the Subcommittee of Five (the United States, the United Kingdom, Canada, France, and the Soviet Union) of the United Nations Disarmament Commission in May 1955. Public interest in the course of the negotiations was active and persistent. A dozen resolutions of the UN General Assembly addressed the issue, repeatedly urging conclusion of an agreement to ban tests under a system of international controls. Efforts to achieve a test ban agreement extended over eight years because they involved complex technical problems of verification and the difficulties of reconciling deep-seated differences in approach to arms control and security. The uneven progress of the negotiations was also a result of regular fluctuations in East-West political relationships during the Cold War.

The Test Ban Treaty was signed in Moscow on August 5, 1963; ratified by the United States Senate on September 24, 1963; and entered into force on October 10, 1963. The treaty prohibited nuclear weapons tests "or any other nuclear explosion" in the atmosphere, in outer space, and under water. While not banning tests underground, the treaty prohibited such explosions if they caused "radioactive debris to be present outside the territorial limits of the State under whose jurisdiction or control" the explosions were conducted. In accepting limitations on testing, the nuclear powers accepted as a common goal "an end to the contamination of man's environment by radioactive substances."

Source: ourdocuments.gov

Aerial Photograph of Missiles in Cuba (1962)

Throughout 1962, in the midst of the Cold War, the movement of Soviet personnel and equipment to Cuba had aroused suspicions in the American intelligence community. In response, U.S. ships and planes began photographing every Cuba-bound Soviet vessel, and U-2 spy planes began regular reconnaissance flights over the island, just 90 miles off the coast of Florida. On September 13, Kennedy warned Soviet Premier Khrushchev: "If at any time the Communist build-up in Cuba were to endanger or interfere with our security in any way . . . or if Cuba should ever . . . become an offensive military base of significant capacity for the Soviet Union, then this country will do whatever must be done to protect its own security and that of its allies." Despite Kennedy's warnings, the Soviets continued to construct the bases, and the United States continued to monitor their activities and take pictures.

Bad weather in the Caribbean the week of October 7, 1962, prevented American U-2 surveillance planes from making more reconnaissance flights over Fidel Castro's Cuba. But Sunday morning, October 14, was cloudless, and the U-2 flight took photographs that, over the next few days, were analyzed and reanalyzed. They provided positive proof of what the United States had for months suspected: that the Soviet Union was installing medium-range nuclear weapons in Cuba, capable of striking major U.S. cities and killing tens of millions of Americans within minutes. With the October 14 photographs, the United States caught the Soviet Union building offensive nuclear missile bases in its backyard, and the two superpowers were now joined in the first direct nuclear confrontation in history.

In a televised address on October 22, 1962, President Kennedy informed the American people of the presence of missile [sites] in Cuba. When the United States put a naval blockade in place around Cuba, tensions mounted, and the world wondered if there could be a peaceful resolution to the crisis. Kennedy's speech drew wide support in Latin America and among United States' allies. The Pentagon continued plans for possible air strikes and a land invasion. Several Soviet vessels turned back from the quarantine line set by the navel blockade, and during a televised confrontation with the Soviet Union in the United Nations, the United States presented photographic proof of the missiles.

On Sunday, October 28, the Soviets agreed to remove the missiles from Cuba. Negotiations for final settlement of the crisis continued for several days, but the immediate threat of nuclear war had been averted. On November 20, Kennedy announced, "I have today been informed by Chairman Khrushchev that all of the IL-28 bombers in Cuba will be withdrawn in thirty days. . . . I have this afternoon instructed the Secretary of Defense to lift our naval quarantine." In addition, the United States agreed that it would never participate in an invasion of Cuba, and Kennedy ordered the dismantling of several obsolete American air and missile bases in Turkey.

Source: ourdocuments.gov

31. What was an initial catalyst for the Test Ban Treaty?
    (A) Concerns about nuclear fallout
    (B) Concerns of a dirty bomb
    (C) Concerns about World War III
    (D) Testing on the moon

32. What did the U-2 surveillance planes observe?
    (A) Soviet installation of nuclear weapons in Puerto Rico
    (B) Movement of nuclear materials to the Soviet Union
    (C) Soviet installation of nuclear weapons capable of reaching the United States
    (D) Soviet planes heading toward the Pentagon

33. According to the passage, in late October 1962, the Soviets _____ President Kennedy's warnings.

Extended Response

DIRECTIONS: Read the following passages. In your response, compare and contrast the court case and the executive order. Discuss both the negative and the positive impacts of the court case and the executive order on African Americans. Cite specific examples to support your position. Develop your answers fully. You have 25 minutes to complete this section.

Executive Order 8802:
Prohibition of Discrimination in the Defense Industry (1941)

In early July 1941, millions of jobs were being created, primarily in urban areas, as the United States prepared for war. When large numbers of African Americans moved to cities in the north and west to work in defense industries, they were often met with violence and discrimination. In response, A. Philip Randolph, president of the Brotherhood of Sleeping Car Porters, and other black leaders, met with Eleanor Roosevelt and members of the President's cabinet. Randolph presented a list of grievances regarding the civil rights of African Americans, demanding that an Executive order be issued to stop job discrimination in the defense industry. Randolph, with others, threatened that they were prepared to bring "ten, twenty, fifty thousand Negroes on the White House lawn" if their demands were not met. After consultation with his advisers, Roosevelt responded to the black leaders and issued Executive Order 8802, which declared, "There shall be no discrimination in the employment of workers in defense industries and in Government, because of race, creed, color, or national origin." It was the first Presidential directive on race since Reconstruction. The order also established the Fair Employment Practices Committee to investigate incidents of discrimination.

Source: ourdocuments.gov

Executive Order 10730:
Desegregation of Central High School (1957)

On May 17, 1954, the U.S. Supreme Court ruled in *Brown v. Topeka Board of Education* that segregated schools were "inherently unequal" and ordered that U.S. public schools be desegregated "with all deliberate speed." Within a week of the 1954 decision, Arkansas was one of two Southern states to announce it would begin immediately to take steps to comply with the *Brown* decision. Arkansas's law school had been integrated since 1949, and seven of its eight state universities had desegregated. Blacks had been appointed to state boards and elected to local offices. It had already desegregated its public buses as well as its zoo, library, and parks system. In the summer of 1957, the city of Little Rock made plans to desegregate its public schools. Little Rock's school board had voted unanimously for a plan that started with the desegregation of the high school in 1957, followed by junior high schools the next year and elementary schools following. In September 1957, nine African American students enrolled at Central High School in Little Rock. The ensuing struggle between segregationists and integrationists, the Governor of the State of Arkansas and the Federal Government, President Dwight D. Eisenhower and Arkansas Governor Orval Faubus became known as the "Little Rock Crisis."

On September 2, the night before school was to start, Arkansas Governor Orval Faubus called out the state's National Guard to surround Little Rock Central High School and prevent any black students from entering. The Governor explained that his action was taken to protect citizens and property from possible violence by protesters he claimed were headed in caravans toward Little Rock. President Eisenhower, who was vacationing in Newport, RI, arranged to meet Governor Faubus to discuss the tense situation. In their brief meeting in Newport, Eisenhower thought Faubus had agreed to enroll the African American students, so he told Faubus that his National Guard troops could stay at Central High and enforce order. However, once back in Little Rock, Governor Faubus withdrew the National Guard.

A few days later, when nine African American students slipped into the school to enroll, a full-scale riot erupted. The situation was quickly out of control, as Governor Faubus failed to stop the violence. Finally, Congressman Brooks Hays and Little Rock Mayor Woodrow Mann asked the Federal Government for help, first in the form of U.S. marshals. President Dwight D. Eisenhower, as the chief law enforcement officer of the United States, was presented with a difficult problem. He was required to uphold the Constitution and the laws, but he also wanted to avoid a bloody confrontation in Arkansas. With Executive Order 10730, the President placed the Arkansas National Guard under Federal control and sent 1,000 U.S. Army paratroopers from the 101st Airborne Division to assist them in restoring order in Little Rock.

Source: ourdocuments.gov

SOCIAL STUDIES EXAM

1. D
2. B
3. C
4. D
5. D
6. D
7. A
8. D
9. A
10. D
11. property, or similar word
12. A
13. A
14. A
15. knowingly, or similar word
16. C
17. A

18. b, e, a, d, c
19. A
20. C
21. A
22. interpreted, or similar word
23. C
24. C
25. D
26. C
27. A
28. A
29. A
30. C
31. A
32. C
33. heeded, or similar word

EXTENDED RESPONSE

Answers will vary.

SOCIAL STUDIES EXAM ANSWERS EXPLAINED

1. **(D)** The law was intended to suspend laws temporarily but only to assist in economic recovery. Options A and B are incorrect because no evidence supports these answers. Option C is incorrect because NIRA was not intended to give businesses an advantage over customers.

2. **(B)** Both laws were focused on economic recovery, and both dealt with regulating industries. Option A is incorrect because no evidence supports this answer. Options C and D are incorrect; these are ways in which NIRA and NRA are different.

3. **(C)** The passage indicates that the act was met with widespread criticism. Options A, B, and D are incorrect because no evidence supports these answers.

4. **(D)** A Japanese flag is on the left bomb and a Nazi emblem is on the right bomb. Japan and Nazi Germany were two of the Axis Powers during World War II. Options A, B, and C are incorrect because no evidence in this poster supports those answers.

5. **(D)** Option A is incorrect; not *all* males age 21 and older have the right to vote. Option B is not the central idea of the section. Option C lists a different age than that listed in Section 2.

6. **(D)** Options A, B, and C are incorrect because none of these groups benefited as much from this amendment as African-American men who could no longer be denied equal protection of the laws.

7. **(A)** The section indicates that certain crimes would preclude someone from running for office. Options B, C, and D are incorrect because no evidence supports these answers.

8. **(D)** According to the key at the bottom, a solid square is a gain while an open square is a loss. Dallas is the only city shown with a solid square for domestic migration.

9. **(A)** According to the key at the bottom, a solid square is a gain while an open square is a loss. New York has the largest solid square for international migration, meaning it saw the greatest increase in immigrants.

10. **(D)** The passage indicates that in 1893, the act's provisions were extended to the territory inhabited by the Cherokees, Seminoles, and Creek.

11. "Property" or a similar word would be the best answer.

12. **(A)** The second paragraph indicates that various-size allotments of reservation land would be granted to individuals. Options B, C, and D are incorrect because no evidence supports these answers.

13. **(A)** The passage indicates that Trist went ahead with the negotiations in defiance of the president. Options B, C, and D are incorrect because no evidence supports these answers.

14. **(A)** The loss of the capital city signaled the end of the war. Options B, C, and D are incorrect; these occurred after the end of the war.

15. "Knowingly" or a similar word would be the best answer.

16. **(C)** According to the graph, the 1840s are just short of 50%. Options A, B, and D are incorrect.

17. **(A)** The 1820s has the longest bar, indicating the greatest amount of growth. Options B, C, and D are incorrect.

18. (b, e, a, d, c) First, women began to organize and picket for the right to vote. Then nine western states had women's suffrage. Next, most suffrage organizations backed the goal of an amendment. Then the House passed the amendment. Finally, the Senate passed the amendment.

19. (A) The passage indicates there were many women's organizations, which is aligned with freedom of association. Options B, C, and D are incorrect.

20. (C) According to the passage, 36 states constituted $\frac{3}{4}$ of the total number of states. So the United States must have consisted of 48 in all.

21. (A) The cartoon depicts Wallace talking out of two faces and saying opposite things, one in 1948 and one in 1941. Options B, C, and D are incorrect.

22. "Interpreted" or a similar word would be the best answer.

23. (C) The first paragraph says that Article III deals with the judicial branch.

24. (C) The second paragraph indicates that the first Congress decided that it could regulate the jurisdiction of all federal courts. Options A, B, and D are incorrect.

25. (D) According to the map, Miami is ranked number 4 out of 25, putting it in the top 25%. Options A, B, and C are incorrect.

26. (C) According to the map, San Antonio is number 25 of 25, making it the least urbanized city shown. Options A, B, and D are incorrect.

27. (A) According to the graph at the bottom, the year 1800 recorded the greatest percentage of the U.S. population living in a coastal population. Options B, C, and D are incorrect.

28. (A) According to the bar graph, initially a high percentage of the population lived on the coastline. That percentage declined through the mid-1800s, leveled off, and began increasing again.

29. (A) The average of 4.6, 4.6, and 5.8 is 5.0. First add the three annual values together: $4.6 + 4.6 + 5.8 = 15.0$. Then divide by the total number of values: $15.0 \div 3 = 5.0$.

30. (C) The range is the highest annual value minus the lowest annual value: $9.6 - 4.6 = 5.0$.

31. (A) Option A is correct. The passage indicates that countries were worried about the effects of nuclear radiation. Options B, C, and D are incorrect because no evidence supports these answers.

32. (C) The passage indicates that the Soviets were installing nuclear weapons in Cuba, only 90 miles from the United States. Option A is incorrect because the weapons were not installed in Puerto Rico. Option B is incorrect because the nuclear material was being moved to Cuba, not to the Soviet Union. Option D is incorrect because no evidence supports this answer.

33. "Heeded" or a similar word would be the best answer.

Extended Response

Answers will vary.

When reviewing your extended response, make sure you have asked yourself the following questions:

- Have I responded to the prompt?
- Do I have enough evidence?
- Do my ideas follow a logical order?
- Are there any misspellings?
- Have I confused any homonyms?
- Have I used proper punctuation, including periods, commas, semicolons, apostrophes, and so forth?
- Do I need to break up any run-on sentences?
- Can I combine any strings of short, choppy sentences?

The prompt asks you to discuss both the negative and positive impacts of Executive Order 8802 and Executive Order 10730 on African Americans. It also asks that you compare and contrast these orders. Make sure that you have discussed the most important positive and negative effects in one paragraph and compared and contrasted them in another. Be sure to cite specific evidence from both of the passages that you feel supports your position. Finally, make sure you have restated your position in the conclusion.

ANSWER SHEET
Model Test 2

SCIENCE EXAM

1. Ⓐ Ⓑ Ⓒ Ⓓ

2. Use lines below for your answer.

3. Ⓐ Ⓑ Ⓒ Ⓓ

4. Ⓐ Ⓑ Ⓒ Ⓓ

5. Ⓐ Ⓑ Ⓒ Ⓓ

6. Ⓐ Ⓑ Ⓒ Ⓓ

7. Ⓐ Ⓑ Ⓒ Ⓓ

8. Ⓐ Ⓑ Ⓒ Ⓓ

9. Ⓐ Ⓑ Ⓒ Ⓓ

10. Ⓐ Ⓑ Ⓒ Ⓓ

11. Ⓐ Ⓑ Ⓒ Ⓓ

12. Ⓐ Ⓑ Ⓒ Ⓓ

13. Ⓐ Ⓑ Ⓒ Ⓓ

14. Ⓐ Ⓑ Ⓒ Ⓓ

15. _____

_____

_____

_____

16. Ⓐ Ⓑ Ⓒ Ⓓ

17. _____

18. Ⓐ Ⓑ Ⓒ Ⓓ

19. Ⓐ Ⓑ Ⓒ Ⓓ

20. Ⓐ Ⓑ Ⓒ Ⓓ

21. _____

_____

_____

22. Ⓐ Ⓑ Ⓒ Ⓓ

23. Ⓐ Ⓑ Ⓒ Ⓓ

24. Ⓐ Ⓑ Ⓒ Ⓓ

25. Ⓐ Ⓑ Ⓒ Ⓓ

26. Ⓐ Ⓑ Ⓒ Ⓓ

27. Ⓐ Ⓑ Ⓒ Ⓓ

28. Ⓐ Ⓑ Ⓒ Ⓓ

29. Ⓐ Ⓑ Ⓒ Ⓓ

30. Ⓐ Ⓑ Ⓒ Ⓓ

31. Ⓐ Ⓑ Ⓒ Ⓓ

32. Ⓐ Ⓑ Ⓒ Ⓓ

33. Ⓐ Ⓑ Ⓒ Ⓓ

34. Ⓐ Ⓑ Ⓒ Ⓓ

35. Ⓐ Ⓑ Ⓒ Ⓓ

2. _____

_____

_____

_____

_____

_____

> **DIRECTIONS:** This practice exam contains various stimuli, which you will need to analyze in order to answer the questions that follow. This exam has 35 questions. You will have 75 minutes to answer the questions.

QUESTIONS 1 AND 2 REFER TO THE FOLLOWING INFORMATION:

Properties of Selected Solar System Objects			
Object	Radius (km)	Volume ($\times 10^9$ m^3)	Mass ($\times 10^{21}$ kg)	Density (g/cm^3)
Sun	696,000	1,412,000,000	1,989,100,000	1.41
Mercury	2,439.70	60.83	330.20	5.43
Venus	6,051.80	928.43	4,868.50	5.24
Earth	6,371	1,083.21	5,973.60	5.52
Mars	3,390	163.18	641.85	3.94
Jupiter	69,911	1,431,280.	1,898,600	1.33
Saturn	58,232	827,130	568,460	0.70
Uranus	25,362	68,340	86,832	1.30
Neptune	24,622	62,540	102,430	1.76
Pluto	1,161	7	13.11	2

1. Which of the following lists the planets in descending order from most dense to least dense?
   (A) Venus, Mercury, Earth, Mars
   (B) Mars, Venus, Mercury, Earth
   (C) Mercury, Venus, Earth, Mars
   (D) Earth, Mercury, Venus, Mars

2. In the table above, Volume is defined as the amount of 3-dimensional space an object occupies, Mass is the amount of matter (solid, liquid, or gas) that makes up an object, and Density is the amount of Mass per unit of Volume in an object. A comparison of the planets Earth and Jupiter shows that Jupiter's Volume and Mass are much greater than Earth's Volume and Mass, while the Earth's Density is more than three times greater than that of Jupiter. A comparison of the planet Jupiter with the Sun, however, shows that while the Sun's Volume and Mass are much greater than the Volume and Mass of Jupiter, the two objects are almost equal in Density, differing by less than 10%.

   In the space provided, give a brief explanation of why an object much larger than Jupiter in Volume and Mass (the Sun) can have an almost equal Density to Jupiter, when an object much smaller than Jupiter in Volume and Mass (the Earth) can have a greater Density than Jupiter.

TIP

On the computerized test, a question like this would have you drag and drop the answers into the correct order.

TIP

On the computerized test, a question like this would simulate a short-answer question.

MODEL TEST 2

TIP

On the computerized test, a question like this would have you click on the diagram to indicate your choices. This would be a hot-spot question.

3. Which two siblings from the third generation are not affected by the inheritable trait?

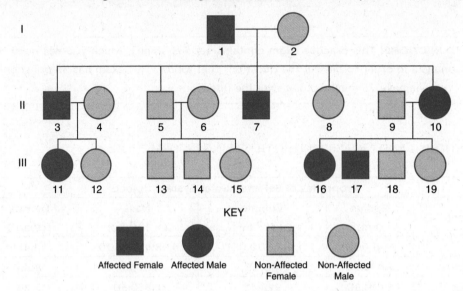

KEY

Affected Female   Affected Male   Non-Affected Female   Non-Affected Male

(A) 11 and 16
(B) 5 and 6
(C) 14 and 19
(D) 13 and 15

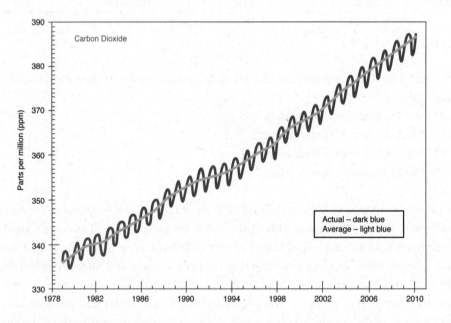

4. Based on the graph above, what was the average annual increase in atmospheric CO_2 between 1980 and 2010?
(A) Between 1.0 and 1.4
(B) Between 1.5 and 1.9
(C) Between 2.0 and 2.4
(D) Between 2.5 and 2.9

5. Which of the following is an example of a learned trait?
   (A) The ability to learn to speak
   (B) Height
   (C) The ability to speak French
   (D) Sharpness of vision

6. Niemann-Pick disease is a recessive genetic disorder. A person must be born with two copies of the gene to develop the disease. People with only one copy of the gene are carriers. Which of the following couples could potentially have a child with Niemann-Pick disease?
   (A) One parent has Niemann-Pick disease, and one parent is not a carrier of the disease.
   (B) Neither parent is a carrier of Niemann-Pick disease.
   (C) One parent is a carrier, and the other is not.
   (D) Both parents are carriers of the disease.

QUESTIONS 7 THROUGH 10 REFER TO THE FOLLOWING INFORMATION:

Jim heats his home by burning firewood. His wood shed can hold up to 5 cords of wood, and the shed floor can support up to 16,500 pounds. He will select firewood for the winter from the types listed in this table.

Type	Density (lb/ft^3)	Weight of Dry Cord* (lb/cord)	Heat Value of a Dry Cord (BTUs** $\times 10^6$/cord)
Apple	48.7	4,100	26.5
Elm	35.9	3,050	19.5
Red Maple	34.4	2,920	18.7
Red Oak	44.2	3,760	24
White Ash	43.4	3,690	23.6
White Oak	47.2	4,010	25.7
White Pine	26.3	2,240	14.3

* Unit of measure for dry stacked wood = 128 cubic feet of space

** British thermal unit

7. Which one of the following should Jim choose if he wants to produce the greatest total amount of heat without exceeding the capacity of the shed?
   (A) 5 cords of apple
   (B) 5 cords of elm
   (C) 4 cords of apple
   (D) 4 cords of white oak

8. Which one of the following could be a list of the dimensions of the wood storage portion of Jim's shed?
   (A) 8 feet × 10 feet × 8 feet
   (B) 8 feet × 8 feet × 8 feet
   (C) 6 feet × 10 feet × 8 feet
   (D) 8 feet × 8 feet × 6 feet

9. According to the table, how many BTUs are produced by burning 2 cords of white pine?
   (A) 28.6
   (B) 28,600
   (C) 2,860,000
   (D) 28,600,000

10. Which type of wood has median density of the woods listed in the table?
    (A) White oak
    (B) White pine
    (C) White ash
    (D) Red maple

_____

QUESTIONS 11 AND 12 REFER TO THE FOLLOWING INFORMATION:

As part of a survey expedition to South America, Charles Darwin visited the Galapagos Islands. While there, he collected fossils and live specimens of plants and animals from each of the islands, and he documented their characteristics. He noticed that several species of finches seemed to have descended from a common species that had come to the islands from the mainland. He also noticed that the different species of finches differed in their food sources and the shapes of their beaks. Each had a beak shape that was different from the ancestor species and was well-suited to a local source of food. For example, some new species had larger, stronger beaks well-suited to cracking nuts. Another new species had a long, narrow beak well-suited for digging into cactus fruit. After consideration, he decided that there was a relationship between the available food sources in the various islands and the adaptations in each new species.

He knew that, within a given species, there are always individuals whose traits (like beak size and shape) are not similar to the majority of the members of that species. He imagined that, in a new environment, these new traits might provide an advantage by improving the individual's ability to find sources of food. Over time, he reasoned, the new trait would become much more prevalent. Individuals with the new trait would not have to compete for food with individuals without it, and a larger food supply leads to a larger population. For example, only finches with large, strong beaks can crack and eat nuts. So finches with beaks more similar to the ancestor finches would not be able to use nuts as a food source, which would mean less competition for nuts. The "adapted" finches would have a better chance of surviving and reproducing, because they would have more food available than other finches. This is called *natural selection*, and it is one of the core concepts of Darwin's theory of evolution.

11. What is Darwin's view that reduced competition for food led to the development of different finch species an example of?
    (A) An inference
    (B) An experimental result
    (C) Observational data
    (D) A conclusion

12. The information that Darwin gathered about the finches, as described in the passage, is primarily which of the following?
    (A) Quantitative
    (B) Experimental
    (C) Qualitative
    (D) Simulation based

QUESTION 13 REFERS TO THE FOLLOWING INFORMATION:

Invasive species are species of animals, plants, microorganisms, and other living things that are not native to an ecosystem, but are introduced into the ecosystem by an external agent. A large cargo ship can move and discharge millions of gallons of ballast water and the organisms it contains. The ballast tanks of cargo ships have been identified as the largest single contributor to the global movement of aquatic species.

Source: NOAA, GLERL

13. Which of the invasive species below is most likely to have been introduced from the species movement described above?
    (A) *Euonymus fortunei* (winter creeper vine)
    (B) *Solenopsis invicta* (red imported fire ant)
    (C) *Rattus norvegicus* (brown rat)
    (D) *Silurus asotus* (amur catfish)

A "nonindigenous" species is an organism (plant, animal, microbe) found living beyond its historic native range, which is usually taken as the area where it evolved to its present form. Executive Order 13112 of February 3, 1999, defined "alien" species as "any species, including its seeds, eggs, spores, or other biological material capable of propagating that species, that is not native" to the particular ecosystem in which it is found. Thus, alien can be used interchangeably with nonindigenous. The terms exotic and non-native are both synonyms for nonindigenous. So nonindigenous = alien = exotic = non-native.

Public Law 101-636 (Nonindigenous Aquatic Nuisance Prevention and Control Act of 1990) defined an aquatic nuisance species as a nonindigenous species that "threatens the diversity or abundance of native species or the ecological stability of infested waters, or commercial, agricultural, aquacultural or recreational activities dependent on such waters." Similarly, Executive Order 13112 defined invasive species as an alien species whose introduction does or is likely to cause economic or environmental harm or harm to human health. Thus, invasive and nuisance species are synonymous and can be used interchangeably.

An invasive species is also, by definition, nonindigenous, but not all nonindigenous species are invasive. For example, coho, chinook, and pink salmon are favored nonindigenous sport fish in the Great Lakes, but are not considered invasive or a nuisance. These salmon could also be called alien or exotic with respect to the Great Lakes. The zebra mussel, on the other hand, is an invasive (or nuisance) species, as well as nonindigenous. In an interesting case of turn-about, the alewife, a nonindigenous fish that was first reported in the Great Lakes in 1873 was considered a costly nuisance species in the mid-20th century. Now it is considered a valuable (but still nonindigenous) food source for salmon and lake trout, which support a multi-billion dollar sport fishery.

The term "invasive" is severely overused—very often we see reference to "invasive" species when the subject is actually nonindigenous or non-native species.

Source: NOAA, GLERL

14. Based on the passage, the history of which of the following is most similar to the history of the alewife?
    (A) A species of rabbit was first considered invasive because it destroyed food crops but then became a popular source of fur.
    (B) A species of plant was first considered invasive because it grew rapidly, choking sewage and drainage systems. After some new herbicides were developed, the plant came under control.
    (C) A species of berry was first considered invasive because it threatened to make a native berry plant extinct. Then it was discovered to be a better source of nutrition for deer than the native berry plants were.
    (D) A species of mussel was first considered invasive because its population grew rapidly, reducing the overall food supply for native fish. Then another species of mussel was introduced and the population of the first invasive mussel declined.

15. Select the word or phrase in each bracket that correctly completes the sentence.

    All [invasive, indigenous, mussel] species are [alien, native, aquatic], but not all [nonindigenous, native, nuisance] species are necessarily [native, invasive, indigenous].

TIP

On the computerized test, a question like this would have you select your choice from among a column of drop-down choices.

16. Based on the passage, which of the following is true about Executive Order 13112 (EO13112) and Public Law 101-636 (PL101-636)?
    (A) The definition of "invasive" species in EO13112 applies to all the species defined in PL101-636.
    (B) The language in PL101-636 defines as a "nuisance" all species covered by EO13112.
    (C) The definition of "invasive" species in EO13112 is the opposite of the definition of "nuisance" species as defined in PL101-636.
    (D) The two apply to completely different species of animals.

17. Based on the passage, which species is considered to be exotic as opposed to being invasive?

18. What is the main point of paragraph 3?
    (A) Exotic species are not always nonindigenous species.
    (B) Nonindigenous species are not always invasive.
    (C) Native species are always indigenous.
    (D) Alien species are always invasive.

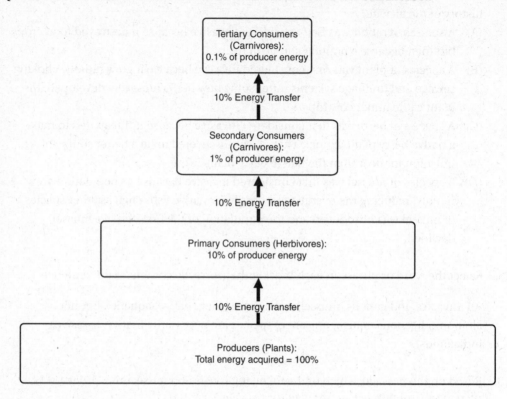

Food webs and chains are organized into hierarchies, with each tier providing a source of food to the next tier above. Plants capture energy from the sun, herbivores eat plants, some carnivores eat herbivores, and some carnivores eat other carnivores. Each kind of organism gets the energy that it needs to live from this process of eating and digesting its food source. It is estimated that, on average, only 10% of an organism's energy is transferred to the next when it is consumed. This is referred to as the "pyramid of energy" because the total amount of energy that is transferred from one tier to the next gets smaller as the tiers go higher. A similar phenomenon occurs with the populations of the tiers in the pyramid. Each tier's population is much smaller than the tier that provides its food source. For example, there are many more plants than herbivores, and there are many more herbivores than carnivores. This is called the "pyramid of numbers."

19. In an ecosystem, the producers capture a total of approximately 8,000 kcal/m^2/yr of energy from the sun. According to the information, how much energy would likely reach the tertiary consumers?
    (A) Between 700 and 900 kcal/m^2/yr
    (B) Between 70 and 90 kcal/m^2/yr
    (C) Between 7 and 9 kcal/m^2/yr
    (D) Between 0.7 and 0.9 kcal/m^2/yr

	List A	List B	List C	List D
Producers	7,562 units	5 units	8,500 units	4,800 units
Primary consumers	6,500 units	48 units	4,250 units	475 units
Secondary consumers	589 units	490 units	2,125 units	46 units
Tertiary consumers	8 units	4,875 units	1,062 units	5 units

20. In the table, which of the following data lists best reflects all levels of a pyramid of energy?
    (A) List A
    (B) List B
    (C) List C
    (D) List D

21. Select the word or phrase in each bracket that correctly completes the sentences.

    The pyramid of [energy, numbers, producers] shows that a small amount of energy is passed from one level of [consumer, producer, plant] to another. This creates increasing limits on the populations at each level, which results in a pyramid of [energy, numbers, producers].

TIP

On the computerized test, a question like this would have you select your choice from among a column of drop-down choices.

QUESTIONS 22 THROUGH 24 REFER TO THE FOLLOWING INFORMATION:

In the stratosphere, the region of the atmosphere between about 10 and 50 kilometers (6–30 miles) above the Earth's surface, ozone (O_3), plays a vital role by absorbing harmful ultraviolet radiation from the sun. Stratospheric ozone is threatened by some of the human-made gases that have been released into the atmosphere, including those known as chlorofluorocarbons (CFCs).

Once widely used as propellants in spray cans, refrigerants, electronics cleaning agents, and in foam and insulating products, the CFCs had been hailed as the "wonder chemicals." But the very properties that make them useful—chemical inertness, nontoxicity, insolubility in water—also make them resistant to removal in the lower atmosphere.

CFCs are mixed worldwide by the large-scale motions of the atmosphere and survive until, after 1–2 years, they reach the stratosphere and are broken down by ultraviolet radiation. The chlorine atoms within them are released and directly attack ozone. In the process of destroying ozone, the chlorine atoms are regenerated and begin to attack other ozone molecules . . . and so on, for thousands of cycles before the chlorine atoms are removed from the stratosphere by other processes. . . .

[Most] of the ozone is in the lower stratosphere, at an altitude of about 20–25 kilometers (12–15 miles) above sea level. This is the so-called "ozone layer." It acts as a shield by absorbing biologically active ultraviolet light (called UV-B) from the sun. If the ozone layer is depleted, more of this UV-B radiation reaches the surface of the earth. Increased exposure to UV-B has harmful effects on plants and animals, including humans. The chlorine and bromine in human produced chemicals such as the ones known as chlorofluorocarbons (CFCs) and halons are depleting ozone in the stratosphere.

Source: NOAA ESRL Chemical Sciences Division

22. Based on the information above, which of the following is the most likely harmful effect that ozone depletion could have on humans?
    (A) Skin cancer
    (B) Pneumonia
    (C) Obesity
    (D) Asthma

23. According to the passage, if the amount of CFCs in use globally today was immediately reduced by 50%, when would ozone depletion likely begin to slow down?
    (A) Within 2 months from now
    (B) Between 3 and 10 months from now
    (C) Between 12 and 24 months from now
    (D) More than 26 months from now

24. Based on the information above, which of the following would increase the rate of ozone depletion?
    (A) Restrictions on the use of CFCs
    (B) An increase in the use of propellants in spray cans
    (C) An increase in the use of halons in industrial processes
    (D) An increase in the amount of UV-B radiation reaching the surface of Earth

QUESTIONS 25 THROUGH 28 REFER TO THE FOLLOWING INFORMATION:

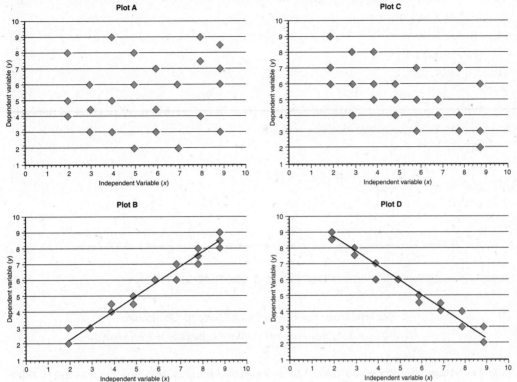

In a certain ecosystem, the population of a native shrimplike organism decreased sharply during the same 15-year period when the population of an invasive species of mussel increased sharply. Scientists plotted measurements of these two populations over the 15-year period, using the mussel population as the independent variable and the other population as the dependent variable.

25. Which of the plots above is the best match for the plot made by the scientists?
   (A) Plot A
   (B) Plot B
   (C) Plot C
   (D) Plot D

26. All of the following statements about the plots above are true EXCEPT:
   (A) Plots B and D show strong correlations between the variables.
   (B) Plots C and D show negative correlations between the variables.
   (C) Plots A and B show strong correlations between the variables.
   (D) Plot D shows a stronger correlation than either plot A or plot C.

TIP

On the computerized test, a question like this would have you click on the graph to indicate your choice. This would be a hot-spot question.

27. Which of the following lists the previous plots in order from weakest to strongest correlation?
    (A) D, C, A
    (B) A, C, B
    (C) B, A, D
    (D) B, C, A

28. Which of the following lists the previous plots in order from most positive to neutral to most negative correlation?
    (A) D, A, C
    (B) A, C, B
    (C) B, A, D
    (D) B, C, A

QUESTIONS 29 TO 30 REFER TO THE FOLLOWING INFORMATION:

Excerpt from *An Elementary Study of Chemistry*
by William McPherson and William Edwards Henderson

How to distinguish between physical and chemical changes. It is not always easy to tell to which class a given change belongs, and many cases will require careful thought on the part of the student. The test question in all cases is, Has the composition of the substance been changed? Usually this can be answered by a study of the properties of the substance before and after the change, since a change in composition is attended by a change in properties. In some cases, however, only a trained observer can decide the question.

Changes in physical state. One class of physical changes should be noted with especial care, since it is likely to prove misleading. It is a familiar fact that ice is changed into water, and water into steam, by heating. Here we have three different substances,—the solid ice, the liquid water, and the gaseous steam,—the properties of which differ widely. The chemist can readily show, however, that these three bodies have exactly the same composition, being composed of the same substances in the same proportion. Hence the change from one of these substances into another is a physical change. Many other substances may, under suitable conditions, be changed from solids into liquids, or from liquids into gases, without change in composition. Thus butter and wax will melt when heated; alcohol and gasoline will evaporate when exposed to the air. *The three states—solid, liquid, and gas—are called the three physical states of matter.*

Physical and chemical properties. Many properties of a substance can be noted without causing the substance to undergo chemical change, and are therefore called its *physical properties.* Among these are its physical state, color, odor, taste, size, shape, weight. Other properties are only discovered when the substance undergoes chemical change. These are called its *chemical properties.* Thus we find that coal burns in air, gunpowder explodes when ignited, milk sours when exposed to air.

Definition of physics and chemistry. It is now possible to make a general distinction between physics and chemistry.

DEFINITION: *Physics is the science which deals with those changes in matter which do not involve a change in composition.*

DEFINITION: *Chemistry is the science which deals with those changes in matter which do involve a change in composition.*

Source: gutenberg.org

29. According to the passage, which is an example of a chemical change?
    (A) The change from ice to water
    (B) The change from water to steam
    (C) The melting of butter
    (D) The exploding of gunpowder

30. According to the passage, what is the difference between chemistry and physics?
    (A) Chemistry studies changes that affect matter, and physics studies changes that do not affect matter.
    (B) Chemistry studies changes that affect the composition of matter, and physics studies changes that do not affect the composition of matter.
    (C) Chemistry studies changes that do not affect matter, and physics studies changes that do affect matter.
    (D) Chemistry studies changes that do not affect the composition of matter, and physics studies changes that do affect the composition of matter.

Excerpt from *An Elementary Study of Chemistry*
by William McPherson and William Edwards Henderson

Two factors in all changes. In all the changes which matter can undergo, whether physical or chemical, two factors must be taken into account, namely, *energy* and *matter*.

Energy. It is a familiar fact that certain bodies have the power to do work. Thus water falling from a height upon a water wheel turns the wheel and in this way does the work of the mills. Magnetized iron attracts iron to itself and the motion of the iron as it moves towards the magnet can be made to do work. When coal is burned it causes the engine to move and transports the loaded cars from place to place. When a body has this power to do work it is said to possess energy.

Law of conservation of energy. Careful experiments have shown that when one body parts with its energy the energy is not destroyed but is transferred to another body or system of bodies. Just as energy cannot be destroyed, neither can it be created. If one body gains a certain amount of energy, some other body has lost an equivalent amount. These facts are summed up in the law of conservation of energy which may be stated thus: *While energy can be changed from one form into another, it cannot be created or destroyed.*

Transformations of energy. Although energy can neither be created nor destroyed, it is evident that it may assume many different forms. Thus the falling water may turn the electric generator and produce a current of electricity. The energy lost by the falling water is thus transformed into the energy of the electric current. This in turn may be changed into the energy of motion, as when the current is used for propelling the cars, or into the energy of heat and light, as when it is used for heating and lighting the cars. Again, the energy of coal may be converted into energy of heat and subsequently of motion, as when it is used as a fuel in steam engines.

Since the energy possessed by coal only becomes available when the coal is made to undergo a chemical change, it is sometimes called *chemical energy*. It is this form of energy in which we are especially interested in the study of chemistry.

Matter. Matter may be defined as that which occupies space and possesses weight. Like energy, matter may be changed oftentimes from one form into another; and since in these transformations all the other physical properties of a substance save weight are likely to change, the inquiry arises, Does the weight also change? Much careful experimenting has shown that it does not. The weight of the products formed in any change in matter always equals the weight of the substances undergoing change.

Law of conservation of matter. The important truth just stated is frequently referred to as the law of conservation of matter, and this law may be briefly stated thus: *Matter can neither be created nor destroyed, though it can be changed from one form into another.*

Classification of matter. At first sight there appears to be no limit to the varieties of matter of which the world is made. For convenience in study we may classify all these varieties under three heads, namely, *mechanical mixtures, chemical compounds, and elements.*

Source: gutenberg.org

31. According to the passage, how are matter and energy similar?
    (A) Both matter and energy can be created or destroyed.
    (B) Neither matter nor energy can assume multiple forms.
    (C) Neither matter nor energy can be created or destroyed.
    (D) Both matter and energy possess weight.

QUESTIONS 32 AND 33 REFER TO THE FOLLOWING INFORMATION:

Excerpt from *An Elementary Study of Chemistry*
by William McPherson and William Edwards Henderson

Elements. It has been seen that iron sulphide is composed of two entirely different substances—iron and sulphur. The question arises, Do these substances in turn contain other substances, that is, are they also chemical compounds? Chemists have tried in a great many ways to decompose them, but all their efforts have failed. Substances which have resisted all efforts to decompose them into other substances are called *elements*. It is not always easy to prove that a given substance is really an element. Some way as yet untried may be successful in decomposing it into other simpler forms of matter, and the supposed element will then prove to be a compound. Water, lime, and many other familiar compounds were at one time thought to be elements.

DEFINITION: *An element is a substance which cannot be separated into simpler substances by any known means.*

Kinds of matter. While matter has been grouped in three classes for the purpose of study, it will be apparent that there are really but two distinct kinds of matter, namely, compounds and elements. A mechanical mixture is not a third distinct kind of matter, but is made up of varying quantities of either compounds or elements or both.

Alchemy. In olden times it was thought that some way could be found to change one element into another, and a great many efforts were made to accomplish this transformation. Most of these efforts were directed toward changing the commoner metals into gold, and many fanciful ways for doing this were described. The chemists of that time were called *alchemists,* and the art which they practiced was called *alchemy.* The alchemists gradually became convinced that the only way common metals could be changed into gold was by the wonderful power of a magic substance which they called the *philosopher's stone,* which would accomplish this transformation by its mere touch and would in addition give perpetual youth to its fortunate possessor. No one has ever found such a stone, and no one has succeeded in changing one metal into another.

Number of elements. The number of substances now considered to be elements is not large—about eighty in all. Many of these are rare, and very few of them make any large fraction of the materials in the earth's crust. Clarke gives the following estimate of the composition of the earth's crust:

Oxygen	47.0%	Calcium	3.5%
Silicon	27.9	Magnesium	2.5
Aluminum	8.1	Sodium	2.7
Iron	4.7	Potassium	2.4
	Other elements	1.2%	

Physical state of the elements. About ten of the elements are gases at ordinary temperatures. Two—mercury and bromine—are liquids. The others are all solids, though their melting points vary through wide limits, from cæsium which melts at 26° to elements which do not melt save in the intense heat of the electric furnace.

Source: gutenberg.org

32. According to the passage, oxygen makes up approximately what portion of Earth's crust?
    (A) Three-quarters
    (B) Almost half
    (C) One-third
    (D) Less than one-tenth

33. According to the author, how can you prove that a substance is an element?
    (A) You can show that it cannot be separated into simpler substances by any known means.
    (B) You can transform it into gold or silver.
    (C) You can find a sample of it in Earth's crust.
    (D) You can find the temperature at which it melts.

QUESTIONS 34 AND 35 REFER TO THE FOLLOWING INFORMATION:

Excerpt from *An Elementary Study of Chemistry*
by William McPherson and William Edwards Henderson

Occurrence of the elements. Comparatively few of the elements occur as uncombined substances in nature, most of them being found in the form of chemical compounds. When an element does occur by itself, as is the case with gold, we say that it occurs in the *free state* or *native*; when it is combined with other substances in the form of compounds, we say that it occurs in the *combined state,* or *in combination.* In the latter case there is usually little about the compound to suggest that the element is present in it; for we have seen that elements lose their own peculiar properties when they enter into combination with other elements. It would never be suspected, for example, that the reddish, earthy-looking iron ore contains iron.

Names of elements. The names given to the elements have been selected in a great many different ways. (1) Some names are very old and their original meaning is obscure. Such names are iron, gold, and copper. (2) Many names indicate some striking physical property of the element. The name bromine, for example, is derived from a Greek word meaning a stench, referring to the extremely unpleasant odor of the substance. The name iodine comes from a word meaning violet, alluding to the beautiful color of iodine vapor. (3) Some names indicate prominent chemical properties of the elements. Thus, nitrogen means the producer of niter, nitrogen being a constituent of niter or saltpeter. Hydrogen means water former, signifying its presence in water. Argon means lazy or inert, the element being so named because of its inactivity. (4) Other elements are named from countries or localities, as germanium and scandium.

Symbols. In indicating the elements found in compounds it is inconvenient to use such long names, and hence chemists have adopted a system of abbreviations. These abbreviations are known as *symbols*, each element having a distinctive symbol. (1) Sometimes the initial letter of the name will suffice to indicate the element. Thus I stands for iodine, C for carbon. (2) Usually it is necessary to add some other characteristic letter to the symbol, since several names may begin with the same letter. Thus C stands for carbon, Cl for chlorine, Cd for cadmium, Ce for cerium, Cb for columbium. (3) Sometimes the symbol is an abbreviation of the old Latin name. In this way Fe (ferrum) indicates iron, Cu (cuprum), copper, Au (aurum), gold.

Chemical affinity the cause of chemical combination. The agency which causes substances to combine and which holds them together when combined is called *chemical affinity.* . . . [Heat] is often necessary to bring about chemical action. The distinction between the cause producing chemical action and the circumstances favoring it must be clearly made. Chemical affinity is always the cause of chemical union. Many agencies may make it possible for chemical affinity to act by overcoming circumstances which stand in its way. Among these agencies are heat, light, and electricity. As a rule, solution also promotes action between two substances. Sometimes these agencies may overcome chemical attraction and so occasion the decomposition of a compound.

Source: gutenberg.org

34. According to the passage, which of the following elements was named for a location?
    (A) Copper
    (B) Scandium
    (C) Gold
    (D) Carbon

35. According to the passage, which of the elements listed below takes its symbol from Latin?
    (A) Iron
    (B) Chlorine
    (C) Carbon
    (D) Nitrogen

ANSWER KEY
Model Test 2

SCIENCE EXAM

1. D
2. Answers will vary (see Answers Explained).
3. D
4. B
5. C
6. D
7. C
8. A
9. D
10. C
11. A
12. C
13. D
14. C
15. invasive, alien, nonindigenous, invasive
16. A
17. coho, chinook, or pink salmon
18. B
19. C
20. D
21. energy, consumer, numbers
22. A
23. C
24. C
25. D
26. C
27. B
28. C
29. D
30. B
31. C
32. B
33. A
34. B
35. A

SCIENCE EXAM ANSWER EXPLANATIONS

1. **(D)** The density of Earth is 5.52 g/cm^3, of Mercury is 5.43 g/cm^3, of Venus is 5.24 g/cm^3, and of Mars is 3.94 g/cm^3.

2. A 3-point response to this question might include the following:

   Cause of phenomenon: Density is the amount of matter present in a given amount of space. When comparing objects, the similarity or difference in Volume and Mass between two objects is not a factor in the relationship between their Densities. Rather, the similarity or difference in Density between two objects will be determined by how similar or different the relationship is between each object's Mass and Volume, which can be determined by dividing each object's Mass by its Volume. This is based on the provided definition that Density is the amount of Mass per unit of Volume.

   Relevant evidence: Data from the table comparing the named objects.

   Scoring Guide

   3-Point Response

   Provides an explanation of the relationship between Mass, Volume, and Density AND uses the definition of Density to compare Jupiter with the Sun and Earth and explain their relative Densities.

   2-Point Response

   Uses the definition of Density to compare Jupiter with the Sun and Earth and explain their relative Densities but DOES NOT provide an explanation of the relationship between Mass, Volume, and Density.

   1-Point Response

   Provides an explanation of the relationship between Mass, Volume, and Density but DOES NOT use the definition of Density to compare Jupiter with the Sun and Earth and explain their relative Densities.

   0-Point Response

   Provides no explanation or an inaccurate explanation of the relationship or provides specific evidence without an identifiable explanation.

3. **(D)** The question requires that the selections be siblings (brothers or sisters) and be in the third generation (the row marked III). Blue symbols represent nonaffected males or females. Choice A is incorrect because 11 and 16 are affected and are not siblings. Choice B is incorrect. Although 5 and 6 are unaffected siblings, they are in the second generation, not the third. Choice C is incorrect. Although 14 and 19 are unaffected and in the third generation, they are not siblings.

4. **(B)** The total increase was approximately 50 ppm. To find the average annual increase, divide that value by the 30-year period: $50 \div 30 = 1.66666\ldots = 1.67$.

5. **(C)** Being able to speak a specific language (French) must be learned. This ability has no genetic component. Option A is incorrect because humans are born with this ability. Options B and D are purely physical traits.

6. **(D)** In order for an offspring to inherit two copies of the gene, one copy must come from each parent. So each parent must have at least one copy of the gene. Option D is the only case where each parent carries 1 copy (both are carriers). In all the other options, at least one parent does not have a copy of the recessive gene.

7. **(C)** 4 cords of apple will produce the greatest amount of heat (106 BTU) without exceeding the weight limit of 16,500 pounds. Option A is incorrect because 5 cords of apple is too heavy. Options B and C are incorrect. Although they don't exceed the weight limit of the shed, they produce less heat than 4 cords of apple.

8. **(A)** According to the first footnote beneath the table, a cord of wood is 128 cubic feet in volume. The shed can hold 5 cords of wood, which is 640 cubic feet: $8 \times 10 \times 8 = 640$.

9. **(D)** Burning 1 cord of white pine produces 14.3×10^6 BTU. So burning 2 cords produces 28.3×10^6 BTU. Moving the decimal point 6 places to the right gives 28,600,000.

10. **(C)** When the set of densities is listed in ascending order, white ash is the 4th wood out of 7, making it the median (middle) of the set.

11. **(A)** At first, Darwin's view was a realization that agreed with his observations but lacked sufficient supporting evidence to "prove" it. Much more work would be done in order to develop the now accepted theory of evolution. A realization based on observation that leads to further investigation is an inference.

12. **(C)** Darwin gathered plants, animals, and fossils. Then he documented their characteristics, particularly beak shapes and food sources. Although some numerical (quantitative) measurements were probably involved, most of the information mentioned in the passage was descriptive and nonnumerical (qualitative). Darwin's work took place in the field and not in the laboratory, so this was not experimental data.

13. **(D)** Of the four species listed, the amur catfish is the only one that lives in water.

14. **(C)** The alewife began as a nuisance but then became accepted because it was a food source for a non-nuisance species. The berry in option C follows the same pattern.

15. **Invasive, Alien, Nonindigenous, Invasive** Invasive species are nonindigenous species that cause harm. Not all nonindigenous species cause harm when they are introduced into a new ecosystem.

16. **(A)** EO13112 defines invasive species as any non-indigenous species that causes or is likely to cause harm to humans or ecosystems. PL101-636 defines aquatic nuisance species any non-indigenous that threatens aquatic ecosystems (waters) The Executive Order includes the Public Law, but the Public Law only refers to aquatic species.

17. **Coho, chinook,** and **pink salmon** would be acceptable answers. The passage says they are all popular for sport fishing. Although nonindigenous, none of these species is harmful. Invasive and nuisance species are harmful. Exotic are only nonindigenous.

18. **(B)** Paragraph 3 provides examples of nonindigenous species that are not considered to be nuisance or invasive. "Exotic" and "nonindigenous" mean the same thing. "Native" and "indigenous" mean the same thing. "Alien" means "nonindigenous," but "invasive" means "harmful." So alien species are not always invasive species.

19. **(C)** According to the energy pyramid, the energy that reaches the tertiary consumers is 0.1% of the energy acquired by the producers. This is the same as dividing the energy captured by the producers by 1,000: $8,000 \div 1,000 = 8$.

20. **(D)** Each level should contain approximately 10% of the level above it.

21. **Energy, Consumer, Numbers** The pyramid shows the transfer of energy from producers to three levels of consumers. The text accompanying the pyramid says that "this is called the 'pyramid of numbers.'"

22. **(A)** Ozone absorbs radiation coming into the atmosphere from the sun. Skin cancer is the only harmful effect listed that is related to damage from increased exposure to sunlight.

23. **(C)** The passage says that CFCs take 1–2 years to travel up to the stratosphere where they can affect ozone levels.

24. **(C)** Halons are identified as another chemical harmful to the ozone layer. An increase in their use would increase ozone depletion. Restrictions on CFCs would reduce ozone depletion. Not all propellants are CFCs, so an increase in propellants would not necessarily increase ozone depletion. An increase in UV-B would be a result of ozone depletion and not a cause.

25. **(D)** The population of shrimplike organisms decreased sharply as the population of mussels increased sharply. Since the mussels are the independent variable, they are plotted along the *x*-axis. This strong negative correlation is shown in plot *D*.

26. **(C)** A strong correlation cluster points along a clear trendline going either upward or downward from left to right. A weak correlation appears as a loose arrangement of points that trend in one direction. When a correlation trends downward from left to right, it is a negative correlation. Plot *A* shows no correlation. Plot *B* shows a strong positive correlation. Plot *C* shows a weak negative correlation. Plot *D* shows a strong negative correlation.

27. **(B)** Of the four plots, plot *A* is the weakest since it shows no correlation at all. Plot *C* is the next weakest since it shows only a loose correlation. Plots *B* and *D* both show strong correlations. (Plot *B* is positive, and plot *D* is negative.) *A, C, B* goes from no correlation to weak correlation to strong correlation. Whether or not the correlation is positive or negative is not an issue here.

28. **(C)** Plot *A* has no correlation at all. Plot *B* has strong positive correlation since it shows a clear trend line upward. Plots *C* and *D* both show negative correlations, with *D* more negative than *C*. *B, A, D* goes from strong positive to neutral to strong negative.

29. **(D)** The other options are all offered as examples of physical changes, not chemical changes. Gunpowder exploding is an example of a chemical change.

30. **(B)** Physics studies physical changes; chemistry studies chemical changes.

31. **(C)** The law of conservation of matter says that matter cannot be either created or destroyed. The law of conservation of energy says that energy cannot be either created or destroyed.

32. **(B)** 47.0% is almost 50%, which is one-half.

33. **(A)** This is the definition of an element.

34. **(B)** The passage states that "Other elements are named from countries or localities, as germanium and scandium."

35. **(A)** The passage states that "Sometimes the symbol is an abbreviation of the old Latin name. In this way Fe (ferrum) indicates iron. . . ."

How to Use the CD-ROM

The software is not installed on your computer; it runs directly from the CD-ROM. Barron's CD-ROM includes an "autorun" feature that automatically launches the application when the CD is inserted into the CD-ROM drive. In the unlikely event that the autorun feature is disabled, follow the manual launching instructions below.

Windows®

Insert the CD-ROM and the program should launch automatically. If the software does not launch automatically, follow the steps below.
1. Click on the Start button and choose "My Computer."
2. Double-click on the CD-ROM drive, which will be named **GEDTest**.
3. Double-click **GEDTest.exe** application to launch the program.

Mac®

1. Insert the CD-ROM.
2. Double-click the CD-ROM icon.
3. Double-click the **GEDTest** icon to start the program.

SYSTEM REQUIREMENTS

The program will run on a PC with:
Windows® Intel® Pentium II 450 MHz
or faster, 128MB of RAM
1024 X 768 display resolution
Windows 2000, XP, Vista
CD-ROM Player

The program will run on a Mac® with:
PowerPC® G3 500 MHz
or faster, 128MB of RAM
1024 X 768 display resolution
Mac OS X v.10.1 through 10.4
CD-ROM Player